CW00430702

This detailed and authoritative volume changes our conceptions of "imperial" and "African" history. Frederick Cooper gathers a vast range of archival sources in French and English to achieve a truly comparative study of colonial policy towards the recruitment, control, and institutionalization of African labor forces from the mid-1930s, when the labor question was first posed, to the late 1950s, when decolonization was well under way.

Professor Cooper explores colonial conceptions of the African worker, and shows how African trade union and political leaders used the new language of social change to claim equal wages, equal benefits, and share of power. This helped to persuade European officials that their post-war project of building a "modern" Africa within the colonial system was both unaffordable and politically impossible. France and Great Britain left the continent, insisting that they had made it possible for Africans to organize wage labor and urban life in the image of industrial societies while abdicating to African elites responsibility for the consequences of the colonial intervention. They left behind the question of how much the new language for discussing social policy corresponded to the lived experience of African workers and their families and how much room for maneuver Africans in government or in social movements had to reorganize work, family, and community in their own ways.

Decolonization and African Society

African Studies Series 89

Editorial Board
Professor Naomi Chazan,   *The Harry S. Truman Research Institute for the Advancement of Peace,   The Hebrew University of Jerusalem*
Professor Christopher Clapham,   *Department of Politics and International Relations, Lancaster University*
Professor Peter Ekeh,   *Department of African American Studies, State University of New York, Buffalo*
Dr John Lonsdale,   *Trinity College, Cambridge*
Professor Patrick Manning,   *Department of History, Northeastern University, Boston*

Published in collaboration with
THE AFRICAN STUDIES CENTRE, CAMBRIDGE

A list of books in this series will be found at the end of this volume

Decolonization and African Society

The Labor Question in French and British Africa

Frederick Cooper
University of Michigan, Ann Arbor

CAMBRIDGE
UNIVERSITY PRESS

Published by the Press Syndicate of the University of Cambridge
The Pitt Building, Trumpington Street, Cambridge CB2 1RP
40 West 20th Street, New York, NY 10011-4211, USA
10 Stamford Road, Oakleigh, Melbourne 3166, Australia

www.cambridge.org
Information on this title: www.cambridge.org/9780521562515

© Cambridge University Press 1996

First published 1996

A catalogue record for this book is available from the British Library

Library of Congress cataloguing in publication data

Cooper, Frederick, 1947–
Decolonization and African society: the labor question in French
and British Africa / Frederick Cooper.
    p.   cm – (African studies series: 89)
Includes bibliographical references
ISBN 0 521 56251 1 hb
ISBN 0 521 56600 2 pb
1. Labor – Africa – History – 20th century.   2. Labor movement –
Africa – History – 20th century.   3. Trade-unions – Africa –
History – 20th century.   4. Labor laws and legislation – Africa –
History – 20th century.   5. Decolonization – Africa – History – 20th
century.   6. France – Colonies – Africa.   7. Great Britain – Colonies –
Africa.   8. Africa – Colonial influence.   I. Title.   II. Series.
HD8776.C66   1996
331′06–dc20   95-46203   CIP

ISBN-13 978-0-521-56251-5 hardback
ISBN-10 0-521-56251-1 hardback

ISBN-13 978-0-521-56600-1 paperback
ISBN-10 0-521-56600-2 paperback

Transferred to digital printing 2005

KS

Contents

Tables

Figure

Preface

My friends and my publisher tell me this is a long book. I think it's too short. It is primarily a book about connections: the ways in which movements among Africans and colonial interventions shaped each other, the relationship of social movements to political struggles in Africa, the interplay between the conceptual schemes of officials and their actions, and the tension of the empire-wide interests and perspectives and the local focus of colonial agents confronting immediate struggles on a daily basis. Focusing on these lines of connection, the book necessarily cannot examine each component part in depth. My analysis recognizes the importance of contexts but does not delve into them; it attempts instead to explain why in a particular moment such movements had a profound impact at the imperial level and how colonial states' efforts to regain the initiative in the 1940s redefined the terrain of struggle, creating new openings and new constraints in which local movements operated in the 1950s. Similarly, a full analysis of the intellectual framework in which labor was discussed in the imperial capitals would require a depth of analysis of metropolitan social movements, social policy, and social science that would make this book even longer. The main concern of this book is how changing structures of ideas both reflected and affected changing struggles in different parts of empire.

This is a book I would not have dared to write until now. I wouldn't have dared to do so had I not already gone through a long period of writing about the social history of a particular African region – the East Coast of Kenya. My coming of age as an African historian in the 1970s occurred at a time when we were anxious to distinguish ourselves from an earlier tradition of "imperial" history and to show how focused on Africa we were. The price of this was that most Africanists of my generation were willing to assume that colonialism could be taken for granted, that we could probe the complexity of African initiatives and responses to outside intrusion without examining the colonial side of this ongoing encounter in similar depth. The success of African historians in showing the importance and integrity of Africa's history now allows a return to questions about colonial regimes that acknowledges their complexity and contradictions. But the pendulum should not – and indeed cannot – swing back, for colonial thinking and policies can neither be considered determinant nor independent of the agency of their erstwhile subjects. European policy is as much a response to African initiatives as African "resistance" or "adaptation" is a response to colonial interventions.

It was while doing research on a spatially focused topic – the series of strikes in Mombasa between 1934 and 1947 and the startlingly large impact this had on British thinking and policy – that I became convinced that Mombasa could not be understood simply by studying Mombasa. British rulers could easily have dealt with this city by other means had officials not been thinking in terms of an entire empire. I view colonial apparatuses – not to mention European settlers, missionaries, entrepreneurs, and intellectuals – as not only cut through by uncertainties about their power and disagreements among themselves, but unevenly focused on immediate and long-term concerns, on the local and the imperial.

The risk of any study this broad is that the variety of contexts which both shape and were shaped by colonial regimes disappears into empty acknowledgements of variation and complexity. I have tried to confront this problem by frequent changes of focus, moving from the Ivory Coast in the days of the forced labor debates on francophone Africa to Dakar when taming urban strikers became the issue, to Mombasa or the Copperbelt to talk about stabilization, to the Gold Coast to look at the relief with which British officials greeted Nkrumah's efforts to discipline the Gold Coast labor movement. In doing so, one not only appreciates the diversity of contexts but the eagerness of many colonial officials, especially at the top of the hierarchy – to act as of that complexity were not there. "African society" emerges as a construct of colonial discourse, unevenly related to different struggles and initiatives. The way such a construct was set against the simplified and sanitized vision the colonial officials had of labor and class in European or "modern" society turns out to be an important aspect of this study, and I have tried to set it against the politics of specific instances. My goal has been neither to recreate the world of colonial bureaucrats nor to unveil the ways in which African workers talked among themselves, but I am interested in what went on at the interface: a limited space of mutual intelligibility and interaction.

My decision to make this a comparative study of French and British Africa – after over a decade of work on anglophone East Africa – was a result of my wanting to open up questions about colonialism that went beyond the particularities of any one empire. It is obviously not a full comparative study, but the comparison is I think a suggestive one.

Among French colonies, my focus is almost exclusively on French West Africa – considered at the time the more "advanced" of the regions – while among British Africa, I emphasize in various contexts Kenya, the Gold Coast, Nigeria, and Northern Rhodesia. Parallel studies of Belgian and Portuguese empires would be extremely valuable, and I give some attention to the efforts of these and other powers after World War II to develop a consensus around the conception of "standards" for social policy just as they had tried to forge a consensus around the idea of "free" labor earlier in the colonial era. Both among and within the different institutions concerned with these issues, major differences of opinion developed, and my aim is not to look for a single "colonial conception of labor" as to follow the disputes and fault lines, to see how differences within power structures were pried open by people outside, to see how partial consensuses emerged and laid the basis for further conflict.

Studying these questions makes it clear how complex it would be to study all the effects of policy shifts: how the lives of workers and their families actually changed in the 1940s and 1950s. Such questions are already being studied, by, among others, graduate students at the University of Michigan: Timothy Scarnecchia's completed dissertation on housing and gender in post-war Harare, Lisa Lindsay's dissertation (in the writing stage) on railway workers and their families in Nigeria, and Martha Baker's research (now beginning) on retirement in Kenya. A new generation of Senegalese scholars, whom I have been fortunate to get to know, will be writing new histories carefully rooted in a regional context, and a preliminary indication of what they are uncovering can be found in the masters theses of Mor Sene, Oumar Guèye, and others. I have already learned much from these students. My own contribution is set out in the hope not only that others will add to it but that they will take its ideas in directions I never would have thought of.

Translations from the French are the author's, and I have tried to simplify esoteric colonial terminology. Colonies are referred to by their names during the era in question. I call the top administrators of individual French territories "governors" even though in part of the period they were called "lieutenant-governors," and the head of the French West African Federation is called the governor-general even though in some contexts he was called the high commissioner. There are some inconsistencies in citations to Public Record Office material, since the classification numbers of some series changed in the midst of research, but the reader can convert old numbers to new using the file lists at the archives.

In moving toward an anglophone-francophone comparison, I had a lot to learn and in so doing I have acquired a wide range of debts.

Boubacar Barry, Mamadou Diouf, Babacar Fall, and Mohamed Mbodj deserve much of the credit for whatever grasp I have acquired of the context in which labor and politics were played out in Senegal. Catherine Coquery-Vidrovitch generously helped me in France. The archivists at the Archives Nationales du Sénégal – particularly the Director, Saliou Mbaye – and at the Archives Nationales – Section Outre-Mer (before and after its move from Paris to Aix-en-Provence) helped me learn the ropes. Babacar Fall of the Ecole Normale Supérieure of the Université Cheikh Anta Diop and several of his students – who joined me in a workshop in Dakar in 1994 on the oral history of the recent Senegalese past – included me in interviews with participants in the processes described here. A special word of thanks to Mor Sene, Aminata Diena, Oumar Guèye, and Alioune Ba for their work on these interviews.

A principle risk of writing a long book is the burden one imposes on one's colleagues in asking them to read it: I am grateful for the comments of Mamadou Diouf, Laura Downs, Myron Echenberg, Lisa Lindsay, John Lonsdale, and Luise White on drafts that were even longer than the final version. Working with Ann Stoler on another project about colonialism has taught me much of value to this endeavor, and she gave me a helpful reading of the introduction. Jane Burbank has helped me to see that the empires of Western Europe were part of a broader spectrum of imperial conquests and imperial systems and that the categories of capitalism and colonialism must be used with specificity; her reading of the introduction to this manuscript and various papers related to it have provided insight as well as encouragement.

This book has been written on four generations of computers (8086, 286, 386, 486) and in settings ranging from a dingy dormitory room in Moscow State University to the beautiful Center for Advanced Study in the Behavioral Sciences. Besides the archival staffs mentioned above, those at the Public Record Office in London and Rhodes House in Oxford deserve a word of thanks, as do librarians at the Library of Congress, the Hoover Institution, and the University of Michigan and research assistants and support staff at the History Department and Humanities Institute of the University of Michigan, the Woodrow Wilson Center in Washington, and the Center for Advanced Study in the Behavioral Sciences at Stanford. My first research trip devoted to this study occurred (in 1982) when my work on Mombasa was still being written, and I am grateful to the Joint Committee on African Studies of the Social Science Research Council and the American Council of Learned Societies for supporting this new direction in my research. They also funded my first trip to Senegal in 1986. In between, I was able to do research in England and France in 1984–85 thanks to a Rockefeller

Humanities Fellowship. Subsequent research in Europe and Senegal benefitted from a Faculty Recognition Award from the University of Michigan. I began writing in the fall of 1987, with the help of a fellowship from the Woodrow Wilson Center, continued in the aforementioned Moscow dorm room (where the sensory deprivation of late communism focused my concentration and my wife's IREX fellowship proved ample to keep two scholarly projects going), and moved back into bourgeois comfort (and a more collectivist atmosphere) at the Center for Advanced Study in the Behavioral Sciences in 1990–91, where the National Endowment for the Humanities and the Andrew Mellon W. Foundation also contributed to my support. I did more revised drafts than I care to count in the interstices of classes and search committees at the University of Michigan. I began a new project (about development and decolonization) at the University of Michigan Humanities Institute while still doing a not-quite-final round of cuts and revisions in 1993–94. I am extremely grateful for all this support over a twelve year period.

Various parts of this project were tried out in the form of lectures and seminar papers at the Program on Comparative Studies of Social Transformations of the University of Michigan, the Davis Center of Princeton University, the Wilson Center and the Center for Advanced Study, the Ecole des Hautes Etudes en Sciences Sociales, Université de Paris VII, Centre de Recherche et d'Etudes Internationales (Paris), the University of Wisconsin, Howard University, the University of California at Los Angeles, the University of Pennsylvania, Northwestern University, the Université Cheikh Anta Diop and the Council for the Development of Economic and Social Research in Africa (Dakar), Institute for Commonwealth Studies and University College (London), the University of Leiden (Netherlands), Queens University (Ontario), University of the Witwatersrand, University of Natal, University of the Western Cape (South Africa), and Kalamazoo College, not to mention various pubs, cafes, and dinner tables. Friends and colleagues from these places may recognize the contributions their questions and comments made to my rethinking earlier formulations; this project has gone on so long I know longer know what ideas came from where. Jane Burbank has been with me throughout this period – in Ann Arbor, Cambridge, Santa Barbara, Oxford, Paris, Aix-en-Provence, Dakar, Moscow, and Stanford – and I thank her for sharing these places and those years with me.

Abbreviations

AMWU	African Mine Workers' Union (Northern Rhodesia)
ANC	African National Congress (Northern Rhodesia)
AWF	African Workers' Federation (Kenya)
BDS	Bloc Démocratique Sénégalais (Senegalese political party)
CCTA	Combined Commission for Technical Cooperation in Africa South of the Sahara
CFTC	Confédération Française des Travailleurs Chrétiens (French Catholic trade union federation)
CGT	Confédération Générale du Travail (French and African trade union federation, affiliated to Communist Party)
CGT-FO	Confédération Générale du Travail-Force Ouvrière (French trade union federation that seceded from CGT)
CGTA	Confédération Générale du Travail-Autonome (Autonomist African trade union federation)
CPP	Convention People's Party (Gold Coast Political Party)
EARC	East Africa Royal Commission
EATUC	East African Trade Union Congress
EMU	European Mineworkers' Union (Northern Rhodesia)
ENFOM	Ecole Nationale de la France Outre-Mer
FEA	French Equatorial Africa (Afrique Equatoriale Française)
FWA	French West Africa (Afrique Occidentale Française)
GFTU	Ghanaian Federation of Trade Unions
IALC	Inter-African Labour Conference
ICFTU	International Confederation of Free Trade Unions (anti-communist global trade union organization)
ILO	International Labour Organization
KAU	Kenya African Union (Kenyan Political Party)
KFL	Kenya Federation of Labour (successor to KFRTU)
KFRTU	Kenya Federation of Registered Trade Unions
MEU	Mine Employees' Union (Gold Coast)
MRP	Mouvement Républicain Populaire (French Social Catholic party)

PCF	Parti Communiste Français (French Communist Party)
PDCI	Parti Démocratique de la Côte d'Ivoire (Ivory Coast branch of RDA)
PDG	Parti Démocratique Guinéen (Guinean branch of RDA)
RDA	Rassemblement Démocratique Africain (African political party)
SAA	Société Agricole Africaine (Ivory Coast planters' society)
SFIO	Section Française de l'Internationale Ouvriére (French Socialist Party)
TUC	Trade Union Congress
UGCC	United Gold Coast Convention (Gold Coast political party)
UGTAN	Union Générale des Travailleurs de l'Afrique Noire (autonomist African trade union federation)
WFTU	World Federation of Trade Unions (communist-affiliated global trade union organization)

Note: For archival file references used in notes, see bibliography. Additional abbreviations used in notes: IT (Inspection du Travail), IGT (Inspection or Inspecteur Général du Travail), AR (Annual Report).

French and British colonial Africa

1 Introduction

> "Everything is permitted, but nothing is possible"
> Graffito, seen on a Parisian wall, fall 1984

The era of decolonization was a time when the range of political possibilities seemed to open up, only to close down again. When Ghana became an independent state in 1957, followed by Guinea in 1958 and others in the ensuing decade, Africans could, in theory, organize their governments as they wished and use them to transform their lives. Leaders – western educated, but rarely more than one generation removed from their milieux of origin – saw themselves as choosing the best of what Europe and Africa had to offer. A wide populace participated in the sense of triumph which attended the transition. In the new Africa, much was permitted, and something was possible. Yet within a decade or so, African writers were portraying societies disillusioned with the fruits of independence, with power-hungry leaders who sought to neutralize the social movements which had once helped them to challenge colonial rule, with the indifference of civil servants to the problems of ordinary people, with elite cultures overly focused on the West.[1] Were new states and new political and social organizations finding themselves constrained by the paths they took toward political independence just as they had been by the structures of colonial rule?

This book is about the changing definition of the possible in the era leading up to decolonization. It focuses on the intersection of French and British colonial bureaucracies with African labor movements and the way in which their conflict and connection both expanded and limited the labor question. From the mid-1930s onward, previous ways of thinking about African labor proved incapable of providing a guide to the social problems that increasingly forceful collective action by African workers thrust upon the colonial state. Before then, the question of colonial labor was limited to the numbers issue – how many low-paid workers could be obtained? – to the issue of compulsion – how much coercion could a "civilized" government legitimately deploy to make people with little interest in wage labor perform work for public or

1

private employers? – and to the issue of disruption – was the delicate fabric of African "societies" rent asunder by the temporary removal of workers from them?

Both imperial regimes moved in a little over a decade from a conception of the African worker as very African – as a temporary wage earner at risk of becoming "detribalized" if allowed to stay away too long from his village – to a vision of the African turned into industrial man, now living with a wife and family in a setting conducive to acculturating new generations into modern society. Colonial bureaucracies began to ponder the range of questions about labor familiar to their colleagues in the metropole, and they began to reproduce in Africa the legal and administrative institutions used to manage labor problems in France or Great Britain, hoping that treating African males as if they were industrial men would create the kind of predictable, known being who could make Africa into the orderly, productive, controllable society that seemed so vital in the post-war conjuncture.

Industrial man, in officials' eyes, was indeed a male. That most migrant laborers who came forth in the early colonial years were male may have had more to do with whom African communities felt they could do without for a period of time than European hiring preferences. But when European officials sought to build a more stable, more acculturated, more experienced labor force, the complexities of African life were of much less concern to them than their own gendered imagery. What was critical to the reformers was the social reproduction of the labor force: that the new generation be brought up adequately nourished and familiarized with urban and industrial environments so that its members would be more productive and predictable than their fathers. Stabilization, as the new policy was called, implied that women should leave their villages to join their husbands near their places of work, and take up the reproduction of the labor force – under the watchful eyes of nurses, teachers, and bureaucrats. Ideas about society, as is so often the case, had their material consequences: jobs that came under formal regulation were coded masculine, while the kinds of things women did were more often labelled "customary labor" or the "informal economy," with all the insecurities and vulnerabilities that such a status implied.

While colonial officials saw this as an effort of social engineering – using up-to-date European knowledge – the entire process was in fact carried out in dialogue with African labor movements. French and British officials were batting around plans for colonial reform in the 1940s, but the actual initiative in the labor field was a response to African agency: the wave of strikes that began in the mid-1930s and reached a climax in the late 1940s and the beginnings of political movements that challenged officials' exercise of power. Imperial governments wanted to confine the labor question to a set of institutions and practices familiar to them from the "industrial relations" experience of the metropole, to treat labor as separable from politics. The threat of a labor crisis becoming unbound – linked to people other than wage workers in countryside as well as city – made governments especially willing to pay the costs of resolving labor issues. As they did so, African labor movements seized the new discourse of administrators and turned assertions of control into demands for entitlements: if colonial officials wanted Africans to work like their idealized European workers, they should pay them on a similar scale and bargain with them in good faith. As African labor leaders participated in this dialogue, they became caught up in its terms: their very success encouraged them to think of trade unionism and collective bargaining as a "normal" way of organizing economic life. They too were part of the gendering of the labor question, and while women had participated in some of the general strikes of the 1940s, the formal labor organizations that followed in the 1950s were largely masculine affairs. For their own reasons, African unions demanded that men be paid a "family wage," enough to support a dependent wife and children.[2]

A careful study of late colonialism will hopefully be a step toward future analysis of how social issues were framed and reframed in the post-colonial era. The new states of Africa were constrained by their small size and military weakness, by the limited options available to primary-product exporters in the world market, and by their dependence on aid from former colonizers, other donor nations, and international agencies. But there were constraints of the imagination as well. Social scientists and policy makers outside Africa generally thought about social policy issues within the categories that emerged in the process of decolonization – with their insights and blind spots. Inside post-colonial Africa, political leaders and high level civil servants brought a variety of experiences and influences to bear, but they participated in this global discourse as well: most early leaders received their experience in defining and implementing social policy in the era of imperial reform after World War II; some were educated in Europe; some participated in organizations like the United Nations and the International Labour Organization. These connections immersed leaders in certain discussions and debates, which, while themselves shifting, also tended to separate a discussible issue from one which lay outside the boundaries of international political discourse.

In the present book I only begin to address such issues. My focus is on the final years of colonial rule: on the way a crucial set of social policy issues was framed within the administrative and political structures of the colonial state, on the way that framework responded to challenges from African workers. These responses both reflected and affected the ability of officials to maintain the "colonial" nature of the state itself, caught as they were between their claims to a right to rule over the colonized and their insistence that their knowledge of managing social change had a universal validity apart from their status of colonizers. Indeed, the very idea that work was work and a worker was a worker made it less evident why rulers had to be white. This line of reasoning also suggested that when Africans ruled, their options would be shaped by the same universalistic nature of work, of economic development, of agricultural modernization. This set of ideas was simultaneously universalistic and ethnocentric; a basis for claims to control and claims to entitlement; a liberating reference point for Africans to deny the claim of one nation or one race to dominate another and a constraining pattern of ideas that defined different kinds of social organization as "modern" and "normal" or "backward" and "inconceivable."[3]

Thus if colonial governments' rethinking of the labor question reflected an active engagement with certain African actors – and an effort to exclude others – the way in which this and other social questions were framed had long-term effects. This process also was subject to challenge: the meanings of a concept like "development" or "equal pay" were shifted as new actors made their voices heard. Meanwhile, African labor organizations found that they could achieve concrete and important gains for their members if, instead of constituting themselves as organizations clearly and irrevocably set against the forces of colonial and capitalist domination, they engaged substantively with the labor specialists of the colonial state, and subtly turned the assertion of authority into a claim to rights.

African labor unions played this sort of politics with sufficient results, in some colonies more than others, that officials by the mid-1950s were wondering if Africans were more effective in using official ideology to claim entitlements than were governments in asserting control over social and economic processes. By the late 1950s, both French and British officials were looking beyond the aura of normalcy and entitlement attached to imperialism toward a hard examination of the costs and benefits of colonial rule.

This book is not an explanation of the language of labor mobilization within African communities, although a study such as this would not have been conceivable were it not for a considerable body of scholarship that explores Africans' involvement in wage labor, the material conditions they faced in cities, mines, and railways, the efforts they made to build family and community life in places of work, and the attempts to

organize collective action.[4] There is still much to do along these lines –
particularly in exploring the forms of expression and ways of defining
collective identity among workers in different parts of Africa – and such
studies will almost certainly reveal a variety of languages of labor in
different African contexts. Research is already revealing the variety of
moral discourses among Africans – popular beliefs as well as those of an
activist leadership – faced with the dilemmas of living in colonial cities.
Indeed, colonial officials' fears of a strange, dangerous, violent African
world beyond their intellectual grasp made the demands of groups
phrased in familiar language more compelling.[5] My emphasis is on the
intersections of European and African discourses about labor, on the
portion of what was said in both camps that was mutually intelligible.
The goal here is thus to get part way toward understanding the boundaries of the possible – in the interaction of bureaucracy, politics, and
labor movements – at the end of the colonial era.

My account seeks to preserve a tension between political projects and
social projects, assuming neither that labor movements naturally lined up
with other social forces toward a more inclusive quest for national independence nor that a movement for political independence is an entirely
separate category from a movement to foster the interests of workers. If,
in certain circumstances, labor's claims against foreign capitalists and the
colonial state facilitated other attacks on the colonial state – and if at
times unions and parties were strong allies – in other circumstances the
two movements clashed.

Looking at such tensions lays the ground work for understanding how
Africa ended up with the kind of independence it for the most part got:
politically assertive and socially conservative regimes focused on their
control of the coercive, patronage, and symbolic apparatus of the state,
distrustful of and hostile to the continued influence of social movements
that had once helped challenge the colonial state, fearful of groups that
might make claims.[6] I am concerned as well with the power of the idea
of "modern" social policy in African states: how new leaders – before and
after independence and in dialogue with "experts" of the "developed
world" – came to define social policy around an imported future more
than the extension of an observed present, around a package of institutions like labor unions, minimum wage regulations, and industrial relations machinery rather than around the complex, category-crossing social
processes that had been going on around them.[7]

The comparison of French and British Africa suggests that colonial
states' labor policies were not solely determined by one empire's structures or habits: confrontation with the labor question was part of colonial encounters themselves.[8] The comparison also suggests that the way

bureaucracies tried to frame the labor problem and regain control was, however, directed and constrained by particular institutional structures and discursive patterns. Neither imperial regime was free to stake out a unique path; both found themselves pursuing transformative agendas that could not be realized and confronting African labor movements that themselves reflected and challenged the evolving structures of the two regimes. France and Great Britain could not find a durable answer to the labor question within their colonial frameworks.

The attempts of both French and British officials to incorporate labor into the institutional fabric of the post-war colonial system seems at first a stark contrast to the direction chosen by the government of South Africa. The apartheid regime's fetishization of Africans as inherently distinct peoples, each with its own separate destiny, contrasts with the quest of French and British bureaucrats for the universal worker. Upon a closer look, the patterns appear to converge around the mid-1940s as South African officials – faced with the realities of an African presence in cities and the growing dependence of industry on African urban labor – contemplated variations on a stabilization policy. Then the policies diverged after 1948 as a new South African government opted instead for massive expulsions of Africans from cities and the vigorous policing of influx and residence to maintain a labor force while insisting that workers remain in an essentialized category of tribal African. Even so, South Africa found that it was not free to imagine its own labor policy, but had to allow some Africans to develop relatively secure access to jobs and urban residence in order to distinguish them from others and to respond to the pass demonstrations, bus boycotts, strikes, youth revolts, and mass movements that countered its own efforts at control.[9] This comparison is a crucial reminder that neither the post-1948 South African pattern nor the post-war French and British one was the natural unfolding of social forces but that each represented political choices made in related and interconnected historical conjunctures.

On colonialism and decolonization

One of the problems in writing about decolonization is that we know the end of the story. Whether self-government is seen as the outcome of a process of preparation carried out by a colonial state or as a triumph wrested from the colonizers by nationalist movements, the story lends itself to be read backwards and to privilege the process of ending colonial rule over anything else that was happening in those years.

The metanarrative of nationalist triumph usually takes two forms. One, the narrative of social mobilization, claims that inchoate, often local, resistance to colonial rule which had been evident since the conquest was channeled into a unified anti-colonial movement in the years after World War II by a western-educated elite. Mobilizing people through a wide range of organizations – from ethnic associations to trade unions – and bringing them into political parties, these leaders forged a movement that attacked the intrinsically racist nature of the colonial state and claimed its territory, its symbols, and its institutions to bring material progress and a sense of national identity to the people of each African colony.[10]

The second version is the revolutionary one, most powerfully articulated by Frantz Fanon: the anti-colonialism of western-educated intellectuals – and indeed of wage workers, aspiring only to become a labor aristocracy – was false, and the revolutionary dynamic lay in a peasantry and a lumpenproletariat willing to face up to the absolute denial of identity that colonialism entailed and to use violence to overthrow the colonial regime.[11] Fanon had little sympathy with the rhetoric of racial unity or the invocation of symbols of the African past which "bourgeois nationalists" embraced and later used as they set themselves up as brokers between African "tradition" and post-colonial "modernity." His imagined future came out of the struggle itself: "'The last shall be first and the first last.' Decolonisation is the putting into practice of this sentence."[12]

Both versions show nationalism subsuming all other struggles. Both miss a lot of history, notably the tension – at times a creative one – between the national question and other sorts of social questions, and both have dangerous political implications, positing a True Cause against which opposition has no legitimate place. In post-colonial Africa, stolidly "bourgeois" regimes like that of the Ivory Coast and radical regimes born of peasant mobilization and violence, such as those of Mozambique or Zimbabwe, have shown a similar impatience with formal opposition and autonomous organization; the single-party state is but one manifestation of this tendency.[13] In practice governments lack any such unity or autonomy from social groups within the "nation" and they are in constant dialogue with the "western" world. But official ideologies focused on the integrity of the nation cannot speak to the dilemmas which the state's porousness implies or open up a wide debate on what states, social movements, and individuals can and cannot do to reform poor and unequal societies and on ways of permitting wide dialogue and common action by people with diverse pasts.[14]

The narrative of decolonization from above, meanwhile, has the same singularity of focus as the narratives of nationalist triumph but from the other side. Ronald Robinson, for one, argues that the impetus for decolonization originated within the British bureaucracy before nationalist parties arose to challenge it, as a result of calculations of British interests and power and consistent with an older conception of colonial rule, based on the trajectories of Canada or New Zealand, as a stepping stone to self-government. By 1947, Africa had been set on the road to decolonization, and the effect of subsequent nationalist agitation – particularly the Gold Coast riots of 1948, which the Colonial Office took to be more serious than they were – was merely to accelerate the time table. This is a classic bit of Whig history – rereading history to conform to a subsequent notion of what constitutes progress – and has been rightly criticized by other British historians of empire in these terms. By detaching discussions of political institutions from their social and economic context, Robinson misses the extent to which the British government in the 1940s was actually intervening more deeply into the lives of its colonial subjects than before, and he ignores the serious challenge to these interventions coming from groups – labor included – that were not specifically nationalist. The contention that self-government was well launched by 1947 ignores the question of whether the colonial imagination could see at the time any group of Africans who conformed to its notion of what an acceptable successor class would look like; in fact the Colonial Office saw potential leaders as either demagogues or school boys, the first unfit to rule, the latter unready.[15]

France's eventual surrender of its colonies, Jacques Marseille argues, stemmed from a cold calculation of their value. The protected zone of colonial economies had been most valuable to weak sectors of the French economy and especially when world markets were depressed. But in the 1950s, France's economy was growing and its focus was increasingly on Europe: the colonial business lobby became increasingly marginal and the sentimental imperialism it had once inspired became increasingly burdensome. Marseille's focus is so resolutely metropolitan that he does not ask what inside of colonies accounts for the fact that they didn't pay and couldn't adjust. The question is not just one of whether rule can be preserved or even if the economic balance sheet is positive or negative, but whether an imperial vision of a subordinate society modelled in accordance with the metropole's needs and conceptions can sustain challenges and whether alternatives are actually imaginable.[16]

The metahistories of decolonization imply particular readings of colonialism itself: top-down interpretations take colonial projects at face value, nationalist ones either accept the goal of modernizing society while denying that colonial regimes were bringing it to Africa or insist that colonialism was destructive of the very personality of the colonized subject. The danger lies in centering colonialism too much in people's lives, leaving them no room to see themselves in other ways and no possibility of selecting and adapting symbols or elements of European domination in calculated, instrumental ways or in acts of creative cultural *bricolage*. Much is lost by reducing the life worlds of people into the category of colonized subject and shoehorning political action into the category of "resistance" or "nationalism."[17]

Much recent work has broken down monolithic views of colonialism, to see the divisions among colonizers, the deflection of colonial projects against the complexity of the societies they intended to transform, and the insecurity of colonial officials about their own social coherence and power.[18] Whereas some colonists in some circumstances wanted to create an abject, obedient colonial servant, who could be coerced into agricultural labor, others sought to "colonize minds" in a more active way, to reshape the way Africans thought about themselves and their futures.[19] But much of this scholarship has been more persuasive in showing what kinds of identities and ideas missionaries, teachers, traders, and administrators tried to "inscribe" on colonial subjects than in showing how such individuals actually thought of themselves.

A collective of innovative scholars of India, the Subaltern Studies Group, challenges scholars of colonialism by tying together a series of important questions: to what extent can the consciousness and actions of ordinary people be recovered? Have narratives of universal progress defined the framework in which even opposition to colonial rule was asserted? Do the categories in which colonial knowledge was collected – labelling people "peasants" or "communal groups" and their actions as "fanaticism" – continue to entrap scholars? Their work is a reaction not only against elite nationalism but also against a Marxism which reduces the colonial subject to a stick figure in a drama written elsewhere.

Ranajit Guha has argued that colonialism's transformative project was necessarily incomplete, for it needed to preserve social and cultural difference to constitute and justify external rule, and it therefore left a realm of subaltern "autonomy" which he seeks to explore in all its complexity.[20] The problem in this rich and varied approach to history is the concept of subalternity itself: subalterns are to be autonomous and agents of their lives, yet to remain subaltern. Are not structures of power and the idioms in which power is expressed forged and reforged in relationships – unequal as they may be – and does not this give-and-take test, at the very least, the boundaries of groups? In practice, Subaltern Studies historians have shown that the category of subalternity was itself created by colonial and nationalist elites' flattening of the intergroup relations within India, and their work, if not the group's manifestos, reveal the many lines that connect the top and bottom of a power structure. African historians have also begun to document the way people – in daily life and frequent efforts at political mobilization – built diverse networks and combined different cultural idioms, simultaneously engaging with and asserting independence of colonial institutions and ideologies.[21]

Colonialism, Guha argues, went against trends in metropoles to envelope the exercise of power under universal social practices and norms: it was "dominance without hegemony."[22] The claim of a government to rule a distinct people denied the universality of market relations weakened colonial claims to be bringing "Improvement" to India, and led the regime to seek legitimacy by hitching itself to indigenous notions of authority and obedience. Nationalist elites, seeking to displace colonial rulers without undermining their own authority, found their own progressive projects and universalizing tendencies constrained by particularistic and backward social relations and ideologies which were politically impossible to jettison.

The distinction between capitalist universality and colonial particularism is a stimulating one. But it underplays both the limits of colonial coercion and the implications of the numerous attempts colonial regimes made to articulate some sort of hegemony, contradictory as those attempts were. It misses as well the exclusions and violences of twentieth-century Europe. Guha's insight, however, offers an opportunity to explore the tensions of particularism and universality within colonies themselves and in a dynamic interconnection of colony and metropole. As I will argue below, the inability of colonial regimes to maintain "dominance" amidst the uneven effects of capitalism led them to deploy the "universalistic" conceptions of social engineering developed in Europe, only to find that their own hopes for such technologies to work required giving up the beliefs about the uniqueness of Africa on which a sense of "dominance" depended.

Colonial rulers' hegemonic projects, however incomplete, brought colonizers into ambiguous relations with indigenous social structures, with all their tensions and inequalities. Such projects were subverted as much by "collaborators" – chiefs and elders who used "customary law" for their own purpose or who turned agricultural improvement into tribute collection – as by those who "resisted" them. Indeed, and contrary to James Scott's distinction of "hidden" and "public transcripts", effective challenges to colonial authority came not just from groups who had preserved their discrete ideologies and identities and mobilized them at the right moment in the struggle, but from the subtle and ongoing interplay of cooperation and critique, of appropriation and denial.[23]

Such considerations imply a view of colonialism in which its violence and its cultural aggression are located precisely: their limits, contingencies, and vulnerabilities to challenge are central to the analysis. The French and British conquest of Africa, whatever its motivations, was represented at home as an effort to save the continent from its own violence, tyranny, and backwardness and to open it to commerce, Christianity, and civilization. In practice, colonial rulers found themselves forced – if they were to maintain order, collect taxes, and obtain desired crops or periods of wage labor – to make alliances with the old elites who had previously been portrayed as the obstacle to universal progress. The more ambitious projects of colonial conquerors soon proved unrealizable. From roughly the time of World War I to the mid-1930s, France and Great Britain scaled down their ambitions to remake and systematically exploit the African continent, and asserted that their goal was to preserve African societies and culture while permitting only slow change from within. The much celebrated policy of "indirect rule" in British Africa – and its less talked about equivalent in French Africa – represented an attempt to make retreat sound like policy.[24]

Despite the cultural work that colonial regimes undoubtedly did in both the early and middle phases, the hegemonic project of colonialism fragmented into a series of attempts to attach itself to local idioms of authority, often manipulated by African elders and chiefs, which limited the state as much as they provided it with its principal claim to order and stability.[25] Keeping overseas colonials within the fold – preventing them from "going native" or from blurring the sexual boundaries of colonizer/colonized with racially mixed offspring or from crossing an imagined line of colonial respectability – became a virtual obsession of colonial regimes from the late nineteenth century onward. This is an indication that the outward face of the colonizer's superiority did not mechanically flow from the fact of conquest but had to be reproduced continually and vigilantly.[26] Colonial regimes tried to awe the populace – building modernist capital cities, staging elaborate ceremonies – but it is not clear in what circumstances the populations in question found them awesome. Nor is it clear that colonial efforts to define categories by which the behavior of the "natives" could be understood was as meaningful in Africa as it was to the consumers of colonial cartography and ethnography back home.

None of this takes away from the terrorism of King Leopold's rubber collectors in the Congo, the bureaucratized brutality of the labor system of South Africa, or the humiliations to which aspiring African clerks in bureaucracies were continuously exposed. Colonial officials could impose themselves – as tax collectors or labor recruiters or providers of western education – at certain sites and thus enter the life cycle of large numbers of subjects at some point. But the unevenness of power, spatially and temporally, also led to a range of "indisciplines" through which Africans tried to reassert a measure of control over when and how they worked, over what crops they grew and how, over social relationships during the course of a life.[27]

Where the demands of colonial regimes were the heaviest, the regime's reliance on indigenous intermediaries was paradoxically the most acute. John Lonsdale and Bruce Berman have made this clear in the case of Kenya: the settler regime, drawing labor out of Kenyan communities, relied on chiefs to do the work, and thus depended on the opportunity for chiefs to develop their own mechanisms of accumulation. In Kenya and elsewhere, excessive demands – as for forced labor – on chiefs risked undermining their legitimacy and this was a major reason why colonial governments sometimes pulled back from rigorous recruitment efforts.[28] These systems of subcontracted authority could not handle the extent of social change which the uneven development of colonial economies entailed. The very minds imperial powers seemed to be colonizing – mission converts, educated Africans, and wage laborers – caused particular anxiety, and they came to be called "detribalized." Colonial regimes in the interwar regimes were thus only capable of labelling such people by what they were not. After World War II, colonial governments would swing back to the universalistic, progressive project, but then they would find that this hegemonic ideal was even more contradictory and even more open to subversion than the fragmented hegemonic claims of the middle period. That is the central theme which this book will take up.

On labor, power, and discourse

William Sewell, Jr., who has written extensively on labor in France, opens a recent essay by wondering why labor history, for all the intense activity in the field, has not generated the kind of intellectual excitement it once did. His answer is that labor history is too wedded to the meta-narrative of proletarianization. This brings together a number of processes and, while acknowledging variation, treats the overall trend as universal: cultivators and artisans are deprived of access to means of production, they flock to cities or are forced into insecure wage labor jobs on farms, their skills are devalued, and ever tighter forms of managerial control are devised; meanwhile, workers acquire a sense of their collective identity as the sellers of labor power, their traditions of artisanal autonomy or republican assertiveness are rechanneled into class identity, they form organizations, they go on strike, and they collectively challenge capital, either forcing it to deflect its headlong rush toward increasingly massive capital accumulation or bringing about a revolutionary situation.

Sewell argues that this metanarrative pays "insufficient attention to the profoundly uneven and contradictory character of changes in productive relations, not to mention the role of discourse and politics in labor history." The proletarianization thesis presumes that material causes take pride of place over others, and this, Sewell argues, is misconceived, for what is conventionally seen as material – money, for instance – derives as much from its symbolic content as from anything else. If there is no bounded economic sphere, there is no social or political one either, and Sewell thus denies the validity of the conventional divisions of intellectual inquiry. The most interesting theoretical claims now cross these lines, not limiting themselves to any one institutional domain and making "imperialist" claims to redefine the social sciences: rational choice theorists insist that all spheres of life are governed by choice under conditions of scarcity; discourse theorists insist that all social relations are cultural or discursive; power theorists find all aspects of life to be political. Sewell insists that each such theory's claim to exclusivity is as compelling as the others'. Resolution lies in recognition that all dimensions of social structure are mutually constituted, by meaning, scarcity, and power simultaneously.[29]

It is ironic, Sewell's plea for mutual understanding notwithstanding, that scholars' response to the theoretical uncertainties of the current epoch is the assertion of imperial authority. Modesty might be a more appropriate stance.[30] Sewell's critique of the inhibiting effect of the proletarianization thesis is nonetheless persuasive; I have also argued that its linearity does not help one to understand how it was that Africans came to work for wages, the struggles that went on over the nature of that work, or the diverse ways in which wage labor was integrated into people's lives.[31] But if the development of capitalism turns out to be more uneven and complex, and less all-determining than some Marxist interpretations imply, the problem of understanding why and how so many Africans, Asians, and Latin Americans came to depend on wages for their livelihood is not about to go away. Capitalism remains a megaquestion.

As Sewell would emphasize, capitalism's spread has a discursive and political as well as an economic element to it: colonizers had to define and enforce categories like private property and alter notions of time and discipline. Africans were meanwhile trying to give such categories their own meanings and to seek alternatives to wage labor in responding to their growing interest in purchased commodities. The classic questions of Marxism remain highly relevant to this study: can a category of people be made to enter production with nothing to offer but their labor power? Will they become a homogeneous, interchangeable class at the disposition of the owners of the means of production? What kinds of mechanisms translate the purchase of workers' time into the production of commodities and surplus value? What possibilities exist in different structures of production and reproduction that workers can seize to make themselves into something more than anonymous sellers of labor power? The answers to these questions, however, do not fit a linear model of "proletarianization": power, on the shop floor as elsewhere, was rooted in particular cultural structures – from the racially based system of colonial authority to Africans' efforts to use personal relations and geographic mobility to shape work patterns to their own needs. Labor movements were more than automatic responses to becoming a proletarian, but were rooted in specific patterns of affiliation and strategies of mobilization and alliance-building. Government interventions were of great importance precisely because the nature of work and of conflict were indeterminant.[32] The labor question was a question.

In this study, class appears as a contingent, changing set of relationships, and also as an imaginative project.[33] The assumption by colonial employers in the 1930s and early 1940s that the African worker moved rapidly into and out of jobs tended to reduce the wage spread and conflate workers' material conditions. When high inflation hit in the 1940s, workers' conditions were pushed even closer together, overlapping with those of small-scale marketers and other urban dwellers, despite the diverse rural connections urbanites had. The potential unity of wage workers was actuated at certain moments, and strike movements spread beyond individual workplaces to embrace entire cities or work complexes: the copper-mining towns of British Central Africa in 1935 and again in 1940, the port city of Mombasa in 1939, 1942, 1945, and 1947, the Nigerian government and communications system in 1945, the city of Dakar in 1946, the French West African railway system in 1947–48. Officials began to describe what they were encountering as an urban working class.

But the working class was for them an imaginative project as well: by the mid to late 1940s, influential officials *wanted* Africa to have a working class, to separate an identifiable group of people from the backwardness of rural Africa, attach its members to particular jobs and career ladders, and over time make them into a predictable and productive collectivity. Trade union leaders were also imagining a working class, and they were soon caught in a fundamental uncertainty: to accept the boundaries of this class much as officials did and use the shared discourses as a basis to claim better wages and working conditions for this class, or to refuse the boundary defined by wage labor and to tie labor organizations into political struggles focused on a wider community and ultimately on the nation.[34] The national struggle too entailed accepting a unit defined by colonial conquest, not to mention much of its institutional apparatus and the symbols associated with statehood. These alternative possibilities of affiliation and self-definition were hotly and specifically debated within African labor movements in the 1950s; the usefulness to Africans of "class struggle" was, in so many words, both affirmed and denied.

Like class and proletarianization, the concept of discourse has become so overused that one might be tempted to avoid it, except for the fact that it does some very useful work. Discourse does not refer merely to speech acts, but to the range of acts – laden with power – which establish meanings within specific historical contexts: a general strike or the arrest of a striker constitutes discourse, as does a governor-general's speech or a union's newspaper or the rituals of a religious cult. Discourse is bounded: the collectivity within which it takes place as well as the range of meanings permissible within the collectivity are both limited and subject to efforts to extend, contract, or redefine the boundaries. Discursive openings may create possibilities for new networks or alliances to emerge around them or for coercive power to be focused in new ways, just as changes in networks or innovations and frustrations in the exercise of power may pry open the interstices of a discursive formation.

Michel Foucault has tried to show the shift within European history from a state which exercised sovereign power to the "normalizing" state of the nineteenth and twentieth centuries, one whose institutions and discourses shaped the kinds of human activities possible within the body social and marked as excluded those categories of people who fell outside. Hospitals, schools, factories, and prisons placed people inside an apparatus of surveillance, turning their bodies into measurable, analyzable, controllable entities. The possibility of respectability was defined against those categories – in class and race terms – which constituted the "social enemy" within European society. Power, Foucault argues, is "capillary" – pervading all human relationships, exercised and felt in all aspects of daily life.[35]

But Foucault is often vague about questions of time and agency, and there is a need to understand how and in what contingencies disciplinary regimes were forged, as well as to ask how much the disciplinary notions of elites actually shaped the behavior of those being disciplined. His conception of capillary power is particularly problematic in analyzing a phenomenon such as colonialism, where power is within certain limits crudely deployed, in others only vaguely evident, in others mediated through institutions that were seemingly local. Until the late colonial era, governments were for the most part content for Africans to be part of non-individualized collectivities, little known and unknowing. Only then were colonial regimes intent on turning Africans into Foucault's "docile bodies" – objects of surveillance and objectified knowledge, individuals defined in relation to the social body as a whole, people expected to find their own place in a set of normalizing social practices.[36]

This change will be the focus of much of this book: one can begin to see the emergence of, in Foucauldian terms, a power/knowledge regime. Colonial regimes went to some length to articulate the knowledge upon which their power claims lay: commissions of inquiry into major strikes were used to try to delineate and bound the problem area and reveal the state's command of the techniques and resources to set things right. Institutions like the Inspection du Travail and the labour offices became apparatuses of surveillance, shapers of discourse, definers of spaces for legitimate contestation set apart from arenas of danger that were policed in a more heavy-handed way. The wives and children of workers became – through programs targeted to the families of wage earners – the objects of surveillance as they became the recipients of benefits.[37]

Even in post-colonial regimes, where the overtly external basis of power is removed, assistance intended to make Africans healthy and better educated, incorporated into more effective governmental institutions, also makes them subject to the monitoring of international organizations and therefore to the unevenness of global power. The World Bank is a major artery, not a capillary, and its power comes not only from its command of money, but also from the command of discourse: to specify the limits of policy.

In claiming knowledge to be the justification for continued imperial rule, the governments of Great Britain and France were also saying that Africa's forms of knowledge were irrelevant. What is remarkable about the post-war era of reform, particularly in its most vigorous years right after the war, was that it demanded little actual information about the complexities of African life in cities or the nuances of labor mobilization and control on actual farms. The knowledge of African elders – male elders for the most part – had once been important for developing systems of authority in a variety of local milieux, but now such knowledge was less useful: the European-trained economist, agronomist, or labor relations specialist, armed with universal, technical knowledge, was the guiding light. Relatively recent developments in the management of social processes in Europe – notably the welfare state and industrial relations – became both the model for concrete policy interventions and the basis of the late colonial states' claim to represent modernity.[38]

The words "African society" or indeed "society" are used in this study as if the quotation marks were built in. Michael Mann, in his sociological treatise on power, admits, "if I could I would abolish the concept of 'society' altogether." He objects to its implication that state, culture, and economy coincide in a single unit and limits his use of the term to spaces where social interactions within its boundaries are closer than those with the outside.[39] But one should not commit the opposite error and assume that only isolated individuals and self-generated networks exist: the point is that the boundaries of collectivities and the criteria for inclusion and exclusion are problematic, dynamic aspects of history rather than fixed units of historical analysis.

Few of the colonial leaders discussed in these pages worried about such questions. They were willing to generalize not just about distinct African "societies" but about African Society: a particular set of structures, values, and habits common to and unique to Africa.[40] What was obviously behind this way of characterizing Africa was the thought that they were common to and unique to a particular race. The constructs of "African society" or "African culture" or "traditional society" – often used interchangeably – enabled colonial officials in the 1940s and 1950s to make an argument about culture with the same structure as one they were no longer willing to articulate publicly about race: African culture and African societies were now portrayed as obstacles to the progress toward which all races could now aspire. To get there, however, Africans would have to give up everything that was distinctly African.

European officials, however, were not the only ones trying to portray Africa as a region sharing common and unique social structures and belief systems: nationalists were imagining their Africa too. Different invented Africas clashed and influenced one another.[41] In the end France and Great Britain found that the only way to preserve a part of their visions of reforming Africa was to come to accept that they would have to give up what was distinctly colonial about the colonial empire.

The argument

Caught between political and ideological limitations on the use of coercion and their limited ability to do without it – trying to hitch their authority to the continued existence and legitimacy of African modes of authority – colonial officials could not directly pose the labor question.[42] Part I of the book, "The dangers of expansion and the dilemmas of reform," analyzes British and French officials' gradual coming to grips with labor as a social issue. In some contexts, officials tried to push workers back into categories they understood, villagers only temporarily in an industrial milieu. In French Africa in 1936, officials briefly contemplated using European social legislation to mold an urban working population whose numbers they insisted must be kept to a strict minimum. Yet their interventions were constrained by a conception, shared with opponents of reform, of Africans as natural peasants and their uncertainty about whether Africans, after decades of the civilizing mission, would work without direct coercion. In the British empire, officials were faced after 1935 with a profound challenge: a wave of strikes and riots in the West Indies, plus a violent strike in the Copperbelt. Realizing existing colonial policy offered no plausible guide to restoring control, British officials tried to reframe the problem into one of "development": better social services and economic growth would remove the causes of disorder. But during World War II, they confronted the specificity of the labor question, for the wartime conjuncture led to continual tension and numerous strikes. For the first time, official reports began to write of an "urbanized African working class," whose presence they had not sought but whose reality had to be faced. The decade 1935–45 was a break point in colonial thinking: the idea of "tribal" Africa was losing its usefulness, and officials were casting about for conceptual tools to regain their sense of control.

As the war ended, both France and Great Britain sought new visions of empire, to make their colonies more productive and orderly and to find a stable basis for imperial ideology in an era when self-determination was being proclaimed a basic principle of international relations. Part II, "Imperial fantasies and colonial crises," juxtaposes the new ambitions of the colonizers against the social crises they had to confront. British planning remained within the development framework, constrained by the old notion of "traditional" Africa from drawing upon the dynamic social forms which Africans had already adapted to markets and export production. Economically, a modern city and countryside had to be built from scratch, while politically Africans were seen as either dangerous primitives or demagogues, the latter threatening to mobilize the inchoate grievances of the former. French officials, meanwhile, hoped for a time that Africa's communities could be helped with better infrastructure, training, and support services to become more productive without creating the kind of proletariat that their British counterparts were now acknowledging. They insisted – as British officials did not – that colonies and metropole were part of an indissoluble whole, the French Union, and they thought that extending citizenship to all, while limiting representation to a small number of elected deputies, would channel the energies of the "évolués" into the imperial system, without upsetting the life of the "paysans."

Both projects were submerged in a series of strikes and urban outbursts, which decisively put the urban labor question on the imperial agenda. Now officials turned to the models they knew, industrial relations as conceived of in the metropoles. Interpreting the crises as the action of an ill-formed, ill-differentiated urban mass – moving into and out of jobs and between city and country – they sought to break up the mass into units differentiated by occupation, seniority, and income, and thus into a structured working class, clearly separated from peasants and urban riffraff. In both empires, the new policy went by the name of stabilization.

Part III, "The imagining of a working class," spells out the way officials sought to define and shape this segment of the population.[43] The French government sought to do so through a systematic codification of labor practices, based on metropolitan precedents and termed the "Code du Travail." The British government avoided such centralized solutions, but they too felt the situation required the payment of wages sufficient to cover the costs of raising a family near the workplace and thus incorporating a new generation directly into industrial culture. Both powers now saw trade unions as desirable, for they would seek benefits for a well-defined body of workers and could be partners in orderly negotiating. In both cases, African labor organizations seized the discourses colonial officials were deploying and turned the assertions of control on the model of European industrial relations into claims to entitlements, whose legitimacy could not be directly denied without calling into question the ideological basis of post-war imperialism. In both cases as well, considerable conflict and disagreement emerged within colonial establishments, but groups like white settlers – whose wisdom had once passed for conventional – were less able to shape discourse or policy and could at best obstruct and deflect.

The first serious studies of Africans in cities only began in the 1950s, after the crucial change of direction in official policy had taken place. On-site investigations complicated the picture officials wanted to believe in – revealing diverse patterns of rural–urban connection and cultural adaptation – but most scholars of the era were sympathetic to stabilization policies and to the idea that the world of work had its own trajectory. Some were willing to leap beyond the complications to posit that "industrialism" was a way of life with its own universal logic that would enforce enormous but predictable transformations on cultures throughout the world. These theorizers of the 1950s and 1960s were echoing a quest colonial bureaucrats had begun on their own: to separate the modern from the traditional.

But the modernizing ideal did not have the effects its bureaucratic originators sought. As Part IV, "Devolving power and abdicating responsibility," explains, officials were bombarded with escalating wage and benefit demands made in reference to European standards, while no such breakthroughs attended productivity or social structure. At first, officials hoped that by confining their reformist ambitions to a bounded and relatively small working class, they could be realized. But that working class took advantage of the hopes vested in it without proving to be so bounded and so malleable. Nor was the labor question separable from the political question. In London and Paris officials – facing mounting costs and potential conflicts without corresponding benefits in the colonies and diverse pressures internationally – began a coldly calculated assessment of the value of colonies. In Africa, officials began to think that African politicians, more in tune with the actual social relations of their societies, might be better equipped than the distant embodiments of European knowledge to handle labor conflict.

Here, their calculations proved more accurate, for African politicians, eager to seize the opportunities of the decline of colonial authority, most often wanted to rechannel the autonomous labor movement into something that could be managed by political parties and in their language of nationalism and solidarity. In the end, officials' belief in the universal value of European social knowledge did not serve to preserve empire, but instead to convince French and British officials that they could give it up, believing that they had molded some Africans to the norms of modernity and that they could bequeath to that elite the task of superintending those who had not made the transition.

Part I
The dangers of expansion and the dilemmas of reform

Introduction

Before the mid-1930s, British and French officials were unable to sustain a straightforward discussion of the labor question, even in the secrecy of government correspondence. The quest of European governments to define a progressive mission for themselves in the colonizing of distant peoples and the long history of anti-slavery movements led – through international conferences and humanitarian agitation – to a focus on free labor as the basic test of the responsible colonizer. But the dichotomy of free and coerced labor offered little guidance to the daily practice of colonial administration and left in the shade an enormous and ambiguous terrain where colonial governments exercised power over how Africans worked.

The questions colonial officials had most difficulty posing in the 1920s and early 1930s concerned work as a social process: the relationship of how people worked to the way they lived, to the expectations they brought to the workplace, to the ways in which they experienced the power of employers and colonial officials, to the relationships they formed and the aspirations they acquired through employment and urban life, and to the ways they reproduced themselves. By this time, colonial thinking was so deeply caught in the conception of the African as immersed in "tribal" culture and obedient to "chiefly" authority that they could only conceive of a wage worker outside a village framework as "detribalized." They did not ask precisely what it meant for workers and for a colonial order to have men shuttled back and forth between wage labor on mines or in cities and their families in villages or examine the possibility that working and raising families near the place of work could become a normal part of African life, with its own innovations, adaptations, hopes, and dangers.

Meanwhile, European elites were developing an entirely different framework for understanding labor within their own societies. National leaders were trying to come to grips with the social consequences of industrial capitalism, debating the need for protective legislation and public insurance for certain categories of industrial and agricultural workers. At the International Labour Conferences in the 1920s, European governments annually compared notes about issues of the minimum wage, the standard of living, housing, social security, and workers' organizations. Capitalists had new ideas about managing labor in their factories, and governments had new ideas about managing class conflict in their societies; Taylorism and Fordism were widely discussed in Europe.[1] But when it came to colonies, such issues dropped from the agenda of conventions, from the contents of articles and books, and from discussions within government bureaucracies.

But for Africa, a different sort of question was crucial: could free labor, so much praised by the European powers as slavery was condemned over the course of the nineteenth century, triumph over what Europeans generally saw as the peculiar nature of the African – his easy life and modest wants, his sensitivity to seasonal rhythms and distaste for regular work? The issue of what was free labor and what was coerced, and how narrowly to limit the legitimate use of the latter, would be the focus of international discussions in the 1920s and 1930s. These discussions had little to do with the lives of African workers or even the daily decisions that colonial officials and African chiefs had to make except to make clear what could not be said, what could not been seen, and what could not be asked. The languages of high-minded principle and of silence and euphemism coexisted uneasily, and made discussion of labor in Africa as a many-sided social process very difficult to begin.

2 The labor question unposed

The French and British governments participated in a European discussion about themselves as colonial powers and about Africans as subjects, even as they competed with each other for territory and trade. They quickly encountered the limitations of imposing change on people with wills of their own. The following pages explore the tension between frameworks for thinking about labor and colonialism among officials and Europeans concerned with questions of empire and the messiness of an historical encounter.

Free labor ideology codified

The argument that blacks needed the stern supervision of a civilized state before they could embark on the "natural course" of market rationality helped European powers to acquire a sense of themselves as progressive imperialists in the course of the late nineteenth-century conquest of Africa. Africa as a slave-ridden continent – oppressed and kept off the path to civilization, Christianity, and commerce by its own tyrants – became the central image of missionary propaganda and later a key basis of pro-imperialist argument. The turn to state intervention overseas was consistent with the increasing social interventions of regimes in Europe itself – state efforts to transform the "residuum" of capitalist development into "respectable" working classes. Although the old Europe had profited from and stimulated African violence, the new Europe preferred that economic expansion be predictable and orderly and that social structures be capable of extending and reproducing themselves.[1]

In the midst of their rivalries, the imperial powers met in the 1880s and 1890s to set out the rules of the game, and they insisted that colonizing powers suppress the slave trade, as well as traffic in arms and liquor. In defining themselves as civilizing powers, they defined Africans as slavers, as disorderly, as incapable of self-control. European powers would hold each other to creating the structures for an orderly and rational utilization of African resources and labor power.[2]

Colonial regimes immediately came up against the complexity of applying such a vision. Although in this era many colonial leaders explicitly argued that European economic models – including private property in land and wage labor – should be imposed on African colonies, the immediate reality was that revenues depended on the export of crops grown by slaves and peasants. Colonizers' political hold depended on alliances with African leaders who had at times had an interest in slavery. Most regimes moved promptly against the slave trade, but wavered about slavery in its agricultural and domestic forms. Their temporizing was criticized by the anti-slavery lobbies and challenged by many slaves who used the disruptions of the conquest to flee their owners or resist their exactions. Slaves' actions fed anti-slavery propaganda back home and undermined the usefulness of slave production to export-minded regimes. By the end of the first decade of the new century, the British and the French had in most of Africa ended the legal status of slavery, and its practice was in rapid decline.[3]

If officials fantasized that freeing the slaves would create a pool of labor power which new sorts of employers could tap, they were failing to appreciate the subtlety of the relations of power necessary to maintain a subordinate work force. Slaves sometimes found vacant land to farm – now freed from worry that they might be reenslaved or killed by marauding slavers – while at times they established new relations of clientage with labor-hungry agriculturalists or reconstituted on more favorable terms forms of tenancy with their former owners.[4] Meanwhile, even where African slavery was not an issue, colonial officials found that the task of remaking Africa in a European image was impossible, and while they attempted various experiments in directed social change – trying to remake indigenous economies or encourage white settlers – they also learned to profit from African systems of production and not to ask too many questions about how they functioned.

The other consequence of the moral construction of the new colonialism was the way in which colonial powers examined each other's practices. The key test of their seriousness came in King Leopold's Congo. Leopold granted concession companies the right to collect rubber, and they did so by terror – brutalizing people who failed to meet quotas. In the 1890s, missionaries and traders mounted an international campaign against such practices, and in 1908, Leopold was finally forced to change the Congo from his personal fiefdom into a proper Belgian colony.[5] On the ground, this action may have been less influential than the exhaustion of rubber supplies, but in Europe the cession of the Congo showed what kind of colonialism was not acceptable in polite company.

The reformist critique of imperialism gone wrong emphasized the morality and normalcy of colonial rule. As a French crusader against forced labor argued, "It is precisely because we accept the general and abstract justice of colonization that we desire, in the specific and concrete instance, to purify it of all that soils it." His argument was rooted in an important tenet of Catholic thinkers on social questions at the time: God had endowed the world with rich resources which it was humanity's duty to use in a productive and progressive fashion; colonial interventions were justified only in so far as they served a wide interest.[6] In such terms, it was easier to condemn forced labor per se than the more subtle forms of constraint and discipline used for example in South Africa, and the obvious economic growth of South Africa made it harder to argue about the anti-progressive nature of its labor and racial policies. In the 1920s, and despite the arguments of some principled critics, South Africa remained within the boundaries of acceptable practices, while the scandals of Leopold's Congo, Portuguese Angola, and Liberia showed where the European community drew the line.[7]

France and Britain themselves faced criticism from the purists of the labor market. The critics frequently used the word "slavery" – and images of death and dehumanization echoing those of anti-slavery propaganda – to dramatize policies that strayed beyond the bounds. Wide publicity was given to forced labor scandals in Kenya in 1919 and in French Equatorial Africa in the 1920s.[8] All regimes defended themselves by evoking public purpose, above all the need to develop transportation networks to "open" Africa, to justify the provisional use of forced labor.

Most Africans faced more indirect pressure.[9] The actual operations of labor recruitment took place in a subterranean world, where relations between chiefs and people were nested in a web of affinity and power far more subtle than the distinction between slave and free. For their part, opponents of forced labor usually phrased their critiques narrowly – against the use of official coercion for private profit or against the abuses of government recruitment – and did not penetrate the patterns of land seizure and power that actually shaped the conditions of labor.[10]

Patterns of production in the 1920s were varied, ranging from areas where African producers achieved a modest prosperity (the Gold Coast) to areas where the loss of resources and marginalization from outlets for crops drove Africans into wage labor (Upper Volta, western Tanganyika, eastern Northern Rhodesia) to areas (central Kenya) where states, white settlers, and Africans trying to balance labor migration and their own farms engaged in long and shifting struggles over the terms on which labor would be obtained or exacted. Outside of South Africa, wage labor was found in specific areas – the mines of Southern and Northern

Rhodesia, the settler farms of Kenya or the Ivory Coast, and various port cities – but each was surrounded by larger labor catchment areas on which it depended. Labor came forth, and not simply because Europeans wanted it this way, for relatively short periods of time. Household heads often tried to insure that young men would leave and also return, bringing back fruits of their labor. Young men, and at times women, often used wage labor to obtain a measure of independence from patri- archal authority or to set up their own households or invest in new, more marketable, crops. A small demand for manpower required large numbers of potential laborers, and worked most predictably when large regions became so impoverished that wage labor was a necessary part of the life cycle.

In the early 1920s, colonial activists in both the British and the French governments called for new efforts and new metropolitan investments to shake the colonies out of economic mediocrity. Despite the stature within the colonial establishments of Lord Milner and Albert Sarraut, they failed: their colleagues thought domestic investment more promising and feared stirring up more African resistance than fragile colonial states could handle.[11] As colonial powers accepted that their early ambitions would not be fulfilled, they began to celebrate the conservation of African culture as a hallmark of wise colonial policy. That Africa's peasants were making modest contributions to imperial or world markets, within the apparent context of their own "traditional way of life," was now heralded. French officials maintained a delicate balance between their claim that France itself represented universal human aspirations and their insistence on the picturesque integrity of each of the empire's component parts. Even better than the French label for such a policy, "association," was the British version, "indirect rule," which serenely distanced officials from the messy world in which power was brought to bear on young men deciding whether or when to seek wage labor.[12]

It was in the context of a long free labor tradition and the still open question of whether free labor was practicable in colonial societies – and in the aftermath of scandals over forced labor in the Congo, Angola, French Equatorial Africa, and Kenya – that the League of Nations passed in 1926 its "Slavery Convention." It was a highly formalistic docu- ment, almost entirely in the framework of the anti-slavery ideology of the late nineteenth century, which mainly committed European powers to doing what they had already done: suppress vestiges of the slave trade entirely and "bring about progressively and as soon as possible, the complete abolition of slavery in all its forms." Uncertain of how far the consensus against coerced labor could be taken where European govern- ments were themselves involved, the League asked the International

Labour Organization (ILO) to conduct an investigation of "the best means of preventing forced or compulsory labour from developing into conditions analogous to slavery."[13]

The League was accepting the possibility that a practice of a member government could be analogous to slavery. The problem now was to define where labor became unfree. Considerable ideological weight was attached to the dichotomy: whatever was not declared coerced was not analogous to slavery and was thus exonerated. The ILO duly appointed a Committee of Experts who undertook this task.

Their labors produced a set of recommendations which went before the International Labour Conference in 1929. Colonial bureaucracies anxiously studied them, and the 1930 Conference passed its Forced Labour Convention. The Committee of Experts faced close debates and divided votes on key provisions, and the International Labour Conference voted the final version by 93 against 63 abstentions, including France, Belgium, and Portugal. The French delegation was itself divided, as government and employer representatives opposed the outright ban on forced labor for private purposes while representatives of French workers supported it, allying themselves on this point with the British government – which thought it had weaned itself from forced labor – and most noncolonial nations.[14] But no delegations could bring themselves to a principled defense of forced labor.[15]

The convention, while comfortably within the free labor tradition, pledged ratifying governments to specific international standards. Its goal was the suppression of "forced or compulsory labour in all its forms within the shortest possible period." Effective immediately, such labor could not be used "for the benefit of private individuals, companies or associations." Forced labor meant "all work or service which is exacted from any person under the menace of any penalty and for which the said person has not offered himself voluntarily." Such labor – temporarily and "as an exceptional measure" – could be used for public purpose, and the convention set out terms: they could work for at most 60 days per year, for limited hours, and at going rates of pay. The detailed regulations went on for 33 articles. Military service, "minority communal services," and certain emergency services were exempted. Member governments had the burden of implementing these regulations while striving to abolish the practice altogether.[16]

Perhaps the most revealing insights into the assumptions behind this convention came from a French opponent, René Mercier. He objected to the "assimilation of obligatory labor to slavery," while he wondered what free labor really was. The Convention "visualized above all 'man in himself,' like an entity, and not the native as he is, with his inheritance, his psychology, his customs, his social life, his 'climate'."[17] He was in effect saying that banning forced labor assumed there *was* such a thing as free labor, and that assumed – although he would not have said it this way – that capitalism had already triumphed. Mercier claimed to know "colonial reality," and that meant he knew that the African was not the acultural, universal being the ILO assumed.[18] Such an argument was as essentialist as that of the ILO but it had a point. The liberal moralizing of the ILO meetings was not about to examine the social and political contexts of colonial labor.[19]

The French government refused until 1937 to ratify the Convention, not for Mercier's reasons but because it objected to international meddling in what it regarded as a national military matter: its use of conscripts in public works projects. The British government ratified promptly. The conventions of 1926 and 1930 were mainly used to justify international pressure and at times intervention, through League and ILO auspices, against the weaker governments in Africa, whose practices were blatantly coercive and blatantly for private purposes – Liberia and Portuguese Angola in particular.[20] But one major power, France, was at least embarrassed, and the Convention plunged the labor question within its colonies ever more deeply into a subterranean world.

French leaders had been worried even before the convention passed. Governor-General Carde in French West Africa was sensitive to the international dimension of the problem: "More and more, the major colonial questions go beyond the purely national domain... [this] is an accepted fact that no-one now dreams of contesting." He thought current labor legislation in French West Africa was consistent with the "broad lines" of ILO thinking. But the principle – already accepted in the Geneva discussions – that administrative authority should not supply labor to private enterprises forced him into a contorted position:

This question is very delicate; the strict application of this rule could in effect have disastrous consequences for numerous established enterprises in French West Africa. It is thus necessary for us, while respecting the accepted principle, to push ourselves to avoid the deplorable effects which its pure and simple application would not fail to provoke.

The problem was really in the "hands of the employers," who should dispense with old habits of treating workers "as an easily replaced quantity" and offer "normal wages" and good treatment. But his carefully chosen words left implicit what the government should do if employers did not suddenly shape up: accept the "principle" of no recruitment for private enterprise and handle the practice with great delicacy.

Forced labor for public works was delicate too, and he feared the danger of finding his administration without possibility "of putting right the economic infrastructure of our possessions and this would mean stagnation in the job of developing enterprise." Here, Carde favored a solution that the ILO was to reject: using military labor for public works.[21]

But in insisting that it was following the principle although not the letter of the ILO Convention, France put its own civil servants in a difficult position. Many of them, particularly in the Ivory Coast and Upper Volta, were called upon daily to round up labor for private enterprises. Throughout French West Africa, public works, from road maintenance to large-scale new projects, were absolutely dependent on recruited labor. Everyone knew it and no-one could talk about it.[22] When under the Popular Front government elected in 1936, the French government at last took serious steps (chapter 3) to eliminate recruitment for private purposes and reduce its use for public ends, and when in 1937 it finally ratified the convention of 1930, it did so with the clash of administrative practice and international discourse very much in mind. Governor-General Marcel de Coppet worried about the effect of this clash on the morale of civil servants as well as on the moral posture of France as he called for a new labor policy:

These abuses, these injustices, these hypocrisies, these lies must cease. Because we are lying. We are lying in France, in Europe, in the entire world, in Geneva and the International Labour Organization when, regulations and circulars in hand, we speak of the organization of public works labor in the colonies. We dishonor our colonial administration and we demoralize our civil servants by asking them to apply, on paper only, regulations inapplicable in practice.[23]

A governor-general in 1930 had accepted international principles in name and emphasized their "delicacy" in practice; a governor-general in 1937 found his administration corrupted by such distinctions. In these conditions, it is hard to know what officials were thinking and doing between those dates: they were supposed to write reports in the international language of free labor, while day by day they exercised power in ways that could not be discussed.

French Africa: grand visions and invisible realities

In 1928, the Director of Political Affairs of French West Africa wrote to a colleague who had requested information about labor, "I have the honor to inform you that Political Affairs possesses no documentation, properly speaking, on the question of manpower."[24] The year before, officials had roughly estimated that there were 60,000 wage workers in all of French West Africa – under 1 percent of the population. A larger number – perhaps 100,000 – seasonal workers, went to the peanut fields of Senegal or British Gambia or to the cocoa farms of the British Gold

Coast; whether they were truly wage workers would remain in question for many years. About half the wage workers of the Federation in the late 1920s and early 1930s were in the Ivory Coast, another third in Senegal and Guinea. The large majority of workers were unskilled, and most worked for six months, at most two years, before returning to their villages; the number of people affected by work was thus considerably larger than the number of workers at any one time. Nonetheless, wage labor existed only in a series of tiny islands: the plantations of the *colons* (white settlers) of the Ivory Coast and to a lesser extent Guinea, and commercial and administrative centers, most notably Dakar. Even in that city, workers arrived after each harvest season, often to load the peanut harvest onto ships, and most vanished when the agricultural cycle again called them. The first inquiry into how Dakar's workers lived – a budget survey – took place in 1936.[25]

The tiny labor force and official ignorance of it were symptomatic of a related problem: France had not harnessed the vast quantity of labor power its conquerors had earlier fantasized in West Africa, and it had not done enough with Africa's soil and its peasants to keep very many dockers or commercial workers busy. In 1923, the Colonial Minister, Albert Sarraut, began his book *La mise en valeur des colonies françaises* from the premise that France, four decades after it entered West Africa, had yet to profit from it. He was a frank imperialist: the government had to locate "the capital points where France can appropriate to the maximum the resources which are useful to it." He wanted a plan to assign each region two to four products which it could best produce. He was willing to break with the old colonial doctrine that each colony should be self-sustaining, and commit France's own funds to developing the colonies. In his view, "the entire work of colonization, all the necessities of creation of wealth are dominated in the colonies by the question of 'manpower': there is the centerpiece of the economic edifice that must be built." Curiously, Sarraut had little to say about labor, other than to comment on the importance of sound administrative and sanitary policies to his developmentalist ambitions.[26]

But even the minister, like his British counterparts in these same years, could not persuade his government to break with the constricting policy of colonial self-financing and to plan systematically. His ambitious plan stood – for some decades it turned out – as an epitaph to past ambitions of remaking colonial societies. Even in acknowledging that France had not yet brought itself significant rewards from Africa or transformed its peoples' ways of life, Sarraut was failing to come to grips with the problems of mobilizing its human resources. Other visionaries of the 1920s and 1930s – seeking to use the "innumerable riches" of Africa's soil to build Europe's economies while "making in her turn Africa in her image" – ignored the labor question. Africa appeared in this genre of colonial literature as space, not people, and certainly not as society.[27]

The other pole of the argument within the colonial establishment of the 1930s accepted the lesson of experience in a cynical form: Europe should take what it could from Africa and set aside its transformative visions. Edmond Giscard d'Estaing, doyen of colonial bankers, complained in 1932 that colonial policy had erred in thinking it was possible to "make perfect what wasn't perfectable." He favored drawing a line around the continent's edges that marked off its accessible and useful regions, concentrating French economic activity on key points within those areas. "[The] rest of the countryside would at the same time continue its autonomous life, would develop its own cultivation and its own trade and would slowly climb the steps of economic progress in so far as its purchasing power and local exchange facilities increased."[28] Here was a program for draining parts of Africa of cheap produce and writing off the rest of the continent.

Sarraut, back in the Ministry of Colonies, was now arguing for a social retreat parallel to Giscard's spatial retreat. He too would not press for the "total development" of French West Africa but would concentrate on "islands of prosperity," well situated for exporting produce, well equipped by the colonizing power, and capable of attracting population "in so far as the customs of the inhabitants and the necessities of native policy allow." Sarraut was still advocating "mise en valeur," but the grandeur of the vision had given way to a calculated call for exploitation as he concluded: "We can now sketch a map of useful Africa..."[29]

Attached to Sarraut's letter of 1932 was an even more interesting note prepared by the Economic Service, which finally began to think through the labor question in the light of assumptions about African society:

In fact, truly free wage workers, those who come to the European plantation of their own will, who have not submitted to the influence of traditional or administrative authority, are only recruited easily in seasons of agricultural unemployment... One deals in Africa with backward races, deprived of judgment and morality as soon as they are removed from their ancient patriarchal armature. Become a wage worker for a European, the native peasant hardly waits to degrade himself... His familial and religious respect disappears. His own family disintegrates. Thus thrown out of orbit, the honest and satisfied black of the day before is nothing more than a malcontent given over to his freed inclinations toward nonchalance and rapine. Direct exploitation, which for the European settler is the most expensive formula, is thus also the most dangerous...

Black Africa is an ensemble of peasant societies. Give the black peasant new tools, more modern instruments of work, make his field bigger, open new and fertile land, give him the sense of prosperity, taste for savings and foresight, the desire for work which returns something, give value to his fields, improve his village and his diet, dig him wells, attach him to the soil that he lives on and which he knows as the nourishing Mother, bring him out of the era of hand culti-vation to the age of plow cultivation, this is not an impossible enterprise; it is to produce a human work of education and balanced progress, to lead the black peasant to a new type of life.[30]

Here was a dichotomous choice that would define French debates on the labor question for the next fifteen years: between *helping* the African become a more productive peasant and *forcing* him to be a worker.

Such a pro-peasant argument was founded on premises about the nature of the African at least as denigrating as the argument that Africans had to be forced to conform to the "higher" discipline of wage labor. A few advocates of the peasant road had a more positive view of what African cultivators could accomplish: one influential member of the colonial establishment, Robert Delavignette, published a novel of rural life, *Les paysans noirs*, in 1931 to illustrate the point that it would be possible "to equip Africa in the future without proletarianizing it."[31] Delavignette stood for a "colonial humanism," espoused by a number of Catholic thinkers at the time and which was highly critical of forced labor and other excesses of colonial rule and which sought to find new forms that a "legitimate colonialism" could make the world's wealth available to all.[32] Certainly, officials were as happy to enjoy the revenue produced by Senegal's African peanut growers as by the Ivory Coast's colons. In the high-level government debates over economic policy, the peasant alternative acquired a certain grudging recognition but only as a comple-ment to settler agriculture; officials were still searching for ways to extract wage labor from reluctant Africans.[33]

Even as policy makers retreated from the reformative arrogance of Sarraut's 1923 book, the colons of the Ivory Coast were going about their business, and French agents were grimly supplying their manpower. The discussion about fundamental directions of colonial policy went on with only occasional glimpses into the labor question as it was actually faced by African men and women and by European district officials on the ground.

The historian can obtain little more than glimpses into the sordid world of labor recruitment. Knowledge was contained and sterilized even when it was generated. Governor-General Carde, arriving in Dakar in 1923 with no illusions that Sarraut's developmentalist approach would be implemented, set out to do what he could with the tools he had. He shared in the myth of the lazy African, and he did not oppose involun-tary recruitment for "the strictly humanitarian goal of protecting the native against his own nature" as long as it was done judiciously and with attention to public purpose. He did not want to regulate obligatory labor in any detail, fearing that this would merely entrench the system and discourage Africans from growing export crops or supplying labor voluntarily in certain instances.[34]

Even when the first labor regulations since the beginnings of French colonization in West Africa were introduced in 1925, largely at the instigation of officials in Paris, they remained ambiguous on the issue of recruitment. As Alice Conklin notes, "On the one hand, the code appeared to be an attempt to move toward a free labor market, since it explicitly stipulated that the contracts in question were to be voluntary. On the other hand, the code did not actually deny administrators the right to continue recruiting wage laborers by force in the face of labor shortages..." For Carde, white settlers, notably in the Ivory Coast, were not an inherently desirable feature of colonial development, but a necessity in the absence of any other source of capital; he signed his Faustian bargain and accepted a labor code that was "ambiguously silent" on the most delicate issue.[35]

Forced recruitment was thus not an issue for discussion within the bureaucracy or oversight by a judiciary. Occasionally, a colonial official argued for a policy which both explicitly legitimated and limited its use, and even more occasionally a crack opened in the facade of silence and indirection. Most interesting is the report of a junior inspector named Maret – part of the inspectorate from outside individual colonies sent to check up on the local administration – who not only brought the language of the anti-slavery and Congo reform movements home to French Africa, but who recognized the process of bureaucratic obfuscation. The Kong district of the Ivory Coast had been subject to a "razzia" (raid) between 1928 and 1931, shortly after the complaints of colons had forced out a conscientious governor, who was replaced by Governor Lapalud:

in the interest of a handful of entrepreneurs pushing to earn immediate profits he sacrificed an entire population... He did it *through dissimulation*, without having the courage to bring into daylight an economic conception, cynical perhaps but frank. No written instruction was ever addressed to administrators on the conduct to follow in this matter. And yet everyone knew what the desire of the chief was, everyone trembled for his advancement and dared not formulate explicitly any criticism whatsoever. For five years the administrators committed crime upon crime to satisfy a chief who did not have the "gumption" to bring out their responsibility by a precise order.[36]

Hidden from view, recruitment reached "a new level," as much as 10 percent of the male population in a single year (1928). Agents of the administration rounded up workers and delivered them to employers, "just as the traders had delivered, before our arrival, their sinister human merchandise to the slave traders who carried them toward the islands of America... The only difference is that today they are delivered for six months ... only." And therefore not treated as well, added Maret. If laborers deserted, the administration helped find and punish them; family members or other people from their villages could be forced to replace them.

Maret did not fail to notice that the customs statistics showed that in this period in the Ivory Coast "economic development followed the fastest rhythm" of any colony in French West Africa. But he called not just for "human pity" but for "political prudence": an "insurrectional movement" had appeared in Kong. Equally significant, this method precluded any long-term notion of colonial education and progress: the African, "far from acquiring if not the taste at least the willingness to work, saw his natural horror grow each day and one finds oneself facing subjects as primitive as the day after pacification."[37]

The labor regime of the Ivory Coast led to the neglect of food crops and pastoralism and to planters' lack of interest in mechanizing cultivation. Moreover it encouraged the annual migration of an estimated 30,000 people from Upper Volta to the British Gold Coast. To redeem itself, the administration had to work by stages: a "progressive suppression of recruitment" giving way to government propaganda, accompanied by higher wages and better conditions, as well as increased taxes on Africans and lower ones on planters.

The inspection procedure required that reports receive comments from responsible officials before transmission to Paris.[38] Conveniently, the nefarious Lapalud was gone, and the governor-general under whom he served – Carde – and the minister could blame him for the "abuses." Nonetheless, Lapalud's successor, Governor Bourgines, thought that one could only proceed "bit by bit to free labor... The native living in a rich country without having to make much effort to procure himself the necessary subsistence, does not understand the necessity to constrain himself to continuous labor."[39]

The new governor-general did not think this a sufficient response, although he thought that the "disastrous methods" used in the Ivory Coast government reflected more "a failure of supervision" than inadequate regulations. He sent a labor inspector to the Ivory Coast, whom he thought would exercise "severe control over employment of labor." This would be the first time – seven years after the enactment of the supposedly comprehensive labor legislation of which Carde was so proud – that anyone would be on this scene to enforce it.[40]

Carde's career was unhurt, and the issue became less salient for a time as the demand for labor cooled off during the Depression. The inspection reports and the controversy they set off disclose not just the hypocrisy of the "mission civilisatrice" – after half a century Africans seemed to need as much education in the virtues of wage labor as before – but the local administrator's entrapment in a world where careers depended on keeping quiet.

There were labor scandals in French Equatorial Africa as well, publicized by the writer André Gide and the journalist Albert Londres, and – along with colonial abuses elsewhere – giving ammunition to the first anti-imperialist movements in Europe in the late 1920s and 1930s. The horrific conditions and frightful mortality brought about by companies given concessions to cut trees or grow crops in Equatorial Africa as well as the government's own contractors on the Congo-Océan railway led to charges that forced labor was bringing about a demographic as much as a moral disaster; the future was being mortgaged for the profits of the present.[41]

Inspectors raised the demographic issue in regard to the Ivory Coast as well: coercive recruitment had reached "the limit of availability" of manpower and was leading to risks of depopulation. But the 1932 inspection report seemed to be accepting the basic premise behind the frightful practices, arguing that recruitment could not be given up altogether, for that was "to abandon this backward country to its own fate, to leave it to waste away slowly without changing its ancestral habits..."[42]

France had to face its labor question conscious that it was a member of the imperial club and that forced labor was under discussion within it. The ILO's questionnaire sent to member states in anticipation of the debate in the 1930 Labour Conference led to inquiries from the colonial ministry in Paris to officials in Africa. We now know why Governor-General Carde was so cagey in his statements about the use of forced labor.[43] The Economic Affairs section of the government-general simply lied: "Forced labor for the profit of private firms does not exist." The administration of French West Africa accepted the convention's ban on recruitment for private enterprise as already consistent with policy. Governor-General Carde, as we have already seen, asserted that such labor would not be supplied to individuals while warning of the dangers that "strict application" would entail.[44] The government of the Ivory Coast was at this time conniving in virtual slave raids for public and private enterprises, and the banana plantations of Guinea were in their great period of growth, based on forced recruitment which its governors avoided describing in detail.[45]

As for labor for public purposes, Carde and other officials insisted that the most important uses of compulsion were not part of the labor question at all, but questions of taxation and military recruitment and hence issues of "national sovereignty" which were none of the ILO's business.[46] Carde was referring to the two forms of compulsory labor which were the most common, and which he deemed vital for building an economic infrastructure: prestations and the "deuxième portion du contingent." The former he regarded as a tax: each subject was liable to a certain number of days' labor each year, most often for the development and maintenance of local roads. Eventually, people could avoid this labor by paying an additional tax in money. The deuxième portion, created in 1926, was an offshoot of compulsory military recruitment. Once recruiters had drafted men from a district, they could hive off a section not needed for the army – hence the name "second portion of the contingent" – for something theoretically analogous to military service, including the three-year duration and the pay, but for public works. These contingents were used mainly on railway projects, and – with particularly bad effect on the health of the workers – in the ageless attempt to bring water and cultivation to the Niger valley. Between 1928 and 1936, an average of 1,900 men per year were recruited in the Soudan alone for the deuxième portion.[47]

The deuxième portion was a metaphor, an attempt to create an association of compulsory public works labor with military duty. The association was in effect an admission that wage labor required military discipline and the detachment of the soldier-worker from the daily life of his own community. Carde, in fact, wanted to expand the role of the deuxième portion, and organize more effectively its "rational and practical utilization."[48] His successors, under rightist and leftist governments, remained attached to it even after all other forms of forced labor were abolished in 1946.

It was with these forms of public labor in mind that Carde's Economic Affairs section, replying to the ILO's questions about whether France could look to abolishing all forms of forced labor, replied, "No, there can be no question of suppressing the use of forced or obligatory labor in all its forms." These and other officials feared that without prestatory labor chiefs – who rounded it up for local roads and other projects – would lose their "traditional prestige" and the motives for their "collaboration" with the French government. The government would then be forced to move to "direct administration," which would not only be undesirable but would require more civil servants and hence "fiscal charges infinitely more onerous for the Africans than the prestations which are required of them." Officials tried to keep the deuxième portion completely out of the discussions at Geneva.[49]

The ILO questionnaires, meanwhile, revealed quite a bit about what governors and other officials in French West Africa thought about labor and African society. The Governor of Senegal feared that the ILO was proclaiming the "right to idleness" before "primitive races" who were "naturally inclined to do nothing" and insisted that failing to teach the virtues of work would constitute negligence of colonizers' "duties as educators."[50] The Ivory Coast government thought that forced labor could perhaps be eliminated over thirty years. The governor of Dahomey claimed it had already been suppressed in the private sector, but that "a certain pressure, a certain constraint are still necessary to complete this *work of liberation*" which an improved infrastructure was bringing Africans.[51] The governor of the Soudan claimed public works could not be completed without deuxième portion labor, but admitted that "Soudan is very close to having attained the limit" of extracting men from agriculture. And the governor of Senegal called this quasi-military labor a "demi-failure" there.[52]

But in Geneva, the very process of debating a set of regulations on forced labor that specified how long people could be made to work and what provisions had to be taken for their housing and medical care left a certain impression, which was why French officials and colonial lobbyists had been so worried about the ILO's intervention in the first place. A French delegate to the meeting reported, "We are present at the elaboration of an international native Labor Code whose first stone had been the regulation of slavery and which can bit by bit embrace the diverse branches of social legislation."[53]

France, in the end, was unable to narrow the Geneva discussion as it wished; the majority of the delegations saw all forms of forced labor as part of a single phenomenon which should, albeit gradually, be eliminated.[54] Blaise Diagne, the first (and at the time only) African elected member of the French legislature in Paris, was trotted out to defend France's position by his presence as much as his voice, but in vain. French delegates insisted that they accepted the principle of free labor but abstained from the vote on the ILO Convention, and the government did not ratify it until 1937. In the period between 1930 and 1937, officials admitted the "high value from a humanitarian and social viewpoint" of the ILO texts, but noted that they "necessarily entail a significant aggravation of production costs."[55] They worked on, without in the end implementing, their own regulations on forced labor, designed to show that France was trying to follow the general principles of the ILO Convention without accepting the supposed infringements on its sovereignty.[56] But no-one was prepared to mount a principled defense of forced labor before the ILO. Even the private musings of Carde or the public writings of

Mercier only indirectly defended its use for anything but public works and above all avoided any discussion of what the practice was really like.

In the early 1930s, nonetheless, a widening stream of correspondence suggests that officials on the front lines realized that the existing labor regime was compromising their integrity as administrators and offering no hope for an economic breakthrough.

The inspector-general of Sanitary and Medical Services, Sorel, warned in 1931 of the "immediate danger of depopulation that excessive and badly distributed recruitment is bringing French West Africa" – a theme also sounded in French Equatorial Africa. Doctors were rejecting as unfit 60 percent of labor recruits examined, and too much recruitment was exacerbating what he saw as the deficiencies of Africans themselves: undernourishment and poor agricultural techniques, leading to low bodily strength and low resistance to disease.

This led Sorel to question the standard figure, itself arbitrary, of what percentage of a local population could safely be sent away to work – 2 percent. Nor could one use the population base of 12 million people, the estimated figure, because ethnic groups like Peuls and Maures would not work, and those living near the borders of foreign colonies might flee. So his base was 9 million, and because the population was so "physiologically diminished," the recruitment percentage should be only 1.25 percent, that is about 100,000 men per year for both military service and labor in all of French West Africa. In contrast to this standard, he cited Kong, where 5,000 workers per year were taken from a population of 79,000. The governor of Upper Volta – prime hunting territory – believed levels were excessive. "One exhausts bit by bit the reservoir of vigorous men, which is worrying for the development of the country and *the future of the race.*"[57]

Not only was death reaping the harvest of African labor, but so too was Great Britain. High emigration to the Gold Coast had been noted since the early 1920s. Estimates of the loss from Upper Volta ranged up from 55,000 to 100,000 per year.[58] Voluntary movement to the Ivory Coast was "almost insignificant," according to the governor of Upper Volta, and "the odds of rerouting or stopping this current directed for a long time toward the Gold Coast are very problematic and in any case fairly remote." Only conditions comparable to those of the Gold Coast would attract workers to French planters. Given the Gold Coast exodus, "military" recruitment (including the deuxième portion), and administrative recruitment for private concerns, Upper Volta was losing much more than the 40–50,000 that it could give up "without damaging the social and economic life of the country."[59]

The notorious "African reservoir" of Upper Volta was being drained:

statistics (at times what officially doesn't exist can be officially recorded) showed that in 1927–28 between 45,000 and 50,000 workers were recruited each year, between 25,000 and 31,000 in 1929–31, for both private and public purposes.[60] Officials from the governor on down were talking the language of limits and disastrous effects.[61] But no-one in power thought Upper Volta – land-locked, arid, and poor – had anything else to offer France than its manpower, and no-one had any more plausible suggestions of where the Ivory Coast would get its workers. Even a minister's skepticism, expressed in a circular to governors-general in 1929, about the utility of "la grande colonisation" (settlers using wage labor), his fear that French West Africa would soon exhaust its manpower potential for such enterprises, and his preference for "familial forms" of labor did not lead to a change of course.[62] Settlers were both a political and an economic fact, and any other possibility of exploiting the Ivory Coast's rich potential was at best theoretical. Indeed, in 1933, Upper Volta was incorporated into the Ivory Coast, the better to coordinate their two economies, which in practice meant that officials whose careers depended on good production statistics for the Ivory Coast were now in charge of all levels of the manpower problem.

The Inspection du Travail was subtly complaining, as the colons demanded more labor in the early 1930s, about being asked to do an impossible job: "the local government has always brought itself, in the framework of the labor regulations in vigor, to favor the recruitment of workers destined for forest worksites and for planters. However, the disproportion between the demand and the supply of hands is felt further each day." They felt trapped between the African's desire "only to cultivate his own fields" and the colons "who think that the Administration must substitute for them in recruiting manpower. They try in addition to extract the maximum output from engaged workers and treat these men as a quantity easily replaceable".[63]

The Gold Coast migrations were only a partial contradiction to this view of African resistance to wage labor, explainable by the fact that the African cocoa farmers who employed Upper Volta's Mossi people were themselves easy-going, let Mossi recreate their own village culture with their own chiefs, and let them grow their own food and share in the cocoa harvest. Implicitly, European planters were thought incapable of following this lower but more suitable form of cultivation. The Gold Coast exodus would remain one of the great themes of discussion of the Ivory Coast labor question for another fifteen years, but rather than see the possibility that Africans might labor for others in a variety of ways, officials dichotomized the possibilities into an African agrarian life and a European work regime. In the end, "turning the current" toward the

Ivory Coast would come about only with the kind of qualitative change in the work regime on cocoa and coffee farms that officials in the early 1930s were unable to visualize.[64]

Most labor inspectors and local officials, when critical of being cast as mancatchers, were not accepting Delavignette's argument that African peasants could bring about progress in their own ways; they were instead saying that dislike of wage labor was part of the nature of the African. Their cultural relativism was an argument for lowered expectations, that Europeans had to adapt to the physical and mental limitations of their colonial subjects, whereas the advocates of forced labor argued from the same premises that there was only one way to get something out of the African. The argument would remain stuck within these boundaries until 1946.

Within the rigidities of official thinking, circumstances were changing. The Depression did not encourage a new address to labor problems. The social costs of decline were sloughed off onto African rural communities, while the continued willingness of Africans to supply crops as prices declined revealed the extent to which *some* involvement in the money economy had become a necessity. In the Ivory Coast, Africans dependent on the money economy suffered a decline in standard of living while a settler economy depended on force rather than incentives to maintain its labor supply. Commercial firms and settlers survived in their narrow and protected niches; the empire, as Jacques Marseille shows, had a counter-cyclical effect, buoying up metropolitan consumption and providing captive, if low-level, markets for vulnerable French firms in the Depression.[65]

Official frustration with the labor system becomes clearest in the period around 1933, when the Depression was bottoming out and colons were trying to get more labor while keeping wages at their Depression lows. The question officials faced was whether the structures that had performed adequately where the colonial economy called for mediocre output at low prices would function so well when demand rose.

The early 1930s, in both British and French Africa, witnessed some rural political agitation, but very little on the labor front. "No strike, no strike threat to record," wrote the Inspecteur du Travail of French West Africa in 1934.[66] The inspectors also remarked on the absence of unemployment, but they had a circular definition of it: since the African family took care of its members and had access to land, only the most "detribalized" Africans, notably urban artisans, could be unemployed.[67] Such an argument is indeed a telling instance – typical of official discourse in the 1930s – of how belief in the peculiar nature of African society could define an entire problem out of existence.[68]

Wages, both legal minima and average, fell during the Depression. In Dakar, regular workers lucky enough to retain their jobs may have seen a modest increase in real wages in the early 1930s as prices fell too, but the hardships of the countryside increased the "floating population" of the city and gave such people less control over the terms under which they would accept labor.[69] This underemployment may well have kept wages down even when prices began to rise in the mid-1930s. In the Ivory Coast, meanwhile, wages were cut in the Depression and in some regions in 1935 stood at half their money value of 1929.[70]

The nadir of wage employment was 1932. In French West Africa, 120,000 people were in official employment in 1933, plus 39,000 migrant peanut laborers in Senegal: 1.1 percent of the population. In 1935, these figures reached 179,000 wage workers and 59,000 peanut workers – still only 1.6 percent of the population.[71] But, in the Ivory Coast, planters had no intention of raising wages to attract more workers; they had other techniques in mind. In 1933, 61,000 workers were recruited. It is then that the annual reports on labor cautiously record the inspectors' resentment and anxiety over the increased pace of forced recruitment, suggesting that administrative concerns about the limits of coercion (as described above) were becoming more acute.[72]

The recovery from the Depression would bring out the resentment of African workers at what the labor market was offering them and the anxiety of officials that additional labor forcefully extracted from African societies would endanger the political security of the colonial regime. The tenuous situation of workers in French West Africa's most advanced city and the growing reliance on forced labor in its most important region of agricultural employment stood as markers of the failure of the colonial regime to build solid social bases for its own economic future. It was in the shadow of this systemic failure and in a difficult conjuncture that the Popular Front would enter power in 1936 and begin a brief experiment in socialist colonialism.

British Africa: indirect rule and indirect recruitment

One of the most insightful comments about British labor policy in the interwar years was buried in a report from an assistant district commissioner in coastal Kenya in 1918: he remarked that success in getting labor for white settlers from an African chief "depended on how far he could be induced to exceed his instructions."[73]

The importance of carefully chosen words was clarified the very next year when the governor of Kenya, in a lapse of judgment, told district officials to "encourage" young men who might be willing to work for white settlers. This crossed the boundary of what the British anti-slavery lobby had been calling "slavery by another name." The public outcry resulted in the word, at least, being taken back.[74]

The critics nonetheless chose their ground carefully. The missionary broadsides invoked memories of the anti-slavery crusade, criticized the harsher side of colonial exploitation, but also extolled the virtues of hard work and the role of empire in bringing Christianity to Africa; they did not contest the underlying structures of an economy in which Africans labored for a "vigorous and enterprising European community."[75] When the colonial secretary, Lord Milner, replied that he was trying to steer "a middle course between allowing the natives to live in idleness and vice and using improper means to get them to work," the missionary critics had no useable vocabulary to take the issue deeper.[76]

Meanwhile, more and more Kenyans were going to work, because of chiefs who exceeded their instructions, increased land pressure after the alienations of the past two decades, the need for cash to pay taxes, or their desire for cash to capitalize their own farms. In the gold mines of Southern Rhodesia as well, a period of highly coercive recruitment gave way by the early 1920s to a situation where Africans came themselves to the mines, while recruiters devoted their dubious attention to getting labor for white farmers. The government had all along been careful to call what it did recruitment, although its methods were sometimes closer to kidnapping. But Africans in the region used the word *"chibaro"* – meaning slave in local languages – to refer to such workers. Recruitment, like slavery, implied an approach to discipline distinct from the "sanction of the sack" that underlay capitalist work discipline. Workers on fixed contracts were held in place by penal sanctions against "desertion" and had few positive incentives. Requirements for passes, withholding of wages, and the very architecture of the compound – with chibaro workers located in the middle and "voluntary" workers on the edge – were designed to restrain desertion, just as corporal punishment, fines, and the strategic provision and withholding of food, alcohol, and access to prostitutes conditioned discipline on the job.[77]

In the 1920s, labor was easier to obtain in Central Africa because in key regions – but not all – Africans had less access to resources that generated food, or even more often, cash. This often was, particularly in the Rhodesias, deliberate policy: not only did white settlers take much of the best land, but railroads were sited to serve them and to bypass regions where Africans might otherwise exchange the maize they could still grow for cash. Sometimes it reflected the failure or the unwillingness of the colonial state to undo previous ecological disasters, especially the havoc of the slave trade, the tsetse fly, and rinderpest in the late nineteenth century. Patterns also reflected shifting conditions across a wide region, as workers ventured – sometimes "deserting" a job for one further along the way – as far south as the Witwatersrand in search of slightly better wages.[78]

Thus British labor policy evolved in a complex spatial structure: small islands of wage labor, dependent on the poverty, induced or otherwise, of surrounding areas. Labor power usually came forth in small units, returning frequently to home villages. Migrant labor meant that it was theoretically possible for employers to pay workers less than the true social cost of their subsistence, leaving it to African subsistence production (and especially to the unpaid labor of women) to subsidize the raising of children and care for the elderly. But it is far from clear that, historically, migrancy and its attendant administrative structures arose from a cost-cutting conspiracy of European employers. They, in any case, had little choice in the matter, for African labor power in the early twentieth century was only for sale in small time units. Young Africans sought to use capitalism even as it used them – to obtain money in order to build up herds or invest in agricultural improvement, to marry and to set up a household independent of patriarchal constraints. It took some doing on the part of governments to make sure that pre-capitalist economies served as the mode of reproduction of capitalism, rather than the other way around. It was in South Africa – where white farmers, white mine managers, and white bureaucrats subjected Africans to control far more pervasive and systematic than was possible by a purely "colonial" state – that the relationship was the most one-sided, and even there capital's victory was far from complete.[79] In British Africa, in the mid-1930s, officials were asking themselves precisely this question: would the improvement of an economy from its fragmented and mediocre levels mean that Africans would work more for whites or work more for themselves?

When the copper mines of Northern Rhodesia came on stream in the late 1920s with their 16,000 workers, many officials and managers accepted the doctrine that a rapidly circulating labor force reduced the burden of social costs on capital, maintained tribal authority, and forestalled the social risks of proletarianization. But some mining companies mildly questioned the wisdom of high turnover and male-only urban residence which followed from such an approach. As George Chauncey, Jr., has shown, they thought a controlled program of bringing wives to town would make workers less likely to desert and more likely to be better fed and healthy. The precedent of the copper mines across the border in Katanga, in the Belgian Congo, was relevant here: the Union Minière d'Haut Katanga was already trying to reduce labor turnover by settling a portion of its work force with their families around the mines, where they would be subject to tight regulation and control in most aspects of their lives. The Northern Rhodesian program was modest and limited to certain mines, but it envisioned urban family life for a segment of the work force for a portion of their lives. In practice, women were not the passive, homemaking creatures the mine managers expected them to be: for some, being in a mine town created opportunities for an autonomy consistent with neither African nor British notions of patriarchy. Whether mine companies wanted it or not, a significant portion of miners – 31 percent according to one estimate from 1931 – lived with their wives in the mine towns; circular migration was never as strong on the ground as in official minds. Meanwhile, officials and African chiefs tried to reassert patriarchy in this changing and contested terrain, prosecuting women for alleged sexual misconduct in courts under indigenous authorities.[80]

A window briefly opened for a more serious discussion of stabilizing the labor force. H. S. Munroe, Chairman of the Native Labour Association of Northern Rhodesia and a mine executive, hoped for a controlled transfer of population from the neighboring British colony of Nyasaland to the Copperbelt, claiming that the movement of people from a poor and densely populated region to a potentially rich but lightly populated area would benefit all concerned. He went on to argue,

From the point of view of the mining industry, it would be much more satisfactory to have a permanent supply of labour settled at its own doors and permanently employed than to be dependent on a system of periodical recruitment and repatriation; and it is evident that the permanent employment of a given number of natives involves a much more economical use of their labour than a system which calls for three times as many natives as are actually being employed at any given time.[81]

The argument struck some responsive chords in London, where officials worried about the effects of "barracks" life on African men and feared that some of South Africa's social problems would arise in the new mining region.[82] But the governor of Nyasaland, Sir Shenton Thomas, shot down the idea, not just because of the hardships group migration might entail but because of the immutable nature of the African mind:

The average African is very deeply attached to his home... I wish to place on record that it would be absolutely incredible to any native in any country in which I have served that the Government should wish him to uproot himself, his wives, and his children from the place consecrated in his eyes by age-long associations, to abandon his relations to whom by native custom he is so closely tied, his plot of land, his flocks and his herds, and to betake himself to a new country.

The Colonial Office was suspicious that the governor was actually trying to keep "cheap labour" inside Nyasaland, but accepted his verdict as definitive.[83] A skirmish had been fought between the African as a factor of production to be moved about as capital saw fit and the African as a being fixed forever in his own culture. The latter had prevailed.

Limited and inconclusive as the actual experiments in family life were, both they and the Belgian ones were reversed in the Depression. The instability of labor force proved convenient in a slump as the burden of the crisis was passed onto rural Africa. Only with the revival of copper production and the return of workers to the towns would serious thinking about labor organization begin. Even when the "detribalized" raised their voices in a strike movement in 1935, officials would first react by trying to reinstate more effectively miners back into their villages and culture.[84]

In other places, the forms in which African labor power was tapped gave rise to problems and unease, but little attempt to follow through. In Kenya, from the beginnings of white settlement to the 1920s, settlers and officials thought of the labor problem as quantitative – the need for more black bodies to toil for white farmers. Problems surfaced in another form: the settlers, many poorly capitalized, with larger farms than they could themselves put into cultivation, often relied on something other than pure wage labor. Squatting was of particular importance: an African family, not just a male laborer, would be paid little but given access to land and grazing rights. In the Rift Valley, this process attracted vigorous Kikuyu pioneers who saw squatting as a way to get access to more extensive and better land; it temporarily eased the tensions of the settlers' land-grabbing. But it soon created a basic issue: time. Both the extent and quality of labor time devoted to the settlers' crops were in question, and the least output-minded whites were likely to attract labor from their more vigorous brethren. Whites had to discipline each other, and the state stepped in, limiting the entourage of squatters a settler could attract and, through increasingly restrictive legislation in 1918 and 1937, curtailing squatters' grazing rights and setting a floor on the labor a settler had to require of them. But it was only after World War II, when settlers in the Rift Valley had the incentives to expand, rationalize, and mechanize production, that the final and fateful assault on the squatting system occurred.[85]

The time question surfaced in another way in the Kenyan port city of Mombasa. Like other ports, Mombasa relied on workers paid by the day, insulating port companies from the risks of irregular arrival of ships and from paying the true social costs of their labor. This irregularity was, however, what attracted laborers from the coastal region to such work: both ex-slaves from the once rich and oppressive coastal belt and peasants from nearby areas could combine small-scale agriculture, as squatters or otherwise, with irregular wage labor. From the beginning, officials had misgivings about the irregularity of casual laborers' lives. Several times the number of workers needed on a given day had to be kept in town – consuming scarce urban resources and creating risks that the vital labor force would overlap and become indistinguishable from elements officials called "idle" and "criminal." The balance of such a system was delicate and tended to alternate between shortage and surplus. Once again, officials acted on their misgivings only when faced after World War II with the fact that dockers could organize themselves to withhold labor collectively.[86]

Nothing in French Africa corresponded to the concentration of labor in the Copperbelt; the Rhodesian and Kenyan settlers achieved a more dependable system of recruitment than the Ivory Coast colons; only Dakar had a "floating population" at all comparable to Mombasa's; African farmers in the Gold Coast could attract labor from French Africa; and the commercial sectors of British West Africa generally obtained needed manpower without recourse to administrative intervention. Still, British officials, getting labor by whatever means they could in different situations, left unposed basic questions about time and discipline, let alone the possibility of acculturating and habituating Africans and their families to wage labor.

Such workers constituted, however, a small percentage of the people of British colonies, and the failures to build wage labor sytems, particularly in agriculture, stand alongside the partial successes. In Zanzibar, coastal Kenya, Uganda, and Northern Nigeria, British officials had fantasized around the turn of the century the possibility of turning African slave-owners or militaristic ruling classes into landlords, and their slaves or subjects into wage laborers. This had not happened: various forms of squatting, family farming units – with ruling classes extracting portions of the surplus through part-time labor service, rent, debt payments, taxation, or extortion – arose instead.

As with wage labor production, the successes of the rival economic model – cash cropping – were concentrated in islands of productivity. The most important of these came about, more so than British empire itself, in a fit of absence of mind. The cocoa farmers of the Gold Coast and Western Nigeria began with little knowledge of officials; the farmers of Northern Nigeria grew peanuts when officials were trying to get them to grow cotton; palm oil production along coastal West Africa was part of the precolonial economy.

Calling all this "native" agriculture, rather like calling it "peasant" today, concealed more than it revealed. The cocoa farmers of the Gold Coast, for example, required considerable nonfamily labor, and they got it, eventually, from the drier, less productive north. Here too, labor was not the labor of Marx's *Capital*: the laborer expected not only wages, but access to land to feed himself, a share of the crop, and in many cases long-term relations with the landowner, who might one day help him to acquire land and plant trees himself. In the Gold Coast – the first of the cocoa systems – this was changing in the 1930s, as good cocoa land was used up. But this complex and changing organization of production was set off in official eyes from the labor question.[87]

In some circumstances, British officials found themselves with as much difficulty finding labor for large scale enterprises – as in the gold mines of Rhodesia or the Gold Coast – as their French colleagues in the Ivory Coast. They were not above administering a hefty dose of forced labor. Large public works projects, notably early railroad construction in West Africa, also required official recruitment, while in East Africa, building the railway required massive imports of indentured Indian laborers.[88] But overall, labor for ports, railways, and commercial operations became part of increasingly differentiated patterns of migration and urban settlement. Small urban labor markets grew up; migratory patterns took in urban jobs as well as cocoa fields; mission-educated men filled clerical and teaching positions (and were beginning to found mutual aid societies and trade unions in the 1920s). British officials did not yet put together the various dimensions of these processes – or link them to the politically volatile numbers question in settler colonies – into a single concern.

Unwilling to spend metropolitan funds in any significant initiative to restructure colonial economies, frustrated in its hope that African slaves and peasants would turn themselves into wage laborers, the government in London – like that in Paris – became increasingly absorbed in the 1920s in the myth that Africa was and must remain a continent of tribes and tradition. With high policy, reinforced by the best anthropology of the day, focused on indirect rule and maintaining order through ethnic structures, the label "detribalized" was now attached to people who might otherwise have been called workers or town-dwellers. Ambivalence about migratory labor could be overcome by arguing that this system allowed Africans to continue to live traditional lives and remain subject to the authority of traditional chiefs, even when they were making their periodic contributions to the empire's copper supply. Within such terms, it was hard for officials to undertake a focused examination of the labor question.[89]

When the Depression struck British Africa, the possibility of sending wage laborers back to the security and invisibility of their villages and the continuing supplies of modest quantities of export crops even at low prices – without the cries for government assistance emanating from white settlers – made indirect rule and periodic migrancy appear to have been an especially wise approach. In fact several colonies which had labour departments in the 1920s dropped them during the Depression, transferring their functions to the provincial administration, assisted by medical departments, reaffirming the bureaucratic domination of the apparatus of indirect rule and the ideological power of "tribe."[90]

Recovery and rethinking in French and British Africa, c. 1935

"The whole affair came so entirely unexpectedly," wrote the governor of Northern Rhodesia shortly after the massive strike on the Copperbelt in 1935.[91] It was not that local officials had never thought about African laborers – they worried about numbers – it was just that the terms in which officials thought did not allow them to imagine the possibility of an African work force acting like workers in Europe. The Colonial Office's future labour advisor, Major G. St. J. Orde Browne, put it this way in 1938: "The whole group of problems connected with labour was thus ignored, or treated only in conjunction with other matters."[92] The posing of the labor question in British Africa would be a consequence of African workers, through their collective action, confronting officials with their existence. I will take up that theme in the next chapter.

Another worry was in the long run not to prove as serious as workers' collective action, but it came directly from the mode of thought outlined above: that Africans' natural attachment to their ways of life implied the labor supply would be inadequate to sustain economic growth. Even as they had shed labor during the Depression, the copper companies of Northern Rhodesia feared that when the expected revival occurred they would face "another acute labour shortage."[93] Orde Browne, in an undated paper written during the Depression, also predicted trouble with economic recovery: "Unlike the rest of the world with its long-standing unemployment problem, tropical Africa suffers in normal times from a constant shortage of labour to a degree that renders it a perpetual brake on the wheels of progress." Africans did not like to leave their tribal economies, and the standard ways of extracting labor from them, such as raising taxes to make people work more, were "crudities" that produced only "fictitious and ephemeral results."[94]

French officials also feared that recovery would mean labor shortages. Noting that the the labor force had risen sharply from 1934 to 1935, the Inspecteur du Travail of French West Africa saw this as "an indication that the moment is not far away when the demand for manpower will become higher than the supply." He was saying this at a time when under 1.3 percent of West Africans were working for wages. The problem was

Table 2.1. *The labor force of French West Africa, 1935 (not counting prestatory and deuxième portion labor)*

	Private		Public	
	Contract	No contract	Contract	No contract
Senegal	175	26,794	34	3,441
Guinea	1,235	16,014	1	5,645
Ivory Coast	20,880	51,330	480	11,528
Dahomey	43	3,077	272	2,071
Niger		10,267	7	4,322
Soudan	445	6,500	29	9,700
Mauritania		131		
Dakar		3,720		790
Totals	22,785	117,803	823	37,497
Grand total				178,908

Source: AOF, Inspection du Travail, AR, 1935.

African society: "Our black Africans are cultivators or pastoralists, cultivating their own fields, maintaining their own herds." The next year, the inspector in the Ivory Coast thought that the worst fears about African responses to recovery were coming true:

The increase in the prices of all products has just in effect benefited the native with wealth and resources they had not hoped for and just when one counted on a movement of populations toward the Lower Coast [site of European plantations] the opposite has come about and the precipitous return of independent workers toward their villages imperils all harvests, above all that of coffee which could not be completed on time.[95]

Even if wages were increased, the problem would get worse, not just because short-term workers would reach their desired cash earnings too soon, but because higher wages and increased income from cash crops would reinforce another *kind* of economy, allowing Africans to solidify their attachments to soil and cattle and move out of the wage economy instead of into it.

The 1935 annual report on labor in French West Africa included the statistics in Table 2.1, revealing a small known labor force.[96] Here, although the inspector claimed that the current labor regulations dating from 1925 were working well, was evidence that it was not. The 1925 rules were built around the labor contract, which was supposed to be a free agreement specifying terms of employment. But few hirings – even recorded hirings – were based on contracts. Even they were poorly enforced.[97] As in several British colonies, the French Inspection du

Travail, created in 1932, had been allowed to lapse as an independent body in 1934, and the government-general's only labor inspector was dependent on each territory's government for information.[98]

The inspector's 1935 report said little about forced labor for private interests in the Ivory Coast, defended the necessity of deuxième portion labor, and thought Africans were no longer upset about having to do prestatory labor.[99] He did not worry about the "floating population" of urban centers, insisting that port labor functioned smoothly as "these dockers, yesterday cultivators" farmed in the growing season and loaded the produce onto ships in the dry season. Not everybody was this smug: other officials, like their counterparts in Mombasa, feared that "serious problems could result for the security of the city" when irregular laborers and criminals could not be distinguished from each other, and forced labor kept appearing and disappearing from official discussion.[100] Of more concern was an old issue, the tendency of workers from French Africa to flee to British.[101]

A half century into the colonial era, neither French nor British officials thought they had developed a secure labor supply and neither had created an apparatus capable of close observation of the labor force it had created. They had, however, come to a common awareness that taking labor power in bits and drabs from African societies whose integrity remained intact left enormous uncertainties about the quantity and quality of the labor that would be supplied, especially when colonial regimes needed it most.

Outside official circles came the beginnings of a critique of the labor system that went beyond the free labor ideology. A book published in 1933 under mission auspices, edited by Merle Davis and entitled *Modern Industry and the African*, began to push beyond the usual.[102] Davis agonized that industrial labor and migrancy were "shaking the foundations of Bantu life" – leaving workers vulnerable to disease and anti-social behavior in cities and leaving their communities economically vulnerable by their absence. The writers accepted as a fact that Africans were backward, impoverished, and helpless.[103] Migration disrupted the one strong asset Africans had – the "integrated solidarity and mutual dependence" of African communities while back and forth movements made the efforts of missionaries to educate them all the harder. "It is a striking inconsistency to encourage tribal integrity on the one hand under the system of indirect rule... and on the other hand to encourage its disruption by the present chaotic economic system." The authors' originality came in an argument for "stabilization" at two levels: insuring the conditions for sustained life in the village, allowing for agricultural improvements and education, and turning mine labor into a long term proposition, allowing Africans "the advantages of family life, of a permanently raised standard of living, of education and outlook."[104] Writing in the Depression, the team worried that too permanent an attachment to wage labor would lead to insecurity and unemployment – the village still seemed like a refuge – but considered that industrialization was both inevitable and in the end desirable.[105]

The argument had begun with the old theme of the disruption of African life by greedy outsiders, a tradition still carried on in much of the muckraking journalism about forced labor or by the peasant advocates like Delavignette.[106] But this study went further, accepting that mining had come to take a central place in the lives of some workers and arguing cautiously that the social consequences had to be faced in the mine towns themselves, by stabilizing the labor and building social institutions needed for their new life.[107]

This was precisely the point British official thinking avoided in the mid-1930s. Official circles recognized two sides to the argument that migration was disruptive of rural communities.[108] But they did not want to make the further leap that the Davis study did and look at urban society and permanent wage labor as a normal and positive part of social change. More generally, the fact that Africans routinely suffered from poor health, poor food, and other poor working conditions was most often seen in the official milieu as a consequence of their being primitive, not as a consequence of empire or a reason for imperial intervention.[109] In the early 1930s, governments felt obligated to intervene in cases of drought and famine, or to take minimal measures for individuals who had become detached from their social unit (including lepers and other outcasts). They were getting more and more interested in health issues and providing minimal medical services, and there was an argument in medical circles between those who blamed African backwardness and those who feared that migration and other aspects of social change led to "degeneration." But indirect rule implied that the fundamental social and economic structures of the continent were deeply rooted in African culture and could only slowly and subtly be changed without endangering the very basis for social and political stability.[110]

There were faint stirrings in government circles in the mid-1930s about this conception of colonial administration. The idea for an authoritative African survey, to be conducted by Lord Hailey, was first suggested in 1929; Hailey accepted the task in 1933, began his investigation in 1935, and published the results in 1938. Although conditions had continued to evolve during this interval (see chapter 3), his focus remained on Native Administration, and his basic message was that the institutions of indirect rule had to be modified, given the changing nature of African society and politics. He recognized that Africans left the tribal unit to work for wages, and that they sometimes remained in urban centers. He talked about them in the old category of "detribalized," but he recognized that this much-invoked term embraced different degrees of separation from the tribe. Back-and-forth migration, he recognized, implied for the government "a savings in that outlay on social services which in other circumstances might have to be incurred on behalf of industrialized labour, a fact which may be taken as reinforcing the claim for expenditure on the improvement of the reserves." Hailey, aware of the complications, still wanted to keep alive a conception of Africa based on apparently indigenous political and cultural units. Insisting that government should guard against coercion and exploitation, Hailey had little to say to the labor question beyond a generalized paternalism, acceptance of the fact that the economic contribution of African workers "carries an equivalent obligation by the community of its social responsibilities towards them."[111]

A break out of this framework was not evident in the colonial thinking of either the Socialist Party in France or the Labour Party in Britain. They joined criticisms of forced labor or other instances of uncontrolled capitalist exploitation in the colonies, but neither undertook a more fundamental critique of imperialism. Léon Blum, future prime minister under the Popular Front, took the civilizing mission seriously; like other socialist leaders before him, he saw a socialist France as capable of bringing progress to backward peoples, and had little faith in the cultural relativism of other leftists in his own party. The Communist Party had previously taken an anti-imperialist stance, arguing – in more Leninist than Marxist fashion – that the struggles of colonized peoples and of the European proletariat were parallel. But in 1935, when the Comintern line switched from "class against class" to the "popular front" against fascism, anti-colonialism slipped from the agenda: western European communist parties were now fearful of weakening their states and wanted to make common cause with the noncommunist left.[112]

In Britain, Labour's Lord Passfield (Sidney Webb) had run the Colonial Office for a time. In retrospect, commented Norman Leys bitterly in 1939, "The Labour Government of 1929–31 left scarcely a mark on Africa."[113] Even the most obvious reformist gestures – recognizing trade unions, preventing racial discrimination – remained unmade except in the most formalistic way, and no real challenge to the settlers of Kenya or the Rhodesias came from London. Passfield also left unchallenged the argument of the governor of Nyasaland that Africans could never leave the sacred and familiar villages of their ancestors. There was an extraparliamentary group of critics of empire. Even there, as inside the

Labour Party, the anti-slavery tradition – carried onto critiques of capitalist greed, land grabbing, coerced labor in its various forms, and the
social disruption caused by labor migration on rural communities –
remained the most telling. Keeping Africans out of the proletariat still
seemed a higher priority than forging a proletarian movement in
Africa.[114]

In Geneva, meanwhile, the ILO kept shoving complex social issues into
the strictures of free labor ideology. Following the League of Nations
Anti-Slavery Convention of 1926 and the ILO's forced labor convention
of 1930, the "Recruiting of Indigenous Workers" Convention of 1936
was the ILO's response to migration, organized recruitment, and contract
labor. The convention defined "recruiting" as "operations undertaken
with the object of obtaining or supplying the labour of persons who do
not spontaneously offer their services at the place of employment or at a
public emigration or employment office or at an office conducted by an
employers' organisation and supervised by the competent authority."
Behind these words lies a contrast between recruitment and the freest of
free labor: a worker presenting himself at the factory gate, and facing the
daily question of keeping, giving up, or losing his job. In the absence of
such a process, it was the duty of government to see that workers enrolled
at a distant location not be rounded up like slaves. Governments were
asked to ensure that the "possible effects of the withdrawal of adult males
on the social life of the population concerned" not be severe; that chiefs
not bring their authority to bear in the recruitment process; that
recruiters be licensed and controlled; that workers be given medical
examination; that families be encouraged to join the trip; that transportation be organized; and that repatriation be provided for. ILO
members were asked to "direct their policy where necessary and desirable
towards the progressive elimination of the recruiting of labour and the
development of the spontaneous offer of labour."[115]

Even at the end of the 1930s, the ILO's interventions into the colonies
remained focused on issues like contracts with "Indigenous Workers"
and penal sanctions. The latter issue proved as awkward to Great Britain
as the forced labor convention of 1930 had been to France. The use of
the state's criminal apparatus to ensure that workers did not break
contracts remained a key apparatus of British colonial legislation,
reflecting the notion that Africans did not take contractual obligations
seriously and had no property which could be seized under a civil action
for breach of contract. But penal sanctions came dangerously close to the
use of governments' coercive powers for private interests, and the ILO
agreed in 1939 that they should be phased out. Although Great Britain
went along with the new convention – and its humanitarian lobby saw

penal sanctions as a relic of the "bad old days of slavery" – there was considerable doubt even in the Colonial Office that the government could actually do without such sanctions.[116]

None of the pre-war ILO regulations applied to situations which that organization considered universal and normal in the noncolonial world, such as regulating working hours or providing for social security. Labor had a juridical significance – it was supposed to be "free" – and it had a social meaning in that it came *from* indigenous communities, so that pulling it out risked damaging their social fabric.

The critique of forced labor, as heard at the ILO or from humanitarian lobbies, accepted that European imperialism could do immense harm. This discourse focused on the conduct of European governments as the most relevant issue in colonial societies.[117] The labor process, and the ways in which workers built their lives as they labored, were not yet amenable to international discussion and regulation. The possible innovations that Africans might bring to work were not being examined. Opening up the labor question in all its complexity remained stymied by the fact that in France, Great Britain, and international organizations, the notion of an "African worker" seemed like two concepts incompatible with each other.

3   Reforming imperialism, 1935–1940

British officials were jarred from their complacency by the Copperbelt strike of 1935 and most importantly by the series of strikes and riots in the West Indies. French West Africa, unlike North Africa and Indochina, experienced no generalized or intense challenges. The Popular Front, however, self-consciously repudiated the colonial policies of previous governments, and when a strike wave came to French West Africa in 1936–37, it was more a consequence of reform – as African trade unionists saw and used a limited opening – than a cause of it. Yet whether the initial moves came from below or from above, French and British governments, trying to turn a new leaf in labor policy, strove to keep their initiatives within frameworks that remained thoroughly imperial. Both governments had great difficulty thinking about labor as a normal social category in an African context; faced with workers' troublesome presence, they wanted the labor question to be something else.

The most obvious explanation of why the period after 1935 opened up the labor question was the recovery from the Depression. As manpower needs rose, workers found that little had been done to improve resources, to make markets work more effectively, to provide decent housing. On the contrary, employers who had cut wages in the Depression were keeping them low even as prices of food and imported commodities began to increase.[1]

Such trends caught up first with British Africa: labor forces were more concentrated in mines and cities. French officials, meanwhile, faced an important piece of unfinished business: forced labor. The politics of growth were relevant here as well, for Popular Front leaders, convinced that the old system had reached its human and economic limits, felt they had to make a departure. Both regimes tried to assert control over the changing meanings of wage labor: the British government by subsuming labor under the question of development, the French by a dual strategy of minimizing the wage labor force while selectively using metropolitan methods for handling workers who remained necessary. Most important, neither government was able to keep the labor problem in its assigned boundaries.

Disorder and development in the British empire

The shock from below

The West Indian disturbances of 1935–38 shocked the Colonial Office and Parliament, and pushed policy makers toward drafting what became the Colonial Development and Welfare Act of 1940. Yet the relationship of African and West Indian events is important as well. The Northern Rhodesia strike of 1935 – and later the Mombasa general strike, the Dar es Salaam dock strike, and a series of notable strikes in the railways of the Gold Coast, all in 1939 – showed that the problem was empire-wide. All these events involved wage workers, all took place in critical communications or productive centers, each capable of shutting off the narrow channels responsible for colonial exports.

The disturbances in St. Kitts, Trinidad, and British Guyana in 1935, in Trinidad and Barbados in 1937, and in British Guyana and Jamaica in 1938 had begun as strikes organized by unions as well as less visible ties of affiliation. Strikes became violent and spread throughout urban areas, and often into the countryside. These movements touched a population where the boundaries of work and unemployment, of regular jobs and insecurity, were porous.[2] The Northern Rhodesian mineworkers strike of 1935 was organized without benefit of trade unions, and it spread from mine to mine, from mine town to mine town, by personal networks, dance societies, religious organizations, and eventually mass meetings. The movement embraced nonminers in the towns, women as well as men.[3]

British officials first reacted to African workers' actions by reaffirming tribal authority. The governor of Northern Rhodesia, Hubert Young, had only just remodelled his colony's system of government in line with the theory of indirect rule. He was surprised by the strike: agitators must be the cause. But the strike produced fatalities and worries that it might be repeated; a commission of inquiry set out to investigate.[4]

These post-mortems were to become key formats in which British officialdom would face the realities it had helped to create. The first time around the commission was determined to strengthen old structures against new pressures. The conflict, it realized, was serious, and the administration had failed to handle it effectively. It pointed to the spread and wide appeal of the strike movement among "natives" living in mine towns. The commission noted an "increasing amount of stabilisation of the native mining population, involving detribalisation and industrialisation." These African workers were living in town without chiefs and the constraints of tribal organization. That they shared the space with "unemployed or unemployable natives who are not under any effective control is one of the most important predisposing causes of the temper which led to the strikes." If such a population seemed like a "labour reserve" – a seemingly normal aspect of capitalist development which mine companies were loath to discourage – it also created "a fertile ground for subversive doctrines."

The commission saw its options in terms of two modes of authority: "The choice lies between the establishment of native authority, together with frequent repatriation of natives to their villages; or, alternatively, the acceptance of definite detribalisation and industrialisation of the mining population under European urban control." The commission could not accept the second option. It wanted instead to reaffirm the authority of rural chiefs and reinvigorate – via frequent repatriations and rigorous policing – the system of migrancy which brought workers to town on a temporary basis only.[5]

Governor Young now acknowledged that detribalization and industrialization were "the most important problems that confront not only Northern Rhodesia but other parts of Africa." He was willing to combine his system of native authority and the reinforcement of tribal life with "some system of detribalized life for those who have already severed or may subsequently desire to sever that connection." His choice of words is revealing: the initiative for urbanization was coming from Africans, not colonial policy, and tribal life constituted the norm from which deviations occurred. The Secretary of State for the Colonies, J. H. Thomas, agreed: "stabilisation of the native mining population" and "a degree of detribalization" were indeed taking place. "In those cases, however, where the miners continue to return frequently to their home districts, it seems desirable that the influence of tribal authority should, as far as possible, be preserved."[6] He too did not want to think about this question any more than Africans made him.

But the strike meant that the labor question could not remain unexamined. In November 1937, Major G. St. J. Orde Browne arrived in the colony to examine the labor situation, admitting that neither he nor anybody else knew much about it: the last annual report on economic and social progress had contained 28 lines on the subject of labor, under the heading "Health." The colony lacked administrative machinery and staff to focus on labor questions, and there had been "no detailed or consistent examination of the progress of industrialism and the sociological effects on primitive native society." But that last phrase itself constituted a social analysis of sorts, and Orde Browne argued for the preservation of primitive native society while facing the reality of labor migration. He favored a more closely regulated version of the status quo:

the appointment of labor officers, contracts, better identity documents, medical supervision, judicious official use of penal sanctions to enforce discipline, the withholding of a portion of wages to ensure that the worker would bring something back to his native community. The exercise of colonial authority was his hope for preventing labor migration from becoming "an industrial bleeding artery draining away the vitally necessary manhood of the country."[7]

Still, the fact that migrant workers would retain access to rural resources – rendering uncertain the urban labor supply – worried him:

An outstanding peculiarity of the African labour market must here be emphasized . . . the worker has almost complete control of the situation owing to the constant demand for his services. He is almost always able to find another employer anxious to engage him, so he can at any time leave his job and find another where conditions or type of work are more attractive... Briefly, discharge carries no threat for the African worker. Consequently 'desertion' is a common and demoralizing offence, so common that it handicaps any attempt to improve the labourer's lot by adding to the employer's responsibilities.

More vigorous managerial discipline only drove away workers, so that a "vicious circle is formed, where pay is very small, but cannot be raised owing to the miserable return offered."[8]

Here was the conundrum: Africans, in official eyes, were shaping the labor process as well as the labor market, and increasing demand for their services would only limit work discipline further as well as curtail the ability to control movement. Some years later, officials would argue that breaking through this vicious circle meant separating workers from the rest of African society, but for now Orde Browne had no solution beyond the authoritarian structure of the colonial state, enforcing through penal sanctions contracts on desertion-prone Africans and imposing minimal standards of treatment on greedy employers.[9]

The desire to reinsert the labor problem into the typologies of African society and African administration was even stronger outside the Copperbelt. Some months after the Northern Rhodesia strikes, London sent around a circular to colonial governments asking what they were doing in order to supervise labor conditions in their colonies and whether they wanted to create labour departments to focus on this task. Several colonies which had once had such specialized services had abandoned them during the Depression (chapter 2).

Not a single African governor wanted a separate department. Kenya had dropped its special service and considered labor "part of the normal duties of District Officers," backed up by labor officers who belonged to the native affairs department. Nigeria and the Gold Coast both admitted inadequacies in their inspection system, but did not want a specialist department to remedy them. Even in Northern Rhodesia – where "lack of contact" with workers had been recognized as a cause of a deadly strike – "it is the function of the district officers, not of a special department, to create and preserve" that contact. African labor was the domain of the Africa hands.

The Colonial Office was not entirely happy with this. P. V. Vernon noted that the economy was improving, prices and profits were up, and African workers should get some benefit. He thought labour departments could study problems of housing, transport, and "the relations between master and servant"; he feared continued reliance in some colonies on penal sanctions to enforce contracts meant that Britain risked being "held up at Geneva as a bad example"; and he thought restrictions on labor unions were "altogether obsolete" and likely to drive industrial organizations underground or "into the political field."[10] This memo aroused another Colonial Office official, J. E. W. Flood, to reassert the all-determining peculiarity of the African. Even considering doing away with penal sanctions, he claimed, would cause people to think that the Secretary of State "must have taken leave of his common sense." Africans were "not mentally suited" for trade unions. He even objected to the word workers: "One reason for this is that the so-called lowly paid 'worker' doesn't work."[11]

Higher-ups decided Africans could be called workers and they thought the Colonial Office needed to "keep pegging away" at ending penal sanctions, but should not insist on it. The Secretary of State himself told Parliament in July that, at least in some cases, he favored keeping labor matters under the rubric of native administration, because "that is the only way the natives understand it."[12] Nevertheless, the despatch that went out over Secretary of State Ormsby-Gore's signature in August of 1937 called labour departments the "ultimate aim" of the Colonial Office and asked colonial governments to "consider them." Vernon's concerns ended up in a suggestion that now that the economy was improving, governments should "take all steps in their power to ensure that a fair share of this benefit is passed on to the workers in their territories," although it did not propose how this was to be done. It reminded governments of ILO thinking about contracts and other matters, and warned them about the dangers of driving trade unions underground. It asked for reports on the situation of "lowly paid workers" and other matters.[13]

Between the time that the governors had pooh-poohed the idea of taking special administrative interest in labor and Ormsby-Gore's despatch of August 1937 asking them to think about it, the politics of the situation had changed. In late June, another wave of West Indian strikes and riots had occurred, in oil-rich Trinidad this time, leading as usual to parliamentary questions and the appointment of a commission of inquiry. Ormsby-Gore expressed complete surprise at "the sudden and unexpected outbreak of these disturbances."[14] The Trinidad strikes showed that the 1935 strikes had not been a fluke and that vital imperial resources could be put in jeopardy by the rag-tag army of the miserably employed. Rumblings were being heard from the Labour Party and the Trade Union Congress.[15]

So the circular went out, and by 1941 33 colonies had labour departments, up from 11 in 1937. Some colonies, Kenya for instance, waited until strikes began on their own territory before acting. In March, 1938, Orde Browne was appointed labour advisor to the Colonial Office. Ormsby-Gore told his new advisor, "You and I have got to be rather radical specimens of Tory."[16]

Creating labour departments implicitly recognized that a labor question existed, requiring specific attention and particular sorts of expertise. Orde Browne's vision was anything but an original one, but he brought a certain focus to labor. In 1939, he participated in a "course of instruction on labour problems in the Colonial Empire," the most revealing part of which consisted of metropolitan specialists telling colonial officials how they handled labor issues, from factory inspections to trade unionism. The colonial secretary expostulated about the recent "disturbances" and the "dangers of a policy of laissez faire." He looked toward the growth of trade unions and conciliation and arbitration machinery and stressed above all the need for "officers possessing knowledge of these delicate problems."[17] The Colonial Office was, however, already moving in a different direction, not toward confronting the labor problem as such, but in subsuming it under another category of analysis – the idea of development and welfare.

The old tendency had been to treat poverty and ill-health as inherent in the primitive nature of African society. Some research, notably by anthropologists, was opening up more complex ways of thinking about this.[18] Audrey Richards' *Land, Labour and Diet in Northern Rhodesia: An Economic Study of the Bemba Tribe* (based on research in the early 1930s and published in 1939) insisted that nutritional questions – the poor diet of the Bemba – required an integrated analysis of a social system. But at what level was one to seek a holistic answer? Richards wondered if the Bemba "were always indifferent agriculturalists, or whether their present attitude is something specific – the result of economic changes at the present day." She then asked whether the absence of young males at the mines did not shape the way farm work was valued and the material possibilities for doing it. The village was becoming a place "to rest," while men's sense of collective identity and the values which underlay it were shaped at the mines.[19] Richards did not fully answer her own questions, but she had set the "labor" field alongside the "tribal."

That the colonial economy might have something to do with malnutrition slowly entered the official mind. The Committee on Nutrition in the Colonial Empire, reporting in 1939, blamed the dietary deficiencies of colonial people on both "ignorance coupled with prejudice" – the old argument – and the fact that the standard of living was too low, that is, people ate badly because they were poor. Most interesting, the report decided that among urban wage laborers – seemingly part of the advanced sector of the economy – the situation was "nutritionally disastrous." The committee was carving out an area where the knowledge and power of an imperial government could be focused on an imperial problem.[20]

The most direct confrontation with the tribal model of Africa and the clearest effort to study a new social field was Godfrey Wilson's 1940 monograph, *The Economics of Detribalization in Northern Rhodesia.* He saw the presence of African men – and above all women – in the mine town he studied as a fact to be analyzed calmly and carefully. His survey showed that 40 percent of men were living with their wives in town; 70 percent of men in the town had spent two-thirds or more of their time in town since first leaving the village. Wilson criticized the imbalance between economic and social change and between the capital investment in the mines and the rate of improvement of rural conditions: this made for low wages and indifference to the conditions of labor, leading to tensions over class and race: "stabilization, rural development and increased trade would resolve those maladjustments and tensions." The solution, as well as the problem, lay in the modern economy. Here was a decisive step out of the narrow debate between those who blamed Africa's ills on the backwardness of its people and those who attributed them to degeneration in the face of western influence.[21]

But the next serious studies of the Copperbelt – largely thanks to mine-owners who did not want to know too much about their workers – were a decade away (chapter 9). Nor, as we have seen, was the government of Northern Rhodesia ready yet to accept stabilization as the reality Wilson had shown it to be or to see it as a desirable policy. African miners, in yet another strike, would be the next to add their voices to the discussion.

As bureaucrats and scholars, in their own ways, slowly began to come to grips with a reality that kept ahead of them, the parliamentary left in Great Britain was only showing hints that it was ready to get out of its older ideological framework. The West Indian riots forced the Labour Party to think more directly about labor in the colonies, but the party was still inclined to focus on criticisms of imperial coercion: the selfishness of white settlers, archaic labor practices like penal sanctions, bad working conditions, or suppression of trade unions. Some defended the so-called West African system of indirect rule and peasant production. Others, Fabians in particular, put less faith in peasants and markets and more on the British state, which would, in its role as "trustee" for backward peoples, guarantee their stake in the land, protect them against the vagaries of the market, and stimulate a new kind of development.[22] Some Labour Party leaders feared that industrial development in the colonies would cost British workers their jobs. Labourites more concerned with colonial affairs, notably Arthur Creech Jones, were forced to argue within their own party that "we must not condone the exploitation of native consumers for the benefit of British exporters."[23]

The strikes of the late 1930s provoked not only sympathy for West Indian workers but a concern that the colonial labor movement not stray too far from the British model of trade unionism. The TUC – heretofore little interested in the problems of workers in the colonies – organized in 1937 its own colonial labor committee, which worked closely with the Labour Party's imperial advisory committee. Its voice ensured that issues like trade union freedom and decent wages would be discussed in relation to colonies. Thus in 1939 the TUC wrote of "the persistence in many British Crown Colonies and Dependencies of deplorable conditions of native labour which are entirely incompatible with present-day social and industrial standards."[24] The Labour Party and the TUC agreed that the latter should itself take a role in providing "advice and watchful care" to fledgling colonial unions and discourage them from "spontaneous action at the grass roots."[25]

Trade unionism, at least, implied that one of the basic institutions of modern industrial capitalism was appropriate for colonial peoples. A few intellectuals on the moderate left – W. M. Macmillan most prominently – were willing to make a comprehensive case for the rapid application of British social and political models to colonial societies, especially in the West Indies and India.[26] Creech Jones, who came out of British trade union politics to become the party's leading colonial spokesperson, became a cautious critic of indirect rule and advocate of democratic institutions in the colonies. His most penetrating insight came in a parliamentary speech in 1939 in which he noted that officials' insistence on calling labor problems in the colonies "disorders" rather than "simple industrial disputes" made them harder to solve.[27] That was an important glimpse into the nature of official vocabularies: Creech Jones was trying to make the labor question in the colonies seem like part of the normal pattern of political life. But he did not quite convince himself: years later,

he too would argue that the backwardness of Africans required government to make many of their decisions for them (chapters 4 and 5). In fact,
Africa – "inhabited by peoples of primitive culture" – was for much of
the left a limiting case in regard to self-government and a prime case of
the need for a progressive government to offer protection against
marauding capitalists or the ignorance of the Africans themselves.[28]

The Labour Party's view of colonialism, in short, was not neatly distinguished from that of other dominant segments of British politics. As with
the Conservatives, only a few leading Labourites were interested in colonial issues. The more radical critics of empire were outside the party,
above all in the organizations of African or West Indian intellectuals that
were becoming increasingly active in London in the 1930s.[29]

Even as the strikes of the 1930s forced Labour Party leaders to notice
that "native workers" were workers as well as natives, they tended to
think of the issue more in terms of colonial poverty than in terms of the
labor question per se. Creech Jones put the problem in the West Indies
this way in 1940: "The unrest of recent years is fundamentally due to
economic causes and the absence of any wide means of political expression. The surplus population and unemployment issues can only be recti-
fied by bold economic and social planning."[30] That was how the Colonial
Office was addressing the problem too: the misery and the anger which
the strikes and riots had forced onto the British political agenda in the
late 1930s were being framed in terms of the question of "development."

The development framework

Malcolm MacDonald, who succeeded Ormsby-Gore in the Colonial
Office in May 1938, skillfully waved the spectre of more colonial disorders in front of his Cabinet colleagues who were loath to spend British
funds in such places. Whether MacDonald was using the crisis to accomplish goals he already had firmly in mind – using metropolitan funds to
improve the colonial standard of living – or whether he and his advisors
conceived of the development idea in their desperation to find a positive
response to the West Indian disorders is less than clear.[31] What concerns
us here is the way the question was posed: how a complex issue became
clarified, simplified, and symbolized within the decision-making apparatus of the British government.

It was fitting that all this occurred one hundred years after the emancipation of slaves in the British empire in 1838; indeed, the colonial secretary wanted to avoid marking the occasion for fear of "serious
disturbances in connection with the celebration of the centenary of the
ending of slavery."[32] Emancipation had been the central symbol of

progress in British colonial politics; in the late 1930s that symbol had become too dangerous to invoke.

Miserable wages, delapidated housing, woefully inadequate sanitation, and terrible anger were part of what the century of emancipation had brought to the descendants of slaves. This suffering was not producing much wealth for others – the islands produced too much sugar of which the empire had little need and not enough of anything else. The exception, Trinidad's oil, proved the rule: even an imperial resource vital "for the defence of London" was in the hands of miserable, grudging, potentially angry people of another race. Ormsby-Gore asserted it was therefore incumbent on the government "to prevent the causes – and especially any legitimate cause – of trouble arising."[33]

The misery of a Northern Nigerian peanut farmer might not be news, but strikes, riots, and fatalities led to parliamentary questions and commissions of inquiry. The investigatory reports – even such mild ones as Orde Browne's on Northern Rhodesia – documented the low wages and poor living conditions. In Africa the reports raised the puzzling question of why Africans were leaving the rural paradise of indirect rule for an urban hell against which they were now rebelling.[34] The West African model – production without wage labor – was meanwhile tarnished by the cocoa hold-ups in the Gold Coast in 1931–32 and 1937–38, where even the relatively prosperous African cocoa farmers and traders refused to sell their crops, protesting against low prices and the imperial system of cocoa buying.[35] The Gold Coast's railwaymen and other workers joined the empire-wide wave of strikes in 1939, and its governor thought that publicity about the West Indian situation had contributed to the "under-current of unrest making its insidious way through the labour ranks." A strike wave in Sierra Leone in 1939 was linked to the radical political organizer I. T. A. Wallace Johnson and his West African Youth League – posing threats of cross-colonial linkages and political mobilization which the government vigorously intervened to repress.[36] Looked at across the empire, the disorders seemed even more disturbing and dangerous than they did individually. Colonial governments used considerable force – Northern Rhodesians, Trinidadians, Jamaicans, and others had been shot to death – against some "disturbances," but handled some strikes – Mombasa in 1939 – delicately. But Creech Jones' idea of treating strikes as normal parts of a wage labor economy had not gained clear ascendancy over colonial officials' tendency to see them as disorder to be put down.

In this atmosphere, the Colonial Office awaited with trepidation what they knew would be the most important and the most negative report of all – that of the Royal Commission on the British West Indies.

MacDonald and his staff had been working on recasting the old Colonial Development Act of 1929 since the middle of 1938; the Royal Commission had been appointed at around the same time, and the next round of disturbances, in Jamaica in May–June 1938, had prodded the process along. As the date of release of the report approached in late 1939, MacDonald decided he wanted his new development initiative to be announced on the same day. Eventually he decided not to publish the commission's report at all, but only a summary of its recommendations and the announcement of the new act.[37] The key words in the title of the legislation reveal that this publicity stunt could not be separated from a more basic restructuring of political language: the Colonial Development and Welfare Act.

Development, before 1940, was not a word regularly associated with government policy toward the poverty of colonized people. Joseph Chamberlain's late nineteenth century image of developing the "imperial estates" represented a landowners' conception. The Colonial Development Act of 1929 was for an explicit project of social imperialism: to improve the capacity of colonial economies to trade with the United Kingdom in order to bring down unemployment in the metropole. In practice, the 1929 Act accomplished even less than intended: only £5 million was spent over a decade in all the colonies.[38]

But in 1940 "development" was linked to "welfare." And "welfare" meant rather a lot in the domestic politics of Great Britain. Health, education, water supplies, the administrative machinery to resolve industrial disputes and settle wage claims, all of these issues – unlike questions of traditional authority and customary law – crossed the line between metropole and colony. These were among the headings under which money in the new act was to be spent – up to £5 million per year.

Nowhere did the act say that the standards of colonial welfare – wages, schools, housing – should *equal* those recognized in England. But merely talking about welfare standards – and the discussions in the Colonial Office touched on this point – raised the possibility of comparison. The government did say that money intended for welfare eventually had to be covered by the improvement of the economic position of the colonies; but for the moment, they were too poor, and the British Treasury had to assume some of the costs of *both* welfare services and economic development, on the assumption that improvement on both scores would one day lead to self-sufficiency.[39]

The discussion of the act thus put on the table the question of what was the relationship of social welfare and economic development, and the relationship of both to preventing disorder. What is interesting about this particular debate was how open the discussion was: later, Colonial Office leaders would become so eager to assert that development meant welfare that they could no longer ask what the connection might be.

MacDonald decided early that he wanted some kind of dramatic gesture – underscored by the provision of funds from the British Treasury – explicitly repudiating the doctrine that each colony's budget had to be met with its own resources. He had to convince the Cabinet and above all the Treasury to go along: parsimony was their rule, the empire not their priority. The war broke out in the middle of the debate – ordinarily a sufficient excuse to defer any nonmilitary expenditure – but MacDonald made shrewd use of this too to weave development, welfare, and disorder into a fabric that looked far tighter than Colonial Office intimates knew it to be.

When MacDonald in June 1938 persuaded the Cabinet to send the Royal Commission to the West Indies, he warned that "the Government would have to be ready to spend more money on the West Indies than at present... It would be disastrous to send a Royal Commission and then reject its proposals purely on financial grounds."[40] The Cabinet entered the process knowingly, but the Colonial Office wanted to broaden the scope of spending as well as increase its amount. MacDonald made clear that "unprecedented" intensity of unrest in the West Indies was the issue, and it was "symptomatic of more than purely local and temporary discontent":

Elsewhere there has been evidence of similar unrest in the form of labour strikes which, in the present condition in the Colonies, may at any time develop into serious trouble... [The] primary cause underlying the unrest is the very low standard of economic and social conditions among the colonial communities.[41]

By defining the colonial problem in terms of welfare, the Colonial Office was setting aside many other possible definitions. The West Indies in particular posed a question of class: to what extent did the poverty of the masses derive from the monopoly of most land by a small planter class? The Colonial Office knew that the landowner-dominated Jamaican legislature "could hardly be expected to take a strong line in the interest of the inarticulate and disorganised native cultivators." This was held to be a reason for a centrally directed development program, bypassing the input of local elites as much as peasantries. But the class theme dropped out of the discussion quickly: centralization was justified in the name of British scientific knowledge and the need for coordination rather than by the opposition of class interests.[42]

Outside of the Colonial Office the class argument was being made, most interestingly by a young West Indian graduate student, W. Arthur Lewis, who was eventually to be a founder of the discipline of development economics, a leading advisor to the Colonial Office, and in the end a winner of the Nobel Prize in economics. While still a student at the London School of Economics, Lewis offered his services to the Fabian Research Bureau as a pamphleteer. He wrote *The British West Indies* in 1935 and *Labour in the West Indies* in 1939.[43] Lewis' dislike of the West Indian planters was strong and stuck with him even as his economic theorizing evolved. He saw them as an obstacle to progress. Lewis thought that the movements of the 1930s had brought together the educated and the working classes of the West Indies, showing issues of race and poverty to be intertwined. For the Labour Movement to seek its objectives by constitutional means required changing the constitution, giving ordinary people a greater voice in electoral politics. The Labour Movement in the West Indies "has already behind it a history of great achievement in a short space of time. It will make of the West Indies of the future a country where the common man may lead a cultured life in freedom and prosperity."[44]

But Lewis' contention that West Indians should seize the initiative through *politics* contrasted to the Colonial Office's attempt to seize it through administration. Seize it was what officials thought they had to do: the strikes and riots had been a blow to their sense of control. A senior Colonial Office official now summed it up this way: "There have been two motives behind this proposal, the one a desire to avert possible trouble in certain colonies, where disturbances are feared if something is not done to improve the lot of the people, the other a desire to impress this country and the world at large with our consciousness of our duties as a great colonial power."[45]

The discussion within the Colonial Office – none of it for public consumption – was filled with this kind of language. "Social services" became a watchword, the sign that something *new* was being done. A new social services department was created within the Office in early 1939, charged with looking after labor conditions, nutrition, public health, education, housing, and so forth and to demonstrate that Britain "acts as a beneficial trustee for its subject peoples."[46] Meanwhile, as new drafts of possible legislation were discussed, officials tried to sort out the differences between what they really wanted and what they had to say to convince the Cabinet and in particular the Treasury.

Up to then, colonies that could not pay their bills from revenues they generated could ask the Treasury for a grant-in-aid, and the metropole would issue loans for initiatives like railways if they met certain investment criteria. Spending money merely to improve the standard of living of colonial peoples was new. And that is what officials wanted: "The crux, as I see it, comes when we have to consider social services... The general objective, to increase the well-being and happiness of the

Colonial peoples is clear, but it is about the only thing that is clear."[47]

The Colonial Office strategy was to make the new development act look like a modification of the old, but more generous and adding a social services component to an economic one. So officials argued that, particularly in time of war, Britain needed empire resources, and that capital spending that would increase the output of raw materials, and a healthier, better educated work force, would be more productive. The pay-off would be longer term than the old idea of colonial self-sufficiency allowed. The Colonial Office insisted that social, economic, and political objectives were all consistent. But in the midst of one drafting round, George Creasy of the Colonial Office wondered if the pandering to the Treasury's productionism had gone too far. The draft which called for increasing the productivity of the empire

appears to me to lay too much emphasis on the desirability of making the African (or West Indian etc.) into a more efficient producer or labourer for the needs of the country. This is a point which may, of course, well appeal to the Treasury... I feel, however, that so far as the Colonial Office is concerned, our real aim should be the more general one of turning the African into a happier, healthier and more prosperous individual, in which case all the other subsidiary objects will automatically be attained.[48]

The Colonial Office memorandum sent on 11 October 1939 to the Chancellor of the Exchequer under MacDonald's signature was a marvelous combination of imperialist sentimentality, hard-nosed realism about the need for resources for the war effort, and above all a play on the fear of disorder, which goes so far toward confessing the Colonial Office's sense of vulnerability that it is hard not to believe the fear was genuine.

The strikes, general strikes, and riots, the memorandum argued, reflected "a similar sense of grievance" stemming from "unsatisfactory economic and social conditions," unemployment, bad housing, bad government services. Bigger dangers lay ahead:

if we fail to take action in the near future, there is a strong probability of criticism reviving and increasing and leading to unruly conduct by masses of people in the West Indian Colonies and elsewhere, which our reputation could ill afford in peace time and still less in war. We know what form such trouble takes. On some pretext or other there is a strike accompanied by rioting and sometimes even by murder; as often as not our police have to fire on the crowds; troops are even called out; and occasionally it is necessary to summon a war-ship in aid to land marines.

A new Colonial Development and Welfare Act would show that Britain had "a policy of reasonable development of schemes for employment and social services," intended "to confirm colonial peoples in their general attachment to us and to bind them more closely to us throughout the troublesome period of war." The program was to be funded at the rate of £1 million per year, just what the Royal Commission had said it would recommend. Some would be spent on "the services which are now normally a part of civilized government": medicine, health, education, social services. More would go to agriculture departments, to basic infrastructure, to immediately productive projects that would yield more raw materials, and to labour departments to help them deal with "labour disputes and disturbances." The Colonial Office was unsure – with good reason – that its administrative machinery could handle this level of development spending during the war. But it was to be a symbol to colonial peoples that their own material concerns would at last be addressed and to British opinion that a sense of imperial mission had been restored.[49]

The Treasury's reservations came straight from the debate over metropolitan welfare: "it is not very far short of amounting to saying that the only thing to do is to put the Colonies on the dole from henceforth and forever." The breaking of the precedent of colonial self-sufficiency might imply, officials feared, that a given level of social services would become the minimum that a self-consciously civilized and benevolent power could accept, regardless of the capacity of each colony – or perhaps colonies in general – to pay for them at any point in their future.[50] The Treasury staff probably did not realize that they had come up with an argument for decolonization.[51]

Here was an argument which the Colonial Office wanted to fudge. They insisted that it was "impossible to draw any logical dividing line" between economic and social services in that "certain social services were in themselves economic development, i.e. they were necessary for the mise en valeur of the Colonies."[52] Why the French expression was used in this meeting between Colonial Office and Treasury civil servants is not apparent, but the argument was in many ways a sound one. It became known later as human capital theory: improving the productivity of manpower promoted growth. It could, but would it? And by how much compared to other ways in which the money could be used, abroad and at home? The steps in this argument were not filled in: the Colonial Office *wanted* to believe that workers who had better housing, better medical care, and a better water supply would be more productive. But they were not going to look too carefully at the question.

The Colonial Office, in the climactic days of drafting the bill in January 1940, feared that the Treasury "will not have any mention of the word 'welfare' or 'social services'." That was exactly what the Colonial Office could not allow, as Henry Moore made clear: "Politically the whole point is that we should be able to make a big thing of the 'Welfare' side. If it is just going to be 'development' on the old lines it will look merely as if we are going to exploit the Colonies in order to get money to pay for the war!" MacDonald backed up his officials by assimilating the argument to the defense of the British Empire: "My only comment is that if we are not now going to do something fairly good for the Colonial Empire, and something which helps them to get proper social services, we shall deserve to lose the colonies and it will only be a matter of time before we get what we deserve."[53]

The Colonial Office won the argument, and the next month the new bill was announced to the world bearing in its title the word "welfare" separated from "development" by that powerful and ambiguous "and." Before Parliament, MacDonald made a passionate plea for doing something right for the colonial people in the midst of a war in which they were proving their loyalty. But he seemed anxious to refute any inference that their standard of living be brought to an unrealistically high level:

it would be a profound error to suppose that economic and social standards which are established here and which are rightly considered as a minimum standard by our people in this country, can be translated at once, suddenly, to the many different peoples in the many different countries of the Colonial Empire.

Colonies now needed to go beyond their resources so that they could later develop into "self-supporting units" that could support a wide range of social programs. He carefully avoided promises of long-term support for the social services of even the most poorly endowed colony or providing any colony with services equivalent to those of the metropole.[54]

For all the tying together of increasing production, providing social services, and generating employment, the internal argument over the bill made it clear that the cause of this new approach was African and West Indian protest. Here too was a sociological theory no more clearly specified than the human capital approach to economic growth: protest was caused by objectively bad social and economic conditions, and disorder would be remedied by direct action to improve those conditions.[55]

Even the promise of improved welfare, the Colonial Office hoped, would quiet disorder. In fact, the war overwhelmed the new initiative, and Great Britain's needs for its colonies' resources outstripped its willingness or ability to devote resources to them. Nevertheless, the symbolism of the act was even more important than its authors envisaged. It had been intended as a reaffirmation of empire: that the imperial power was in control of complex and difficult events, that it could acknowledge and remedy its own weaknesses, that its sense of mission was restored, and that it could set forth its principles for others to acknowledge. The discussion had moved the meaning of the imperial mission beyond vague and inherently ethnocentric concepts like civilization and trusteeship toward something more seemingly specific but one which raised questions that could be dangerous to open. After acknowledging how little had been accomplished in the century since emancipation in the West Indies and the half century since the partition of Africa, could officials fashion and pay for a program that addressed the magnitude of the problem? What record of material progress would justify a continued British presence? How much inequality in social services could an empire accept? Would striking workers in colonial cities be proof that the British Empire was not fulfilling its mission and would colonized people demand different standards from those officials deemed appropriate?

Socialist colonialism and labor in French Africa

The implicit admission that past goals had not been met, so evident in the discussions within the British Colonial Office in the late 1930s, was echoed across the Channel, but in a different way. The election of the Popular Front in 1936 owed little to colonial issues but brought to power people willing to note the mistakes of past regimes and to think about empire in new ways. Although the British Labour governments of 1929–31 and 1945–51 largely left innovation to the Colonial Office, French colonial policy – particularly in regard to North Africa and Indochina – was the subject of more direct political controversy. When the new colonial minister, Marius Moutet, appointed a man who was both an experienced colonial servant and a socialist, Marcel de Coppet, to be governor-general of French West Africa, it was a signal that he would try to shape a colonialism that was simultaneously socialist and within the boundaries of colonial professionalism.

Some scholars have argued that the Popular Front's plans, let alone its accomplishments, constituted a less radical break with past policies than their architects pretended. The Popular Front did not question colonialism per se. On the contrary, it saw a socialist government bringing its message beyond metropolitan France: "I am truly the missionary of revolutionary France..." Moutet told the Chambre des Deputés, associating – as French socialists had before him – the legacy of the French revolution with the colonizing impulse of the missionary.[56] Nor did the Popular Front break from the old "pacte coloniale," a state-controlled division of labor between an industrial metropole and colonies devoted to primary products.[57] Such criticisms, to a certain extent, measure Popular Front thinking against a later era, when fostering political independence and industrialization became the markers of progressive policy. In regard to

Africa, such issues had barely been raised in the mid-1930s, by African politicians any more than radical Europeans.

It is more useful to ask precisely where Popular Front colonial policy broke out of older frameworks, where it remained caught in them, and where it reshaped discourse for future regimes. The labor question is a case in point: Moutet, de Coppet, and their colleagues tried to think through questions which their predecessors had pretended did not exist. They discovered that the subterranean structures of labor recruitment had so deeply penetrated the meeting point of laborers, chiefs, local administrators, and colons that Paris could only partially enter it. The following pages probe the limitations on a self-consciously reformist project in a colonial situation; they explore the constraints of knowledge, of imagination, and of the ability to exercise control at ground level.

The Popular Front's attempt to get to tackle the issue of forced labor was part of a two-pronged approach to the labor question. First, Moutet and his advisors insisted that heavy-handed intervention into African society – through demands for labor and taxation – had done more harm than good, and that the answer was to permit Africans to evolve in so far as possible within their own communities. This neotraditionalism was romantic – it was rooted no doubt in the pastoral fantasies of rural Frenchmen who had gone to Paris – and did not address in any substantive way the particular structures of affiliation that existed in French Africa.[58] Labor policy was based on a critique of colonialism gone wrong, and so it offered Africans relief, if not a blueprint for the future. The labor problem could best be approached by minimizing it. Moutet made this policy explicit to the Chambre des Deputés: "our entire colonization program is based on the indigenous peasantry and all that we can do to facilitate the task of the black or yellow peasant constitutes the true work of colonization." True colonization was not compatible with forced labor: "that man can work, he must have liberty, that is that he can apply himself to his own cultivation... It is also necessary to free the workers from certain corvées, the corvée of transport, of porterage, of road-building, or bridge-building." After his trip to Africa in 1937, he repeated: "we have no interest in developing a wage labor force. We must on the contrary allow Africans to cultivate their own land."[59]

The Popular Front saw the "equipment" of Africa – improved transport, mechanization of production, better health services, and education – to be the key to reconciling economic development with peasant society through reducing the demand for labor and raising the efficiency of the needed workers. It proposed a new development fund – hoping to make the same break with the doctrine of colonial self-sufficiency that the British government made in 1940.[60] A vigorous development initiative –

with government planning assuring that it would reflect the "general interest" of colonies as well as the metropole – would at the same time show that France had found a progressive colonial policy, "une politique altruiste."[61] But the upper house of the French legislature, like its predecessors, proved unwilling to spend the money, so that in practice Popular Front reform had more to do with what the government stopped doing than its active promotion of development.[62]

Second, the Popular Front believed that in so far as a modest number of workers came into being, they really were workers, with the same human attributes and needs as workers in France. No sooner had new legislative reforms, including the 40-hour week and paid holidays, been applied to workers in France in the summer of 1936 than the Colonial Ministry began to contemplate applying them to the colonies. The government did in fact extend trade union rights, with limitations, to Africans. Legally – and for the most part in practice – the government in these two years treated union organizing and strikes as ordinary events. The discussion itself created an important analytical precedent: African workers and even protesting African workers could be a normal part of social life. In this regard, de Coppet was quite clear what his reference point was: he was trying to "provide the wage labor force with a professional organization analogous to that of the metropole."[63]

De Coppet also thought that Africans could be socialists, those few of them who qualified for the franchise, that is. He politicked with them, and encouraged pro-Popular Front political associations to include educated Africans as well as metropolitans.[64] As political activity heated up by 1937, most notably in Senegal, a curious pattern of alliances emerged: Lamine Guèye, the socialist mayor of Dakar, and his trade unionist supporters acted as allies of the governor-general, while Galandou Diouf, deputy and rival of Lamine Guèye, intrigued both with right-wing, anti-Popular Front business interests and with certain African groups left out by the elitist African socialists. All this came to a head in the tragic incident at Thiès in September 1938, which revealed that the division of African society into the educated, workers, and peasants failed to address the complexity of Africans' circumstances and aspirations.

In its first months in office, the Popular Front self-consciously undertook a series of inquiries into colonial policies. The upshot was a plan to shift the emphasis from European colonization to "la colonisation indigène," encouraging increased production and indigenous prosperity via improved transport, the organization of cooperatives, and other forms of assistance. On the labor front, a report prepared for a never-completed inquiry left a revealing diagnosis:

For a long time we said, instead of peasantry, manpower, and we in effect considered our native populations as a mass reservoir of manpower, and not as a peasantry organized socially into a community of workers and delimited geographically into nations. In reality, there is no manpower for European colonization that does not come from a native peasantry.

The report noted how little European colons had to date accomplished – 200,000 hectares brought under cultivation in French West Africa. "And yet, the indigenous peasantry is already profoundly disturbed by such a feeble colonization. And the European colonist already has great difficulty in finding labor and he seems from the point of view of labor, in the coastal regions, very nearly to have attained the *limits of extension.*"[65]

That wage labor for Europeans had reached its limits when so little had been planted and when less than 2 percent of the population was working for wages, was an admission of a failed approach. The rhetoric of limits coming from local officials had jostled before with extravagant claims to an imminent *mise en valeur*, and similar differences would appear again; but now the limits to wage labor were to be a central presumption of policy.[66] Moreover, the commission acknowledged the role of compulsion in obtaining what labor there was, arguing that it hurt African societies, put the administration in a hypocritical position, and was not leading to a freer labor system:

It is a position that is fairly badly defined: without administrative pressure, no manpower for the colons but this pressure has no juridical base and no sure rules. Most often the Administration furnishes labor under the table while guarding against possible excess by hiring through the Inspection du Travail, by regulations regarding both treatment of recruited laborers and by a delimitation of native reserves, where colons cannot acquire concessions.

The remedy was to stop trying to extract individuals from communities. The communities should come first, and the extension of export agriculture into zones should take the form of "veritable villages, *villages of colonization*," around European plantations. The villages should be given help from a "fonds colonial": basic infrastructure, the organization of sociétés de prévoyance, and rural schools.[67]

This was the basic plan: those Africans who could be classified as workers should be treated as such, even while others should be thought of in their communal and traditional roles. The most important concrete action taken early on – in November 1936 – was to restore the inspectorate of labor, as an independent office and with Pierre Tap occupying the role of inspector for French West Africa as a whole.[68] Whereas only the Ivory Coast had an inspectorate in early 1936, the other colonies were soon to get theirs. This meant more information – especially with a Ministry in Paris that now wanted to know. This too suggests a particular mode of thinking about labor: a regular bureaucratic apparatus would focus on a normal administrative problem.

From Gouverneur Providence to Apostolat du Travail: the case of the Ivory Coast

As Moutet, who had virtually no knowledge of Africa, got to work, there was little indication that he realized how far French Africa – including the potentially rich Ivory Coast – was from a world of "normal" workers and productive peasants.[69] Even de Coppet, installed in Dakar in September 1936, was not yet talking openly about forced labor. He had, however, good reason to be sensitive to the issue; earlier in his career, as lieutenant-governor in Chad, he had opposed recruitment of labor for the Congo-Océan Railway.[70] But the colons of the Ivory Coast soon precipitated a crisis: believing that their labor supplies were diminishing as Africans began to get more cash for their own crops, and unwilling to raise wages, they loudly demanded more vigorous recruitment from the administration. Their timing was not wise, and in late 1936 and early 1937 the subterranean world in which labor recruitment had taken place was opened up for a time to closer scrutiny.

The problem originated the previous December when the governor of the Ivory Coast had agreed to lowering the minimum wage, claiming it was "too high" given the low prices of the Depression. The lowest wage was reduced from 2 francs a day to 1.25. Moutet, in July 1936, wanted to know why this was done. The governor-general – de Coppet had not yet taken office – replied with some embarrassment that he had gone along with the governor because his decision had been made after "wide consultation" and was justified by lowered prices, the need to reduce production costs, and the improvements in working conditions labor inspectors were imposing on employers.[71]

The wage reductions came as prices and demand for labor were rising again and as observers were noting that higher crop prices meant less labor was forthcoming.[72] But the colons were not counting on wage incentives. They expected to be provided with workers – a point that could hardly have been misunderstood in Abidjan and Dakar, but which could not be discussed. The governor-general, however, knew that Moutet's concern could mean trouble, and he sent a circular to the colonies informing them of Paris' anxiety about "the modesty of minimum wages." He wanted them to be examined systematically in the light of "the normal budget capable of assuring the worker the satisfaction of his minimal needs and those of his family."[73]

De Coppet was warned of the *sub rosa* recruitment in October via a briefing paper from a relatively progressive official of the colonial ministry, Henri Labouret. Local administrators were receiving "imperative telegrams" from headquarters telling them "to procure for such and such a firm the workers that it asks for" and they "have furnished in the past and continue to furnish in the present recruits who are neither free nor voluntary." In the margin, de Coppet noted, "Send soon an imperative circular on this burning subject because I want to take a very clear position in this regard."[74] In early November 1936, de Coppet wrote a circular letter to his governors stating, "According to information reaching me in regard to certain colonies of the Group the error of direct intervention of administrative authority at the occasion of recruitment of labor for private individuals has been repeated. These are practices which I would not accept." Labor offices should facilitate relations between employers and employees, centralize requests for labor, and publicize job offers – in accordance with the 1926 legislation – but no more. "No hesitation is possible, administrative authorities, whatever their place in the hierarchy, should not intervene directly to procure labor for any enterprise or any individual who wants to recruit it." He cited the 1930 forced labor convention of the ILO.[75]

The governor of the Ivory Coast insisted in reply that the Ivory Coast already did things this way: "at no moment has administrative authority had to intervene either directly or indirectly in labor recruitment." He enclosed a circular to Commandants de Cercle, dated 25 September 1936, suggesting that they allow employers into their cercles "to find, by their own means and without administrative intervention, the workers necessary for the proper functioning of their enterprises." The governor-general did not quite believe him, saying he had a report from the Inspecteur du Travail which referred to both voluntary and recruited labor "which leads one to suppose the exercise of administrative pressure at the moment of engagement." He reminded him that administrative recruitment for private purposes was now banned.[76]

Before this reply, however, the governor sent his boss a second letter, saying that during a time of "transitions" the current coffee harvest was at risk and asking "that you authorize me, *by the intermediary of the Office du Travail*, to take dispositions so that the harvest is assured, it being understood that minimum wages of workers will be raised to rates corresponding to a just remuneration." In the margins of the Dakar copy of this letter is written, "yes, certainly, m. de Coppet." The governor continued, "I am moreover convinced that, the day when the workers will be sufficiently compensated, the labor question will no longer be posed in the Ivory Coast," and here the marginal note says, "exactly, m.c." De Coppet, having sternly warned against administrative intervention in recruitment, now wrote the governor to permit the intervention of labor offices "to facilitate relations between employers and employees..."[77]

De Coppet was thus clearly complicit in ordering the government labor bureaucracy to assure the harvest of 1936-37 through rather suspicious means. The new governor of the Ivory Coast, Mondon, had only arrived there in December 1936. He later claimed that local administrators, apparently sensing the change in atmosphere, had abruptly stopped recruiting in September and October. He argued that the period of forced recruitment – when treatment was bad, wages low if paid at all, and food and lodging inadequate – was followed "without transition" by this period of official refusal to do anything. On his arrival he found an "agonizing" situation: "It was a total work stoppage on the majority of plantations" at the moment of the harvest, threatening to ruin both white and black planters. He met with the Chamber of Commerce and administrators on the day of his arrival. Two days later, he came up with an entirely new organization of recruitment.[78]

Mondon's plan raised wages to close to where they had been before the cut – 1.75 to 2 francs per day – and established "regional committees" to assess the ability of each cercle to provide men. Mondon claimed that employers did the actual recruiting themselves, but he did not say how.[79] Six months after his reform, Mondon insisted that "The harvest was saved by men *freely* hired, usefully counseled I will not deny, by the Commandants de Cercle. And it was thus that we were able to see unfold the harvest which was the most beautiful that the Ivory Coast has ever known." The reforms, he claims, benefited black planters as well as whites.[80]

De Coppet was skeptical. He did not see that employers were doing much to make work more attractive – nothing was being done to set precise standards for working hours or housing. Instead of leaving recruitment to employers themselves, the plan had shifted the initiative from the Commandant de Cercle to the Office Régionale du Travail. "But after as well as before, the Administrator is the working mainspring of intervention and the system, in these conditions, can only be considered as a transitory regime. I would be happy to know what measures were taken to make a reality of recruitment by the efforts of the employers, a question to which *I attach great importance.*"[81]

The Inspecteur du Travail of the Ivory Coast, in a detailed chronology written later in 1937, declared, "All this is painful to write." Caught between orders to "proscribe *constraint*" and the "brutal lack of hands" for the coffee harvest in October and November 1936, "there were no other remedies than to resume recruitment with administrative intervention, the loss of laborers having been observed even on indigenous plantations."

When, according to the chronology, the governor-general's circular of November banning official participation in recruitment arrived, some officials took this to mean they were "totally rid of the trouble inherent in the hiring of workers in their territory." The situation "was grave; it threatened to become tragic." Here the report noted the change of vocabulary: "The so called 'authorizing' telegram was moreover radically suppressed." Instead, circulars went out betwen January and March 1937 stressing the role of the administrator "to incite the native to work in view of his well being." Available labor was inventoried, demands for it centralized by the regional committees. Now in August, 2,500 laborers were being requested for the cocoa and coffee harvests. This would be difficult, for Africans were engaged in their own harvests. Officials were contemplating new methods – for example paying workers a share of the harvest (as in the Gold Coast) – or trying to find foreign laborers, from Guinea, the Soudan, or even Indochina. There was hope that the completion of the railway from Abidjan to Ougadougou would help.[82]

The Chief Inspecteur du Travail of French West Africa, Pierre Tap, was less ambiguous: "As to 'recruits' by contract, none are really voluntary, they respond by desertion to the pressure of which they have been the object." Mondon countered by asserting that Tap was out of date and too pessimistic. But he was not about to claim that the invisible hand of the market had taken over, and he quoted Tap's own praise for the administrator as "counselor and guide" back at him. In a series of letters, he continued to claim that the lot of workers "is clearly satisfactory and tends to improve every day" and that planters were "flourishing."[83]

The uncertainty behind the assertions of successful transition is obvious, but the administration was no longer united in trying to pretend that forced labor did not exist. The humble local administrator was no doubt even more unsure than before what he should do.

De Coppet had no way of penetrating what went on in the rural districts where the fine line between encouragement and pressure was or was not being crossed. His respect for the hierarchy of administration meant that his questions had to be channeled through the governor of the territory in question. Firing Mondon might have made the confrontation between colons and the Popular Front too direct and might have risked an immediate harvest for a distant future of peasant production. It wasn't certain that Mondon was lying.[84] What is clear in the correspondence in the first half of 1937 is that the carefully chosen words of administrators – de Coppet's as much as Mondon's – did not fully illuminate processes more complex and more nuanced than the dichotomy of free and coerced labor.

Mondon found a phrase to make vivid his new policy: "apostolat du travail," preaching the virtues of labor. As he exhorted his Commandants de Cercle in February 1937, "In the apostolate of work which we must undertake, it is better to convince than to impose, to persuade than to constrain." But he did not seem to be talking about a labor market functioning without administrative assistance: he wanted administrators to inventory the manpower in their cercles; he had expectations for the crops that should come forth; and he was sure that Ivory Coast Africans could provide 25,000 to 30,000 workers for private and public enterprise and still grow more crops. Mondon also lectured the employers on the need to mechanize and therefore reduce their labor demands.[85]

In July, he again circularized – in capitals – for his "APOSTOLAT DU TRAVAIL," also naming it "the great school of work by consent." Local officials were the teachers. They were to assure workers that they would be "well and regularly paid" and well fed. Administrators were told to "issue unceasing publicity so that work will no longer be considered in the Ivory Coast as a fall from grace but as an elevation" and as a step toward "so many material satisfactions that it would be easy to obtain."[86]

By this time, Mondon was already proclaiming success for his version of free labor. The Bureau Permanent du Travail likewise claimed victory for "the new methods of recruitment based on persuasion and gentleness." The administrator was no longer a "purveyor of labor," but was fulfilling his role "to incite natives to work." Wages were up again: varying between 2.5 and 4 francs per day. Laborers were now agreeing to contracts, and noncontract labor was flowing toward indigenous planters, who were now coming to labor offices to get their share of the fruits of the "placement" effort.[87]

At the end of 1937, the governor reported that 49,993 men had entered into contracts, up from 23,136 in 1936. The labor inspector claimed that the contracts' clear terms had obtained the confidence of the African. The system, he concluded with a curious caution after the previous extravagance, had moved toward freedom but not so fast as to allow forced labor to be replaced by "barbarism." The language recalls that of British officials in the 1830s, who had advocated a slow transition from slavery in the West Indies to free labor so as not to allow a reversion to "barbarism" or "savage sloth."[88] Nevertheless, a special report to the governor-general by Mme Savineau, Technical Counselor of Education, based on investigation in February–March 1937, used the relative form of adjectives: "now the laborer is better treated, better fed, better paid, freer." "Too many whites demand men," she was told. Africans in some districts were complaining about extensive recruitment: "The recruits, they say, are slaves."[89]

Others, including Inspector Tap, doubted whether enough labor was coming forth, and wanted a transitional regime more responsive to planters' needs. This de Coppet refused to do, fearing the return to "former abuses to which we justly wanted to bring to a definitive end." He wanted instead to remind planters that the system "is essentially transitory," giving planters "the necessary delay to adapt to the new state of things and take appropriate measures in order to obtain the voluntary labor which they need."[90] It seems that free labor was both less free and less plentiful than Mondon was saying.

The governor lobbied the highest Mossi chief, the Moro Naba, to carry on the apostolate, and the chief assured the Governor that he could count on "a relatively large number of workers." The regional committee in Upper Volta claimed this had all been done without constraint, but that obtaining workers in former Upper Volta "is due, without question to the good will of the Moro Naba." In this same region, a European merchant transmitted reports of Mossi chiefs receiving orders to deliver men and complying with them.[91] These reports unleashed a long correspondence and more denials of impropriety from Mondon. De Coppet, forwarding the documents to the Minister, was notably tentative:

Reading these different items should give you all assurances; however, taking account of misguided past policies regarding the Ivory Coast we cannot hope to see all the abuses disappear from one day to the next, however eager the struggle undertaken to make them disappear. The latter were profoundly anchored in customs and they are slow to be transformed. The recruiters, the canton chiefs, could say that they were sent by the Administration and in some way mandated by it. It is difficult to suppress such schemes.[92]

The same day, de Coppet wrote Mondon an even more tentative letter, broaching the most delicate question of all: what constituted administrative complicity in recruitment by a chief?

It is certain, in effect, that if a recruiter operated in Mossi country without the aid of the French Administration, *but after agreement with the very centralized organism represented by the Moro-Naba* and his lieutenants, there would exist as a consequence a certain and unacceptable pressure on indigenous populations. This example, we have to admit, only has the value of a hypothesis since your reports are categorical in so far as they concern the absence of *all* intervention.[93]

But then, in August, de Coppet wrote to express confidence in Mondon, acknowledging the "essential role" of the Moro Naba "under the aegis and control of French territorial authorities," and praising his "spirit of cooperation." The minister in turn expressed his relief that "the intervention of 'the Administrator' in the matter of recruiting labor for individuals no longer exists, except for exceptional mistakes... I was particularly happy to learn that, contrary to interventions of which I am still the object, all administrative constraint has ceased to be exercised in this regard."[94]

Skepticism virtually leaps from de Coppet's and Moutet's letters, and we know (see below) that Moutet periodically received direct reports of alleged misdeeds from low-ranking officials or private individuals. But neither Moutet nor de Coppet was about to overturn the chain of command, and they lacked the means to find out what power really meant where a traditional leader and a Commandant de Cercle held sway.

All the talk probably did matter. Wages rose.[95] The multiplication of local labor offices meant that it was perhaps more likely that employers who did not pay their workers at all or whose sanitary provisions were grotesquely awful might get in trouble. Administrators had to be cautious in their recruitment work.[96]

That public language had changed is made clear from a letter from one of the stalwarts of the colons, Jean Rose, president of the Chambre d'Agriculture et d'Industrie de la Côte d'Ivoire, in late 1937. Rose favored – and he would be saying the same thing until 1946 – government recruitment for the benefit of planters, so he argued that the ending of that system meant that private recruiters came to a district, bribed chiefs, and then got the chiefs to do the dirty work. "At present, we have returned to slavery. The employers buy men from the chief who 'sells' them as dearly as possible, without caring if they have sleeping sickness, leprosy, syphilis, tuberculosis or other diseases." So anti-slavery language could be invoked in favor of forced labor. Mondon considered Rose's charges absurd: he "wanted moreover to see the return, without a doubt, of the period of the 'Gouverneur Providence' and of the Administrator purveyor of labor..." The local administrators duly furnished Mondon with affirmations that private recruiting was generally honest and free of chiefly coercion, and de Coppet backed up Mondon.[97]

If this correspondence reveals the attempt of a diehard colon to use new language for his old purpose, it also suggests that the Ivory Coast administration was willing to go only so far to pacify labor-hungry colons. Rose's letter was one of many he was writing – "campaigns of denigration" de Coppet called them – and officials dismissed them. Mondon added, "That one reconciles the needs and aspirations of everyone, that's our role, but that it is necessary to sacrifice the native to the European, we cannot consent to that."[98]

A few officials were beginning to understand the complexity of work itself, not just the ambiguities of the hiring process. Pierre Tap, in charge of the Inspection du Travail for French West Africa, remarked in mid-1937 on the fact that the Ivory Coast, needing some 20,000 workers annually, was suffering "this long crisis of manpower" at the same time that "120,000 men expatriate themselves *voluntarily*" to the Gold Coast.

In the Gold Coast, work and community were adapted to the African's way of life – Mossi chiefs looked over him, and the government ignored him, whereas in French Africa people feared "the military and the tax agent."[99] Even African planters in the Ivory Coast presented a better model than European colons: their workers arrived in families or in groups and established themselves "like at home," planting their own food crops while working on the landlord's cocoa farm and adjusting work hours "to their will." They were paid either a set sum at the end of the harvest – say 500 francs – or else one-third of the harvest.

The French plantation, on the other hand, provided too much discipline and too little attraction: "But work at precise hours, the call of the bell or the whistle, the militarized existence of the night bell, he is in horror of that." The French plantation regime erred by not letting the migrant come with wife and children, and by insisting that a large proportion of the wage (the *pécule*) be withheld and paid only on return to the home village where there was nothing to spend it on. He stressed wages most of all: "with a free labor force that was well paid and well fed, one would have fewer enterprises, but those that would be found and maintained would be healthy, sure of the future." It was necessary "to consider the black worker not as a would-be soldier and malingerer but as a free man." Tap indeed had a point: contract labor in many ways resembled the military more than the enterprise of advanced capitalism, and malingering was the flip side of military discipline.

Tap in the end was uncertain whether Africans' prior work habits were a fact to which Europeans had to adjust, or whether despite everything Africans could simply be treated as nothing more than "free men." Perhaps he meant that the model of the income-maximizing individual was best to follow even when it was not accurate.[100] But whichever approach was taken, it would take European control to make it work: "But I have the absolute conviction that all these anarchic and naturally enemy races would return to the forest and to their savage life, abandoning fields and shops, if they were not strongly contained by the French."[101] Neither Tap nor his colleagues discussed the way labor was organized in the Gold Coast as an alternative means of solving the problem of mobilizing labor; it was seen as intrinsically African and hence more attractive than something intrinsically European. The African work ethic was innate, a part of the African's essential being, whereas the European work ethic was taught and learned.[102]

However Africans might have responded to a pristine labor market, in the actual conditions of recruitment workers frequently did not serve out their contracts. Some deserted collectively. In November 1937, a hundred men engaged on a public project went on strike seven months into a year-long contract, leading another hundred men working from a second public works project off work. They complained of excessive tasks, but were cajoled or threatened to return to work a day later. The next year, 192 workers half way through a year-long contract left a public works site, complained of unpaid wages and other abuses, and asked to be repatriated. Chiefs intervened and got the men to return.[103] Such confrontations were behind the long-held dislike of free labor ideologues toward contract labor: the freeness of free labor was relevant only at the time of hiring and not during the time of work. When Mondon tried to dismiss the incidents as "due to the inconstancy of which natives frequently give proof," insisting that they did "not merit the name of strikes," he was revealing more about the system than about the workers.[104]

By mid-1937, nonetheless, the labor question in the Ivory Coast moved into the administrative background, not because it had been resolved, but because it had disappeared behind walls of impenetrable ambiguity. Popular Front officials moved on to the modern project of reforming social laws; Mondon still sang praise songs for the "apostolat du travail" and for the "beautiful physical appearance" of workers at the end of their contracts.[105] De Coppet publicly congratulated Mondon for superintending the transition to "free recruitment," while saying yet again, "The recruitment of workers must be absolutely free. Imposed or forced labor for private enterprises is absolutely forbidden, as much by our laws as by the generous tendency of the French spirit."[106]

But in 1939, after the Popular Front had fallen, the topic came up again in a way that revealed how much remained of the problem. Moutet – now a Deputy in the Assemblée Nationale – was given reports from low-level officials in the Ivory Coast that labor recruitment was still coercive, despite what high officials said. Moutet warned his successor at the ministry, Georges Mandel, of the "grave peril that there is to go back on a situation considered to have been resolved." He insisted,

I have in effect accepted the conviction that free labor is much more productive than obligatory labor, and that the regime of long contracts is an evil regime, because the planter, assured of the support of the Administration for recruitment and for keeping the native on the plantation, does not take care to provide the latter with either the necessary conditions of housing, of food and of leisure... If forced recruitment is added to military recruitment all the effort to reattach the people to France risks being compromised, under the pretended pretext of "apostolate of work."[107]

There is much pathos in these words: a former minister having to defend the superiority of free labor ninety years after France abolished slavery in its colonies. His inquiry had the same effect as his inquiries when in power: Mandel asked the governor-general for comments, who asked the governor, and the usual denials came up the channel.[108]

Moutet had been tipped off by Robert Delavignette, then head of the Ecole Coloniale and a proponent of the peasant path to development. He in turn was getting information from two local administrators whose identity he was protecting. Delavignette claimed that Commandants de Cercle "are menaced with being transferred and as a result downgraded ... if they do not turn over labor to planters in the South." Recruitment, he claimed, was reaching a level of 1,000 men per 100,000 population – and if one counted adult males only that meant "1 man of 12 who is pulled from his village to go 600 kilometers away to 'earn' 2 francs per day." The labor inspector, was "the planters' man"; the interim governor at the time "sacrifices everything for the desire he has to be named governor, by the power ["piston" was the image he used] of the so-called planters."[109]

Delavignette's informants were two young administrators, one of whom had directly refused an order to make chiefs bring forth workers when volunteers had not appeared, and was given a patronizing talking-to by the interim governor. The other wrote that labor regulations were a "dead letter," and "the Governor favors the exploiters and closes his eyes to all abuse."[110]

A new governor, Crocicchia, found all charges "without basis." He insisted that the government was trying to "convince" the African of his interest in working in the Ivory Coast, and claimed success in getting men to leave behind their "dark habits of laziness in which they are too often led to stagnate."[111] Governor Crocicchia claimed that contract workers never numbered over 30,000. But this turns out to be around the maximum of the pre-Popular Front days – which had been criticized as dangerously high – and at the upper end of the 20,000–30,000 the Vichy regime in its much franker discussions of forced labor believed it could recruit. All this suggests that in 1939 the administration was cranking up the pressure on the Ivory Coast's population.[112]

Mandel was in fact worried that labor migration might have gone too far. Reports from the Ivory Coast made him fear that villages might become "deprived of too large a number of healthy men." Officials should

take care of that fact that the prolonged absences of these men from their households could cause in the future grave problems from a demographic point of view. If it is necessary to facilitate the recruitment of manpower necessary to private enterprises, and this recruitment should encounter the minimum of difficulties, the wages paid should be comparable to those paid in the neighboring colony, the attitude of the administration never should be interpretable as a return to methods of coercion in favor of private individuals.[113]

Governor and governor-general as usual claimed "the problem of manpower is in the process of definitive resolution on optimal terms" for all concerned. Migrants returned with a

small fortune allowing its beneficiary to constitute a herd or to found a household in exceptionally favorable demographic conditions. Right away, he can in the fullness of robustness forged by work and rational diet, pay the bridewealth of a healthy and robust girl, while it would have required several years of village toil to put together the meager bridewealth of a widow unsuited to reproduction. The temporary exodus of the small contingents of cultivators, in assuring the villages of an unexpected growth of wealth and increase in natality, thus reenforces their social stability and their potential.[114]

This was the classic defense of migratory labor, drawing on a conception of a traditional way of life shared with officials who favored the peasant path over wage labor. Wage labor undoubtedly had become woven into marriage relations. But something was clearly wrong with all of this: somebody in Dakar penciled in the margin next to the word "potential" the word "genital?" and added, "This is the conclusion of a veterinarian." And Crocicchia didn't seem entirely at ease, for he reported issuing a circular saying that all migration from a village, including military recruitment, should not surpass 10 percent of able bodied men – double the figure the pre-Popular Front regime (and Vichy) thought the maximum.[115]

All this suggests that things had gone too far, that village life was being disrupted in 1940 as officials had thought it was four years previously. Mandel's lumping together of labor migration with military recruitment – which was hardly voluntary – suggests that the labor question was slipping into a conceptual domain where free will was not even an imperfectly realized ideal. Crocicchia reduced social life to cash and biology.

What had clearly changed since the Popular Front fell was attitudes at the top. Mandel's ministry had one paramount concern: mobilization for national defense.[116] Officials were instructed to inventory manpower again, to determine how many men could be sent to France or contribute in various ways to bringing colonial resources to bear in the struggle. One can thus read with a sense of ominousness the circular of Governor-General Cayla in May 1940:

At the moment when an intense and sustained effort imposes itself on all the Nation, it would be extremely regretable that a part of physically able and available manpower could remain insufficiently employed. I ask you therefore to please ask the Chefs de Circonscription under your orders to push themselves to obtain, by an active propaganda, the largest utilization of local resources in labor.

Enterprises benefiting from this effort were supposed to obey labor regulations, but Cayla did not bother to repeat the ritualized warnings against coercion or the abuses of the past.[117]

The circular, issued weeks before the fall of France, was a license for a manhunt. A manhunt did in fact take place under Vichy, but the impetus for it had come before.[118] The flowery language of 1939 which alerts the later reader that something is not being discussed honestly gave way to frank demands for labor, with both safeguards and apologetics kept to a minimum (chapter 4).

The Popular Front effort itself did make concrete differences: wages rose and for a time local officials received signals that their role was not simply to round up laborers. The very defensiveness of Mondon or Crocicchia, and their inability simply to shroud recruitment with silence, suggests that the Popular Front had for a time changed bureaucratic discourse. Peasant production briefly emerged as a serious developmental strategy in 1936–38.[119] But governors and lower level bureaucrats had not fully accepted that Africans could be workers, and they did not think of forced labor as something inconceivable in the twentieth century.

Slaves of the Commandant: the Popular Front and labor for public purpose

Throughout the 1930s, two forms of "travail obligatoire" – prestations and the deuxième portion du contingent – were above board. They had a statutory basis and France defended them in international fora. The French government, officially at least, had refused to ratify the 1930 Convention not because it opposed in principle the ban on forced labor for private enterprise, but because it wanted to set the terms on which the government used it.

Popular Front officials, like their predecessors, insisted that these forms of compulsion were transitional: Africans should not be deprived of the infrastructure that would improve their well being because they were unwilling to build it. They wanted to minimize prestatory labor and military recruitment and hoped that mechanization – requiring increased capital spending – would reduce the need for such practices. But when de Coppet actually saw what prestations meant in practice, he was shocked.

On tour in December–January 1936–37, he observed that the idea of modest community service implicit in the notion of prestations was everywhere abused to make up for the administration's own inadequacies. In theory, all adult males were to pay prestations in either labor – four to ten days per year, depending on the district – or to pay instead an extra tax, "le rachat," wherever the population was thought sufficiently advanced to exercise this option. Their duties were not supposed to conflict with local agriculture. But de Coppet concluded: "These rules, acceptable and perhaps even equitable in theory, are in practice constantly and everywhere violated." Children and sometimes women did much of the work. They were often made to walk long distances to their work site, and the time this took was not counted toward the days owed. The Commandant de Cercle understood that if roads were bad he would not be promoted, but if prestatory labor were abused, no-one would know the difference. "One abuse engenders another and the population becomes, literally, corvéable at will." It was in this report on the abuses of labor for public purposes that de Coppet made his case (chapter 2, p. 31) that the abuses and lies in which local officials had to engage were demoralizing his administration.

But, he wondered, did recognizing this mean that France should give up its systems of roads "which bring to the native wealth, civilization and even happiness, as we conceive it, that is in work. No assuredly." He wanted instead to push the earlier policy of replacing prestatory labor with a higher tax.[120]

The governor-general and his governors became almost equally disillusioned with the practice of using the deuxième contingent for public works. In theory, as officials argued at Geneva, the use of military recruits was justifiable for "large-scale works of general interest." But in practice, noted the Political Report for 1937, "The institution is complicated and costly." Recruits had no military training – and so would be useless in war – yet recruiting the second portion along with the first (the soldiers) made meeting the quotas of the latter more difficult. It was not clear how the "hybrid" deuxième portion should be supervised: should they be under military discipline or treated like civilian workers?[121]

The most important consumer of the men of the deuxième portion throughout its long and dubious history was the Office du Niger, a large-scale project to bring irrigation works to the Niger valley in the French Soudan, and then to bring African settlers from other regions to make the desert bloom with cotton, rice, and other food crops. There, the deuxième portion acquired particular notoriety. A 1935 report on the conditions of 2,595 recruited laborers (plus 1,987 volunteers) then at work had cited evidence of beatings and brutality by administrators who felt that sending men to prison would be insufficient punishment for offenses, since jail would seem like a "place of rest" in comparison to working under the sun. The government officials running the Office abused the government's own regulations about rations, lodging, medical care, and working hours.[122] In early 1938, de Coppet wrote scathing reports of the Office du Niger: the "one concern of the Office is output, the one rule, constraint." His emissary, Mme Savineau, put the issue in Popular Front language: the Office wanted to "destroy this admirable spirit of liberal cooperation which is that of indigenous societies and *fascicize*. Like other dictators of the largest scale, the Director of the Office du Niger freely gives this policy the colors of socialism. In reality, he is reconstituting slavery."[123]

But officials couldn't quite bring themselves to give up all of this. They hoped to find better ways to build roads and other instruments of civilization, but they saw the work ethic as a consequence of the improvement efforts – attainable by Africans, but not quite yet. The communications system of French West Africa was truly a problem: it depended on a small number of major axes, each of which required the concentration of laborers along routes with small populations. Nor was the government willing to give up the Office du Niger, for it was one of the few ongoing projects that promised – however implausibly – to bring something *new* into the agricultural picture of the interior of French West Africa.[124]

So the administration tried amelioration instead of abolition, insisting that its long-term goal was to wean itself from its addiction to forced labor. The regime of prestations was reformed by extending the system of rachat, allowing cercles to collect more money in taxes and use it to pay for labor. They hoped to create teams of workers specializing in road work, who would be more efficient than the forced laborers and who would create "a new class of small-scale consumers" helping to stimulate economic activity in rural areas. In early 1938, the system of rachat had been established in 25 of the 109 districts in French West Africa. At the same time, the governor-general noted that "the suppression of prestations does not at all liberate [our subjects] from traditional tasks inherent in village life that they performed all the time according to the rules of custom and without our having to intervene, except in case of collective negligence in the very interest of the collectivity." Custom would still have its reign, but that would be distinct from the reign of French officials.[125]

The problem with reforming the deuxième portion was that it was needed most where it was most likely to lead to deplorable work conditions: big projects in isolated areas. This included work projects along the Dakar–Niger railway, and of course the Office du Niger. In 1937, de Coppet ordered that recruitment for the deuxième portion in the Soudan be dropped from 3,000 in 1936 to 1,000, although the governor noted that even this number was hard to find (especially since the première portion, the soldiers, grew). He ordered the work day cut to eight hours and other reforms. But this didn't solve the basic problem, and no sooner had the changes been made, than the governor of the Soudan was in the awkward position of realizing that the smaller contingent of 1937 and the shortened work day meant more workers would be needed in 1938: he asked for 4,750 and settled for 3,000. Like soldiers, they were all expected to serve a three-year term. One third of their wages would be held as the "pécule" payable "at the time of their liberation" – an interesting choice of words.[126]

So a few thousand men each year (not to mention the larger contingent of soldiers) had to suffer the miserable fate of lengthy service, while a larger number suffered through a few days (if the rules were obeyed) of hard work nearer their homes. Officials were caught in a dilemma within the terms in which they thought about Africa: a poor continent, made up of distinct communities, desperately needing French help to improve their standard of living without destroying the social fabric, and needing for such gradual improvement to be integrated to the wider world by communications systems whose construction with wage labor presumed that the goal for which they were being built had already been attained.[127] Popular Front officials, like their predecessors and their successors, occasionally contemplated bringing in foreign laborers for big projects or as colonists within such ventures as the Office du Niger. The logistics of such movements were difficult and the political implications of bringing foreigners into Africa uncertain. And doing so would not necessarily be a step toward bringing Africans into a world in which wage labor made sense.[128]

Despite the limits of reform, the Popular Front felt sufficiently confident that it had set itself on a course away from forced labor that it decided in 1937 to ratify the ILO Convention of 1930 on forced labor. The French government attached reserves to its ratification, which it claimed pertained to "forms of forced or obligatory labor whose maintenance are currently indispensable to the material and social progress of the populations of our colonies." This referred to the deuxième portion, prestations, and forced cultivation for instruction or experimentation in agricultural techniques, all of which were alleged to be consistent with the ILO's intention of moving progressively toward the elimination of forced labor. France claimed in mid-1938 to be in compliance with the convention and de Coppet kept reminding his subordinates until his departure to refrain from recruiting for private purposes and be vigilant about any public use of forced labor.[129]

What the Popular Front accomplished here was modest: less forced labor, slightly better conditions for those who had to do it, and above all a sense among officials that whenever they coerced Africans into the workplace they were endangering future progress. The most dangerous continuity in colonial ideology across the Popular Front period was the fear that Africans had a dislike of wage labor that was somehow fixed in their culture: such a notion was both argument for a peasant-based strategy of development and a rationale for the use of forced labor.[130] It was only in 1946, when African political actors entered the debate, that the French government got out of this ideological trap.

Africans as workers: social legislation and the labor movement, 1936–1938

The new thinking which the Popular Front contributed was less about getting Africans into the workplace than about accepting the reality of their being there. One of its first actions was to raise the question of applying new social legislation in France to the colonies. Officials took the question seriously and were not alarmed when African workers began to participate actively and collectively in issues that concerned them. To a significant extent, they reacted as Creech Jones lamented British colonial officials had not – treating conflict as industrial disputes rather than as "disorders." But by luck, or because France had done so little to develop commerce and industry in West Africa, the disputes themselves were narrower, threatening less to spill into a broad social realm.

In June 1936 Moutet requested opinions on how to implement the new legislation on the forty-hour week, paid vacations, collective bargaining, and the legalization and regulation of trade unions.[131] The Syndicat de Défense des Intérêts de la Côte Occidentale d'Afrique saw no benefits from collective contracts and thought the forty-hour week "inconceivable." The Chambre de Commerce of Dakar claimed that the "natural evolution" of Africans rendered contracts and trade unions out of the question, that Africans worked too slowly for the forty-hour week to make sense, and that they "take their holidays automatically." Others denied there was a working class to regulate.[132] The governors agreed: Africans were not in general ready for the forty-hour week, paid holidays, and especially trade union rights.[133] It was up to the administration, not trade unions, "to protect the native masses..."[134]

By then, two African unions had organized themselves sufficiently well in the legal limbo in which they existed to add their opinions. The Syndicat des Ouvriers du Bâtiment de Dakar (Abdoulaye Diop, secretary-general) sent its "thanks" to Moutet and thought that the social laws would "deliver the worker from the rigors of their bosses." It claimed most workers lived in misery and submitted a sample budget of a mason or carpenter with three children and a wife: expenses came to 22.33 francs per day, compared to a rate of pay of 15 francs. The union of Employées du Commerce de l'Industrie et des Banques (EMCIBA, Doudou Sakho, secretary-general) also praised the Popular Front for its "eminently French achievement," supported the collective contract, the forty-hour week, paid vacations, and paid medical care, and warned against the machinations of the *patronat*. The Dakar newspaper *Périscope Africain* ran articles supporting the application of the social laws.[135]

A comprehensive and in some ways far-reaching draft of labor legislation was prepared in early 1937 by Inspector Tap. After this was shot down by business interests and officials, a second, more cautious, draft was prepared by his successor, Pierre Casset, and sent around for comments in May 1938. But by then it was too late, for the Popular Front was about to fall. However, the commentaries (discussed below) on the two drafts reveal much about how officials thought about the intersection of the category of worker with the category of African.

Meanwhile, Paris issued several decrees representing small steps toward protecting workers against the hazards of selling their labor power. In August 1936, legislation of 1932 was applied to French West Africa giving workers limited protection against the consequences of industrial accidents.[136] In September, metropolitan laws regulating the "labor of women and children" were applied. This rubric would persist – it can be found in the Code du Travail of 1952 – and reveals that the effort to think of African workers as normal applied to males only. As the governor-general told his governors, the goal was to insure

effective protection of women and children, inside the indigenous family, without conflicting with, as far as possible, local customs and traditions. Working women will remain for a long time the exception, compared to the immense majority of them, in the country as in the city, who are only called to do family labor.[137]

The ministry described these actions as part of its conception of "modern colonizing action," and its goal of "the admission of workers to the benefits of metropolitan social laws." It wanted to apply labor legislation "wherever the modalities of work can be assimilated to those of the Metropole," but at the same time it wanted to take account of special conditions in native societies. All this, plus the ratification by the French Senate of the 1930 Forced Labor Convention, was thought to put France in the international labor vanguard.[138]

The most important practical gain was trade union legislation. Moutet himself pressed for quick action on laws permitting unions to organize and be registered. From the start, officials wanted to limit union membership to Africans with a "minimum of competence of which the criterion could be sufficient knowledge of the French language." For Africans not meeting the criterion, "their union is the Administration."[139] No doubt officials' desire to act quickly was accelerated in December 1936 when a series of strikes broke out in Dakar. Their immediate cause, as local officials readily acknowledged, was inflation: prices, as exports and economic activity in Dakar picked up, rose sharply, but wages did not. Still, the process took the form it did because Popular Front officials did not try to suppress the strikes, but negotiated with workers – in the absence of official unions – and in most cases put pressure on employers to make concessions. In some cases de Coppet developed cordial personal relations with union leaders.

That workers took advantage of this window of opportunity owes something not just to workers' very real grievances, but to particular conditions in Dakar and to the initiatives that had slowly been building up. Like the neighboring communes of Rufisque and Gorée, Dakar was part of the old "Quatres Communes" (the fourth was Saint-Louis), whose African inhabitants had been given citizenship rights. They included significant numbers of families engaged in trade or in professional activities: law, teaching, service within the bureaucracy. They had political protection: Blaise Diagne came from their ranks and had not only served in the Assemblée Nationale in Paris since 1914 but ran a political machine in Dakar. His successor in 1934, Galandou Diouf, was also a machine politician *par excellence*, and he was hostile to the Popular Front, which was allied with Diouf's rival Lamine Guèye – Saint Louisien, French educated, lawyer, mayor of Dakar, and leader of the Parti Socialiste Sénégalais.[140]

The line between the Dakarois petty bourgeoisie and the more permanent, skilled workers was not a clear one, particularly in regard to wage employment in the civil service, where African advancement was not as narrowly constrained as it was in most of British Africa, and in commerce, where literate Africans worked for French firms. They were able to form "amicales" – associations nominally for social purposes but which created the potential of collective discussion and occasionally action. Such amicales existed above all in the civil service, and since 1929 on the Dakar–Niger railway. This association, centered in the railway junction of Thiès, was led by François Gning, an immigrant from the French Congo, army veteran, and trained accountant.[141]

The record of known strikes in Dakar goes back to 1919, and the most significant included a railway strike in 1925, which was harshly suppressed, and a month-long walkout of seamen based in Dakar in 1928. From the latter emerged a clandestine union, led by Magatte Codou Sarr, who had worked in France as well as Senegal. There had been a few strikes and strike threats in 1930–33, but 1934, 1935, and early 1936 were quiet throughout French West Africa.[142] The new season began on 30 June, 1936, when 150 sailors who worked on boats along the coast went on strike. Administrators at Dakar intervened, obtained wage concessions for the sailors, and the strike ended the next day.[143]

As soon as the Popular Front raised the possibility of legalizing unions, there was a flurry of activity. European commercial workers formed their own professional association, and in August 1936 African commercial employees organized EMCIBA and – despite the absence of relevant legislation – deposited papers with the government. Articles about trade unions appeared in the local press – another sign that the boundaries of the educated and the working population overlapped. Civil service organizations were formed, theoretically open to blacks and whites but in practice along separate lines. There were strikes – all short – in the summer and fall, and the threat of a railway strike at Thiès which did not come off.[144]

In December, the peanut export season began, and with it a well-timed strike wave. It began with a dock strike on the morning of 21 December. Apparently some port companies had raised wages while others had not, and a group of workers "erupted" onto the docks to get workers who had accepted lower wages to stop work. Nearly the entire dock labor force eventually left work. Magatte Sarr, the veteran maritime trade unionist who presented himself as the representative of the (unrecognized) dock workers' union, joined the Inspecteur du Travail in vainly trying to get the strikers back to work. After a mass meeting, a rejected offer of a wage increase, a brief involvement of workers in industry and building in the strike, a plea by the inspector to employers to acknowledge the higher cost of living, and finally a higher wage increase, the dock strike ended the next day. Wage rates of 8–10 francs per day went up to a standardized 15.[145]

There rapidly ensued in December and January a series of strikes among seamen, bakers, commercial workers, factory workers, workers at an oil company and the electricity and water company, tugboat crews, painters, gardeners, cooks, and domestic workers. Some strikes were more organized than others; one lasted several weeks. Intervening rapidly in each case to try to get employers to grant wage increases and settle, labor inspectors were realizing that well-organized unions had their virtues: "If the workers have an interest in being defended by a powerful organization, the employers, to consider everything, have on their side as much interest in dealing with representatives who, after an accord, will have enough authority to ensure that it is respected."[146]

These strikes were not conducted by trade unions – above-board unions at least – which the Inspecteurs du Travail and the Sûreté thought disorganized and inactive at that moment. The Sûreté remarked that in previous years workers obtained raises during the frenzy of the "traite" – the period when the peanut harvest was brought in and exported. But this year the pattern seemed more like a "movement of collective demands."[147] In the relatively small world of workers in Dakar, especially in the "advanced maritime milieu", the knowledge of the success of some workers may well have given rise to similar claims for others. This pattern of the rolling strike, passing day by day to new groups of strikers, who nonetheless carried out and settled their strike individually, was found elsewhere in Africa.[148]

The governor-general took the strikes to indicate genuine problems, and he cabled his governors to take a lesson from the Dakar strikes and insist that employers raise "low wages without delay." Meanwhile, administrators and the police should "proceed to discreet inquiries on the state of workers' spirit." Now that the labor question was being forced into the open by African collective action, de Coppet's administration needed knowledge, contact, and awareness.[149]

His secretary-general, Geismar, saw in the "sudden outbreak and relatively large scale" of the strikes "the awakening of a common consciousness of rights." The emergence of trade union organization from these events was "an opportunity." It was important for the administration and employers to be able "to address themselves to effective representatives of workers."[150]

The strike wave had spread into other parts of Senegal. It involved boat crews and dockers at the peanut ports, the electrical generating company, and truckers in the peanut shipping areas, as well as the ports of Rufisque and Saint-Louis. So worried were officials over some violent incidents that they contemplated calling on "influential religious personalities" to counsel moderation. But it took wage increases to get the strikes settled. On New Year's Eve, the indigenous railway workers at Thiès threatened a strike when the director refused their demands for a raise. Workers paraded through the town, and government officials scrambled to get the railway to make an acceptable offer, which it finally did.[151] The Senegalese government was inclined to blame "the diffusion of ideas emanating from Dakar," while de Coppet and his staff kept reminding them of the genuineness of the grievances. But officials agreed that this was something new in the colonial context: "Never," said one high official, "have work stoppages reached an amplitude comparable to that which they reached these last few days."[152]

The rolling strikes, with their significant victories, petered out in mid-January. They had been a phenomenon of Dakar and the peanut basin although there were smaller labor conflicts at Conakry, and one in the Ivory Coast.[153] Given the embryonic union organization, success had very much depended on momentum and the pressures of the season of the traite.

The strike wave of December–January reinforced the Popular Front's inclination to channel demands into visible, regular structures. In March

1937, with the debate on other social laws very much unresolved, the French government took the plunge and enacted comprehensive trade union legislation that would define the framework for union activity in Africa until the Code du Travail of 1952. The March decrees established the principle of trade union freedom, but limited to people "capable of understanding trade unionism" – that is, meeting an educational qualification – and providing procedures for union accountability. A second decree provided that people not eligible to join a union could join a "professional association," which lacked the civil status of a union. Another established procedures for arbitration: only after exhausting a series of steps, leading up to a judgment by a "surarbitre" that either side could accept or reject, was a strike legal.[154]

De Coppet's defense of restricting trade union rights to literate workers was both evolutionist and political: it was necessary that union members have a "degree of evolution giving them the ability, a priori, truly to participate effectively in union life, that is to follow and control with full knowledge, should the case arise, the management of their professional interests confided to their directors." He feared that illiterate union members might be exploited by "swindlers, agents provocateurs and other fishers in troubled water."[155]

He was challenged by a number of quite literate Africans: Périscope Africain criticized the legislation for excluding nine-tenths of all workers. The radical Paris-edited journal Africa noted that railwaymen, sailors, carpenters, drivers, shop employees, weavers, tanners, agricultural workers, cooks, and domestics would have no means of collective defense. The mayor of Saint-Louis, Paul Vidal, pointed out that since most already existing unions had members who met the standards and others who did not, the legislation simply gave local officials the power to ignore or enforce the provision. The real risk was that discontent could lead to "the general strike of crossed arms to express discontent. This risk can be prevented by giving generously and with good grace, in the French style, that which it would be necessary to concede with bad grace to a justified revolt."[156]

De Coppet maintained his position, insisting that the "benevolent understanding" of the administration was the best antidote to discontent.[157] Within the administration, Tap, the Chief Inspecteur du Travail, argued that the issue was not evolution, but stability: union rights should be available to anyone who had spent a specified length of time in "a skilled or specialized trade or proof of a certain stability in an enterprise."[158] It is not clear that the administration took its evolutionist perspective as seriously in practice as in theory: it negotiated with unions that included ordinary laborers.[159]

The flourishing of unions in 1937 and 1938 went the furthest among civil servants, and they were decidedly centered on Dakar: 30 of the 42 unions enumerated were based there, most of the others in Senegal and Ivory Coast; 41 of the 55 recorded strikes occurred in Dakar or Senegal in 1936–38. In the Ivory Coast, labor protest – given the recruitment system – most often took the form of mass desertions.[160]

The two most active unions in mid-1937 were EMCIBA, the union of commercial and industrial workers, and the railway union. EMCIBA negotiated a contract in 1937 with the principal association of commercial employers in Dakar. It specified large numbers of job categories and a wide range of wages: clerks earned from 450 to 1,100 francs per month, an ordinary laborer's wage being from 7 to 12.50 francs per day. These hierarchical scales were to be critical to French labor policy for many years, for they – along with clauses on working hours and benefits – provided a well-defined framework for negotiation; they also reassured management that it could control the differentiation of the work force, and gave workers a sense that they had something to aspire to. These wages were 10–65 percent above the old rates; EMCIBA nonetheless had shown restraint by not joining the strike wave in December–January, when its participation might have led to something close to a general strike.[161]

The administration had extended the contract to the rest of Senegal – its right under the March decrees – with adjusted wage scales, but the commercial firms used procedural complications and stonewalling to render it ineffectual. In the end, the Dakar unions were too concerned with their own wage gains to risk the total collapse of the agreement, and their provincial comrades had to settle for a good deal less. Procedure, it became quickly clear, was no substitute for collective struggle.[162]

The railway union had talked strike in December 1936, and had obtained a raise. Union head François Gning was able to get audiences with de Coppet, and he insisted against rank-and-file criticism that patience and connections were the best strategy. Gning opposed organizing the "simple temporary laborers," claiming that such workers might be pushed to "a too violent conception of union action." His narrow conception was soon to lead to bitter conflict.[163]

De Coppet was also thinking about railway workers as special: they represented the "very special mentality among Senegalese," born of the citizenship rights given Africans in the Quatres Communes. They resented "in a particularly lively fashion every inequality of treatment in relation to Europeans." Most important, "if the Administration were obliged to give in, and everything leads me to believe that it would in the end be obliged to do so, it would result in a very large loss of authority for it." De Coppet visited Thiès, spent two days with the railway workers, convinced himself that concessions had to be made to them, and convinced the railwaymen not to strike. He also ordered the governor of Senegal "secretly" to make sure local officials let railwaymen know how much he had done for them. Gning, for his part, obsequiously thanked the governor-general.[164]

The two most interesting elements of this interaction are the fragility of the government's sense of its own authority – the fear that it could not win a railway strike – and the fact that the government and the union could carry on a dialogue about past and present favors. In 1938, the limits of such relationships would come to the fore.[165] But in the fall of 1937, the rolling strikes that had begun the year had given way to a pattern of demands, bluff, and concession – within the new industrial relations machinery.[166]

The government extended the industrial relations machinery of the March 1937 decrees throughout French West Africa, and indeed to French Equatorial Africa, where forced labor was still a more timely issue than strikes and trade unions. Inspecteurs du Travail were now stationed in all territories, with their own bureaucratic interest in standardizing procedures and pressing a model of industrial relations which recognized the importance of what they did: they kept track of unions and contracts, advised the governors on setting minimum wages, and had the right to inspect work sites. Some of the agreements negotiated in Dakar were extended further – with the numbers changed to reflect alleged differences in the cost of living – but even in Senegal, as EMCIBA learned, such contracts meant considerably less when a labor movement was not active. The common framework of labor relations established throughout the Federation in 1937, and the transterritorial linkages of the railway and civil service, remained a potential that would be realized after the war.[167]

The rise of the labor movement in Dakar changed the labor question fundamentally: it led to rapid wage concessions and to dialogue.[168] While addressing workers as political actors through the labor movement, officials were simultaneously trying to put a more scientific gloss on the labor question. Part of the impulse came from the social sensibility of the Popular Front. Moutet in 1937 had decried the "famine wages" of "the very large majority" of unskilled workers in the colonies, and asked, "How, in any case, can one not admit that a decent minimum wage is the indispensable condition of social progress?" A family should be able to live from wage labor.[169] But if the minimum wage were a test of social progress, the Popular Front had a long way to go. In Dakar, in June 1937, the minimum wage was fixed at 7 francs per day: it had been set at this figure in 1929 but it had been unenforced, with wages falling to 4 or 4.50 francs in 1933 with administration approval. But with dockers getting twice that (although they did not work every day), skilled manual workers 10–25 francs, and the workers on the EMCIBA contract (manual and clerical) from 210 to 1,200 francs per month (7–40 per day) there was considerable differentiation within the labor force, accelerated by the varied level of strike activity. Wages outside of Dakar increased as well, but stayed well below Dakar's levels.[170]

The first budget survey done in French West Africa was carried out by the administrator of Dakar, Ponzio, in October 1936.[171] He added up the totals for food, rent, laundry, clothing, and lights, and came up with 200–300 francs per month for a bachelor, 523–577 for a married worker with four children. At the legal minimum wage, a worker might earn just under 200; at what Ponzio thought was the average – 15 francs per day – a full month of work would bring around 400. The budget study concluded apologetically, noting that women had gardens and carried out "small tasks," while a child could earn 3–4 francs per day, so that "despite the comparison of figures between the wage and the expenses of a head of family, I sincerely believe that current wages permit the native to live honorably." The government itself was giving its manual laborers 7 francs per day in mid-1937: they must have been the honorable poor, and they certainly were not meeting Moutet's standard of a family living from work.[172]

The minimum wage, however, stayed minimal: it went from 7 to 8 francs per day in Dakar in 1938.[173] The next official study of the standard of living in Dakar, in early 1939, found that prices had risen 50 percent in the past two years. Calculating the budget of a bachelor worker, officials found he fell short, and "It is without question that the wage does not cover the needs of a family. But it is equally beyond discussion that the laborer is in most cases a bachelor." Only the top of the EMCIBA scale, for example, would support a family. But by early 1939 the Popular Front was out. Pierre Boisson was governor-general, and it was his turn to comment on the new study: he decided to think of the unskilled worker as a bachelor who worked when he was not farming, and he declared that the skilled worker who earned 350 francs if single and 650 if married as "living almost in ease." Most Dakar workers, he concluded, lived in "good material conditions." Boisson had equated a skill category with a family category and assumed a relation to rural resources that allowed him to consider the majority of workers not to be truly workers at all. And he had changed vocabulary: the "honorable" life of 1936 – which admittedly could not be led on wage income alone – had become "good material conditions" or "ease" in 1939, although inflation had at least erased the gains made in between. The Popular Front had not solved the problem of balancing urban incomes and living costs; its successors simply declared it not to exist.[174]

Unionization and wage setting represent concrete ways in which the Popular Front entered the labor question. Equally important is the debate it unleashed, the questions it opened. In a climate changed by the first flurry of African trade union organization, strikes, and collective bargaining agreements, the Popular Front from 1937 until its fall kept trying to enact its overall social program. In June 1937, the government circulated a revised draft decree on labor. Inspecteur du Travail Casset asserted that it not only proclaimed "freedom of work" but also promoted "labor stability":

> The concession of paid holidays after a year's presence in the same establishment, the allocation of a retirement pension to old workers, constitute extra payments capable of attaching the black to the firm that employs him. The allocation of food to members of the worker's family, in the form of a ration or a family allocation, will contribute to the result in assuring the improvement of the physical condition of the race and will also have the effect of maintaining at as stable a level as possible the buying power of the worker and his family.[175]

Employers, he insisted, might face higher costs, but they would have a more productive and willing labor force. This was the stabilization argument that was to be heard from French and British officials for the next fifteen years. A stable linkage of workers and families to particular enterprises was the alternative to forced labor. The idea of family allocations was the most radical part of the formula: it meant a supplementary ration for a worker's wife and up to three children, plus an adjustment of wages to cover "the other needs of the worker and his family." The draft decree provided as well for an eight-hour day and for the replacement of the pécule by a savings certificate redeemable at a network of facilities.

This proposal was subject to withering fire, just like the initial proposals of 1936. Business interests thought it too costly; the eight-hour day, higher ration requirements, and vacation pay, would add 25 percent to labor costs. But the family ration (and it was clear that the family allocations now meant little more than that) was attacked with a vigor that revealed not only the unwillingness of the patronat to pay higher costs for stability, but its fundamentally different conception of what sort of beings made up the African labor force. A sisal planter explained in detail that in cargo handling, plantation labor, and in general, employers wanted a "young and vigorous labor force, these workers are bachelors." In agriculture, "whether the man works [for wages] or not, the wife, SHE, works. It is she who cultivates dry season rice, manioc, potatoes and most often as well peanuts and millet." Giving workers' families food would reduce food production: "the concession of three free rations creates three lazy people. The family agricultural economy is reduced to nothing." The Chambre d'Agriculture et d'Industrie de la Côte d'Ivoire similarly argued that women and children, "far from being a burden on the native ... constitute rather a significant asset." In any case, Africans changed wives too often and declared too many other relatives to be their children for family wages or rations to be workable. In general, natives "are not evolved enough to get the most profit from the money they receive."[176]

As before, such views were partially shared in official circles. Some thought the plan too complicated and costly to administer. Others claimed that their work forces were too "provisional" and "variable" for such measures. The governor of the Ivory Coast thought planters would not accept anything which increased their costs after their recent sacrifices in adapting to free labor. The governor of Senegal reported that most local officials and consultative bodies opposed family wages and rations, but he himself thought they would be a step toward putting the family under "the influence of modern ideas."[177]

The question of who was a worker, and hence subject to labor regulations, arose in this debate and was to remain controversial through the passage of the Code du Travail in 1952. An employer organization demanded that navétanes – the seasonal workers who went to the peanut fields of Senegal each year – be included, so that their employers, all Africans, would face the costs as did European planters. The governor disagreed: the navétanes were caught up in "native customs relative to working conditions" which he did not want to disturb.[178]

De Coppet read so many negative reports – he was not making any attempt to collect the opinions of Africans[179] – that he dropped the family benefits. He dropped paid holidays as well, and the idea of a savings scheme. As the Inspecteur du Travail noted, "the truth is that the current project with the suppression of the family wage, caisses de compensation, paid holidays, retirement pay for old workers, is hardly revolutionary."[180]

The family wage had fallen victim not only to the fact that it cost money but to the widespread conception that African families were large and unfathomable. The issue would return after the war. Meanwhile, the idea of family allocations for Africans proved not so strange in the 1930s as long as it was associated with the category of "évolué" rather than the category of "worker." "Evolué" was of course an old term in French colonial parlance, and it was meant to identify those Africans who had gone over to something like the "European" side. Officials, much more so than their British counterparts, had long for the most part accepted that – just as African peasants should be allowed to live within their own communities – African évolués should be given some voice within French institutions.

In the bureaucracy, Africans were not put in a separate racial classification as much as shunted into positions in lower levels of an intricate hierarchy. The top ranks, the *cadres généraux*, were all white, but the *cadre commun secondaire* and above all the *cadres locaux* were mixed. French civil servants always got a special indemnity for serving overseas. Beyond that, the Popular Front favored equal treatment within each rank, although in practice the numerous special indemnities paid for variations in local costs of living were highly discriminatory. Family allowances were part of the French system of compensation in government service, and their application to African civil servants – true évolués – did not seem so strange. As of January 1937, following recent increases, the "cadres autochtones" within the *cadres commun secondaire*, *locaux*, and *spéciaux* received upward of 360 francs for each child.[181]

After the Popular Front was gone, a civil servants' union tried to push family allowances back into the domain of labor. When family allocations in France were increased in January 1939, the Fédération des Fonctionnaires and the Union Fédérale des Fonctionnaires Indigènes du Gouvernement-Général chimed in with their own requests. But the African union's demands were rejected decisively: "The level of life of native agents is not comparable to that of European civil servants."[182]

As for laborers, the issue never got beyond a modest proposal about family rations. Retreating on that front, the government produced a new, weaker draft of the other social laws by May 1938, and a new round of comments came in toward the end of the year. By then, the Popular Front was gone. The proposals went before a hostile Commission des Lois Sociales of the Conseil Supérieur de la France Outre-Mer (one of the endless consultative bodies in the way of decrees and laws) in December 1938, and it debunked the entire Popular Front project: "even in France, it is important now to make an assessment of this generous experience" of the social laws, in the light of "a world [that is] unhappily more and more aggressive." It added,

It is from the point of view of the productivity of the Empire which must above all be the base for the examination of this so-called social legislation, for which we would prefer to reserve, in so far as it concerns the subjects of our Empire, the old name of native policy.

One had to take account of "the slowness of the evolution of indigenous mentality," and the danger that the native population was likely to interpret social laws as "an invitation to relax its effort and diminish its spirit of discipline." The commission concluded that new legislation should wait for "the necessary evolution to be accomplished."[183] The commission's willingness to put everything aside before the new imperatives of production stands out alongside the even more striking attempt to redefine the labor problem back into "native policy."

This was the end until after the war of the project of bringing French social laws to the colonies. The frank defense of exploitation and the stereotyping of "indigènes" after the Popular Front's fall is a useful reminder that the colonial politics of that movement were in fact different from what went before and what would come after. Although de Coppet took a paternalistic view of Africans who were insufficiently educated to belong to trade unions, he did insist that other Africans could do so, and he was able to work with trade unionists like Gning and politicians like Lamine Guèye. The government, in practice, negotiated with the strikers of 1936–37 as if they were making normal, indeed reasonable, claims. Inspecteur du Travail Tap, author of the legislation that attracted such vehement hostility, thought that African work habits and rhythms were quite distinct from those of Europeans, but he believed one had to act *as if they were not*. Africans could become better workers if they were freed of administrative constraint, paid better wages, accorded the same kinds of social protection as other workers. After the Popular Front fell – even before Vichy – the dogged opponents of thinking of the worker as a worker showed their alternative: treat the native as a native, and restore forced labor to make him work.

The limits of labor reform: Thiès, September–October 1938

The last act of the Popular Front's performance was a tragic one: a strike ended in shootings and death. The people excluded from de Coppet's conception of a working class separated from the rest of African society insisted on being heard; a young labor movement proved too divided and inexperienced to control a complex situation; and opportunists and obstructionists, opposed even to the slow pace of Popular Front reform, seized an occasion to embarrass it at whatever human cost.

The Syndicat des Travailleurs Indigènes du Dakar–Niger, under François Gning, had made good use of its relationships with de Coppet and the director of the Dakar–Niger railway, Giran. The Sûreté considered this union to be the "avant garde, if one can say so, of the union movement in Senegal."[184] The railway union made its strike threats, but – with other lines to the top – it had so far pulled its punches. Just whom the union represented was in question. Gning, in 1937, had expressed doubts about recruiting "simple temporary laborers" to union ranks. His real interest was in the literate, skilled workers in the cadres, the regular hierarchy of railway workers.[185]

By the summer of 1938, the "auxiliaries" and "journaliers" – auxiliary and daily workers, whose actual employment pattern was frequently long term – were so aggrieved by Gning's disinterest in their situation that they began to organize their own union. A delegation of auxiliaries led by Cheikh Diack, himself an auxiliary at Dakar, went to see the director to complain that auxiliaries' wages were lagging behind both the cost of living and the wages of the lowest level of the cadres, the cadres locaux. The director replied that wages had been raised 6 to 20 percent in 1937, and that the workers had been exempted from seasonal layoffs, awarded paid holidays, sick pay and other benefits. He made no new promises. On 9 August, 300 auxiliaries at Thiès demonstrated in front of the director's office, and later spoke to the acting director, in Giran's absence.[186]

Meanwhile, Gning wrote to de Coppet complaining of the "continual menace of disorder fomented by certain daily employees." They had demanded "unjustified wage increases." He sent along a list of twelve men active in organizing the auxiliaries and suggested that "sanctions" be applied to them. "It is a question of elements new to the Railway whose past is more or less doubtful, who worked upon by political agitators of the town, aspire to create a union that is more political than professional in the sole aim of sowing at any moment disorder in the Railway, which *our current union does not accept*." The acting governor-general, Geismar, wrote in de Coppet's absence to thank Gning for his "confident collaboration" and sent the letter on to the railway, which he hoped would "lead the protesting daily workers to a more exact comprehension of realities."[187]

Gning was betraying worker solidarity, but something political was afoot. The auxiliaries' movement, legitimate as its grievances were, apparently was being used in a political ploy. Galandou Diouf, deputy and rival of Lamine Guèye, appears to have been seeking a way to counter Gning's close ties to Guèye; Diouf was not particularly known for his support of the working man. In any case, the auxiliaries were apparently taken under the wing of Menekh Seck, an associate of Diouf, who let them meet at his house and accompanied their deputations to railway officials.[188]

Whether the momentum toward a strike that developed in August and September 1938 was the result of the machinations of Seck and Diouf or a more spontaneous outburst from a marginalized section of the work force is not clear. The two explanations are not incompatible. The split in the workers' ranks, the hostility of European agents toward all African workers, and the temporary absence of de Coppet and Giran added to the tension. [189]

On 27 August, 300 daily workers in the machine shop left work and unsuccessfully demanded a raise. The railway made things worse by transferring Diack from Dakar to an isolated railway station on 26 September.[190] So there assembled on 27 September an angry group of auxiliary workers. Of 1,975 men in these categories, 1,410 were absent from work that day; the members of the cadres remained at work throughout. The government had received an anonymous telegram saying "Services will be suspended if we do not receive Diack on the noon train tomorrow. RAILWAYMEN." It responded by sending troops to Thiès. Soldiers and 200–300 strikers confronted each other. Stone throwing by strikers – as near as one can tell from the accounts – led the inexperienced soldiers, apparently without an order, to fire. Six strikers died.[191]

After the shooting, the workers were visited by Galandou Diouf, who urged them to remain calm but not to return to work. The Muslim leader Seydou Nourou Tall came to them and preached peace. The next day, as the strike continued, the governor of Senegal urged that everything should be done to expedite the disposition of the auxiliaries union's documents, since he regarded union recognition as the principle aim of the strike. Negotiations began and agreement was reached with the daily workers of Dakar and Thiès on the 29th, despite, if railway officials can be believed, the efforts of Diouf to prevent it. The agreement provided for de facto recognition of the union, conditional amnesty for strikers, indemnities for victims of the shooting, and a sympathetic hearing for the claims of the auxiliaries. The same day as the strike at Thiès, the auxiliaries at Dakar had struck. There was strike action at Guinguinéo and Louga – all coordinated, apparently, with the help of telephonists and others who used the railway's own communications mechanisms to their advantage. The strike ended throughout the system on the 30th. The Popular Front's successors did not honor the agreement and fired some workers who had participated.[192]

In agreeing to work with the union, the governor of Senegal, who regarded its members as "simple natives of the bush for the most part", ignored the educational qualifications of the March 1937 decree on unions. De Coppet himself, guilt-stricken by what had happened, visited Thiès on 4 October, spoke with auxiliaries, and convinced them to try to work things out through government conciliation procedures. He also sent a note to a union activist, "In order to show you how much I desire to see you form rapidly and regularly The Association of Auxiliaries that you intend to create, I am sending you, enclosed, not for you, but to be placed in the treasury of this budding association, a sum of 2,000 francs."[193]

The aftermath was as ugly as the incident was tragic. Diouf attacked de Coppet for condoning brutality, while members of the European business community attacked him for not being brutal enough. White railwaymen campaigned successfully for the removal of the director, Giran, whom they felt encouraged indiscipline among Africans by listening to their grievances, while Gning's union supported Giran and commiserated with him when he was sacked. Lamine Guèye's newspaper, *L'A.O.F.*, blamed the entire problem on Diouf, claiming that auxiliaries were well paid and well treated and that they had been provoked by "Galandou, agent provocateur."[194]

The new minister, Mandel, used the occasion to fire de Coppet on 15 October. Strike rumors flew again in November and December, but this time the new regime in Paris made it clear that it had no ambivalence about repression. Mandel telegraphed to Dakar to be prepared to "replace instantly absent personnel in case of interruption of service"; the police followed Gning and Diack around Dakar, fearing they might patch up their differences and call a general strike. Soon Diack became as hesitant to act as Gning, although Sûreté insisted that "an order or any incident skillfully exploited" would be enough to start a strike on the entire line.[195]

The shock of the deaths, the removal of de Coppet and Giran, and the harsh stance of Mandel and the new administration in West Africa appear to have subdued the railway unions. The auxiliary union – now turned into the Association Amicale et Professionnelle des Auxiliaires du Dakar–Niger – became "much moderated and for the past several months its influence is exerted toward maintaining calm and discipline among the most numerous and least favored workers of the Network." Gning, trade unionist ally of a leftist colonial administration, also got along with its successor: he was praised in 1939 for having "shown devotion toward the Administration on different occasions."[196] In general, the trade union movement seems to have been shocked into quiescence. In 1939, there was not a single strike reported in Dakar, in 1940 a few minor ones. All these strikes, commented a report, were "purely professional," and had kept away from "racial struggles or political terrain."[197]

On reform and the labor question

In the late 1930s, British and French colonial officials began in a serious way to question their pasts. Senior officials and ministers – Moutet and MacDonald – had noted the poverty that remained after years of colonial rule. Their comments on African work habits and African resistance to labor markets implicitly admitted that a half-century of teaching Africans the value of work had ended up conveying rather different lessons.

In 1940, this period of reform in French Africa was over. In French colonial policy, there was a difference between left and right. But the Popular Front left an important legacy on the statute books, the decrees of March 1937 legalizing trade unions and providing machinery to resolve disputes, and it opened up two kinds of issues – forced labor and social legislation – for debate.

The British Colonial Office in 1939 acquired the most important piece of reformist legislation it had been given in years, but officials themselves readily admitted that its immediate value was largely symbolic and that its material impact would have to await the end of the war. The war, in the meantime, would exacerbate some of the problems the Act was supposed to solve, dragging down the urban standard of living in much of British Africa.

The Popular Front had not been pushed so hard by African strikers as were British regimes, but it more explicitly acknowledged that Africans could be workers. It had sought to minimize the labor question – by reducing forced labor and encouraging peasant production – but it began to face the labor question where it was posed. Officials were led into this by their belief that even a small working class was after all a working class and needed the same *kinds*, if not the same *level* of protection as one in France. That social legislation was under consideration at the time of the Dakar strike wave of 1936–37 made it easier for officials on the scene to respond to the strikes *as* a labor problem and to try to resolve them in those terms. The gains of the workers were temporary – inflation ate up much of what was won in the first wave of strikes – but the process showed that a French industrial relations framework could channel conflict into fora where movement could take place.

The British government had been confronted with a labor problem before it was ready to think about it. Indeed, officials transposed it into a problem of development and welfare, positing a plausible but unexplained and unproven relationship between the improvement of a colony's productive capacities, improvement in its population's material welfare, and the taming of disorder. Words like "disturbance" kept turning up in reference to the actions of workers demanding a better life: on the Copperbelt, in the West Indies, in Mombasa. The principal recognition of the labor question came through the establishment of labour departments and the labour advisor; like the Inspecteurs du Travail in French Africa, these individuals and their reports would help to make labor issues more visible.

Most important, both colonial bureaucracies started to learn that the labor question was an intimate one. The labour officers and the Inspecteurs du Travail were beginning to supply information. In British

Africa, colonial surveys and the work of independent scholars or missionaries were only starting to describe labor migration and the formation of communities of workers as a part of colonial reality, while in French Africa progressive scholar-administrators were more interested in arguing that African peasants could make a positive contribution to an imperial economy.[198]

The will to end forced labor, to foster conciliation procedures, and to make work organization more efficient did not mean that such tasks would get done. Indeed, old ways of doing things had created subtle relations of power that were hard to see, let alone to change. The Popular Front discovered this in the Ivory Coast – where the difference between forced labor and the "apostolat du travail" proved elusive, just as the controversy over "encouragement" in Kenya in 1919 had for a moment let out the fact that people in British Africa made their decisions about seeking wage labor in a power-laden environment that fit uneasily into a category labelled "free." Popular Front leaders, despite having recognized that Africans could be workers, were still unable in 1938 to appreciate how complex the African labor force was. The British government, in 1935, had failed to realize that events like the Copperbelt strike could not be willed away, and they had yet to learn that labelling "detribalized" the people who had escaped their vision of traditional Africa – by calling them what they were not – only made it harder to figure out what they were.

4 Forced labor, strike movements, and the idea of development, 1940–1945

The governments which ruled French West Africa and British Africa during the early war years had one characteristic in common: both were planning for futures that did not exist. Looking beyond the war itself, London's and Vichy's colonial leaders envisioned a rational, planned world, where the concept of development would rule supreme. London looked toward evolutionary economic and social change leading eventually to political devolution; Vichy thought in terms of top-down control utilizing every resource to an optimal degree to make the French empire a coherent and prosperous whole. As the central bureaucracies enjoyed their imperial dream, African workers – facing heightened demands for labor, fewer goods to consume, and escalating compulsion – were living a colonial nightmare. Local officials were frightened themselves.

The difference between the dream and the nightmare would soon prove central to the collapse of the colonial project: empire was not, after all, such a good laboratory of modernity. The will of colonized people kept intruding itself into the apparatus of control. African workers forced colonial planners who wanted to think about development think instead about the labor question.

This came about in quite different ways in the two empires. In the European war, France fell quickly. Its African empire split, as officials in Equatorial Africa remained loyal to de Gaulle while those in West Africa submitted themselves to Vichy. Vichy, in line with its *fascisant* conception of a rational order in which each social group took its place, set out its coordinated development program allocating investment to each region in accordance with its particular advantages. Industry would have a place in the colonies, and Vichy scornfully set aside fears that creating an African proletariat would have consequences a French colonial government could not control. But from Dakar, Vichy's governor-general, Pierre Boisson, kept warning that the limits of labor mobilization had already been reached. The reality of the war years was that, in trying to preserve an export economy while imports were curtailed by war, Boisson's government escalated the use of forced labor to the point that Boisson himself feared demographic and political disaster.

The British government, meanwhile, was searching for a formula for colonial policy that would appear – or even be – progressive while avoiding precipitate commitment to self-government. Concerned that the legitimacy of colonialism was being questioned in the United States and elsewhere, London increasingly linked the future of empire to the idea of development. Officials insisted that economic and social development was a necessary prerequisite to political progress. Yet from Mombasa to Lagos, officials on the scene were reporting that African workers, in a series of strike movements, were pushing them in another direction. The issue being forced was that of workers' standard of living, despite the economic planners' contention that this was undiscussable in wartime and would have to be deferred in peacetime in favor of raising productive capacity. Those who had to face the struggle at first hand – local officials and boards of inquiry into the inevitable confrontations – pioneered a different analysis: a working class had emerged in African cities, and its ability to survive and to reproduce had to be assured before the colonial economy could become more productive and orderly.

All this happened during a conjuncture shaped by war. French West Africa was relatively cut off, its production artificially maintained by the state. Vichy's labor recruitment by terror led to resistance in the form of "desertion"; workers wanted to be left alone more than to have higher wages which they could not in any case spend. At the same time, British Africa had become more vital to its metropole than ever before, the loss of Asian colonies making African ones the only sources of tropical commodities. But shipping was short and imports into colonies had low priority, so workers were getting less as they contributed more. The result was a strike wave in the most active commercial centers: in ports like Mombasa and Dar es Salaam, on railways in the Gold Coast and mines in Northern Rhodesia, and in colony-wide movements in Nigeria.

Development and labor conflict in British Africa

Development and the Africans

In 1939, the labor question was assimilated into the development question. And in those terms it remained. The development framework was elaborated in two contexts during the war years: the debate over constitutional structures and political evolution and the debate over production and the standard of living. Part of the pressure to devise a systematic way of thinking about colonial progress came from the Allies. President

Roosevelt and other American officials assumed that the Atlantic Charter, when it referred to peoples' rights to determine their own government, applied universally; Churchill thought that applying such a concept to colonies was absurd. Meanwhile, the United States pulled Great Britain into a long and worrisome discussion in 1942 over the possibility of international agreements specifying minimal standards for colonizing powers to meet, rather like those of the ILO Conventions in the labor field. In the end, the American government pulled its punches: its worries about the dangers to security of the sudden appearance of new and weak states exceeded its concern for the consistent application of the principle of self-determination. But meanwhile British officials – fearing American self-righteousness as well as possible designs on imperial markets – sought ways of making explicit the justification for empire.[1]

What concerns us here is the social dimension. British policy makers were anxious to deflect the discussion from progress toward independence to a broader consideration of the responsibilities of imperial trusteeship.[2] Africa acquired the dubious distinction – along with New Guinea from time to time – of being a test case: when would independence be appropriate for people as primitive as Africans? Lord Cranborne, then Secretary of State for the Colonies, said in 1942: "We all know in our heart that most Colonies, especially in Africa, will probably not be fit for complete independence for centuries." He castigated the Americans for insisting on implausible goals when they "do not understand the conditions under which we have to work" – in other words, that they did not appreciate how primitive primitive people were. From within the Colonial Office came the opinion: "A good many years (perhaps a good many generations though it would be impolitic to say so openly) must elapse" before even the first stages along the road to self-government were completed.[3]

A vain attempt by British and American policy makers to agree upon a joint statement on the future of colonial rule had the effect of deepening British attachment to the policy of colonial development. British drafts kept stressing "improved labor standards, economic advancement and social security." They insisted independence would be meaningless without economic self-sufficiency.[4] Colonial powers, redubbed "parent states," should bring about "rising standards of life" and be sure that the territories' natural resources would be used "not for the promotion merely of commercial ends but in the best interests of the peoples concerned and of the world as a whole."[5]

Colonial Secretary Oliver Stanley had this in mind when – partly in lieu of the failed Joint Declaration – he delivered a statement to Parliament on 13 July 1943.[6] He insisted "we are pledged to guide Colonial people along the road to self-government within the framework of the British Empire," but he kept the meaning of self-government vague and said little about the process of getting there and nothing about the time table. He emphasized what had to be done before self-government could be an immediate object:

if self-government is to succeed it has to have solid, social and economic foundations, and although without them spectacular political advances may draw for the authors the plaudits of the superficial, they will bring to those whom it is designed to benefit nothing but disaster. [To] my mind the real test of the sincerity and success of our Colonial Policy is two-fold. It is not only the actual political advances that we make, but it is also, and I think more important, the steps that we are taking, economic and social as well as political, to prepare the people for further and future responsibilities.

Stanley pledged British help to establish an economic basis "to meet the needs of Government and peoples and which will give a reasonable standard of life. It is pretty clear that unless we succeed in doing this any talk about self-government is really humbug."[7]

Stanley's linkage of social progress to evolution toward self-government served both to push claims for political autonomy into the future and to distance him from possible claims that minimum social standards should be empire-wide. *Each* colony should become "self-supporting." He was careful to distinguish his view from "the old, rigid system of Colonial financial self-sufficiency," which prevented any colony from preparing for a better future unless it could finance it from past savings. The Colonial Development and Welfare Act would allow "those reforms and developments which alone held out any promise of increasing its permanent wealth." But only for a time.[8] The self-governing former colony would eventually have to fund its social services by its own means. Stanley's statement – at the very beginning of the development effort – was an effort to avoid what came to bedevil the French government, whose explicit insistence of France as a reference point for its colonies made it the object of claims to the material entitlements of French citizens as soon as social and economic development became a subject of discussion.

Nonetheless, Stanley's use of the word "test" pointed to the ideological vulnerability of his position. Development spending was quantifiable; economic growth was measurable; social services could be assessed and incomes calculated; and any renewal of mass discontent could be read as a sign that the state was not doing enough. The old idea that Britain exercised a "trusteeship" on behalf of dependent peoples had the virtue of being untestable; the new claims for a progressive colonial policy were not so insulated from their consequences.

Here is where the debate within the Colonial Office over production and the standard of living raised questions about what the commitment to economic and social development actually meant. The linkages assumed in the statements of MacDonald in 1939 and Stanley in 1943 – that increased productive capacity would lead to improved standards of living and to political evolution – were so tenuous that they were quickly debunked in the privacy of the Colonial Office. The head of the Colonial Office's Economics Department, Sydney Caine, minuted in 1940, "In many Dependencies the natural poverty and/or the over-population is such that it is very doubtful whether any economic development will ever be able to maintain the inhabitant in anything like the standard at which we are now aiming."[9]

Caine's point was not about wartime conditions; it was about aboriginal poverty. In wartime, increasing colonial people's standard of living was simply out of the question.[10] But such words could not be spoken aloud, not so soon after the great gesture of the Colonial Development and Welfare Act. Indeed, the act was premised on an improved standard of living and improved social services cooling colonial anger and restoring imperial honor. After much discussion, the Colonial Office came up with a circular to all colonies, signed by the then secretary of state, Lord Moyne, on 5 June 1941, specifying that the wartime sacrifice should come from "those inhabitants of the Colonial Empire who enjoy a comparatively high standard of life." For those who did not, "it is an imperative duty to do all that is practically possible to raise the standard of living of such people, even during the war period, alike for humanitarian, political, economic and administrative reasons." Colonial governments should use local resources and savings from deferred consumption during the war; they should plan; they should address "social development in health, education, rural welfare, and so on."[11]

That did not settle the issue. Caine was insisting in late 1941 that wage increases in the colonies should be avoided. Given that manufactured commodities were in short supply (allocating more to the colonies was not discussed), raising wages would simply raise prices. He wanted wages and prices to be kept in check, and if something had to be done, he preferred subsidizing the prices of basic commodities. Orde Browne, the labor advisor, warned how risky this could be: "The avoidance of friction and grounds for legitimate grievance is of great importance in war time." He too wanted to avoid increases in basic wages, but favored a bonus system that would compensate for the increase in costs of local food and imported goods. He hoped that objectifying the problem would take it out of politics: pegging bonus rates to published cost of living figures would "go far to reduce any press agitation, or threat of strikes."

To Caine, such an argument was outside the limits of the discussable: "your approach and that of the Economics Department are so different that it would be preferable not to attempt to produce an agreed memorandum" on the subject.[12]

The head of the Africa department, Arthur Dawe, reminded his colleagues that if Great Britain were serious about improving the standard of living "of the mass of the colonial populations," this "can only mean a rise in *basic* wages: and in many places it is quite clear that, apart altogether from war conditions, there is a strong case for raising the basic rate." But Caine insisted that this was economically unsound: "However much we may talk therefore, there is no real possibility of a general increase in the real standard of living of the whole population of the Empire in present circumstances." He did recognize that he had made a major assumption, that the existing distribution of commodities was fixed. But here he turned to a political argument: the people of Great Britain would not accept that the standard of living of colonized peoples be raised "at the expense of this country."[13]

The Colonial Office could not agree within itself whether or not to declare publicly that it would strive to raise the standard of living in the colonies.[14] The best it could do was reaffirm the circular of 5 June, but point out that "the fundamental basis, however, of such a rise in the standard of living must be an increase, by greater local productivity or otherwise, in the quantity of goods available for purchase and consumption." For now, its goal was much more modest: to avoid "depreciation in the standard of living of the working classes." Price controls and bonus schemes – linked to measured changes in the cost of living – were the best ways of handling the problem. Increasing basic wages – the logical implication of the earlier circular, as Dawe had argued – was changed from a government policy to a hoped-for consequence of economic processes, that is the raising of productivity.[15]

In 1942, real wages in African cities were in fact plummeting, and in Nigeria and Kenya protests and strikes took place. Whether or not Caine's economics were sound was becoming irrelevant. The economics and social services departments of the Colonial Office, where this argument had been taking place, did not handle the consequence of the strike waves. They were deemed political issues, and the Africa department made sure that the wage increases necessary to settle the strikes went through (see below).[16]

In London, Caine's argument presaged a swing toward a productionist view of development: policy should center on increasing output, not on a specific attempt to raise the standard of living of the poor or the working class. But to stress productivity was to return to African workers in another sense: how could particular people, in particular ecological and social environments, be induced to produce more? In 1942 and 1943, officials were thrashing about: their images of Africa and their images of efficient production were hard to reconcile. And so in 1942, an attempt to provide guidance to Colonial Governments on how to reorganize production had to be dropped because neither Caine nor anyone else in the Colonial Office knew what to say.[17]

They had great difficulty in focusing on what labor, production, and consumption actually meant. Caine and others insisted they were not after improving subsistence farming – that meant only the continuation of "abject poverty."[18] On the other hand, most officials agreed with Lord Swinton, resident minister in West Africa, when he insisted that the producer "should not rely only on export. He should live 'on' as well as 'off' his holding; producing food for himself and for internal sale." Swinton couldn't make up his mind whether larger units of production were a good idea, and he was leary of the formation of a class of Africans who had gone beyond peasant production: "Africa for the Africans does not mean Africa for *some* Africans." Large units "would be vigorously resisted by Africans" and "accelerate the creation of a landless class which in times of depression will provide an unemployment problem." Gerald Clauson too had previously warned against the danger of creating "a class of plutocrats" in Africa, whose privilege would be a new cause of "social upheaval."[19]

To see plutocrats as the alternative to subsistence cultivators was on the face of it bizarre. But officials like Lord Swinton were caught in their model of the tribal African and this impoverished their ability to analyze the possibilities of class formation. He invoked a common British conception of how its approach differed from that of France: "Broadly the French aim at making Africans into good Frenchmen; we aim at making them good Africans." He was actually reproducing the French dichotomy of évolué and paysan as the only two social categories necessary for analyzing African society. This classification left out workers – not to mention the dynamic Hausa merchants who criss-crossed West Africa or the market-oriented farmers of the cocoa belt or the energetic coffee farmers of Mt. Kilimanjaro.[20]

The discussion of plutocrats and subsistence cultivators also suggests that the economics specialists of the Colonial Office had trouble thinking about capitalism. Certain enterprises clearly filled the image of the capitalist: white settlers and mining enterprises. But outside of that, did economic development mean capitalist development? Would the use of wage labor by certain Africans lead to the long-term accumulation of capital in their hands and thus to an ongoing process of mobilizing and concentrating economic power? Were there particular forms of capital accumulation and wage labor exploitation that Africans had already devised and which could affect the future of development in specific ways? The official architects of development were not thinking about anything so specific; they weren't sure whether Africans could manage capitalism and whether it would be a good thing if they could; they talked about plutocrats instead.

Orde Browne, whose job it was to think about workers, was relatively isolated in bringing labor as a social concept into a discussion of development: labor had to be carefully considered not only because development required "the manual worker," but because the way labor was organized could endanger the entire effort: "a discontented labour force is a constant danger as affording a permanent basis for political agitation of the unscrupulous type." Equally important, "urban overcrowding, slums, and similar questions, are also largely labour problems, since they are bound up with wage rates, rotational employment, cost of living, credit system, and so forth." The conflicts of Mombasa and Lagos appear between the lines: the way Africans lived and the way they worked were part of the same problem. Orde Browne conceded to Caine that wage increases would not solve urban distress. The tribal framework of social control would not help here; he looked instead to urbanites becoming involved in "practical activities," even voluntarily, in sanitation, surveying, medical work, and social welfare, that would "occupy the energies and capacities of the better educated class in a far more useful fashion than political agitation." Orde Browne was taking refuge in a Victorian fantasy – tame little societies taking care of local problems for themselves and not raising questions of class or of politics. But along the way he had pointed to the reciprocal relationship of urban development and labor. Unlike some of his colleagues, Orde Browne hoped to see African workers as part of a more complex class system than presently existed:

the African plantation owner, mining prospector, shopkeeper, factory manager, skilled mechanic, etc., should be encouraged, for they are at present deplorably rare. The development of this class would go far to give the African the feeling that he owned his country and exploited its resources, instead of seeing these constantly in the hands of the white man.[21]

Frederick Pedler, one of the Colonial Office's bright young Africa specialists, was flirting – although no more than that – with even more radical ideas. Pitching in on the standard of living debate in 1942, he commented that increasing a very low wage by a modest amount might do no good at all: raising wages from Shs 15 per month to 17/6 would raise labor costs but not significantly affect output. But increasing the wage by a factor of four – to Shs 15 *per week* – might produce four times the output. The worker would now be able to bring his wife and children to town and would not frequent bars and prostitutes. Caine shot that idea down with a more conventional argument: given the current shortage of imported goods, paying four times as much in wages would reduce output to a quarter its former level rather than increase it by four times.[22]

Pedler's argument was essentially a call for stabilizing the labor force. He agreed with Caine and Clauson that to reinforce subsistence production was to reinforce African backwardness, but he did not want anybody to dodge the fact that moving away from an Africa of "peasant production" meant "urbanisation and industry."[23] Pedler was anticipating the focus of attention after the war: he was not only arguing for a quantum leap in wages for workers, but he was also putting the worker's family at the center of the labor question, insisting that the orderly reproduction of a labor force was a necessary condition to increasing production.

These ideas sat on the table. If labor unrest had shoved the Colonial Office into its development mode, its development efforts were not leading it back to a careful consideration of the labor question. The latter discussion took place mostly in reaction to events, such as the strike movements of 1942 and 1945, to which front-line officials had to respond. The social services department monitored progress in organizing labour departments and promoting trade unionism, admitting that shortages of funds and personnel slowed the initiative.[24] Calls for "greater permanency of labour" occasionally surfaced, but received no sustained discussion. The highest officials seemed unable to draw lessons from their subordinates' experiences: at the end of 1942, a particularly tense time, Secretary of State Lord Cranborne felt able to tell the other noble lords, "The relations of employers and employed are better than they have ever been."[25] In Parliament, both sides of the aisle seemed to agree that the founding of labour departments represented the right sort of action – Labour spokesmen said this could be done more vigorously – and both were content to posit that following ILO Conventions in the colonies amounted to a kind of "labour code" that addressed major issues facing labor.[26]

There was a weak consensus among politicians and senior bureaucrats that trade unions were a good thing; the Colonial Office made some efforts to appoint trade union advisors to certain colonies and to encourage them to register unions and help them get organized.[27] Many governors, including Bourdillon in Nigeria, who had responded positively to the demands of African workers (see below), wanted to handle the problems by correct administrative action rather than through union participation in wage setting. In Northern Rhodesia, only three years after the second major mineworkers' strike, the governor put aside a trade union bill even as he talked of his desire to maintain "industrial peace": "the African workers are not yet thought to be sufficiently advanced to be able satisfactorily to organize a Trade Union and take a proper part in Trade Union activities."[28] So in the midst of an active period of labor unrest and despite Colonial Office endorsement of the principle of unionization in the colonies, little was done along these lines.[29]

Meanwhile, the economic policy makers could no more talk about industrialization as a social process than they could address the complexity of African agriculture. When an advisory committee on which the brilliant young economist W. Arthur Lewis sat tried to discuss different approaches to industrialization and the desirability of large or small units of production, Caine shut off the discussion by arguing, as Lewis put it, that discussing them "would raise political questions outside the Committee's terms of reference." Lewis resigned in frustration.[30] Lewis had run into an issue of discourse: the boundaries of what could and could not be discussed. Caine complained that Lewis' proposals were "revolutionary."[31] The issues – in Caine's version as much as Lewis' – of course had a political dimension: deciding whether to foster small farms, big plantations, or industries involved issues of wealth and power. If problems of labor and welfare were to be shoehorned by the Colonial Office into the problem of development, and development was to be defined in such a way that Lewis' issues were excluded, the discursive boundaries were being narrowly drawn.

Unable to specify with any complexity what kinds of social structures were relevant to Africa and how they could be transformed, officials had trouble thinking through exactly what their pride and joy, the Colonial Development and Welfare Act, was supposed to do. During the war, neither colonies nor London had the manpower, the supplies, or the funds to give much substance to the initiative.[32] In 1944, Stanley noted that of the £20 million authorized for the first four years, only £4 million had been spent; under the wording of the act, unspent balances in any year went back to the Treasury.[33] As colonial officials pondered whether London and individual colonies should have broad plans for economic change or narrow objectives to improve infrastructure and how social services and economic investments should be weighted against each other, Stanley brought attention back to the fundamental political importance development and welfare had to the future of empire.[34]

Stanley was about to ask Parliament in 1944 to refund the Colonial Development and Welfare Act, providing over double the annual funding set in 1940 and lasting ten years: that is £10 million per year rising slightly each year toward a ten-year total of £120 million. The ten-year period would allow for long-range planning. He thought that the capital which colonial governments had set aside during the war amounted to roughly double this amount. This was, Stanley claimed, as much money as could be absorbed, "without dislocating the whole social life of the Colonies, which would be disastrous to them."[35]

Stanley's thinking in 1944, compared to MacDonald's in 1939, reflects the influence, but not the triumph, of Caine's efforts to narrow the meaning of economic, as well as, no doubt, the more powerful concern with output that war engendered. But it also cemented the anxiety that commitment to development not be taken as commitment to an empire-wide set of social standards:

It was easy to allow oneself to over-emphasize the welfare side, as in some ways it was so much the easier to tackle. But if it was easy it was also fatal: the whole object of the Colonial Development and Welfare Act – not always understood... at the moment in the Colonies – was that at the end of the period... the Colonies' own resources would have increased sufficiently for them to maintain a decent standard of life... Nothing could be worse than to give Colonial peoples the impression that the Colonial Development and Welfare Act was a permanent subsidy to their social services which the taxpayer of this country would undertake to pay without thought either of return, or indeed of supervision.[36]

Nonetheless Stanley – like MacDonald in 1939 – saw what Great Britain was doing for its empire as a necessary rationale for imperialism. He told the Cabinet:

the Colonial Empire means so much to us that we should be prepared to assume some burden for its future. If we are unable or unwilling to do so, are we justified in retaining, or should we be able to retain a Colonial Empire?... If these sums are wisely spent, and the plans devoted to increasing the real productive power of the Colonies, there will in the long run accrue considerable benefit to us... But I am not basing my argument on material gains to ourselves, important as I think these may be. My feeling is that in these years to come without the Commonwealth and Empire, this country will play a small role in world affairs, and that here we have an opportunity which may never recur, at a cost which is not extravagant, of setting the Colonial Empire on lines of development which will keep it in close and loyal contact with us.[37]

Development was a statement about empire: that it had a future, and it was a long one and a just one. Social services were clearly going to be funded, even if the rationale for doing so was now more likely to be some kind of human capital theory – better social conditions would raise productivity – rather than the argument made in 1939 that social conditions should be improved for their own sake and for the sake of tranquillity in the British empire.[38] For all the uncertainty about the social meaning of development, at least welfare and the standard of living were discussable issues: they would not necessarily remain that way.

A revealing exchange took place in the parliamentary discussion of the 1945 Colonial Development and Welfare Act between Stanley and Creech Jones, the future Secretary of State for the Colonies. Debunking American criticism of "British imperialism," Creech Jones argued that the development act was really a step to achieve the "liberation of the Colonial peoples" and "disintegrating" the empire:

It will contribute to training the Colonial people for complete and responsible self-government and fitting them, socially and economically, to discharge their responsibility in the world. They will thus, in due time, make their own independent decisions, in regard to their future inside the British Commonwealth. I believe, of course, that we are helping to unify the Commonwealth by the Bill before us. Nevertheless, it is important that we should realise that there can be no real political liberty unless the economic and social conditions of the Dependencies are built up.

Stanley replied, "I believe that the effect of these provisions and of this new outlook will be not to disintegrate but to consolidate the 60,000,000 people in the Colonial Empire." Creech Jones was unifying the Commonwealth, Stanley the empire. Both insisted that economic and social accomplishments would first have to be made. Both agreed that individual colonies would have to pay for the services they provided their people. As Creech Jones said, "there should be the fullest development of the economic resources of the separate Colonies, in order that they may be able to sustain their social services and economic development, and carry on should some British Government, at any time in the far-off future, be obliged to withdraw any of the grants..." Stanley and Creech Jones were giving themselves an escape clause against too exacting and too long-term a conception of imperial social policy, guarding against the danger of creating a colonial "dole" that the conservative Treasury officials had expressed in 1939. Creech Jones was also making it clear that the argument about self-sufficiency and self-government cut two ways: if economic and social progress was touted as a more meaningful approach to helping colonies than was promoting immediate independence, the eventual possibility of self-government was an argument against raising economic and social standards too high.[39]

The Labour Party had policed the empire for signs of "exploitation," but the idea of development allowed it to reconcile its sense of a progressive mission for Great Britain in the colonies with the view that planning and government vigilance would protect Africans from the excesses of capitalism. Such a position was related to that of the Labour Party in domestic affairs: planning and welfare were the basis of compromise and consensus among different tendencies within the Labour Party, making capitalist development reconcilable with the social goals most party leaders shared. Creech Jones drew his conclusion strongly in 1943: "The economic development of our dependencies in my judgment can't properly be left any longer to chance or individual enterprise. It must be a planned and controlled development."[40]

The virtue and the flaw of the concepts of planning and development were their ambiguity. Just how planning would reconcile profit and welfare was unclear, and Creech Jones and his compatriots were in the position of constantly attaching caveats to growth-oriented policies rather than presenting another vision of development.[41] Creech Jones, like Stanley, was anxious to distinguish current policy from "the old Imperialism with power and profit," but neither made clear how Africans could be sure that public-spirited British imperialism would be better for them than the self-interested variety.[42]

What Labour shared above all with the Conservatives was a conviction that African society itself offered no path forward and that it fell to Great Britain to bring progress to it. In 1944, he visited West Africa and reported on his experience in words that suggest he was taken aback:

I saw great areas where tyrannical and cruel despots until quite recently imposed their will on the people. There were districts where once barbaric rites and superstition brought death to innocent victims. Great stretches of the country were either devastated by disease or denuded by slavery. In darkest Africa men lived with superstition, cruelty, pestilence and famine haunting them.[43]

He was seeing the Africa of the Anti-Slavery Society in 1895. His view of progress was similar: government building roads and stopping "barbaric customs"; traders and missionaries bringing commerce and education; and more recently the government improving social services and working to raise the standard of living. But the present still embodied the African past:

In many villages I saw the primitive conditions of the people's lives, the miserable hovels they live in and the wretched food they eat. I jostled with them in the markets, saw them sweating at their work on their farms and toiling down the roads. I became painfully aware of how huge and how difficult is the task that Britain had assumed in co-operating with these Africans to enable them to stand on their feet in the strenuous conditions of the modern world.

He had met Africans doctors, lawyers, chemists, and teachers. Still, "Most of the people of West Africa live in villages... Agriculture is still very primitive." He had noticed workers: "Some of them have in recent years been taught to work on the railways, make roads, build bridges, run motor lorries, and exploit minerals... Labour conditions are often very poor and there is not too much welfare provision. But even that is beginning to come." He spoke of Africans' desire for change and their interest in seeing that "tribal institutions are being adapted to carry the strains of social services" and in participating in British governmental bodies. But his main point was that "our system cannot be transferred ready made or quickly to African soil. For millions of Africans it would be unfair to break suddenly their methods and traditional ways of doing things."[44]

It is less the apologetic tone of Creech Jones' discussion of British policy that stands out in this text than the starkness of his imagery of primitiveness in African society. From him and colleagues, the "tribal" cultivator was a much more vivid image than the complex social process by which Asante farmers mobilized labor and land and produced cocoa for the world market. From such a stand point, Great Britain appeared as the only way out of backwardness, and whatever skepticism a Creech Jones might have about self-serving notions of development he was unlikely to question very deeply the meanings of the concept of development itself. Development and planning were terribly important fetishes.

But the entire discussion of development during the war years has to be set against the experience of imperial economic policy at the time. The empire – India above all – played a critical role in financing the war through the accumulation of sterling balances. Exports outside of the sterling block were not balanced by imports, which were limited by allocation of shipping and by controls on sterling, as exports were encouraged and imports constrained. British military spending in the colonies generated balances which could not be spent either. Here was the economic meaning of colonialism: independent countries could not have been restrained in such a way, and the sacrifices of the British consumer – which were considerable – were made against the promise of being redeemed after the war; the British consumer voted and the Nigerian did not.[45] A planning apparatus was set up to keep control of Africans' export earnings and their access to capital goods and other imported commodities at the very time London was talking about the beneficial effects planning and capital spending would have on African economic development.[46]

The lack of imports or local substitutes contributed to the declining trend in real wages, except when strikes forced them back up; the war years were a time of serious hardship in much of urban Africa. Meanwhile, agricultural producers had much of their income confiscated by marketing boards.[47] Even with much of their incomes denied, farmers seemed to be doing better than urban workers. As a Colonial Office official commented in regard to Nigeria at the time of its 1945 general strike, "the peasant farmer for once has the advantage over the clerk and the industrial worker on fixed wages. The former now has more cash than he can spend, and can grow his own food; the latter have to pay stick up prices."[48]

It wasn't quite that neat, but even farmers involved in export production could fall back on their food growing capacities – as well as the strength of local and regional marketing networks – to insulate themselves somewhat from export markets; some could sell food crops to urban workers or military personnel. Urban workers could not do this: the urban infrastructure, and housing above all, was import-dependent, and even the markets that supplied local food and other produce were constrained by transport and organizational difficulties.

As the Colonial Office prepared itself for a new effort at planned development after the war, officials recognized that the most important instances of wartime planning would continue in effect after the war: currency would be strictly controlled, and imported commodities would be scarce and rationed.[49] As the war ended, a Labour government was elected by British voters determined to make good on the promises of a better society made to them during the war. The government faced enormous obstacles to delivering on its promise. Its position on colonial affairs had been a minor part of its electoral platform and was not fundamentally distinguished from the ground carved out by Stanley during the final years of the war. In any case the constraints of personnel and capital goods on colonial development would be enormous.

But the commitment embodied in the renewed Colonial Development and Welfare Act of 1945 still stood, with its promise that something would be done to improve colonial peoples' material welfare under the evocative but elusive concept of development. What the Labour government did not know as it took office was that the pressures from African workers would continue as they had during the war. The protests would in their own way be compelling, perhaps not enough to topple an empire but enough to challenge fundamentally the imperial rulers' beliefs in their own benevolence and their own control.

An unsettling presence: workers and strikers in wartime British Africa

In Africa itself, British officials confronted two questions and had little confidence in the answers: would Africans work when and where they were wanted and would those who did respond to the disciplinary authority of employers and the state? The British government had been warned that the labor market, as it existed at the end of the Depression, might be incapable of responding to the pressures of economic expansion (chapter 3). As the war began, officials believed the prediction to be true. Fearing that Africans in most of their territories could still assure subsistence and sell crops, officials fell into their older military model for labor mobilization. If labor did not enlist, it would be conscripted. The word conscription – unlike recruitment or even encouragement – allowed officials to overcome their scruples about ILO Conventions and to direct supplies where needed for the war effort, to sisal plantations, pyrethrum farms, and tin mines as much as to the construction of military bases.

The Colonial Office initially thought Africans less useful as troops than as laborers, but as the war proved ever more demanding it kept widening the areas of recruitment within Africa and the places and the roles – including fighting – they served. In the end, British colonial governments recruited over half a million men from all colonies in Africa. Officials invented such titles as Military Labour Corps, the East African Military Labour Service, the African Auxiliary Pioneer Corps, and the West Africa Military Labour Corps for what was essentially forced labor. By 1943, Kenya, Northern Rhodesia, and Nyasaland were considered "virtually dry" of men, and recruiters turned to West Africa. Skilled laborers and truck drivers – literate men who intensely disliked what befell them – were conscripted, along with so many farmers that local officials feared shortages of food and valuable crops. Conscription and military discipline were seen at times as the answer to low productivity as well as unresponsiveness to wage incentives. Many Africans responded exactly as they had to other forms of forced labor – with high rates of desertion.[50]

Conscription for private farms became increasingly important as labor shortages increased after 1941. In 1945, Kenya and Tanganyika had nearly 40,000 conscripts at work – the same order of magnitude as that of forced labor in the Ivory Coast. Mauritius and the two Rhodesias employed forced labor in agriculture. The tin mines of Nigeria, which had to take up the loss of tin production in Malaya, soaked up 100,000 conscripts over two years, causing great disruption of local agriculture and high mortality in the poorly prepared camps. Productivity was low and conscription, as David Killingray writes, was a "brutal failure." All of this provoked doubts in the Colonial Office and occasional protests in Parliament.[51]

Thinking about labor in military terms reinforced old conceptions of the labor question. The Colonial Office's labour advisor was himself a former officer, Major G. St. J. Orde Browne, and his extended visit to West Africa in 1939–40 revealed how upsetting any deviation from regimentation could be. Observing that most workers in West African cities, farms, and mines took themselves to their place of employment, arranged for housing on the open market, and returned to a home village if not permanently settled there at the place of work, he termed this situation "theoretically admirable," but in fact he disliked it. "In practice," he wrote, "the worker is at a great disadvantage and in a far worse position than his brother in a country where adequate arrangements exist for the collection, transport, care, and subsequent repatriation of the worker." He thought that the absence of the "rationing system" meant that the laborer's diet was "markedly inferior to the well-balanced generous ration supplied on the Rand, the Rhodesian Copper Belt, or the mines of the Congo," and that African "taste or prejudice may lead to unwise expenditure of the available money." Nor did he like the housing which African entrepreneurs provided; he preferred "municipal housing schemes." He was appalled by "mushroom villages" near Gold Coast mines where one found side by side "comparatively repectable petty traders down to gamblers, prostitutes, drug-sellers and criminals." What he really did not like was Africans building their own towns and living their own lives: the more ordered life of Central Africa was his model.[52] His advice thus helped the Colonial Office to underestimate three major labor problems of the coming years: Africans, he thought, were too imbued with tradition and enterprises, too uninterested in having a stable work force for "detribalisation" to be an issue; employment was too intermittent for the wage level to be a major concern; and unions were not a worry because labor organization was "still at an elementary stage."[53]

Only a few officials on the scene anticipated the struggle that was about to ensue. Governor Bourdillon of Nigeria thought, "this is not a country in which labour problems are likely to attain serious proportions."[54] The labour department of the Gold Coast noted some minor strikes but believed that "any general upheaval in labour in unlikely." Governor Sir Arnold Hodson was more anxious about social conditions in the Gold Coast: real wages had declined, and there were more "largely detribalized Africans living in towns." He reasoned, "improvements will in time be forced if they are not readily conceded."[55]

The strike movements of the Gold Coast should not have been a surprise. Railwaymen had struck there as early as 1918; in 1921 they had stayed out a week and won a wage increase; a Railway Association was founded in 1928. In 1939, railwaymen demanded union recognition and a wage increase. The government's first instinct was to refuse to negotiate until the union went back to work. But officials reconsidered, because, as Governor Hodson noted, the grievances were real and the world situation dangerous. Most important, he recognized the underlying problem: railway workers at the bottom ranks shared their low rates of pay with "unskilled labour throughout the Colony." That meant that the potential of the railway strike was unlimited: "our first duty was to settle the strike as soon as possible and get the men back to work to avoid its spreading to other public services and the mines which it very easily might have done."[56]

So after the reflexive resort to police intervention, wage concessions were made to the railwaymen and, on the same basis, to other government workers.[57] All was calm for a time, but meanwhile inflation ate away the gains; the urban cost of living rose 51 percent between 1939 and December 1941. The railway workers led the way in another strike movement in their headquarters city of Sekondi in November 1941: they took with them harbor workers, public works department employees, and workers at the water department and conservancy. Workers in the port of Accra struck too. Perhaps connected through the bush telegraph were a brief strike at a gold mine and a longer one at a manganese mine. The police arrested the secretary-general of the Railway Union and other strike leaders; they attacked workers who were allegedly armed with sticks. After a week, the harbor workers in Sekondi-Takoradi returned to work, the railwaymen a few days later.[58]

The workers received a 20 percent increase for their pains, and the comments in London on the process reveal how caught officials were between their desire to appear firm and their sense of their own impotence in the face of strikes. After the arrests, Governor Burns indicated a willingness to rescind the sentences if there were a general return to work and he telegraphed London that he would recommend a 15 percent wage increase at the lower ranks. The Colonial Office, concerned about the movement of war supplies, recommended Burns' proposal be accepted, as long as the 15 percent raise was made to appear the result of the investigatory committee's work and not of the strike and would be termed a cost of living bonus rather than an increase in basic wages. Then the committee report came in recommending a 20 percent raise, and Burns – "in view of the ugly and serious situation" – approved.[59]

On one of the telegrams in the midst of the strike appears the minute, "Surely they should return to duty and submit the case to arbitration. How is it that the Governor has let this all develop?" initialled, W.S.C., 2 December 1941. When it was over, Churchill minuted, "Not a good story."[60] But the strikes were showing the limits of a colonial regime's authority, as disciplined unionized workers in key sectors shared with urban workers generally common conditions of life.[61]

This sequence of events was echoed on the other side of the continent, where it seemed to jar officials' concern with their own sense of control even more. In Mombasa in 1938, labor officials thought things were going smoothly. In late July of 1939, however, a rolling strike – a fast version of what had happened in Dakar in 1936-37 – began with public works department laborers. They returned quickly with a Shs 3 housing allowance. The pattern repeated itself with other groups of workers until, between 1 and 3 August, the dockworkers struck and roamed the city in bands. They returned with an hour lopped off their workday – which perhaps created more employment among these casual workers.[62]

But the significance of the Mombasa general strike of 1939 was less what workers won than the anxieties it evoked. "Casual labour is the danger point," noted the Mombasa district officer. Casual work, ruminated the *Mombasa Times*, meant that workers were part of a rough world with men "sleeping in odd sheds and even in cow sheds and other crudely made shelters, these natives are a source of crime, ill-health, and economic discontent." The principal labour officer was arguing within days of the strike that "the regular worker should be substituted for the irregular worker."[63]

In the Colonial Office, Frederick Pedler immediately drew a quite radical conclusion that he would shortly thereafter develop (above) into an argument for stabilizing the labor force: "Before very long East Africa will have to change over – probably very suddenly – from low grade labour and very low wages to something much nearer the standard of European manual labour and the European labourer's wage." After the reports made the rounds of Whitehall, Secretary of State Malcolm MacDonald concluded that cities like Mombasa were

unnecessarily crowded by large numbers of persons who are only intermittently employed. A policy of grading up wages and performance concurrently might so far reduce the number of African employees as to make it possible to ease the housing situation, through the return of large numbers to the native areas.[64]

These comments were given a more solid basis by the report of the investigatory commission issued in December. It argued that housing was at the root of workers' legitimate grievances, and that casual labor was at the root of the housing problem. Not only was housing expensive, but it was of low quality and unsupervised. So the commission recommended that workers immediately be given a Shs 5 per month housing allowance over their wages and that over time controlled housing be built for regular workers. The corollary to this was that the dockworkers had to be turned into a more compact and disciplined body of men. The commission called for the "decasualization" of Mombasa's docks, for making its workers into a full time proletariat.[65]

The conclusion was radical enough to attract the vehement opposition of the cargo handling companies, who were not yet ready to accept its costs and who insisted that casual labor was inevitable in dockwork. But many officials were now ready to believe that they had to distinguish a class of regular dockworkers – to whom more resources could be given and from whom more work expected – from the idle, the criminal, and the dangerous of the city. Meanwhile, MacDonald reprimanded Kenya's administration for letting the labor situation get out of hand, and he urged the creation of new institutions to handle "industrial disputes." The founding of Kenya's labour department in 1940 was a direct result of the general strike.[66]

As in the Gold Coast, a second round of agitation occurred, this time in October 1942. In between, more workers came to Mombasa, putting great pressure on housing, and the supply of imported commodities was at its worst. Casual workers were getting more work as port activity grew, and the new episode centered on monthly workers: another rolling strike went through the city, beginning with a four-day strike of 2,000 railway workers and extending to the public works department, the Shell Oil Company workers and other major employers. Its spread was facilitated by the fact that 77 percent of the workers for "large employers" – mainly government departments – received wages within a narrow and low range: Shs 23–40 per month. Treated as so many interchangeable units of labor power, Africans recognized their common situation. In the absence of African labor unions in Mombasa at the time, the strike movement passed along the communications networks among the city's workers.

This time, officials, aware that inflation was a genuine issue, tried to put a potentially wide-spread political conflict into a box of economic issues defined narrowly and, they insisted, objectively. A long series of investigatory committees and wage tribunals convened and sought formulas for "war bonuses" based on taking old price figures for commodities Africans needed and adjusting them for inflation. These official bodies were saying that the needs of workers could be objectively and scientifically determined. Maintaining the fiction that the basic wage remain the same – African labor was really worth only so much – committees put together sample budgets and decided how to assess prices. But the only government body that actually awarded money in 1942 did so under the duress of strike action.[67]

This attempt to objectify the labor question was characteristic of British policy during the war and early post-war years. It acquired an academic imprimatur from South African scholars such as Edward Batson at the University of Cape Town, who pioneered techniques for measuring poverty in Africa, and who directly influenced investigatory commissions in East Africa in 1945.[68] Perhaps it was the inability of officials to address directly the structural issues behind the general and rolling strikes – the little-differentiated, footloose quality of the urban work force – that made them so anxious to see the problem as amenable to adjustment mechanisms that were asocial and acultural, universal and quantifiable.

The basic problem had first been encountered in the Copperbelt, with the 1935 strike. In 1940, there was a repeat performance. Following a strike by white miners, to whom wage concessions were made, black miners walked out on one mine on 22 March, setting off a movement that spread to other mines and lasted in some instances to 8 April. Once again, the miners were not led out by a trade union. Workers assembled in a football field, slept there, and turned physical togetherness into a mechanism of solidarity. Again, there were confrontations and loss of life – seventeen miners died from police bullets.[69] Even more this time, the government felt it was in a situation it could not control. The governor – not quickly enough – decided he would send the dispute to arbitration. He regretted having to face off with 15,000 strikers "wholly unversed in trade disputes procedure." There were no accredited representatives and "talk took place at large meetings where any native who suggested any reduction of the demands was shouted down. We felt that if the strain continued much longer danger of disturbances and clashes with police and troops was serious and that some effort to effect settlement was needed." The governor would not go to the site of the strike himself, for fear that "I might be treated with disrespect and that failure would prejudice effort which I might have to make later."[70]

The investigation was notable for its recognition of basic problems and its unwillingness to act on them. Real wages were lower than they had been before the Depression ten years previously, but workers' demands were considered unreasonable and only a modest adjustment was recommended. Even thinking about paying Africans wages equivalent to Europeans was ruled out because of "the wide gulf between the standard and outlook upon life of the European and the African worker" and fear that with equal wages mines would not employ Africans. The commission acknowledged that there was no effective mechanism for articulating the workers' quite real grievances, but insisted that Africans were "not ripe" for trade unions. Admitting that the existing system of relying on "elders" to communicate between management and workers had failed and "Elders were then repudiated by their followers," it could only recommend strengthening the system as "natural and consistent with native custom and habits of thought." It noted that Africans could only aspire to a very low level of supervisory post, "boss boy," but accepted only the most minor tinkering with the racial hierarchy. It noted that many workers' wives came with them – and companies encouraged this – and realized that children would be appearing soon, but did not recommend basic changes in a system that assumed rapid turnover – six to eight months on average.[71]

As noted in chapter 3, "stabilization" – in the sense of declining labor turnover and the movement of families from villages to mine towns in the expectation of living a life based on wage labor – was a de facto tendency before it was an official policy. The aftermath of the 1940 strike witnessed a slow movement on the part of mining companies to try to control this reality, with the provincial administration sticking stubbornly to its tribal conception of African society.

But for now, the strike posed an issue of control: a migrant, rapidly circulating, poorly differentiated labor force had pulled off a second strike that had affected an entire, extremely valuable, region. A year after the strike, the Colonial Office was still focused on the issue of control in the region. "If a strike develops we may not be able to confine it to the dimension of a mere trade union dispute."[72] As worried about change as about its absence, the British government hoped to encourage Africans to move into better jobs "without saying too much." The mine companies, meanwhile, organized themselves into the Chamber of Mines in 1941 to present a united front. More investigations took place, which disclosed an alarming extent of urban poverty, especially among non-miners in the mine towns. Miners, meanwhile, were staying longer on the job.[73]

Thus, in the early years of the war, in West, East, and Central Africa, the British government faced the actuality of workers in action: their very lack of long identification with particular trades, the narrow range of wage scales, and the constant juxtaposition of economic issues with the role of the state and the question of race meant that such disputes were difficult to contain. In 1942 – the nadir of wartime inflation and therefore of labor struggle – the labor question as seen in Africa ran into the development question as seen in London. Caine, among others, had been trying to argue that development did not mean paying workers more, even when the evidence was that their standard of living was abysmal. But the wartime strikes intervened: workers' standard of living had to become a focus of attention, for the fragile control of colonial governments was at stake.

The connection was drawn most explicitly in correspondence between London and the field in a dispute in Nigeria. It all happened without an actual strike. In mid-1941, the government had issued new salary scales for the civil service, but had been greeted with an "outcry" in the press and from the African Civil Service Association. It withdrew the proposals, agreed to raise the minimum salary of a clerk from £36 to £48 per year, and appointed a committee to study the cost of living. The committee sat, and kept sitting. By the beginning of the year, railway workers were adding their demands to those of civil servants and strike threats were in the air.[74]

Governor Bourdillon put the issue squarely in terms of the Colonial Office's development paradigm. After discussing the need to improve farmers' output and incomes, he wrote,

But there is another class of inhabitants of Nigeria, a large class, whose ability to make their needs known and to insist on their recognition is rapidly growing, whose position, none too good before the war, is deteriorating as a result of war conditions. I refer to the daily wage earner and to low-salaried employees. An amelioration of their position is essential.

He cited recent labor disputes at the government coal mine and on the railway; he considered their demands "not only reasonable but modest." And he feared that "we shall in future be compelled to pay adequate wages and salaries to Africans as well as Europeans, whether we can afford to or not; it would surely be wise to assume the obligation voluntarily rather than at the point of the bayonet."

Bourdillon saw the problem as imperial, not as limited to the bounded economy of a colony. He attacked the "fetish of the Balanced Budget," and insisted that paying adequate wages in the British empire was an imperative: "the inadequacy of local funds must never again be taken as a sufficient excuse for paying the Government labourer or employee an inadequate wage."[75]

But the Secretary of State, Lord Cranborne, set aside the issue of how to finance wage increases by writing "I have decided not to pursue the subject further at present." The cost of living committee continued to sit. Then in May came new demands from unions, campaigns in the press, and threats of demonstrations and strikes. The underlying problem was that Nigerian workers needed commodities, not just cash, and Britain did not want to give them more. Frederick Pedler figured it all out through a brilliant non sequitur: "We must not be hurried into wage increases and cost-of-living bonuses. Any concessions will increase the demand for imports; on the other hand if concessions are necessary to keep African labour from striking etc they will have to be made."[76]

They were. At a meeting with union representatives on 14 May, officials offered a interim bonus pending the committee report: the current 3d per day bonus would be increased to Shs 10 or 15 per month depending on the wage. After discussion, these amounts were increased further. Even this was not accepted by the unions and agitation continued. African civil servants for a time refused to work overtime – the custom in Nigeria – and a mass demonstration was planned for Lagos on 30 May but banned by the government.[77]

Alan Burns, acting as governor while Bourdillon was in England, warned that unions did not see the issue in the narrow terms of a cost-of-living adjustment, but as a question of "accelerating the rate of improvement in general living standards of the African population." Most important, he noted "the solidarity of all classes of Government servants in the demand for an improvement in their living conditions generally." The cost of living commission, which had an African majority, might "not have the moral courage to resist pressure," and if the government did not accept its recommendations "labour trouble will certainly result."[78]

The breadth and solidarity of the movement defeated London's attempt to rule the standard of living question out of bounds. In the end, Governor Bourdillon promised that any award from the committee would be made retroactive to 1 October of the previous year, a move which annoyed the Colonial Office – since the sudden dispersement of all this cash could be sucked up in instant inflation – but which may well have prevented a Nigeria-wide strike.[79] Finally, in July, came a decision for a substantial increase in the cost-of-living bonus and pay adjustments to bring the bottom of the scale up to the "lowest desirable minimum." Bourdillon decided to call all raises cost-of-living bonuses, but he fiddled the figures so that the money workers received corresponded at least to the lowest desirable minimum wage suggested by the committee.[80]

The unions grudgingly accepted the award. No sooner had they done so than demands for a similar retrospective cost of living award came from other workers. A strike at an oil storage facility led to eighty-eight arrests under an act prohibiting strikes in essential services. One shipping company promptly agreed to a retrospective award – which "weakened the whole position" according to the governor – and dockworkers who did not get similar raises struck briefly. The demand for retrospective pay raises spread from Lagos to other towns.[81]

While the dispute was still on, Governor Bourdillon had suggested that the Colonial Office pledge to appoint a commission at the end of the war to take a comprehensive look at civil service salaries. He was jumped on by numerous London-based officials who feared that this might carry the issue that had become so hot in Nigeria to other West African colonies, and the Secretary of State refused to be stuck with a pledge to study the adequacy of civil servants' wages.[82] Governor Burns too thought that the malaise in the West African civil service needed radical rethinking: he went so far as to recommend in 1942 equal pay for equal work (with a substantial expatriation allowance for Europeans) for such positions. This was a can of worms London did not want opened; it was in effect defending racial privilege so as not "to establish the civil servant as a privileged class of the community." Despite recurrent tension throughout West Africa, civil service reform was put on ice until after the war.[83] Meanwhile, when Bourdillon pursued his thoughts of January regarding the spending of funds outside of the individual territory's budget for meeting just and threatening demands from government workers, he was shut down. Colonial Office minutes refer to Bourdillon as "querulous" and acting "like a child who cannot get the toy he wants."[84]

This nastiness was a sign that Bourdillon had a point. The costs of keeping government workers adequately fed and housed – let alone educating their children and catering to their aspirations for self-improvement, let alone creating a civil service without racial discrimination – were not necessarily determined by the same factors which defined an individual colony's budget. Bourdillon was discussing the standard of living question with a directness that London did not welcome, and he had opened this issue because he saw the limits of his own power in the face of social disorder. His fellow governors also handled their own workers gingerly in some key tests, and in London officials sought face-saving formulas for concessions. The insistence on objectivity – the tiresome string of committees on the cost of living – was a thin veneer over the politics of strike threats, demonstrations, and press campaigns.

Such give and take is typical of union-management relations, but there was nothing normal about any kind of union-management relations in British Africa. Governors, the substance and symbol of colonial authoritarianism, had not usually confessed their impotence. The rhetoric of limited power and the repeated wage concessions showed how basic were the challenges to colonial authority and how potentially far-reaching were any attempt to address the underlying social issues. Colonial governments tried to push the issue into the category of objective determinations of the minimum standard of living, but it wasn't staying there.

Nigerians and Kenyans still had more lessons to teach. In 1945, they reversed their roles, as Nigerian workers pulled off a month-long general strike, and their Mombasan counterparts, who had done the striking in 1942, stopped short but provoked a serious reexamination of labor policy.

The Nigerian strike of 1945 enveloped the railways and the civil service. Over 18,500 railwaymen, 5,500 to 6,800 public works department employees, 2,900 workers for the Lagos town council, and numerous other public sector workers – a total of 31–33,000 people – struck, and most of them stayed out with rigorous discipline from late June to early August. After the panicked wage concessions of 1942, officials had done nothing on their own and inflation again produced great hardships for wage earners. The strike followed open activity by the unions, especially the railway workers union and civil servants' organizations. The government, however, insisted in June that "the men behind the troubles are, as might have been expected, Macauley and Zik" – that is, the venerable Lagos politician Herbert Zachary Macauley and the younger leader from Eastern Nigeria, Nnamdi Azikiwe, press lord, businessman, and populist politician. When the strike began, the acting governor called it "a political weapon" in Azikiwe's hands and suspended publication of Azikiwe's newspapers, *Pilot* and *Comet*.[85] Officials seemed rather less concerned with the man who was more important in organizing the strike, Michael Imoudou of the railway workers' union, and they were diffident, as was also the case in Mombasa, about using the repressive apparatus of the colonial state against the strikers even though the strike was technically illegal. They did not arrest the quite visible strike leaders, and the inevitable suggestions that strikers be dismissed and replaced were set aside by the Colonial Office as being a "bluff" too easily called.[86]

The strike gave rise to the revealing spectacle of one of Britain's leading Labour politicians – himself a former trade unionist – Arthur Creech Jones, writing a "Dear Comrade" letter to the general secretary of the African Civil Servants and Technical Workers Unions telling him that the strike was "unofficial and illegal and conciliation was rejected. In the eyes of the world the strikers put themselves in the wrong." Just as revealing in a different way was the confession of the acting governor, G. C. Whiteley, who, after having claimed that his predecessors had shown "weakness" by their concessions in 1942, now admitted his own:

there is very little more I can do in the way of positive action to end the strike... [The] mood of the people of Lagos in general is such that there are few lengths short of violence to which they would not go to secure greatly increased wages. With a population which is largely either uneducated or semi-educated, among which an anti-European Press has had considerable license, it is of no use to appeal to reason.[87]

The acting governor gave way, ordering an investigation into wage demands that both sides knew would result in substantial increases. The workers were offered in anticipation a 20 percent increase in the cost of living allowance, and although the unions eventually rejected this, the government gave them the 20 percent anyway, retroactive to 1 August.[88]

The inquiry, as in 1941–42, took months, and as it went on rumors emerged of a new general strike or of a plan by Nigerian labor leaders to meet with their counterparts from other colonies to plan a strike for all of British West Africa. Governor Richards feared violence and "great dislocation of trade"; he thought the "real object" was political. Creech Jones, now serving in the Colonial Office, contemplated sending a naval vessel to Lagos, and he wanted the labour department to use its contacts to convince trade unionists of "the folly and wickedness of a general strike."[89]

The second general strike never happened, but the cost of living commission duly – and slowly (in April 1946) – produced a recommendation that the cost of living allowance be increased by 50 percent, retroactive to August 1945. The governor thought the investigation contained "many inaccuracies and mistaken assumptions which in my view reduce its value almost to nothing." Officials in London thought the money would be better spent on development projects. But the governor also warned that a general strike might spread across all of West Africa, and concluded "political considerations alone dictate acceptance." He added that publication "would be disastrous." So the workers got their 50 percent.[90] The unfortunate commissioner, Tudor-Davies, was in fact stepping through mine-fields of inequities: the salary scales discriminated between Africans and Europeans in equivalent posts; other Nigerians were worse off than civil servants; real wages for all had declined since the 1942 concessions. He recognized the politicization of the urbanized government workers, but wanted "to maintain a proper ratio between wages and the real earnings of peasant producers." Actually, the government was at this moment keeping down prices paid to cocoa, palm oil, and other export producers, so that this argument for restraining urban wages was utterly hypocritical. Tudor-Davies, however, weighed his alternatives in old and confused terms: "It is, therefore, incumbent upon the Commission to strike the mean, i.e. to close the gap between the too progressive and the too primitive."[91]

The fact was that the wage increase granted reflected fear of social and political disorder, not any of the ideas of what a correct wage should be. The broader problems of hierarchies in the civil service was left to another civil service commission, which the Colonial Office had appointed with great reluctance for fear that too much light might shine on the racial basis of government wages in West Africa.[92] Between the commissions came a brief attempt by the unions to get onto the table an issue that would occupy officials throughout the 1950s: family wages. Union representatives brought this before the Tudor-Davies Commission, arguing that bad urban conditions and civil service posting practices forced Nigerians to maintain two homes and that a family allowance for African workers was justified on similar grounds to the separation allowance for Europeans working in Africa. Tudor-Davies didn't quite buy the comparison, but realized the problem of civil servants being posted away from home. More important, he acknowledged that in principle it would be better if the "male ceases to rely upon the economic contribution of the female to the family exchequer."

Unions subsequently tried to get the separation allowances into practice, only to be met by a government assault on both the specific demands and the wider "male breadwinner" argument. In Africa, officials insisted, polygamy and extended families made such policies impossible. In the end, the civil service commission paid lip service to the needs of Africans to raise families, but accepted that the African family structure prevented addressing such concerns explicitly. The unions were disappointed, but could not mobilize on a wide scale around this issue (as unions in French Africa did in the 1950s). The question of family wages remained a marker of the confusion between scientific wage determination and politics, between universalistic claims to what the family should be and assertions of what the African family actually was.[93]

Kenya's 1945 troubles followed a similar period of hardship. The strike movement began at the other end of the narrow transportation corridor that linked Mombasa to Uganda. A number of small strikes in early January in Uganda – hard hit by the decline in real wages – led to more serious strikes in the Kampala region, and then moved beyond the workplace to crowd violence, looting of shops, and assaults on shopkeepers and police. The disturbances were quelled with force, and four alleged rioters were killed; the movement as a whole lasted seventeen days. Both the governor and a subsequent inquiry tried to blame the whole thing on political agitators, a move which one scholar calls "evidence of the Protectorate Government's dwindling grasp of reality."[94]

The strikes were still on when news of them reached Mombasa. A newly founded railway union provided a venue for a series of meetings over the next few months, although its leaders opposed striking. Officials, meanwhile, feared that dockers and other Mombasa workers were ready for a repeat performance of their 1939 general strike. The leaders of the strike were mainly Luo and Luhya from Western Kenya – long-distance migrants who were the core of the monthly workers in Mombasa.

The railway refused officials' suggestion to raise wages, and the situation was extremely tense. The strike was defused by the timely intervention of two Luo and Luhya chiefs, who cajoled or intimidated workers into turning the dispute over to another investigatory commission. But officials were convinced that they had to take this part of the bargain seriously. Even before the committee, under Crown Counsel Arthur Phillips, began its inquiry, it awarded the low-paid railway workers an extra Shs 5, bringing their minimum pay to Shs 35 exclusive of housing.[95]

The Phillips Committee report was the most thoughtful such study of its era. It showed that the anger of Mombasa's workers was inseparable from the structure of work in colonial Kenya. Its central discovery was highlighted in the title of its focal chapter: "Emergence of Urbanized

Working Class." Railway workers were often staying for five to ten years in Mombasa, and 80 percent of the lower-paid workers were married, and two-thirds of that group lived with their wives in Mombasa. The majority were not the "raw migrant" of official rhetoric, but family men with a growing desire for a "civilized standard of living."

This meant that the single-male basis of all the complex budget calculations of 1942 and thereafter was false. Yet, the committee found, the "different classes of African workers" were paid relatively similar wages – mostly below Shs 43 per month – and the long-term worker had little more to show for his years of stability than the casual laborer. The committee saw in Mombasa "the beginnings of class-consciousness, complicated by race-consciousness." The committee recognized that treating workers as interchangeable created the potential of unified action. The same factor made it impossible to achieve discipline on the job: the "'sanction of the Sack' is largely inoperative." Phillips then turned on its head the old argument about the dangers of detribalized natives: "There seems to be no escaping the fact that the evils which are commonly attributed to 'detribalisation' can only be cured by more complete detribalisation."

This meant identifying "the more decent and progressive elements" in the work force and paying them enough to raise their families amid the healthy and civilizing environment of the city. Seeking the causes of unrest, the committee's logic pointed to the problems of migratory labor generally. The Phillips Committee thought through the problem so comprehensively that Kenya's labour department decided it was too "contentious" to publish.[96]

In these arguments, the creation of a working class was discussed as a *fait accompli*. The entire question of class had arisen because of a challenge to order, but Phillips carried it into issues of productivity: good nutrition and a civilized upbringing would make the working class more efficient. In both regards, thinking of workers as a class that had distinct needs and posed a distinct danger of collective action was essential for the state to shape future possibilities. If the state were to take an active approach to workers' classness, it implied "stabilizing" the work – another term used by Phillips and others and soon to be the key concept of post-war labor policy.[97]

By the time the argument was put in such a clear form, officials were trying a different route to separating the true worker from the idle and the dangerous: police action. Regulations from 1944 were used to expel unemployed and nonworking people from Mombasa and Nairobi. Even that colonialist action had social implications: in Mombasa they only made sense if the "legitimate" casual worker – who did the most essential work of all in the port city – could be identified. So in August 1944, officials began to register casual workers and require employers to hire registered casuals only. Anyone not "a bona fide casual labourer" could then be repatriated to his rural place of origin.

In fact, the procedures were leaky and officials reluctant to enforce them too vigorously for fear of driving away the men from coastal districts who made up the large majority of the stevedores. They had allowed the pool to expand to 7,200 in mid-1945, even though only 1,500 or so dockers worked on an average day. Even when the pool was later cut down to around 4,000, only 5 percent were working over twenty days per month. Decent wages, but not steady labor was what dockers wanted.[98] Officials were still not ready to attack casual labor as such, partly because the port firms were not yet willing to decasualize and partly because the administration did not feel ready for a full scale assault on the work habits of Mombasa's dockers.

But the questions which the conflicts in Mombasa and elsewhere had posed were about the kind of life African workers were to live. Would the British government build – using the Colonial Development and Welfare Act and other resources – an urban infrastructure capable of socializing and acculturating a new generation to a European vision of urban society? Would employers pay the costs of reproducing its work force – including raising children and caring for old people? Or would leaving workers to reproduce themselves in their own social and cultural idiom lead to a society that colonial rulers could not understand, let alone control?

These questions came up with particular acuity in Southern Rhodesia, where a relatively advanced urban sector demanded more African labor during the war and where a large white-settler population insisted that African workers be segregated into "locations" and "compounds." Housing policy in effect denied that Africans had a legitimate place in the city except for the immediate tasks they performed.[99] The two tendencies coexisted uneasily – as they did to an even greater extent in South Africa during the war years.[100] A committee chaired by the native commissioner, R. Howman, set out to study the question of African urban employment and ended with an even stronger focus than Phillips on issues of family:

African life in the urban areas can be characterised as casual and precarious and nourished by roots that go no deeper than the daily contingencies of living; community life has been shattered; the family suppressed... As a result an abnormal social structure has been erected in which there is an overwhelming preponderance of men, and almost complete absence of old age and the moderation and guidance old age provides, and a coming and going which cuts away the roots of every association, society and personal leadership that might crystallise out of the fluid mass of the irresponsible 18–35 age group.

The problem was not just the number of men in town but the kind of women who were now "flocking" to join them: they were getting into "all sorts of domestic arrangements, prostitution, illicit beer brewing. Their children would pose a future danger, threatening social chaos and conflict."

The consequences were political danger and economic uncertainty. "It will be impossible to build up an efficient, reliable, first-class labour force out of the vagrant bachelor. In the absence of the married man, industry cannot expect to compete with the products of other countries." The remedy, however, lay well within the controlling habits of the colonial mind: "co-ordinate planning and deliberate control of urban life." One had to look beyond "the narrow confines of a classroom, courthouse, or gaol" – the old institutions of colonial acculturation. The focus had to be on making families and making communities – under the eyes of the state. Hostels should be built for single women and houses for married couples; schooling for children should be compulsory; efforts had to be made to control disease and delinquency. This meant a rejection of "our segregation policy" which seeks "to keep the African a tribal peasant, in a peasant's home with haphazard peasant standards and attitudes with an occasional spell in industry." It meant a higher minimum wage intended to discourage the hiring of "the casual, inefficient rural visitor" (although the committee rejected family allowances or paying higher wages to married men).[101]

This was a radical indictment of colonial policy in many parts of Africa, and it presented on the basis of observed social conditions the argument for stabilizing family life that Pedler (above) was beginning to make in the Colonial Office. The problem was that the politics of implementing it were most difficult precisely where the labor question was particularly acute. Southern Rhodesia would indeed try to move hesitatingly toward a policy of urban stabilization, but would pull back in the name of segregation and low wages – both demanded by white settlers – and the issues raised by this 1944 report would still be unresolved when colonial Rhodesia became independent Zimbabwe in 1979. And Howman's idea of reproduction required a degree of state surveillance and policing likely to make it intolerable to those whom it was allegedly to benefit.

In Africa as a whole, far-reaching questions about urban conflict and urban culture were being raised at a time when the daily reality facing most workers was harsh and most often getting harsher. They arose in the context of wartime demands to make production more intense and more predictable, and wartime constraints on consumption. Elliot Berg's wage statistics from West Africa show "the universality and severity of the decline in real incomes" during and immediately after the war.[102] But

Table 4.1. *Real wages, Lagos, Nigeria, 1939–46 (1939 = 100)*

	Real wage Unskilled laborer	Import purchasing Power of wages	Textile purchasing Power of wages
1939	100	100	100
1940		75	80
1941		73–87	67–79
1942	116–132	105–120	102–116
1943	120	90	82
1944	123		89
1945	122–135	96–107	84–93

Source: Elliot J. Berg, "Real Income Trends in West Africa 1939–1960," in Melville J. Herskovits and Mitchell Harwitz (eds.), *Economic Transition in Africa* (London: Routledge, 1964), p. 205.

they show something more too: a reversal of the downward trend in 1942 and a lesser one in 1945 (Table 4.1).

Mombasa's workers also got their wage hikes in 1942 and 1945, when they demanded them. The economic circumstance of the war was thus not the only determinant of how workers lived. The demands were not routinely made in a long series of small industrial relations disputes. They came in bursts, through movements. In Nigeria, in 1945, trade unions were instrumental in organizing the movement and the general strike. In Mombasa in 1939, 1942, and 1945, unions played no significant role.

The lack of organization made it hard for workers to consolidate gains, to insure that they would get routine adjustments of wages and to be sure that other issues would be tackled. But that lack was part of what made the disputes potentially far-reaching. They did not have neat boundaries. A class of workers in the broadest sense of the term – the sellers of labor power – shared the most basic conditions of life. Movements spread through these bodies only at certain times, but when they did, they did not necessarily stop. And the unorganized strike could be even more difficult for officials to get under control than an organized one: there were no responsible representatives with whom to negotiate.

Development and coercion in French Africa

Vichy's visions: corporatism, modernity, and development

The gap between a vision of future social organization and the practice of labor was even wider in French Africa than in British. Like the Popular Front, Vichy's planners recognized the mediocrity of past

economic performance and wanted to use metropolitan funds and expertise to build up Africa's ability to produce. Unlike its leftist predecessor,
Vichy was uninhibited by suppositions that Africans would not – or
could not be made to – work. Some of Vichy's leading economic minds
thought that the corporatist ideas being applied to French workers
should be applied to Africans as well: they should face an "obligation to
work," but should be guaranteed decent wages, working conditions, and
a family life at the place of work. Yet such ideas were pure fantasy, part
of a grand vision of a disciplined French empire, rationally organized and
productive. Vichy's ten-year plan for building up the colonies' capital
structure never was implemented: what the development effort actually
meant was a more vigorous and more overt recruitment of forced labor.

The interest of Vichy's fantasies lies in the relevance of the thinking
behind them to future generations of planners. As Robert Paxton has
argued, the Vichy period cannot be dismissed as an isolated aberration
in French history.[103] There was a considerable overlap in personnel as
well as ideas: Jules Brévie, René Barthes, and Hubert Deschamps served
previous and subsequent governments; the first two played important
roles in colonial debates in Vichy, the last (also known as a socialist and
an Africanist scholar) was impresario of its program of labor recruitment
in the Ivory Coast.

Much of Vichy ideology – a desire to make the world rational and free
of class conflict, submerging distinct interests under technocratic planning and corporatist organization – had a longer life than Vichy's four
years. At one pole of the leadership were the "dirigistes," technically
oriented planners. At the other were social Catholics, enemies of communists and socialists, yet people with their own conception of justice for
the lower classes based on state authority and the corporatist unity of
capital and labor. After 1940, new Comités d'Organisation were developed in each branch of industry and commerce, charged with invento-
rying its resources and regulating competition. A "charte du travail" was
implemented, under which all the old unions were destroyed and replaced
by syndicats within each "organized profession." Employers and
employees would be part of the same professional grouping, and strikes
and lockouts would be forbidden. A central planning organization for
France would coordinate the use of national and colonial resources and
ensure decent housing and higher wages as the counterpoint to strict
labor discipline. Both the planners and the social Catholics would be
around after Vichy was gone.[104]

In fact, the focus on intensified and planned production had been articulated earlier in the name of national defense by a man who was to be
murdered by Vichy's collaborators, Georges Mandel. As colonial

minister, he decreed a plan intended "to intensify production to the maximum"; each colony would be instructed to produce what would best contribute to the metropolitan effort; a "summary industrialization" would conserve supplies and foreign exchange without conflicting with metropolitan industries. This thinking justified for Mandel a renewed vigor in recruiting forced labor.[105]

Vichy put colonial planning into the hands of the kind of corporatist bodies it developed in France, the Groupements Professionnels Coloniaux (GPC). The colonial economy was divided into branches – agriculture and forests, mines, industry, commerce, credit, and transport – each of which was to be organized by its GPC. They were supposed to subordinate the particular interests of narrower groups toward the greater whole. In practice, they were dominated by larger corporations who could exert considerable influence over policy without worrying about contrary voices from *petits blancs*, let alone African workers.[106]

A typical Vichy theorist, Bertrand Mounier, argued in a book published in 1942 that the GPCs would help create a true "imperial economy," run by "the association of competence with authority" – of the GPCs and the state. The GPCs would bring "method" to work organization; they would "pull out of the indigenous masses an elite of foremen and masters." It was important above all

to attach the indigène to his trade, give him the sense of the profession, fill him with the mystique of work and of progress... That no-one escape from obligations to work, that no-one will be held outside of common profit... Proud to belong to a trade, a profession, conscious of the profits and advantages he gets from it, the indigenous wage worker will no longer be a deracinated person, an isolated person having broken with the indigenous community without entering the European community. He will be integrated in a new social cell...

In his corporatist dream-world Mounier had even abandoned the myth of the backward African: the African worker would inhabit a similar – Mounier did not say the same – social cell as the European worker, content with his role and his allotted share of the imperial wealth.[107]

Under Vichy's ten-year plan, each colony was to concentrate on doing what its soil, climate and "little evolved manpower" could accomplish "for the needs of the Empire." Vichy wanted to do what the Popular Front had vainly attempted, break with the doctrine of colonial self-sufficiency and use metropolitan funds to get colonies out of their poverty. In the end, this plan suffered the same fate as the Popular Front's version: it was not funded, a victim of wartime financial difficulties and the conservative leadership surrounding Pétain.[108]

While the plan was in the offing, the central committee of the GPC decided to create a Commission des Questions Sociales, which promised to give the range of questions surrounding African workers and African society specific attention. Meanwhile, the governor-general of French West Africa, Pierre Boisson, had ordered a wide inquiry into the availability of manpower and the possibilities that existing labor organization in Africa posed for the development plan.[109]

The theorists thought they could navigate between the crudity of the demands placed upon them and their progressive views. In September 1942, a Vichy position paper took on the African labor problem, claiming it could go beyond the selfishness and shortsightedness of colonial business interests. It recognized colonial business's "waste" of manpower and the lack of incentives provided workers. Instead, the employer "counts on the Etat-Providence for manpower, as for everything else." Vichy's "planned economy," however, would insure a sufficient profit margin so that employers could attract labor:

To unite to produce becomes today the common rule. This union must become *natural* for it to be fertile: the African should come voluntarily to the enterprise, the latter must attract and keep him freely by conditions of existence superior to those in his village of origin. He must live with his family and his hours of work must leave him a minimum of leisure time (during which the worker becomes consumer). He must have the possibility of having a garden, cattle, etc. The enterprise will watch over his health, his hygiene, and his comfort... The administration will develop its plan of production by favoring the voluntary movement of workers toward the richest regions.

For a time, the European consumer would pay more, but a more stable work force with better equipment would raise productivity and "a return to world parity will be easy." The transition from forced to free labor would take ten years, under the watchful eyes of "the professional organization" and the government.[110] Here was free labor, stabilized labor, well paid labor, being pushed by a right-wing regime without all the fears of disrupting African society expressed by previous French regimes or by Great Britain.

The Commission des Questions Sociales wanted more accurate statistical knowledge of the colonial population and "centralizing organisms to procede to operations of recruitment and distribution of workers." Members spoke contemptuously of the "hypocrisy" of the present system which presumed that labor was free but used "disguised requisition" when something more was necessary. A planned and explicit use of force, giving way to a planned transition to free labor, was its preferred approach. The commission was scornful of the peasant alternative:

It is a formula à la Jean-Jacques [a reference to Rousseau's bucolic romanticism] which does not pass the test of realities. The condemnation of wage labor in favor of the peasantry is the condemnation of the development of new countries.

Indigenous agriculture does not lend itself to improvements which only are brought by large enterprises and European techniques: mechanization, use of fertilizer, etc.[111]

Then came the fundamental problem: "to struggle against the repugnance of the indigène to wage labor." The president of the commission, Saurin, began in France: the law of 4 September 1942 had imposed the "obligation du travail" on Frenchmen. Such an obligation was "sanctioned by the necessities of existence in all civilized countries." The answer then to indigenous peoples' alleged dislike of wage labor was to require it legally of all men 16–40 years old: they had to show they had a permanent occupation "or be sent to a public works site." He also favored "civil conscription" for public works, paying slightly below the free market wage so as not to compete with private enterprise.[112]

In Vichy, compulsion was a discussable topic. As the Comité Central of the GPCs took up the theme, its vice-president, E. du Vivier de Streel, denounced "obscurities, equivocations, and demagogic influences. The problem of labor must nevertheless be studied seriously, scientifically." He supported the social commission's desire to proclaim the "principle of obligatory work imposed in civilized states" and to revise labor legislation both to make clear that obligation and to provide workers guarantees in regard to wages, food, and housing. He agreed that economic development would depend largely on European entrepreneurs and African laborers, and that the GPCs and the government should regulate all labor questions. This would eventually lead to the "generalization of progress in the entire world." He thought that one could "extract in the near future from every human being the same output" from all 2 billion people in the world, not just the 500 million of the civilized countries.[113]

To expect equal productivity from French and African workers (although he said nothing about equal pay) was to carry the universalism and progressivism of European thought to a high degree. Except that the entire argument was as blatant a hypocrisy as the pretenses and silences beneath which forced labor had been practiced in the past. In the "civilized world" an obligation to work had emerged from the history of capitalist development itself, and Vichy was putting the state's authoritarian and moralistic gloss on what the economy entailed anyway. Its legal significance was at most comparable to an anti-vagrancy statute. In French Africa, people had other ways to live than what du Vivier de Streel considered to be work: "obligation au travail" was in practice nothing but forced labor. And in the absence of any discussion of how and why Africans worked and how Vichy's policies could effect *that particular social milieu*, the promise that this time forced labor would be temporary was an empty one.

Some participants in the Vichy discussions in early 1943 were skeptical. Paul Bernard, President of the Comité d'Organisation des Productions Industrielles, thought there was too much uncertainty in the world to plan "a sort of ideal regime"; the colonies above all were short of manpower.[114] The Inspecteur Général des Colonies tried to be more realistic: the administration was already struggling to supply unwilling laborers to existing European enterprises, as well as to public works.[115] The Comité Central toned things down a bit, but stuck to its fantasy of the rapid growth of "production and income of peoples, not only the advanced people but the two billion individuals who inhabit our planet."[116] But the entire argument had become divorced from political reality: West Africa had gone over to the Free French in November 1942.

The commission, undeterred by its irrelevance, unanimously agreed (based on a proposal from Barthes) to recommend that the "moral obligation" to work meant requiring the indigène to show that each year, for a specified time, he worked on tasks of interest to the collectivity, as fixed by the administration, or worked on a public or private worksite, or produced a given quantity of a specified product on his own farm. The administration, advised by the GPCs, would allocate wage laborers. The commission was eager to assert that "it in no way intends to reinstate the institution of forced labor." But it noted that "a certain use of administrative constraint" was already in effect covertly, and it wanted to avoid "all the equivocation or all the running from responsibility which this procedure in certain cases involves."[117]

Vichy had already – when it had the power – escalated the use of forced labor. The colonial ministry in Vichy was besieged via the GPCs by representatives of various planters' organizations (bypassing Dakar) to help them round up labor. Thus the banana planters of Guinea complained that the local administration was not doing enough to supply labor, and they wanted penal sanctions to be used against workers who were "refractory to the agricultural effort which is demanded of them."[118] Some GPC leaders took this seriously and accused the administration in French West Africa of being overly fearful of using pressure and of creating an indigenous proletariat: "These objections of fact are frequently reinforced, explicitly or tacitly, out of a shady doctrinal position in regard to any intervention suspected of 'capitalism' in the colonial economy."[119] This could be read as a scarcely veiled threat against Governor-General Boisson.

But all the talk about a stable African work force, organized along similar corporatist lines to the labor force of Europe, paid livable wages, and living in families, is nonetheless significant. It opened up such possibilities to an audience that included powerful business interests and future administrators, such as Barthes. Vichy's version of the Popular Front's approach to wage workers – treating the modest number of workers who qualified as such in similar ways to workers in France – was grander, and it was only fantasy, but it was playing before an audience devoid of leftist sentiments. Perhaps this episode played a role in making ideas such as family wages or stable work forces become conceivable to more conservative administrators and to some elements of the business community.

The most intriguing figure in the Vichy debates was Governor-General Pierre Boisson. He was no clandestine leftist. He had decisively dismantled political and union organizations in French West Africa, and he superintended the supplying of large numbers of unwilling laborers to the French planters. But this colonial ruler par excellence knew the limits of his power, and that was the basis of his argument against Vichy's plan to remake Africa with European enterprise and African wage labor.

Much of his thinking emerged before his experience as French West Africa's chief labor recruiter. He had claimed in a speech delivered in 1938 that the necessity to choose between "European Colonization or Indigenous Colonization" had confronted him when he became governor of Cameroun in 1937. Struck by the "lively repugnance of the indigène against industrial or agricultural wage labor," he came to the view that the African was a "peasant in all his fibres," eager above all "to cultivate his land for his own account, exploiting its possibilities for his profit." The alternatives, then, were stark: "In Black Africa, one must not dream of extending without control European colonization if one has not at the same time decided to institute more or less directly forced labor. In our French possession, I repeat, the limit of extension has either been reached or is close to being reached." For this reason, he had suspended new concessions of land in the Camerouns to European planters, and pinned his hope on peasants for economic advance. This did not imply lack of control: "indigenous colonization should be closely oriented, supervised and guided by our efforts."[120] Whereas the men of Vichy viewed Africans as empty vessels to be molded, their man in Dakar saw an essentialized African nature to be guided by colonial authority.

In his circular as governor-general to governors and other top officials in August 1941, Boisson repeated this theme: "Africa is peasant. She should, in her necessary evolution, remain peasant." The limits of European colonization were encountered "relatively early" because of the "poverty of Africa in manpower." In some ways, this lack of labor required more capital expenditure: road work, plantations, forest cutting, mines, and ports should be mechanized. Agricultural products could be processed and mines exploited by making use of the dead seasons in the agricultural cycle; a core of permanent and seasonal laborers could be the basis of a certain industrialization. That meant – although he did not put it this way – adapting the labor process to the African as much as the African to the labor process. Boisson's peasant idyll remained linked to an authoritarian approach: "It is necessary to show and to demonstrate, to counsel, to order and to control."

He was willing to talk frankly about coercion, but it appears in his texts as an undue burden placed on his administrators: "The indigène comes to workplaces or to plantations under the effect of administrative pressure more or less direct. Moreover the employers do only a little to attract him, to satisfy him and to keep him. They count on the Colonie-Providence..."[121]

His rhetoric was one of limits: "local administrations affirm that they are at the limits of the effort of recruitment."[122] In the present context, the needs of "our imperial or national economy" was putting "multiple constraints" on Africans: demands to cultivate or gather certain crops, to build airports and roads, to carry loads. At the same time the demand for African products gave peasants "relatively large monetary disponibilities while the purchasing power of money does not cease to decrease and imported merchandise is in deficit..."

In effect, the black peasant who remains in his homestead, surrounded by his people, succeeds today in assembling, in continuing to work on his own time and according to his ancestral habits, sums of money out of reasonable proportion with the wages of skilled workers, with more reason of a laborer, held to another discipline and another regularity in the effort not counting the different conditions of life that they experience far from their native village. It is thus inevitable that the raising of contingents of essential workers runs into growing difficulties.[123]

These remarks on the rural–urban wage gap – in favor of the rural – echo views expressed by British officials. In both cases the argument stressed the qualitative difference of social structures: rural Africans could take advantage of markets without suffering all the pains they doled out.

The constraints of war led Boisson to repeat in French West Africa the decision he had made in the Camerouns before the war: ban new concessions to European planters, proclaiming again that "Africa is peasant" and extracting more labor would put "in danger at the same time the existing plantations, the execution of our programs of public works and the political climate of the Federation." He would, however, continue "the maximum of efforts" to bring to existing workplaces and European plantations "the number of laborers indispensable to their rational exploitation."[124]

Meanwhile, industrialization posed another political danger: "Finally, for the political stability of Africa, nothing would be more dangerous than to proletarianize it by generalizing wage labor." Peasants, however, were immune to the "propaganda which menaces so gravely the working classes and so easily influences them."[125] Village life avoided yet another danger: demographic decline. He stressed the imperative of natality: "faire du Noir," in his charming phrase.[126]

This was not, indeed, what Vichy wanted to hear from Dakar. The GPCs representing West African planters, after lobbying Boisson for more labor, accused him of going back on his promises to them, stating categorically, "for reasons which are poorly discernible, it appears that in the majority of cases, the Administration does not favor the recruitment of labor."[127] Boisson defended himself, insisting he was doing his best for existing plantations, but that expansion was impossible. In Guinea, 39,000 laborers were at work – despite their "repugnance" for wage labor – and providing more for the banana growers would hurt all other efforts as well as create risks of an exodus of population to Sierra Leone and deterioration of the "favorable political climate of the colony."[128]

Vichy's point man on industrialization, Paul Bernard, predicted "grave consequences" for his program from Boisson's reservations. Dakar officials stuck to their guns: labor was available for developing the "indigenous economy," but not for "a program of industrialization for the West African economy."[129]

Bernard kept insisting that systematic inquiry was necessary, that it should reflect "an intimate collaboration of private initiative with the Administration," that the very labor shortage which Boisson kept stressing made it all the more imperative to use "the most modern techniques." Boisson wanted the GPCs to obtain "a more just view of the effort imposed on the indigenous mass" and try to get employers to live up to their responsibilities. Boisson demanded that he be consulted before any industrialization program went into effect; Bernard demanded "obligatory consultation of professional groups before the authorization or refusal, by the public powers, of any new installation or extension of an older industry."[130] The battle over turf between the administration and GPCs was also a battle over industrialization and wage labor.

What was left of the GPC's plans was the demand that government recruit labor. GPCs were still insisting in 1944 – when French West Africa was no longer Vichy's – that the problem with forced labor was that it was "clandestine," that a "Governor-General cannot legally give his subordinates precise instructions on this subject; all must pass by suggestions and by allusions" and so local officials or chiefs who did not get the hint allegedly could not be punished. They were advocating forced labor to be "organized and controlled."[131]

Diligence and discontent in the colonie-providence

What was actually happening in French West Africa was the expansion of forced labor, not for the benefit of a new, forward-looking structure of production, but for the benefit of the same old colons of the Ivory Coast and Guinea. In the Ivory Coast, officially registered labor contracts – which the governor contended were entirely voluntary – had risen unsteadily from 33,000 under the Popular Front regime to nearly 35,000 in 1939. After a temporary decline in 1940 when colons were mobilized for war, recruitment rebounded to 31,000 then shot up to 41,000 in 1942, then 55,000 in 1943. In early 1940 officials in Haute Côte d'Ivoire noted that the exodus to the Gold Coast, which had slowed in recent years, had picked up again. Even Governor Crocicchia, who had been insisting that recruitment was going satisfactorily and without coercion, worried in the face of these reports that recruitment in the Voltaic region had reached "a degree close to saturation" and that there was danger of recreating the impression of "systematic constraint."[132]

Over 90 percent of the recruits were for private enterprise, slightly under half of them for coffee and cocoa plantations. Everyone concerned now admitted that virtually all these workers were involuntary: "Truly 'voluntary' labor has become entirely exceptional, even for public works and modest establishments," read a report in 1943; "labor destined for works of public utility, as well as for private enterprises is, in its immense majority, *recruited by administrative measure*," reported Governor Hubert Deschamps in late 1941.[133]

Deschamps, the socialist governor, duly sent his recruits off to colons, following distribution patterns established by the Comités Régionaux.[134] But his reports were filled with the rhetoric of limits and the impossibility of progress within the forced labor framework. He would not exceed the accepted (if arbitrary) recruitment quota in each subdivision – 5 percent of the population designated as liable to prestatory labor. He cited "the danger new administrative pressure would represent in the upper Ivory Coast" and wanted it limited elsewhere because the indigenous population was itself producing valuable commodities.

Even Africans' resigned acceptance of this "inevitable corvée" depended on the absence of alternative sources of cash. The new railway line to the north would open agricultural markets and, as in southern regions, make chiefs' efforts more difficult. Demography was the ultimate constraint: It was necessary to "faire du nègre," to avoid wasting manpower resources through mechanization and better organization, and to "educate the indigène, to give him the taste for work, and in the future free the labor market of its current constraints. This is a work of long duration..."

Deschamps totted up the demands of European plantations and lumbering companies, public works, railway constructions, the military, plus the ten-year plan (which never came to be), and came up with a grand total of 66,000. The 5 percent rule meant that 36,876 were available: "This number, which responds only barely to the needs of European colonization, *should not, without grave consequences be exceeded.*" European colonization – Vichy's hope for the future – had reached "the limit." Effective 1 January 1942, new concessions to Europeans were stopped, and African planters, who produced more coffee than whites, and almost all the cocoa, were denied access to recruited labor.[135]

Reports from the field noted the "large difficulties" chiefs faced in meeting quotas, the extent of "discontent," the "terrible resistance" of men who had no desire to work for wages.[136] An intercepted letter from a low-level administrator was particularly revealing:

I am disgusted to fill, and at the price of some difficulties, the role of slave trader. We recruit laborers to a terrible extent in this god forsaken place and we have come to exceed the maximum possible. Headquarters remains obstinately deaf to our cries of alarm and obstinately kills at a rapid pace all possibility of a future in this country with its magnificent landscapes and rich in all possibilities if we did not take away from it its hands and its reproducers.[137]

Even the main planter organizations knew the limits of recruitment were being reached, and they had a brilliant solution: increasing the length of contracts from 12 to 18 or 24 months would cut recruitment by half and "reduce by as much the palavers and meetings of the population which each recruitment occasions."[138]

Forced labor – sordid as it was – could be fit into a quite conventional vision of colonial administration. Because labor was "recruited entirely by the Administration," wrote Deschamps' successor in the Ivory Coast, Georges Rey, it was officials' duty to insure that workers were treated properly, and to guard against the "diminution of authority" that planters' abuses and workers' resistance to them engendered. If the administration must protect black workers, it could not tolerate the questioning of white employers: "The employer is a chief. He constitutes a step in authority accepted by the Administration in so far as it recruited for his benefit. The laborer owes him respect and obedience, in other words, an always deferential attitude, and good will in the execution of orders received." Labor inspectors were told not to criticize employers in front of workers, and to insist that complaints be brought first to the employer. "In no case, can the desertion of a laborer be tolerated. Recruits must know: first, they will be searched for and pursued before courts; second, their family will be constrained to furnish a replacement and to pay the costs of his transport."[139] Managing forced labor was pushing officials more deeply into a notion of society and of politics focused almost exclusively on command: on the authority of the official and the derivative authority of the white employer.

Shortly after French West Africa went over to the Free French side in November 1942, a colonial inspector, Pruvost, toured the Ivory Coast, noted the misery and disruption experienced by African populations, the "disorder" that ensued, the massive desertions and the growing exodus of Africans to the Gold Coast, and the "disarray" and "resentment" recruiting induced within the administration. But for all the force of his critique, Pruvost could only see free labor as a long-term remedy. For now, he wanted excessive recruitment reduced, plantations with a proven record of abuse excluded from labor supply, no more sanctions on the families of deserters, and closer vigilance exercised by a revivified corps of inspectors.[140]

The story was similar in Guinea, the Ivory Coast's younger and faster growing sister. Expanding banana cultivation meant by 1939 the "apostolat du travail" was insufficient, and the governor came under pressure for more direct recruitment. Governors recruited while insisting on the limits of what they could do. Demands escalated and the governor claimed again that the limit of what could be done without political danger "has already been reached."[141]

Officials, much as they complained about acting as mancatchers for the colons, would not give up their own reliance on compulsion to recruit labor for public projects. When the ten-year plan fell by the wayside, work on public projects was still unredeemed by the mechanization and rationalization Vichy had promised. Boisson told officials that they had to be ready "to ward off any insufficiency of voluntary labor." They were to keep up census lists, noting men "able to work" and act according to the situation. The labor demands of Vichy's grand "plan d'équipement" of 1942 was a major reason behind its call for an "obligation au travail."[142]

The Office du Niger, given a new life under the Vichy regime, upped recruitment in the Soudan (via the deuxième portion) to 4,700 in 1941 and 8,000 in 1943, compared to an average of 2,700 in the period 1928–46. The governor of the Soudan, like his colleagues in richer colonies, thought the limits of recruitment were at hand.[143] Predictably, laborers deserted public worksites at a high rate. A senior official frankly admitted that this was so because the "true interests" of Africans was to devote themselves to farming, which was both more remunerative and less arduous. Recruitment for the deuxième portion and other public projects once again fell back on "the authority of autochthonous chiefs" and desertion had to be "severely repressed." Nothing diminished the legitimacy of an indigenous chief more than mancatching.[144]

In a poor country like the Soudan, where the administration was practically the only significant employer of wage labor, officials accepted as inevitable the disarticulation of the economy: a large "indigenous economy" that worked in its own way and a small official economy that worked by force. No labor market conveyed price signals between the one and the other.[145] In fifty years of colonization, wage labor had become neither a desirable nor a necessary part of African life.

Aware that shortages of imports discouraged the sale of crops as it did the offer of labor, Boisson emphasized to his administrators that meeting metropolitan demands for particular commodities depended on them:

Your action should thus be constant and direct. It also will be nuanced, following the milieux and the regions: here more persuasive, there clearly more authoritarian. [The] chiefs of administrative circumscriptions have the authority to apply the code of the indigénat to repress the refusal, the manifestations of bad will or interference with the execution of measures of economic or agricultural nature having for their object to assure the subsistence of the populations.[146]

Boisson and his governors were saying that Africa was very African, its people peasants to their very souls. Therefore a colonial regime had to be very colonial: the men who knew their natives and knew their own power had to control its economic destiny as much as its political order. And they had to know where to stop.

What was new about the position at the end of the Vichy era was the frankness of official discourse. In 1936, forced labor existed in a world of tacit understandings and euphemisms, so much so that when the Popular Front leaders decided to attack it, they could not find the object of attack. In 1943, forced labor existed in the open, but it loomed so large and appeared to officials so necessary that they could not see an alternative to it.

Labor unreformed: the case of Senegal

All this should have been least true in Senegal, the oldest of the African colonies, with self-conscious évolués in its cities and experienced peanut farmers in its countryside. Dakar was an urban center, the site of government, maritime facilities, repair shops, and a modest agricultural processing industry. Senegal made little use of forced labor while exporting more than the Ivory Coast; it had a significant wage labor force – roughly 5 percent of the economically active population, much higher in Dakar. But Vichy's vision of industrialization and labor discipline did not apply here any more than in the fields of the Ivory Coast.

Senegal's administrators also proclaimed the limits of the possible, and admitted that the possible was defined by Africans' unwillingness to subject themselves to the regular work rhythms of capitalist production and their ties to the soil. Officials in Senegal argued they had to live within the limits of the colonies' values. Governor Rey wrote in 1942, "The attraction of work on the land is still very great among Africans, which the city and even at times a poorly assimilated European education have not corrupted. One even sees truck drivers and office workers periodically becoming cultivators again." Much of Dakar's working population came and went with the seasons, while even the rural reflux left Senegal's peanut farms with insufficient labor, so that still more itinerant laborers – the navétanes from the Soudan or Guinea – had to add their uncertain and irregular efforts.[147] Rey went on to say:

private and public places of work, mines and industries should adopt themselves completely to the agricultural rhythm of the country. With the exception of the skilled and maintenance worker, labor should be liberated at the beginning of the agricultural season... It will still require a long time before the indigenous mass is physically and intellectually capable of working in the European rhythm. Do those people who sometimes dream of an immediate development of industry in French West Africa imagine to themselves the Wolof working on an assembly line in an automobile factory?

Vichy's hopes were thus dismissed in a rhetorical question whose sarcasm depended on the assumption that being Wolof and building a car were incompatible. Rey was trying to remove directed industrialization from the realm of possibility: "there is now in Senegal no manpower available on a permanent basis." It would have to be the European who adapted to the way of life of the African.[148]

Senegal's industrialization was not about to be. Agricultural processing plants (manufacturing peanut oil in particular) was mainly what there was, but Dakar's industries only employed 1,502 permanent and 1,537 temporary workers in 1939. In 1942, the European sector in Senegal employed 0.3 percent of the economically active African population in "productive" activity (as opposed to government and commerce). Production rested "almost entirely" in the hands of peasants and herders. In French West Africa as a whole only 178 industrial firms, 108 of them treating agricultural products, were counted in a 1943 survey.[149] In Dakar, the war, the Allies' attempted blockade, and the shortages of imports reduced port activity in 1943 to a quarter of its 1939 level.[150] Boisson actually tried to send many residents of Dakar and other French West African cities back to the villages, thinking that the "solidarity of the autochthonous milieu" would be a sufficient antidote to wartime decline. The post-Vichy regime continued this policy, without notable success.[151]

Official skepticism about the possibility of creating anything like a modern wage labor force – for agriculture or industry – in West Africa's most sophisticated colony still left the question of the small but regular working force that had already come into existence. In theory, Vichy's modernizers wanted to do what the Popular Front had in its own way attempted: to treat the small African urban labor force as a working class under the same legal framework as any other workers. The GPCs in Vichy contemplated applying the corporatist "Charte du Travail" over-seas, a move with affinities to the past efforts of the Popular Front and the future struggle for the Code du Travail. But officials – notably in Indochina – objected, finding this conception of labor organization (much like the earlier socialist version) inappropriate in a situation "where the administration has assigned itself the role of tutor of indige-nous wage workers..."[152]

The Charte du Travail did not come to Senegal.[153] Vichy's social policy extended to people of "metropolitan origin" working in Africa, but when improvements were made in the program of family allowances in order to encourage natality, Boisson and others made clear that this measure was intended to propagate the "French race," and that even Senegalese with French citizenship were excluded.[154]

If Vichy's industrial and social policy came to little, one problem of the urban labor force which it did attack – bequeathing its approach to its successors – was the disarticulation of the labor market, a simultaneous overabundance of people who worked irregularly and indifferently and a shortage of skilled or steady workers. There were numerous complaints about the "bad quality of this labor" and its lack of stability. "It is prac-tically impossible to recruit skilled personnel and even often laborers." Part of any solution was "to attach existing indigenous manpower," but firms were loath to pay the costs of training – finding Africans "difficult to improve" – or the higher wages that might affect an attachment.[155]

If this argument on the need to "attach" labor presages what later was called stabilization, the immediate reaction to the problem of the scarcity of reliable or skilled workers took another direction. A report asserted, "This absence of manpower has led certain employers with few scruples to practice *le débauchage et la surenchère*." These two words – bandied about in Dakar for a time – mean, in the first case, hiring away another employer's workers and in the second bidding up wages. Although such practices might be considered a normal part of a labor market, in this context they were thought to have "grave" consequences. Given officials' perception of a disorganized labor market, bidding away workers was thought to discourage increasing the skill of the work force, for any firm investing in training was likely to increase a rival firm's productivity.[156]

Government officials worried about losing their own skilled workers to private enterprise. The remedy proposed was requisitioning such workers for the public service. This would oblige them to remain at their posts under threat of a jail sentence of six days to five years.[157]

Just before the Free French triumph in West Africa, Boisson proposed legislation against débauchage and surenchère, making it illegal for a worker to leave a job in order to accept another one with a higher wage.[158] The decree was still in the works when French West Africa went over to the Free French side, who (see below) took quite a similar interest in this little piece of coercive labor control.

If some Dakarois and Senegalese – mainly those with skill – found employers bidding for their services, virtually all experienced the war as hardship, struggling to move between an urban economy of shortages and irregular employment and a rural economy filled with uncertainty over the marketability of export crops. Wartime inflation was rampant: in 1941, according to official figures, an African "living African style" faced a cost of living 1.9 times what it had been in 1938. It rose again in 1942 and 1943.[159] In Dakar, the minimum wage of 8 francs per day in 1938 rose 25 percent by 1941, whereas prices had increased closer to 100 percent. The official ration of rice had been cut in half because of shortages and the administration was trying to get people to eat millet and maize grown within French West Africa: the overall food supply for Dakar was down 25 percent although the population of the city was rising. Officials were trying to keep wages down and control inflation instead, at which they achieved little success.[160] Dakar and other cities, at the dawn of the Free French era, still contained a highly irregular work force, sharing crowded living space, poor services, and suffering from a war that was not theirs. The new regime would initially share the old one's inability to imagine the African worker – Dakarois or Voltaic – as really a worker, until they learned otherwise from the workers themselves.

The Free French and unfree labor

The ideas of Boisson – although certainly not those being espoused among the GPCs in Vichy – were actually not that far from the ideas of his opposite number: Félix Eboué, governor-general of French Equatorial Africa. Eboué had rallied his Federation to the Free French cause, and he became the architect of the Brazzaville Conference of 1944, being hailed as the embodiment of liberal colonialism. Eboué was an Antillian, often cited as evidence of the French colonial system's openness to men of color who played by the rules.[161]

Eboué's circular of November 1941 revealed him as more Lugardist than Lugard, anti-assimilationist, pro-chief, pro-peasant.[162] He believed population was declining and linked this to social degeneration, caused by excessive labor recruitment and the creation of a proletariat: "it is a mass which disaggregates itself and disperses, it is voluntary abortion and syphilis which spread in an embryonic proletariat, it is all the evils of absurd individualism inflicted on the ensemble of the colony."

He saw reproduction as a social process which had to take place within a particular milieu, within the African community. The African, he wrote, should not be treated "as an isolated and interchangeable individual, but as a human personage, bearing traditions, a member of a family, of a village, and of a tribe, capable of progress in his milieu, and very probably lost if extracted from it."[163]

Politically, this meant that local affairs should be run by chiefs and not by French functionaries: "The chief is not a functionary, he is an aristocrat." Economically, it meant peasant production – the "fixation of the African on the soil... in the midst of collective traditional institutions." He held the concession companies that had made much of Equatorial Africa into their private domains responsible for much of the region's woes; like Boisson, Eboué wanted officials to assist, cajole, and often coerce peasants to grow cotton and other crops. Socially, it meant that France should concentrate on health measures, on the "social enrichment of the village and the tribe," and keep urbanization and proletarianization to a minimum.[164]

The urban population, limited as it was supposed to be, needed some fixation too. Cities all had "a socially stable element, composed of civil servants, former soldiers, artisans, and commercial employees, and an unstable element (servants, laborers, families of soldiers) properly named a 'floating population.'" The problem was that the two shared space:

Neighborhoods juxtaposed at random, without each constituting a distinct village do not have, moreover, the community of tendencies and habits where the urban spirit would be born... [Next] to useful inhabitants, a band of half-unemployed and half-vagrant people live at the expense of Europeans and Africans, lost to their villages and farms that they have abandoned, lost to repopulation for lack of a household, physically lost through venereal diseases and morally lost by the practice of getting by and neglect of all social discipline. There, without doubt, is where one recruits servants and laborers, but for one who works there are five who rest.[165]

Sending Africans back to their villages was "the best solution" but wouldn't work for all. The other possibility was "discipline, and only discipline." He meant not only the police and the indigénat – although he meant that too – but "equally the ameliorative discipline of sporting societies, scouting, military preparation and recreational circles." He meant above all discipline through steady employment and a life structured around it: employers had a "duty to fix as much as possible the labor which they utilize and to avoid recruiting temporary personnel." People from the same ethnic group should work together, creating "a true village" at the worksite. In this way, the stability of work and the stability of traditional life would balance and reinforce each other.[166] Eboué's corporatism, while its urban manifestations paralleled Vichy thinking, also reflected an idealized conception of an African village.

Eboué shared with Boisson a belief that the mobilization of wage labor had already gone too far. Eboué saw a more peasant-oriented approach as part of a recreation of traditional society in all its dimensions, including the political – although he did not explain how village harmony and traditional authority had survived the labor round-ups of the past decades – whereas Boisson emphasized the authority of French officials over chiefs and through them peasants. Boisson was concerned with demographic constraints on economic growth, Eboué with demographic decline. Both feared what they called "déracinement" and which the British called detribalization, and both believed that minimizing wage labor would keep that process in check. Eboué went further than Boisson in sketching a corporatist solution for the urban life that was inevitable: Boisson wrote about the need to keep an eye on the "jeunesse évolué."[167]

These pro- and anti-Vichy leaders, then, shared the myth of the African traditional community. Their version smacked less of bucolic romanticism than that of Moutet or Delavignette in Popular Front days, and more of a sense of the limitations and dangers of the present. Neither thought of a working class as a normal and desirable part of African society.

In French West Africa, such broadly held conceptions were to have a strong effect on the post-Vichy years, to be reversed only when African workers and African politicians forced a new agenda onto the table. Boisson's successor as governor-general of French West Africa, Pierre Cournarie, was still arguing in mid-1945, two years after his arrival, that the problem of labor was made difficult because of

grave problems... inherent in the way of life of autochthones... Little habituated to work fixed hours, little interested in improving their situation by a painful discipline, they easily slip away to any prospects... It is impossible in such conditions to think of implementing a development program based solely on the principle of free labor.

He noted the "shocking and inhuman character" of forced labor, and wanted to make an effort to undertake public works with free labor. But he wanted to be prepared for "a partial failure" that could only be eased by some kind of obligatory labor service.[168]

The decision of French West Africa's government-general in November 1942 to switch to the Free French side (once it became clear who was likely to win the war) and the replacement of Boisson in July 1943 thus did not have a great and immediate impact on the lives of West Africa's workers. Two policies are emblematic of this continuity: forced labor and "surenchère et débauchage." The major differences were over trade unions and, later, political rights: the unintended consequence of these differences was that the voices which forced a sharp break in French policy would be African ones.

These continuities were conditioned by a wartime concern with production that survived a change of sides. Governor-General Cournarie, in his first address to the Conseil de Gouvernement in late 1943, made clear that the first priority was production for the war effort, and in particular "the battle of the peanut." The economic future depended on the "intensification of production of vegetable oils, rubber and all products useful for the war." Like de Coppet, Boisson, or Eboué, Cournarie intended "to exercise trusteeship over the indigenous populations, to raise them in the framework of their traditional societies, of their particular tendencies and of their own genius, toward a better civilization, materially more profitable for them, morally superior and more useful for all of humanity." What he had to say about labor was vague: "Abusive practices must disappear... if we should demand a proper output from the worker, we should also formally assure him satisfying conditions of life and equitable treatment."[169]

The Free French Commissaire des Colonies, René Pleven, also invoked the imagery of "the *battle of production*," and called on West Africa to make "a maximum economic contribution to the effort of liberation and general relief after the war." The war had hurt African exports and reduced imports to under a third of their pre-war volume. Pleven knew that it would be necessary to send more goods – "these stimulants to labor" – to French West Africa. The "problem of labor" remained unsolved.[170] Pleven realized how tenuous was the government's control over a population that could partly remove itself from marketed production: peanut growers had become millet growers when the the price of rice relative to peanuts had gone up three-fold. Pleven now recommended increases in the price of peanuts: given peasants' control over their labor time, he had no alternative.[171] What would attract men to wage labor?

At the very time – late in 1943 and in early 1944 – that officials in the Ivory Coast and elsewhere were documenting the calamity of forced labor, the top administration came to the conclusion that it could not be stopped abruptly. The dilemma was exposed with remarkable frankness in the speech the new governor of the Ivory Coast, André Latrille, gave to the Conseil de Gouvernement in Dakar in December 1943. He described how "so-called recruited labor" was obtained: an administrator received a notice: "recruitment of X laborers for employer Y authorized in such and such a subdivision." The head of the subdivision was notified; he told the chiefs and sent out the guards, who brought back two to three times as many men as were demanded to allow for high percentages of men judged unfit. When the requested number had been reached, they were sent off with an agent of the employer, accompanied by guards and the henchmen of the chiefs. Latrille described conditions of work on the colons' plantations as terrible: bad food, bad housing, bad medical care, and wages often held back. In 1943, 55,000 had been recruited for the private sector, 15,000 for government work. Latrille called this "half slavery for sole profit of private interests."

Then came his plan: a "progressive return to the free labor market" by reducing official recruitment each year until it was brought to zero at the end of five years. Meanwhile, a "service obligatoire du travail" would be created by reducing the period of service of the deuxième portion du contingent from three to one years and making it more general. These workers would be used exclusively in public service, but anyone who had worked a year for a private employer would be exempted. The idea was to encourage Africans to seek wage labor "to escape from the work camps with a slightly military style." For the African, wage labor would become "a sort of refuge to which he would be accustomed little by little."[172] This was not exactly free labor ideology.

The basic ideas of his plan – the five year weaning period and the "service obligatoire du travail" – were endorsed by the Brazzaville Conference the next month and governors were ordered to plan their schedules of reduction promptly, demonstrating "a commencement of execution sufficient to affirm our sincerity, calculated however in a manner so as not to undermine the war effort in the domain of production."[173]

The story of the self-consciously reformist drive that emerged at Brazzaville, and the ambiguities of its implementation, will be taken up in chapter 5. For now, the point to be emphasized is that for all the repulsion which Latrille, Eboué, and their Free French colleagues felt toward Vichy's brutality, their sociology of Africa was not remarkably different. Their Africa was a peasant society and a tribal polity, and their own role was one of commandment: to use colonial authority and "traditional" authority to make Africans act in their own interest, while protecting them from the dangers of social change. French West Africa, after the Vichy nightmare, was in some sense back to where it had been when the

Popular Front decided it would do something about forced labor in 1936. The main difference was that the issue had come up from underground. The system before 1936 had operated by winks and nods and Governor Mondon was able to declare forced labor transformed into the "apostolat du travail" while leaving a wide area of ambiguity. In 1943, forced labor was larger scale, probably more brutal, and no-one was pretending it did not exist. Rural areas of the Ivory Coast, in fact, were suffering some of the "worst hardships of the war" under the Free French "effort de guerre."[174] So Latrille was trying gradually to wind down something identifiable. He was, however, about to get a lesson in sociology and politics from the Ivory Coast's cocoa planters, whose own approach to ending forced labor would replace the governor-general's.

The Free French urban sociology was also not sharply distinguished from Vichy's. Both regimes worried that the urban labor market was too disarticulated to function properly, and the new administration took over Boisson's project for a decree to prevent the hiring away of workers and the bidding up of wages. Although Algiers recognized the seriousness of the "manpower" problem and wanted action to improve the labor supply and the condition of workers, its first specific intervention was to keep Africans' wages down. In March 1943 it approved an ordinance intended "to break the increase in wages on the indigenous labor market" by providing that any employer hiring a wage worker other than an unskilled laborer could not, without authorization from the government, pay him for a period of one year wages and benefits superior to those paid him by his previous employer. The regulations did not apply to the government, but Boisson shortly before his departure ordered officials not to bid away workers from private firms.[175]

Free French officials, like Boisson, did not like the spectacle of Africans in a colonial society doing well in the job market: "Their attitude manifests itself more each day by an absence of respect toward the employer and his proper duties, by the absence of professional conscience, by laziness and by an effrontery of bad faith reaching often to insolence." The government would study the labor market and come up with tables of "normal" wages for particular occupations, to be used by both public and private sectors.[176]

But one element of this discussion had changed. The government approach was contested. Unions had sprung back into existence within months of the fall of the Vichy regime in Dakar, having been banned by the Boisson administration in December 1940. By the end of 1943, officials knew of eight unions of Africans and two professional associations, including one of laborers and dockers. There was an umbrella organization for Africans, the Union des Syndicats et Associations Professionels de la Circonscription de Dakar et Dépendances, and another central organization of European trade unions.[177]

In August 1943, the Syndicat des Travailleurs Indigènes du Chemin de Fer Dakar–Niger – one of the major unions of the pre-war period – wrote to the new governor-general protesting the measure which restricted the right of railway workers, including auxiliaries, to seek better employment. The union asked for reconsideration of this "measure dictated by the former Government being far from compatible with the democratic spirit of the Comité de la Libération Nationale to which we are infinitely grateful for having permitted the return of trade union freedom." Cournarie wrote back that the measure was part of the war effort; it was intended "to clean up the labor market."[178]

Officials had reason to worry about the railway workers' protest. Even before the fall of Vichy in May 1942 there had been a strike threat among railwaymen in Dahomey, broken by firing twelve participants.[179] Early in 1943 there were angry meetings of workers at Thiès, confrontations with railway officials over wages, and a cooling off of the conflict only after concessions had been granted.[180]

Between March and October 1943, the government, acknowledging the increased cost of living, set about revising wages. The railway promised to do likewise. Calm returned for a time, but the ensuing wage increases passed major categories by and left others annoyed with the de facto racial discrimination that kept them in the *cadres locaux* instead of the largely white and better paid *cadres communs*. There were meetings at Thiès and talk of a strike or public protest. The government-general revised its own wage scales to correspond with what its study of the private sector showed to be "normal." Some officials thought the increases unwise but admitted that for "political and psychological" reasons they were impossible to reverse.[181]

In Dakar in 1943, the Inspection du Travail was meeting – as it had in 1937–38 – with representatives of unions and employers to discuss wages. Faced as well with a growing need for labor as Dakar became involved in the Allied supply system and with continued shortages of imported goods, French firms felt they were losing control. The leading French cargo handling firm, Manutention Africaine, complained of

a crisis of manpower such as we have not seen in the last twenty years, as much for laborers as for skilled workers, a crisis caused on the one hand by new firms and industries which, in the last two years installed themselves in Dakar or its environs and on the other hand, by an almost total lack of training apprentices. *The indigenous element understands very well that enterprises need it and becomes more and more exigent*; thus, when it demands with insistence a wage increase, we will be obliged to accord it.

Manutention Africaine, like the government-general, thought the proper response to a market moving in workers' interest was to pay all workers in the same category the same wages and benefits, with a set indemnity to compensate for inflation.[182]

What officials seemed to want above all was some escape from the anarchy of the market, in Dakar above all, an anarchy that was partly the result of immediate economic conditions – shortages of imports – and partly the result of what they took to be the nature of African society. The administrator of Dakar – a man whose 1941 report had included a praise song for Pétain's National Renovation – was writing in 1943 about the need for better organization and the usefulness of trade unions and collective bargaining agreements. He noted the "massive departures" of workers each agricultural season, the absence of training systems, the irregularity of working hours, the indifference of employers "to their social, colonizing and educating role," and the "habitual nonchalance and insouciance of Africans." He saw unions as part of the solution:

Union activity has never been as necessary as it is today... [It] is to be encouraged, because given the impossibility of following some 20,000 employees and workers in Dakar alone, it is necessary that shop stewards in enterprises act in constant liaison with the offices of their respective unions, the latter having to work in their turn in close collaboration with the Inspection du Travail.[183]

Thus in 1943, as officials in the Ivory Coast or Guinea hoped that chiefs would keep an eye on unwilling, desertion-prone workers, officials in Dakar hoped that trade unions would keep an eye on workers who were likely to leave one job for another. The first way of thinking led nowhere, and officials knew it. A recruited laborer was no more likely to be a willing worker the next year.[184] The second situation offered the hope that workers might become attached to their jobs, to their regular incomes, to the new institutional structure which defended their interests. All this was dangerous – the line between unionization and political mobilization was a thin one – but some officials realized that Eboué's concept of "fixation" meant something only if it occurred through organizations that workers might actually take seriously. The Vichy's GPCs or Eboué's sporting organizations and scouting came to nought. Unions, in Dakar at least, showed their attraction as soon as they were given a little space in which to operate.[185]

The Inspecteur du Travail in Dakar noted in 1944 the continuing efflorescence of unions: commercial workers, municipal workers, the metallurgists, bakers, printers, dockers, and port laborers now had their unions. The unions of civil servants and auxiliaries were allegedly "much more agitated and violent" than those of the private sector. The inspector argued that the government had to anticipate demands for adjustments

Table 4.2. *"Normal" wages, June 1943*

Category	1939	Current	Proposed
For "ouvriers" (hourly)			
I	2.60–4.00	3.00–6.00	3.00–8.00
II	2.00–3.00	2.50–5.00	2.50–6.00
III	1.50–2.00	2.00–3.00	2.05–4.00
For "employés" (monthly)			
Superior	1,200	1,200–2,000	1,350–2,500
Subaltern	500	850–1,000	900–1,500
Auxiliary	450	300–600	450–800

Source: Conclusions de la Commission d'Evaluation des Salaires Normaux, 23 June 1943, K 273 (26), AS.

to the rising cost of living, which could escalate even higher if they led to a strike.[186]

Where did this leave workers? Inflation continued into the Free French period. In Dakar, the minimum wage for a laborer in 1944 had increased 50 percent from 1938, compared to a 258 percent inflation. At the top, the wage increases for government workers in 1943 did not entirely make up lost ground.[187] The commissions studying "normal" salaries and wages set forth the standard for "ouvriers" shown in Table 4.2. The significance of the wage figures lies not only in their modesty relative to the increase in prices since 1939, but in the very fact of the classification system; indeed, each of the categories listed here was broken down into two classes plus a "hors catégorie." Particular jobs were classified in different categories. There were places for interns and apprentices, and employers would determine passage, if relevant, from one category to another. The list of classifications was based on the EMCIBA accord of 1938 in the case of employees: it would now provide an official basis for classifying workers and creating homogeneous salary structures.[188]

At the same time that wage hierarchies and unionization were being advanced as measures to tame the anarchy of the labor market, old methods were brought to Dakar as well. A camp was set up in 1943 for up to 600 workers of the deuxième portion, and they were put at the disposal of the cargo handling firms. By 1944, although the camp was still in use, it was in decline. The immediate crisis of port labor passed.[189] Perhaps the supplementary involuntary workers helped, perhaps the growing migration to Dakar helped: officials thought – based on data from the issuing of ration cards – that Dakar in 1944 was inhabited by 145,000 Africans with ration cards, and another 15,000 Africans "poorly identified and deprived of ration cards," compared to 120,000 the year before.[190]

The easing of the shortage of laborers in 1944 coincided with an improvement in peanut production: the relationship between such labor and farming was clearly not inverse. And even as urban migration increased, the migration of navétanes *into* the rural areas of Senegal for peanut cultivation began to creep upward toward its pre-war levels: having fallen from 70,000 in 1938 to 25,000 in 1941, it rebounded to 42,000 in 1944. Officials still thought – despite efforts to repatriate nonworkers – that there was still a large "floating population" in Dakar and little sign of evolution toward a stable working class.[191]

But the experience of 1943 had been bad enough that at least some employers began to look toward a more systematic approach to the labor question. The president of the Syndicat des Entrepreneurs Français des Travaux Publics et de Bâtiments de l'Afrique Occidentale Française wrote in December 1943 that they had been willing to go along with the government's decision to raise wages, but expected in return more from their workers. After the predictable complaints about the low quality of African labor and claims of declining productivity since before the war, he concluded: "We demand that a code du travail [labor code] be prepared and that the rights of our personnel correspond to duties and that failings in regard to these duties be followed by just, but severe sanctions."[192]

This section of the *patronat* was peeking beyond colonial employers' usual tendency to pay little, know little, and expect little from their workers. It was willing to consider something like the great compromise of the class struggle in Europe – more control for employers, more money for workers. But the Dakar businessman gave the class compromise a colonial twist: state regulation and state punishment to enforce labor discipline.

The idea of a labor code would be at the center of the labor question in the ensuing decade, and workers and state officials would bring quite different perspectives to this common focus. The Popular Front and Vichy had in their own ways sought to apply French models to parts of the African labor force, only to find that local officials and employers decidedly rejected universalistic conceptions of labor beneath their overwhelming belief in the peculiarity of the African. The Dakar businessman's intervention was an early hint that the encounter of employers and officials with African workers would pose problems that a colonial framework could not solve and that the experience of regulating class conflict in the metropole was the imaginable alternative.

But for now, the simultaneous discussions of the problems of the Dakar labor market and the issue of forced labor in agriculture and public works revealed how confused and contradictory discussions of the labor question in French Africa remained. Accepting Africans as urban laborers, in need of trade unions, wage setting machinery, social security, and collective bargaining agreements and conceiving of Africans as peasants unable and unwilling to work for wages unless coerced implied very different conceptions of the role of the state, of production, and of the laborer. One problem evoked a set of experiences in Europe, the other an authoritarian vision of colonialism.

The contradictory images were being applied to aspects of African life that were not necessarily as disarticulated as the official vision of them. In the region of Dakar, to take the most striking example, workers were part of a regional economy that did not starkly separate the world of urban labor and of the rural peasantry. Vital workers, such as dockers, often kept their links with the rural economy, moving between Dakar and the peanut fields, even as people from distant parts of the Soudan and Guinea moved into and out of the peanut fields of Senegal. Perhaps such patterns could give rise to social networks linking city and countryside and to cultural adaptations to a complexly articulated milieu. But for French officials at the time, African rural life represented something wholly distinct from urban and industrial society. They worried on the one hand that the apparent cultural wholeness of the African village could be disrupted by wage labor, and on the other hand that increased crop sales and prosperity within the village would reduce the flow of labor to enterprises that needed wage labor. The city itself, divided between a stable kernel whose integration into French institutions could at least be imagined and a "floating population" that brought African backwardness into urban life, seemed more like a source of social and political danger than the possible site of a creative synthesis. French officials, however, would not enjoy the luxury of their contradictory thinking for long: African political mobilization would bring the forced labor issue to a head just as the collective action of African workers forced officials to focus on the social conditions of urban labor.

Conclusion: posing the labor question

After November 1942, French and British Africa were officially on the same side of the great struggle of the day, and both sought to mobilize their African populations for the "battle of production." Up to that point, those populations had experienced the war quite differently. British Africans had fought in a long war, and larger numbers were mobilized – by force, by the attraction of wages, or by pressures that lay somewhere in between – to produce for it. Vichy Africa had been cut off, much of its production bought up by the state so as not to cause the entire market economy to shut down. British officials wanted to expand exports and minimize imports, and they faced more directly than the French the social consequences of directed economic mobilization.

Vichy and London ardently planned for what both came to call development, and they did so in ways that were strangely detached from what their officials on the scene were facing. Vichy's planning took place in a dream world, set off by the gap between its rhetoric of a coordinated and prosperous French empire and the tawdriness of what it actually did. Vichy's *fascisant* language aside, its thinking on development was perhaps only a step further removed than London's from the messiness of colonial Africa in the 1940s, but in both capitals the wartime efforts to think about development would have long-lasting consequences. The Vichy government's attempt to bring colonial business groups into its corporatist structure may well have made development planning appear more plausible and useful to the right of the political spectrum, just as the British Labour Party's dialogue with the Colonial Office on colonial development made the left more amenable to new forms of economic expansionism after the war.

Thinking about development, especially in the British case, became more muddy as it was made to bear increasingly varied weights. It was – in its initial conception – supposed to prevent colonial people from becoming angry, to improve their standard of living, to raise their output for the benefit of the war effort and the metropole, and to demonstrate to the entire world the progressive and benevolent nature of British imperialism. It provided a framework for a British response to the first waves of labor protest in the colonies, turning the labor question into a matter of providing social services and raising the standard of living of workers. But the Colonial Office's lengthy debates over these issues could not focus on production as a social process or give any indication of whether economic growth would lead to less social conflict or to more or suggest whether the enhanced role of the technologically and socially advanced metropole in economic and social development would be conducive to or contrary to eventual self-government.

The familiar assertion (quoted in chapter 4) that the goal of British colonial policy was to make Africans into good Africans, while the French sought to make Africans into good Frenchmen, reveals little about the relationship of two colonial policies. The good Africans for whom British officials took credit were colonial inventions – officials were more ambivalent about the real ones – while the French administration had long shrunk before the implications of its assimilationist tendencies and balanced it with a neotraditional view of colonial societies quite comparable to that of British authorities. In both bureaucracies, the Africans officials thought they saw had little in common with the Africans they sought to create.

In both cases, the clearest thinking about labor came from the field, not from the metropole, and the Inspection du Travail in French Africa and the labour departments in British would soon become loci for a new departure. In 1939, when London was hoping that its new development initiative would be the antidote to colonial disorder, local officials in Mombasa put their finger on a more specific kind of social transformation than was being discussed in the Colonial Office: turning casual labor into permanent and focusing urban social services on a core of steady workers. Elsewhere, as in the Copperbelt, some provincial officials still clung to their hopes that Africa's problems could be pushed back into the realm of tradition and authority. But as strikes continued throughout the war years, local officials had to live with the unsettling presence and activism of urban workers. Local investigatory commissions and labor officers were beginning to raise complex questions about the nature of work, of urban society, and of possible ways of controlling it. In 1945, they had done little to change workers' lives, but had made possible a discussion of social processes that the development idea obscured and which policy makers in London could not even begin to examine. French officials, as of 1944, faced the problem in less acute forms, and their thoughts on it were contradictory. Both the apologists for forced labor and the defenders of peasant production thought in terms of an essentialized African nature that made the growth of wage labor appear unlikely and potentially disruptive and peasant life as deeply engrained, either to be encouraged or confronted with authoritarian methods. Yet in 1936–37 the officials in French West Africa had proposed decrees that would take into account the fact that workers had emerged as a distinct social category, and attention was again turning to this possibility as the war ended. Still, most leading officials hoped that the labor question could be kept to a minimum, as peasants took up the main burden of production and mechanization eased the burdens of transportation.

British officials in London shared with their French equivalents a sociology of Africa that divided its population into peasants and educated elites and treated everyone else as a residual – "detribalized Africans" or a "floating population." They were beginning to see the inadequacy of this thinking as guides to the problems they confronted and were being drawn, step by step, into facing more complex realities in African cities.

When they became allies, British and French colonial officials realized that they should cooperate, and by 1943 they were talking about doing so. Both powers strongly opposed tentative American initiatives toward greater international accountability over colonial empires and they needed each other's support. As the war wound down, both thought that they could work together to demonstrate the possibilities of a modernized imperialism for the post-war world, although they somewhat distrusted each other's designs on the trade of West Africa and feared that too overt cooperation might only invite more vigorous international supervision.[1] Actually, the most immediate social question which crossed colonial borders – the migration of Voltaics to the Gold Coast – was a sign that something was wrong. French officials were annoyed that different colonial practices, notably their own use of forced labor, gave Africans options.[2] Eventually, French and British officials would begin to assimilate social problems of labor and health to scientific questions which could be solved by the application of universal knowledge and would thus become more readily discussable at international fora.

For the time being, the consensus among European powers on labor in colonies was limited to the principle that labor should be "free." Not only had free labor ideology in the decades before the war obscured the conditions under which Africans decided whether or not to seek employment as well as those which conditioned production and reproduction, but during the war its limited vision was sufficient to show how much the strains of wartime production plunged French and British officials deeper into the authoritarian patterns of their colonial histories. Even the critics of forced labor were drawn into a mode of argumentation that led them to distance a supposedly African peasant nature from the modern world of wage labor. The actions of African workers in ports, mines, railways, and cities would soon confront officials in France, Great Britain, and international organizations not only with the fragility of colonial power, but with the inadequacies and inconsistencies of their ways of thinking about Africa and about themselves.

Part II
Imperial fantasies and colonial crises

Introduction

At the end of World War II, political leaders in Western Europe faced what seemed to be an open future, perhaps a dangerously open future. The old structures of power and habits of discourse had been shaken and it was not clear what would take their places. The ascendancy on the global stage of the United States and the Soviet Union – whose imperial visions and ambitions took quite different forms – reshaped the nature of the international community within which the morality and the politics of imperial rule were being discussed. Great Britain and France found themselves on the defensive in the colonies in the moment of victory in Europe. Domestic politics affected the way in which colonial issues were addressed: the end of the war brought about a dual focus on the politics of production and of welfare. In conditions of acute material hardships, cross-class bargaining centered on management efforts to increase output in exchange for social protections for workers.[1] Both international and domestic contexts fostered among high officials a conception of society as something to be managed, as something with a general logic that could be understood and controlled. The old claims to colonial authority based on superiority of race and civilization were thoroughly discredited by the experience of Nazism and fascism, whereas universalistic notions of social progress – based on knowledge and capital resources – offered a seemingly more plausible basis for assertions of imperial hegemony.

None of this explains – certainly in regard to the labor question – why France and Great Britain changed their entire approach *when they did*. The answer to that question may be found in Africa itself – a new discourse was brought to Africa in response to challenges raised by African workers. The key efforts at rethinking may be found in investigatory reports on strikes and in the work of Inspecteurs du Travail. Transitions from unease about the failures of past policy to explicit interventions occurred in the heat of strike movements, as in Dakar in 1946 or Mombasa in 1945 and 1947 as well as in response to African political mobilization in the Ivory Coast over the forced labor issue in 1945 and

1946. The metropolitan and international context suggests why French and British officials were intellectually and politically open to rethinking policy, aware as they were of being at a turning point in the history of colonialism, but collective action within the colonies is the reason why something actually happened.

The range of possible approaches to social issues in colonies and former colonies would in time close down again, leaving the issues defined in quite different ways.[2] It is vital to understand the opening up of questions as much as the closing down, for the alternatives taken were not necessarily inevitable. In the many-sided struggles – political, military, ideological – of the post-war years, global problems were framed and reframed, and what came to be excluded from international debate was as much part of the redefinition of global power as what came to be accepted fact.

It is tempting to read the period backwards, as the progressive enlarging of the meaning of self-determination and independence in the modern world. But in 1944 or 1945, it was not obvious in London or in Paris – let alone in Dakar or Accra – what progress was. To get a deeper understanding of this period of ideological flux and contestation, and to appreciate the limits of the conceptual framework which eventually emerged, requires keeping the political, economic, and social elements in tension with one another. They should not all be collapsed into a trend toward European decolonization or African nationalism. At the same time, one must decode the implicit social visions behind plans and projects. Just as the understanding of the compelling drive of nationalist movements requires seeing the "imagined communities," in Benedict Anderson's telling phrase, through which leaders and followers saw their future, it is necessary to see the imagined world which the leaders of colonial regimes, contesting and negotiating those futures, saw for themselves.[3] On the one hand, the deeply ingrained images in colonial officials' consciousness of Africans as tribal people, as backward, as ill-suited to the pressures of the modern workplace or the modern city did not disappear overnight; the wave of strikes and urban violence in African cities in the 1940s confirmed the images of urban Africa as the terrain of primitive masses and dangerous demagogues. On the other hand, European officials came to Africa with strong, if inaccurate, images of the social order of the metropole – often conflated with "civilization" or "modernity" – and these offered them a prefabricated social order that served as a beacon on the hard road to directed social change. The two sets of images existed in close and contradictory relationship to each other, and the eagerness with which officials sought to imagine a modern future for post-war Africa and the depth of their anxiety over the weight of its backward past accentuated each other.

It is not enough to analyze labor policies in the post-war era. One needs to come to grips with the subjective conceptions of African society and of "modern," industrial society that were as much part of the policy-making process as the drafting of legislation. The very processes of imagining and codifying framed problems for some time to come, even if the consequent policy did not resolve basic social and economic problems.

This part of the book, then, will seek to go behind the daily questions of managing crises and implementing new policies to examine the changes and continuities in official thinking about work and Africans. What Africa could officials imagine?

5   Imperial plans

French and British governments, as the war was ending, thought through their imperial futures in different ways. The British government stayed within the framework of development, the breakthrough they had made in 1939–40. To the extent that they looked to expanding African roles in politics, they did so by claiming this was established policy and they tried to shoe-horn African politics into "local government."

The French government made its own major breakthrough to using metropolitan funds for development projects in 1946 with the inauguration of the Fonds pour l'Investissement en Développement Economique et Social (FIDES). This in a sense put money behind the plan that Albert Sarraut had been pushing since 1923, and the importance of capital spending to improve the colonial infrastructure, broaden possibilities of production, and palliate the much-discussed shortage of labor had been vainly advocated by Popular Front, Vichy, and Free French leaders. But French officials were not so centered on development as the framework for colonial policy. They were caught up in redefining the structure of the French empire – rechristianized as the Union Française – and entered into a heated debate over the constitution of that entity. Whereas in Great Britain, post-war policy was debated above all within the Colonial Office, the French legislature engaged actively in debating the relationship of colonies to metropole, and the fact that Greater France was assumed (in different ways by left and right) to be a lasting entity made the stakes in such structural debates particularly high. At the same time, social policy in French Africa was dominated by a nagging bit of unfinished business, a reminder that officials were still trapped by their belief in the peculiarity of African economic behavior: the issue of forced labor.

Both powers were caught between their own need for empire and their belief in the political necessity of doing something for their empires, as well as between their desire to see colonial societies as plausible objects of reform and their fear that they were hopelessly backward. African society, in most officials' eyes, inspired both anxiety and a sense of purpose. René Pleven, leading colonial spokesman of the Free French, applauded "colonizing action, that is freeing people of the grand scourges which ravage primitive society, whether they be called superstition, ignorance, tyranny, corruption, exploitation of cruelty." To him, "To colonize, in other words, is in the final analysis to project in space one's civilization." Arthur Creech Jones, Secretary of State for the Colonies in the post-war Labour government, believed that "our work in many areas of Africa" is "to disturb the conservatism of ignorance, to break through the crust of custom, magic and superstition, and to revolutionise the whole approach to conduct and convention."[1]

In both empires, however, the attempts of officials to work through their contradictory images of Africa and of imperial reform ran quickly into a series of crises brought to the fore by African workers and city dwellers themselves. The labor question, as chapter 6 will explain, was soon to be posed in unexpected ways, plunging both regimes deeply into the complexity of labor as a social process.

The French Union and the contradictions of forced labor

In 1943 and 1944, French leaders were preoccupied with imagining the future because in the present they did not possess France. French Equatorial Africa remained loyal to de Gaulle and the Free French; the progressing Allied conquest of North Africa gave them a new headquarters city in Algiers; and French West Africa, as its leaders saw the inevitable, went over to Free French control in November 1942. The Algiers-based Commissariat aux Colonies du Comité Français de la Libération Nationale – and de Gaulle himself – saw clearly the need to anticipate a return to power and a need to rethink past policies. The one point which was an absolute, from de Gaulle on down, was that the empire would remain French. The war had proven the value of the empire to France, and the post-war recovery would require both an efficient empire and one whose legitimacy was secure. It was in this light that the Commissariat, led by Pleven – a highly regarded *résistant* and Gaullist – laid plans for a conference of officials with African experience to be held at Brazzaville, in French Equatorial Africa, at the beginning of 1944.

Brazzaville, January–February 1944

The assembly was in some dimensions a narrow one: all top officials – governors, governors-general, leading luminaries of the Algiers headquarters – all male, all but two white (both West Indian). The group included some who had served Vichy in France or in Africa before seeing the light and some who had resisted; there were Gaullists and socialists.[2]

It is easy to dismiss Brazzaville as an exercise in hypocrisy, as only a surface break with the colonialism of the past. Claiming a desire to give Africans, or at least évolués, representation in the governance of the French empire, the conferees conceded only minority representation in the centralized bodies in France that made decisions while devolving little power to the territories where Africans actually lived. Claiming a desire to improve the African standard of living, the conferees would not break with the past division of imperial labor, under which Africans produced primary products, the French industrial goods. But that is to measure Brazzaville's departures by later standards. In fact, the most progressive implications of the Brazzaville doctrines derive precisely from its most "imperialist" position, that the unity and continuity of the French empire must remain unquestioned. There was an implicit universalism in such a claim, and however much officials resisted this implication in any domain, French society itself set the model for its empire, and France – anxious to convince itself and the world that French imperialism was progressive – set itself the task of living up to its own standards.[3]

The quest for a progressive imperialism brought to the fore crucial tensions and contradictions in official thinking. Most basic was the argument between those, including Félix Eboué, who favored something akin to indirect rule and a social policy that gave wide space to production and reproduction in a "customary" milieu, and those, like several governors, who feared such policies would condemn Africans to permanent backwardness and who instead put most emphasis on a metropole-directed process of planning.[4] The final resolutions ended up closer to the assimilationist position: calling for "une économie dirigée et planifiée," insisting that education be entirely in French rather than in vernacular languages, and promising improved access to positions and increasing levels of political responsibility to those Africans who acquired French forms of knowledge.[5] Economic planning became one of the key elements of a centralizing, universalizing approach to colonial policy, however much that contradicted making government more representative of colonized peoples.[6] The most serious reservations about assimilation occurred in relation to labor.

The administrators at Brazzaville knew that heavy-handed past policies – notably forced labor -- had been a catastrophe. André Latrille and Pierre Cournarie, governor of the Ivory Coast and governor-general of French West Africa, brought now familiar critiques of forced labor before the conferees: the suffering and resentment of the workers, the damage done to families, the undermining of administrative authority.

Eboué brought up his old concern with Africans' dislike of "regularity and discipline in work."[7] Here was the conundrum: given the peculiar nature of the African and the demands of production, forced labor was both an impossibility and a necessity. The only logical way out was evolutionist: the hope that a little more time, a little more civilization, slightly higher wages, and a few more manufactured goods – France in 1944 could sell little that an African might need cash to buy – would create voluntary labor. Latrille, who knew perfectly well that the past fifty years had not done the trick, proposed taking another five: phasing out forced recruitment, reducing the numbers recruited by 50 percent annually until the final year, with an "obligation au travail" replacing "travail obligatoire" (obligatory labor becoming an obligation to work), now in the form of one year's public service. The final resolution, following Latrille, proclaimed the "absolute superiority of free labor" but phased out recruitment over five years and called for the creation of "un service obligatoire du travail" to do work in the public interest.[8]

Officials could still not envision wage labor as a normal part of African life: Africans were both resistant to it and endangered by it. To the director of political affairs in Dakar, wage labor appeared more as a disruption of African society than as a step toward something new:

In French West Africa, the limit beyond which the taking away of workers' risks to damage indigenous society has generally been attained or even passed in certain territories... The problems of work are not measured here by the number of individuals who depend solely on a job but by the size of the population whose conditions of life are modified by wage labor.[9]

Meanwhile, those who did work were not sufficiently skilled or committed to their jobs to do them adequately:

He [the wage laborer] does not attach himself to his work and above all doesn't fix himself there with his family, striving to organize himself better materially. In the inverse sense, to be sure, the employer is practically disarmed against the instability of a labor force which does not respect labor contracts and against the laziness and inertia of the laborers.[10]

The conferees saw these limits as major obstacles to any program of industrialization, whatever the merits of such a policy. A vigorous argument occurred between those who feared industrialization would compromise agriculture or lead to the dangers of a "black proletariat" and others who insisted on the "educative value of industrial labor" and the risk of colonial dependence on metropolitan industry. The debate reached no consensus, and the best the group could do was to accept a draft recommendation for a "prudent industrialization."[11] Calling again for something like the Popular Front's economic development fund, officials argued that better equipment and precise planning would allow for more export production while making less demands on Africans to leave their villages; even development spending was seen as socially conservative.[12]

In the end, some officials felt, the limits placed on the growth of wage labor were not altogether a bad thing:

The risk of a proletariat does not present, at this hour, any gravity, the African rarely expatriating himself without the intention of returning, most often to his milieu of origin. One should encourage this tendency, and for this limit to the maximum the number of workers transplanted in urban centers.[13]

Wage labor agriculture – the source of so much agony over forced recruitment – received virtually no support at Brazzaville. The colons were reviled for their inefficiency and greed and for putting officials in the position of "slave traders."[14]

The same paradox as in the pro-peasant days of the Popular Front appeared: to the extent that wage labor had come into existence, it should be legally regarded in similar ways to the French working class. A number of position papers, while expressing the hope that European-style "class struggle" could be avoided, acknowledged that workers did need protective legislation. But the focus of attention was on an elite of literate workers. Growing numbers of Africans in commercial firms needed to come under "metropolitan social laws," and the conditions of appointment for white and for black white-collar workers should over time converge. In the civil service, positions of "command and direction" would remain in the hands of "French citizens," but subordinate positions should increasingly go to Africans: "The personal status, for subject or citizen, means little, the African has only to furnish proof of his competence, his training, and his credentials. For equal competence, equal remuneration and analogous advantages."[15] These statements go further than official discourse in British Africa toward invoking the concept of equality – or at least convergence of conditions of employment and remuneration – in regard to whites and blacks in certain domains. But the domains in question are those of the "employées du commerce" and civil servants, and these both fall in or close to the conventional French sociological category of "évolué." The logic of assimilation posited that once Africans entered a French social category, the universality of French law and French sociology applied to them, but the logic of African society, in French eyes, suggested that few would enter those categories. The argument in these texts was to serve, however, as an opening wedge for African leaders, and French officials would find the assimilationist position thrust back upon them.

A few parties to the discussions of the future of empire were ready to make the intellectual leap to uniform social legislation in spite of – or precisely because of – the backwardness of its objects. At a meeting of the French Assemblée Consultative Provisoire (the pre-liberation legislative body meeting in Algiers), one delegate, M. Poimboeuf, intoned,

We remain the most universalistic people... it is necessary, by all appropriate means, to teach about the fertility of work to populations who have lived up to now in idleness... The social laws must be extended to our overseas possessions keeping in mind, obviously, local particularities, but taking inspiration from our principles and even reproducing, as far as possible the letter of our own legislation.[16]

In effect, he was saying, implementing laws and institutions as if colonials were normal Frenchmen, even if one knew they were not, would make it so. It was a bold synthesis of claims to French universalism and assertions of African peculiarity, tempting enough – as the attempt to implement a Code du Travail for the colonies in 1946 (see below) indicates – to be acted upon, but complicated enough so that it would actually take until 1952 to devise the code of social laws for the colonies.

But what resonated in Brazzaville was still the old sociology of Africa that divided its population into a large group of peasants, who should be relieved of coercion and allowed to live within rural communities and by African customs (whatever that meant after fifty years of colonial rule), and a very small number of évolués, whose political participation now had to be encouraged and who deserved some protection under French social laws. High economic hopes for economic progress rested on a conservative conception of the social organization of production.

Hopes for social progress rested on an even more conservative conception of reproduction. This was an old concern of Eboué's, and the low population density and birth rate of French Equatorial Africa were cited as evidence of the demographic dangers of the "disorganization of the indigenous family by unregulated wage labor." West African officials thought "the demographic problem dominates and conditions the process of colonization in French West Africa" and that "the first task, the most urgent, is thus to develop and improve the race." Although health and sanitation services received significant attention, key officials insisted that demographic reproduction could only be restored by African communities themselves, freed of the excessive constraints of past regimes: "the necessity imposes itself to consider for many years the application of a demographic policy, giving a very large place to the agricultural activity of the African, freely exercised in the family, social, and customary context."[17]

Wage labor, as Henri Laurentie told the conference, involved migration and raised concerns about "the influence of the labor system on the condition of the family and the woman. If the worker is married, he is generally obliged to leave his wife in the village." Such conditions led to the spread of venereal disease. If the worker were unmarried, he needed to earn enough to pay bridewealth, but in present conditions this was rarely possible. "If he leaves the workplace assured that on his return he would have the financial means to marry, work will become attractive to him, because he will see in it the means to realize one of the dearest goals of the young man: marriage." Laurentie, at least could *imagine* that wage labor, by males, might become part of a normal African life, even if he could not see African families living and reproducing anywhere but in their villages.[18]

Brazzaville's social and economic policy – resurrecting themes of the Popular Front days with a touch of Vichyite planning – were thus a tangle of contradictions along with a wish for an Africa that would be simultaneously better off, more productive, socially stable, and politically secure.[19] The problem of labor appears as a black hole of anxiety: Africans wouldn't work for wages, but if more than a small percentage of men did so, they would jeopardize food production and population growth. It is another sad commentary on the Vichy years that this program, particularly the proposed end to forced labor, actually offered some solace to Africans. French officials would discover over the next two years that the social category they had wanted not to think about – the worker – would prove critical to their aspirations and fears. At the same time they would find that some of the promises they had spelled out at Brazzaville would develop a political weight greater than they had imagined.

The emancipation of colonial workers

The influence of Brazzaville lay not so much in the new departures in its resolutions, but in the fact that the French government desperately wanted to think it was making a new departure. In late 1945 and much of 1946, the issue of defining the colonies' place in France's future had to be faced explicitly, for the new constitution was being debated, while the Indochina war was starting up and the massacre by French soldiers in response to the Sétif insurrection in Algeria was polarizing opinion. The assimilationist language of Brazzaville helped insure that French society would be a continual reference point for discussions of social questions, and French officials would constantly be confronted with the progressive implications of their own doctrines in an international situation where progress seemed the only defensible rationale for colonial rule.[20]

France wanted to use Brazzaville to assert itself in international discussions. It did so at the ILO Conference in Philadelphia later in 1944, promoting its new-found resolve to end forced labor and racial discrimination, proclaiming its goal to raise the "African's standard of living, to lead him toward modern life, to bring ourselves to raise him to our level."[21] France thought it would look good under the ILO's proposed international "standards" of labor policy for colonies (see below). In so doing, French officials were willingly subjecting their reformist agenda to a measure of outside scrutiny.

The next year, de Gaulle made much of the Brazzaville reforms while in Washington. The commissaire of colonies, however, added a warning to his claims of a propaganda triumph: "Our colonial policy thus receives a stunning consecration and becomes an element in the international situation of France. Hesitations or restrictions in the execution of our will, thus proclaimed, would however produce absolutely disastrous effects."[22]

This dialectic of national initiative and international reinforcement for taking reform seriously was sufficiently worrisome to the colonialist right that some of its leading lights warned the minister of the dangers of being pulled along by the idea of "the social" as formulated by people who are "incompletely informed on the mentality and daily needs of native populations." The peculiarity of the African had to be reasserted against the enthusiasm for the universal.[23]

Meanwhile, the promise of improved political representation had to be given some concrete meaning, however disproportionate to the numbers of people in Overseas France. Citing Brazzaville, the provisional government of France, at the end of 1945, brought African and other colonial representatives into the Assemblée Nationale Constituante, which was to draft a new French constitution and temporarily carry on legislative functions. With that, the French government had brought to Paris people very likely to call them on the contradiction between their vision of African progress and their obsession with the backward tendencies of its people. What happened next illustrates the relationship of one set of discourses and institutions – about constitutionalism and the French Union – to another – about labor and social policy – and the way in which the definition of an issue changes in the course of debate.

How Overseas France was to be represented in French government structures was debated at length by the Assemblée Constituante, with the participation of colonial deputies.[24] These members had been chosen in October 1945 in separate colleges, for citizens and non-citizens, and the franchise for the latter was extremely restricted. Some of Africa's most important future nationalists – Léopold Senghor, Lamine Guèye, Gabriel d'Arboussier, Félix Houphouët-Boigny – took active roles in the committees working on proposals affecting the colonies.[25] So too did the other side – representatives, in effect, of the colons and colonial businesses. For most deputies and much of the public, colonial issues were not of great interest, but for this reason the white and non-white colonials, who cared very deeply, could make themselves heard in a closely divided assembly where alliance-building was crucial.

Opinions fell loosely into three camps: some, including most African deputies, favored relatively autonomous political bodies, including legislatures, within each territory, as full participation as possible of colonials in both an assembly concerned with Overseas France and in the Assemblée Nationale itself, and elections within a single college and with a wide franchise. They thought of the Union as an association held together by free will, and sought a formula which would give territories the right to go their own way at some future point. A second position was also federalist in nature, but with quite opposite intent: the old colonialists favored strong institutions in the individual colonies, an assembly for Overseas France, no role for non-citizens in the Assemblée Nationale, and a narrow franchise. They wanted, above all, to insure that white Frenchmen would control the institutions of the colonies – whose ties to France would be permanent – while protecting themselves from the intrusion of French universalism (including the idea of free labor) into colonial affairs. The third position, found among metropolitan politicians with a zeal for reforming the empire, reflected the universalism the old colonialists feared, favoring powerful central institutions, capable of legislating and implementing economic planning for the empire as a whole, and in which colonial people would participate. Territorial institutions would be weak but the franchise broad, and representation in a powerful French legislature would not be equivalent to overseas population – a point as sore with African deputies as it was inconsistent with universalistic claims.[26]

Advocates of the first and third positions could talk to each other, even if they seemed at opposite poles of the federalism to centralism spectrum. That proved to be a basis for compromise on constitutional questions and opened up common ground on social issues. The proposed constitution of April 1946 was a relatively liberal one, giving significant voice to African opinion in elections on all levels. But that constitution was rejected in the May referendum in which only citizens could vote (although the real reasons for the defeat were not connected directly to colonial questions). France had swung to the right in the early months of 1946, and the next draft – by a newly elected assembly – was a step backward, and showed the influence – mobilized in a vigorous campaign in the summer of 1946 – of the colonial right. It was, nonetheless, a compromise (and inconsistent) document, guaranteeing that representatives of Africans, Asians, and North Africans would have a voice in all levels of government but insuring that it would be a minority voice. The constitution – reluctantly backed by African colonial deputies and accepted this time by French citizens in a referendum – proudly proclaimed itself to be giving all the peoples of France "freedom of administering themselves" as well as "equal access to public offices and to the individual or collective exercise of the rights and liberties proclaimed or confirmed above." Colonialism ended by declaration; the empire became the French Union. It remained a single entity, with no clear right of secession, and ultimate sovereignty over colonial matters rested with the Assemblée Nationale in Paris.[27]

Whatever the inequalities of access to power, the idea of citizenship extended throughout the empire contained – as an African legal scholar put it in 1951 – a centralizing, unifying, assimilating tendency.[28] It was therefore consistent to declare "It is necessary that colonies cease to be colonies," and that "Africa does not have and cannot have an African future." Colonies and Africa would both disappear into France; they would become "a living part of the mère-patrie." The power-laden relationship of colonizer to colonized now became "a pedagogical problem."[29] But in Africa, such language could be liberating as well as demeaning: it provided an ideological and legal basis for empire-wide claims to equality in all sorts of domains.[30]

Two debates, one looking to the future and another to the past, reveal the slippage of the language of political assimilation and imperial unity into the realm of labor: the questions of the Code du Travail and forced labor. The code debate picked up where the debate over the Popular Front social laws had left off in 1938. As noted above, even colonial business occasionally expressed interest in bringing legal order to the labor question and Vichy had briefly considered extending its corporatist "Charte du Travail" to the colonies. In April 1944, a committee of the liberation government in Algiers began to discuss which parts of the metropolitan Code du Travail could be applied to the colonies. Within the Inspection du Travail in Dakar a draft labor code, to apply specifically to "indigenous" workers, was also considered.[31] It was to be a comprehensive code applied to indigenous populations throughout French Africa. Following upon Popular Front ideas, the new code contained the central idea of "social security." But within limits: "If one wants, in practice, to promote social security in A.O.F., it is necessary to limit its application to workers who are identifiable and findable." They did not want to do anything to complicate the flow of seasonal labor, but would issue cards, giving rights to certain social security measures to people "whose work presents a character of permanence sufficient that they believe it useful to establish a contract... It favors permanence of work, at least seasonal stability of labor, repaying that stability by the advantages of Social Security."[32]

A draft provision read, "Given equal conditions of work, of professional qualifications and of output, remuneration is equal for all workers." To say that was to presume a certain universality in what work means which had been very much in question in French Africa. The presumption was also evident in the carrying over – to a situation where its meaning was quite ambiguous – of the French code's notion of work obligation: "The new Code du Travail Indigène being elaborated, presumes the principle that work is a social duty for man whose accomplishment should be watched over by the Administration."[33]

Obligation and labor of course had their sinister linkage in France's colonial history, and such a conception was not necessarily reconcilable with the universalistic conception of social rights that also permeated the draft codes. The political cornerstone of the 1945 draft code was an evasion: the idea of "free labor and its quality as a social duty."[34] If the relationship of freedom and duty were unclear in theory, they were even more difficult in practice.

In June 1945 a code was proclaimed by decree, although it was not implemented pending further elaboration. Forced labor was the sticking point: there were still four years to go on the Brazzaville time table, but acknowledging forced labor – even as a temporary measure – in this progressive document would take away its punch. So the intended code posited an early end to the phase out: 1 April 1946. But as officials discussed how to implement the code, the governor-general, following the visit of his Chief Inspecteur Général du Travail to the Ivory Coast and objections from governors that harvests would be ruined without recruited labor, anxiously telegraphed Paris, "total return to free labor impossible in time anticipated by decree that is 1 April 1946." This would lead to "grave perturbations" of economic life.[35]

Here Félix Houphouët-Boigny, new deputy from the Ivory Coast, intervened. He came to Dakar, and "declared himself a firm partisan of an *immediate* application of free labor," that is on 1 April 1946. He warned of "a real exodus of black peasants by entire families" in opposition to forced labor. Officials now had to admit that the population "accepts more and more painfully the regime of constraint," and that the Gold Coast exodus as well as massive desertion from plantations were bedevilling current recruitment efforts. Houphouët-Boigny was developing a mutually useful relationship with Governor Latrille (see below) and officials put considerable weight on his opinion. The result was a compromise on the implementation of the free labor provisions of the new code: a 12 month delay.[36]

Then officials lost control over the entire code debate. The general strike of January 1946 in Senegal fundamentally changed official conceptions of the problems they confronted: the united, disciplined action of workers in Dakar and Saint-Louis made it unclear that African workers would tolerate a separate labor code for "indigènes." More important, the strike clinched the argument over whether Africans were really capable of acting like workers and convinced officials and business that an effective system of industrial relations had to be brought to Africa (chapter 6). Meanwhile, Houphouët-Boigny and other African deputies took the issue of forced labor out of discussions over labor codes and worries over harvests and forced the Assemblée Nationale Constituante into a stark choice between voting for or against forced labor (see below). Soon thereafter, in May, the Constituante – following through on the idea of a Greater France – passed a law extending citizenship to all inhabitants of Overseas France. Now a code specifically for "indigènes" was legally impossible since the category no longer existed. A new code would have to apply to all citizens, black and white; debate over its contents would drag on for six years (chapter 7).

But it was already clear in 1946 that the African labor question had exploded out of its boundaries, as much because of the presence of African voices in French politics and the activism of African workers as because of the universalistic rhetoric of citizenship. Yet the forced labor question still festered in the midst of the debates about democracy and constitutional reform going on in Paris in early 1946.

In February 1946, a group of deputies – Félix Houphouët-Boigny, Fily Dabo Sissoko, Lamine Guèye, Sourou Migan Apithy, Léopold Senghor, Félix Tchicaya, and Tacine Diallo – wrote the colonial minister, the Popular Front veteran and socialist Marius Moutet, serving notice that: "Millions of men have sent us here giving us a precise mandate, to struggle with all our might to abolish the slavery which is still practiced in Black Africa by men, civil servants and civilians, who are traitors to France and her noble civilizing mission." The astutely worded letter invoked the authors' personal ties to Moutet and the high purposes of French colonial policy, but developed the analogy to slavery with force and at some length.[37] Moutet, in reply, thanked the African deputies for their "generous sentiments" and insisted that he was already working on the problem and that "liberté du travail" was part of the labor code he hoped to implement in the colonies.[38]

This was too little, too late. The step of going public had already been taken. The above group, on 1 March 1946, joined by the West Indian Deputy Aimé Césaire and a number of metropolitan deputies, submitted a proposed law abolishing forced labor in all overseas territories. The group's preamble argued:

Forced labor, which undermines the race and provokes total disaffection of natives in regard to France and an increasingly massive exodus, has endured long enough. It is necessary, right now, to give political significance to the French union. It should not have masters or slaves.

The proposed law was simple:

Article 1: Forced or obligatory labor is forbidden in the most absolute fashion in the overseas territories. Article 2: All means or procedures of direct or indirect constraint with the object of hiring or maintaining at places of work a non-consenting individual will be the object of a legal text forbidding it and provided correctional sanctions. Article 3: The present law abolishes all previous decrees and regulations on the requisition of labor, in whatever regard.[39]

This was what electoral representation, however unequal, was all about: if the assembly wanted to retain forced labor, it would now have to vote on it.

The proposition was duly sent to the Committee on Overseas Territories. Meanwhile, as the Constituante went about other business, Gabriel d'Arboussier, deputy from Moyen Congo, wove an attack on forced labor into a general discussion of "the situation of Overseas France," opening the possibility that criticism of forced labor could be the entering wedge of an attack on "the capitalist regime which submits them to ferocious exploitation which we do not want to accept any more." Other delegates tried to confine the debate to the specifics of the movement to free labor; none defended forced labor.[40]

When the committee report on the proposed law was put before the assembly by Houphouët-Boigny on 30 March, it linked forced labor to the corvée of the Ancien Régime in France and to slavery. Houphouët-Boigny warned that in the Ivory Coast, Madagascar, and New Caledonia, "the situation has become singularly worse since the war... Never has forced labor been practiced on a greater scale..." Forced labor imperiled the future by driving workers to leave French colonies, by spreading disease, by hurting African producers – who were responsible for most crops exported from the Ivory Coast – by leading to political disaffection, and by compromising the work of administrators. He cited himself as a "large landed proprietor who has voluntarily renounced forced labor," and held before the Assembly a positive view of African production and free labor. He astutely used the rhetoric of post-war French imperialism:

In suppressing forced labor, a unique occasion is offered to us today to prove to the world that the France of the rights of man and of the citizen, the France of the abolition of slavery, remains always true to herself and could not contest or limit the liberty of any of the people living under her flag.[41]

On 5 April, the assembly approved the proposal without debate, and later that day, it began a long and vociferous debate on rules for elections in the overseas territories.[42]

The colonial administration in Dakar and in Paris did not oppose what became known as the "loi Houphouët-Boigny."[43] While the bill was pending, Moutet wrote to the governor-general referring to it, and he took the initiative to order a halt to the forced cultivation – a longstanding practice of local officials to order particular groups to grow particular crops. He added, "I will not tolerate any exception to the principle of free labor and I will not hesitate to reassign civil servants no matter how highly placed who put the brakes on this imperative rule."[44] The five-year plan for phasing out forced labor, defended since Brazzaville, had fallen from favor in only two.

What had changed was political mobilization in Africa as much as political rhetoric in Paris. For over a year after Brazzaville, the policies and opinions of the government-general of French West Africa remained neither more nor less than what had been promised. Prodded by the Commissaire des Colonies in Algiers and concerned with the international opinion Brazzaville and the ILO meeting had helped to start up, the government-general notified all governors in April 1944 that the five-year countdown on ending forced labor would begin on 1 July and they should come up with a plan, whose first steps were "sufficient to affirm our sincerity but calculated so as not to undermine the war effort in the domain of production."[45] It superintended the annual reduction of recruitment quotas and tried, in various ways, to make wage labor more attractive, but remained so committed to increasing production and so skeptical of African work habits that it would not give up constraint.[46] As late as the summer of 1945, Governor-General Cournarie still wondered whether French West Africa could do without forced labor, and he was still unsure that free labor was such a good thing for Africans after all. He feared that "they would lose the ancestral contact with the land and this would mean the creation, full of hazards, of an indigenous proletariat, having lost its sense of landed property (in the customary sense), only counting on wages to live."[47] In short, he, and most of his governors, could still not imagine a system of wage labor in Africa.

One astute Inspecteur du Travail in Paris pointed out how this reactionary sociology contradicted the government's economic aspirations:

let us declare clearly that to prevent any proletarianization, the 15 million Africans are condemned to cultivate with the *daba* [hoe] and to maintain piously, like their ancestors, the sense of landed property. But what will become of the development of AOF and can one still speak of promoting whatever it is?[48]

The governor-general's imagination was expanded and his anxieties moved in another direction by the advent of a new politics in the Ivory

Coast – long the crux of the forced labor question – in 1945 and early 1946.[49] Africans had been planting cocoa and coffee in the Ivory Coast, most notably in the Baulé region, for years. Even before the war, most of the exports of these crops were coming from Africans, not from the colons who received most official attention and most – after 1941 all – of the recruited labor. At the end of the war, officials realized that the hoped-for increases in production would have to come from Africans. But current production was another question.[50]

The director of political affairs in the government-general in Dakar noted privately that the governor of the Ivory Coast, André Latrille, faced a "permanent dilemma: to produce or to be human."[51] Latrille's plan was to reduce the recruitment level from a current 54,000 to 38,000 the first year, then to 20,000 the second, 10,000 the third, 4,500 the fourth, and zero the fifth, concentrating the early cuts in coffee, which was not deemed necessary for the war effort.[52] This resulted in protest from the colons. Their belligerent leader, Jean Rose, insisted that Africans would never work: "I know the 'Negro," he proclaimed. At two tumultuous meetings in Abidjan, in May and December, this argument was confronted directly with Houphouët-Boigny's insistence that he was already showing that African-owned farms – copying the Gold Coast's system of métayage (a form of sharecropping, discussed below) was already bringing in labor. Still uncertain about who was right, Latrille was willing to accept some delay in exchange for promises from planters that they actually would make an effort to recruit voluntary labor, and officials left the December meeting convinced that "the principle of a return to free labor has been accepted and the voluntariat is 'launched.'" Only white planters would benefit, as before, from recruited labor, but Latrille was convinced that African planters, with their "common affinities" to potential workers and the attractions of métayage, would do well in the free labor market.[53]

In 1944 and 1945 the European planters complained endlessly and acted as if "the Administration will come to their aid as in the past and will take their place again in the recruitment of labor." Meanwhile, the African planters quietly created an alternative organization of labor.[54]

In 1944, African cocoa and coffee planters had organized themselves into what became the Société Agricole Africaine (SAA), seceding from the unsupportive European-dominated planters' organization. By August, they had enrolled 1,600 members, and in the next year or so grew to 5,000 members. The SAA was led by men whom Latrille described as "très évolués" and who manifested "the best state of mind."[55] The SAA leader, Houphouët-Boigny, was both a chief and a doctor, as well as a cocoa planter whose yields were as good as those of European farms.

"One can say," wrote the governor, "that the plantation of Canton Chief Félix Houphouet constitutes one of the model enterprises envisioned by the Conference of Brazzaville. It is particularly satisfying to note that this situation is the work of an African entirely trained by French Civilization."[56]

Houphouët-Boigny, by his own testimony, was from a former slave-owning, elite family. His first step on his path to glory – going to school – had taken place because a French local administrator had refused to let his family send three of its slaves to school in place of the "free" family members officials wanted to see educated. When Houphouët-Boigny later referred to forced labor "as a more or less disguised slavery," he knew what he was talking about.[57]

Latrille, at least in part in response to lobbying by the SAA, extended to African planters – albeit only ones with large holdings – the government subsidy given to white coffee exporters, and he later exempted Africans who possessed a relatively small acreage of coffee or cocoa from being themselves victimized in the labor round-up.[58] Latrille – aside from resenting having his administration serve as man-chasers – realized that the African planters offered him the only way out of his "permanent dilemma," to show that the Ivory Coast could produce for the metropole without forced labor.

It soon became clear that the SAA had established a network and a mechanism for obtaining labor. With good contacts with chiefs, members went around to various districts and recruited labor. Their standard contract was a variant on practices that had attracted so many migrants from the Upper Coast to the Gold Coast – the métayage system, under which the laborer received one-third of the value of coffee harvested and/or two-fifths of the value of the cocoa, with a minimum guarantee of 200 francs per month, plus free transport, rations, and transport for the worker's family if he so desired. In 1944, according to officials' probably understated figures, 3,504 laborers had been recruited. Latrille even accompanied Houphouët-Boigny on one "propaganda tour" to the Upper Coast. Houphouët-Boigny later reported his happy astonishment on hearing an old chief, who had long served the French, say, "We want, with Houphouet, to try the experiment because it is very painful to us to recruit by force, each year, 6,500 of our young men, the majority of whom do not return."[59]

Meanwhile, it was clear in 1945 and 1946 that even the modestly reduced levels of recruitment were leading to administrative breakdown and political danger. Latrille had already tried to adjust recruiting schedules in hard-hit districts. Documents described familiar practices: chiefs and administrators rounded people up on a particular day; chiefs protected "their 'creatures'" and punished enemies; unmarried men fled; less mobile heads of families were caught; and round-ups included high proportions of men unfit to work.[60] In a "very secret" report, Latrille was explicit about the implications:

The workers were engaged by force; firing them would hardly be a sanction; only coercive means, abusive retention of wages or savings [pécule], holding back food (you understand me correctly), and bad treatment are the procedures which most entrepreneurs employ.

Seasonal laborers, including the women and children who participated in the coffee harvest, were treated even worse. He called this a system of "semi-slavery." He concluded that France must "declare unacceptable, humanely, politically and even economically the practice employed until this day." France's actions in this regard would constitute "the test on which one can judge our Empire by the facts themselves." His answer to the test was still the five-year phase out.[61]

Brazzaville had opened up space for others in the administration to add their views. The government-recognized leader of the Mossi of the Upper Coast, the Moro-Naba, protested with particular power in July 1945:

The bad treatments suffered in the Lower Coast are recounted everywhere and produce the worst impression among parents of those who have left and parents of those who died and must be replaced...Thus, they are convinced that they are sold as slaves by their chiefs, because even the Moro-Naba and Province chiefs propagandize in favor of forced labor at each recruitment. They believe this so fully that satiric songs have been invented about the Chiefs and they are sung in the various campments at the time of assembly for recruitment and repeated all over the country.

Meanwhile, returnees from the Gold Coast told happier stories, the exodus to British territory continued, "and one finds sometimes at the time of recruitment villages abandoned by all their habitants including old women [and] still latent hostility everywhere that one goes and which would threaten to have grave consequences."[62]

Latrille forwarded numerous reports on the damage being done to Dakar and concluded, "the recruitment of workers by way of administrative constraint must stop as early as possible, under threat of the gravest political complications." He considered the colons' objection to free labor "puerile." But he and the governor-general still stuck to the Brazzaville formula of annual cuts in the recruitment quotas and a five-year phase out.[63]

Then in January, the Ivory Coast government decided on "the suppression of forced recruitment in the Upper Ivory Coast." The "reservoir" was in such a disastrous state that it could no longer be drained.[64] To ease the immediate crisis and get the harvest in, officials wanted Upper Coast recruits to extend their contracts by two months, in exchange for a bonus on top of the normal wage rate. Mossi – urged (if that is the correct word) by their leader, the Moro Naba – apparently accepted in substantial numbers. The government-general noted the good work of the SAA "with the support of the administration" in moving to voluntary labor. The freedom "to sign up or leave on their own will" was now said to be the key to getting seasonal labor, while enterprises needing a stable labor force would have to pay higher wages, fixed by collective bargaining agreement with the workers. [65]

French officials were no longer the only people debating the problem. The first elections were held in October 1945, and 31,384 non-citizens voted in the second college, electing Houphouët-Boigny to the Assemblée Nationale Constituante.[66] The SAA was already beginning to act like a political party, and it would soon give birth to the Parti Démocratique de la Côte d'Ivoire – the Ivorian section of the Rassemblement Démocratique Africaine – and it has dominated politics ever since. At the time (and through March 1946), Latrille was on leave in France, replaced by the old-guard Governor de Mauduit. This official reported with alarm that the SAA had acquired great influence "in all the milieux of indigenous évolués in the Lower Coast, among canton chiefs, village chiefs, cultivators." He feared that SAA influence on the population would "end very rapidly in the complete elimination of administrative authority" in favor of a kind of authority "of a 'tribal' conception related to that which we found on our arrival in Africa where there reigned blind submission to self-interested and unscrupulous chiefs." He thought that SAA's presence in a cercle led to "a movement against the furnishing of labor," and he fulminated about "the application of liberal measures, seductive at first, but premature and dangerous in a milieu where the African is insufficiently evolved." Cournarie was unconvinced, writing in the margin of this report, "The agricultural Union is a good piece of work as long as it remains under surveillance and within fixed limits."[67]

At the beginning of 1946, political officials in Dakar were quite well aware that the issue behind political mobilization in the Ivory Coast was forced labor; it was "a cause of discontent whose solution we are awaiting." The SAA's expanding network of recruiters – feeding the system of tenancy-cum-labor – were simultaneously a network of political agents, engaged in, as security officials put it, "the organization phase of the conquest."[68]

This story explains why the ministry in Paris and the government-general in Dakar, after years of dithering over the feasibility of ending forced labor, posed no objection when the African deputies to the

Constituante took the issue out of their hands. The SAA had shown both that forced labor was politically impossible and that their own organization could provide an alternative means of preserving agricultural production.

Looking back on the terms in which forced and free labor were discussed between the Brazzaville Conference and the 'loi Houphouët-Boigny', a significant difference separates it from the previous round, under the Popular Front. In the 1930s, forced labor had been an unacknowledged fact. Vichy had been willing to talk about it without either concealment or shame, and Boisson in Dakar had rather skillfully used this discursive shift – and all the bandying about of numbers to be recruited – to inject the notion of limits into the conversation. Now, beleaguered local officials in the Ivory Coast could write about how forced labor compromised their jobs and poisoned local politics. More important still, the development of an African political network in the rural Ivory Coast – itself using the elegant rhetoric of the constitutional debate – created another level of incongruity. Forced labor, machine politics, and political debate do not mix. That is what it took to end – after a half century of brutality and sixteen years after the International Convention on Forced Labour – the practice of rounding up men to be sent to work.

The belated end to forced labor came after the era of development had already begun – when France, like Great Britain, was publicly dedicating itself to improving the welfare of its colonized peoples. The labor question intersected the development question in peculiar ways. On the one hand, development projects – building roads, health facilities, and expanding productive facilities – became an imperative that added to the doubts about the feasibility of ending forced labor. In September 1945, Governor-General Cournarie added to his old argument about African reluctance to work for wages: "It is impossible, in such conditions, to envisage the implementation of a program of development based only on the principle of free labor." Even after the law of April 1946 abolishing forced labor, Cournarie warned that extending "liberation of recruits" to the deuxième portion du contingent (still considered military service rather than forced labor) would "inevitably lead to a slow down of public works and in certain cases total stoppage."[69] On the other hand, the desire not to press too heavily on reluctant Africans became one of the principal justifications for development spending – alongside increasing output and improving Africans' incomes.

From Brazzaville to the passage of FIDES by the legislature, officials cited mechanization as a palliative for labor shortages. Both concerns, as well as the attention given to constitutional questions in early 1946, contributed to the inability of the French government to showcase its development effort in the same way as Great Britain did. In contrast to the long discussions and high-flown rhetoric attendant on Parliament's passage of the British Colonial Development and Welfare Act of 1940 and its refunding in 1945, the French legislature seemed barely awake for the passages of FIDES the same month as the law ending forced labor.[70] The reporter from the Committee on Overseas Territories, Gaston Monnerville, called the investment fund "a very old idea" and moved in barely a phrase from asserting that the act would serve to "develop [mettre en valeur]... the natural riches of these countries" to a claim that it would "promote the economic evolution of our territories." Arguing that development of colonial resources was "in the common interest" of members of the French Union, he was eliding in an unexamined sentence the difficult question of how interests would be balanced – an elision British policy-makers were to make as well, although after vainly and at length trying to think through the problem.

Most interesting, the minister, Marius Moutet, reframed the development question in the light of the labor question: alluding to the wasteful use of cheap labor, he claimed "all this manpower must be replaced by mechanical equipment." The government would no longer have "to pull away from their fields, from their farming, men who must remain attached to them..." The point of metropolitan investment in colonial infrastructure, then, was not to extract Africans from their rural, communitarian ways, but to allow economic growth to take place with less disturbance of African society.[71]

But Moutet's hope for growth without change was contending with more dynamic conceptions of development; industrialization had been discussed, however inconclusively, at Brazzaville, and more importantly the Dakar general strike had sharply revealed the need for up-to-date solutions to social problems. The problem of urbanism posed closely related issues, and engineers in the public works department, like the labor inspectors, realized they were at a crucial conjuncture. More wage labor and more urban migration within existing structures could lead simply to slums, to "taudification." What was needed was good urban design – simple but modern housing, sanitary facilities, and roads. That would imply a change in how workers lived, but also a change in how workers worked in the public works sector. Well organized work with expectation of "analogous productivity in quantity and speed to that of workers from the metropole" was needed. As a leading engineer put it, "*Bricolage* must give way to technique."[72] Between the minister's rural conservatism and the engineer's technique in managing labor lay the contradictory impulses of the post-war colonial establishment.

The emancipation of the Inspection du Travail

The Chief Inspecteur du Travail for French West Africa stated in his annual report for 1946 that the law of 11 April 1946 "emancipated the African workers." The same term was used by Africans, and Houphouët-Boigny could claim to be Africa's Frederick Douglass and Abraham Lincoln rolled into one.[73] There is a sad truth to the language: in the Ivory Coast, at least, the most concrete contribution of the progressive imperialism of the immediate post-war years was probably the undoing of the worst of pre-war imperialism.

The administration itself was also emancipated: a fledgling African political organization freed officials from the way they had framed the labor question. The SAA provided the Ivory Coast government with a way out of the ideological bind, shared by the friends of the peasants as well as the exponents of forced labor, that African nature was incompatible with wage labor. It showed that the question could be avoided, that agricultural labor could be mobilized in ways that French administrators need not probe. By taking most of the agricultural sector out of the realm of work, the Ivory Coast solution in fact allowed the Inspection du Travail to create a modernizing conception of labor in the bounded confines of industry, transportation, commerce, and other essentially urban occupations. As the inspection went about imagining a predictable African world of work modelled after the inspectors' conception of French industrial relations (see chapter 7), it necessarily reinforced a dualistic view of African society, divided between their realm and the realm they had left to African planters and peasants.

The immediate reaction to the end of forced labor in the Ivory Coast and elsewhere was repeatedly described by officials as "calm."[74] In other colonies, there were some desertions of public works laborers and more serious problems in Guinea, but the trouble stopped short of mass desertions of wage labor enterprises.[75] The most difficult situation, as predicted, was in the Ivory Coast. Between May and July, the proclamation of the new law coincided with a period in which agricultural work on Africans' own farms was at its most demanding, and many workers went home, not worrying too much about the "contract" under which they were working. According to authorities in the Ivory Coast, a wave of desertions had begun in November 1945, not coincidentally the period after the elections to the Constituante. The proclamation of the law of 11 April 1946 led to another wave of "desertions," as "workers recruited by the intervention of administrative authorities and those taken in the name of the deuxième portion, abandoned workplaces and services in order to return to their villages of origin." The colons, meanwhile, did virtually nothing to ease the transition, preferring to continue to assert its impossibility.[76]

The first, and essentially only, drama took place near the Abidjan–Niger rail line. The European-owned enterprises which cut wood for the fireboxes of the steam locomotives would not accept government offers, and some officials thought this was a deliberate attempt to sabotage railway traffic in order to demonstrate the futility of relying on free labor. There thus began what officials called the "battle of firewood." With a shut down of the railroad looming, and some traffic reductions already in effect, the administration turned to its new friends in the SAA.[77] A group of African entrepreneurs belonging to the SAA offered to hire workers to cut trees near the line of rail and sell wood to the railroad for an agreed-upon price far lower than what the European contracts had demanded. The government agreed and through the common fund of the Sociétés Indigènes de Provenance provided financial assistance. Houphouët-Boigny and a leading government official undertook a "propaganda campaign" to recruit workers. In July seven African-run wood-cutting operations opened up, employing 1,690 workers. By September, the number of laborers working for African wood-cutting firms hit 9,869, more than offsetting a decline in European employment in this sector from 9,125 in January to 5,046 in June and 2,637 in September. The Régie's own wood-cutting lots stepped up their employment from 327 to 2,366. By September 1946, more wood was being cut than in 1938 or 1945. The battle of firewood had been won.[78]

By fall, the battle of agriculture was not going badly either. The season changed, and workers were again willing to leave their own farms. The SAA was active in labor recruitment, including arrangements with chiefs in the old "reservoir" of labor power in the Upper Coast. With the end of forced labor, Mossi men no longer faced the same painful decision of whether to flee to the Gold Coast, and some even returned from there and became increasingly amenable to the blandishments of the SAA. The African planters, an official commented, arranged an agricultural routine "perfectly adapted to the African mentality which detests mathematic regularity in work, by the clock or in the assembly line." In September, an emissary from Dakar reported that African coffee farmers were getting all the labor they needed for the harvest, while Europeans got enough to ensure half to two-thirds of the expected harvest.[79] By year's end, the government's statistics showed that there were nearly 77,000 wage laborers in the Ivory Coast, of whom 22,000 were unskilled agricultural laborers, nearly 9,000 in forestry labor. This was a higher level than in the final stages of forced recruitment. Exports from Ivorian ports totalled 135,000 tons in 1946, versus 113,000 tons in 1945, and they would soon regain the peak levels of 1938.[80]

The government's contribution was to raise the minimum wage from 11.5 francs per day in the Abidjan region in December 1945 to 35 in May 1946, while the lowest regional minimum wage went to 25. Officials justified the sharp jump by reference to past failures to adjust for the cost of living. But it was also intended as a "psychological shock" to the colons. Officials looked to new work regimes and new capital investment, which would produce a more compact, better paid, more efficient labor force in private and public sectors.[81] The administration underscored its focus on wage labor by creating a "ration card for textiles specially for workers" – allowing them to buy a certain quantity of cloth three times per year. This was intended as a palliative for one of the major obstacles to creating a free labor market – the inability of France to provide much in the way of manufactured goods desired by Africans and its unwillingness to let Africans purchase them in hard currency markets.[82] Other special facilities were targeted at workers: free rail transportation between the Upper and Lower Coasts, centers to provide lodging and food for migrating workers, provisions to allow the purchase of tax-free cola nuts. Regulations to control movement – intended to prevent vagrancy and facilitate tax collection – were repealed on the grounds that "it is better to allow a vagrant to escape than to create distaste forever in a worker of good will en route for the Lower Coast."[83] These measures defined workers as a distinguishable category: the administration was framing the labor question as it tried to solve it.

The myth of the peculiarity of the African did not easily go away: the new version stressed the quality of the work force.[84] "This voluntary labor force has an output below that of the recruited labor force, because of its lack of consciousness of its social duties and its spirit of vagrancy which excludes, for the moment, all possibility of stabilization acceptable for economic activities." The "instability" of labor was seen to be at the root of the problem, but inspectors continued to refer to Africans as "indolent," as content with the modest income of his fields and loath to accept "discipline and the obligation for constant physical effort."[85] Some called the problem of instability and indiscipline "infant diseases" or a "puberty crisis" – the language of child development is not exactly precise.[86] In all of this, the focus on "stability" and "mechanization" as remedies and the use of evolutionary metaphors implied that the problem of the African worker could be separated from the problem of the African. By devoting attention specifically to workers and by emphasizing improvements and incentives to wage labor, officials thought they were addressing whatever aboriginal disabilities kept African workers from working or working well.

Meanwhile, the problem which the Inspection faced had been bounded even further by the exclusion of African-owned farms from the domain of "work": most of the coffee and cocoa production of the Ivory Coast was now being produced by métayage, a form of tenancy. Officials' worst fears in regard to the Gold Coast – that Africans had found a more "customary," more familiar form of work – now became a source of hope in regard to export production in the Ivory Coast. Through the share system in cocoa and coffee and with the guaranteed minimum receipts of about 200 francs per month, workers on the farms of SAA members were returning to the Upper Coast with 2,400 francs after a year's work, which officials thought equivalent to the typical remissions of Voltaic migrants to the Gold Coast – a sum a male migrant could use to marry. By the end of 1946, officials thought that the pace of migration to the Gold Coast had slowed.[87]

French officials were not asking many questions about how the SAA recruited workers or how, precisely, métayage worked. They did not have to. The leading sector of agricultural production was disappearing into a world French officials did not need to know. In February 1946, the administrator of the Upper Coast would only delicately describe the success of the SAA in recruiting Mossi for African farms in the Lower Coast:

One cannot say that this was purely voluntary recruitment because the chiefs used their influence and the duration of the contract was imposed at one year at the beginning; but we have observed that the contingents are currently returning at the end of the contract satisfied with the treatment which was given them; many declare they want to return once they have, according to custom, reestablished contact with their people for a more or less long period.[88]

No-one along the chain of information took up his veiled questioning about how the SAA actually got its laborers; Africans were self-evidently pleased to work for Africans and in African ways. The SAA had shifted a large domain from the category of "work" – which the state had obsessively and ineffectively made its business to control – to the category of "customary labor" – which the state could claim was not its concern.

The colons, meanwhile, had their last attempt at counter-revolution. The colonialist right constituted itself into a group called, with a large dose of hubris, the Etats Généraux de la Colonisation Française, and it met in Paris in August 1946 and proclaimed itself in favor of saving the empire.[89] Its efforts to influence the constitution – seconded by various publications and politicians on the Right – were not without effect, but on the question of labor they had no ground left for a principled defense of forced labor. Jean Rose, the leading light of the Ivorian planters, even insisted that "'administrative recruitment' was always used with repulsion by planters and forest or industrial enterprises." The meeting now called for a declaration that work was a "social duty which translates into a number of days of work which each individual owes the collectivity." They thought that 240 days per year, of wage labor or the equivalent of approved independent work, would nicely define this social duty.[90]

Social duty was not a concept unique to the old colons, but their ploy of using it to reintroduce forced labor went nowhere. The African deputies by now posed an alternative to the colonizers' strongest suit: as the possessors of valuable knowledge about colonial realities and as embodiments of France's progressive role. Houphouët-Boigny sent a telegram to Paris in the summer of 1946 turning around the usual stereotypes to warn officials of the dangers of Europeans provoking disorder in Africa, while affirming his own commitment to the French vision of free labor and development.[91] More astute leaders among the colonial planters and businessmen were now bowing to the inevitable and trying to get what they could out of the administration in exchange for acquiescence. M. Dubled, vice president of the Syndicat des Planteurs de Café et Cacao de la France Outre-Mer, took such a tack, and met with the colonial minister, Moutet, and Houphouët-Boigny in May to promise his "adherence to the suppression of forced labor." Moutet decided to read this, possibly in the hope that the wish would create the reality, as a genuine expression of planter sentiment and told the governor-general to cooperate with planter organizations and to ease the flow of free labor by reducing its own labor demands, providing free transport, propagandizing Africans to seek labor, and other such practical measures.[92]

Officials in West Africa, however, thought their local planters were simply making themselves irrelevant. Some thought the government should buy out the European farms, others thought they would disappear on their own.[93] The colons, who had tied up officials in the Ivory Coast in knots for decades, faded from official consciousness, complaining that they could not get the labor they needed while African planters were busy making the Ivory Coast into French West Africa's leading exporter.

While all this was going on, the administration was slowly weaning itself from its own dependence on coerced labor. Ever since Brazzaville officials talked about replacing the three-year service of the deuxième portion du contingent with a one-year but more universal Service du Travail Obligatoire, but they went on using the deuxième portion. They felt all the more reluctant to give up this form of coerced labor because of the heavy expectations they had of new public works projects, intended among other things to allow a free labor force to work more effectively. The Ivory Coast recruited 2,666 workers this way in 1946; the Soudan, long the heaviest user, went after 4,156; and even Senegal conscripted several hundred for work on roads and airport construction.[94]

Maintaining such unwilling labor in an era of election campaigns, wage labor mobilization, and union organizing soon proved impossible. Near Dakar, officials noted the "large liberty" such workers enjoyed in their time off, observed "acts of generalized indiscipline," and feared – especially after the strike of January 1946 – the "great danger of maintaining at the gates of the city a hotbed of revolt."[95] In the Soudan, work stoppages among deuxième portion laborers occurred in early June, shortly after the Soudan's African politicians, in the May elections, had claimed credit for the law of April 1946 and argued that more still had to be done.[96] In 1947, the R.D.A. newspaper *Réveil* and Lamine Guèye's *L'A.O.F.* ran articles attacking it. By May 1947, Senegal decided to abandon it, and in 1948, rumors circulated that the current "class" would be the last. The deuxième portion was abolished by decree in 1950, but it had already faded from use: pseudo-military labor, like recruitment for private purposes, could not stand the light of public examination. In the installations of the Office du Niger, long the major consumer of conscripted labor, its end did indeed lead to labor shortages, revealing, in fact, how much compulsion had allowed the perpetuation of ill-conceived projects that could not be sustained in any other way.[97]

The solution to the problem of forced labor appears at first glance to have been removing the leaden hand of official authority from Africans' backs and letting them organize a more productive future. The solution was only possible, however, because in the Ivory Coast, where the question was most acute, African planters were neither the communal cultivators of colonial mythology nor autonomous individuals in a labor market. Their web of connectedness and authority had offered a concrete solution to the problem of maintaining production while abolishing forced labor: it had won the battle of firewood and later the battles of cocoa and coffee. What exactly went on when the SAA recruited labor and what "métayage" actually meant was not clear, and French officials did not want to know.[98] They would pursue their own reformist projects in a limited domain, leave other areas under African aegis, and meanwhile claim that the entire labor question fit under a universalistic conception of work and human nature. The lesson Governor Latrille wanted to draw from the year of emancipation was not about the specificity of the social and political struggle that he had lived through but a generalization about humanity:

the old slander which said that the African was an incorrigible idler, incapable of working except under constraint, has been denied by the facts. For the African is not made differently from the rest of humanity. He knows how to appreciate the dignity of work done freely and he comes to offer his labor each time that one offers him remunerative prices.[99]

While helping to liberate the French administration from its constricting belief in the peculiarity of the African, the SAA had also built itself into a powerful political machine. Emancipation was the kind of mobilizing issue officials dreaded, and when the day was over the SAA could lay claim to a stunning victory. Meanwhile, the Dakar general strike – followed by the railway strike of 1947–48 – plunged the Inspection du Travail more deeply into an effort to come to understand and to transform urban labor. An agenda for political and social reform was being established for French West Africa, but it was not the agenda French officials at war's end had had in mind.

Great Britain's Africa: defining the object of development and reform

Great Britain's colonial labor policy was to a large extent pulled along from the periphery, as local officials had to come to grips with the challenges posed by workers. British Africa – more urbanized, more commercially active, with more mining enterprises than French Africa – not surprisingly found its agenda shaped at an earlier date by the inescapable reality of the African presence in places of work and urban residence. It was in the commissions that investigated strike movements and strike threats (starting during the war) where British officialdom began to recognize the social complexity of the labor process and its integration into other dimensions of African life. There was nothing comparable to the legislative involvement in the forced labor question in France to focus political attention on the labor question in England.[100] What London wanted to think about was its initiatives in economic and social development and the gradual process of constitutional change in each of its colonies. As in France, attempts in Great Britain to open new approaches to labor, development, and political organization took place in uneasy tension with visions of African society that continued to emphasize the peculiarity and backwardness of the African in all these domains, and it is that tension which will be explored before turning, in the following chapter, to the front lines of the labor question.

In the late 1940s, colonial secretaries were eager to remind the public that leading Africa toward "responsible government within the Commonwealth in conditions that ensure to the peoples fair standards of living and freedom from oppression from any quarter" was a bipartisan, established policy. [101] Virtually every word in the formula was ambiguous and gave rise to debate at the time and ever since.

The discussion in London of post-war reform seems to take place within a different rhetorical structure from the discussion in Algiers, Brazzaville, and Paris. Some scholars have held that the French assumption that a unified Greater France would persist indefinitely left it brittle in the face of subsequent nationalist movements, whereas the British acceptance of the principle of eventual self-government gave it a more flexible framework for response in which concessions could be portrayed as consistent with original policies.[102] The distinct rhetorical structures may help explain the different ways in which the governments could convince themselves that it was politically and ideologically acceptable to give up empire; they do not explain the differences in how each metropole sought to exercise power when it had it. It pays not just to look at decolonization as a political question, but to ask what imperial governments intended to *do* with their power and the limits they encountered.

Britain, like France, needed its empire more than ever in the immediate post-war years. When the Labour Party, under Clement Attlee, took over the government in July 1945, it was operating within narrow economic constraints: war debts were in dollars, and the British economy – damaged and redirected by the war – had little ability to produce the kinds of commodities that earn hard currency. Africa's primary products offered a likely source of dollar earnings, as well as the most likely means of supplying Britain with necessities without buying them in hard currency markets.[103] There was a political element to this as well: the Labour Party's political base in the British working class, having deferred consumption during the war and having voted Churchill out in hope that its turn would come, had to be fed and the expanding welfare state paid for.[104]

Labour, like the post-war French governments, approached the post-war era convinced that it should move toward a more positive colonial policy – fostering economic and social progress and devolving political responsibility – but severely constrained in what it could do. Unlike the case of France, where past policies had little legitimacy, much of Labour's thunder had already been stolen by the Colonial Development and Welfare Act. In London, African colonies tended to be the concern of senior bureaucrats in the Colonial Office, not of legislators. The Fabian Colonial Bureau, which had played the principled critic of empire, lost its critical edge after the 1940 Act and was further muted when its main man in Parliament, Arthur Creech Jones, became Secretary of State in 1946.[105]

In its own way, British thinking was as brittle as French, caught in the same contradiction between a universalistic conception of human progress and a fear that African society was ill-equipped to partake of it. Both Conservative and Labour spokesmen accepted that economic and social progress were prerequisites for political responsibility, that development would mutually benefit colonies and metropole, that colonies would move *toward* British standards of social services, but not *to* them, and that in time productive forces within the colonies would have to pay for such services.

Between 1945 and 1947, the discussion of development changed in tone. The reason was the dollar crisis: the United States insisted in 1947 that its debt be repaid in hard currency, and Britain's need for American help to meet this American demand gave the United States powerful leverage in redesigning the world financial system, just as Marshall Plan aid led to considerable American influence on a wide range of economic and social policies.[106] It also led to a sense of desperation in London about the need to export more colonial products. Sir Stafford Cripps, the Labour government's minister for economic affairs, told the conference of African governors in 1947, "the whole future of the sterling area and its ability to survive depends in my view upon a quick and extensive development of our African resources." He wanted, "within the next 2-5 years... a really marked increase of production in coal, minerals, timber, raw materials of all kinds and foodstuffs and anything else that will save dollars or will sell in a dollar market."[107] The foreign secretary, Ernest Bevin, plunged into fantasy about the "great mountains of manganese" and other resources waiting in Africa to be sold to the United States: "If only we pushed on & developed Africa we could have U.S. dependent on us, & eating out of our hand in four or five years."[108]

Cripps barely nodded to the old rationale for the Development and Welfare Act – that it would improve the standard of living of colonial peoples. He was sure that interests were "mutual," and that the more the European economy was strengthened "the better of course Africa itself will fare." The capital goods needed for industrialization were most efficiently employed in Great Britain itself, and colonies were asked to "make their contribution... by reducing demands for unnecessary current consumption and devoting some of their own earnings to capital purposes."[109] Creech Jones, in apologetic tones, told the Colonies to curb "unnecessary" expenditures in dollars and limit their own consumption of anything that could be sold for dollars, because of Britain's crisis and the "vital interest" of the colonies in "the economic stability of this country."[110]

It was thus under the Labour government that one sees the triumph of a productionist vision of economic development that Tory ministers had only partially accepted. Officials made it very clear that economic development – as opposed to welfare – was the "more fundamental" goal, that metropolitan support of social services was a temporary effort, and that, as Stanley had first warned in 1943, each colony could aspire to the level of social services that its own output allowed.[111] The government created in 1947 the Colonial Development Corporation, intended to undertake projects that would boost production, yield a return on investment, and earn dollars – as opposed to the more infrastructural and welfare concerns of the Colonial Development and Welfare Act. The ministry of food started its own project in southern Tanganyika, the infamous groundnut scheme, which envisioned the use of heavy equipment and industrial techniques to clear vast acres of supposedly "virgin" bush for the planting of peanuts and whose failure became a classic example of colonial fantasies that went over the edge.[112]

The focus on output was a sore point for Labour politicians who had long pointed out the exploitative nature of various imperial practices, and in defending the CDC and the related Overseas Food Corporation, they contributed strongly to a drift that had begun earlier: using the word "development" as equivalent both to increased output and to increased welfare, avoiding the complex question of what the relationship of the two was. Ernest Bevin worried, "We must be careful that our plans for the development of our Colonial Dependencies cannot in any way be represented as springing solely from our selfish interests. It is above all important that in their presentation there is no possible suggestion of exploitation of the colonial populations."[113]

The government reaffirmed its commitment to raising the colonial standard of living and repeatedly denied that raising output was "a new phase of an old exploitation," but this begged the basic question: who was to decide what would ensure mutual benefit and harmony?[114] In practice, Great Britain in the period 1946–51 maintained sterling balances and West African marketing board balances – exchangeable funds that colonies were not allowed to spend – that were around six times higher than dispersements under the Colonial Development and Welfare Act.[115] Colonial rule mattered.

Creech Jones himself was, in less public fora, distancing himself from giving primacy to direct efforts to raise the colonial standard of living, and arguing, "I consider that there should be greater emphasis than hitherto on *economic* development as the immediate object of His Majesty's government's assistance." Indeed, it had become necessary within government circles to argue – reversing the direction of the Colonial Office argument of 1939 (chapter 3) – that social spending actually had an "economic character":

Development is held up today by the shortage and inefficiency of labour, and the inability of many Colonial people to work with the intensity of stronger races. The number of workers and their ability to work is directly affected by their state of health and therefore by the medical services provided. The efficiency of workers is equally directly affected by their education and technical training. I am fully convinced, therefore, that the inclusion of these 'welfare' services in the ten year programmes is absolutely justified on economic no less than humanitarian grounds.[116]

Success was measured in productionist terms: summarizing his ministry's achievements at the end of 1948, Creech Jones put the "export drive" first, "dollar earnings and savings" second, and social programs in Africa and the West Indies thirteenth.[117]

The rhetorical move being made here is a slippage: the word development starts to take on a new emphasis without its old one ever being discarded. The ambiguity of the word – expressing simultaneously the notion of increasing production and increasing welfare – made it particularly useful in serving multiple political purposes. In 1948, Creech Jones reminded the prime minister of the "importance of a quick and vigorous development of Africa as part of the Western world" and that "our long term aim must be to secure that when the African Territories obtain self-government they do so as part of the Western world."[118] He was circling back to the agreed-upon basis of British colonial policy, but now with a defensive note. The best he could do would be to keep Africa in the West – to build economic structures that would tie Africans into the western economy and give emerging African leaders incentive to maintain ties with the West.

Indeed, African leaders were being drawn into development discourse, and some were trying to use it to make claims for benefits to Africans. But the rare African who got a chance to speak at a policy-makers' meeting had to couch arguments about the welfare of workers in terms of their impact on production. Eliud Mathu, the only African on the Kenya Legislative Council, told one conclave,

My assumption is that any economic development either in this country or in the colonies must depend, other factors remaining constant, on the efficiency of the man-power employed either in the farm, in the factory or in the workshop. If we have not got a contented labour force, a contented worker who feels that it is his duty to contribute to the welfare of the Empire by increasing his output, I suggest, Sir, that we will fail in our effort. In order to treat a worker as a human being it is of vital importance that his welfare should be looked after very carefully, his wages and other conditions of work must be taken into consideration with a view of enabling him to feel that he is a human being, that he is inspired by almost a divine ideal of making the Empire economically independent and to stand on its own in the economics of the world.[119]

Mathu, a year and a half earlier, had persuaded African workers in Mombasa, in the midst of a successful general strike, to go back to work under his guarantee that their grievances would be investigated sympathetically. Just as francophone trade unionists were to make good use of the assimilationist rhetoric of French imperialism to lay claim to entitlements of French workers, Mathu was using the rhetoric of developmentalism to claim attention for the problems of workers. It was not, unlike the French case, a rhetoric which itself contained any premises of entitlement. Kenya's best placed African politician of the 1940s was arguing that workers would be more useable if only they were treated better.

But in seeking to balance production and welfare, particularly for wage laborers, British policy makers were indeed caught in a dilemma. The empire-wide shortage of dollars and the sterling-area shortage of capital goods constrained developmental investment in the colonies. Meanwhile, through at least 1949, consumer goods from the sterling area were in short supply as well, a point Sydney Caine had earlier argued made raising colonial standards of living virtually impossible. In the major markets of British Africa, Nigeria, the Gold Coast, Kenya, and Uganda, consumption of cotton piece goods (often used as a proxy for imports consumed by Africans) in 1948 stood at 63 percent of the 1937 level.[120] Colonial officials were caught in a vicious circle: hard pressed by shortages, workers demanded raises, but the lack of commodities meant that much of what was conceded was eaten up by inflation, making it difficult either to increase the size of the labor force or to improve its condition.[121]

The problem was compounded by imbalances. With high crop prices after the war, farmers – even when gouged by marketing boards – were receiving unprecedented incomes which they had difficulty spending on imports, and so they had less incentive than ever to grow food to supply workers living in cities. The reluctance of farmers to market food and the consequent rise in the urban cost of living was thought to be a cause of the devastating urban riots in Accra in 1948. One of the reasons officials tried to put a lid on producer prices was to keep some wealth out of farmers' hands – particularly in Nigeria and the Gold Coast – and try to make the domestic market more appealing to them; they were taking income away from farmers in part to reverse the rural bias in this conjuncture of the imperial economy.[122]

Meanwhile (chapter 6), British colonial governments were facing a series of strikes and consumer revolts in cities. The timing could not have been worse. Strikes disrupted economic growth; concessions to workers raised the cost of development projects; and the entire process cast doubt on the political legitimacy of colonial development.[123] More subtly than that, the strike wave forced officials to think about means by which they could reassert control. They increasingly tried to imagine for themselves a structure of work in which the African worker would become more predictable, more controllable through effective managerial techniques.

Ultimately, as we shall see, such fantasies focused specifically on workers, as well as on a subset of African cultivators who, officials hoped, could be taught to be an effective farming class. In the early post-war years, officials were still more caught up with their idea of African (or colonial) backwardness than with specific groups who could be extracted from it. It is notable how a variety of officials generalized about Africa and Africans as well as the stark difference between Africans as officials saw them and Africans as officials wished them to be.

Take the following statement in Parliament, alluding to the Colonial Development and Welfare Act, by Ivor Thomas, former parliamentary undersecretary for the colonies:

If the old regime had continued, then the Colonies would inevitably have remained at their medieval level of productivity. I doubt whether the House fully realises the lowness of that level; the hoe is still the chief agricultural implement in the Colonial Empire. There are almost limitless possibilities of improvement. Thanks to this new departure, I think it will be possible to lift the Colonial Empire to something approaching European and American standards.[124]

The transition from medieval to modern took only one sentence, to be paid for by development spending which most members of Parliament admitted was a drop in the ocean.

Creech Jones told a conference of administrators in 1948, "African society in the past has been peculiarly devoid of initiative and enterprise and has left little mark on the African background or shown signs of radical movement from within." But with British intervention, "I see Africans shaking off the shackles of ignorance, superstition and cramping custom, becoming aware and self-reliant and marching with other free people down the great highways of the world to keep their rendezvous with destiny."[125]

At the same time, a governor, Philip Mitchell, who was less sanguine about Africans' future, was equally damning of their present: "How primitive the state of these people is and how deplorable the spiritual, moral and social chaos in which they are adrift at the present time, are things which can perhaps only be fully realised by those who are in close personal touch with the realities of the situation."[126] By contrast, Prime Minister Attlee's condemnation of African culture was merely relative: "it had to be recognised that the African, unlike the Asiatic, had not behind him a tradition of developed civilisation."[127]

Most people of course thought of Africa as a continent of villages, cultivation, and pastoralism, and the rural roots of stereotypes help to explain why officials, once they started to come to grips with wage labor, sought – like their French colleagues – to carve out a distinct domain of urban wage labor. Sydney Caine, head of the Colonial Office's economics department, wrote in a minute in 1946, "Broadly, there can be little doubt that the social structure throughout most of our African territories acts as a pretty heavy brake on change... African systems of land tenure and the cultural routines associated with them, if maintained to the full in their traditional form, would effectively prevent any rapid technical change, possibly any change at all." He thought that in the colonies manual laborers lacked "efficiency" and entrepreneurs lacked "enterprise and organising ability." He would not reject, in explaining this situation, "the possibility of innate racial inferiority" but for now blamed "climatic conditions and a social structure which... is inimical to change, and therefore to enterprise..." The head of the Africa department, Andrew Cohen, noted "the present inefficiency of African labour and the unwillingness of the average African peasant to make the effort which would be necessary in connection with any radical change in the basis of agricultural production..."[128]

These kinds of arguments had multiple implications – besides what they give away about the fundamental attitudes of Colonial Office leaders at a time when they were supposedly leading Africa to self-government. They invoked African backwardness to break with the "general preference for social stability," as Caine called it, that lingered in the colonial establishment, despite the blows of urban disturbances and the discrediting of indirect rule which had been taking place since the late 1930s. Caine went on:

We cannot wholly prevent the impact of modern conditions and modern ideas on Colonial communities, and changes will happen whether they are encouraged and recognised or not... I do not pretend to any great knowledge, but I have a strong impression that many social evils of urbanisation are developing in Africa because of an unwillingness to admit that the urbanised, de-tribalised native has come to stay and must be properly provided for.[129]

The argument – and the language, notably the use of the word "evils" – is very similar to, and quite possibly derivative from, the Phillips report, issued ten months previously, on disturbances in Mombasa (chapter 4). For Caine – who had previously argued that little could be done for workers other than let the economy take its course – this was a significant admission. He was now willing to define urban Africa as a distinct domain and to think about it in social terms. He even came as close as a senior civil servant is likely to get to admitting error in his tiff of 1944 with W. Arthur Lewis: he now interpreted the refusal to consider Lewis' far-reaching questions about the social and political meanings of economic change as a decision "that there was little advantage in pursuing the discussion of 'revolutionary' economic change any further. I suggest that the whole subject should be reconsidered now."[130]

This was opening – in the highest reaches of Whitehall – a place for a labor policy, and the closeness of Caine's words to Phillips' suggest that this place was being defined by the discourse that had taken shape in the reports of investigations into disturbances in African cities: the actual existence of urban society was now a reality that could not be escaped by retreat into a conception of mythic Africa. But mythic Africa was not so much denied in this new argument as condemned.

Thus if this argument opened up an urban labor policy, it suggested a more radical direction in rural policy as well. Indeed, in 1947, Caine and his colleagues were working out such a policy. In a paper for the African governors' conference, they argued,

There is today general agreement that African agriculture cannot secure the improvements in productivity which are necessary by continued dependence on the efforts of the individual family working with primitive tools and that radical changes in the system of agriculture are required in order to permit operations on a larger scale, with increased use of mechanical assistance and with the basic object of increased productivity.[131]

They were thinking positively about "the emergence of a class of larger farmers holding substantially greater areas than the present small holdings on tenures which would enable them to raise capital on the security of their lands," or, as alternatives, "co-operatives" which could share machinery or more integrated groups of cultivators "in some form of collective farm." Larger holdings, as before, gave rise to certain fears about "social evils," but now Caine and colleagues thought that "the emergence of a landless class would not be wholly disadvantageous," since there would be roles for such people to play in a more differentiated economy.

This was what the progressives had to say. The more conservative Governor Mitchell was sarcastic about the whole business: "an ignorant man and his wife with a hoe are a totally inadequate foundation for an enlightened state of society."[132]

This discussion of a new direction for African agriculture was taking place at a high level of generalization and abstraction, with no reference to the adaptability and innovation which should have been evident, for many decades now, in many parts of rural Africa, and which indeed had been noted and at times admired by some members of the colonial establishment. The imposed agricultural revolution was, not surprisingly, implemented in a piecemeal fashion. But post-war governments did, in a number of instances, revise land laws in an effort to encourage the progressive farmer alluded to above. Yet local officials, ever worried about anything autonomous of "traditional" authorities or disruptive of established patterns of food production, did not pursue such policies toward a logical conclusion, and in general new-style farmers were only encouraged in the crevices of older systems. Yet white settlers could still get support from London (and from a Fabian colonial secretary at that) not because they were white, but because they now seemed to offer a model of capitalist farming as well as the possibility of generating capital for economic development. Regardless of the form of land tenure and agrarian structure, post-war governments were eager to send agricultural extension agents to tell Africans what to do. "There was a great need for the recruitment of skilled Europeans to teach and supervise the African," noted the parliamentary undersecretary of state in a discussion of agricultural policy. This kind of thinking accounts for some of the more madcap schemes of the post-war era for centralized production of valuable commodities – notably the groundnut scheme.[133]

The question of compulsion in the name of agricultural improvement opens up a particularly revealing discussion. The British government, which had promptly ratified the 1930 International Labour Convention against forced labor, did not face a forced labor question after the war, as did the French. Yet as long as the image of the primitive African was around, compulsory labor was a temptation in order to meet an objective deemed of sufficient importance. The British government had made extensive use of forced labor during the war, and now it was justified in the name of saving African soil from the ignorance of its cultivators.

In the same minute in which Caine lamented the African peasant's resistance to change, he wrote, "I was struck in this connection with the very general inclination among the officials at the Oxford Conference [the Colonial Service Conference] to accept a quite substantial degree of compulsion in the introduction of agricultural and other improvements." Cohen took up the theme: "Mr. Caine refers to compulsion and I agree that this may be necessary."[134] Creech Jones agreed, and put the authority of the Colonial Office behind a despatch which emphasized the role of a reorganized local government in agricultural change and which argued that in relation to "the African peasant" the use of force was justified "by his unwillingness to adopt improved agricultural methods and by his failure to take proper measures for the conservation of the soil." Creech Jones worried whether compulsion would in fact lead to the use of proper techniques, but concluded that "if this can only be achieved by the use of compulsory powers then the native administrations will have to take such powers, since neither they themselves nor the government can stand by and see the soil ruined, the well being and development of the people prejudiced."[135]

Thus in the period 1946–48, Cohen, Caine, Creech Jones, and other top leaders of the Colonial Office – and several governors in the field – looked upon change in African agriculture not as an outgrowth of ongoing processes, but as something imposed from above, an "agricultural revolution" some called it.[136] The African, all Africans, stood accused of idleness and ignorance in the very domain most central to the lives and experience of the large majority. It was through this door that forced labor reentered a discourse from which it had previously been banned.[137]

In London the agricultural revolution could mean anything from land registration schemes to giant mechanized groundnut plantations, but in Africa heavy-handed intervention had its political consequences. Agricultural schemes often took something like the form it did in Central Kenya: forcing cultivators, frequently women, to work long hours carving terraces out of the hillsides along the contour lines drawn by the experts. Hundreds were prosecuted for refusal, and the attorney general would not relent even when the Labour Commissioner warned him of the political dangers. There were disturbances in 1947 in the regions of the campaign which led to alliances between rural cultivators and the leading political organizations based in Nairobi. Some of the districts hit by terracing became foci of Mau Mau activities in the 1950s.[138]

Given this explicit and generalized assumption of African backwardness, the route to the future did not begin with the dynamics of the African present but with the British imagination. Officials, looking ahead, tended to write in terms of sociological categories such as "the worker," as if using a word that brought with it attributes from a European experience would avoid a more complex engagement with cultural change. In the late 1940s, as will be elaborated later, the switch in emphasis in discussions of the African worker from the first to the second word heralded a major discursive shift. Separating "workers" from the mass of Africans would turn out to be the key move in trying to establish a modern labor force in a backward continent. The vision of primitive agriculture – except where British intervention turned it into something else – was important to the British emphasis on the worker as a bounded category: there was nothing positive to be gained by the worker's village origins or village connections. The modern wage laborers would have to be produced and reproduced in the milieu of work itself.

The labor question was also posed in relation to the question of political evolution, a large topic that can only be alluded to here. In the immediate post-war years, the focus of British hopes was "local government." They were trying to take themselves out of the image of traditionalism associated with indirect rule and to create political and administrative organisms at the local level into which their efforts at transforming agriculture would fit. "I wish to emphasize the words efficient, democratic and local," wrote Creech Jones in his famous despatch on local government.[139]

An unintentionally revealing insight into what Colonial Office officials meant by the words they used comes from a memorandum by G. B. Cartland in 1947 which refers to an educated African elite as the "'ruling class' of the future" – the inner quotation marks being his. He believed that "the whole political future of the African Colonies is bound up with these few men." But Cartland's "ruling class" was a far cry from any of the African politicians now clamoring to be heard. They consisted of African university students in Great Britain. Cartland's main worry was that they would "run intellectually wild during the important formative years at an English University." His remedy was for them to have lectures on political philosophy and more contact with "cultured Englishmen and women and to gain access for them to the best type of English homes." In short, Cartland thought of Africa's future leaders as semi-adults who would probably turn out all right if only members of the English upper classes would invite them to tea.[140]

The colonial government's education policy is, not surprisingly, a complex subject, particularly in the years under discussion. This was a period of considerable investment (often from the Colonial Development and Welfare Act) in educational facilities, including higher education. Education was important as metaphor as well as policy, closely linked to the metaphor of maturation into adulthood. The educational metaphor was deployed in regard to the building up of "local government": experience in more democratic local institutions would provide "some measure of political education."[141] The metaphor was carried to another level of abstraction, as nations were seen to go through a process of education and maturation en route to adulthood, and officials proclaimed their intention to control the timing and process of devolving power so as to create the right kind of self-governing ex-colony within the Commonwealth: "A vigorous, adult and willing partner is clearly more to be desired than one dependent, adolescent and unwilling." And finally, the metaphor was used in comparisons among colonies, flattening the complex political conflicts that separated them to a notion of advancement to adulthood. Thus at one point the Gold Coast and Nigeria were seen as having made progress, but Attlee told the Northern Rhodesian African National Congress that there were "no short cuts to political maturity."[142] Maturization was a collective, not just an individual project: one high official, for example, argued that bringing Africans into responsible posts in the civil service was not just a matter of the candidate's qualifications but "a slow and gradual process governed by the rate of advancement of the general level of the community."[143]

This kind of language was taken up by the most influential development economist of the day, advisor and sometime critic to the Colonial Office, W. Arthur Lewis, for whom education was both a program and a metaphor and was clearly central to his entire conception of progress:

The colonies are poor because the colonial peoples have not learnt how to master their environment. Their techniques and their tools are primitive; their hygiene deplorable; and their attitudes too frequently a fatalistic acceptance of their condition as inevitable. The key to rapid and effective colonial development is mass adult education; education not just in literacy, or even primarily in literacy, but in life – in agriculture, in hygiene, in domestic living, in cultural values, in democratic organisation, in self-help, and so-on.[144]

These were the terms in which the present and future of African people were being discussed. The maturation and education metaphors underscore the centrality of social and economic development – on the achievement of modernity – to post-war colonial thinking.

Such a discussion gives a different focus to the aspect of post-war colonial policy which has been most thoroughly treated in the literature, the move toward self-government. A number of scholars have seen the Colonial Office, and prime credit has been given to Andrew Cohen, taking a decisive step toward the devolution of power *before* the nationalist challenge became serious. The year 1947 is taken as the point at which the Colonial Office, having hesitatingly moved away from indirect rule for some years, firmly committed itself to a modernist project: focusing on educated Africans, bringing them into local government and involving them in development projects, using them as the key agents to bring social change to rural areas. Alongside this local focus was an acknowledgement that Africans had to play an expanding role in central institutions, notably Legislative Councils.[145] This project was seen to be more concrete than the usual claims that self-government was the end-goal of colonization, because it provided a series of steps through which each colony was expected to pass. Timing, however, was vague. The key document in this argument, a paper prepared mainly by Cohen for the African governors' conference of 1947, put it this way:

Prophesy as to the length of this period is idle, but it may be said that in the Gold Coast, the territory where Africans are most advanced politically, internal self-government is unlikely to be achieved in much less than a generation. In the other territories the process is likely to be considerably slower.[146]

In the Gold Coast, we know, the generation-long process actually took four years: Robinson and others argue that this acceleration was an over-reaction to the 1948 riots in Accra, which officials interpreted as a nationalist challenge when it was in fact something more amorphous than that. The nationalist challenge, they argue, was a consequence of British initiatives taken in 1947 and 1948, and not a cause.

There are two problems here. Nationalism was not the only challenge, not the only threat to colonial officials' sense that they were in control of events. The events in Accra in 1948 were powerful not just because they evoked unrealistic fears that the history of the past few decades in India were being recapitulated in an instant in the Gold Coast, but because they evoked an entire series of related events that had been occurring in Africa ever since the Copperbelt strike and disturbances of 1935. It was not yet clear in 1948 that British sovereignty over the Gold Coast was under threat, but officials at that time had good reason to wonder if the narrow and vital linkages between African colonies and the world market could be assured in the face of urban collective action. Africans might submit for some time to come to British rule, but would they perform, in a predictable and orderly fashion, the labor necessary to make economic and social development possible? This is a question to which I shall return in chapter 6.

The second problem is one of imagination. Did British officials, from Cohen to Creech Jones to any of the African governors, have in their minds, as of 1947 or 1948, an African political class capable, within the current generation, of governing, of African civil servants capable of running government services, of African farmers, entrepreneurs, and workers capable of organizing the economic activity of a nation? The private – and even public – words of officials is so filled with generalizations about African primitiveness, and its discussion of African society so lacking in notions that Africans, in different walks of life, could be agents of their own future, that it is hard to see at this time where senior officials thought the social basis of nationhood was coming from. The problem becomes more specific when one thinks of the political class. British officials, in the Gold Coast or elsewhere, did not have a range of candidates for high office they thought of as plausible, and virtually every African politician who acquired a following was labelled a "demagogue." This was not only the case with Nkrumah, but with the more conservative J. B. Danquah – arrested beside his more militant younger colleague in 1948. It was true of Azikiwe, banker and business proprietor that he was. And at a general level, Cohen, Creech Jones, and Pedler often wrote of the "evils of a class of professional politicians," and of an "ignorant and gullable [sic] majority" in danger of exploitation by "unrepresentative oligarchies." Local government was explicitly advanced as a strategy that would minimize the influence of the demagogues.[147]

Demagogues were significant because the masses were significant: without a balanced program of local government, minuted Pedler, "we shall find the masses apt to follow the leadership of demagogues who want to turn us right out very quickly."[148] As for non-demagogues educated enough to aspire to positions at the center, they were discussed through the educational metaphor: they needed to be taught and to mature.[149]

As of 1948, when the Accra confrontation shook the entire framework of African policy, the social vision of the Colonial Office was so limited and so negative that officials in fact had little basis for thinking about their successors – or about the social basis of a new regime – in a coherent and positive way. As the discussion of colonial crises in chapter 6 will suggest, officials' hope that a reasonable political class – like a respectable working class – would emerge in Africa was more an inversion of their image of African society in the present than a projection forward of their assessment of African social structure.

Imperialism internationalized: the ILO and standards for social policy

Great Britain and France were drawn further into portraying themselves as progressive because neither was acting alone. They were in dialogue with each other, with other colonial powers, and through international organizations with non-colonial powers.[150] They participated in the internationalization of the colonial labor question because they thought the progressive tilt of their recent colonial policies meant that they could only benefit from international recognition. In turn the international discussion codified what a progressive policy was and created a venue at which questions could be asked and information obtained about the seriousness with which standards were taken. International fora, notably the International Labour Organization, helped to turn new labor policies into a labor discourse.[151]

Before the war, the ILO intervened in colonial affairs within the limits of free labor ideology; the aim was to protect "dependent" peoples against coercive practices. A convention on migrant labor inched into a broader conception of the social nature of labor, but not very far: it too was designed to protect laborers against deceptive and abusive practices of private and public entities trying to get them to work away from their homes.

The 1944 ILO Recommendation marked a decisive break: it dealt with work as a normal part of life in "dependent" territories and self-consciously modelled its provisions on the social policies which the ILO had for many years been developing in regard to workers in independent countries. Such issues as job security, trade union rights, and social security came onto the agenda. The 1944 Recommendation originated with the governing body of the ILO, was drafted by a committee, and debated at the international labour conference in Philadelphia in April. The ILO claimed its role in dependent territories was part of bringing them into "the framework of an international order." "Rapid political advance" had to be matched by an appropriate social policy, but their dependent status made it necessary for an international body to formulate basic social standards.[152]

The text called international attention to the role of independent states in assuring "the well-being and development of dependent people" and the need "to provide for the extension of the application to such territories of accepted international minimum standards and for the improvement of these standards." The ILO was trying not only to apply its notion of standards for labor legislation to colonies, but to inscribe a wide range of measures to improve the lives of the world's poor into international moral discourse:

All possible steps shall be taken by appropriate international, regional, national and territorial measures to promote improvement in such fields as public health, housing, nutrition, education, the welfare of children, the status of women, conditions of employment, the remuneration of wage earners and independent producers, migratory labour, social security, standards of public services and general production.

A long list of specifics followed: wartime forced labor was to be phased out quickly; "spontaneous offer of labour" was to replace recruitment; governments were to help the "married man" employed on contract away from home to bring his family; the employment of children below the school-leaving age was to be phased out; steps were to be taken "to improve the social and economic status of women" and conditions for their employment were to be regulated. Wage earners and independent producers should be assured "minimum standards of living" and official inquiries should be held to see that this was so; "discrimination directed against workers for reason of race, colour, confession or tribal association, as regards their admission to public or private employment shall be prohibited"; labor inspection services should be established; workers and employers should have their right to "associate" guaranteed and machinery for conciliation, arbitration, and minimum wage fixing established.[153]

Some government delegates saw these provisions as codifying reforms already under way in colonies; others hoped that reforms would "prevent the serious social abuses found in the introduction of industrialisation." French and British governments claimed they had already done much to implement such objectives. The British employers' representative worried that the recommendations were going forward too fast, while the Indian workers' representative feared that there would be a "lower standard" for dependent countries. The report and the Recommendation were adopted by a vote of 81 to 0.[154]

By 1947, the ILO was ready to promote the 1944 Recommendation to a convention, demanding a higher commitment from member nations. It now referred to "Social policy in Non-Metropolitan Territories" – colonies were defined by what they were not instead of what they were. As before, great emphasis was taken on the duty of colonial powers to promote improvement in a wide range of social areas, including wages, the status of women, social security and public services. The text reminded colonial powers that economic development was really about the "improvement of standards of living."

Labor migration was becoming that focus of concern that forced labor had once been. The ILO's experts wanted efforts "to avoid the disruption of family life"; migratory movements should be studied; town and village planning was encouraged; rural living conditions should be improved; terms and conditions for the employment of migratory workers should "take account of their normal family needs."

Most delegates felt that the genie of the wage labor economy could not be put back in the bottle: "it would be vain to imagine that controlling migration can effectively safeguard tribal and family life." The general agreement that migration made stabilization and social security harder to achieve led to dissent: the South African employers' delegate, Gemmill, responded with a defense of the practices of South African gold mines, denying they disrupted family and tribal life because repatriation was compulsory. But other committee members stressed the "evils" resulting from migration, including the lack of "moral support" for workers on the job and the lowered birth rate in their villages of origin. The committee could not recommend an end to migration – both employers and job seekers needed it – but it did want the issue addressed in social terms, considering the effects it had on communities of origin and ways of finding "a more stable form of economy of the social point of view."[155]

The experts were facing a problem they could not solve, but they were inching toward a consensus that "tribal" and wage-labor economies had to be stabilized within their own domains. Not incidentally, the deliberations revealed how little the experts knew: a report submitted to the committee on migration in French West Africa had data on population growth in Dakar and little else; the report on French Equatorial Africa admitted that there were "no precise data."[156] These questions would preoccupy the colonial powers, separately and together, for years to come.

The 1947 Convention moved toward more specific standards for fixing minimum wage levels. Wage rates were to reflect "the principle of equal pay for work of equal value in the same operation and undertaking to the extent to which recognition of this principle is accorded in the metropolitan territory." Progress in this direction was to be made by levelling upward the wages of lower-paid workers – one can read in these complicated formulations the evidence of compromise, particularly British concern that too direct a statement of this principle would be embarrassing for some of its colonies (see below).[157] The conference passed another convention assuring the right of workers and employers to form associations, although in somewhat weak form and only after lengthy debates in committee over the readiness of Africans to belong to unions.[158]

The Indian workers' delegate, Mrs. Mukherjee, noted quite rightly the near absence at the meeting of workers from the "non-metropolitan" territories and asked, "Can any policy which has not freedom as its declared objective secure the well-being and happiness of dependent peoples?"[159] The exception to her rule, Mr. Assalé, an African member of the French delegation, used the occasion to give a strong speech about his "disillusionment" with the results of Brazzaville and the last ILO Conference, with the French repression of the Madagascar revolt, with the incompleteness of the abolition of forced labor, and with the weakness of many provisions of the proposed convention.[160] On the other side, the British employers' delegate, Mr. Gavin, opposed the effort "to apply a whole series of conventions, drawn up expressly to meet conditions in metropolitan territories to non-metropolitan territories." In the end, the convention passed overwhelmingly – supported by both governmental and labor representatives from around the world – although employer representatives from Europe and the United States voted against the extension of labor standards to non-metropolitan countries, while accepting (or sometimes abstaining) on the more general statements about the need for a forward-looking social policy for the colonies.[161]

The French and British governments, from the beginning, took the ILO agenda quite seriously in internal discussions. Both governments felt themselves at risk from "sentimentally anticolonialist" public opinion, above all in the United States. They feared a move to "internationalize" colonies, to put all of them under the kind of supervision which the League of Nations and later the United Nations exercised over Mandated Territories. In the end, American concerns with stability and balance of power – and the risks that weak, newly independent nations might behave in unpredictable ways – blunted the anti-colonialism of the West. But France and Great Britain felt a need to cooperate with each other and with other colonial powers to present a common front of "enlightened" colonialism. They sought to use international fora simultaneously to claim moral high ground through their efforts in economic and social development and to depoliticize the questions involved.[162] Their effort was thus simultaneously technical and moral: the two were closely intertwined.[163]

The Colonial Office sent a "really high-powered" delegation to Philadelphia, studied draft articles at length, and set off for the meeting eager to show their accord with the ILO's "modern conception of social and other responsibilities." The British government backed the Recommendations that emerged from the 1944 Conference. As the ILO turned immediately to more specific items and asked governments to fill out an ILO questionnaire, delicate issues arose. Northern Rhodesia had a color bar, which denied access to certain jobs to non-white workers; this clearly violated the Recommendations. Proposed articles on wage regulation gave rise to worries about whether an explicit resolution on equal pay for equal work could be avoided. Andrew Cohen came up with a clever evasion that made development the cure for racial discrimination in colonies like Kenya or the Rhodesias (and thus vitiated the entire point of the resolution): "But where different sections of the community at present enjoy standards of living which vary widely the immediate application of the principle would not be practicable. The aim of policy should be to raise the standard of lower paid workers by gradually narrowing any difference in wages." In the end, the British government accepted that shortfalls in certain colonies would be made known to the ILO, and it both backed the ILO effort and took refuge behind the decentralized structure of the British empire: "His Majesty's government proposes to accept the general principles set forth... and to bring the minimum standards set forth... before the authorities competent to make them effective in each dependent territory."[164]

The acceptance of international standards and the evasions of much of their import concealed uncertainty within the British establishment over fundamental conceptions of the labor question. The ILO's treatment of migration and recruitment implicitly put the seal of international consensus on the policy of stabilizing labor. The 1944 version of this, still quite tentative, was enough to frighten the Colonial Office's labour advisor, Orde Browne:

The choice between a policy of stabilised or migrant labor is perhaps the most important and also most difficult problem connected with colonial labor; no authoritative opinion can be expressed by any responsible person, and all that can be said at present is that either policy may, in certain circumstances, be advisable, or again, disastrous.

The higher-ups decided that the ILO texts were all sufficiently future-oriented that they did not unduly constrain the British colonies in the present.[165] But the little flap revealed that London at war's end didn't know where it was desirable to have a stable labor force – thereby creating a working class rooted in places of wage employment – and where to rely on migration, with all the social risks that entailed. Serious thinking on that subject was taking place in Mombasa and the Copperbelt. The ILO meetings helped to define "stabilization" as an empire-wide issue and a policy which formally, at least, Great Britain had to accept.[166]

The French government, flush with the excitement of Brazzaville, was even more convinced that it would shine in Philadelphia. French officials thought they did pretty well in regard to the standards being discussed at the ILO – notably the stated goal of improving the standard of living of colonial peoples, the formal denial of racial discrimination, the legalization of unions, the existence of a labor inspectorate, and the impending end of forced labor. They sent a Senegalese trade unionist, Magatte N'Diaye, in their 1944 delegation who eulogized French policy. They thought that at the conference, "France has found again, quite naturally, her place as a great colonial power."[167] As more specific standards emerged over the years, the French administration duly filled out the required annual reports, and – despite a fair number of lamentations about the difficulties of implementing the standards – claimed progress on each of them.[168]

Meanwhile, British and French governments were talking to each other. They had trouble doing so, exaggerating the differences in their methods of rule and fearing that any regional organization they created might be vulnerable to more internationalist plucking. But they also saw the need for a common front against anti-imperialist world powers, the potential of Pan-Africanist or Pan-Islamic organizations, the danger of strikes or political agitation spilling across borders in West Africa, and the possibility of useful cooperation in development projects in an interconnected region.[169] British and French governments thought they shared a progressive attitude toward labor and economic development, and for a time thought the Belgians provided a good model by promoting a relatively stable work force in the copper mining regions of the Copperbelt and concentrating welfare services on workers and their families in that region. They thought (as of 1947–48) that the Belgians' resolutely anti-trade union policy was not appropriate to the modern working class they were beginning to think about, and within a few years sensed that their own rapidly evolving policies had outstripped those of Belgium.[170]

The British and French governments both tried to fit their common actions under the notion of "technical." French officials, of course, saw political evolution taking place within the French Union and British officials focused on the movement of each colony along the path to self-government, but the economic and social fields were precisely where they saw room for cooperation, bringing in Belgium and Portugal as well.[171] Both powers badly wanted to elide the two meanings of development, "to raise the standard of living" in the colonies while allowing "the countries of Western Europe to act to procure the resources in food products and primary materials in regions which do not pose problems of foreign exchange."[172]

Beginning in May 1946, a long series of meetings of delegates from the colonizing powers took place: specialists on public health, communications, trypanosomiasis, soil conservation, pastoralism, and nutrition had their meetings in European and colonial capitals. This pattern – and the inability of France and Britain to agree on more powerful regional bodies – led in 1949 to the creation of the Combined Commission for Technical Cooperation in Africa South of the Sahara (CCTA).[173]

The labor question came under the "technical" rubric. European officials founded the Inter-African Labour Conference, which had its first meeting in Jos, Nigeria, in 1948 and soon became part of the CCTA. Belgium, Portugal, South Africa, and the Federation of Rhodesia and Nyasaland were members along with France and Great Britain. Labour officers, advisors, and their equivalents, got together regularly to exchange experiences and methods of working with labor questions, and to issue ILO-style recommendations for policy norms. The first meeting came out in favor of trade union rights; mechanisms to fix minimum wages; vocational training; programs of social security to insure against all risks facing the working person and "to assist the wage earner in meeting his immediate family obligations"; pensions "where tribal organisation has ceased to be effective"; and efforts toward "increasing the wage-earning capacity and general standard of living of the people of Africa and the creation of a well-balanced state of society."[174]

The assembled government experts on the labor question were clearly thinking about work as a social process and workers as people who were losing access to the presumed capabilities of "tribal" societies to sustain them. The focus was on social security and protection: on being sure that workers could support families and that, over a working life, society could support them. The model was the European apparatus of social security – itself having achieved its full-blown form only at the end of World War II.[175]

There was another approach to labor at the international level. After the war, leftist trade unionists tried to shape an international labor movement, centered around the World Federation of Trade Unions (WFTU). It was, if not controlled by the Soviet Union, heavily influenced by it and by the communist *centrales* in France and other countries. For a time, the British TUC tried to play with it, hoping to combat communist control within the organization, but eventually it dropped out, helping to split the organization in 1948 and foster – along with a substantial effort by the American Federation of Labor and the United States government – a rival international organization, the International Confederation of Free Trade Unions (ICFTU). As the cold warriors of both sides sought to line up the labor movements in various countries into one or the other camps, the fledgling unions of Africa received considerable attention, and the question was posed for a moment of whether they could be part of a global movement.[176]

At the World Trade Union Conference in London in February 1945, delegates heard a speech from I. T. A. Wallace-Johnson, the Sierra Leonean veteran of the early unionization battles of the 1930s, calling for the abolition of racial discrimination in employment, the end of forced labor, and the end of flogging and penal sanctions for contract violations. He called for "equal pay for equal work" and the extension of metropolitan social legislation to the colonies. He spoke of the Atlantic Charter's promises of self-determination, and wanted colonial powers to declare a time limit for their implementation.[177]

Then the WFTU went to Dakar, holding a "Pan-African Conference" in April 1947. Senegal had witnessed a great general strike a year earlier, and the railway strike was in the offing. The CGT-affiliated "unions des syndicats" – the confederations of trade unions at the territorial level – from French West Africa were well in attendance, as were central labor organizations from Nigeria, Sierra Leone, and the Gambia, and union organizations from South Africa, the Belgian Congo, and French North Africa, Equatorial Africa, and Madagascar. Delegates heard reports that in most territories the labor movement was young but making progress; in French West Africa it had relative liberty, while in British West Africa the governments were trying to "channel" it in acceptable directions. Delegates from French West Africa spoke strongly in favor of a Code du Travail, based on metropolitan models and applying to workers (the "permanent worker" in one document) of all races in the colonies. The conference resolved to push for trade union rights, the extension of social security legislation to all without distinction of race, and the raising of living standards, including equal pay for equal work, and equal opportunities for education and professional instruction.[178]

What is striking about this list of topics is how close it was to the agendas of the ILO and to some extent to the issues which French and British governments were raising. That does not mean the contents of the discussions were the same: the dialectic of entitlement and of control has two sides even where it has one object. They shared an aura of modernity and universality. The positions of colonial officials and left-wing trade unionists – as well as the compromises of the tripartite ILO – reflected a wish that the labor question in Africa would take a familiar form. And when the ICFTU split off from the WFTU – to the relief (and with the connivance) of the French, British, and American governments – it too pressed for economic development, trade union rights, fuller labor codes, and social security. The ICFTU, if it was to compete with its rival in Africa, had no choice but to address issues of self-determination.[179] It may have been more anti-colonial than the WFTU, for the latter worked through its member organizations, notably the French CGT, whose position on anti-colonialism was ambiguous at best. In any case, both French and British governments, having welcomed the ICFTU as a bulwark against communist trade unionism in Europe, found themselves the butt of its criticisms in Africa.

Here was the dilemma of the effort to forge a modern imperialism for the post-war world: in so far as British and French leaders looked toward social and economic progress leading Africa toward an acceptable modernity as a welcome antidote to African demagogues mobilizing backward masses for political action, they were opening themselves to claims to the standard of living that went along with European modernity. And in so far as they sought to channel claims toward the least threatening modern western institutions – the ICFTU versus the WFTU – the British and French governments opened themselves up to the fact that colonialism had an ambiguous standing within the political ideology of the West itself.

The strange connections and contradictions of anti-imperialism and class struggle will be taken up later. For now, it is important to stress that, for all its contradictions, much was shared within the modernizing framework in which an international left-wing labor movement, imperial governments, and an established international organization discussed the labor question in the late 1940s. The supposed primitivism of Africans, which had so long preoccupied officials, was no longer being spoken about in public, except by the representatives of South African business. The international labor movement, WFTU and ILO versions, were by 1947 staking out a terrain of struggle that looked like past battlefields in other parts of the world: the struggle for union rights, better pay, and social security. What they would find, however, was not only that the struggles over precisely what equal pay or trade union rights meant would be hard-fought, but that the terrain was not so well defined after all.

6   Crises

The late 1940s was the time when the sense of mission in France's and Great Britain's colonial elites was strongest: officials thought they had given empire a new sense of purpose and they had not yet discovered how difficult it was to translate the development concept and its modest level of funding into actual transformations of social and economic systems. The series of strikes and urban disturbances that took place in these years thus had the critical effect of undermining officials' sense of control on their chosen terrain. And because the colonial regimes were so intent on establishing themselves, in their own eyes as much as overseas, as progressive forces, the range of options they had in countering these challenges to their authority was narrowed. They were constrained as well by the power of the converse imagery: Africa's backwardness implied that its people who worked were not committed economically or culturally to wage labor and hence that too much repression might drive them from the workplace altogether. Taken together, these constraints precluded colonial regimes from acting very colonial – from relying too heavily on repressive force external to the social milieu in question.

African labor organizers soon learned the boundaries of maneuver which they had. The modern form of a labor dispute, even where a strike strayed beyond the legal limits which regimes defined for it, gave workers and their organizations considerable scope for action, whereas at the same time disputes which fell outside this form could be repressed brutally. In the year 1947, the contrast of the vast (and technically illegal) strike of French West African railway workers – which the administration handled with kid gloves – and the bloody repression of the rural revolt in Madagascar makes this point clearly. The "revolt" or "insurrection" in Madagascar was portrayed as the work of primitive rebels stirred up by demagogic politicians to slay Europeans, destroy valuable property, and sabotage order. The rebels were blamed for "an almost complete desertion of the places of work," in almost the same moment that they were accused of insurrection.[1] In British Africa, the idea of primitive violence could be blown into a vast and inalterable evil (some-

225

times confused with communism) and could evoke brutality as well, as in Malaya in 1948 and in Kenya in 1952. Meanwhile, a "strike," as in the technically illegal Mombasa general strike of 1947, evoked a much less coercive response. The Accra riots of 1948 (see below) and the Enugu colliery strike of 1949, which were blamed on a nexus of demagogues and masses, fell in between.[2]

In British Africa, the strike wave of 1946–49 was a continuation of a pattern dating to 1935. The development initiative of 1940 was in part a response, but the post-war strikes – following upon the wartime strikes – revealed the inadequacy of the response and brought officials into a deeper engagement with the labor question itself. Development was not a panacea for urban challenges. All this came at a time when the top administration was taking, in the name of imperial interests, an increasingly productionist, and less welfare-oriented, approach to development: the strikes kept the social in front of a regime which was tending to focus on the economic. In French Africa, the experience of massive strikes was a new one: there was a discontinuity of nine years between the relatively mild strike wave in Dakar in 1936–37 and the sudden advent of the post-war strikes in December 1945. The strikes put a very rapid end to the fantasy of reconstructing French Africa through a "politique du paysannat," and French officials – in the very course of the first major challenge of this sort – embraced modernizing solutions, based on the French industrial relations model, with startling rapidity.

The strikes of the late 1940s were significant not just in number or in man-days lost, but in the quality of the strike process itself: they included general strikes or other such events which transcended the boundaries of a particular industry or location, and they took place in vulnerable nodes of the colonial economies, particularly in transportation. In British Africa, the key events were the general strikes in the port cities of Mombasa (1947), Dar es Salaam (1947), and Zanzibar (1948), as well as the general strike in the key Rhodesian city of Bulawayo (1948). The Gold Coast experienced a major railway strike in 1947, and a strike which effectively shut down the gold mining industry the same year. Nigeria experienced a colony-wide strike of government and railway workers lasting a month in 1945 (chapter 4) and a wave of strikes in 1949–50: 46 strikes resulting in 577,000 man-days lost. A radical central labor organization appeared, and officials feared that organized labor as in the Gold Coast would become the "spearhead" of a popular mobilization against the state.[3] In French West Africa, two large-scale strike movements in 1946 and 1947–48 had an enormous impact on French official thinking. Other general strikes occurred in Conakry, Guinea, and the key cities of Dahomey in 1950, and numerous smaller strikes took place in this period as well.[4]

Each of these strike movements took place in a particular milieu, and it was the ability of workers to draw on the resources and solidarity of communities that made them so effective. Indeed, it was the strikes that turned into an imperative something that officials had either dimly perceived or wanted to avoid – shaping a working class separated from its social milieu. The strikes took place in an economic conjuncture which helps to explain the cluster of major strikes in these years: shortages of imported goods and high inflation, at a time when colonial regimes were trying to step up economic activity. Pay scales, at this time, were relatively undifferentiated and many workers moved into and out of jobs, between wage labor and other urban activities, or between urban and rural areas. The movements were as much city-centered as workplace-centered, and the tendency of strikes to transcend obvious boundaries was especially worrisome to officials. But the pattern was not uniform – not every African worker suffering from inflation became a striker – and the process of mobilization must be understood in the social dynamics of particular situations. These have been studied quite unevenly and much more detailed research is needed. Here, I will focus on four strikes: the Mombasa general strike of 1947, the Dakar general strike of 1946, the French West Africa railway strike of 1947–48, and the series of strikes and urban disturbances in the Gold Coast in 1947–50. These will be necessarily brief summaries, in some cases drawing on work I have published elsewhere and in the case of the Gold Coast on other scholars' publications. I hope to bring out something of the social context in which the movements emerged, but my main focus is on the interface between African strikers and French and British bureaucracies, on the selective aspects of complex social phenomena that entered into different levels of colonial administrations. It was in the heat of events – where officials feared loss of control and sought to reestablish it on a new basis – that a break emerges most clearly in the discursive structures that shaped analysis of colonial policy and representations of colonial situations themselves.

Dakar, December 1945 – February 1946

As late as the end of 1945, the governor-general thought that the problem of a proletariat was an avoidable one. But for those Dakarois who entered wage labor, the post-war regime – like the Popular Front – followed a certain formalism: regular, urban workers should have the protection (and control) of labor legislation. Without much consideration, officials acknowledged the Popular Front decrees of 1937 giving Africans the right to organize and, after going through certain conciliation mechanisms, to strike. They quietly dropped as unworkable the educational standards for trade union membership. Officials thought that they would be able to keep better track of labor issues if they could work through unions (chapter 4). This was a sufficient opening for the trade unions, dormant since 1938 or 1939, to reconstitute themselves in 1944 and 1945, especially in Dakar and especially in the civil service. In Dakar, unlike Mombasa, western educated (*évolué*) families were relatively well integrated into urban life, and the first union leaders (heading unions of manual workers as well as civil servants) came from elite origins; in turn, they were able to establish connections with the Confédération Général du Travail (CGT) and receive some help in establishing French-style trade union organizations.

In the post-Brazzaville atmosphere, the French government took seriously évolué politics, including the demands – posed in their own assimilationist language – for equal treatment for all people of equivalent qualifications. The évolué–paysan conception of society led officials into a serious miscalculation: they failed to realize during the course of 1945 that they faced a labor problem, in which there was risk that all workers, from the illiterate laborer to the civil servant, faced certain basic problems and might act together.

In 1944 and 1945, civil service unions were demanding more pay, while the leading Senegalese politician, Lamine Guèye, was arguing for equality as a fulfillment of promises made at Brazzaville. This was what French officials expected from évolués, and, while trying to hold down demands, they reorganized the civil service hierarchy, assuring Africans access to higher-paid posts while raising the standards which candidates had to meet. The reform, however, led to considerable agitation among civil servants who felt they would fall on the wrong side of the standards barrier. Civil service unions protested throughout 1945 and some boycotted the competitions.[5]

Workers at all levels, meanwhile, were beset by high inflation and poor supplies of imported commodities like cloth. Although there were some wage adjustments during this period, the Free French governments tried both in 1943 and 1945 to block wage increases, arguing that restraint was a necessary condition to revive production.

In December 1945, after a few episodes of "agitation" and short strikes among manual workers in various parts of French West Africa in the previous year, about 2,800 dockers, metal workers, and ordinary laborers struck, demanding better pay and benefits. Officials tried to use deuxième portion workers to break the strike, but they had to make concessions quickly. A week later, the workers went back with a pay scale that was widened as well as raised, from a range of 3 to 7.75 francs per hour to 5.45 to 20.45 francs per hour. At the same time, postal workers went on strike in much of French West Africa, but curiously not in Dakar. In the Soudan and Guinea, this strike lasted until early January. Officials heard the slogan "equal pay for equal work" and complained that "Everyone wants to be assimilated to the European, in salary, in indemnities, in order of precedence, in access to the hospital, etc."[6]

In early January 1946, clerical and manual workers in the Syndicat des Employés du Commerce, d'Industries, et des Banques (EMCIBA) struck, paralyzing commerce and industry. Their strike stimulated the metal workers to go out again. The administration's first instincts were authoritarian: striking workers were "requisitioned," drafted temporarily into the military. But the workers ignored the order. By now, the various unions were acting in concert through the Union des Syndicats Confédérés de l'AOF, under the leadership of Lamine Diallo. At a mass meeting at the race track (Mombasa's strikers used a soccer field), workers heard the call for a "general strike in the most absolute sense of the word" to start in three days. Diallo sent a resolution to the governor-general, telling him that "the growing development of the working class in organization and consciousness permits it to play a decisive role as the motor and guide of all the proletarian forces of French West Africa." He listed the demands of the Union des Syndicats: "equal pay for equal work and output," union participation in classifying jobs, a minimum wage triple that of official calculations, equal rates of indemnities for family and residence for civil servants, regardless of classification, and including daily and auxiliary workers. The Union threatened, "This movement will eventually be extended to the whole of the Federation."[7]

The general strike broke out as proclaimed. It embraced most sections of the working class, except for railwaymen and school teachers. The city was shut down, from the bureaucracy to the port to domestic service and markets catering to Europeans. Two days later, the general strike spread to Saint-Louis, shutting down commerce and the territorial government of Senegal. It spread to the peanut port of Kaolack and to a lesser extent to other Senegalese towns. The Dakar strike lasted twelve days. Officials described the atmosphere as "calm," with relatively few incidents and restraint on both sides.

Even before the strike had become general, the Governor-General telegraphed Paris: There is hardly any more hope of seeing the conflict evolve favorably. On the contrary, some indications appear to allow predicting that the indigenous civil servants will join the current strike... The meeting of the assembly of the United Nations gives me the duty of avoiding all measures of brutal constraint.[8]

The language of powerlessness was coming from French West Africa's highest official. He felt obliged to explain why he could not be brutal – and fear of driving workers away was probably as important as fear of the United Nations – but in any case colonial authoritarianism was not going to work. He pleaded with Paris to release him from earlier instructions to freeze wages; raising pay was both justified and politically necessary.

Not finding a solution in colonial authority, the minister in Paris turned to another type of official, Colonial Inspector Masselot, "specialist in questions of labor conflict."[9] Masselot would push for the negotiation of contracts, based on French models, with each group of workers, hoping to give workers an interest in orderly collective bargaining within their own profession.

Equally remarkable is how quickly African trade unionists mastered the institutions and rhetoric of industrial relations and started to shape the dialogue. Officials had begun negotiating over the *minimum vital*, the calculation of the minimal needs of a worker which would then define the minimum wage. They kept trying to treat the process as a "scientific" one. But Papa Jean Ka, head of EMCIBA, politicized the debate: he argued that the items in the lists which officials used for their calculations assumed there was an African standard of living distinct from a European one, and that this was contrary to reality and French principles. The protracted negotiations blew the cover off the official attempt to objectify minimum wage determination. After a long stalemate, officials had to settle on a compromise figure and work backward to make the numbers add up. The governor-general proclaimed a figure of 7.40 francs per hour, a considerable increase over the 5.45 then in force and the 2.50 before the December strikes. This both helped to settle the strike while setting a precedent for future contestation over the issue of the *minimum vital*.

Union officials in Saint-Louis displayed a similar capacity to turn around French discourse in their negotiations. A negotiator for clerical workers applied the assimilationist justification of French rule to the labor question:

The evolution of this country, the long contact of the African with whites has created needs in him. We have habits that we cannot abandon, needs which must be faced. If we have children we want to give them a secondary education, we don't want them to stay in the cadres locaux, just as we want comfort for ourselves. All this requires a costly course of life and we need the money that we are asking from you.

One of his colleagues added, "Your goal is to elevate us to your level; without the means, we will never succeed." The official negotiators were left speechless by this argument, but they understood it well, reporting it precisely to their superiors.[10]

The strike was forcing French officials to decide if they actually believed that French models pointed the way to solutions to social problems. In the private sector, officials looked toward collective bargaining agreements in the major industries with hierarchical wages, based on multiples of the *minimum vital* and with higher ranks receiving "salaries based on those paid to similar European employees." In the public sector, the crucial issue was family allowances and the indemnity of zone: allowances, based on wages, intended to compensate for the cost of raising a family (calculated on the number of children) and for living in places with different costs of living. Such allowances had crept into the emoluments of the most senior categories of African civil servants, whose numbers were few enough that they were of little consequence. But now the public sector unions were demanding equal rates at all levels of public service, down to a lowly guard at a government office.

This was a tough demand not only because of the money involved, but because of the conceptual breakthrough: paying a government worker – not necessarily an évolué – family allowances implied that the needs of an African family were similar to those of a European one and that the state should accept in an explicit fashion to pay the cost of reproducing its African civil service. Cournarie would not go so far as accepting equality, but even going as far as he went would open the door to demands for equality, which would be conceded, in principle, four years later. Five days into the general strike, Cournarie was willing to concede that civil servants in the lowest category (*cadres locaux*) receive 20 percent of the rate for the highest levels in the colonial service (*cadres généraux* and *cadres communs supérieurs*), and that people in the middle rank (*cadres communs secondaires*) receive 40 percent. In the end, he settled for 25 and 50 percent respectively.

With the help of the visiting specialist, Masselot, officials in Dakar began to work out settlements: public servants would get their family allowances, private sector workers their increased wages, wage hierarchies, and collective bargaining agreements. The unity of the general strike was lost in success, as civil service and other unions went home with their gains and Lamine Diallo announced the end of the general strike on 26 January. EMCIBA held out for more until 4 February, the metallurgical union until 12 February, getting little out of their extra pain. The strike movement as a whole had lasted over two months. The Saint-Louis strike, meanwhile, held together even when Dakar made its settlement and the civil servants stayed out in support of the commercial workers even when their own issues were settled on the basis of the Dakar accords. Finally, on 4 February the Chambre de Commerce de Saint-Louis accepted an agreement with the commercial workers based on the Dakar model. The police conceded grudging admiration: "the mass of indigenous workers led by about a hundred leaders showed itself to be perfectly disciplined." The governor of Senegal took the strike as a serious blow to governmental authority, but one which could have been – or still could be – worse:

If the movement had had the support of the peasants, we would have witnessed the economic and financial collapse of Senegal. But if the danger is put aside for now, it continues no less to exist and we must fend it off. Because the sudden breaking out of this general strike has disclosed the existence of an organization whose ramifications extend to the most remote corners of the bush.[11]

The governor was only a little paranoid; he had no way of knowing what sort of organization existed.

The challenge to colonial power was in any case a serious one. Governor-General Cournarie was more careful to note that strikers had kept the dispute strictly within the realm of labor, that there had not been "the smallest riot, the least disorder," and that the leading political figure, Lamine Guèye, had "disappointed the strikers" by avoiding any situation in which he might have had to take a stand. Masselot, the labor expert, saw the strike as "a movement for profound emancipation," even though it had focused on professional issues. For him, the challenge meant that strikes had to be anticipated, not reacted to, and the collective bargaining agreements he had helped to put in place would limit the boundaries of dispute and define issues in ways that could be handled. The wage hierarchies "will have the effect of classifying the workers of each establishment according to well-determined categories [and] will mark a very clear improvement compared to the previous situation. There is a technique to organizing work, as with everything, and it cannot be improvised."[12]

The inspector's smug faith that social engineering could maintain control of a domain where colonial authoritarianism had proven ineffectual signalled a significant shift in the ideology and administrative relations of French administration. The Inspection du Travail was empowered by the events of early 1946 and by the anxiety lest they repeat themselves or spread to other major centers in French Africa. During 1946, the inspection was beefed up by the appointment of an inspecteur-général to oversee the respective territorial inspections in French West Africa.[13] The inspectors' reports became fatter, and their contents reflected the effort to extend the settlement pattern worked out in Dakar throughout the Federation, and to urban centers in particular. The model wage hierarchies – almost always six levels plus an "hors catégorie" – became frameworks for industry-by-industry negotiations in each colony.

The annual labor report for 1946 devoted four pages to describing the hierarchy in commerce alone, going from 1,540 francs per month to 9,500.

The inspectors, in reports and correspondence in the aftermath of the strike, articulated a clear rationale for their job classifications and wage differentials, as well as for using these models as a basis for collective bargaining with trade unions. They considered a differentiated work force the key to avoid "social trouble and a strike which would rapidly become general" as well as to "separate out an African elite and consequently maintain the attractiveness of superior positions."[14] This conception of stability, incentives, and hierarchy in wage labor was not new in the metropole, but its application to French Africa represents a dramatic and sudden reversal of policy. In subsequent years, the Inspection du Travail pushed for the systematization of labor policy in the Code du Travail (chapter 7).

Meanwhile, the labor movement continued to turn the language of scientific industrial relations into a language of entitlement. It campaigned for better wages, for the extension of family allowances to the private sector, and above all for equal pay and benefits for equal work. The administration could not counter directly the argument for equality, not only because it was a direct application of the assimilationist ideology through which imperial rule was itself justified, but because officials hoped that Africans might, after all, act in the predictable manner expected of industrial men. Governor-General Cournarie wrote in March 1946 – and this was confidential correspondence, not propaganda for public consumption – "The Administration has always pushed for the application of the principle, 'equal pay for equal output.'" He warned against "any difference in juridical treatment" between the races and cited racially specific legislation in East and South Africa as negative examples. "The only criterion," he concluded, "is professional value." This was a self-serving version of labor history, but his assertion of French policy was a contrast to British policy in East Africa, which specifically rejected claims to equal pay for equal work on the ground that Africans, collectively, were "markedly inferior to the Asian of the same educational qualification in such matters as sense of responsibility, judgment, application to duty and output of work."[15]

The Dakar strike, like others of its era, was not exclusively the work of a highly stabilized or skilled proletariat; it cut across divisions of occupation, status, and literacy in uniting most of Dakar's 15,000 wage workers. In response, the government tried to break up the similarity of circumstances, even at the expense of conceding substantial wage increases and developing wider wage hierarchies for each occupational category. By conceding low-level government workers some kind of family allowances, officials were accepting the urban labor force as a complex social entity whose conditions of production and reproduction were crucial to control, order, and productivity. The terrain would quickly be seized by African trade unionists demanding full equality of family allowances in public and private sectors alike.

Mombasa, January 1947

The Mombasa general strike of 1947, like several earlier strike movements in that port city, was not called or organized by a trade union.[16] Mobilization was rooted in the dense network of communications in the Swahili-speaking milieu of Mombasa's *majengo* neighborhood, the principal residence of workers. Once the strike began, a daily mass meeting, held in a soccer field, became the principle focus of coordination and morale-building, and it was during these meetings that a labor organization, the African Workers' Federation, finally emerged. The strikers included dockers – the most critical element in this port, virtually the sole outlet of Kenya and Uganda – workers in light industry in the city, employees of commercial firms, government workers, utility workers, hotel workers, and domestic servants. As in Dakar, the movement was neither that of a definable group clearly tied to wage labor and urban life nor was it the anonymous mass of casual workers moving into and out of jobs and the city, but it was a complex integration of people with different relations to work, drawn together in a particular spatial and temporal context.

On 13 January 1947, after a month of strike rumors, mass meetings of workers, and government efforts to talk groups of workers out of striking, some 15,000 African workers struck. This represented about three-quarters of Mombasa's labor force, and the strikers paralyzed the docks, government operations, commerce, and even domestic service. Taxi drivers went around the city spreading the word; ethnic associations helped to call on their members to strike; mass meetings in the port and government departments took place. The strike spread to a number of plantations in the region.

On the strike's second day, a crowd estimated at 10,000 gathered at a soccer field which was renamed *Kiwanja cha Maskini*, the Field of the Poor. The daily meetings, witnesses recalled, were democratic. Men and women from nearby farming communities brought food for distribution, while others contributed cash for buying maize, which was cooked at the field. Still others went home to rural areas so as not to strain the resources available in the city. The field was the locus of an alternative justice as well: a "tribunal" tried and punished strikebreakers by having their heads publicly shaven into "fantastic shapes." An official later commented, "We had a 'New government,' we had 'People's Courts,' and we had all the town burglars acting as policemen..."[17]

Officials were convinced that the angry masses could only act if led, and the best candidate they found for leadership was Chege Kibachia. Kibachia did, in fact, become the leader of the African Workers' Federation, but they got the chronology wrong. The AWF was organized at Kiwanja cha Maskini as the strike progressed. Kibachia's initial claim to fame came not as the embodiment of proletarian culture, but as someone with connections. He was a graduate of Alliance High School, the entry point to the educated elite, and, like many of his fellow alumni, he was building a career that combined clerical jobs, small businesses, and farming. Although a Kikuyu from central Kenya, he was, in January 1947, a clerk for a clothing factory in Mombasa. From school, he knew Eliud Mathu, the first African to serve on Kenya's Legislative Council. He was sent to Nairobi to try (in vain it turned out) to contact Mathu. Later, as one of the best educated strikers, he served the cause by writing for the local newspaper a statement of the "motives behind the strike":

(1) Indifference toward paying them equally with the other workers of other races who performed identical or same duties. (2) Partiality and disrespect shown to African workers wherever they are employed. (3) Deliberative [sic] devices to keep the African poor that he may keep at his work all the time... (4) Not giving wives and children allowances. (5) Taking no notice of the present high cost of living.[18]

The government tried to convince strikers to return to work, promised investigations, and issued threats – but restrained its repressive hand. Finally, it enlisted the aid of Kibachia's former classmate Mathu, who was able to present a convincing case to a mass meeting on 24 January that he would guarantee sympathetic investigation of workers' grievances. The meeting agreed to end the strike the next day, and the workers duly returned to their jobs in as orderly and systematic a fashion as they had left them.

In the aftermath of the strike the AWF attempted to give institutional form to the solidarity of the general strike. Kibachia became its president and addressed weekly meetings at the Kiwanja cha Maskini, invoking the symbols of the strikers' unity, attacking the "cheap labour policy" of Kenya, and arguing that any response to strikers' grievances should apply to workers as a whole. The AWF attempted to spread throughout the coastal region and upcountry, although with only moderate success.

The strike gave powerful confirmation to the kind of thinking which the Phillips Committee had embraced two years previously: that the working class presence in Mombasa was a reality, which could best be controlled by shaping a differentiated and stable labor force, acculturated to urban life. In mid-strike, the *East African Standard* acknowledged that the migrant labor had "settled in the town" and was now seeking "to make a living and raise his standards on a permanent basis." The first priority must be "the organisation of the various groups of African workers into *their proper categories* and the application to them of the best principles of trade unionism suitable for the conditions of Africa."[19] What the guardians of civic virtue in Kenya wanted was the opposite of what they perceived Mombasa to be. The absence of trade unions, rather than making collective action less likely, seemed only to make it more difficult to resolve.

Slightly more than 4,000 of the 15,000 strikers were dockworkers, the large majority of them working by the day. The dockworkers were indeed a militant force in 1947, as they had been in 1939, but their irregular working habits – 74 percent were working under 15 days per month at this time – seemed in official eyes to epitomize what was wrong with Mombasa. Casual workers did not face the discipline of regular work, and risked the loss of a day's pay, not the loss of a job. A coastal member of the Legislative Council gave casuals an exaggerated role in the general strike and saw an "attempt to decasualize labour in Mombasa" as necessary to prevent future "labour trouble."[20]

The dockers themselves were not demanding an end to casual labor, and they later resisted the loss of control over their work rhythms when it was later imposed on them. There was no evidence and no sustained argument that casual labor was an inefficient means to get ships loaded and unloaded, but the strikes made into an issue the sensibility that had affected officials and civic leaders for years: casual laborers exercised too much choice in the labor process. The tribunal under Justice Thacker, investigating labor conditions in Mombasa after the strike, added its call to that of its 1939 predecessor: that dockworkers be hired on a permanent basis and paid by the month.

For a time, the stevedoring companies refused to pay the social costs of a permanent labor force. They wanted instead some variant of a pool of registered dockers, whose attendance could be recorded. Officials were already moving in that direction, but they were so afraid that dockers – who were mostly from the nearby coastal region – would return to their farms and stay away from the port altogether that they kept attendance requirements minimal. At the end of 1947, around 70 percent of dockers were still working less than 15 days per month. But the longer-term significance of the indictment of casual labor was two-fold: first, it led to a continual tightening of the registration scheme, and by 1954 the port was decasualized in earnest – indeed, Mombasa was decasualized before London. Second, the indictment of casual labor opened up a critique, developed in official circles in the late 1940s, of any form of labor which entailed high turnover, and this included any form of migratory labor. I will return to that point shortly.

The more immediate result of the strike was in the realm of knowledge: virtually the only systematic investigations into the situation of wage laborers in Africa had come in the wake of strikes. Here, the post-general strike investigation had two parts: a tribunal, empowered to recommend wage increases and other reforms, interviewed African workers and officials, and a survey researcher was asked to conduct a "sociological and economic survey of conditions on Mombasa Island." Despite abusive questions from the tribunal, African witnesses told of their daily struggles to make ends meet and the frustrations of long-term workers who found themselves earning the same wage after years of service as they had at the beginning. Veteran permanent workers, it turned out, earned monthly wages similar to the average monthly income of a casual docker. As housing costs went from bad to worse, neither category of worker stood much chance of being able to support a family in the city. The social survey, meanwhile, documented the escalation in the cost of living since 1939 and the clustering of wages near the bottom. These were the conditions which the Phillips Committee had warned against two years before: a working class, conscious of its common situation, was being shaped in Mombasa precisely because the vast majority of Africans who sold their labor power – in whatever form – faced a common situation and a common future.[21]

The Thacker Tribunal gave casual workers a 30–38 percent wage increase and monthly workers in the most vulnerable sectors up to 20 percent increases in wages and housing allowances, as well as guaranteed leave, holidays, and paid overtime. The tribunal also tried – more symbolically than anything else – to address the fact that the existing wage structure did "not provide sufficiently for the normal development of a man's life." New workers got part of their award only after six months on the job. Then, in order to "make marriage financially possible," the tribunal provided that a man with five years' continuous service with one employer must be paid at least Shs 7/50 over the minimum wage.[22]

The other side of Thacker's attempt to put more resources into the hands of a defined and increasingly stable working class was his insistence that "the benefit of the Awards made by it would be very largely nullified unless steps are taken to remove this surplus population and prevent further immigration into the island." The government had previously made a practice of denouncing "spivs," "loafers," and criminals and had occasionally tried to expel them. But a spiv put on the train to his village tended to get off at the next stop and walk back, and in any case, unless casual labor were altogether eliminated, there was no way to distinguish a would-be worker from a would-be vagrant.[23] The attempts to cleanse the city were never successful – they required the kind of bureaucratic system dedicated to following Africans in all phases of their lives, which was no more than a partial possibility even in post-1948 South Africa. But they did reveal a Manichean tendency in official thinking: to separate the domain of reform from the domain of backwardness.

The award, however limited, changed the politics of labor in Mombasa. Both the interim and the final award were vehemently attacked by the AWF, at its weekly meetings and in further efforts at mobilization, for introducing distinctions within a working class which the federation wished to unite. That was precisely the point. Most workers did gain quite substantial wage increases from the award, and they knew that their gains were a direct consequence of their collective action. The AWF was unable to respond to the differentiated but valuable award that constituted the government's countermove; attendance at the weekly meetings at Kiwanja cha Maskini dwindled.

Kibachia wrote a letter to the Colonial Office with an astute critique of the "cheap labour policy." Rural impoverishment was leading to urban migration without mechanisms to sustain a laboring population: "This low pay policy is also responsible for many of the vices that prevail such as moral and culture decline, crime and destructivity of the African economic machinery, pauperism, mental and physical deterioration due to malnutrition." These were some of the points that officials – in their own ways – were beginning to worry about, but they were not about to see their emerging agenda taken away from them by a perceptive labor leader with a mass base.[24]

At that point the government, sensing that the AWF was vulnerable, was willing to do what it had refrained from doing in the strike and in its immediate aftermath: crack down. A decision to detain Kibachia was made at the highest levels of the Colonial Office, and on 22 August he was arrested. His comrades in Mombasa failed to mount an effective protest. There were reports from Nairobi – where Kibachia was trying to extend the influence of the AWF – of bitter anger, but the organized forces of Kenyan politics decided to pull back. Jomo Kenyatta denounced illegal strikes and meetings and counselled workers to bring grievances to their individual employers. The event symbolized a parting of the ways in Kenyan politics, as Kenyatta and the constitutionalist wing of the Kenya African Union became increasingly isolated from the more militant labor and youth leaders.[25]

The repression of the AWF and the state's cautious moves to foster the establishment of a more stable working class organized along occupational lines were two sides of the same coin. A British trade unionist sent to Kenya to advise fledgling African trade unions later wrote, "I am firmly convinced that at the present moment workers in Kenya must confine themselves to separate Unions for different occupations."[26] In fact even the last point remained problematic: the Kenya government theoretically supported unionization, but in practice could not seem to find trade unions it approved of (chapter 8).

The general strike, following a barely averted strike two years previously, had exposed the fragility of state power in the domain of work. It is not clear how much officials appreciated the significance of the fact that the only government connected individual who was able to exercise influence over the strikers was a Kenyan politician, Eliud Mathu.[27] The contributions of two African legislators in the Gold Coast (see below) to settling a strike in that same year would also hint that the day-to-day management of social and economic relations might be stronger if the state was represented by people more connected to the local milieu than British civil servants.

At the same time, the strike strengthened the arguments of those officials who had, since at least the 1939 general strike and the 1945 strike threat, been rethinking the labor question. Not only had the general strike revealed the spectacle of mass collective action spilling across the boundaries of industry and occupation, but once it was over the majority of workers were no longer quite so poorly paid. Barely had the January strike ended when the general manager of the railway told the port manager that output must be increased as a consequence of the wage increase.[28] Thus a question of order and control also became a question of productivity. It became more so as the decade wore on, and the concern with productivity translated into a concern with the conditions under which a working class lived and reproduced itself. Two months after the strike, Creech Jones took up the productivity theme, asserting that increases could be achieved "by increasing the incentive to work and by making the actual conditions of work more attractive. Greater efficiency should follow from the health, educational and social services provided for in the long term programmes now being made..."[29]

The Kenyan labour department soon embraced stabilization for the colony as a whole. Labour Commissioner E. M. Hyde-Clarke told the Legislative Council in 1949 that "in order to increase production we have got to have either more labour or better labour, and I have a very firm conviction that the answer lies in the second." Better labor meant a "stable and contented labour." It required "very much better supervision," and only if the laboring population was attached for the long term to its place of work would the effects of good supervision on "a fairly primitive people" have any cumulative effect. That in turn implied "housing on a family basis" and "as great a degree of social security at his place of employment as he gets in his own native reserves."[30]

Production and reproduction – the nature of social life in and around the workplace – were thus tied together. So too was culture and social life within rural Africa. But linking the two via migration threatened to reproduce the wrong kind of working class. This was the gist of the analysis of the influential "African Labour Efficiency Survey," conducted among Kenyan railway workers in 1947 and published in 1949. The argument began with nutrition – inadequate food in childhood, a consequence of ignorance as much as poverty, made African workers sluggish and inefficient for life. This argument then became a condemnation of African society in an industrial age: "He [the African worker] is ineffective in many industrial techniques by the very nature of his birth, his upbringing, and his native culture."

The survey was adamant that Africans *could* be efficient workers, but this required a total remaking of culture. Within the workplace, the idea of time-discipline had to be taught:

The East African has not been bent under the discipline of organised work. In his primitive economy, the steady, continuous labour is carried out by women... Though the tasks he performed were prescribed by tribal law and custom, he could do them in his own way and at his own speed, for to him time had no economic value... To work steadily and continuously at the will and direction of another was one of the hard lessons he had to learn when he began to work for Europeans.[31]

Those lessons could not be taught on the job alone: a stable body of workers had to be separated out from the African masses, socialized and acculturated, given the conditions necessary to live a "respectable" life and to reproduce itself within the industrial milieu.

The British labor experts were extending to migrant labor in general and systematizing arguments already voiced by newspapers and government tribunals in relation to the Mombasa strike: migration and casual labor were shaping the wrong kind of labor force. The conclusions were both underscored and criticized in these terms. Skeptical of the survey's argument that Africans should be given increments and promotions to foster their long-term attachment to their employer, the general manager of the railway wrote that the real causes of high turnover and inefficiency lay in the "workings of the African mind."[32] This was the old argument about the peculiarity of the African, espoused by anti-reform elements in

British as much as French Africa. The progressives differed above all in their willingness to change the workings of the African mind.

The expert from England charged with the survey had reproduced an argument about the nature of industrial society quite conventional in the European context. Social policy for decades in England – from issues of housing to factory hours to education and to motherhood – had focused on the relationship of social reproduction to production and social order.[33] The break came in applying them to Africa. The hope expressed after the Copperbelt strike of 1935 that more rigorous repatriation of workers and reinforcing traditional authority would keep industrial action in check was no longer credible, after the massive strikes in Kenya, Tanganyika, Southern Rhodesia, the Gold Coast, and elsewhere in 1947–48.[34] Labour departments, like the French Inspection du Travail, were ever more closely identifying themselves with arguments for stabilization, confronted as they were with the social consequences of migrancy and city-wide strike movements and given their inclination to see labor as an issue amenable to professional and scientific analysis.

The other side of the contention that an African – via stabilization, discipline, and socialization – could be made into an efficient industrial worker was the denigration of Africans who had not made such a transition. By decasualizing dock labor and seeking, however partially, to tie Africans to their urban jobs, officials were trying to separate the African worker from what they thought of as African society.

The French West African railways, October 1947–March 1948

The strike of railway workers which began in October 1947 involved nearly 20,000 workers, their families, and their communities and lasted, in most regions, for five and a half months. It was an epic event by any standards, but it has been made larger by the novel of Ousmanne Sembene, *God's Bits of Wood*. The novel portrays the strike as a giant step in a wider popular struggle against colonialism. My interpretation is more ambiguous.[35] The politics of decolonization and the labor question certainly need to be examined in relation to each other, but the tension between the two should be preserved. The irony of the railway strike is that its success was contingent upon the integration of railwaymen into wider, supportive communities, but its goal was to achieve equality with railwaymen from metropolitan France, in effect to link their life chances to a structure separated from the rest of African life. The partial success of the strike certainly gave African workers a sense of collective empowerment – and in this way it contributed to the anti-colonial struggle – but the very process of striking and negotiating framed the struggle in a very particular way.

The strike was about the *cadre unique*, the demand of African railwaymen for a single, non-racial job hierarchy, with the same benefit package for all members, including the complicated supplements for local cost of living and family obligations. The demand followed from the victory which the civil servants had won in the Dakar strike of 1946 – including family allowances – and which had been generalized over most of the civil service in French West Africa. The *cadre unique* was conceded early in principle; the actual strike was over implementation, and it was really about power, whether African workers would actually have a voice in a formally nonracial work structure.

The government had in 1946 made the Régie des Chemins de Fer de l'Afrique Occidentale Française into a parastatal corporation run by a board weighted toward government officials but including representatives of railway unions and commercial interests. The effect – if not the intention – of this move was that workers no longer automatically qualified for the status and perquisites of civil servants, notably those won in the strike of 1946, and that the Régie could claim that its own resources, not those of the French government, set an upper limit on labor costs.[36]

The Fédération des Travailleurs Indigènes des Chemins de Fer de l'AOF brought together the unions on each of the regional lines that made up the railway system: the Dakar–Niger (Senegal and Soudan); Bénin–Niger (Dahomey), Conakry–Niger (Guinea), Abidjan–Niger (Ivory Coast).[37] The Dakar–Niger was the most powerful branch, and the Fédération's headquarters were in Thiès, a railway junction and major maintenance center inland from Dakar. The Syndicat des Travailleurs Indigènes du Dakar–Niger dated to the late 1930s (chapter 3). It had been the most conspicuous absentee from the 1946 general strike, largely because its leader François Gning was affiliated to the socialists then in power in France and hence in the government-general in Dakar. His stance led to a revolt of younger trade unionists, who installed as secretary-general Ibrahima Sarr, graduate of an elite secondary school, railwayman since 1935, clerical employee in the *cadre local supérieur*. Sarr's first speech showed he too could turn the rhetoric of imperial reform in a direction it was not necessarily intended to go, calling for "the abolition of antiquated colonial methods condemned even by THE NEW AND TRUE FRANCE which wishes that all its children, at whatever latitude they may live, be equal in duties and rights and *that the recompense of labor be a function solely of merit and capacity.*"[38]

Sarr broke out of Gning's évolué-oriented way of thinking and brought the auxiliaries into the union in a meaningful way. As of 1946, the railway employed 478 Europeans, 1,729 Africans in the various cadres, and 15,726 auxiliaries. Many auxiliaries – treated as temporary workers even if they had years of service – did the same work as members of the cadres, but they lacked job security, paid housing, and other indemnities.

The railway union, under Sarr, put forth a two-dimensional claim in August 1946: for the *cadre unique* and for the integration of the permanently employed auxiliary into the cadre. The claim went to the Commission Paritaire, the negotiating body specified by French industrial relations law, and by April 1947 it had not emerged. The outright rejection of the *cadre unique* by the unions of white workers did not make the situation any easier. Then, the union pulled off a theatrical coup. At the moment of a visit to Senegal by the president of the Republic and of the colonial minister, Marius Moutet, it organized a strike.

Under the looming presence of Moutet, Governor-General Barthes, Lamine Guèye, Léopold Senghor, and other political luminaries, the government-general could not publicly go against principles of equality. The Commission Paritaire accepted the *cadre unique*, while the union accepted the Régie's demand to rationalize the structure of the railway by reducing the number employed. The commission was to regulate the details.

For "details," one can read power: much was at stake in how many auxiliaries were to be integrated and how scales were to be combined into a single cadre. In the end, the board of the Régie rejected the proposed settlement of the Commission Paritaire. The union felt betrayed by the rejection and mobilized for a strike set in advance for 10 October. The union's final list of demands – all rejected by the Régie – included making the integration of auxiliaries retroactive, revising the table of equivalences which slotted people into the wage hierarchy of the *cadre unique*, revising certain barriers to promotions within the cadre, allowing leave for family emergencies in addition to annual vacations, making company lodging available to auxiliaries rather than just to the cadres, and providing uniform, rather than hierarchical, rates for the indemnity which compensated for local variations in cost of living. The strike would take place not over the grand principles of the *cadre unique* or equality, but formally over a narrower set of issues.[39]

The strike of 10 October was virtually total. Governor-General Barthes insisted that it was illegal while an arbitrator, whom he had appointed at the last minute, was considering the case. He would therefore not negotiate but insisted on enforcement of the arbitrator's eventual decision, which was favorable to the Régie's position on how to implement the *cadre unique*. Three weeks into the strike, thirty-eight Africans were at work. The strike would remain remarkably solid until January, when the Abidjan–Niger region broke away and went back to work. Even this did not lead the rest to lose heart, although there was a small drift back and considerable hiring of strikebreakers. The strike ended, finally, on 19 March 1948.

More research is necessary on how strikers survived, but even the evidence of the security forces points to the importance of workers' integration into town-centered and family-centered networks. Through family connections, workers had access to agricultural products and fish: the strike, probably deliberately, took place after the harvests. Some railwaymen returned to their villages of origin to lessen the strain on urban resources. Women played a crucial role in pulling together such resources, although there is no evidence that the women's march which climaxes Sembene's novel ever happened. Merchants in railway towns contributed money, food, and transportation vehicles to strikers. The journal *L'AOF* gave much publicity to the strike and collected donations, and the French CGT gave the union a major donation, although only enough to keep such a huge labor force supplied for about a week. The union itself had opened and stocked a cooperative at Thiès, and for three months it gave strikers needed items on credit. One strike committee member boasted sardonically that the strikers were now like a marabout: "we do not work but we have our provisions..."[40]

This was the optimism of the early strike days. There is no question – *God's Bits of Wood* is on the mark here – that by the end, the hardships were severe. This was, by any standard, a long strike. The comment made by the Inspecteur Général du Travail, Pierre Pélisson, in January is extremely revealing: "Here the means of defense are very different – and singularly more effective – than in the case of metropolitan strikes."[41] It was, Pélisson noted, the incompleteness of workers' integration into proletarian society that gave them more diverse roots than their French comrades. Over five months, workers of various origins, working on quite different terms for the railway, managed to stick together, hold to union discipline, and keep their support networks in railway towns and surrounding villages together.

According to security reports, the question of calling a general strike in support of the railwaymen came up at union meetings in Dakar, Abidjan, and Conakry in November 1947. But each time a solidarity strike was rejected, although several unions supplied money to the strikers. At Dakar, some of the veterans of 1946 – Abbas Guèye and Lamine Diallo – argued for a general strike, but the Commission Administrative of the Union des Syndicats de Dakar refused to go along. There were three reasons for the failure of working class unity: the railway union had itself failed to join the general strike of January 1946; the railway union was "autonome", while most other unions and the major federation were affiliated to the CGT; and the unions of Dakar and elsewhere were at the time in the midst of renegotiating their own collective bargaining agreements. In fact, the post-1946 policy of the Inspection du Travail was paying off: each occupation had a great deal to gain by working within professional boundaries.

The story is similar in relation to organized politics. The French West Africa wide political party, the RDA played no role in the strike, and its newspaper, while indicating sympathy with the cause, insisted that Sarr "is not RDA," and "It was the business of the railwaymen and the railwaymen alone to take up their responsibilities." Senghor is remembered by former strikers as having come privately to the strike committee on the eve of the walkout to indicate his support, but he is also remembered for having given the strike no public support.[42] Only in December did the leading African politicians act: on the occasion of the meeting in Dakar of the Grand Conseil (French West Africa's legislative body), Houphouët-Boigny and others tried to get the governor-general to intervene to effect a settlement. They were careful to make clear "their concern not to mix politics with an affair that must remain strictly professional and simply to bring their purely obliging support to settle a conflict whose importance to the country is considerable."[43] The governor-general would not budge, and the Grand Conseil itself, in two attempts to discuss the issue, was so torn by partisan bickering that it could not even pass a bland appeal for a settlement.[44]

At home, Houphouët-Boigny was criticizing the strikers for failing to consult him, bad timing, and acting inopportunely in not accepting a settlement and working for their demands later. When the Ivory Coast strike ended in early January 1948, over two months earlier than elsewhere, officials noted, "According to our information, this result is due to M. the Deputy Houphouet who succeeded in persuading the African railwaymen to return to work despite the counter-propaganda of M. Sarr."[45] The importance of the Ivory Coast's farmers within the Ivorian RDA was undoubtedly relevant here: they stood to lose by the continuation of a post-harvest strike. Senghor, meanwhile, wrote an elegant letter on the union's behalf to the minister of Overseas France appealing for a solution based "on the equality of rights and duties, without discrimination based on race or religion," but he shied away from engagement with the mundane details of a labor dispute.[46]

But the strike committee, noting the lack of forthright support, took a jaundiced view of the political leaders of Senegal, and criticized both Senghor and Lamine Guèye "for having placed themselves on the side of the Administration and for their support of Cunéo [Director of the Régie]."[47] In January, the Soudanese Deputy Fily Dabo Sissoko intrigued with government officials to try to split off the crucial Soudanese workers from their Senegalese comrades on the most militant branch, the Dakar–Niger. Sarr was sufficiently shaken by the danger of a split that he thought briefly of taking up Sissoko's initiative, but his strike committee instructed him to reject it. But when Sissoko, angered by the Union's refusal, tried to get the Soudanese railwaymen to go back to work, only seven railwaymen in the Soudanese capital reported. It was only after the strike, when the influence and importance of the railway union had been made clear, that the most astute of the political elite, Senghor, moved to bring Sarr and other union leaders into his orbit.[48]

The government side of the strike has its puzzles too. Why did officials allow a disruptive strike to drag on so long without either resolving the less than enormous issues or using its power systematically to break the strike? The government did not requisition strikers into the military; it waited a month before beginning to hire replacement workers and did so diffidently and to little effect. Only in mid-November did they begin to prosecute Sarr for ordering an illegal strike, and despite being convicted Sarr never served his sentence. Nor did the Régie play another card it had: it did not fire its workers nor – despite occasional threats – expel the large number who lived in railway housing.[49]

The caution of the Régie and the administration was very much a product of the post-war conjuncture. Railway workers represented the best hope for the kind of stable, increasingly skilled, work force officials wanted to build. But the very prolongation of the strike revealed that railway workers had another foot in a different sort of social entity, and the Régie feared – probably more than was actually the case – that railwaymen, including skilled workers, would leave the labor market altogether. The issue was conceptual as well as practical. Having committed themselves to an industrial relations model of labor control, the colonial regime found it hard to go back to the old-style colonialist methods. Robert Delavignette argued this specifically: "the strong style directed at the strikers will not itself resolve the problem... if the government gives the impression of going back, after a detour, on trade union freedom and on the abolition of forced labor."[50]

But the one point to which the administration stuck with utter stubbornness until near the end was its interpretation of the rules of the new industrial relations order. Governor-General Barthes had taken his last opportunity before the strike to lecture the union leaders on "the terms of the law and my intention of insuring that it is respected." As late as 3 February, the administration insisted that the affair "end by the total execution of the arbitration ruling," refusing to let an inspector to talk to the union about negotiated alternatives.[51]

The strike came to an end when a new governor-general, Paul Béchard, a socialist politician rather than a colonial functionary, succeeded Barthes at the end of January and made a series of proposals in early March. He sustained the Régie's hierarchical scale of indemnities and its refusal to house auxiliaries, but compromised on the starting date for integrating auxiliaries, some details of reclassification, and on leave policy. There would be no punishment for striking; all workers in the cadres would be rehired; and striking auxiliaries would be taken back until the staffing levels had been filled, keeping in mind that workers hired during the strike would be kept on if qualified. After a positive but still critical response from the union, Béchard agreed that the union would be involved in the process of coming up with a new staffing table – as agreed in April the staffing structure was to be rationalized and reduced – and in deciding which workers would not be rehired. Workers also received a 20 percent wage increase, officially to compensate for the increased cost of living. Agreement was finally reached and work resumed on 19 March. "It left no victors, no vanquished," Béchard concluded. "We will resume work calmly, and with discipline," were Sarr's final words, and they, like his previous appeals, were systematically followed.[52]

In the aftermath of the strike – even more prolonged than the main event – came the negotiations over staff reductions. The process must have reminded the railwaymen why they had fought so hard to make clear their collective strength. The railway had initially claimed that it needed only 13,500 men, not 17,000. After discussion, it settled on a figure just under 15,000, and, after further debates and attrition among the strikebreakers, relatively few auxiliaries were left at risk. In the end Pélisson acknowledged that the union "had done its duty in defense of the railwaymen."[53] The process of integrating auxiliaries into the *cadre unique* went on as slowly as the compressions. But the union again had something to show for its efforts: in 1950, over 30 percent of the railway workers were in the cadre, as opposed to 12 percent on the eve of the strike.[54]

The administration now knew that restructuring the colonial labor system would involve African agency as much as imperial design. When a hard-nosed inspector later complained that the cost of integrating auxiliaries into the *cadre unique* was driving up freight rates on the railway, a senior official reminded him that good labor relations in the region's largest enterprise were "necessary, as the strike of 1947 proved, for the sound functioning of the Régie itself. I believe that technical progress and social progress cannot be separated."[55]

The 1947–48 railway strike was above all a contest over power within a system of industrial relations that had only just come to French Africa. The break toward accepting work, workers, and workers' organizations as part of African social reality had been made in the 1946 general strike and the April 1947 agreement. The railway job structure would look like a French job structure rather than the racial structure of backward colonialism. But the question of how power would be exercised *within* this structure had not been settled, and that was what the strike was all about.

The railway workers proved that their voices would be heard. The government made its point too: African unions could fight and win, but within certain legal and institutional structures. The very battle brought both sides deeper into those structures, and the strike did not become a popular liberation struggle or an exercise in colonial repression. At the end of 1948, a government report applauded the form in which the two sides had joined their conflict: "Social peace can only profit from such a crystallization of forces around two poles, certainly opposed but knowing each other better and accepting to keep contact to discuss collective bargaining agreement and conditions of work."[56]

The Gold Coast, 1947–1951

Whereas the French West African strikes of 1946 and 1947–48 – which threatened for a time to become truly emancipatory events – were put back into the category of labor dispute, the Gold Coast strikes and riots of 1947–48 were not. In Mombasa, with a less politicizied atmosphere than Accra, officials were able to keep a labor dispute a labor dispute, although only by restructuring dock labor. In the Gold Coast in 1948, political leaders were able to do what the Colonial Office feared: to take the labor question out of its boundaries.

The 1948 riots in the Gold Coast are a key moment in virtually all accounts of post-war politics: for some they represent the moment when mass nationalism arose from the pressures a popular uprising put on elite parties; for others they represent a moment of panic when the Colonial Office's clear but stately progress toward self-government turned into a headlong plunge (see chapter 5). But 1948 was not just an episode in political history. It emerged from a decade of strikes and trade union mobilization, as well as the overlapping of efforts of a specific segment of the urban population (ex-servicemen) and a general movement of urban consumers (a shop boycott). For nationalists, the social pressures defined an initiative they needed to seize, yet they couldn't quite pull it off: the relationship of the political and the social remained ambiguous. The tension of the political and the social was equally crucial for the government: it now needed more than ever to find "responsible" political elements with which to cooperate and to build a "respectable" working class separated both from unruly masses and dangerous demagogues. But it was precisely the mass-demagogues model of African society that became a trap that increasingly narrowed the way in which officials saw their options.

The responsible leader was only of use if somebody would follow, and the urban unrest in the Gold Coast kept forcing officials to relabel the individuals involved. In 1948 Danquah and his United Gold Coast Convention were the demagogues, and they were blamed for the riots. By 1949, they were the moderates and Nkrumah the demagogue, leading a "rough" element of society and subverting state efforts to make trade unions respectable. In 1951 Nkrumah became the moderate, and the section of the labor movement which had been closest to him now threatened a still more radical politics. The very danger of demagogues mobilizing masses lent an element of desperation to officials' quest for the Man of Moderation and Modernity. If decolonization were even to be an imaginable policy, the men of the Colonial Office would have to convince themselves, Parliament, and a sufficient portion of the public that their current version of who was responsible and who was dangerous was sound.

In 1947, the Colonial Office was sure that "in the Gold Coast, the territory where Africans are most advanced politically, internal self-government is unlikely to be achieved in much less than a generation." It wanted to set aside political distractions to focus on preparing for "efficient government" and "ordered development" of social and economic institutions.[57]

The Gold Coast, in comparison to the other cases discussed here, had a longer history of strikes and trade union organization, but there still remained in the government and above all in the mine industry a reluctance to see work, workers, and industrial disputation as normal parts of a colonial society. In the wake of a strike wave in 1937–38, the Gold Coast government had created a "skeleton" labour department and it inched toward acceptance of African trade unions while retaining the usual colonial anxieties about detribalization. In 1941, a two-week long strike hit the railway and the railway towns, resulting in wage raises and establishing the railway union as a force to be reckoned with. Between 1939 and 1947, the population of the Gold Coast's major towns, Accra, Kumasi, Sekondi-Takoradi, and Cape Coast increased 55 percent. Some 45,000 African soldiers ended their wartime service and, for the most part, sought to enter urban labor markets. As in most of Africa, the war and post-war years were difficult for established as well as would-be laborers: in Accra, real wages – relative to an index level of 100 in 1939 – fell to 66 in 1945 and recovered only to 86 in the fall of 1947.[58]

In the second half of 1947, the Gold Coast experienced a "wave of strikes," involving twenty-six different industrial concerns and 46,105 workers. Government workers benefited from retroactive awards consequent upon the 1945 strike of government workers in Nigeria, and "demands for similar treatment came thick and fast from employees in every branch of commerce and industry."[59]

The two key strikes were on the railway and in the gold mines. "The Railway Union," Richard Jeffries writes, "was essentially the creation of a dynamic, elementary-school educated, labour elite of artisans." The Gold Coast railways moved somewhat in the direction of stabilization and improved working conditions even before the war, and in the coastal region they had a population with significant rates of literacy and familiarity with British ways to draw on. But the largely Fante artisans also had their traditions of political association and their ties to other segments of the region's population, particularly in the crucial railway town of Sekondi. Union leaders needed to cater to a diverse constituency, and in the successful railway strikes of 1939, 1941, and 1947 they did just that. Even this limited experience of stabilization suggested that it was no panacea against labor militance, but it did give officials hope that they could direct union militance into a "peaceful, apolitical model of unionism." In 1945, the Railway Union was instrumental in setting up the Gold Coast Trades Union Congress, which would play a key role in post-war politics. In October 1947, with militant workers pressing against a more conservative union executive, railway workers struck for fifteen days.[60]

The strike was well timed – there was a shortage in world cocoa markets and even the Colonial Office could see the argument that "with cocoa prices so high, it ought to be possible for demands of railway workers to be met." The acting governor replied ruefully, "Unfortunately those in control of the Unions realise as clearly as I do how inopportune is the strike from the economic point of view." He saw the railway strike in the context of a broader discontent on the part of all but the civil service workers – "a spontaneous, widespread and barely coherent demand for more money." He blamed the "intransigent attitudes" of the railway and mine unions, but more so the shortage of consumer goods and a public perception, fed by British propaganda about the sums that were to be invested in development, that money was available: "it is important to recognise present labour troubles not as 'labour' matter in the restrictive sense but as part of a general economic disorder affecting the country." He was pleading for action within the framework of the development idea, but also for a more politically sensitive handling of the restrictions on access to consumer goods in British colonies.[61]

The railwaymen's demands for wage increases ended in a compromise, but one negotiated in a portentous way. Two African members of the Legislative Council offered to do what the labour department had failed to do – to mediate the strike. They persuaded the strikers to return to work, as Eliud Mathu had done in Kenya. In London, Creech Jones commended the legislators' "ability and... real sense of responsibility" and noted that the railway and mine strikers were settled "largely due to their efforts."[62] In neither Kenya nor the Gold Coast were officials ready to say on paper – although they may have thought it – that Africans had accomplished an act of governance where white officials had failed.

The mine strike of 1947 involved 33,000 men. It was organized by a union of recent origin – 1944 – and one torn by an important cleavage. Most of the surface workers in the mines were from the southern Gold Coast. Like the railwaymen, they were in touch with political currents in the cities and with the growing trade union movement. Most underground workers were northerners, who worked for limited periods and returned to the poorer and more isolated parts of the colony or adjacent French territory, although by the late 1930s some, especially those in skilled occupations, were settling with their families near the mines.[63]

Miners had been caught up in the strike waves of the late 1930s. Even as the Gold Coast government slowly moved to encourage unions in some contexts, officials still discouraged unionization among the "inarticulate and illiterate labour" of the mines.[64] The mines, meanwhile, felt sufficiently threatened to try to preempt workers' action by building new housing estates to replace the "mushroom villages" in which many miners lived a physically deprived but socially autonomous existence, allowing them land to grow food, improving health facilities, trying to organize the employees' leisure, and appointing committees to discuss work-related questions.[65]

The leaders of the Gold Coast Mine Employees' Union (MEU) were southern, skilled, and educated, notably J. N. Sam, a Fante carpenter and former teacher. But in the context of the Africa-wide inflation and strike wave, the fledgling union had trouble keeping up with the militancy of its men. A two week strike over wage issues took place in 1945, other strikes in 1946. After government workers got their raises in 1946, the MEU demanded retrospective raises and a union check off. The ensuing strike lasted thirty-five days and ended with an arbitration award – a stunning victory for the union. It achieved a substantial wage hike for both underground and surface workers, a 45-hour week, overtime, annual paid leave, sick leave, and a gratuity scheme for workers who left the mines after five years' service. The Chamber of Mines was forced to accept the legitimacy of the union and to negotiate with it. The union, however, held the surface and underground workers together only in so far as it could deliver the goods.[66]

The mine owners tried in response to recruit more workers from the north on a migrant basis, but were frustrated by labor shortages. Then, like the copper mine companies in Northern Rhodesia, they began to try to make a more stable, better paid, work force more productive. Jeff Crisp describes the new approach as "scientific management," a Tayloresque approach to dividing up the work force into finer units, defining tasks more precisely, and exercising close supervision over workers. Consultants from Southern Rhodesia and South Africa were brought in. The obstacles they faced included not only the resistance of African workers to tighter discipline, but also managers' tendency to make their low expectations of Africans into a self-fulfilling prophecy. Most of the numerous strikes were not instigated by the union, which had initially cooperated with the productivity drive, only to find that it was losing touch with its rank and file.[67]

The issues raised in the 1947 railway and gold mine strikes would not stay in the workplace. They coincided with a considerable degree of rural anger, as farmers – although benefiting from high cocoa prices – reacted against heavy-handed government attempts to cut out allegedly diseased cocoa trees. Then came the boycott of urban commerce, which focused on the sorest spot of all, the acute commodity shortage and galloping inflation.

There was no question of the legitimacy of the grievances, as the post-riot Watson Commission acknowledged.[68] Inflation reflected the state of world markets in the aftermath of war, British efforts to avoid sterling expenditures, lack of incentives for local food producers, and the monopolistic structure of import–export and wholesale trade in the colonies, dominated by the United Africa Company (UAC). Local businessmen felt cut out of the action while urban workers, petty traders, and other city dwellers bore the brunt as consumers.

The boycott was organized by Nii Kwabena Bonne II, an Accra chief of minor standing, former worker, and businessman, the kind of figure cutting across social categories – a wealthier and less educated version of Chege Kibachia – who turns up in populist movements. He formed a committee which kept watch on the practices of storekeepers and, beginning on 24 January, persuaded Africans in Accra, Kumasi, and other cities to boycott European- and Syrian-owned businesses. Nearly a month later, the government engineered an agreement among the boycott committee, the Chamber of Commerce, and the Joint Provincial Council of Chiefs under which the firms in question cut their gross overall profit margins from 75 to 50 percent on certain items – an agreement which suggests that the charge of excess profits was well founded.[69]

The boycott ended on 24 February, just when a group of ex-servicemen in Accra, encouraged by the United Gold Coast Convention (UGCC), were planning a protest march against the government's failure to help them find jobs and the difficult conditions facing urban dwellers generally. They marched on 28 February, the same day that the price cuts that the boycott movement had negotiated went into effect. Apparently, people in Accra mistook the agreed-upon cut in the merchants' mark-up to be a 50–75 percent cut in prices, and felt cheated when they learned the reality.

The collective actions of the consumers – a "cost-of-living" riot – and the ex-servicemen came to a head together. The typically undermanned and poorly led police contingent protecting government headquarters panicked, fired into the marchers, and caused fatalities. As news spread, a full scale riot was underway in downtown Accra, directed above all at European-owned shops. The UAC offices and shops were burned; looting was extensive. Fishermen and market women were apparently active among the looters.[70]

The looting and rioting spread to other towns, in some cases after the arrival of what the governor called "irresponsible elements from Accra" by lorry or train. There were more casualties: a total of 29 deaths and 237 injuries.[71] The UGCC was not the instigator of either the servicemen's march nor the consumer boycott, but it moved quickly to seize the initiative: Danquah and Nkrumah sent off telegrams to the Colonial Office and to newspapers around the world. The Secretary of State was told

Unless Colonial government is changed and new government of the people and chiefs installed at the centre immediately conduct of masses now completely out of control with strikes threaten in Police quarters and rank and file Police indifferent to orders of officers will continue and result in worse violent and irresponsible acts by uncontrolled people. Working Committee United Gold Coast Convention declare they are prepared and ready to take interim government.[72]

The UGCC was using the same rhetoric about mass disorder as officials were to adopt, and they were offering themselves as controlling intermediaries. The offer was not appreciated.

The UGCC leadership clearly took this as a moment in which the legitimacy of British rule could be called into question, but at no point did it mobilize revolutionary action to effect such an end. Nor, despite administration fears, did the hot-beds of trade union activity in the mines and railways mobilize in the month after the Accra riots. The international follow-up was in some ways more impressive: anti-imperialist groups issued statements, and Africans and West Indians organized a protest meeting in Trafalgar Square, London, on 7 March.[73] Officials took the threat to British rule very seriously: an emergency was declared; troops were called in from other colonies; warships were sent to the area; Nigerian troops patrolled the streets; the prime minister was kept informed. Officials in adjacent French colonies were warned that the movement might spread, and Nigeria was prepared for a similar eventuality.[74]

In the aftermath of February–March 1948, officials constructed an image of disorderly masses and unscrupulous demagogues. They asserted that the the UGCC was responsible, and that it had egged the ex-servicemen on, and in turn the masses: "The greed and baser feelings generally of the rougher types of the population have been stimulated but the consequential thieving and destruction has been attributed to the outraged feelings of the ex-servicemen." The allegation of "communist influence" surfaced in almost the same breath.[75] Ten days after the event, six leaders of the UGCC, including Danquah and Nkrumah, were put in detention without charges, leading to a brief flare up of protests. Governor Creasy made a radio broadcast to justify his action: "the restrictions on these men are in no sense a punishment or a reprisal, they are purely a preventive measure in the interest of the peaceful, the progressive, the democratic element in the country. They are like the quarantine which is imposed on people who have caught a dangerous infectious disease."[76]

It was a powerful simile: the political leader as disease vector within a vulnerable body. Creech Jones, responding to Creasy, focused on the role of

illiterate and semi-literate population in the towns and urban areas... I imagine that it is very largely among such people that the followers, as opposed to the leaders, in the recent troubles have been found. It has seemed to me for some time that many of our most serious difficulties in Africa are going to lie on relations with these detribalised urban people... [The] Gold Coast government will be considering possible means of securing more effective representation of actual working populations and at the same time more effective contact with them.[77]

Breaking the demagogue-mass connection was to be the key: workers would have to be brought within a framework of institutions, and the government would seek "the sympathy and goodwill of responsible and educated elements."[78] The word "responsible" would recur again and again in official writing.

What colonial officials had constructed immediately after the 1948 riots – based on longer experience of disorder in the colonial empire –

was a set of images of demagoguery attached to actual political figures, and a set of images, which were truly imaginary, of their polar opposite: the "responsible" political leader. The label "communist" was sometimes attached to the former – although its contents were usually no more than a set of contacts and friendships Nkrumah and other leaders acquired around anti-imperialist circles in London.[79] The "responsible" element existed only as a logical antithesis to the demagogues: the British government put the moderate Danquah in jail alongside the more radical Nkrumah. Similarly, in Nigeria at this time, the businessman Azikiwe and his youthful (and rather independent) followers the Zikists were being described as radical, violent, dangerous, and demagogic, as was the leftist labor leader Nduka Eze.[80]

Governor Creasy applied the vocabulary of demagogues and masses to union leaders and the rank and file:

There is no doubt that certain extremists and hot-heads, particularly in Sekondi-Takoradi, have been trying to foment real trouble, especially on the railway, and if they were to get the upper hand there might well be further violent disturbances, the consequences of which elsewhere in the country, in the present stage of general unsettlement, might well have very serious effects.[81]

He was not altogether without a point: the educated, politically-attuned, and militant leadership of the Railway Union and the TUC were ready to take on the colonial administration on many fronts. But intelligence reports were already revealing that unions were hesitant and divided on the issue of striking for "a purely political objective." Northerners, notably in the Mine Employees' Union, did not identify their own cause with that of the more politicized southerners. The union of public works department employees decided not to strike.[82]

The official analysis of the riots and their significance, the Watson Commission Report, only partly deserves the billing of "radical document" which some historians bestow on it.[83] It did declare that the rule of chiefs was "on the wane," that the achievement of self-government in India, Burma, and Ceylon could not go unnoticed in Africa, and that many Africans were deeply suspicious of colonial government. It looked to the creation of more modern institutions of local government and toward central legislative bodies with real power, although with "a probationary period of ten years."[84] Watson represented above all a new earnestness in the ongoing search for the responsible African politician.

The commission did not actually find any. The leaders of the UGCC were condemned and mocked. It noted that of the 1,300 or 1,400 senior civil servants, only 98 were African. There were 171 students in Great Britain whose training might make them eligible in the future for such appointments.[85]

The commission, acknowledging that Africans had legitimate grievances regarding agriculture, education, and labor, stuck to a development-minded framework. It, for example, thought the Cocoa Marketing Board was justified in withholding a significant proportion of the currently high world price from producers, in order to prevent inflation and to insure that the money was used constructively. It was disparaging about Africans' calls for industrialization, considering it merely a "vague desire for something that promised wealth and higher standards of life." But it backed the Volta River dam and investment in secondary industry. It had nothing very innovative to say about labor, although one of its members, Arthur Dalgleish, was a trade union expert who around this time authored a report about Africanization in the Copperbelt (see chapter 8). It claimed that its witnesses, the Gold Coast TUC included, had said "very little...about wages and working conditions." It supported the reformist thrust of the commissions which had studied civil service salaries and backed the principle of equal pay for equal work in the civil service. Like other commentators on labor – in French as well as British Africa – it treated agricultural labor as a mystery, saying "that employment of labour in the cocoa industry takes a variety of forms which meantime admits of no general recommendation."[86]

The constitutional reforms pressed by the Watson Commission, the aspect of the report most often stressed, were thus part of a generalized developmentalism, a measuring of progress around European institutions and categories. But the commission did not seem convinced of its own argument: its progressive views on representative institutions and Africanization in the civil service were counterbalanced by its apparent belief that most of the people capable of serving in such contexts were still in school. It did not get very far from the government's demagogues-mass model, with a touch of communism thrown in. The commission thought it appropriate to write of the "peoples of the Gold Coast": "We found them a lovable people whose hearts were in the right place."[87]

The implications of this ambivalence and anxious embrace of development and constitutional advance were contradictory. Socially, tight control from London was needed to insure that colonies got serious about building a responsible trade union movement but that such a movement be prevented from becoming "political" – I will take up this theme in chapter 8. Politically, there was no choice but to devolve some of that control. The quest for the responsible African politician to save the Gold Coast from the masses led officials to convene a new constitutional commission, the Coussey Committee, representing as wide a spectrum of moderate, educated African opinion as officials could tolerate. That included five of the UGCC six, with the conspicuous exception of Nkrumah.

The strategy insured two results: the Colonial Office would not be in a position to reject any consensus recommendation of the Coussey Committee and this, as one would expect from the modernizing Africans on the committee, led to another step away toward a system focusing on elections as the source of legitimacy. And it gave Nkrumah, unlike his rivals, a position from which to criticize the incomplete nature of proposed reforms. Nkrumah used the opportunity brilliantly to forge his own support base, rooted among urban workers, young men with only a limited education, and other "popular" (and very largely urban) elements, which eventually broke away from the UGCC and became the Convention People's Party (CPP).[88]

In official eyes, the UGCC turned from the demagogues of February–March 1948 into the moderates of 1949, while the CPP took on the mantle of irresponsiblity. Intelligence reports kept warning of "roughs among the young men," of new rumors of boycotts and strikes, and of trade union activists who were trying to find political collaborators more radical than "Dr. Danquah and Company."[89] In May 1949, officials worried that their attempt to isolate the radical intelligentsia from the (presumably traditionalist) will of the people was backfiring:

Nkrumah and his party continue to catch the public imagination... Nkrumah's influence is now spreading not only into the countryside but also into the trade unions. His declared object, in the event of a degree of self-government satisfactory to him not being granted, is to adopt the tactics of non-co-operation, to bring about a sit-down strike and make the work of the present Administration impossible by non-violent methods. That these methods can be operated by the African temperament in the present political temperature of the Gold Coast without degeneration into violence seems unlikely, and it is at least probable that Nkrumah realises this.[90]

Trade unions – intended to be the voice of a defined social category – risked instead bringing workers into a different sort of mobilization. The fear of the mass made it imperative to bargain with the responsible: "The worst is that the [Coussey] Committee or a majority of it may be stampeded either by conviction or expediency or even fear into producing recommendations which go far beyond anything which H.M.G. are likely to accept."[91]

This is pretty close to how things turned out. From mid-1948 to mid-1949, the labour department reported twenty-seven strikes, most small, but some – particularly in the mining sector and in the Sekondi-Takoradi region – quite significant. In the next year, there were fifty-five strikes involving 39,000 workers; many of these strikes were successful. If gaining a measure of control meant paying workers more, officials now wanted to pay up: the "gold mine industry must do something urgently

to improve the position of their labour, if they wish to avoid a strike..."[92]
The acting governor, in June 1949, attributed the "labour unrest" first to
continued inflation and tight food supplies for the cities and second –
"the chief reason" – to Nkrumah's influence. The radical leader was
engaged in an "intensive drive to forge organised labour into the spearhead of his attack on ordered government." Creech Jones told the
incoming governor, Sir Charles Arden-Clarke, before his arrival in
August that he feared the colony was "on the edge of revolution."[93]

The government was not entirely paranoid when it came to the Gold
Coast's oldest and most militant unions, in the railways. Anthony Woode
and Pobee Biney, both educated southern Gold Coasters, led the railway
unions into a militant, nationalist politics. When the TUC tried to follow
the British-backed vision of non-political trade unionism, Biney and
Woode seized the initiative within that organization and brought it into
an alliance with Nkrumah.[94] The labour commissioner, G. N. Burden,
thought Nkrumah was working with "irresponsible malcontents in the
trade unions" and with their help was "working up the illiterate and semi-
literate elements of the town populations to a trial of strength with
government." The labour department had been "encouraging counsels of
moderation and constructive effort in the T.U.C. and the big Trade
Unions, but I know that we all feel that at present we are waging a losing
battle and the forces of disorder are gaining all the time." Burden and
others thought that Nkrumah had a following among junior civil servants,
and that their "subversive influences" threatened the government.[95]

At the end of 1949, the TUC was contemplating a general strike and
Nkrumah was building up support for a campaign of "positive action,"
a program of civil disobedience intended to make it impossible for
government to function. Ever since the middle of 1949, the government
had feared that "a series of strikes or a general strike that would cripple
essential services" would be a vital part of Nkrumah's positive action.[96]

But officials underestimated the extent to which their policy of encouraging trade unions as autonomous bodies devoted to "industrial" issues
had succeeded. The trade union movement was divided over "positive
action." The large Mine Employees' Union in particular was split
between its southern, educated leadership, which favored cooperation
with Nkrumah's CPP, and largely northern underground miners who
were deeply involved in struggles over very particular sets of work issues.
Nkrumah himself vacillated on the subject of a general strike. In the end,
the TUC acted in response to the firing of government workers from a
member union which had led a brief strike, but the general strike – 6 to
19 January 1951 – proved to be less than general, particularly outside of
the Sekondi-Takoradi and Accra regions.[97] It was in the context of this

division, that the government – as it had when Kenya's African Workers' Federation lost its initiative – stepped up its repression. The urban demonstrations were countered with strong police measures – plus official talk comparing their action to the anti-guerrilla actions in Malaya – and Nkrumah and other leaders were arrested for fomenting an illegal strike.[98]

The corollary to taking on the extremists was embracing the moderates. This meant accepting, in essence, the new steps toward the devolution of legislative and executive power recommended by the Coussey Committee, which indeed went further than officials would have liked to go. In urging in October 1949 the British Cabinet to accept the proposed constitutional changes, Creech Jones brought out the contrast of responsibility and moderation versus extremism and disorder:

During the past eighteen months there has been considerable political agitation in the Gold Coast and the extremists have been conducting a campaign for immediate responsible government, which has attracted support among the less responsible elements. There is, however, a large body of moderate opinion which, while recognizing that the country is not yet ready for full responsible government is convinced, as the governor and I myself are, that immediate constitutional advance is necessary. If we are not prepared to accept it [the Coussey Report] broadly, moderate opinion will be alienated and the extremists given an opportunity of gaining further and weightier support and of making serious trouble.

In handwritten notes attached to a copy of this Cabinet Paper in his papers, Creech Jones had written, presumably for his presentation to the meeting, "Continuous political agitation. Disturbances." He concluded, "Delay and irresponsible elements come to surface. Act now and opportunity of getting the responsible moderate opinion."[99]

Creech Jones convinced his fellow Cabinet members, but he could not convince the people of the Gold Coast that his moderates were what they wanted. With Nkrumah in jail, the CPP won the election of February 1951 under the new constitution. Nkrumah went almost directly from jail to state house, as leader of government business, a sort of junior prime minister. Governor Arden-Clarke had, in the run up to the election, realized what was about to happen and that there was little alternative but to accept it. But the Political Intelligence Report on the Gold Coast for February 1951 included a long justification for this decision, which amounted to an epitaph for the politics of demagogues and masses:

In the present political circumstances it is not expedient to keep in jail the leader of a party which commands the enthusiastic support of such a large section of the electorate and who has himself had an overwhelming victory in Accra. His Excellency would have been faced with an ultimatum and widespread agitation if he refused to accept it. There would not of course have been the remotest chance of securing C.P.P. co-operation in the working of the new Constitution in the latter circumstances, and it is obviously desirable to avoid if possible a situation in which the governor is faced with either yielding to an ultimatum or jeopardising the working of the Constitution and evoking widespread agitation.[100]

These words were, among other things, a confession of powerlessness. This text also deferred to popular opinion, acknowledging its preference for a man the state had chosen to jail. The next ideological task for the British bureaucracy began immediately: to reconstruct the Apostle of Disorder as the Man of Moderation and Modernity. By June, the Colonial Office was writing about the need "to keep on good terms with the more responsible political leaders such as Mr. Nkrumah."[101]

Conclusion: modernity, backwardness, and the colonial state

At the end of World War II, colonial officials in France and Great Britain self-consciously put forth new conceptions and new justifications for colonial policy for the post-war years. A few years later, their policies and the thinking that lay behind them were indeed quite different from pre-war patterns, but not in the way officials expected. They found that they were facing not just a long-run problem of directed social change, but an immediate question of control. The challenge occurred at a time when imperial regimes were unusually open to the intellectual implications of policies and concerned about international scrutiny of their words and actions, and when the metropoles needed the imperial economy more than ever.

The challenges combined, at the same moment, colonial officials' best hopes and worst fears. From the Assemblée Nationale Constituante in Paris to the mass meetings of Mombasa and Dakar, officials not only heard their own words turned back at them, but they also saw the possibility that Africa's workers might express themselves through a familiar institution like a trade union. The social movements described in these pages seemed balanced on a knife's edge, taking modern forms but also revealing elements of a truly mass revolt, threatening at times to bring in the riff-raff of the city and the peasants of the countryside. Should the masses be mobilized by a Chege Kibachia or a Kwame Nkrumah, the danger could spill far beyond the context of urban workers and consumers, threatening the colonial state, and worse still its modernizing projects. However much colonial officials feared trade unions as a locus of power, the alternative was worse.

French and British colonial officials haltingly moved to think of the world of work as having its own structures, its own rules. Past colonial policies, in this context, were an albatross around officials' necks: coerced labor grudgingly performed, migratory and casual labor, the small extent of wage differentials, the lack of job security, the absence of housing suitable for families, all this blurred the boundaries between workers and farmers, between workers and urban low-life, between workers conscious

261

of their profession and their skills and the footloose, between the diligent and the lazy, between the orderly and the dangerous. Officials, in the heat of struggles, made moves – tentative or decisive – to separate workers vertically and horizontally into hierarchies and occupations and to separate workers from other Africans.

The attempt to turn the recognition of the labor problem and the rapid adjustments made to the crises of the late 1940s into coherent policies – focused on the idea of "stabilizing" labor – will be the subject of the following chapters. Even in the heat of conflict, it was clear that efforts to delimit a terrain for labor disputes would sometimes be more successful than others. The 1947–48 railway strike in French Africa remained a railway strike; the strike wave in the Gold Coast in 1947–48 did not remain inside such boundaries. Some unions and workers became caught up in a political process that pushed them together with other urban inhabitants and a "mass" threat remained acute in 1951.

The contrast of these two cases cannot be attributed solely to differences in labor policy – although the institutional clarity of the French system gave organized workers a larger stake in keeping their particular grievances inside the industrial relations machinery – for the political moment was quite a different one in the Gold Coast. But two patterns of institutionalizing labor organization were in play: the French system made it easier for trade unions to strengthen themselves as institutions. This did not necessarily make unions less political, and indeed the very process of state regulation gave the unions a reason and a means of posing political demands in the name of workers in general. The less clear-cut British industrial relations system and the more fragmented unions made it unlikely that a generalized claim for, say, family allowances for all workers, could emerge. The catch for British officials was that in the Gold Coast, Nigeria, Kenya, and elsewhere the problem of the inchoate but militant mass emerging out of the general strikes of the 1940s did not get resolved.

The obvious contrast to these initiatives is South Africa, and the differences are a clear warning that one should not posit a mechanical connection between the conjuncture of the post-World War II years (or even the escalation of labor conflict) and policies to stabilize labor and incorporate it into political institutions; these are ultimately political choices. South Africa for a time seemed poised to lead a shift toward stabilization, and with its large mining industry and rapidly growing manufacturing sector it was in a position to do this on a larger scale than any other part of Africa. It did not. After the Nationalist victory in the 1948 elections, the South African government made determined use of police powers to reinvigorate the migratory system and to expel massive numbers of city dwellers to rural areas and to a life deemed to be "African."

South Africa's confrontation with the labor question, like that of Great Britain and France, came about not just because of increasing numbers of workers in wage labor, but because of workers' collective action. In South Africa, this had happened first around 1920, but an escalation of urban strikes during World War II and the gold mineworkers' strike of 1946 sharply confronted the government and the voting white public with urban and industrial labor as a question of order. The Fagan Commission – like various commissions in British Africa – appeared to be bringing official sanction to the notion that the African urban worker was a reality that had to be accepted and controlled within urban space itself.[1] South African experts on welfare, meanwhile, pioneered the notion that social issues could be treated as technical problems, solvable by European social engineering, and they contributed to the efforts of the Kenyan government in particular to face the labor question.[2]

The divergence, then, appears as a direct consequence of the South African electorate's decision to embrace apartheid, with its notion of separateness, and reject stabilization. But on closer examination even that appears too simple, for South African government policy – whatever its formal ideological basis – in fact sought to fracture the working population into segments with different access to urban legal status and housing, and these fractures were manipulated in a pragmatic way to accomplish goals not altogether dissimilar from those of the post-war colonial powers: to transform an unpredictable mass of labor power, moving into and out of employment, into distinct components that could be more readily controlled.[3] One clear contrast, however, was that the post-1948 era in South Africa witnessed the enormous growth of the native affairs department bureaucracy – for it was there that the necessary policing functions were concentrated – whereas in British and French Africa, the provincial bureaucracies strikingly lost prestige in favor of the "technical" departments, including labor.[4] That had extremely important ideological implications, for the South African approach, however mixed its material results, was to push African workers back into the essential category of "African" (or "Bantu" or "Xhosa" or "Zulu"); whereas the French and British approach, however incomplete the reforms it envisaged, pushed African workers into the acultural, asocial, and ahistorical category of the wage worker.

South African politics reflected a quite differentiated capitalist system: mines, white farmers, manufacturers, and others were not so much trying to choose between "migrant" and "stable" labor policies as to insure access to particular segments of the African laboring population and to balance their needs against others, and against the white working class as well. Colonial regimes – in their original projects and in their responses to the challenge of labor – also were acting in complex relationship to capital. The colons of the Ivory Coast, the settlers of Kenya, the commercial firms of Dakar, the gold mine corporations of the Gold Coast, and the shipping companies of Mombasa were not the sources of initiative after World War II; all, to at least some degree, opposed the way in which officials reframed the labor question, and in particular the governments' willingness to pay higher wages and benefits in exchange for stability and, in some cases, to cooperate with trade unions (although the roles were to some extent reversed in Northern Rhodesia, as noted in chapter 8).

In a capitalist society, as some theorists argue, the state should stand above the immediate interests of capital, not only refereeing disputes among capitalists but ensuring that too much profit maximization or too much competition does not impede the reproduction of the system. The most obvious and important action of the "semi-autonomous" state is to coopt labor – something which would go against the interests of any one firm or sector to do – in order to contain conflict. The distinctive institutional and symbolic apparatus of the state – its impersonal bureaucracy, its emphasis on the autonomy of judicial institutions, its cultivation of patriotic symbols – all separate its authority from capital accumulation and make it possible for such a concept as "private property" to be defined socially as a natural right and not the result of a process of class appropriation and coercion.[5]

The colonial state is a special kind of state, a component of a more broadly situated imperial state. Its political base, and the point from which the cultural and social background of its officers emanates, is distinct from the social formation in which it acts. In Africa, the population was at most partly alienated from the means of production, and in this fundamental sense colonial states did not preside over capitalist economies. Notions of free markets and free citizenship did not provide a rationale and legitimation for the way colonial states dealt with their subjects, even when such constructs were invoked in debates in imperial capitals.[6]

Bruce Berman and John Lonsdale's studies of Kenya emphasize that colonial states were constantly caught in the contradiction of accumulation and legitimation, oscillating between coercive intervention in the interests of capital and restraint of capital in the name of paternalism.[7] But these issues came to the fore in the late 1940s in a particularly pointed way in French and British Africa. Part of this has to do with the problem of forced labor. It was only in 1946 that the French government, with help from African politicians and an African farmers' organization, freed itself from undertaking direct coercion in the labor market; the British government, despite its tendencies to be sanctimonious on this subject, had relapsed into such coercion during the war. The banishing of the forced labor question freed officials to distance themselves from direct service to capital and to take up the regulation of the labor question from a loftier perch in the labour departments and Inspections du Travail.

But the colonial state could not abstract itself from an overtly power-laden intervention into social and economic life by virtue of the fact that it was colonial. It could not legitimate its autonomy from capitalist firms, despite all the very real conflicts between officials and capitalists, because both had political representation in the metropole, from which governmental authority derived, while Africans (except a limited number in France) did not.

The working populations of Europe experienced social questions in relation to a highly contested and complex involvement in politics itself. The kinds of rights and protections that labor acquired – accident insurance, unemployment compensation, retirement pensions, the right to organize, free and universal public education – were not so old and not so secure in 1945. Labor regulation and welfare reflected specific combinations of mobilization by organized labor and attempts of middle classes to assure themselves against the risks of industrial civilization and of capitalist interests to balance competition and security.

In the colonies as in the metropoles, the initiatives of governments and international organizations constituted the objects of their policies in a particular way. The "worker" – who might be entitled to certain rights – was envisioned against the "mass" – which was dangerous and backward – and against "traditional society," whose cultural backwardness necessitated the intervention of colonial powers in the first place. The theoretical acceptance, partial as it was, of the African as a worker was set against the increasingly negative terms in which the African who did not choose to participate in this framework was held. This led not only to belittling stereotypes of Africans invoked in public and private discussion or the willingness to use forced labor in soil conservation projects, but to some of the ugliest instances of colonial violence in the twentieth century, as in Madagascar in 1947 and Kenya in 1952, let alone Algeria, Malaya, or Indochina, all set in contrast against the delicate handling of the strikes described above. Even as colonial governments came to imagine for the first time an urban worker as a rational being located within institutions of family, workplace, and trade union, their authoritarianism remained strong in the areas they deemed to be backward.

The gendering of the African worker was so profound it was barely discussed. The entire discussion of danger and of promise – of the African worker becoming productive – assumed a male worker. But the role of women was crucial to changing perceptions. The male wage earner, after all, would remain a wage worker under migrant or stabilized regimes. What made the difference was where the wife and child were located, in the rural village or near the urban worksite. At an extreme, as in Southern Rhodesia, urban housing regulations denied women a right to live in the city except as a dependent of a male – whose rights came from his job – or in quite closely defined job categories. Women – and the evidence is becoming steadily richer – in fact occupied diverse economic roles in cities, including small-scale commerce, the provision of services (legal or otherwise) to workers, providing access to housing.[8] As Luise White has shown, colonial regimes in the early twentieth century could tolerate women's initiatives in colonial cities, on the grounds that their services helped to reproduce without official effort a badly underpaid migrant labor force, but it was in the era of labor reform when they cracked down on independent women for fear that they would reproduce the wrong sort of labor force.[9] Women appeared in official narratives of the 1940s strikes as people linking male strikers to a wider African community, denying, as market sellers, food to whites, and providing it through their own networks and rural connections to strikers. In the imagination of post-war officials, this kind of connectedness was threatening. As the following chapters will show, both French and British officials believed women's presence *as wives* living with and off their wage-earning husbands could bring forth the next generation of workers in an atmosphere removed from the primitiveness of the African village. Women stood for both a danger – what was truly African about Africa – and a hope, for a new generation of Africans who would represent officials' imagined Africa rather than the one they then saw. Meanwhile, the complexity of what actual women did in cities, in workplaces, and in markets was not something officials were eager to investigate.

Governments dealt with Africans as collective actors because they had no choice; the strike wave made that much clear. Much more ambiguous were the relations between Africans as the objects of social reform and as political actors. Both British and French governments, in quite different ways, were trying to construct some kind of junior citizenship through which colonized people could partake of some, but not all, of the qualities of a metropolitan citizen. This not only took the form of the flurry of constitutional inventions which characterized the late 1940s, but also entailed a recasting of the way in which the state presented its authority. The paramount authority of the wise white man who knew his natives, the district officer or the commandant du cercle, lost credibility in the face of the challenges of the 1940s – conflicts over restructuring agriculture as well as labor – and instead the state claimed authority in the name of abstract, universal principles applied to a collectivity of individual subjects.

In the case of France, the eagerness to define colonial subjects as citizens in 1945 and 1946 opened up political space for an assertion, evident in the forced labor debates and the follow-up to the Dakar strike of 1946, that labor also had to be discussed as if the African worker were a rational human being, similar to other workers. In British Africa, the opening appeared in the other direction, as efforts to control strikes beginning in the late 1930s led officials to think of the African worker as someone amenable to forms of negotiation and discipline familiar from the metropole even before they were willing to think of the mass of Africans as rational political actors. But in both cases, the quest for the responsible worker, the responsible voter, and the responsible politician – and the responsible mother – influenced each other.

The problem was that officials didn't quite believe what their own developmentalist position assumed. Even as the colonial state escaped its former association with coerced labor, the men who made it up retained, for the most part, their notion of the peculiarity of the African which had formerly justified direct coercion. The myth of the backward African coexisted with the myth of the universal worker in considerable tension, which crept into numerous commentaries quoted above and which underlay the fear that workers would either desert the workplace altogether or foment mass violence. But, in redefining their own authority through possession of knowledge of how to run a society and in constituting the African laborer as an individual subject, officials placed themselves where their claim to superintending a universal social process stood in uneasy relation to the lingering fact that they ruled a colony. The language with which French and British officials discussed their numerous crises was laced through both with notions of wise men supervising backward peoples and with a simplified view of the European past, of an idealized managed capitalism that offered solutions to problems of the workplace or of urban living.

The profound – although not uncontested – move toward developmentalism and social engineering after the war might have evolved even without the challenge of the post-1935 and post-war strike waves in Africa and other challenges throughout the empires. Perhaps they would have got to the stage of the 1945 British development initiative or the French development fund – or to the kinds of actions labour departments and the Inspection du Travail were taking – a few years after they did, or perhaps decades. But in the event, the challenges of the 1930s and 1940s forced the issue, denied officials any hope of approaching African societies as organic and peaceful backwaters, to be protected or plundered but not to be reformed, and led them to bring to Africa their knowledge of how a state under industrial capitalism contained social problems and directed change.

In the case of French West Africa, the transition occurred very rapidly, when the striking workers of Dakar confronted the government with an immediate problem with no solution in the colonial past but an apparent one in the European present. The transition in British Africa can be charted in investigations into strikes from 1935 to 1947, but it was no less profound for its less precipitous pace.

The profound racism of colonial rule remained evident in officials' fear that African workers were always on the verge of deserting the labor market, fomenting "mass" violence, or reverting to the backwardness of village life. The depiction of African cultural backwardness had long been a part of racial ideologies, and remained part of official thinking even when colonial governments formally repudiated racial discrimination and looked increasingly toward the incorporation of Africans into a world of wage labor, economic rationality, generalized education, and citizenship. The fact that "capital," whatever it was in theory, generally came with white skins, as did the people who constituted the "state," was still an important fact. The commonality of language, social connections, and participation in metropolitan politics underscored the racial division that derived from conquest itself.[10]

But it was far from unmediated. A comparison of the way two colonial states in the 1940s, the Ivory Coast and Kenya, dealt with their colons and settlers illustrates how post-war ideas of progress intersected the racial structure of colonial society. By 1946, the colons of the Ivory Coast had nothing to offer except casting the state indefinitely in the role of man-catcher. The Société Agricole Africaine removed its last claim to a necessary role, providing an alternative source of fuel for the railway, exports, and revenue without raising questions about the integrity of the state. The settlers of Kenya, however, had something to offer which seduced even the Fabians who had criticized white privilege for years: agricultural development. Weaned from forced labor and understanding the interplay of capital and labor, they undertook the mechanization, rationalization, and expansion of agriculture in the favorable market conditions of the late 1940s. In their own ways, the settlers were no less brutal than the colons: the massive expulsion of squatters in the name of more efficient production caused the destruction of a way of life. But within a developmentalist framework, this meant exports, revenue, and a model of progress for Africans to follow.[11]

As soon as one takes seriously the role of human agency in making states work, and as soon as one examines contradictions of differing projects, differing interests, differing conceptions of change, the functionality of outcomes appears contingent rather than necessary. In the case of the colonial state from the 1940s onward, a profound question was raised: could the state assume a detached, abstracted role, distancing itself from any particular form of capital, fostering what officials conceived of as a universal form of progress, arbitrating conflicts that developed along the way, and still remain a colonial state?

Part III
The imagining of a working class

Introduction

Much of what has been written about African labor history conforms to a master narrative: more and more Africans went to work, their lives became increasingly dependent on wages, they became conscious of the extent of their exploitation and their vulnerability to the whims of capitalists and the vagaries of markets, and they formed trade unions and conducted strikes, making themselves into a working class. The story's power – the linear momentum that sustains it and the way it ties an African tale into a global one – is also what is problematic about it. The strike wave occurs too soon, among casual and migrant workers as well as relatively long-term ones, and the strikers' success is as much a phenomenon of communities – and complex ties of affiliation and support linking urban and rural areas – as it is of a class of people who can be specifically identified as workers. The general strikes of the 1940s were a class phenomenon in the broadest sense – collective acts of sellers of labor power in general and those closely tied to them. But as such the strike wave is a conjunctural phenomenon, not a pathway to ever deeper unity, and class mobilization occurred most powerfully when it was simultaneously mass mobilization, a populist rising of petty traders, unemployed or semi-employed youth, and of people with strong connections to agricultural and fishing communities. The Mombasa general strike of 1947 was the last event of such scope in that city, similarly with the Dakar strike of 1946 and others. There were to be sure different sorts of general strikes later on – notably those led by a highly organized Federation-wide union movement in French West Africa in the 1950s (see below), and some post-colonial regimes allowed elements of the postwar conjuncture to be repeated in the 1960s, with similar results. But the wave of general strikes of the late 1940s did not prove to be a stepping stone to a broader proletarian unity.

That was to a large extent a consequence of the fact that colonial states had their own kind of class consciousness. In the late 1940s and early 1950s, an African working class became for officials something to mold rather than to avoid. The 1945 report on labor unrest in Mombasa had referred to an "emergent urban working class," and argued that its emergence should be the basis of a new labor policy. When the wartime strikes continued into 1947 and 1948 and at times threatened to embrace entire urban populations and perhaps rural ones as well, the possibility that the sellers of labor power, as a whole, could be separated from the rest of Africa became an attractive one. French and British officials saw the bounded and potentially differentiated class as a positive alternative to the unbounded mass. And they saw a working class as something that could be socialized and tamed by techniques that were familiar in Europe.

This part of the book explores this imaginative process – set against the shifting terrain in which actual African workers strove to shape the work process in their own ways. It examines two variants on the theme: the systematic approach to conceptualizing African workers in relation to African society found in the debates on and the implementation of the French Code du Travail and the equally characteristic efforts of British policy makers to muddle through, a process which frequently got them into more muddles than they got through. But neither colonizer could escape the elusiveness of its object – the African worker, with all that he brought into the workplace and all that he invented and learned while he was there.

British and French governments, by 1946, had different styles of operation in colonial affairs, but similar institutions for handling the labor question: the Inspection du Travail and the labour department.[1] A brief word is needed about these organizations, whose expertise helped to influence the framing of the labor question as well as the implementation of policy. They inspected worksites to make sure labor laws were enforced, registered trade unions and kept an eye on their activities, intervened to set up negotiations and resolve disputes and strikes, monitored minimum wages and advised governors or wage boards on their revision, compiled data on the labor force, and advised on labor legislation.[2] Both institutions were born in the 1930s, although the French version lapsed under Vichy, and was resurrected under decrees dating from 1943 and 1946. Its influence got a great boost from the Senegalese strikes of 1946, which shook the entire administration and revealed it had a basic problem which only expertise and attention could solve.[3] The British version was a child of the disorders of the late 1930s (earlier departments having lapsed during the Depression), and expanded during the era of tense labor relations during the war itself. By 1946, 33 of the 35 colonies had labour departments, and 200 officers were trying to solve the labor problem, as were a labour advisor and a colonial labour advisory committee in London.[4] The French government created after the war the Inspection Générale du Travail, with an inspector in Paris and others in Dakar and Brazzaville, to superintend the work of the inspectors in each territory. These structures constituted a locus for new arguments about labor, and they had a bureaucratic interest in giving the labor question a specific focus and prominence.

Repeated insistence that the labor question be taken seriously was not always welcomed by provincial administrations, loci of the idea that ruling Africans required its own sort of expertise. The strike waves gave the specialists a strong impetus – the men who knew their natives did not have the relevant answers. The labor experts were part of the technical services within both colonial services, and these were undergoing a large expansion in the post-war years, as colonial administrations focused on development and on the control of knowledge as the raison d'être of colonialism.[5]

But ambiguity did not just disappear. In 1946, the Colonial Office's labour advisor, Orde Browne, wrote about labour officers in language that reproduced the ideology of the provincial administration. He admitted that the African colonies had workers in railways, mines, factories, and commercial firms who could be "regarded as largely industrialized" and for whom labour officers with "European experience" were necessary. But the large majority were occasional wage-earners, and

To be of service to such workers, a Labour Officer must have a wide experience of Africans, their habits, customs, and idiosyncracies. He must be familiar with scurvy, beriberi, ulcers, and the other diseases of tropical labour; he needs a good knowledge of diet, and the accompanying tribal practices, prejudices and vulnerability; and above all, he must have a comprehension of African psychology and mentality.

Orde Browne, himself a military man, thought he knew where to find the ideal candidate for a labour officer: the Army. He wanted men with "experience of campaigning with African troops."[6] Giving orders to Africans was apparently what it took to be a labour officer.

Other opinion emphasized the need to make the position of labour officer as attractive as any other. Recruits usually came from the ministry of labour, from trade unions, or from some line of work where they had previous experience with labor; they were to be made to "feel that they can make a career in the Colonial Service."[7] They went through the short courses organized in England for the Colonial Service and, if that is not where they came from, served internships with the ministry of labour in order to imbibe metropolitan approaches to industrial relations and union organizing.

The Inspection du Travail of French Africa was underfunded but less insecure in its status. Although in the 1930s its duties were performed by administrators temporarily assigned to it, after the war a corps of inspectors was recruited in parallel to the other administrators, given special training, and sent on internships in France under a metropolitan labor inspector.[8] As of 1946, there were supposed to be fifteen full-fledged labor inspectors in French West Africa; there were in fact four, plus eleven others on secondment from other branches or interns. These numbers gradually improved, and a special track in the Ecole Nationale de la France Outre-Mer (ENFOM, formerly the Ecole Supérieure Colonial) was set up to train Inspecteurs du Travail, insuring that they would be schooled in colonial administration as well as metropolitan approaches to industrial relations. When the task of implementing the Code du Travail of 1952 befell the Inspection, it had grown to sixty-five inspectors plus seventeen trainee labor inspectors from ENFOM.[9]

In French West Africa, the institution had been taken in charge in 1946 by Pierre Pélisson, who had experience in the West Indies and with Indochinese workers in France.[10] Soon, an assertive inspectorate got into conflicts with governors – normally considered "le roi de la brousse"(king of the bush), but evidently not "le roi du chantier" (king of the workplace) – usually over such questions as whether the administration should go the extra yard to appease strikers or whether they should draw the line firmly at maintaining the law.[11]

Meanwhile, the rise of the specialists within the bureaucracy, and the election of Africans to political office, compromised the prestige and authority of the provincial administrators and of chiefs. By 1949, the minister was feeling the need to reaffirm the "principle of authority" in political administration, reassuring officers that the intervention of elected politicians would not affect their careers. African chiefs, meanwhile, were buffetted by their loss of the power to use forced labor, by the interventions of technical departments, and by interventions into their constituencies by political parties.[12] The ultimate sign of a shift in the nature of authority was that "traditional chiefs" in the 1950s tried to organize themselves into trade unions.[13]

Such was the changing structure of colonial authority in relation to which the labor question of the post-war years was posed.

7 The systematic approach: the French Code du Travail

French and British administrations could not possibly have approached the resolution of the labor question in the same ways. The administrative and political structure of the British empire made it difficult to enact comprehensive change in any policy domain while that of the French empire necessarily put corresponding issues into the lap of the legislature in Paris. Yet both regimes were responding to crises that could not be analyzed, let alone resolved, in the context of colonial authority as previously constituted. In trying to channel labor movements into imaginable directions, French and British officials achieved contradictory results: the labor legislation they enacted created an aura of reassurance that Africans would act within familiar boundaries, even as the appeal to the universality of work provided a basis for African unions to make more claims.

Imperial politics and labor reform

At first, it appeared as if the labor question after the war would be revived in exactly the same form that the Popular Front had left it in, both by revising the *politique du paysannat* and by seeking to bring legislative clarity to the small working class. In 1944, a first attempt was made to systematize and extend existing labor legislation into a Code du Travail, focused on workers who were "identifiable and locatable" and "permanent" (chapter 4). In 1945, two codes were issued for white and European workers. That effort quickly fell apart, a victim of two major events in 1946: the Senegalese general strike and the Parisian debate over citizenship within the French Union. The rhetoric of equality coming out of Dakar's labor movement went against any racially defined code, even if the labor movement welcomed the codification of its rights. French rhetoric about the unity of greater France – crucial to its defense of imperial power – made separate codes equally illogical.[1] The citizenship construct left a major question unanswered: would citizenship be limited to the political domain, or would the expanding realm of social citizenship – the protections French people received from the state by virtue of their nationality against the risks of modern life – be extended overseas? Labor legislation, social security, and family promotion policies lay at the heart of the question of social citizenship, and would be debated for the next ten years.

In France itself, the labor force had only recently achieved a substantial measure of stability; Vichy had been a disaster for labor and social regulation; the social security regime only achieved its modern form in 1946. But none of this mattered in the colonial context: stabilization and social security were talked about in the overseas ministry as if they were timelessly "French."[2]

The Inspection du Travail was an eager advocate of codification, and settling the 1946 strike had given its experts a sense of importance within the administration. When the dual codes were dropped in mid-1946, the Inspection had to write one that would apply to whites and blacks alike. That immediately raised the stakes of the question of who was to be defined as a worker in any future code: such a person would attain the entitlements of the white worker overseas.[3]

Hence the very argument that linked African workers to French workers also separated them from the rest of Africa. The chief labor inspector wrote in 1949 of the need "to select this work force and to improve its training, inspired by methods tried out elsewhere." The colonial minister, Coste-Floret, saw things the same way: "For the overly large masses of unskilled workers, it is important to substitute progressively a class of workers responding to the diverse specializations required by the modern economy."[4]

The inspection stressed the "goal of provoking stabilization of manpower," and advocated higher wages and seniority bonuses – up to 15 percent of wages – for long-serving workers. They wanted to raise the admittedly inadequate skill level of the work force. Such a program would not only "facilitate better output from labor" but would change a mode of life. Stabilization in labor would "make the family situation less unstable"; it would lead Africans, especially skilled workers, to "orient themselves progressively toward the European way of life."[5] Such changes not only justified higher wages, but implied that urban wages in general should be decoupled from rural incomes. The urban wage in Senegal, noted a special report on wages in 1949, should not be based on comparison with the potential earnings of a farmer, but on the necessity to "lead the African worker to a decent material level of life."[6]

Whereas as late as 1945, the governor-general and other high officials were hoping to avoid the creation of a proletariat, after the strikes of 1946 and the creation that same year of a metropole-funded development program, the consensus was reversed:

The worst error that we could commit would be to refuse Africa such an industrialization under the pretext of breaking the evolution of the masses and conserving as long as possible the peasantry in a primitive state that we believe to be tranquil. Frightened by the beginnings of African proletarianization and by that class struggle which inflames race struggle, certain Europeans have tended to oppose industrialization in order to maintain the peasant world of the savannas in what they call the good old times.[7]

At their most visionary, senior West African officials saw their mission was "to modernize," and not just industry. "No, the true modernization of Africa, this must be the industrialization of all methods of work, including agricultural methods."[8]

Officials would soon admit that they simply could not undertake so vast a task as "modernizing" the entire countryside. On the contrary, such forms of labor as practiced by the cocoa workers of the Ivory Coast or the *navétanes* of Senegal were being defined as not being work at all; they would be excluded from the purview of the Code du Travail (see below). That was why the experts, the labor inspectors, used the word "stabilization," which separated the workers who were transformed from those who were not.

The inspectors disparaged Africans who were unwilling to make the transition. The inspector in Senegal warned in 1951 that the "social prejudices and ancestral prejudices" of the Wolof and Serer peoples of his colony were an obstacle to "the promotion of the black worker to the standing of modern man." The inspector in Guinea wrote in 1946, "the native has a general repugnance for wage labor, for which he has no taste. He flees regular work, with its fixed hours." Such a work force was a "heavy handicap for the harmonious development of the country."[9]

The point, then, was to get African workers out of their customary milieu.[10] There were dangers if such a process was not carefully managed. Governor Roland Pré of Guinea, one of the most influential of the French governors, warned of the dangers of the "floating detribalized mass" in African cities, which past policies had been unable to stop or even slow. Like his British counterparts in the Gold Coast, he feared that such a mass would be taken in hand by "agitators" and lead to "the worst social or political adventures." But for him, the solution was to "deproletarianize this mass by educating it and raising its standard of living, thus integrating it into the urban social fabric which will naturally replace for it the customary tribal group from which it issued." By making labor more productive such a policy would not only solve a social and political problem but would "permit them to win the battle of production costs, that grand battle which the new Africa must win."[11]

In the late 1940s, the Inspection du Travail advanced its agenda to superintend the world of work. Factories were inspected and changes ordered. Employees brought complaints about employers' delinquencies. Inspectors arranged bargaining sessions and rushed off to a worksite when a wildcat strike took place.[12] Minimum wages were proclaimed for individual territories, albeit with a level of conflict – including a major strike in Guinea in 1950 – that belied attempts to pretend that wage setting was a "scientific" matter.[13] If the government's vigilance kept minimum wages on an uneven but upward course (see chapter 13), the more fundamental achievement was in the collective bargaining process. As of 1948, 152 collective bargaining agreements had been signed, 53 in the previous year alone. By 1951, the inspection was claiming that almost all enterprises in commerce, industry, and transport in FWA had signed such agreements, and that many firms which had not signed them followed their rules anyway. There still were some bitter strikes, but the containment mechanisms were working.[14] Collective bargaining and the labor market – particularly the shortage of skilled workers – made firms willing to do what the inspection hoped they would: reward stability and skill with substantial wage differentials. Outside of Senegal, the Inspection du Travail worked hard to extend model agreements to areas where unions were less well organized and the *patronat* less willing to anticipate demands.[15]

Despite the inspectors' belief that their approach to labor was making modest progress, they knew better than anyone else that anything they did stood on shaky legal footing. Most of the labor legislation – dating back to 1925 – referred specifically to "indigènes," but the citizenship legislation and constitution of 1946 rendered that category obsolete.[16] Officials were anxious as well to remove certain basic questions from the arena of contestation: the maximum work week, procedures for overtime payments, the principle of paid holidays, all these were regulated in France and officials wanted to see them regulated in Africa. The answer for them was a comprehensive Code du Travail de la France Outre-Mer.[17]

For one governor, from the Soudan, the case for the code was part of a regulatory impulse: citing past French achievements from the abolition of slavery to wage-hour regulations, he added, "It remains to insert the relations between employers and workers into rules and into still narrower limits, leaving to the arbitrary and to each person's fantasy a less vast framework."[18] Alongside the apparatus to regulate labor was the question of "social security." The term had been used at ILO conferences since 1944 in reference to nonmetropolitan countries and was coming up repeatedly in the meetings which the colonial powers had begun to hold on labor questions in 1948. In France, social security, revamped in 1946, was justified less on the notion of "insurance" than on that of "solidarity": French citizens were entitled to protection, paid for through a redistribution of the nation's income, against risks which they faced. The French system, as the Inspecteur Général du Travail interpreted it, aimed at "unity and universality." The law provided that the French system would at some unspecified time and in an unspecified way be extended to the colonies.[19] A committee within the ministry of Overseas France was thinking in 1946 about an effort "to install a system of social security, very large in regard to risks and beneficiaries and strongly resembling the current system perfected for the metropole."[20]

Officials in Dakar noted in 1947 that the "customary milieu" could not take care of people who had fallen victim to industrial diseases and that the question of retirement pensions had to be faced since "the worker, at the end of a certain number of years as a wage-earner, has lost all attachments with his milieu and can only with difficulty be reclassified as a peasant." But officials were worried about the implications of the universality of the French system, and the aspect of the system which brought out the most anxiety was family allowances. Officials had two sorts of fears: the costs "for a still embryonic economy" and the peculiarity of African family structure.[21]

The government-general in 1948 was of two minds: "The conditions of life and work of wage-earners will shortly lead to the elaboration of systems adapted from the metropolitan organization of Social Security..." However, "the current form of the traditional African family and its modes of existence, independent of wages properly speaking, has not permitted, until the present, the organization of an extended program of social assistance and security."[22] The problems with family allowances – or social security generally – were family parisitism and polygamy: the African extended family could diffuse the benefits intended to make workers' nuclear families autonomous and workers might themselves dissipate new resources by marrying more wives.

The issue, then, was whether the nature of African society made it possible for Africans to be citizens in a social sense as well as the constitutional one. Equally uncertain was just how universal universality would be: would the wealth of the metropole, the individual colonies, or French territories as a whole determine what level of social services could be paid for and hence how much belonging to the French Union actually offered?[23]

Family allowances were a recently acquired right for workers in France, at first provided by some employers, since 1932 by law. Before and during the war, few officials thought this issue relevant to Africans: family allocations were intended to promote the race, and Africans were neither of the right race nor did their race need promoting. The social security legislation of post-war France emphasized redistributing a certain amount of revenue in proportion to the burden of child care on particular families.[24] In Africa, the top ranks of the civil service were entitled to such payments, but that applied to an insignificant number of Africans, and evoked in official minds the category of "évolué" rather than "worker." The abortive labor code of 1945 referred to family allocations as a future possibility, when an état-civil (registry of marriages, births, etc.) had been established, but no-one seemed to think that was likely to be very soon. Some inspectors made clear that they did not think family allocations for Africans were practical.[25]

The break occurred in the 1946 strike. The civil servant unions had demanded the extension of family allocations to all ranks of government servants. They had won a partial victory: 25 and 50 percent of the top rate of family allocations for the two lower cadres. The principle that the family needs of even a lowly clerk fell into the same category as those of European civil servants had been won. But an anomaly was becoming apparent: even the top categories of workers in the private sector were not entitled to family allowances, whereas all workers in the public sector were. The railway strike – taking place in an industry ambiguously placed between the two – suggested that such anomalies could acquire political salience.

Meanwhile in the highly unionized public sector, it was hard to defend holding the line at unequal rates for certain categories, rather than having a single rate (the absolute amount varying with salary) for all. Governor-General Barthes, as early as February 1947, recognized that Africans in the civil service were in effect demanding a *cadre unique*, open to qualified applicants of all races and on similar terms. He supported such a goal in principle, and claimed to be making progress toward making the cadres simpler and more open.[26] The issue was pressed by civil service unions, and it was debated in the legislature as well. In 1950, the so-called Lamine Guèye law (sometimes the second Lamine Guèye law, since the citizenship act of 1946 also bears his name) established the principle that benefits, as well as wages, were to be equal for all civil servants. The decrees implementing this law, discussed in the Grand Conseil of French West Africa, where many of the legislators were veterans of the civil service, made clear that equal family allocations would be among the consequences of this act. There was opposition and predictions of dire consequences to budgets, but in such a context inequality proved indefensible.[27]

Officials now worried about "the dangers that could be provoked by a social disequilibrium resulting from the differences in resources between a privileged class which receives family allowances, the civil servants, and the rest of the population." A civil servant with three children received three to four times, in salary and family allowances, more than the ordinary wage earner, and the Inspecteur Général du Travail worried about having created a "mandarinate" of 30,000 to 40,000 civil servants.[28] Nor were the unions about to let this issue stay within the boundaries of civil service reform (see below).

Meanwhile, the very desire of the inspectors to mold a self-reproducing working class was weakening the argument about the peculiarity of African family life. In 1949, the Inspecteur Général du Travail in FWA argued that promoting "evolution" required taking urban workers out of the support mechanism of "customary life":

It would be regrettable if because of the state of mind of certain workers the evolution of the African family were stopped and if workers wanting to improve the material and moral conditions of life of their family were deprived of the support facilities which family allocations provide. The institution of a regime of family allocations becomes in current conditions necessary if we want to give the family the best chances of access to a less constricted social level.

In rural families, he noted, children were more of an asset than a burden. But urban families tended to "adopt a mode of existence approaching European life." It was the urban, Europeanized family – where the mother could afford to stay home – that should be encouraged. Therefore, family allowances would be limited strictly to "families of wage workers whose principal resource is limited to the wage of the worker" and further limited to "workers who are stabilized in a profession." Those only "temporarily separated" from families remaining in the "customary milieu" would be excluded. Allocations would thus be both a means of reproducing the working class and an incentive to enter it on a permanent basis. The argument also reveals – and this is only one such dimension – how starkly the urge to stabilize the urban working class implied a desire to treat it as a wholly different world from rural Africa.[29]

The governor-general, however, worried that workers would not really spend the money on their children, that the facilities on which workers were to spend their allocations were inadequate, that limiting family allocations to stabilized workers was wrong in principle, and that they might foster urban migration. He wanted the issue put off until after the Code du Travail was in place and more studies had been done.[30] The ministry entered into a frank and revealing debate on the subject in 1950 and 1951. Louis-Paul Aujoulat, secretary of state for Overseas France, an influential representative of social Catholicism, and a leading architect of the Code du Travail, sent a circular to high commissioners in Africa asking for a careful study of the problem. He was already pushing his view that the "family of European type" should benefit from cash aid funnelled through the wage packet and financed by employer contributions. He had no doubt that he was on the side of the future: "the evolution underway leads and without doubt will lead more and more to African society approaching the European type." Family allowances would promote monogamy, stability in employment, and a family life focused on raising children.[31]

The argument amounted to a virtual assault on African culture and a claim that European supervision was needed to remake it:

The disaggregation of the traditional family corresponds to an emancipation, a liberation of its members... The extended family must be succeeded by the household (and even the monogamous household), established by the reciprocal consent of the spouses, just as one can hope that the village or the tribe will little by little become the rural commune. And the African collectivity, organized, protected by the public French power, will in its turn be able to assure total and effective protection of the family and the child.[32]

Such evolutionist arguments not only made the case for family allowances, but they explained why such allowances should in Africa be limited to wage laborers, despite the fact that France provided them to the population as a whole. Such limitations were also advocated for practical reasons: "The wage earning sector has in effect a homogeneous structure, easily identifiable, generally monogamous and whose life style tends to approach the European mode."[33] To say that was less to state a fact than to offer a program: to define a class and its life style and to make it identifiable.

If one did not promote the right sort of families, the danger was demographic regression. Now the concern wasn't so much population decline in general, but the failure of a particularly desirable portion of the population – the working class – to reproduce itself. A survey done in 1949 in French Equatorial Africa – long the focus of demographic worries – showed that less than 40 percent of wage workers were married and only 15 percent had children. Officials explained this by arguing that wage workers' resources were so "reduced" as to "prevent the majority of them from founding a household."[34] They were expressing a *particular* anxiety about workers, "their abstention in the domain of nuptuality," as if workers constituted the best stock for the reproduction of the African population.[35] The argument sounds almost eugenic, but it was cultural as well: indeed, the entire program of stabilization – and the hope that new generations of workers would be socialized in the modern milieu of the workplace – would be jeopardized if workers disproportionately abstained from reproduction.[36]

As of 1951 there was still no consensus on family allocations. Skeptics worried that they would be expensive and drive up the cost of exports;

they would lead to an administrative nightmare in the absence of an état-civil; they might encourage polygamy and drive up bride-price; and if awarded to workers alone – and the idea of awarding them to all Africans seemed inconceivable at the time – they would create a gap between wage earners and cultivators as wide as that then existing between civil servants and private sector workers.[37] Opponents, notably among employers, insisted that the peculiarity of the African rendered the evolutionist hopes of proponents futile: "there is no possible assimilation of the autochthonous family to the French family of the metropole." Some claimed to know of Africans with fifteen wives and seventy-four children, and they insisted that whatever social problems existed could be best solved by direct intervention by the state in the realm of health, for example, rather than by employers in the form of payments to African men who would be likely to dissipate whatever sums they received.[38] The debate would go on for years, but it was already clear that employers were going up against top officials who very much wanted to believe that treating the African worker as if he were almost a European would make him become that way.

Much as discussions of labor regulation, social security, and family allowances reflected officials' desire for a predictable, modern working class, similar concerns resonated with the labor movement as well. This movement had come into its own in the aftermath of the Senegalese general strike of 1946. Within each territory of French West Africa, trade unions (*syndicats*) grouped themselves into a *union des syndicats*, affiliated (again following the Dakar model) with one of the major French *centrales*. In the post-war climate of high inflation and political opening, security agents and labor inspectors in Dahomey, the Soudan, Guinea, and the Ivory Coast, reported "great activity" among unions as well as "continual demands," "permanent strike threats," and a steady stream of strikes in the major towns, none of the magnitude of the Dakar events, but enough to make officials quite conscious that unions had become a factor to be reckoned with.[39]

By 1948 there were active West African organizations affiliated to the communist-led CGT, the government-supported CGT-FO, and the Church-connected CFTC. The railway union remained autonomous. The CGT got the jump in this process, and in 1948 had 42,500 adherents, versus 17,500 for the "autonomes," 8,500 in the CFTC, and 1,000 in the CGT-FO. In 1948, 20 percent of the wage labor force of French West Africa was unionized, in 1956, over a third.[40] Senegal remained the best organized territory in both public and private sectors, but Guinea – Conakry in particular – emerged as a second pole of trade unionism. Sékou Touré, dynamic leader of the Guinean CGT unions, and David

Soumah, the most effective CFTC leader in Africa, sometimes competed and sometimes cooperated, and neither *centrale* could politically afford to appear less militant than the other.[41]

African leaders were quite adept at using the protection, legitimacy, and logistic support of their French comrades without losing their focus on issues that mattered in Africa.[42] The French CGT, meanwhile, was trying to link colonial workers to a world-wide working class movement, and through it the African CGT unions were affiliated to the World Federation of Trade Unions (WFTU).

The global struggle of the proletariat was another universalist model, embodying a clear vision of the worker as having made a definitive leap from his ancestral social formation into the capitalist order, from which yet another social order would be constructed. The left was in its own way imagining a working class and assuming that Africans were on a path that Europeans had trod before. Some African trade unionists, like Abdoulaye Diallo of the Soudan, took up the internationalist approach – Diallo becoming a vice president of the WFTU – but even those who did not share the entire package took public positions in favor of the equivalence of the needs of workers of all origins and saw union organization as the basic means to fill those needs.[43] The revolutionaries and the industrial relations bureaucrats were locked in serious struggle, but they shared similar views of the battlefield. Both parties saw the Code du Travail as a goal which could mobilize Africans as workers conscious of their future, a framework which would define what being a worker entailed.

The African unions turned an official discourse on stabilization, productivity, order, and French civilization into a discourse on entitlements. In union and leftist newspapers, in May Day rallies, and in other public fora, leaders talked about equal pay for equal work and claims to benefits; year by year, piece by piece, they tried to get parts of this program written into collective bargaining agreements.[44] When the Union des Syndicats Confédérés de Dakar, for example, met in November 1948, it demanded revision of the minimum wage, immediate promulgation of the Code du Travail, the conditional right to strike, a single minimum wage for Africans and Europeans, a single system of family allocations for all, systems for social security and worker compensation, committees for discussing work issues within firms, payment of transport costs to places of work, a single *cadre fédéral unique* for civil servants, and a *cadre unique* in the private sector.[45]

At the Conférence Syndicale Africaine of the CGT in Bamako in 1951, denunciation of "colonial exploitation" and "racism" was followed with a resolution identifying "the most urgent and the most tangible demands of African workers": "1. Immediate and definitive passage of the Code du Travail... 2. Unification of the indemnities of zone and family charges for all civil servants. 3. Extension of these indemnities to auxiliaries and employees of the private sector."[46] A Soudanese trade union newspaper called for the implementation of a social security system in Africa, arguing with particular vehemence for family allowances by citing the universality of such problems as infant mortality: "In effect, in the face of danger, there is no difference between a FRENCHMAN born near the banks of the Seine or the Loire and a FRENCHMAN born near the banks of the Senegal or the Niger."[47]

Officials, ever since January 1946, were well aware that small strike threats might become large. They argued for concessions to prevent strikes that might have "grave consequences for the political and social climate of the country where certain elements seem to be trying to provoke social malaise for anti-French political ends." They warned of general strikes and opposed efforts from Paris to restrain wages on the grounds that efforts had to be made to ensure "social peace."[48]

By 1949, officials thought that the era of the "disorderly strike" was passing and an age of "systematic organization" and orderly collective bargaining opening up. There had, however, been large-scale strikes in Senegal, Guinea, and Dahomey in 1949–50.[49] While very much worried about the connection of the largest African trade unions to the French CGT and the WFTU, officials thought that the French West African trade union movement also showed opposite tendencies which needed to be encouraged. Collective bargaining at the local level on the one hand and the weakening of radical international trade unionism by the WFTU split in 1949 and the founding of the government-supported International Confederation of Free Trade Unions (ICFTU) on the other raised hopes for a more focused trade unionism.

Colonial officials' approach was temporarily cross cut by a toughening of government attitudes toward the left following the end of communist participation in the government coalition in 1947.[50] In Africa this implied a period of confrontation with the CGT – and even more strikingly the RDA, which had allied for parliamentary purposes in France with the PCF and which in Africa stood ambivalently between *communisant* versions of anti-colonialism and a "bourgeois" politics of pressing for a greater political voice and greater economic participation within the structures of Overseas France. The hardening manifested itself, ironically, in a campaign against the most bourgeois of the RDA branches, in the Ivory Coast, where intimidation, arrest of RDA militants at the local level, and blatant cheating in elections were used to try to break a potent political machine. This strategy created considerable conflict. Eventually,

Houphouët-Boigny, who had no more than a tactical interest in the legislative alliance with the PCF, proved willing to negotiate with the colonial minister, François Mitterand. In 1950 he broke the alliance in exchange for a relaxation of administrative harassment and the entrance of Houphouët-Boigny into closer relations with the French government itself.[51] Not surprisingly, the already ambiguous relationship between the RDA and the West African branches of the CGT became even murkier. I will return in chapter 11 to that question.

But around 1950, the divisions and tensions within African and international labor movements were read in Paris as offering new hope for what they called "a true trade unionism" – as much within the CGT as among its rivals – opposed to the "partisan trade unionism" they saw as so dangerous.[52] This assessment was questionable, for CGT dominance would be challenged more by an alternative form of "political" trade unionism – a nationalist one at that – than by any desire to surrender the political field. But the perception had important implications: the possibility of shaping a labor movement within certain boundaries meant that something had to be done to give that form of the movement a positive basis and to discourage wavering trade unionists from thinking that they had nothing to lose from following the most militant or the most explicitly anti-colonial line. The legacy of old-style colonialism – the unequal wages and benefits, the insecurity of jobs, the heavy-handed and racist management style for which the French *patronat* was notorious – was an obstacle to such a strategy: French officials were facing a barrage of demands, appealing to the very claims toward progress and equality through which the government was asserting its own legitimacy. Given the wide gap between the ideology of progressive colonialism and the grim realities of daily life in most African cities, officials were in a position where they had to take their own ideology seriously, where they had to make a plausible case that operating within the framework of nonpolitical trade unionism and the rules of an industrial relations system would bring concrete benefits to workers and a secure position to trade union leaders.

The Inspection du Travail thus brought before French lawmakers a double argument about the centrality of labor to the entire project of colonial modernization and control:

Without doubt, the latter [wage workers] represent only a small part of the population; they nonetheless constitute one of the most important groups, if not the most important, because they are more receptive to new ideas, the most dynamic, the most manipulable because of their concentration in cities and industrial centers. Removed from customary discipline, the mass of wage earners would rapidly become a redoubtable element of social agitation, if, seriously discontented with their lot, they were taken in hand, supervised and guided by clever people without scruples... The moral and material situation of these workers should necessarily remain among the most fundamental preoccupations of all...[53]

Against the threat of a militant labor movement stood the opportunity to shift the discourse on labor onto territory which both the colonial administration and the majority of the labor movement could accept, isolating those who refused to work within the frame.

So, when right-wing legislators, in the midst of the code debate, charged after a one-day general strike over the code, that the government was being intimidated, Paul Coste-Floret, a former colonial minister, countered by invoking the shared ground:

what demands does one find constantly repeated? Free labor, explicitly formulated and without dispute; the free exercise of trade union rights, firmly guaranteed; a healthy conception of inspection services; immediate regulation of family security. Nothing in these motions overthrows our law or the principles on which it is based, but, on the contrary, they recall the most authentic principles of our democracy.[54]

The French colonial elite – bureaucrats and politicians – were not entirely misreading what the labor movement was saying, but they were reading selectively, projecting their own view of what mattered most onto the priorities of African workers.

The colonialist right – the organizations of settlers and businessmen – had their own vision of a Code du Travail, born of a belief in discipline and order. Indeed, in France the Vichy government had its "Charte du travail," and there had been some talk – never implemented – of applying it to the colonies. In August 1946, the Etats Généraux de la Colonisation, meeting in Paris to try to "save the Empire" and restore a de facto form of forced labor, pronounced itself in favor of the "general principles of a labor code adapted to the territories of the French Union."[55] The last phrase pointed to the line that was to be taken by the *patronat* and its apologists throughout the debate on the code: it should be adapted to the realities of the situation – meaning the peculiarities of the African worker and the needs of the European employer. The proposals of the Etats Généraux revealed the colons' need for government help to recruit and discipline labor as much as its rejection of ILO standards and the reasoning of the government's Inspection du Travail.

The Dakar general strike of 1946 had been a formative experience for employers as well as labor inspectors. "It was chaos," an employer organization was told later in 1946, "With so many different rules, one risked getting lost." The *patronat* wanted to bring order to the anarchy, but to stop short of "excessive centralization," and it was thus sympathetic to the idea of some sort of labor code or codes.[56]

When Moutet, as colonial minister, tried again in 1947 to come up with a code by decree, the "parti colonial" protested that it was too specific and too "draconian." They thought it took insufficient account of the supposed fact that the African "is not led by either heredity or by moral rules or by material needs to furnish continuous and constant labor." The Comité de l'Empire Français and other patronal organizations argued in 1948 and 1949 for a code to make clear the social obligation to work, but for the code to be flexible enough so that the governor-general, not French decrees, would determine the "modalities of application."[57]

But the right was losing its ability to frame the problem, faced with the powerful universalism in which the defense of colonial rule was being made, its own desire for economic development, and the fervent hope that the unpredictable and conflict-ridden social situation in French Africa could be brought under control. It was caught between the politics of keeping the empire and the politics of exploiting it. The discursive shift had covered so much ground when the debate on the code began in Paris that the stalwarts of the right found themselves falling back on an argument that would have appalled them a few years earlier: equality. Seeing that the draft code was defining the worker in a restrictive way, so that the labor which most Africans performed for other Africans would be labelled "customary labor" and excluded from the code, while the labor which Africans performed for Europeans would certainly be regulated, some representatives of the *patronat* became defenders of the rights of African peasants. Luc Durand-Réville, a colon from Gabon who would organize the employers' case before the Conseil de la République, published an article in January 1951 entitled "No Racial Discrimination in the New Code du Travail." He noted that the code then being debated would "deprive of the advantages and guarantees provided at least 80 percent of the working population." The code would subject European employers to "extraordinarily meticulous legislation" while leaving the "exploitation of man by man in these little evolved countries" outside its "field of application."[58]

There was nothing wrong with Durand-Réville's logic. But separating wage workers from people engaged in other forms of economic relationships was precisely what the code's supporters wanted to do. Its opponents feared that African employers' relations with their workers would in practice slide into the category of customary labor, giving them a competitive advantage vis-à-vis European employers. The irony of the situation lay in hearing the defense of the exploited African coming from the defenders of white privilege.

Another set of actors in the debates was moving into more productive terrain. These were the social Catholics, found within the centrist

Mouvement Républicain Populaire (MRP) in the legislature – a member of most governmental coalitions in the post-war decade – and well represented within the bureaucracy. Alongside the social engineering of the Inspection du Travail or the proletarian universalism of the unions and the left parties, they pioneered another intellectual route toward the Code du Travail. Robert Delavignette, at various times head of Affaires Politiques, a governor-general, and director of the Ecole Supérieure Coloniale, exemplified social Catholicism within the colonial establishment, as did Louis-Paul Aujoulat, a parliamentarian from the Cameroun who served as Secrétaire d'Etat in the ministry during the years of the code debate and who was one of its public defenders.[59] Their rhetoric stressed the need for social harmony, for family stability, for "the liberation of the human personality," and for protection of workers, all as alternatives to both the unmediated exploitation of workers and class struggle. The Vichy regime had attempted to appeal to such a tendency, with some success, but its version of harmony in fact subordinated the workers to the *patronat*. The social Catholic position after the war is not so easily dismissed, and they helped to bring about the belated consolidation of the French welfare state after the war in a manner which put support of the family at the center.[60] Although identifying French civilization, and particularly its religious aspects, with social progress, a number of social Catholic thinkers were often quicker than socialists and communists to realize that the French empire could not necessarily contain the progress it was fostering and that appeals for autonomy or even independence had to be taken seriously.[61]

In one of the early debates on the code, the Abbé Paul Catrice, an MRP delegate to the Assembly of the French Union, told his fellow legislators of "the considerable role played by the Catholic Church in the social movement," and of the role of MRP in "the avant garde of family allocations, funds for family social insurance, profit sharing, co-management of enterprises, low income housing." He saw the proposed Code du Travail for the colonies as another step towards "social progress," and part of a "message of social peace..."[62] When the MRP, led by Joseph Dumas, deputy and a former leader of the Catholic *centrale*, the CFTC, joined its legislative proposals to those of more left-wing organizations, it pronounced the draft bill "a veritable declaration of the social rights of man."[63]

The social Catholics brought to the debate a particular concern with the question of the family. Sister Marie-André du Sacré-Coeur, who sat on a committee advising the ministry, published an article in 1951 arguing that "the family problem is, at the present time, the key problem of Black Africa." She juxtaposed African societies' "sacrificing the individual to the clan," with Christian "notions of moral responsibility, and as a consequence individual liberty and respect for the human self."[64]

There was common ground shared by social Catholics, by the bureaucratic modernizers of the Inspection du Travail, and by the progressivist and universalist French left. African trade unions were themselves making masterful use of assimilationist and universalistic rhetoric in turning imperial claims to hegemony into demands for entitlements. The ultimate aims of these groups were diverse, but they were overlapping when it came to seeing the central importance of a comprehensive labor code and when it came to the underlying vision of a working class as a distinct social and cultural entity marking a step forward in human history. In their own ways, these groups were imagining an African working class.

The great debate, 1947–1952

Marius Moutet tried to push through a Code du Travail by decree just before he left office in November 1947, but his successor as colonial minister, Paul Coste-Floret, pulled it back, arguing that it should have first been discussed by the Assemblée de l'Union Française and other deliberative bodies in the colonies. He was influenced by the vociferous complaints of the colonial *patronat* as well as by uncertainty over whether a decree – as opposed to a law enacted in the French legislature – was legally sufficient.[65] Coste-Floret's action unleashed a wave of protest in Africa – including threats of a general strike – and the Assemblée de l'Union Française and the Grand Conseil of French West Africa voted strong resolutions demanding the code be implemented immediately pending further legislative action and warning that it would be "dangerous" to allow African workers to feel betrayed.[66]

The upshot was that the government decided that a legislative debate over the contents of a code was necessary. Legislators from the major factions duly submitted their proposals.[67] They went first for advice, approval, and revision to the relevant consultative bodies, the Conseil Economique and the Assemblée de l'Union Française. The MRP, the SFIO, and the RDA-PCF submitted detailed proposals; the minister submitted a new version. Luc Durand-Réville, representing Gabon in the Conseil de la République (the French equivalent of the US Senate), submitted a proposed labor code that embodied the *patronat*'s argument that substantive regulation should be left to the territories. Even the colonialist right wanted to create a "régime du travail" and paid lip service to equal base pay "given equal conditions of work, qualifications, and output" (a significant qualification). Durand-Réville couldn't help getting a dig at French universalism with a remark on the absurdity of applying the same regulations to colonies of white settlers "and to the still savage tribes of the most backward countries of the equatorial forest."[68]

This line – not so far removed from ideology and practice for the past fifty years – was immediately ruled out of consideration by a committee of the Assemblée de l'Union Française on the grounds that the right's proposal "does not constitute a code du travail."[69] The other proposals entered into a process of criticism and synthesis. The committee acknowledged the crucial polarity between extending the metropolitan code overseas and gearing regulations to local situations, but left no doubt that subsequent discussion would be framed by universalistic principles:

Thus, the proposal of the committee extends to workers of the overseas territories, the majority of the social advantages accorded to metropolitan workers – that is only just. In so far as a modern work regime is affirmed overseas, the social legislation which has passed the test in the metropole must, without delay, bring its benefits there.[70]

It was February 1949 by the time that the Assemblée de l'Union Française as a whole began to discuss the version which its committee had put together, March by the time it approved an amended draft. It was November 1950 before the Assemblée Nationale took up (after committee deliberations) the effort. The Commission des Territoires d'Outre-Mer, led by the social Catholic Joseph Dumas, laid out a draft code considerably closer on several key points to the position favored by the trade unions than was the government's own proposal: it gave the government less scope to interfere with trade unions and contract negotiations, put fewer obstacles in the way of strikes, and guaranteed workers in industry a 40-hour week.[71] Rightist deputies tried again to get their kind of code on the agenda, and some African delegates tried to get yet another version discussed. The Assemblée debated the code off and on until April 1951, approving a modified text by a vote of 463 to 110.[72]

Once passed by the Assemblée Nationale, the code went to the Conseil de la République, where it was discussed in committee and then by the conseil as a whole from December 1951 to April 1952. The right, Durand-Réville in particular, did a great deal of damage to the code although the Conseil kept the basic structure of articles and the detail of the regulations rather than accept the right's preferred general code. The more conservative upper house whittled away enough of the guarantees and protections accorded workers that most delegates from the colonies, as well as the communists, voted against the final version, in order to send a message to the Assemblée Nationale to restore its earlier version on second reading, as was the Assemblée's prerogative.[73] By this time, the trade union movement in FWA was alarmed at the delays and the

changes and organized (see below) to put pressure on the Assemblée
Nationale. The Assemblée went over the Conseil's changes one by one,
and the final code resembled its earlier version more than that of the
Conseil de la République. The Assemblée finally passed the code 353 to
1 on 22 November 1952. It was over seven years since the first attempt
had been made to issue a Code du Travail by decree, four since the
legislative process had begun.

The legislative process left a paper trail as long – and often as arid –
as a trans-saharan trade route. All I can do here is focus on those parts
of the debate which reveal the most about the shifting boundaries of
discussion.

Joseph Dumas introduced the bill, noting the impossibility of simply
extending the metropolitan code to the colonies – it was necessary to take
account of "particularities." But he still claimed, "wherever we have
introduced wage labor, the relations between employers and workers
offer common characteristics. Only the law can provide this generality
and guarantee the right which it installs."[74] Louis-Paul Aujoulat insisted
on the "invariable character which modern forms of wage labor assumes,
in all latitudes and among all people." Workers and employers, "from
Shanghai to Pointe-Noire" had the same "preoccupations," and therefore
"regulations can hardly vary in their overall lines. The necessities of
hygiene and security, the general dispositions regarding the labor
contracts, the very conditions of work and the regulation of conflict are
practically universal norms."[75]

African deputies agreed. "Work itself does not change," said
Mamadou Konaté. The key question, Léopold Senghor concluded, was
"to define le salariat, that is the worker." And the main problem was to
distinguish wage labor from customary labor. The committee draft
specifically excluded people "from whom the regime of wage labor has
not substituted for the customary relations of their traditional society."
Senghor wanted to drop that phrase, leaving only the committee's positive definition of a worker as any person "who has engaged himself to
put his professional activity at the disposition of another person, physical or moral [i.e. a corporation], public or private, in a manner so as to
exercise it for hire under the direction and authority of the latter." This,
Senghor argued, would limit the purview of the code to true wage
laborers, but would be sure to include seasonal or temporary laborers
who worked for wages for a time but who had not left the traditional
milieu.[76] His argument persuaded the drafting committee and the
Assemblée Nationale.

This (and the original text) left a certain ambiguity about the status of
people like the navétanes, migratory workers from the Soudan who came

to the peanut fields of Senegal, exchanging their labor against a diverse package of remunerations – access to land to grow their own crops, personal relations with the landlord, shares of the crop, and, at times, cash. Senghor's definition, centered on cash, gave grounds for excluding the *navétanes*, or others working for African landlords under arrangements more complex and ambiguous than pure wage labor.[77]

Senghor and his colleagues were giving the Inspection du Travail what it wanted; the labor inspectors did not have the heart to take on the immensity of African agrarian life. This office – the great defender of the universality of the worker – did not deny the peculiarity of the African; it wanted to separate the two constructs. An inspector then in the Paris office, Combier, put it this way:

In regard to family labor, it is worth remembering that the immense majority of cases of this do not fit the mold of wage labor, but are regulated by custom... The framework of the family, which comprises a true system of social security, is, as you know, much larger overseas than it is here. It draws its principal force from ties of a religious nature, which have not been unaffected as a result of contact with western civilization, but whose value and solidity we must be careful not to underestimate. It is possible that under cover of these ties abuses can be committed. At the same time, the possible victims are far from being disarmed. They retain the freedom to leave the family circle when they want to... There is in consequence no need for the help of the law in this domain, where it would only be detrimental.[78]

In defining the boundaries of the working class, the inspectorate was saying something about the realm which lay outside; it was a strange world, and one which – now that France was not extracting labor from it by force – could remain that way.

The white deputies representing settler communities in Africa argued that this definition forced white farmers to abide by the regulations of the code while allowing blacks to avoid the stipulations of the labor law. Jules Castellani charged, "In effect, under the cover of an obviously less shocking expression, which you call customary rights, you have consecrated these feudal rights and, thanks to you, it is still possible to exploit workers in the overseas territories."[79] This forced African deputies to defend the non-exploitative, communal nature of customary labor, while communist deputies claimed that they were only concerned with the exploitation of colonial capitalists and Africans could be left to settle their own affairs among themselves. Senghor interjected "We are against all bourgeoisies, whatever their color," but he presumably did not think bourgeoisies could be built on customary labor. Dumas admitted that the problem was worrisome, but insisted that the courts could make the necessary distinctions. It was, however, not a problem that anybody but the right wanted to solve: Senghor's definition passed 448 to 147.[80] The right tried again in the Conseil de la République, and Aujoulat defended the government position, coming close to admitting that much of the issue was to define a terrain of action that was manageable: putting customary labor under the code would require "an apparatus of control so numerous, so large that it would exceed in size the political administration." The legislators were asked to concern themselves with the "wage labor force properly speaking" and "to leave it to the Africans to take care of this question [customary labor]."[81] After some compromising, a somewhat more ambiguous version of the Assemblée's text passed the Conseil and the second reading in the Assemblée, where the legislative record affirmed, "we have clearly specified that the dispositions of this code du travail would not apply to customary labor."[82] The bounded domain of work – le salariat – had been demarcated. Within these boundaries, egalitarian and universalistic principles would obtain: Article 1 specifically applied to workers "whatever their sex or nationality may be" and to workers and employers without regard to "juridical status."[83]

Those dispositions amounted to a comprehensive set of guarantees and procedures. All workers, as defined above, would have the right to a weekly day off and paid holidays (with certain provisions made for employers' paying costs of transport for workers who lived away from home); places of work had to meet certain standards of safety and sanitation and in some cases provide on-site medical care; the right to organize unions was made clear and procedures for conciliation, arbitration, and legitimate strikes or lock-outs were laid out. The code ended up with 241 articles, although someone felt called upon to note that the metropolitan labor code had 491.[84] Its most conspicuous omissions were unemployment insurance – officials still thought that African society provided alternatives to wage employment – and insurance against industrial accidents, held up while the metropolitan codes were being revised.[85]

One of the most revealing, and hotly contested, debates was over the length of the work week. The norm in major cities like Dakar was 48 hours, but elsewhere it was highly irregular and often longer. Beginning in the Assemblée de l'Union Française, communist, RDA, and other colonial deputies favored the 40-hour week, above all because, "We promised in the Constitution that France accorded to all inhabitants of the Union the same rights and the same duties as to the inhabitants of the metropole." Actually, the shorter work week – like much of French social legislation – was hardly a long tradition in the metropole, won in 1936, lost in 1938, only regained after the war. But a convoluted French history was being compressed into a clear-cut metropolitan model by both sides in the code debate, and African deputies insisted that the principle be enshrined in the code, since territorial officials could not be trusted.[86] They also argued that long hours reduced productivity, and "scarce manpower" had to be conserved. The ministers thought the 40-hour week was a desirable, but presently unattainable goal, when productivity was so low. African productivity was said to be below European standards, and therefore longer hours should be expected; local officials who knew the peculiar work habits of their peoples should be entrusted with setting the work week. Senghor argued that in this debate productivity issues were "false problems" – they could be dealt with by emphasis on training, equipment, and nutrition – and that the point here was that the *minimum vital*, the amount of money a worker was calculated to need to meet basic needs, should be met by a 40-hour week, and that overtime should be paid, at a higher rate, for work beyond the 40th hour.[87] Others proposed that the 40-hour week be applied in industry, while seasonal variability in agriculture should be taken into account via the specification of a 2,400 hour work-year, equivalent to a 48-hour week over 50 weeks.[88]

The Assemblée de l'Union Française accepted the 40-hour week/2,400-hour year proposal. The Assemblée Nationale, despite the government's opposition, voted for the 40-hour week. The Conseil de la République rejected it in favor of giving local authorities authority over the work week. Back went the debate to the Assemblée Nationale, and its committee now called for a 2,000-hour work *year*, with anything over 40 hours per week paid at 25 or 50 percent overtime. The debate focused on the issue of whether overtime should be paid at a fixed rate or one determined by governors, whom African and communist deputies feared would set them lower than metropolitan rates. Senghor once again got to the heart of the debate: "As you know, Africans now have a mystique of equality. In this domain, as in others, they want the same principles to be applied from the first in the overseas territories as in the metropole." Senghor indicated that he would accept to have the actual rates omitted from the law if the government would assure him that governors would follow metropolitan rates. This the government would not do: they wanted governors to be able to take into account the economic conditions of the territory. But some African deputies were willing to seek a compromise, one which enshrined the 40-hour week and made higher wages for overtime compulsory, but left the rates open: this would be a victory on the principle, a compromise on the fact. Mamadou Konaté, proposing such an amendment, stated, "The worst outcome would be the absence of a text at the end of these debates." He clearly feared that the votes of the center parties, essential to the left and colonial deputies, could be lost over this issue and the entire code could be put in jeopardy.

The advocates of fixed rates accepted this argument, and voted for Konaté's text. The 40-hour week had been won, and as the struggles of the next year or two would reveal, the law gave African trade unionists a framework in which they could work to assure that the victory would be in fact as well as in theory.[89] The real reason for the victory was that the 40-hour week was the norm in France, and the only real case why the figure was any less valid for the colonies assumed the inferiority of Africans. The "mystique of equality" triumphed over the peculiarity of the African.[90]

Similar legislative battles were fought over a range of related issues. The code went into such details as requiring employers to pay an indemnity covering some of the transport costs for an annual paid vacation of a worker and family working away from their normal residence, and Castellani tried to argue against it by citing the apparently outrageous case of one of his own workers whose family included eight wives and forty-seven children. He got laughs but not his way. As each such instance became a focus for debate, the idea of the comparability of the working situation of the African and the French person was reinforced.[91]

The code thus gave substance to the idea of equal pay for equal work, and its opponents conceded that the principle should be written into the law even as they tried to void it of substance. The principle was explicitly acknowledged in relation to gender as well as origins: women were supposed to get equal pay. But here the code gave mixed signals. At every stage of the legislative process, a section entitled "The labor of women and children" appeared, and no-one seemed to question whether these two categories belonged together. While the code included provisions for maternity leave – 14 weeks at half pay – which female workers in some more "advanced" economies have yet to obtain, legislators spent an inordinate amount of time debating whether a doctor had to verify a pregnancy (there were few doctors in much of the continent) or whether obvious appearance would do.[92] That the legislators were more likely to give more thought to women as beings who, like children, needed special protection because of their physical vulnerability than to women as workers is not exactly astonishing, but the fact that most provisions of the law were sex-blind and denied explicit discrimination in wages and benefits is a reminder that formalism is not such a bad thing. When (see below) the question of family allocations came up, it was clear from the debates that officials had in mind the male wage-earner and the female homemaker.

Labor unions and the question of strikes were a major focus of attention, and some considered the provisions on these matters the heart of the code. The government spokesmen and members of the centrist MRP

worried about the newness of African trade unions and the need to keep
a watchful official eye over them, and their anxieties mediated their usual
universalism. All the same, the very process of devising the code reinforced the *normality* of African labor organization. Even such relatively
uncontroversial measures as those creating certain kinds of consultative
councils assumed that there were labor unions to nominate one portion
of the membership.[93] Politicians wanted to believe that unions would be
a force for the good: "It is a fact, in any case, that trade unionism overseas has very rapidly proven its possibilities and its utility... they [the
unions] occupy themselves, in addition to their usual claims, in exercising
a true and positive influence over the economic and social influence of
their country."[94] The situation in French Africa thus differed substantially from that in British, where the normalcy and significance of trade
union organization remained in question well into the 1950s and where
battles over such questions had to be fought out in each colony.

Opinions differed over whether and to what extent governors were to
review collective bargaining agreements. The Commission on Overseas
Territories of the Assemblée Nationale followed the metropolitan model:
a collective bargaining agreement was a contract between two parties,
and the government had no right to review its terms. Even before the
Assemblée Nationale as a whole took up the code, this provision was the
subject of an anxious and revealing correspondence within the administration.[95] Aujoulat believed that unions "had not yet attained a sufficient
development" and were prone to demagogy. In some sectors, where business was booming and labor in short supply, private firms might not
necessarily oppose high wage demands, but in a backward economy this
could distort the labor market in other sectors as well as drive up prices
to the detriment of workers who were not so well organized. Aujoulat
worried about the effects of radical upward pressure on wages on development projects, on which so much hope rested: "There is no question
that the administration has exercised a check on the movement of wages,
preoccupied as it was with general considerations of the economy and
also because of the fact that it is a very large, if not the principal,
employer."[96]

Here one sees a distinction between fixing certain rights for workers –
including rights (such as paid vacations) which raise labor costs – and
procedures which empower workers themselves to organize to force
wages upward. Political leaders like Aujoulat accepted the first – they
were granting these rights – but balked at the second – they did not know
where the process would end.

But Aujoulat did not get his way. He made his argument to the
Assemblée Nationale – the Assemblée de l'Union Française had already

rejected the principle of governmental assent to contracts – but its Committee on Overseas Territories, led by Aujoulat's fellow social Catholic Joseph Dumas, stuck to its position in favor of free exercise of the right of contract, while communist deputies pointed out explicitly the danger that governors would intervene on the side of employers.[97] The Assemblée Nationale voted to allow governors or the governor-general to generalize agreements within certain boundaries, but not to reject ordinary agreements. This position held up in the final version of the code.[98]

A similar debate raged over the government's attempt to make strikes illegal until the dispute had gone through a long procedure, including conciliation, arbitration, and appeals of an arbiter's ruling. The communist and overseas representatives objected that this amounted to an infringement of the right to strike, and more or less restrictive versions were voted up and down as the code went through different legislative bodies. Once again, government spokesmen revealed themselves more reluctant to concede on issues of power than on issues of textually defined rights, but African and communist deputies countered by threatening to deny legitimacy to the code – by voting against it or abstaining – unless an issue as important as the right to strike was resolved in an acceptable manner.[99] This put the centrist MRP on the spot, and its leaders were anxious for a strong code and for trade unions capable of guiding African workers in acceptable directions to be encouraged.[100] The final version included compulsory conciliation procedures and the appointment of an expert to investigate any dispute that could not be resolved, but set strict time limits and guaranteed the right to strike after such procedures had been followed.

The most revealing controversy of all was over family allocations. This was dangerous terrain: the ministry and the Inspection du Travail were still unsure, even as late as 1951, what they thought about this issue. The issue surfaced quietly, in a section of the code called "transitory dispositions." The Assemblée de l'Union Française passed with barely a word an article saying that any previous regulation already in vigor "in regard to work, social security and family prestations will continue to be valid" until new procedures of the present and future laws went into effect. The Abbé Catrice, MRP member and a leading exponent of social Catholicism, along with a colleague, proposed an additional article stating:

Until the establishment of a system of social security, the heads of territories [governors] are empowered to issue decrees on the advice of representative assemblies provisionally instituting family prestations for all workers under the present code and to institute compensation funds to insure the payment of these prestations.

The article was voted without debate. A similar article, differing by a preamble reading "until the intervention of a law in this regard", was passed with no debate by the Assemblée Nationale. Such a provision had been included in the government's draft as well as the more liberal version of the Commission des Territoires d'Outre-Mer.[101] Perhaps the right, seeing an example of an article giving the relevant power to governors, thought this measure would respond to trade union demands for legislative action but lack all substance.

The Conseil de la République thought otherwise. Durand-Réville insisted, "We are not *a priori* against the principle of family prestations." But, he argued, the demographic development of Africa was better addressed by programs in infant hygiene; the African family was already "prolific"; costs had to be taken into account. The government accepted Durand-Réville's motion to remove this article. The other side undoubtedly felt it was, in this forum, a lost cause, and without further argument the family allocations clause was removed by a vote of 216 to 89.[102]

Once it was clear that the article was not just going to slip through, the debate was joined with vigor, for this issue had already become a focus of attention from organized labor. The Committee on Overseas Territories of the Assemblée Nationale, sticking to its universalist position, recommended putting the clause back in. A group of deputies from the Radical Party moved to take it out. They claimed to be willing "to give to our brothers overseas what I would call their social majority," but "[unhappily], we cannot give them at the same time the security which follows from a prosperous economy." Senghor replied that the clause only established the principle of family allocations overseas, not the rate, and he pointed out that the working population of Africa was not large and most workers were bachelors or childless. The issue was one of principle, and it was also an issue of politics. His side had compromised on the question of overtime rates:

It is up to you now to take a step toward us. What concerns me now is the future of relations between Africans – to speak of Africa which is my native land – and Europeans. If you do not follow us in our willingness to compromise, the code du travail will not be approved. The disappointment of the African workers will be terrible. You will push them to gestures of despair.

Senghor clearly had read the trade union demands, the May Day resolutions, the union press of the last several years, and was warning the Assemblée that African politicians could not come home without some progress toward bringing family allocations to African workers.[103]

The minister, Pierre Pflimlin (the sixth man in that post since the time of Moutet's abortive code), now took direct part in the debate, calling this question "one of the most difficult." He did not think there was a difference of opinion on the question of "the necessity of aid to the African family." The question was whether a metropolitan approach would work in Africa, as well as a question of economy. The development plan had already brought other sorts of social achievements, but that plan itself was, for now, burdening the territories with expenses before having brought about a comparable improvement in production. The costs of French African exports were going up, while world prices were coming down. He wanted to pause and reflect before taking another step that might "end up in a disequilibrium, which could be dangerous, between economic progress and social progress." He came close to acknowledging a difference of opinion within the administration: Aujoulat, the social Catholic, "gives this problem of family policy the very highest importance" and had started a number of studies of it, which were not yet completed. He wanted the Assemblée to wait and consider legislation on overseas family policy in the future.[104]

The reporter of the Committee on Overseas Territories, Dumas, who had much at stake in the code, now appealed to the government to reverse its position: the article, after all, gave it the power to implement family allocations or not. But he had been told that the socialist deputies – and Jean Silvandre immediately confirmed this publicly – would vote against the entire code if this article were taken out. He asked the political question:

Has one sufficiently reflected on the situation which would be created in the overseas territories? Is one really aware of the drama that will take place? In shouting a cry of alarm, I will have done my duty... Is it necessary at the last moment to risk a total failure? The rejection of such a text would constitute, to my mind, the worst of catastrophies for the overseas territories.[105]

The Assemblée Nationale voted 308 to 302 to remove the article on family allocations from the code. Senghor immediately moved for reconsideration, and after a tense procedural wrangle, the Assemblée adjourned for an hour so that the committee could reconsider. It returned with new wording that appeared stronger than the original, dropping the allusion to a future law on family allocations and the provisional nature of the decrees that the governors might issue. Then, the government dramatically changed its position. Pflimlin acknowledged that the Assemblée was divided in two, and he emphasized "What appears indispensable to us is that the code du travail be approved and that, tomorrow, the overseas workers do not register the immense disappointment of watching an edifice so laboriously constructed collapse." The government "puts itself before the wisdom of the Assemblée."[106]

Challenged again by the opponents of the family allocations clause, Pflimlin claimed that the government had not changed its mind about anything other than methods: the minister's approval was required for any decree on family allocations, and he would consider "all circumstances, including economic circumstances" in any future decision. He did not mention political circumstances.

The second vote went the other way: the revised article giving the government the authority to implement family allocations in the overseas territories passed by a vote of 314 to 268, with 30 abstentions.[107] The African deputies and their allies had played tough, and they had won. The Assemblée Nationale immediately went to summary statements from each party on the code as a whole, and that evening voted for it 365 to 0.[108]

But the culmination of the code debate in the Assemblée Nationale, and particularly the drama over family allocations, cannot be understood without reference to an event in Africa. Another of the great strikes of French West African history took place on 3 November, three days before the Assemblée Nationale began its final round of debate. African trade unions and African newspapers had followed the lengthy code debate through its many ups and downs. The efforts of the Conseil de la République to weaken its major provisions caused great anxiety.[109] Then, in July 1952, while waiting for the Assemblée Nationale to take up the draft of the Conseil, the Senegalese deputy Abbas Guèye wrote a letter to the Comité de Coordination des Unions Territoriales des Syndicats de l'AOF et de l'AEF and to several of its constituent unions, giving a "true alert" in regard to the code. Guèye had led the metalworkers – the group which held out the longest – in the 1946 Dakar general strike. He had since allied himself with Senghor in Senegalese politics, and been elected as the junior deputy to Paris. Now, he communicated to his comrades in West Africa that the delays were insufferable and that the code had been "emptied of its meaning" by the Conseil. He went on, "I think it my duty to call your attention to the necessity that it will no longer do to confine ourselves to passive waiting as we have done for five years." He suggested that the central trade union organizations call a "Special Assembly" and ready themselves "to use the means which the law authorizes."[110]

Abbas Guèye's intervention led to a series of initiatives in the Soudan, Dahomey, the Ivory Coast, and Senegal, plus coordination at a pan-West African level, notably an interunion conference in early October.[111] Nearly seventy trade union leaders from the CGT, the CFTC, and the independent unions met in Dakar, formulated resolutions, and planned a three-step protest: a "Journée de revendications" of demonstrations and speeches on 28 October, a one-day general strike throughout FWA on 3 November 1952, and if necessary a three-day strike on 12-14 January 1953. The conference demanded a return to the version of the code passed by the Assemblée Nationale at its first reading. It also resolved that more active measures be taken to implement the Lamine Guèye law equalizing the benefits of civil servants. A Comité d'Entente

CGT-CFTC-Cheminots was formed to coordinate the effort. The governor-general, learning of these plans – which had been brought before a public meeting of 3,000 at the Parc des Sports in Dakar – thought that local unions were on board for the campaign and that it reflected a "profound malaise" in West Africa. He wanted the attention of the Assemblée Nationale to be drawn to these events.[112]

On 28 October, meetings were held in the major West African cities, from Dakar to Porto Novo. Then, on 3 November, the general strike was a stunning success. The governor of Senegal commented on the effectiveness of the strike in Dakar, Thiès, and Kaolack, but also in lesser towns like Ziguinchor and Tambacounda: "This success resides principally in the coalition which was created among the still distant union *centrales*, such as the CGT and the CFTC. Unity of action was not a vain word, and it has borne its fruits." He noted as well the importance of common action between the union coalition and the BDS, the political party of Senghor and Abbas, and the role of local politicians in cities in mobilizing strikers.[113] The BDS newspaper noted that the strike was "quasi-total" among Africans, but that European workers had not participated at all, and it accused the latter of putting "trade union demands on a racial plane."[114]

In the Ivory Coast, the railway workers, led by the bloodied veteran of the railway strike Gaston Fiankan, spearheaded an impressive strike, with other unions, CGT and CFTC, joining forces. The Inspecteur du Travail concluded, "On the side of the workers, the success of the strike can only make them conscious of their power and, in regard to trade unions, of the advantages of concerted and firm action." Even in an inland city like Bobo-Dioulasso in Upper Volta, the strike was 100 percent effective in industry and construction, 95 percent in road transport, and 87 percent in commerce. There were strikes in every colony of FWA except Niger.[115]

When the Assemblée Nationale met three days later, the right-wing deputy René Malbrant grumbled about beginning the debate under the "menace" of African unions. The other side alluded carefully to the "pressing appeals" of unions and the merit of their case.[116] The experience of 3 November – and the three-day strike already scheduled for January – undoubtedly made the African deputies' threat of scuttling the code over the issue of family allowances a credible one.

So a real fear that social peace might be immediately at stake hung over the final debate on the code, leaving the government, caught between claims to entitlements and warnings of threats to the economic development of Africa, all the more convinced that it had to make clear gestures guaranteeing basic rights to colonial workers.

The form, as well as the contents, of the code and indeed of the debate did much to insure that in future debates about the colonies African workers would be viewed as part of the universal category of worker, that African trade unions would be treated like any other trade union, and that the families of African workers would be considered to have the same sorts of needs as other families. Aujoulat defended in just such terms the principle of a code that applied universally within a bounded domain: "let us recognize that this code responds to an undebatable reality: that of the profound and present-day unity of the wage labor force." The foes of the code fought and lost the battle in these terms, attacking the "pseudo-universalism" behind the extension of metropolitan entitlements to Africa, and warning that, "Universalism presents... fearful consequences."[117]

Perhaps the consequences of the Code du Travail would be fearful. The code was an assertion of control as much as it was a concession to demands. In some ways, the struggles that ensued turned out to be as vigorous as skeptics had warned and would put the government in a position of having to make concessions which it regarded as contrary to other interests, including its supreme interest in fostering economic growth. But, at the same time, as the proponents of the code had argued, the struggles of the ensuing years would draw African workers and trade union leaders deeper into the framework the architects of the code had fashioned.

Implementing the code

A few days after the final vote on the code, the Minister, Pflimlin, sent a telegram to Dakar stating:

The application of the Code du Travail must not entail increases in hourly wage rates. Wage increases will correspond only to overtime rates according to scales which you are supposed to determine under conditions to be defined in the texts of applications. Article 227 of the code anticipates providing governors with authority to institute a regime of family prestations. It is necessary to use this authority only with great circumspection, taking account notably of economic circumstances... Be sure to make workers' representatives understand the necessity for delays to put in place serious and carefully adapted modalities of application. Warn them against the illusion that the application of the Code du Travail could modify rapidly and profoundly their conditions of life.[118]

The workers of Africa had put faith in the code – and the legislative process – because they thought it would profoundly affect their conditions of life. Pflimlin was right in one respect: the two issues which would be the focus of contestation were the work week and family allowances.

That the labor movement had succeeded in getting the code would hardly discourage them from insuring that they received its substance. The very effort of the state to frame the labor question as the object of state regulation in fact led to its politicization.

Even before the final vote on the code, colonial business lobbies demanded caution in its implementation. The president of the Chambre de Commerce, d'Agriculture et d'Industrie de Dakar petitioned the Grand Conseil of French West Africa; the Comité de l'Empire Français, and the business periodical *Marchés Coloniaux* lobbied and editorialized against raising hourly pay as a consequence of the shortened work week. Admitting that African trade unionists were well organized, they feared that in the consultative bodies discussing implementation "the European delegates seem drowned by the African delegates."[119]

The West African unions were indeed preparing to bring home their victory. Political leaders from the colonies were claiming credit and promising that "everyone will be able to benefit from family allocations and social security."[120] The Conférence Intersyndicale Territoriale of Senegal and Mauretania – continuing the cooperation among *centrales* mobilized during the campaign for the code – resolved, "this victory, as important as it is, is only the prelude to the true struggle that we are about to conduct in favor of the just and progressive application of the Code du Travail." As in the previous battle, plans were made for a "journée revendicative" later in March, and strikes in May and August, as well as a press campaign, lobbying of deputies, and developing committees inside firms.[121] Meanwhile, public sector unions protested the slowness of reforms deriving from the Lamine Guèye law and possible staff cuts, organizing a number of short strikes in Senegal and the Soudan and attempting to coordinate action again across West Africa.[122] A general strike, led by the CGT, took place in the cities of the Soudan beginning on 3 August. The administration, this time, fought back, punishing striking civil servants and allowing private firms to do likewise. Chiefs apparently mobilized a campaign against the strikes, accusing workers of being "aristocrats of wage labor" – a rather nice touch given who was making the accusation.[123]

The Direction des Affaires Politiques in Senegal thought that the government was losing control:

The CGT leaders have succeeded in locking the public powers and the rival union federations into a sort of cycle from which it is difficult to exit. If in effect one satisfies the claims, these become the point of departure for new claims, even more extravagant, which risk at such a pace to break open the structure of the country and lead to a crisis, with unemployment, misery, and mass discontent... If on the contrary one refuses the demands, it is easy for leaders of Marxist tendency to line up the workers against the public powers and the employers, with the familiar slogans even more dangerously effective in that they lay claim to anti-colonialism and that the class struggle, following local conditions, can quickly lead to painful demonstrations...[124]

The political analysts were pointing to a fundamental dilemma: giving way to union demands meant giving up government control of economic planning, while resisting them risked bursting the labor question out of the frame into which it had so carefully been squeezed, uniting class struggle and anti-colonialism. Officials now took solace that the majority of the population were peasants, "insensitive to anything which doesn't directly interest them," not mentioning in this context what such conservatism implied about the government's entire project of development.[125]

Officials hoped that the FO and the CFTC would stand in the way of the CGT, but these union federations could only do so if they brought concrete gains to their members. So the other *centrales* were drawn into matching the CGT's demands.[126]

By November 1953, the unions were focusing on the "affair of the 20 percent": if the work week went down by 20 percent, hourly wages had to rise by the same amount. They argued that the minimum wage was supposed to cover necessary expenses of a worker and that a legal work week would mean little if workers had to work overtime in order to get by. As the Guinean trade unionist David Soumah pointed out in the Conseil Supérieur du Travail – the advisory board to the inspection in Paris – the law required maintaining this minimum income level and admitted no other considerations, including the state of the economy at the time.[127]

The Grand Conseil of FWA voted to recommend a decree implementing the 40-hour week while maintaining the minimum earnings of the previous 48-hour week.[128] But the government did not act, and in the November session the issue came up again amidst an atmosphere of "social trouble" (see below). Governor-general Bernard Cornut-Gentille was stuck. He acknowledged that the reduction of the work week by the code implied a 20 percent increase in the minimum wage. That wage was supposed to be adjusted for inflation as well, and that in Senegal was 6 percent, so that a 26 percent increase in the minimum wage was called for. This he insisted was impossible: as it was, FWA was having trouble gettings its products into export markets, paying for its imports, and meeting the charges of development loans. He put this in language previously used by the colonialist right: the fact that "70,000 workers [the official figure for union membership] spread out in the Federation, make their grievances known with a certain noise" should not negate the "aspirations of the 16 million country people of FWA." Cornut-Gentille wanted to accomplish the goals of the minimum wage revision by other means: increase the wage by 16 percent but roll back government-set prices for food and other basic commodities so that the cost of living would drop by an estimated 10 percent, thereby preserving the workers' standard of living. But he was all too aware of the union's potential show of strength, predicting serious economic consequences from strikes and aware of the threat to the government's control: "in so far as authority reinforces itself by unbending firmness when menaced by irresponsible pressure, the same authority commits suicide if it pulls back from devoting positive efforts at relieving evident inequalities."[129]

The union's interpretation of the code, unfortunately for Cornut-Gentille, was sound – a point emphasized later that month by some of its authors in the Assemblée Nationale.[130] The elected members of the Grand Conseil in Dakar saw any retreat on the 20 percent as "a violation of the law," and warned of "social troubles capable of dangerously compromising the order and the economy of the Federation." Mamadou Dia noted that the *minimum vital* could always be adjusted downward if prices did fall; this was a separate question from adjusting hourly wages to conform to the new work week. On the other side, Louis Delmas claimed that with such policies "we would kill the industry of FWA." But the Grand Conseil resolved by a vote of 27 to 4 that the government should decree a 40-hour week with a 20 percent hourly increase in the minimum wage.[131]

Meanwhile, unions in each territory put in their claims for minimum wage increases of 20 percent plus whatever the rate of inflation was. The debate within the government was only over the minimum wage; as long as a worker's earnings in a 40-hour week did not dip below the *minimum vital*, wages were a matter for collective bargaining. In most territories, unions were willing, after hard negotiations, to settle for less, believing that most workers would earn enough overtime (at 10-25 percent over the regular rate) so that they would emerge better off. In Guinea, where a general strike in 1950 over the minimum wage had been bitterly fought, no agreement was reached, and on 21 September a wide strike broke out, bringing together workers (skilled and semi-skilled but not laborers, for whom the government-set minimum wage was the relevant point) in construction, industry, public works, as well as office personnel.[132]

With the Conakry strike still on, a one-day strike took place on 13 October, in both private and public sectors of Senegal, 80-96 percent effective in its various components. Then came a series of strikes in the private sector in Senegal in early November, including a general strike from 3–5 November over the application of the code. Unions were rejecting the employers' offer of a 16 percent wage increase, and it was in this light that the governor-general proposed to try to lower prices by 10 percent, making minimum wage and negotiated wage policies consistent. The governor of Senegal went on the radio to try to get workers to accept lowered prices in lieu of the wage increase. The Senegalese strike ran its planned course, and another one – to be a week long – was planned for December. The political parties joined the campaign and "every man of politics had to show that he was acting." In Dakar, according to a political officer with a short memory, "for the first time was realized the unity of the working class." Meanwhile, the demand for the 20 percent plus cost of living adjustments spread to the Ivory Coast and a strike was threatened for 3 December. A strike was being prepared in the Soudan.[133]

The situation was sufficiently tense that the IGT (Colonna d'Istria) urged that the unions' demands for meeting the *minimum vital* within a 40-hour week be promptly conceded before the logic of universality and equality gave rise to questions about the standards of food, shelter, and clothing used in determining the *minimum vital* itself. If that door were opened,

there would no longer be any reason for claims to cease, along with agitation, until a minimum budget identical to that of the metropolitan worker were accepted, a budget already proposed by certain unions in the Ivory Coast and Guinea, under the pretext that this basic document for the determination of the minimum wage cannot be tainted by racial discrimination and thus must respond to the minimum needs of the European as well as the African.[134]

Receiving reports of strike threats from across French West Africa, the governor-general lost faith in his own solution based on reducing the cost of living. His compromise had been "overtaken" by events, and he wrote to the minister in language echoing one of his predecessors' confession of impotence during the 1946 general strike:

there would be very grave difficulties if the final decision to apply completely the Code du Travail were to appear here as having been imposed on an executive suspected of wanting to violate the law... It would be better that the Executive accepts and takes on his own account the inevitable rather than let it be imposed on him.

He recommended the "immediate and complete application of the 20 percent..." And he added, "I allow myself to express to you these views from my soul and conscience and with the conviction that this, in regard to FWA, is the only possibility to retake the initiative in extremis and to avoid worse developments of the situation."[135]

A few days later Cornut-Gentille warned that a general strike would break out throughout FWA and that the question of the 20 percent had taken a "racist turn." Presumably he meant anti-colonial turn. He thought that some employers were now ready to accept the 20 percent but were awaiting administrative action. Three days later, on 28 November, the minister announced that he had accepted the 20 percent increase in the minimum hourly wage.[136]

This was how the workers of French West Africa won a 20 percent increase in the minimum wage. In Guinea, the Conakry strike had lasted sixty-seven days, with workers getting their 20 percent and Sékou Touré being remembered over the years for his "remarkable personal success" in leading the strike.[137] It may well be that Cornut-Gentille had panicked – his own political reports exposed the disunity among the *centrales* – but he no doubt feared inchoate agitation as much as a coordinated campaign.

It is not clear that the labor movement was at this time pressing an anti-colonial stand as well as its case for the 20 percent. The interest of a strong block of voters in the Code du Travail did not make a seamless anti-colonial/pro-labor web: labor's stand in the code debate focused on the French connection. In Senegal, where a strong CGT union movement existed, as well as a branch of the RDA which stuck to a *communisant* position even after the 1950 split, Senghor succeeded in partially detaching the two, by astute alliance-building with Ibrahima Sarr and Abbas Guèye, leaders of the two great strikes of 1946 and 1947–48. Sarr became the representative of Senghor's BDS to the Assemblée de l'Union Française and Guèye joined Senghor in the Assemblée Nationale in Paris. Guèye played an important role as liaison between the deputies and the unions during the crucial period before the second reading of the code in November 1952. In 1953 he played more the role of moderator, helping to broker the agreement by the Senegalese unions to accept the employers' offer of 16 percent increases.[138]

Elsewhere, the split between the RDA and the French Communist Party led the African CGT to focus quite specifically on work-centered issues, while "the indifference of the RDA–Houphouet for union questions" struck some officials even as others worried that the labor movement was bringing about anti-colonial mobilization.[139] Houphouët-Boigny, according to security services, invited a group of Ivorian trade unionists to his house just after the code was passed to deny his indifference to it. But he apparently did say that he considered the strike of 3 November 1952 – the great triumph of trade union unity – "an error," and he left the trade unionists skeptical.[140] Officials reported in 1953 that

M. Houphouet does not conceal that from his point of view the situation of wage earners in Abidjan does not constitute the basic problem. The union leaders would soon be brought to hold a grudge against him for what they call his anti-social attitude and it is necessary to note that the RDA has not supported, in any manner, the most recent work stoppages noted in Abidjan. For M. Houphouet, the planters constitute the real economic armature of the Ivory Coast.[141]

Houphouët-Boigny, French officials were noting, was answering the question, which side are you on? He had chosen the correct side, they felt, and he was credited with persuading the militant Ivorian trade unionist Fiankan to work against a strike over the minimum wage in early 1953.[142]

The most difficult case of all to read is that of Guinea, and only more research will provide answers. Sékou Touré was the hero of the Conakry strike of September–November 1953, which ranks along with Dakar in 1946 and the railways in 1947–48 as the longest major strike in the region. He was a CGT stalwart, known for his fiery speeches and his militance in favor of the standard CGT issues: the Code du Travail, improved wages, and family allowances. He told his union officials, "*Résponsable*, your bedside reading is the Code du Travail, which you can never study enough."[143] But French officials were convinced that his own political ambitions were causing him to side with the RDA–Houphouët and indeed to try to find a tone for his statements that would not displease Houphouët-Boigny. When the Ivorian leader apparently didn't want Sékou Touré to attend a CGT meeting in Abidjan in early 1954, Touré – still wanting to have it both ways – told him that "he was not an agent of communism," which could be taken as an affirmation of support for Houphouët-Boigny in his break with the French communists. Touré went to his meetings, swearing that he would keep out of political discussions, the turf of the RDA. Cornut-Gentille credited Sékou Touré for the "strictly professional character of the resolutions adopted."[144] As chapter 11 will make clear, Sékou Touré would soon help to take the French West African trade union movement toward a nationalist position rather than take nationalism toward an identification with the labor movement.

The governor-general's words suggest a growing official awareness that a domain of "labor relations" could be separated off from a domain of "nationalist politics." Whether it was more strategic for a colonial government to use narrowly focused trade unionism against mass political agitation or conservative political leaders against labor activism was not yet clear. Undoubtedly, it was Houphouët-Boigny's break with the PCF in 1950 that gave officials hope that an African political party could be a conservative force on social issues. Houphouët-Boigny's opponent on the left of the RDA, Gabriel d'Arboussier, seemed quite well aware that the break with the French left could also mean a break with the African trade union movement.[145] Sékou Touré seemed poised on the edge: he could either remain a militant *cégétiste* or ally himself with the RDA–Houphouët faction and push for a widening political voice, but one which was not necessarily going to speak to social issues. Senghor, meanwhile, emerges from official reports as someone shrewdly taking leaders and issues away from the explicitly left-wing Senegalese parties, placing them on the "cégétiste wing" of his own BDS.[146]

For the government, the difficulty with a strategy intended to separate trade unionism from politics was that taming union militance required meeting expensive demands. The business-led Comité de l'Empire Français kept emphasizing this point: "If our products are expensive, it is partly because of the social laws."[147] The high commissioner, as noted above, was very worried about the effects of higher labor costs on development programs. His directeur général des finances, Erhard, reported early in 1953 on the likely incidence of the code provisions in terms that were as polemical as those of the *patronat*. The provision for equal pay for equal work implied the creation of a "single classification of workers," and it would be impossible to find places low enough within the existing contract structure for Europeans in which to place most Africans. The reclassification would in effect upgrade African wages by, Erhard claimed, an average of 35 percent. Of course, this calculation was actually a damning admission of long-standing failure to implement a policy of non-discrimination to which officials had laid claim since the end of the war. And it was not apparent that anyone in the government, including the labor inspectors, had any intention of redoing job classifications in such a systematic way, even if that was what the law implied.[148]

Erhard calculated that the 40-hour week and overtime provisions could add 23 to 27 percent to wages, and social security provisions and family allocations would add some more. Private sector wages for Africans, depending on how various provisions were implemented, would go up at least 30 percent and perhaps 100 percent. More labor inspectors would have to be hired to administer the code. Although civil servants were not affected by the code, ordinary laborers hired by the government were, and government contractors would pass on their higher labor costs to official budgets: "We are thus in the presence of a dilemma: either stop the development of the Federation or suffocate the taxpayer." As to the private sector, "it is the entire economy of the Federation which risks being crushed under expenses inappropriate to the resources and the social structure of Africa."[149]

This argument is still used against programs seeking social comparability between African workers and those of industrialized countries. Other officials were not so alarmed. They didn't think that the implementation of the code was going to be quite so rigorous as Erhard assumed, and they made clear that the proportion of total costs accounted for by African wage labor was not very high. Assuming a 25 percent increase in the average wage, the net cost of peanut oil would rise

2.5 percent, that of factory-produced textiles 4 percent. In most cases, agriculture came under "customary labor," and was not affected at all. The costs of transport and commercialization of crops would rise, but probably under 2 percent for Senegalese peanuts or Ivorian coffee and over twice that for Soudanese peanuts which had longer to travel before reaching a port. Bananas, grown on plantations with wage labor, would be more affected. But employers could also respond by improving efficiency and restructuring work time. In commerce, one study suggested, reducing the work week from 48 to 40 hours would have little effect on output, and costs would only go up by one percent.[150] Another study concluded that the effect of wage increases on the economy "remains small given the part of these wages themselves in total costs."[151]

A brief public debate emerged over what other than wages contributed to the high cost of colonial products. Aujoulat replied to an article in *Marchés Coloniaux* which had bemoaned the impact of the 20 percent increases, pointing out, "profit margins in commerce and all the other factors in net costs remain paradoxically high." African wages, he argued, were still "relatively modest," and if anyone was worried about the peril which colonial economies faced, "why not attack nonetheless the problem of rationalizing enterprises and that, no less important, of profits."[152] This, the Comité de l'Empire Français thought, was a low blow: "One cannot allow such inexactitudes in regard to the size of profits get by." But the business community did not offer to open its books to permit a more precise examination of the topic.[153]

Aujoulat's position was supported by the most detailed study of the period, by a professor at a French law faculty then assigned to the Institut des Hautes Etudes de Dakar, Jacques Lecaillon. He too concluded that the effects of increased labor costs would be felt mainly in industry and other factors – notably the "mercantilist" organization of commerce – contributed far more to the economic weaknesses of French West Africa. He argued that workers' real wages had declined until the union movement developed after the war, at which time they began to rise, and the gains under the code were part of that process of collective assertion. These wage increases, however, were at a slower pace than the rise in revenues from sale of the principal crops, and to the extent (far from clear) that workers were gaining at the expense of agriculturalists, it was because the latter were not getting their share of the export price. The impact of rising wages, he pointed out, did not necessarily translate into higher production costs; they could lead to improved productivity. The question was whether employers would reform their heretofore wasteful forms of labor management. He concluded, "A high wage policy (in the broadest sense) can only succeed however if the economic structure does not block it. It is precisely there where one finds the drama of overseas economies."[154]

The supporters of the code and the 40-hour week did not dwell on the fact that their argument for the benign effects of the code depended in part on the assumption that its social effects were not widespread. The reforms of the code could be radical in principle and significant to the workers involved, but have only modest affect on the economy because the realm of work had been so carefully bounded.

From the start, the minister made clear that the legislature's decision about the definition for a worker would be followed closely: only people earning a wage and working in a position of "subordination" to an employer would be covered, and "paternal power" or "métayage" were specifically contrasted to wage labor. Some officials emphasized that excluding "customary labor" from the picture was not an expedient attempt to limit the law's effects, but sound social policy. A senior judicial official wrote,

an extensive application of the dispositions of the Code du Travail – contrary to the clear wish of the legislature – would lead to a rapid disorganization of certain forms of African society whose evolution we should certainly foster, but whose replacement by an adaptive social organization has not yet been realized in all the territory of French West Africa.[155]

The argument for bounding so carefully the terrain of reform thus did not reject the desirability of transforming rural Africa, but merely asserted that such a process was at present beyond the capability of government. The abode of agricultural production would remain hidden.

This continued to enrage representatives of French business, just as it had during the code debate itself. White businessmen felt that the definitions of the code, in effect, applied to them, but not to African employers: they complained of unfair competition from African businesses and lamented that "under the empire of customary law, autochthonous workers will be without defense against their autochthonous employers."[156] Their arguments were not without an element of truth – despite the evident falsity of the new-found sympathy for exploited Africans – but they were no longer being heard.

Officials, trade unionists, and employers soon turned their attention to family allowances. The vagueness of the article in the code – giving power to implement family allocations to governors – reflected the lack of consensus on the issue as of November 1952. Days after the code was passed, the Inspecteur Général du Travail in Paris, Mlle Guelfi, warned the minister that the reason why many workers had campaigned for the code was to get family allocations and without prompt action in this regard there was a risk of being "overtaken by workers' demands."[157] Yet even a pro-code, pro-family official like Aujoulat was openly uncertain after the code's passage about what form family support should take – the "prestation in cash is not the only form, nor the only one capable of assistance to the family. Formulas can be proposed and put into operation in each territory. A good field of action, let us say in passing, for local assemblies."[158] When, after the "quarrel of the 20 percent" was over, the question of family allocations came to the fore, High Commissioner Cornut-Gentille greeted it with little enthusiasm: there were "redoubtable problems" but "according to the wish of the legislature we are getting to work without delay..."[159] The government's attempt to control the discussion would not go unquestioned.

In September 1953, the minister, L. Jacquinot, sent around to his high commissioners and labor inspectors a circular asking for a study of how to implement family allocations. He laid out the case for action: family prestations had become accepted as part of the social entitlements of a worker in International Labour Conventions and in the Code du Travail; demographic regression was a threat, particularly in French Equatorial Africa; the status quo in which only civil servants received family allocations risked creating a disequilibrium in labor markets. Jacquinot's demographic argument took up the quasi-eugenicist concern expressed within the ministry in the pre-code discussions, that workers had a distressingly low birth rate, even though they were "the most able-bodied and, as a consequence, the most desirable elements from a demographic point of view."[160] It was in the family where individuals grew physically and socially, and effort to reproduce a working class had to be focused there.

Jacquinot wanted to proceed from metropolitan models: allocations would apply to all workers (as defined by the code) who had been in service for a certain length of time; they would include a series of payments made during pregnancy and childhood and would be financed by employer contributions to a fund based on a percentage of the total wage bill of the employer.

By the time officials in the field responded to his queries, a year had gone by and the topic had been politicized. Unions were demanding allocations, and officials feared a strike wave in which general mobilization over this issue would bring together a variety of local demands (see below). Meanwhile, employer organizations were charging that family allocations would lead to economic disaster, promote polygamy, and be a less efficient way of improving infant and child health than expenditures on health facilities.[161] But the consensus of officials was that a modest level of support along the lines suggested by the minister would not be extremely expensive. A study of FWA estimated that about 95,000 workers – about a third of the total number – had children, a total of 211,000 of them. The surveys presented a picture of a young labor force, with a high percentage of bachelors, a low incidence of polygamy, and small families. In industries in FWA, for example, 44 percent of workers surveyed were single, 7 percent were polygamous; 61 percent had no children, only 12 percent had more than three children. Civil servants had more, workers in agriculture had fewer. This low reproduction rate for workers was one of the reasons the Inspection du Travail had pushed for family allocations; it also implied, until allocations themselves brought up the rates, that the program was not expensive.[162] They figured that the program could be financed by a surcharge on wages of 3 to 5 percent and that the effect on final costs would in most cases be under 1 percent.[163]

Officials now were convinced that family allocations responded to a genuine need in the African world of work. Pierre Pélisson, having moved from the head of the Inspectorate in FWA to the corresponding position in FEA, argued that whatever differences existed between African and European families as a matter of fact made it all the more desirable as a matter of policy to help African workers' families become more stable:

the African wage earner, as head of a family, above all the urban detribalized wage earner, encounters special difficulties from the necessity of maintaining a family notably when, having attained a certain level of social evolution and stabilization as a worker, he tends to base his living conditions on those of the European worker.[164]

The high commissioner of FWA, still Cornut-Gentille, had a different, but equally compelling concern in mind:

The refusal, pure and simple, on the part of the Authorities to examine in a favorable light the institution of family prestation can only have the effect of social agitation, which will not fail to occur sooner or later in the form of multiple strikes, extending to all sectors of activity...[165]

Meanwhile, in the Conseil Supérieur du Travail, the Paris-based advisory board on labor issues, there was a head-on collision between labor and management. The African union representatives "noted vigorously their support for allocations in cash as a complement to the wage." They insisted that agricultural wage workers be included, although the minister was leaning in the opposite direction.[166] The *patronat* was willing to consider a "network of institutions in favor of the family," such as dispensaries for pregnant women, giving blankets to children, and providing food aid to women and children, but insisted that cash allowances were inconsistent with the "structure of the African family cell" and would add 5 to 15 percent to labor costs. The employers then refused to engage in specific discussion of a plan, since their counter-proposal had failed to move officials. The minister, now Robert Buron, refused to fall for this ploy, saying "Your silence is neutral."[167] Deputies to the Assemblée Nationale kept up pressure, passing a resolution which in effect called on the administration to implement the family allocations provisions of the Code du Travail. Respect for Africans' "profound sense of equality," a key supporter argued, required that French workers' benefits be extended to all.[168]

Family allocations were a key issue behind a new attempt to bring all the unions together at the Conférence Intersyndicale of Conakry, initiated by the CGT in September 1954. This led to plans for a 24-hour strike on 3 November 1954 and a 48-hour version 10–11 January 1955. The delayed revision of family allowances for civil servants under the Lamine Guèye law of 1950 and the slow implementation of the Code du Travail, especially in regard to family allowances, brought together public and private sector unions. But in the context of growing tensions among unions (chapter 11) the strikes were not nearly as unified as the 1952 general strike over the code itself. However, throughout 1955 a series of public and private sector strikes in several territories focused on issues of equality between African and French workers.[169] What frightened Cornut-Gentille was that family allocations provided an issue which crossed different sectors and interested all the rival union confederations. The CFTC, he thought, would cooperate with the CGT for "the sole object of the unification of the regime of family allocations in the public sector and the concession of family prestations to the workers of the private sector."[170]

As another Comité Intersyndicale planned protests for October and November 1955, officials thought that family allocations gave them the one issue for which "unity was not a vain word."[171] In November, as territorial assemblies were giving administration proposals a final look, Cornut-Gentille telegraphed Paris that a 72-hour strike over this issue had just been put off thanks to "moderate elements of the Comité Intersyndical Fédéral" on the government's promise that the regime would be in place by 1 January 1956. If this promise were not met, he warned,

the unanimity of trade union organizations of all tendencies will immediately unleash generalized agitation throughout the Federation and measures of application which are put into effect afterward will appear as if decided under threat of a strike, which can only contribute to increasing social malaise and eroding our authority.[172]

This was Cornut-Gentille's second warning of the need to anticipate union action in order to preserve French authority. Between the dénouement of the battle of the 20 percent and the battle of family allowances, "agitation" was more background noise than a chorus. But he and his advisors saw the threat of mobilization linked to a discourse in which they themselves participated, albeit from a different angle.

By June of 1955, the labor experts had devised a plan; territorial consultations concealed the reality that decisions were made at the center.[173] The labor experts applied allocations to all workers under the code's definition, including those in agricultural wage labor, largely because they wanted to avoid biasing the labor market in favor of urban labor.[174] But agriculture – and this was of particular relevance to the Ivory Coast – would benefit from a separate organization to administer allocations as well as state contributions to reduce the burden on employers.

The prestations themselves would take several forms. New families would be supported by a special allocation at the birth of their first three children;[175] a prenatal allocation would be paid in regard to expectant mothers, as long as they were monitored by health authorities; the maternity allocation would be paid after children were born; and the family allowance itself, on a per child basis, would be paid in regard to young children and to those who remained at school and under the parents' charge. Another indemnity to working mothers – required elsewhere in the Code du Travail – would be taken over by the family allocations fund from the employer. This fund would be built up, as in earlier plans, from employer contributions based on total wages paid; the rate would be kept under 5 percent. The draft plan kept the amounts of each allocation below the figures that had previously been discussed on the grounds that it was necessary to start slowly and get an accurate picture of family sizes and needs.[176] The plan was batted around in the territorial assemblies of FWA, and modified by the minister. By then it was November 1955 and authorities in Dakar were fearing a renewal of agitation. The government-general offered to subsidize the funds to allow the poorer colonies to pay the various prestations. The *patronat* made one last appeal "to the good sense" of officials, but realized that the battle was over.[177]

On 1 January 1956, family allocations went into effect in FWA; they were extended to FEA six months later.[178] In Senegal, a family would receive 4,800 francs "allocation du foyer" for the birth of each of its first three children; each pregnancy would bring the family 3,600 francs prenatal allocation and 4,800 francs maternity allocation; 400 francs per month would be paid as the basic family allowance for each dependent child, through the end of his or her schooling. The 400 francs would be around 8 percent of the minimum wage; the maternity allocation around a month's minimum pay: such allocations would make a considerable difference to the life of a worker. The sums were identical in the Ivory

Coast, slightly less in Dahomey and Guinea, least of all in Niger (260 per month per child).[179]

The corollary to the distribution of revenue was the surveillance of the recipients. Marriages and births were to be registered if allocations were to be claimed; prenatal and maternity allocations were conditional on visits to medical personnel; family allowances were contingent, once the child reached the appropriate age, on school attendance.[180] Since the allowances were being distributed to workers in their pay packets, the entire program tied together the place of work, family life, and the institutions of the state – from the état-civil to the school.

This was the kind of surveillance which Michel Foucault has located at the heart of the modern state and the modern conception of society. It was a far cry from the monitoring of African collectivities by Lugard's indirect rulers as well as Eboué's view of African reproduction as taking place within an "indigenous" community which French officials did not have to know or understand. But surveillance, focused as it was on women, also revealed a fundamental ambiguity in the late colonial vision of gender: women were the key to the reproduction of industrial man, but they had nothing of their own to bring to the project. The proper model for a family and for childraising came from elsewhere and their fidelity in following them was to be observed by bureaucrats.[181]

The decrees provided support for the children of female workers as well as of male; there was even a special provision for benefits for wage earning women who gave birth. But the expectations of the planners was that of the male worker and the female child-care provider. In the studies on which cost estimates were based, the surveyed population in industry included 25,357 African males and no females; in commerce there were 14,045 males and 105 females.[182] The language in which officials addressed the burdens of raising children on a worker's salary was comfortably masculinist, and officials allocated, using their work force data, minimal funds for working mothers.[183]

It was the male worker's position in the work force which officials wanted to stabilize while assuring that his role would be reproduced in the next generation. The gender bias was too self-evident for much discussion. Nor did anyone comment on the fact that the definition of the worker in the Code du Travail placed the kinds of tasks which women most often did outside the law's conception of work. That women were crucial to the commerce of West African cities or that they performed a great variety of income-generating roles, did not enter into the discussion of family allowances – or any other aspect of the code.

The implementation of family allowances got off to a slow start. Although the minister had acknowledged that the surveillance component of the project would have to be phased in slowly – since the numbers of nurses, doctors, and teachers, let alone registrars for the état-civil – were insufficient, the system still took time to begin paying out at anticipated levels.[184] At the end of 1956, 41,796 families in FWA (about half of them in Senegal) were collecting allocations based on 106,599 children. The payout totalled 358 million francs – less than a quarter of the anticipated figure.[185] These figures would come up. Meanwhile, the principle and the mechanism had been established for, in the minister's words, "a redistribution of a part of the territorial income for the profit of workers, as a function of the number of children they have in charge."[186]

Ten years earlier it had seemed unthinkable to the makers of colonial social policy that family allocations should be extended in a systematic way to Africans. It was not unthinkable, however, to the African civil service unions which first raised the issue in January 1946. By 1956, family allocations had been extended to the entire wage labor force of French Africa, and officials now embraced them for much the same reason that they rejected them earlier – the peculiar nature of the African family. But now it was a question of weaning workers away from its debilitating effects, of creating family forms that resembled those presumed to predominate in Europe, of insuring the reproduction of a working class on the basis of workers' earnings and within the milieu of the workplace.

It was less clear that the way African workers' families lived would change as soon as they began to collect family allowances – how workers made use of their diverse material and cultural resources was an open question, one which was only barely being investigated by social scientists and largely ignored by officials at the time. But by 1956, having satisfied themselves that the problems of work could, as a policy matter, be put into the framework of a comprehensive, metropolitan based labor code, and having implemented some of the most materially and symbolically important aspects of the code, government officials had made their move to define a working class and to shape the way it would evolve. In so doing, European precedents became the standard for what was sociologically and morally correct. African trade unions used such a framework – and a language of universal needs and contributions – to put themselves at the focus of debate over labor issues and to win important gains for their rank and file. Meanwhile, the colonial business interests found themselves and their once-compelling arguments about African nature at the margins of policy.

The argument that remained for employers to use was costs: the 5 percent surcharge for family allowances was now added to the 20 percent increase in the unskilled laborer's hourly wage and other mandated social payments.[187] Some commentators argued back that the challenge of the code was for employers to change themselves. "One of the happy consequences of the code," wrote Pierre Chauleur in the introduction to a volume on labor in the overseas territories,

is that the massive and unnecessary use of workers with mediocre output and low pay becomes impossible and that the employer finds himself obligated to make an effort of intelligence and rationalization... The application of the code must result, it would be pointless to dissimulate, in a modification of the very structure of the overseas economy.[188]

Once defined, the working class became the object of more comprehensive attention. A "Service Sociale" was created in 1951 and charged with "the protection of the collectivity, the family, and childhood," in light of the fact that "an urban proletariat has thus been created with all the social problem which this condition implies..." Its offices offered help to troubled families and programs to combat juvenile delinquency.[189]

Most revealing was the "Office des Etudes Psychotechniques," created in 1951 to organize training programs, "to prepare the young worker to hold his own in the Europeanized technical world," and to study the "particular mental habits" of Africans.[190] The office arose from the neo-Taylorism in vogue in certain management circles in France, where a heavy dose of psychology was added to concerns with efficient industrial organization. A newspaper called its director, Raoul Durand, "one of the most powerful French reconstructors of the black man." Asked, "Is the black man malleable?" Durand replied, "He is, at times marvelously."[191]

Durand's remark revealed more about certain white men than it did about any black man. It was an assertion of control, of power, and of the belief that the goal of this power was to make the black worker more like the white. An Office study in 1953 concluded,

It is exceptional that a black accepts the need to carry out his effort beyond the simple task in order to increase his gains. For that to happen, he must have been profoundly Europeanized, he must have adopted our motivations and accepted our own necessities. In a word, he has retained nothing African except the color.[192]

Conclusion

The labor inspectors and reform-minded officials and legislators pushed their models at the very time when their control was very much in question, in the labor field as in others. They had the most success when African trade unionists and politicians saw their own interest in using a similar discourse for their own ends, in ways which simultaneously threatened French power and deployed its language.

In 1953, shortly after the code was put into effect, someone in the bureaucracy, most likely in the Inspection du Travail, wrote a mimeographed memorandum entitled "How does an African worker in Senegal live?" He acknowledged how much needed to be done to bring up the standard of living of those at the bottom of the wage hierarchy and how much of a drag on progress African institutions like the extended family remained. He took it as a sign of improved living standards and advancing civilization that Senegalese workers were eating more imported food. Even the ordinary laborer in Dakar, he concluded, "is infinitely closer, by the totality of his tastes and conceptions of diet, to a worker in Marseille than to a cultivator in the Niger bend." He undoubtedly didn't know that his language had been used a couple of years previously by a Soudanese trade union newspaper in making a claim for family allowances: "there is no difference between a FRENCHMAN born near the banks of the Seine or the Loire and a FRENCHMAN born near the banks of the Senegal or the Niger."[193] What for one participant in this discourse marked a belief that France had set the model for the world's future was for another a claim to a material entitlement.

8   Family wages and industrial relations in British Africa

Something like the French Code du Travail was not a solution available to the British Colonial Office. Legislation had to come from individual colonies and their governors, and Whitehall in the late 1940s was trying to show that it was giving colonies more of a voice in their own affairs. Where settlers were a factor, they got the first chance to use Legislative Councils, whereas in French Africa the influence of colons and commercial was diluted and subordinated to the larger tasks of post-war imperialism. The Colonial Office could often do little more than try to "inculcate a sense of urgency" into colonial governors in regard to his policy initiatives.[1] The tension between imperial center and colonial periphery made it difficult to paper over the ambiguity – felt in London as well as Nairobi – between modernizing reforms and deeply-rooted ideas about race and African culture.[2]

The absence of an institutional capability to act on a pan-African scale was not, for British policy makers, altogether a bad thing. It meant there was no incentive for African trade unionists to organize on a similar scale. The French West African strike intended to influence the code debate in 1952 or those over its implementation would have no anglophone equivalent. No regional trade unions emerged comparable to the West African CGT, and unions had trouble focusing at an empire-wide level on issues of equality with metropolitan workers.

But British officials still faced the same problems that their French counterparts did: how to create an orderly and productive work force. They had the same basic intellectual tools with which to work: the African work force, like its European equivalent, could be acculturated and socialized to industrial and urban life if the new generation of workers grew up in the civilizing atmosphere of the workplace itself. Such thoughts were most clearly articulated in investigatory commissions following strikes (chapter 6), but they helped to convince the Colonial Office that a specific set of policies directed at the labor question had to supplement the emphasis on development as a remedy for disorder. Having recognized that the problem was imperial – that strike waves might wash ashore anywhere – officials faced the question of what they could do within the institutional framework they had.

This chapter will follow how officials in London, working at a high level of generalization, thought through their anxiety about the African present and their imagination of an industrial future. But the government actions which had the most effect on African workers – and revealed the starkest contradictions in colonial policy – were debated within individual colonies, and I will examine two of the most important of those, Northern Rhodesia and Kenya.

Trade unionism and wage-fixing/order and reproduction

Officials were convinced that higher wages were essential to head off trouble and make it possible for a working class to reproduce itself. The Secretary of State, Creech Jones, in 1948, insisted, "we cannot condone colonial economies which are based on cheap labour." He wanted his governors to tell him if wage regulating machinery was being used not only to keep pace with inflation but to bring about "a higher standard of living... [The] matter is of some urgency if we are to tackle subversive propaganda, escape in these new economic plans the charge of exploitation, and give all round satisfaction to the colonial people that their interests are being protected and promoted."[3]

Two approaches to raising wages were batted around through the mid-1950s, embodying quite different assumptions about workers: industrial relations and wage-fixing. The former assumed that workers could organize themselves and bargain, provided that the state recognized the legitimacy of unions and strikes and supplied mechanisms for orderly negotiations. The second assumed that workers had to be helped, that statutory bodies – whose agenda and procedures were set by officials even if workers and employers were represented – would set wages in certain professions or in certain places. Doubts about the first made the second appear more attractive, but the wage fixing solution, it was feared, might make the negotiations model harder to develop.

This, at the end of the 1940s, was what a leading labor advisor in London thought was happening:

much of colonial trade union activity has been directed toward seeking higher wages from government Departments... If the workers are unable to secure a reasonable wage from private employers because of their lack of organisation there seems to be a good field for government action in the way of wage-fixing machinery.[4]

The work of government boards to fix minimum wages – based on a cost of living index – had an aura of objectivity about it. The trouble was that once one went beyond adjusting wages for inflation, the terrain into which officials had tried to confine discussion during the war (chapter 4), it was not clear what principles were to be used. The point, as Creech Jones had stated, was to raise standards of living in a period of favorable economic conditions. A study in 1949 on "Labour's Share in the Product of Colonial Industry" found that wages in copper mining were going up – but not as fast as copper prices – and that wages in gold mining were going up – but not as fast as gold prices. In most colonies, no estimates were available of national income; nor were data on actual (as opposed to the legal minimum) wages generally available, let alone data on taxes and profits. Meanwhile, "On the separate question of whether the wage earner is receiving a 'living wage,'" officials complained of statistical problems as well, but the interesting point about the query is the phrase "separate question." A notion of a "living wage" was being teased out from questions of export earnings and productivity. This came close to saying that the cost of reproducing a labor force could be calculated on the basis of the conditions it encountered in the workplace and independently of such considerations as alternatives (farm income), possibilities for paying higher wages (high profits), or consequences of paying them (driving up export prices). The relation of workers' incomes to those of other segments of the population was to be an issue that would not go away (see below). But for now, a Colonial Office draft memorandum on how to calculate a fair wage was so unsatisfactory that it was never sent.[5] Policy remained where it had been left by a rather vague circular of October 1947 to colonial governments, "asking them to consider the need for the introduction locally of such aspects of [wage-fixing machinery] as might be suitable for the Colony."[6]

On the other hand, trade union organization was not necessarily going to achieve the "living wage" officials had now set themselves as a goal. A British newspaper had proclaimed in 1948 that British policy was "find the Ernest Bevins of the Bush and teach them all they know." But there weren't so many Bevins to be found and they didn't necessarily want to know what British officials wanted to teach.[7] Reviewing trade union policy in 1950, the Colonial Office claimed that it had been encouraging colonial trade unions since 1930. In the empire as a whole, there had been only three unions in 1932, 228 in 1942, 939 in 1947 and now 1,037, with 616,000 members. But they were bedevilled by the lack of informed membership and by the prevalence of "irresponsibles" among the leadership. Increased labour department staffing since 1942 had not solved these problems, which were now accentuated by frequent diversion "from its industrial purposes to serve political ends."[8]

"I have long held the view," minuted a Colonial Office labor expert in

1949, "that the development of *sound* trade unionism in the colonies has not led to improvements we had hoped for." Most important, and again in the absence of reliable data, he thought that only 10 percent of workers in the colonies were organized, a figure roughly half that of French West Africa. Other reports gave the figure as closer to 5 percent, and saw "little prospect of any significant increase in their numbers in the immediate future." And the trade unions that had organized themselves focused more attention on extracting concessions from government than on private sector bargaining.[9] James Griffiths, who took over as Secretary of State from Creech Jones in 1951, admitted that this weakness put the onus back onto government wage fixing: he protested his "faith in the ultimate ability of the unions to achieve improvements by voluntary methods of negotiation," but "where trade unions are poorly organised it is a duty of government to ensure the payment of reasonable wages and the establishment of reasonable working conditions."[10]

Whereas the French system divided the colony into geographical zones, each of which had a wage set for it based on measured variations in the cost of living, British colonies lacked publicly stated wage policies and were covered by a patchwork of minimum wages by industries and localities, some set by employer–employee–government wage boards, some by other means.[11] The British system left large gaps, and gave considerable scope to organized employer lobbies – such as the white farmers of Kenya – to insulate themselves from its effects. In 1951, the governor of Kenya told his Wages Advisory Board that he was "perturbed" at the low level of minimum wages and particularly at employers' insistence on paying only "bachelor wages." The board duly considered his opinion and decided to ignore it on the grounds that the minimum wage

is not intended to be a fair or reasonable wage, but merely the legal minimum which may be paid. The Board therefore thought it wrong to take into account the fact that the worker is probably married, and considered it proper to base the wage on the minimum required for the man himself.[12]

In 1953, as in 1945, wages in East Africa generally made it impossible for workers to separate themselves from the rural economy: "The wage is not, and apparently has not up to the present been intended to be, a living family wage – a family cannot live on it without the 'hidden subsidy' provided by the products of the worker's holding." Officials claimed that wage rates in British West Africa were "very significantly higher" than those in East Africa, and officials attributed the difference to better trade unions and the fact that the government employed a larger percentage of the work force and set the market conditions for the rest. Equally likely, the strength of African agriculture in coastal regions, in cocoa and other products, drove up the supply price of labor, although "northern" workers in colonies like the Gold Coast were in a situation more comparable to those of East or Central Africa. Whatever the causes, the "bachelor wage" appeared to be the norm in Kenya, Tanganyika, and Uganda, while Nigeria, the Gold Coast, Sierra Leone, and Northern Rhodesia made claims to approach the family model – with considerable variation and uncertainty.[13] The Colonial Office's labour advisor, Earl Barltrop, had his doubts about West Africa too: the Nigerian government's "family" wages for its employees were too low actually to cover family needs, and Sierra Leone's mines expected workers to "supplement" their wages from efforts of their wives and children on farms and in petty trade – precisely what London wanted to break away from.[14] Whatever the uncertainties about actual wages in West Africa, it was not clear anywhere that *policy*, as of 1954, had brought about a family wage structure.

The biggest difference between French and British policies was not so much on the wage-fixing side as in the aura of normality that attached itself to most French discussions of African trade unions, and the unwillingness of British officials to make that discursive leap. Most British colonies included the kinds of restrictions which were discussed and rejected in the debate on the Code du Travail, such as the insistence on annual reports to officials of trade unions' financial accounts. But the tone is more significant than the contents: the supposed "immaturity" of colonial trade unions caused French officials to pause – and then to pretend that institutions could be built as if African unions did correspond to the French model – but it induced British officials to agonize over the danger of "irresponsibility" of current unions and the inordinate difficulties of creating them elsewhere.

Like their French counterparts, British officials assumed, without serious consideration of alternatives, that if colonial trade unions were to develop, they would do so on the metropolitan model. "The industrial history of the United Kingdom has been the natural source of the experience and the techniques which have motivated and guided the development of industrial relations in the Colonies," wrote one of the guides in 1951. The word "natural" discloses the most about this way of modelling Africa's future.[15] The British model, the Colonial Labour Advisory Committee (CLAC) concluded in 1951, was "adaptable enough to be transplanted successfully and to provide a sound foundation from which the Colonial movement can develop its own traditions." Still, another report claimed, trade unions weren't there yet: "experience has shown that in many Colonies the development of the trade unions has not yet reached the stage at which it is thought to be advisable to have trade union legislation based entirely upon that of the United Kingdom."[16]

The language in which trade unionism was being discussed abounded with metaphors from child development. "Both workers and employers needed careful nursing before they could enter into joint relations in the right spirit"; trade unions needed "mothering"; trade unions were "in their infancy" or even "embryonic." The language was catching: a Nigerian labor specialist in 1962 deemed trade unions to be in their "adolescence."[17]

The British Trade Union Congress, which cooperated with the Colonial Office on union affairs, was at least as condescending. In East and Central Africa, trade unionism was "in its infancy." West African unions were "fairly mature," but "prey to nationalist political groups." Unions were prey to communists, who were becoming a TUC obsession. Even the TUC's most optimistic projections depended on belittling African workers: "But in the exertion of influence upon their movements the task is at least made easier by one of its weaknesses, the fact that the bulk of the members will follow their leaders blindly, uncritically and largely inarticulately. Influence exerted upon the leaders is capable therefore of a decisive effect."[18] So if the French CGT projected onto African workers their fantasy of the international proletarian, the TUC projected its fantasy of the primitive, with itself playing for the moment the role of chief.

This kind of language was reinforced by the political context in which trade unionism was being discussed. Right after the war, the major strikes – such as that in Mombasa in 1947 – were perceived as actions of an inchoate mass, as movements of people barely incorporated into industrial occupations and urban life; officials saw themselves struggling against African primitiveness brought into the city. A few years later, this worry had shifted form, particularly as a result of events in West Africa: demagogues were mobilizing masses. The British model of apolitical trade unionism was sometimes evoked as a welcome antidote to present dangers. But those unions could themselves be dangerous, and in the early 1950s, the word "communist" as well as the word "nationalist" appeared alongside – although it did not replace – the evocations of unruly masses.[19] Trade unionists in the Gold Coast were thought to be dangerous nationalists, perhaps communists; the East African Trades Union Congress had been taken in charge by the alleged communist Makhan Singh; the Nigerian trade unionist Nduka Eze was thought to be a threat as a mass mobilizer and as a leftist. Danger could lie in organization as well as its absence, and the political threat in West Africa clouded the rather brighter picture – by East African standards – of trade unions engaged in collective bargaining.[20] Officials in the post-war years generally argued that in principle unions in the colonies were a good idea, but they insisted on a measure of colonial authority on industrial relations. I will return to that point shortly through a look at British thinking about the trade union question in one of its most volatile arenas, Kenya.

But the very factors which made officials think that industrial relations required a guiding hand also made them think that trade unions were all the more necessary. As officials increasingly fantasized the modern Africa they claimed to be shaping, the idea of trade unions helped to hold together a number of other considerations that went beyond their specific role in industrial relations.[21] An influential pamphlet written in 1949 by Richard Luyt, an important labor administrator in both Northern Rhodesia and Kenya, linked trade unionism to the growing consensus in favor of stabilization, arguing that as new communities began to form they would need new forms of social bonding and of leadership. Trade unions could replace the "traditional African system of family or tribal mutual aid." James Griffiths, then the Secretary of State, saw this too:

An alternative society must be created for men no longer bound by tribal and village affiliations or else we should be faced with a people without roots, a "lumpen" proletariat. It was essential that a social structure should be erected for these newcomers to industry and urban life in which they would have a "sense of belonging."[22]

Politically, much the same argument was made: unions were part of a modern polity, representing certain interests and providing a forum in which leadership could arise:

great weight should have been given to the need for the development of trade unions not merely to provide a protection for working standards but also to create in time an additional balance and check in the machinery of government; and, to some extent, to lay the foundation of self-government in industry as a step towards a wider degree of political autonomy... It might also be hoped that, in an increasing measure, the movement will throw up its own leaders and bring into the political and public life of the Colonies that leavening of practical common sense and experience of the "man in the street" which is so much needed in some areas to break the monopoly of the professional politician and the lawyer.[23]

This is vintage Colonial Office thinking: the present consisted of masses and demagogues, immature workers, trade unions dominated by irresponsible elements, while in the future trade unions were a vital force for community and responsible politics. The fantasy of the modern and the fear of the backward shaped each other.

Practically, the Colonial Office insisted that trade unions be placed under a series of restrictions: trade unions had to be registered, and registrars were entitled to refuse unions they deemed illegitimate; accounts of trade unions were subject to inspection; the right to strike was restricted in certain areas.[24] Taking their child development language to be more than a metaphor, officials sent British trade unionists to train African trade unionists. Labour officers took special courses in the UK so as to become effective tutors. Meanwhile, the TUC provided advice and aid on a modest scale to African unions.[25]

But, more importantly, the concern with maintaining supervisory authority opened London up to arguments – duly provided – that made the positive goals of officials even more difficult to realize. The Kenyan government argued that the danger of "communist-inspired" general strikes and later the Mau Mau Emergency required legislation restricting the right to strike. Officials in London saw this as a ploy to make trade union development "as difficult as possible," but when the governor played the disorder card, the Colonial Office let him have his way. Secretary of State Lyttleton wrote the governor in 1954:

In the face of your strong conviction... I feel unable to sustain my objections... It is perhaps felt that the present is no time for the governments voluntarily to reduce their legal powers for countering unrest generated for subversive motives in whatever form it appears and I recognise the grounds for this viewpoint; but in my opinion it is inappropriate and may in the long run be harmful to seek to minimise this risk through the retention of permanent legislation which restricts the fundamental right of organised labour in the last resort to use the strike weapon to achieve its legitimate aims.[26]

The same arguments about political demagogues and gullible masses appeared in all regions and resulted in debates about restrictive trade union legislation.[27] The Colonial Office – subject to TUC criticism for denying trade union rights and fearful that too much restriction "might well result in 'unofficial' strikes replacing the 'official' variety" – tried to moderate the restrictive urge, but it basically accepted the argument that the peculiarities of colonized peoples required a restrictive and vigilant government approach to trade unionism.[28]

The old debate over collective bargaining and wage-fixing was getting nowhere in the early and mid-1950s, and colonies in varying ways fiddled with minimum wage regulation, improvised in their relations with unions, and dealt with labor disputes among workers earning well above the minimum wage as well as those living on the margins. At the empire-wide level, officials still insisted that the key to economic advance was higher productivity, which required stabilization, which required paying a family wage.

Meanwhile, the family wage idea had acquired international credibility, and this helped to frame British discussions. There had been a series of discussions at the Inter-African Labor Conference in 1950 and 1953, following upon opening of the agenda of the ILO to include applying the social policies of European nations to dependent peoples, of family wages and family allowances (chapter 9). The French representatives at these conferences, along with those of Belgium, had drawn attention to the idea of family allowances. Having that issue on the table forced British officials within the Colonial Office to come to grips with what they really meant by a policy of supporting workers' families.

Although the British colonial establishment accepted the international consensus in favor of stabilizing workers and even though a form of family allowances was part of the welfare state in Great Britain, no-one wanted to apply family allowances to British colonies.[29] The most telling argument was political, and it was put clearly by the newly appointed Subcommittee on Wages and Family Responsibilities:

It would however be dangerous for us to adopt the Belgian method of approach [family allowances]. In British Colonial territories the amount of any family allowance would be likely to be a greater proportion of a wage-earner's total income than in this country, and therefore, if family allowances were introduced, government would have a say in fixing a significant percentage of a man's total income. The workers could then reasonably conclude that their interests could be better advanced by political agitation than by action in the industrial field.[30]

The committee certainly had a point: family allowances in French Africa had been the focus of mobilization on a wide scale to claim favorable action by the government.

The British approach neither fostered orchestrated, wide-scale campaigns for entitlements nor solved the problems in question. While officials rejected family allocations, they insisted upon the importance of family wages and stabilization. The collective wisdom emerging from a CLAC meeting in 1953 was on both sides of the same issue:

A family wage was needed which would enable the worker to have his family with him near his place of employment... The employer ought to pay to adult male workers an adequate wage for a family of average size and, while it might be difficult to define what an adequate wage was, it was not difficult to see when it was inadequate. The adequacy of the wage had however to be related to the productivity of the community as a whole. All sorts of difficulties would arise if a differential wage were to be paid simply because a man had a family. Wives were regarded as economic assets in most of Africa and it would be difficult to limit payment of allowances to one only.[31]

One problem with this statement was its standard economic conception of the wage as a transaction between two individuals, which gave no room for considering the process of social reproduction.[32] From a transaction-centered logic, it indeed made no sense to pay one worker more than another because the former had children – it might very well lead to discrimination against parents in the labor market. The French plan had solved that problem by dealing with a social problem at a social level: employers hired without regard to family considerations, contributed to a fund based on their total wage bill, and this fund then doled out money based on family configurations. The other problem here was its simultaneously positing an objective for the future – getting workers' families to live with the workers – and held against it a defect of the present – the supposed proclivity of African men to have more than one wife and to live off their labors.

Opinions coming in from the field, requested from London, now generally saw bachelor wages as inadequate but would not accept family allowances. Governors and labour commissioners pointed out that where bachelor wages prevailed family separation lowered the birth rate and that "the urban worker so separated from his family is unlikely to feed or live as well as he would be able to if they had accompanied him." They thought that bachelor workers were unstable in employment and were not learning the values and habits of industrial society, that instability seriously held back productivity. But family allowances were "not appropriate" to local situations; they cost too much; or they had "not yet been contemplated."[33] The subcommittee reviewing the question concluded, "What was needed was rather a general effort to bring the wage up to an adequate level."[34]

That of course had been British policy since before World War II. In those cases, like Northern Rhodesia in 1953, where officials claimed to be getting close, they did so in terms of a rigorously male-centered perspective:

The fact is that African wage earning husbands are able to support their wives and families from the wages they receive and it is immaterial whether the wives and families cultivate the family plot... In fact a high percentage of our industrial workers have no family plot since they live in the municipal or township locations or the mine townships.[35]

More frequently, these masculinist images represented an aspiration. Southern Rhodesia's important Urban African Affairs Commission was still looking in 1958 toward the day when the African would "become more and more divorced from his tribal economy" and more focused on the "European market" and on the "values and aspirations" of Europeans; when workers' wives would devote themselves to "the building up of healthy stable homes" in urban areas; when "the influence of an energetic and proud woman [would] stimulate a man to provide better clothes, housing, household equipment and education for his family and thus inculcate in him a spirit of healthy ambition." And it admitted that inadequate wages, insufficient housing, and residential segregation remained "shackles which prevent Africans from becoming normal urban dwellers."[36]

When doubts were raised along the way on economic grounds they were set to rest by socio-economic arguments. In 1954, some lower level officials in the Colonial Office worried that any wage principles other than the market would not be "economically sound." The Tory Secretary of State,

Oliver Lyttleton, put a stop to that, issuing in June 1954 a circular which reaffirmed government policy for the last decade, putting the principle of family stabilization above the principle of the market: "even where the 'bachelor wage' still represents the supply price of labor, it may be below the level of wages necessary to secure efficient production."[37]

When labor administrators pooled their experience at a conference in 1956, they decided that the governments should stress collective bargaining as the way to raise workers' standards of living, but insure that wages "are not unduly low" and covered family responsibilities. Workers' wages had to meet the contingencies of life and reproduction in an urban, industrial setting and the poverty of rural Africa should not bring them down: "We consider that it is wrong to relate the earning capcity of a wage earner to these peasant standards; his wage rate should rather be related to those factors which influence wage rates in industrial societies."[38] An industrial worker was an industrial worker.

Industrial societies also required mechanisms of social insurance, and the ILO since 1944 had been moving toward a consensus that such systems belonged in colonies. British officials realized that their own policies logically implied that African workers faced the same hazards of loss of income in ill health or old age as any other wage-dependent people, and they opened up a discussion of social security between London and various colonies. But they did so with trepidation. Within the Colonial Office, the discussion was quickly limited to a few forms of insurance and sharply cut off as "not realistic" when briefly raised in a parliamentary question in 1954. As late as 1961, a Colonial Office specialist on social security minuted, "Obviously a genuine insurance scheme is out of the question." A 1954 committee cited England's "high standard of social security" as the obvious model but immediately dismissed it as out of step "with social and economic progress." More practically, it contemplated some measures that would allow a worker who fell on "ill days" to "remain a townsman" and not be "driven by circumstance to return to his rural community and burden them." British officials knew that social problems of cities had to be tackled – and sent a small number of social welfare workers out to Africa – but they would not go so far as the French legislature in writing some principles of a social security system into legislation, even if its substance, as initially with family allowances, was left to be implemented in the future.[39] Trade unionists in British Africa were never able to seize this discursive terrain, such as a claim to equal benefits, and turn it into a sustained theme in a decade-long campaign for entitlements, as did French West African workers.[40]

Having opened the possibility that the African could become industrial man, officials drew back from the implications of their universalistic thinking: the healthy African in his prime of life could, with his family, enter industrial, urban civilization, but African communities, after all, were best suited to handle the predictable crises of the life cycle. But the danger that stabilization would lead to a destitute population of aged ex-workers, who had made the desired move away from Africa's rural backwardness, could not be avoided despite the hope that the stabilized worker would after twenty to thirty years "retire gracefully to the rural area."[41] In the mid-1950s, Kenya, Nigeria, and Northern Rhodesia asked for "expert" help to devise national pension plans – or at least a lump-sum retirement contributary payment scheme known as a Provident Fund – to generalize the efforts some large employers and most governments had made to provide some kind of retirement benefit.[42]

The Kenyan case reveals both the concern and the way in which the problem was caught up in the seeming unknowableness of Africa: local officials called for a social security committee in 1953 to study old-age insurance; it did its work by 1956 and recommended a national pension fund built from employer and employee contributions focused on relatively stable segments of the labor force; officials in London and Nairobi pondered its details between 1957 and 1960 and decided to send two British experts to issue a report on the report; the experts in 1961 recommended a provident fund rather than a pension plan; the Kenyan Council of Ministers decided in 1962 that it needed "further advice" and so a report on the report on the report was done in 1963 and it called for a provident fund to be set up "as quickly as possible," limited for the time being to "male persons" in firms employing ten or more. By then, Kenya was about to become independent, and the colonial file closes with an officer who had followed the case for years minuting, "I have no advice to give... I hope that Kenya will adopt it."[43]

The need for such a scheme was not in question: only 9 percent of Africans working for large firms were covered by pensions, 15 percent by provident funds (compared to 57 and 15 percent respectively for whites).[44] The problem was not employers' opposition – they preferred a national scheme to which they would contribute to the possibility that they would have to organize pension programs themselves – nor was it fear of the effects of the charges on the economy – funds could be invested productively as they accumulated. The central problem, bemoaned in a decade of reports and correspondence, was the lack of actuarial data to enable proper budgeting and absence of identification systems and registers of births, marriages, and deaths to insure that the proper person got the proper retirement payment.[45] The entire morass reveals the colonial inversion of Michel Foucault's vision of surveillance and control in shaping the "social" in Europe (chapters 1 and 7): in the

African colony, the state could not track the individual body or understand the dynamics of the social body. And so it could not lay out the basic structures for shaping the outlines of the life cycle even as it sought to define a working class, and it could not guarantee workers a little bit of security after their years of toil.

French West Africa got a skeletal retirement system in 1958, and as with family allowances officials hoped that these systems would actually drive the creation of an apparatus of surveillance. But the knowledge and the benefits in both empires were sharply bounded, by the definition of work and by gender. The successor states – Kenya among them – would seek to incorporate national provision of old age security into their more expansive conception of citizenship, but limit applicability to the observable "formal" sector and often allow inflation to erode the security which was the quid pro quo of surveillance.[46]

The difficulties of stabilizing African labor went beyond the inconsistency of wage policy or the unfulfilled logic of social security. As Timothy Scarnecchia has shown in regard to Southern Rhodesia, housing was crucial to the entire issue, and the government's professed intention to make African workers and their families permanent parts of the city of Salisbury ran up against the high cost of building adequate housing, the resistance of whites to living near Africans, and the confining and unrealistic nature of the model itself. In the 1950s, the rhetoric of stabilization stressed that women were the key to creating urban man: they would determine the cultural standard of the home and the upbringing of the children. But in concentrating scarce housing on the model family, women were denied the right to live in African neighborhoods – except in narrowly controlled circumstances – unless through a provable marriage to a worker. Personal life is not so neatly organized, and as women tried to make their way in a difficult world they were subject of intense police harassment. For a time, they cooperated with a fledgling political organization to fight for rights to live in the city, but they were eventually pushed aside by male political leaders intent on proving their respectability and their ability to defend men's interests against the job competition of unattached women. What official documents called the "demoralisation of African women in urban areas" – which became a reason to exclude or harass – was for part of the African elite a sign of the danger that they could be pulled down to the level of the masses. For women caught in between, the problem was to live. The model worker's family may have made its appearance in African cities in the 1950s, but for women and men trying to survive as market sellers, small-scale artisans, domestics, or beer brewers, faced with the difficulties of finding and keeping jobs and of sustaining marriages, and confronting inadequate wages and urban resources, the experience of labor bore little resemblance to discussions in London.[47]

In Southern, and to a significant extent Northern, Rhodesia segregation and oppressive policing enhanced the vulnerability of women left out – or opting out – of official family policy. But everywhere, in French as well as British Africa, the resources devoted to housing and urban services were in question. There was much improvisation, by African entrepreneurs who built, sold, and rented houses and by squatters who invaded land and built communities themselves, but such approaches often ran up against colonial policy – paralleling thinking on the labor question – that insisted that the city be a symbol of modernity and order. These are issues that are only beginning to be studied.[48]

The urban influx of the 1950s, however, in part reflected the fact that major changes were occurring in those years. Wages moved unevenly upward (see chapter 13). The growth of trade unions was substantial in most colonies, and in key industries and key cities trade unions had won key victories. In essential industries like the Northern Rhodesian copper mines, the Mombasa docks, or the Gold Coast railways, workers had won substantial wage increases, and the African wage labor force was far more differentiated in the mid-1950s than it had been at the end of the war. Struggles were being waged place by place, industry by industry. Although British officials had fantasized in the midst of the post-war strikes that they could create an orderly city, filled with workers and their families and excluding the idle and the dangerous, they lacked even the theoretical blueprint which the French Code du Travail provided, setting minimal standards for wages and working conditions and spelling out a clear structure for contestation. British officials knew that African unions were generally not strong enough to win family wages for themselves, and they feared so much that unions would become strong in the wrong sort of ways that they held them back; they knew that the government itself had therefore to intervene in setting wages, but they feared that the government's role would politicize the wage question. So in London and in colonial capitals, a vivid image of the working class British officials wanted in Africa's future coexisted with an image of Africa's present that did little to provide the means of getting there.

The dilemmas of "stabilization" and "African advancement": Northern Rhodesia

The Copperbelt was one of British Africa's prime laboratories for stabilization – and with strong copper prices after the war perhaps the most valuable and vulnerable industrial site. But the experiment was immediately caught up in a deeper involvement with local politics than the centralized French system would have permitted, and thus it got caught in just what officials were trying to avoid – the quagmire of race. In the four-way power struggle among officials, corporations, unionized white workers, and a union of African miners, the universalized category of "worker" did not displace the essentialized category of "African." Mine companies and officials could not create the kind of hierarchy of positions that might give Africans a deepening stake in the structure of industry and the African labor movement could not be channeled into a narrowly "industrial" form of disputation. The great experiment was enveloped in confusion and conflict, leaving race in the heart of the labor question.

The struggles of the 1950s need to be set in context. James Ferguson has pointed out that most scholars writing on labor in the Copperbelt, like officials in the 1940s and 1950s, have put their subject into "an over-arching, progressive narrative, in which a 'classic migrant labour system' featuring short-term migration by lone, male, rurally based migrants gradually gave way to a 'permanently urbanized', 'fully proletarianised', settled urban working class."[49] He contrasts the linearity of this modernist narrative to the messiness of the evidence we have of the lives miners lived: "classic" migrants were far more urbanized and "fully prole-tarianized" workers far more tied into rural networks than the narrative allows. Much of the high labor turnover of early years was movement from one mine town job to another by workers who were unable or unwilling to sustain any role in rural production; women, whatever role they were supposed to play, often came to mine towns and tried to build their lives there and either could not or did not wish to fall into the role of "worker's wife" that had been scripted for them.

By the time of the second world war, the mining companies had accepted the long-term presence of workers in the mine towns as a reality which they now hoped to control by recognizing it. They aimed at this time to slow down turnover but to keep rural connections alive, to insure that cultural affinities and respect for traditional authority would still be there when the miner was no longer performing useful work. Tribal authority could, they hoped, be maintained not by periodically sending workers back to villages, but by erecting neo-traditional councils and judicial bodies within the towns – by ruralizing the city – and by linking welfare services to assertions of company and state authority. But by the 1940s it was clear that this form of control was an illusion. Men might leave jobs too soon and not leave the city soon enough. Men and women might go before a neo-traditional authority to perform rites or settle disputes, but they might still create and contest marriage forms in ways that did not fulfill official images of the "stable family." Africans with education or long urban experience might seek "respectability" by trying to regulate marriage and access to housing through city-based structures rather than neo-traditional ones.[50]

By 1949, a trade union was adding its voice to the challenge to paternalistic authority.[51] By then, the central struggle over who was to define the parameters of stabilization within the workplace was focusing on an issue of job access and wages that came to be called "African advancement." From the start of the controversy in 1947, the phrase "equal pay for equal work" was used – contrary to the practice in French West Africa – as a defense of the racial privilege of white mineworkers. The unions of white workers argued that, without such a provision, allowing Africans to enter job classifications formerly reserved for whites would undercut white workers and violate a clause in their contract with the companies which prohibited jobs listed in the European mineworkers' contract from being given to anyone not covered by that contract. The union clearly assumed that given a choice between hiring a European and an African at the same wage, the companies would invariably choose the former. The white union's suspicions of company policy were not without foundation: the companies, with government approval, were seeking more flexibility in assigning Africans to semi-skilled and skilled jobs and intending to pay them less than they paid whites. In line with the progressive thrust of post-war imperialism, the companies now called their goal "African advancement." There is no indication that the companies wanted either to phase out white labor or to hire on a color-blind basis, but they wanted to open up more job classifications through which they could exercise choice, reduce wages, and manipulate racial divisions within the work force.[52]

After a failed conference in 1947, the Colonial Office commissioned a British trade unionist and one of its favorite post-war consultants, Arthur Dalgleish, to lead a study which would focus on "What posts, not now occupied by them, Africans are capable of filling" either immediately or with training, and how wages and other structures could be adjusted. The European mineworkers (as well as the railway workers) refused to have anything to do with Dalgleish, but the commission collected and duly reported the opinions of other Europeans and of Africans regarding the question of what Africans could and could not do. "The average African is still controlled by tribal customs and superstitions," the commission proclaimed, but this could be remedied by education. It carefully noted the allegations of its white witnesses: Africans were irresponsible and had little sense of "duty and ethical standards"; they did not apply themselves "consistently" to their jobs; they had little regard for safety; "the African is capable of performing the physical part of the job, but... he does not fully appreciate the reason for these jobs being done and why they are being done in a particular way." It concluded, "both in quality and quantity the work performed by the African artisan is far below that of the European which indeed in certain aspects is completely outside his present capacity." But it saw all this as part of a "vicious circle": unless Africans could slowly be trained and given positions of responsibility, they would not make progress toward any of these presumed virtues of an industrial working class.

The bulk of the report went through job classification after job classification and decided exactly what Africans, as a race, could do: "The Africans are at present laying light tracks with few curves, etc., and we recommend that he [sic] should not be given the responsibility of more important track-laying. This should be the responsibility of the European, although for certain posts Africans could be put in charge of a gang under the European." Responsibility and understanding were "African" or "European" traits. The problem, as the commission analyzed it, was not just one of training individuals to perform tasks, but of redefining the culture of workers. In the end, the commission listed fifty-four categories of work not performed by Africans that could, either immediately or after suitable training, be opened up to Africans. Implicit in its recommendation was that the types of work not specified were beyond the capabilities of Africans, now or in the discussable future.

The Dalgleish Commission did not accept the white union's demand for equal pay for equal work. It thought all Africans should receive a basic wage sufficient "to maintain himself, his wife and his children in a reasonable standard of comfort... Then as the African advances extra remuneration should be given dependent on service, the nature of the job, responsibility and the efficiency with which the work is performed." But the question of equality was premature:

It is further clear that for some considerable time to come the African will require much more supervision than is at present required by the European. We also have in mind the policy of equal pay for equal work and responsibility, a policy which is frequently misconstrued. In view of all these considerations and on the assumption that the wage at present being paid to the European is equitable and that it requires three Africans to undertake completely the work of the European without any additional supervision, then the wage and emoluments of the European should be divided between the three Africans, provided that this is not less than they were receiving prior to their advancement and is not less than the minimum laid down... Where Africans are promoted to take over the duties of Europeans and as a result there are more Africans required and in addition an increase in the European supervision is required, then a similar arrangement should be arrived at, *viz.* that the cost to the employer should be the same as if the work had continued to be performed by Europeans.

The core of this convoluted argument was a ratio plucked from thin air, but apparently repeated by enough Europeans around the copper mines to take on the aura of truth: that it takes three Africans to do the work of one European. The essentialist assumptions are manifest – the ratio attaches to races, not to any variations in work organization. In theory, as Africans acquired more experience and needed less supervision, their wages would go up.[53] The commission thought that in rejecting equal pay for equal work it was making possible African advancement.

But even this was optimistic. The European union had no intention of cooperating with this program, and the British government had bigger fish to fry. It was trying to put together a Central African Federation, assembling the two Rhodesias and Nyasaland into a more or less coherent political unit, and it was eager to obtain the support of Roy Welensky and other labor-oriented white politicians. Federation appealed to the developmentalist framework of the post-war governments, providing a large unit whose diverse human and physical resources could be used in a planned manner, and it seemed to answer Colonial Office worries that the new Nationalist government in South Africa might have imperial ambitions extending northward via the white population of Central Africa. Federation, however, would give wider power to the white voters of Southern Rhodesia: the developmentalist goals of Federation appeared in stark contradiction to claims that Africans were being brought toward self-government. The contradiction was barely papered over by clauses in the Federation plans about providing mechanisms to protect the interests of the African populations of the region. African opposition would eventually prove fatal, but for now what the Colonial Office really wanted from Africans was quiescence, while what they wanted from whites was active participation in their rationalized regional economic and political system.[54] So the Dalgleish report, such as it was, remained on ice.

In 1951, it showed signs of defrosting. The difference was that the African Mine Workers' Union (AMWU) was now a factor. British officials worried that the paralysis over ending the color bar would lead to a strike, and they thought that an African strike over the blockage of advancement for Africans was a bigger risk than a European one.[55] Attempts at negotiating with the white union failed, while that union apparently persuaded its African counterpart of the justice of the claim for equal pay. The African union most likely thought the principle was worth defending and that the majority of its members would benefit more from efforts, with white help, to improve the general wage level for

Africans than from the efforts of a fraction of the African mineworkers to move upward in the hierarchy. The companies made clear that much as they would like to assign Africans to certain jobs, they had no intention of paying Africans equal wages in those positions and had no desire to provoke a strike of European miners. The removal of the industrial color bar, they insisted, was a problem for the government to solve.[56] The government made some attempts to bring its influence to bear on the EMU, but got nowhere: the white miners had found a formula for protecting their privileged access to jobs on the basis of a principle which African miners could not criticize, and they had correctly calculated that neither companies nor the government were willing to confront them.[57]

By 1952, the governor was convinced that the African union was arguing for a large across-the-board wage increase "to secure for Africans better pay for the work that they are doing, since they cannot advance to jobs which provide better pay." A strike was being threatened, and the companies were now "very anxious" to find a way out of the deadlock over African advancement, "but nothing can be done until the Mine Workers' Union [European] can be induced to change its attitude."[58] The strike turned out to be as hard-fought as feared, lasting three weeks and ending in an arbitration award through which African miners achieved substantial gains. The starting rate for Africans was raised from 45 shillings per ticket to 80, the union having demanded 125 to the companies' offer of 60. The strike made the companies take the advancement issue more seriously: they saw this as a way in which concessions could be made to a segment of the African work force that would, if anything, add to the companies' control, and they feared that pending investigations by trade unionists from Great Britain might uphold the principle of equal pay for equal work and strengthen the EMU's paralyzing grip on the question.[59]

The issue of the color bar came before Parliament in 1953 when the anti-imperialist Labour deputy Fenner Brockway introduced a motion calling on the government to introduce legislation "with a view to the progressive elimination of the colour bar" in the colonies. He and his supporters evoked the Declaration of Human Rights and the abolition of slavery in calling for the elimination of racial discrimination in all forms from the colonies; he warned that the color bar was "largely responsible for the bitterness which has now turned into a vicious movement of Mau Mau" and could lead in the future to "a race war."[60] The rather platitudinous resolution was weakened or opposed by some Tories, notably the Secretary of State, who accepted the principle but thought existing strategies were bringing it about and by a smaller number of MPs who openly defended racial discrimination. Beresford Craddock thought the problems of inequality and racial friction lay with Africans – "the psychological make-up of those primitive people from time immemorial" – and Europeans' consequent and legitimate desire to be separated from such people. Such an argument lay within the boundaries of legitimate debate in Parliament even if it was at one end of the spectrum; the Tory majority, the vote showed, did not think the color bar deserved parliamentary condemnation.[61]

Back in Northern Rhodesia, the government was still allowing the white miners to define the issue. The South Africa based Anglo-American Corporation – more so than the Rhodesian Selection Trust, the other major mineowner – was willing to accommodate the EMU, and the government continued to temporize.[62] The AMWU, meanwhile, was publicly edging away from equal pay for equal work. Its leader, Lawrence Katilungu, argued that Africans should be given training and move into positions of "some responsibility," at pay rates between the average African and the average European wage.[63] The EMU, however, was holding firm, and under its influence, Roy Walensky, whom officials hoped would play a moderating role in the interests of promoting the Federation, was explicitly arguing, "I would never countenance the replacement of European labour with any kind of cheap labour, African or otherwise."[64]

It was now 1954; the debate over African advancement in Northern Rhodesia had already lasted as long as the debate over the Code du Travail in French Africa and had accomplished nothing. Meanwhile, African wages were up, turnover was down, more and more families of miners were installing themselves in mine towns, and new migrants were finding it more difficult to break into urban labor. Although the break with past practice was far less sharp than the stabilization narrative suggests, the reality of African working class life centered in the copper mine towns was becoming inescapable and the idea that this class could be safely confined to the lowest levels of manual labor was becoming increasingly implausible.[65] The best officials could do – another round of negotiations with the white miners having failed – was send another inquiry, this one headed by the same John Forster who had led the inquiry into the strike of 1940.

The Forster Board reproduced the essentialism of its predecessor, and used it to justify the continued existence of what it called the "dual wage structure." Its data made clear just how dual this structure was: the mines were paying 5,879 European miners a total of £9,965,780 in salaries, wages, and bonuses; 36,147 Africans were receiving £4,842,633 in wages and rations. The African – and it was *the* African again – had "but recently emerged from his primitive state." Therefore, the "industrial

standards of the African today fall far below those of the European."
Africans should advance to higher positions; they should receive the
training needed to help them do so; but "advancement will be slow"; and
Africans should not expect equal pay for assuming the same work roles
as Europeans. The board looked positively on the company argument
that African rates of pay should be "related to, though always measur-
ably in advance of, the standards and needs of their own traditional
society." Over time – the board kept repeating how slow Africans would
be to advance – African wages would be adjusted upward. Meanwhile,
the idea of job fragmentation put forward by Dalgleish – that a European
job could be broken into three African jobs – would create "some missing
rungs" on the ladder and enable the advancement process to go forward.
Actually, it would inch forward: the companies (and Forster) were
contemplating Africanizing 300 jobs over a 5 year period, making
"advancement" of relevance to less than 1 percent of African workers.[66]

To Edgar Parry, one of the top labor specialists in the Colonial Office,
the report provided "a strong moral position" for the companies' plan
for African advancement without equal pay. He thought that the real
danger of equality lay in relations among Africans: once skilled Africans
acquired wages equal to those of skilled Europeans, unskilled Africans
would demand pay equal to that of skilled Africans, "and no trouble
should be avoided which would prevent such a lunatic state of affairs ever
rising." Now, he thought, Africans accepted that Europeans had a higher
standard of living than they did. "It is too much to expect that this
grudging concession by ordinary Africans to people whose background
is in a more highly developed culture than they have developed themselves, should be extended to men of their own race."[67] So deeply did
Parry believe in his evolutionist conception of culture that he assumed
Africans must accept it too. Racial inequality, he felt, was less humili-
ating than income inequality. Like the board, he was caught in a
dilemma: the segmented nature of colonial society, the fact that people
within a single industry and a single colony might compare their wages
to the income of the African peasant or the average wage of the skilled
European worker meant it was impossible to bridge one gap without
enlarging another. But neither he nor the board saw this issue as a structural dilemma of a colonial economy; they saw only the contrast of
modernity and primitiveness.

The governor expected "serious trouble... because I think the wretched
Africans, with this behind them, will almost certainly stage a large strike
which may not be on the true advancement issue but rather on a demand
for a general all-round increase in pay." More dangerous still, the
governor thought an African strike would lead to involvement of the

African National Congress, a general strike, and linkage of the Copperbelt struggle "with the Nationalist movement." This, he argued, was a greater risk than a strike by European miners.[68] Here was a new sort of boundary problem: having begun the post-war era hoping to compress the inchoate struggles of urban masses into the category of industrial dispute, they now feared industrial disputes would explode into politics.

The companies tried to gain control of the situation by reopening negotiations with the EMU, trying to limit the number of jobs at stake to fairly low level ones.[69] At this time, copper prices were soaring, companies could afford higher African wages in exchange for stability, and white workers – they thought – had too much at stake in their high wages and bonuses to want to strike. Rhodesian Selection Trust gave the EMU six months' notice that it was breaking the recognition agreement, hoping to force the union to bargain. But the companies could not even agree among themselves: Anglo-American wanted to go further in accommodating the white workers' union than Rhodesian Selection Trust.[70]

Much of what the governor feared came true. In January 1955, the AMWU went on strike; they stayed out nine weeks. The strike came at a time when the union, in part because of the lack of progress over African advancement, was losing support and needed a show of militance over a general wage demand. The union asserted it was asking for a form of "mass advancement".[71] The companies set out to inflict a serious defeat on the unions, hiring new workers and threatening to consider striking workers as having discharged themselves and evicting them from company housing. The government, fearing the effect of angry, unemployed workers in the mine towns on an already tense political situation, tried to temporize.[72] In the end, the companies' hopes for a total victory were thwarted by the arrival in Northern Rhodesia of a delegate from the Miners' International Federation in London and by the menace of international trade union action, including a possible boycott of Northern Rhodesian copper in British ports over the issue of "scab" labor. Meanwhile, the delegate talked the AMWU into dropping its wage claim as long as the workers got their jobs back. From there, an end to the strike was negotiated, with none of the issues resolved.[73]

The companies continued their efforts to undermine the AMWU by recognizing, shortly after the strike, its rival, the Mines African Staff Association which had been set up by the more senior African workers in 1953. But the companies' divide-and-rule strategy had in fact created a problem for themselves: if they were to divide the unionized personnel and separate out the more stabilized, experienced miners, they needed to have enough Africans at the higher levels to make the split meaningful.[74]

By then, the Rhodesian Selection Trust had come up with a new formula: "equal basic pay for work of equal value," which would presumably justify paying an African lower wages in a position than his European predecessor on the grounds that the overall context of his work made it less valuable. The rank and file of the EMU indicated in a vote more willingness to compromise than did its leaders.[75] Finally, in September 1955, an agreement was signed by Anglo-American and Rhodesian Selection Trust with the European mine union which opened up twenty-four job categories to Africans, not subject to EMU veto. Over half of these were "ragged edge" job categories, which were filled by Africans at some mines and Europeans at others and which had long represented an ambiguous terrain. It was not much of an opening, but it was about as far as the door to African advancement was going to be opened. Officials were already worrying that African workers had lost interest in the whole affair – they seemed more interested in raising overall wages than in an agreement that would probably improve the career chances of a few hundred Africans.[76]

The agreement did not restore company control. Tension over the entire range of Copperbelt issues led to a series of strikes in 1956, which overlapped with efforts of the African National Congress to organize boycotts in the region. The government claimed that the rank and file was having trouble distinguishing the numerous strikes – over issues like union recognition and jurisdiction as well as wages – from the ANC actions, also known as "strikes." The government feared that the industrial relations situation was "growing worse and indications are that general strike, including essential services, may be called throughout Copperbelt."[77] By September, strikes were multiplying, Africans were marching to compounds "shouting songs of defiance," and AMWU leader Katilungu was being outflanked by more militant trade unionists. The government declared an Emergency and detained leading members of the AMWU and the ANC (but not Katilungu who was out of the country). A Commission of Inquiry was appointed. With help from Katilungu, the majority of workers returned to work about a week after the declaration of the emergency.[78] Officials and commentators realized, however, that the Emergency had done what officials had hoped to avoid – drive the miners' trade union and the region's leading political organization closer together – and after a brief attempt at weakening the union, government officials decided their best hope now lay in their old strategy of fostering nonpolitical trade unionism and cooperating with the African miners' leader, Katilungu.[79]

As late as 1960, officials were still stuck in the African Advancement framework, still fearing to push it too vigorously for fear of a strike by white mineworkers. In 1962, the companies were still bargaining on the basis of filling in missing rungs in the ladder and it was only in that year that the union finally demanded something like the *cadre unique* which French railway workers had won in principle in 1947 – a unified wage scale "in which the various wage levels are inter-related and [which] has as its sole criterion the comparative value of the jobs performed."[80]

African mineworkers in the 1950s went through a conflict-ridden and frenzied moment of social change, and by decade's end they could compare their material gains with two reference points and see something very different. African average wages in the mines went up 116 percent between 1949 and 1955, compared to a 28 percent increase in prices. Mine wages went from 1.8 times the average in administrative employment in 1954 to 2.1 times that figure in 1960, from over three times the agricultural wage to over four times. Northern Rhodesian copper miners earned 37 percent more than their counterparts in the Belgian Congo, 56 percent more than miners in South Africa. Yet if one looks in the opposite direction, one sees that the *top* wage paid to an African as late as 1962 was 50s 4d, whereas the *bottom* wage paid to a European was 64s. African miners were much better off than other Africans in the region, much worse off than European miners.[81]

Partly in response to higher wage costs, partly in response to changes in the world market, mining companies made an effort to rationalize production and substitute machinery for masses of wage labor. Officials began to admit that unemployment was a real problem, not a contradiction in terms for Africans who always had alternative resources. A year before Northern Rhodesia's independence, officials estimated that 90,000 people were in employment in the Copperbelt; 30-50,000 were unemployed. In this context absenteeism and turnover fell on the mines, a consequence as one investigator put it of the fact that in the new situation African workers "value their job very considerably."[82] There was now a great deal at stake, and a great deal of tension.

Sir Ronald Prain, head of the Rhodesian Selection Trust, was seeking publicly in 1956 to define himself as a progressive capitalist and to position himself in a modernizing discourse. The Copperbelt, he wrote, provided "laboratory conditions" to examine "the conversion of the African from a primitive and semi-nomadic forest dweller into a long-service worker in a very large and very modern industry." Africans were still "by nature vain, cheerful, fond of leisure, drink, and music, and easily amused." But he did not claim complete control over the process of transforming them. He described stabilization over the previous five or six years as a fact, and saw policy as a response to the fact. But the provision of housing, higher wages, and – since 1955 – pensions, "give jobs on the mines a scarcity value they did not have in the early days." He thought policy makers could respond in two ways and refused to come down on one side: "stabilization without urbanization" – long service in mines punctuated by periods of leave and terminated by retirement to a rural area – versus permanent urbanization, which he described as an inevitability which could at best be limited. Permanent urbanization would give people, through home-ownership, the possibility "to put down respectable roots"; stabilization without urbanization would reduce the risks of "slums, vice, and crime" associated with industrialization.

But Prain hinted at a profound disequilibrium that threatened any policy: "The young generation on the Copperbelt already far outnumbers the jobs in prospect for it, the regulation of entry is ineffectual, the number of the African population unknown, the law-and-order outlook unpropitious." He argued, as government and corporations long had, that the African's wages "should be related to, although constantly in advance of, the standard of living he enjoys at home" and "should not be outrageously incompatible with what other industries, including farming, are paying." Yet he recognized that "the violent contrast between the European and African wage structures" led to serious grievances.[83] The copper magnate could not claim control over a social process his industry had initiated, could not see alternatives to a dualistic society and a dual wage structure, and could not get away from a sense of peril.

Those perils were shared with much of the continent. French officials too could only see the possibility of turning the African into a worker by defining an enclave in which he could be enveloped by French legislation and French-based social structures, and so they too faced in one form or another the dangers of social and economic disequilibrium on the African continent. But in a more specific sense, British and French policy makers had carved out rather different problems for themselves. In the mid-1950s, even the most right-wing of French deputies included formal equality of wages and a single, race-neutral hierarchy in civil service and industrial organizations within the boundaries of accepted discourse. In Northern Rhodesia, dualism was accepted *within* the modern wage sector, and virulent attacks on formal equality and the suitability of Africans for a place in modern society could still be made in public.[84]

French officials avoided the knots into which Northern Rhodesian managers and civil servants tied themselves by formally accepting the principle of equal pay for equal work but evading much of its substance. The wage hierarchies of French West Africa were racially neutral – there just happened to be no Europeans at the lower levels and few Africans at the higher ones. There were no industrial color bars, but the top cadres demanded diplomas and other credentials which were obtainable only in the metropole. The kind of politics which paralyzed Northern Rhodesia for a decade did not happen in French West Africa because the centralization of the legislative process distanced the debate from the loci of white power. Even a group of European workers with vital skills, an established union, and strong racial prejudices, such as the white railwaymen of French West Africa, were easily marginalized as officials focused on what they considered the fundamental labor problem, the African worker.

The white workers of Northern Rhodesia could not remain important forever, but their run was long enough to survive to the end of colonial rule. Their defense of privileged access to the labor market forced officials to answer the question of whether they really wanted to assume that an African worker was just like any other worker. The companies did not, in the end, want to pay for African labor as if it was any other kind of labor, and the government would not make them. Northern Rhodesia failed to channel disputes with their most valuable labor force into predictable channels and could not give African workers a sense that their orderly participation in the industry would give them an improving future. The companies could not decide whether they would rather make or break an African union, and in 1956 a strike movement, much like the strike movements of the 1940s, did not remain a problem of industrial relations but became an "Emergency." The issues of the 1940s had not entirely been resolved when Northern Rhodesia became independent Zambia in 1964: the dual wage structure was not formally abolished until 1969.[85]

Colonial development as Manichean drama: Kenya in the Mau Mau era

Although the long dispute over African advancement in Northern Rhodesia constantly recalled the contrast of African backwardness and industrial life, the struggles themselves were conducted wholly in modern forms: demands from trade unions, strikes, commissions. African social networks and the languages of affiliation and contestation in the mine towns were certainly more complex than that, but officials could allow themselves to think that the very aspiration to "advancement" confirmed the existing industrial structure. In Kenya, in the early 1950s, British officials had to listen to an African discourse that fell outside of the framework of modern political contestation: they increasingly came to interpret Kenya's conflicts of the early 1950s as the clash of progress and atavism, of good and evil.

Mau Mau – a name given by whites to a revolt which began in its violent form in 1952 – has been termed by some scholars another manifestation of modern nationalism, similar to those in other African colonies except for the intransigence with which the settler-influenced administration blocked non-violent efforts toward constitutional progress. Others argue that aspiring African capitalists found their path blocked by settlers and a paternalist and authoritarian local administration. The Marxist variants posit class struggle: the revolt of landless squatters and the urban underclass, victims of the rising pace of capitalist accumulation in post-war Kenya and the expulsion of squatters from European and African farms in the process of intensifying production and rationalizing labor management. In such terms, Mau Mau was a civil war among Kikuyu as well as an anti-colonial struggle.[86]

There is truth in all these explanations, and they are not mutually exclusive.[87] The land issue in Central Kenya and the Rift Valley had been festering long before the war and became more acute afterwards. The long-sputtering settler economy was, during the commodities boom of the late 1940s, at last coming into its own – output was growing at 13 percent per year between 1947 and 1954 – and whatever misgivings the Labour government had about white settlers and their continual demands for a cheap labor force, the mystique of economic development made them seem like an indispensable source of export earnings, capital formation, and technical skill.[88] Seeking to gain more control over labor in a period of expansion, farmers expelled thousands of squatters – who had long served the variable labor needs of the settlers while growing crops and keeping herds on under-utilized white-owned land. Meanwhile, in the areas from which most of the squatters originated, an accumulating class of Kikuyu, many of whom were in collaborative relationships with government, were trying to discard old social obligations and rationalize their use of labor as well. The expelled squatters received a rude welcome when they tried to reconstitute older Kikuyu relationships of clientage and tenancy. Many ended up circulating between rural marginality and the urban underclass, for the moderate expansion of industry was far from sufficient to soak up the influx.[89] It was among this stratum that a wave of agitation and eventually violence began in the popular districts of Nairobi, spearheaded by an organization of Kikuyu who were supposed to have passed the rituals of initiation in 1940 and who saw the deprivations and exclusions they experienced as denying them passage to masculine adulthood. They called themselves the 40 Age Group.[90]

There was a strong constitutionalist side to political mobilization in these years as well, led by the Kenya African Union (KAU) under Jomo Kenyatta. Many people were in the middle, and the repressive nature of soil conservation programs in the post-war years – a virtual obsession of officials – extended anti-government militance in Central Province beyond the squatters.[91]

It is hard to understand government actions without appreciating the seriousness with which the post-war governments took their self-definition as progressives, set off against African backwardness, reactionary settlers, and even the past record of the Colonial Office. Developmentalism was a moral discourse – it claimed a universal value to the direction in which government was leading the African people. Philip Mitchell, governor of Kenya during the crucial period 1944–52, saw the issue in these terms: "the African has the choice of remaining a savage or of adopting our civilization, culture, religion and language, and is doing the latter as fast as he can."[92]

The cultural assault of Europe, in its missionary and statist versions, had not gone unopposed in Central Kenya, but it resonated in some quarters. The individualism of Christian missionary discourse and the developmentalism of officials made sense to Kikuyu who were acquiring title to land, finding new opportunities to market crops, discovering that the colonial state had increasing need for people with their skills and self-discipline, and worrying that threats to "order" might affect them even more than white settlers. Kikuyu "loyalists" had their own moral vision, as did the constitutionalist opposition, which distinguished itself from the youthful anger of the Nairobi slums by portraying its own approach as consistent with the discipline and patience of the Kikuyu elder.[93]

For the young men and women on the other side of the divide, the loss of the squatter option, the increasing improbability of acquiring land, and the paucity of jobs which paid a family wage meant that the possibility of creating a family – in Kikuyu as much as in western terms – was all but foreclosed. The urban guerrilla movement was in its own way making claims to responsible adulthood, only in ways which opened up a wide debate over what work and family, gender and adulthood meant in a colonial society.[94]

The victims of post-war development confronted not only interests – bureaucrats, settlers, and privileged Kikuyu – opposed to them, but a moral and ideological edifice which defined them as primitive and their exploiters as progressive. Even their claim to being Kikuyu was threatened. The squatters, having tried to establish their own way of life in the midst of white settlement, were increasingly attracted to an ideology which harked back to a mystic sense of Kikuyu identity, bypassing the recently invented traditions of the senior chiefs or the traditions of kinship units. The oath that began to spread among the deprived sections of Nairobi and the rural areas was constructed like an initiation into the "home of Mumbi and Gikuyu," the mythic founders of the Kikuyu people; the oath-takers' songs and rituals invoked a Kikuyuness unsullied by the ambiguities of the past hundred years. They did not just

demand land, but the land of the founding ancestors.[95] The official interpretation of African anti-modernity, self-serving as it was, was not
entirely wrong.

By 1950, as disorder grew in urban and rural districts, as oathing
spread among the younger, poorer, and more angry sections of the KAU,
the radical particularism of the movement's ideology separated itself
from the universalism of official ideology. The two sides, locked in
unequal combat, shaped each other: the anti-modernity of "Mau Mau"
confronted British officials with all they feared about Africa and the
developmentalism of the colonialists and the loyalists denied the poor
their adulthood as much as basic resources.

When the fighting began, the government was careful to use British
troops and to marginalize the settlers' role: the battle would be fought in
the name of a modernizing imperialism and not a reactionary one. The
core of the repression was the arrest of thousands of Kikuyu, who were
put through psychologized rituals intended to cleanse them of their
collective insanity, accustom them to healthy labor, and reinsert them
into a purified Kikuyu society.[96] The detention camps were put under the
jurisdiction of a "Department of Community Development and
Rehabilitation," under the charge of an officer considered a liberal on
racial matters.[97]

While settlers saw the rebellion as proof that the African could only be
kept down by sustained use of force, such a position offered London no
hope for the future and a contradiction to political thinking applied to
other parts of Africa – Kwame Nkrumah already was a sort of junior
prime minister in the Gold Coast.[98] The Emergency, as it went on, hardened the conviction of top officials that the psychic crisis of transition
could only be solved if Kikuyu were pushed through the dangerous
middle ground to the other side.[99] By 1954, as the rehabilitation camps
went about their ugly work, committees were sitting, imagining for themselves what post-Mau Mau African society and a post-Mau Mau labor
system should look like.

The labor question was being rethought contemporaneously with the
crises that produced Mau Mau. From the official discovery of an "urbanized working class" in 1945 to the "Labour Efficiency Survey" of 1947 to
labour commissioners' efforts to open up a dialogue about stabilization
in the late 1940s, a clear case had been made that orderly and efficient
labor could be obtained from Africans only if urban workers were
enabled to live with families near the place of work and if the next generation of workers was brought up in an urban and industrial environment.
The weak point of the effort was convincing white settlers that paying
Africans higher wages would make it possible to employ fewer of them.

Hyde-Clarke, who had argued for stabilization before the Legislative Council in 1949, commented twenty-five years after having resigned in frustration, "everyone was in favour of a stabilised African work force but no one wanted to pay for it."[100]

The ice was broken – gradually – in Mombasa, where casual dockworkers were made to register and to report for work a minimum number of days per month in order to retain registration. From 1952, as the port became more crowded, the registration rules were enforced in earnest. Whereas at the end of 1947 only 18 percent of dockers worked over twenty days per month, 70 percent were doing so in 1954. These workers were, despite their resistance, forced to earn more money, and the average docker shifted from being in the middle of a narrow wage spectrum in 1947 to a position near the top of manual laborers. With the new hiring system went closer supervision by company officials, replacing the role of African middlemen who signed up and supervised gangs of casual workers with the standard top-down authority structure of industrial capitalism.[101]

The docks were the vanguard of government-enforced policy to create a more steady, disciplined, better-paid work force. They were, not coincidentally, the most vulnerable point in the import–export economy of Kenya. Similarly, railway wages went up 20 percent in 1945 and 50 percent in 1953 – reflecting concerns with both turnover and order – and more slowly Africans made inroads into Indian predominance in artisanal positions. The railway union took up the theme of commitment and family: "From now on thousands of Africans will be forced by circumstances to live and die, like Asians and Europeans, in towns, depending entirely on employment."[102]

Meanwhile, Kenya was in the forefront of arguments in London about wage fixing: in the absence of an effective colony-wide trade union movement the labour department's desire to see the working class paid enough to reproduce itself depended on setting the minimum wage high enough. The settlers resisted this, and real wages in agriculture fell in the period 1946–52, while urban real wages rose slightly.[103] When the Colonial Office's labour advisor, Earl Barltrop, visited Kenya in 1952 he reported that the minimum wage was "the only statutory protection afforded to the vast majority of workers," and it barely provided anything for such basic needs as transport or utensils, let alone support for a wife or savings for marriage payments. The Wages Advisory Board, on which settlers sat, was "unmoved by representations from the government that there should be an increased margin for wants over and above the figure for one man's basic needs."[104]

Not only did the partial devolution of power to settler-dominated legislative and advisory bodies leave the Colonial Office and Kenya's own labour department with weak tools to reform the low wage economy, but officials themselves were too caught up with fear of demagogues and masses to let African trade unions take their own course. In 1947 African workers had shown their interest in a particular form of union: the general workers' union, which sought to bring together, in a poorly differentiated labor market, all sellers of labor power. The Kenya government had deemed this outside of the permissible boundaries of labor organization and had carefully plotted the moment to smash the African Workers Federation (chapter 6). But African labor leaders were not ready to give up this line of organization. Makhan Singh, a labor organizer of Indian origin, tried to revive in 1947 and 1948 an earlier general workers' union, the Labour Trade Union of East Africa. The government had him arrested, although it could not obtain a conviction, and pushed a new law through the Legislative Council giving the government wide discretion to deny registration to unions, as they did in this case. In 1949, the East African Trade Union Congresss, with Fred Kubai as president and Singh as general secretary tried again, offered the same appeal to the unity of the African working class, and suffered the same fate.[105]

African trade unions were regularly accused of following "specious political aims" instead of focusing "on industrial objects"; of toeing the "communist line"; and of trying "to bring about a similar situation here to what was experienced in places like Malaya, Gold Coast and Trinidad." In London, Creech Jones was suspicious of the rationales for restricting unions' rights to organize and to strike, and he rather pathetically pleaded with the governor "to deal with the causes of discontent." Nevertheless, "in face of the threat of a communist-inspired strike" the Colonial Office allowed Nairobi the legislative authority it wanted in its campaign against militant general unions.[106]

Meanwhile, what was supposed to be the proper British approach to responsible trade unionism within specific industries or occupations was not going well. James Patrick, the trade union advisor, wrote in 1949, "I will not agree to mass registration until the people concerned know and understand the meaning of what they do." Of the ten unions that somehow had been registered, Patrick claimed five "can be ignored completely at the present moment as they do not understand what it is all about," one was the general workers' union which he was attempting to destroy, and only one, the Transport and Allied Workers' Union, met his approval, although it was about to come under the influence of the radical Fred Kubai and thus join the ranks of the dangerous. At a meeting with settlers in 1949, Patrick was asked if he had "met one African capable of being a real Trade Union official in this country?" He replied, "honestly – no."[107]

With African trade unionism unable to live up to officials' standards and wage reform blocked by settlers, officials had little to offer against what they feared the most: a downtrodden urban mass, particularly in Nairobi, interacting with an increasingly radical leadership. In December 1949, Governor Mitchell noted that one of Nairobi's important labor organizers, Mwangi Macharia, was a "prime mover" in the 40 Age Group – the kernel of the urban guerrilla movement. Macharia, Kubai, and Singh, he believed, were plotting a general strike aimed at securing the release of Chege Kibachia, the deported martyr of the AWF, and of provoking major "trouble" in Nairobi.[108] Actually, it was by arresting Kubai and Singh for operating an unregistered trade union that the administration provoked the Nairobi general strike of May 1950, although this event also followed a period of strikes and boycotts reflecting the grievances of the poorly paid work force. The general strike lasted nine days and involved 6,000 workers. Nairobi's railway workers, who were of comparable importance to the dockworkers of Mombasa, joined to only a limited extent, and the strike never acquired the unity of the Mombasa strike of 1947. Seeing the strike as "political," officials suppressed it with hundreds of arrests, armed patrols, and tear gas.[109]

The top leadership of KAU was not overly sympathetic to the strike or to trade unionism in general. Kenyatta had pompously told workers in 1947, "Write your demands on paper, give them to your employers, give them notice of intention to strike and then strike if need be – that is the proper way." Tom Mbotela (who was later assassinated by militants) railed against the EATUC, criticized the 1950 strike, and told workers that they "ought to learn to strike in a civilised manner." For their part, the Nairobi strikers of May 1950 shouted down Eliud Mathu, the African Legislative Council member, when he tried to speak to them, crying "traitor, bribed by Europeans."[110] As in French West Africa at the time of its great railway strike, anti-colonial politics and the labor movement did not constitute a seamless web.

The social cauldron of Nairobi was boiling over in 1950, and a little more flexible trade union policy or a family minimum wage might not have cooled it off very much: landless and jobless migrants were flocking to the city, entering a world of casual labor, vagrancy, and criminality. But British policy gave little ground for the growth of a social category that could potentially have stood between elite politicians and the urban underclass: the respectable working class that had been the object of official fantasies since the war. The laborer, unskilled but well established in the city, had little more chance of being able to sustain family life than the casual worker, and the organizations which could have given a focus to issues that were specifically theirs had been repressed as being too "political" before they had a chance to develop an "industrial" focus. When the Emergency came about, the consequences of officials' failure to shape a differentiated, institutionally rooted population was revealed by the crudeness of the measure used to bring Nairobi under control: detaining (in Operation Anvil) *all* members of the Kikuyu ethnic group, and "screening" them to see if they belonged to "Mau Mau." Officials thought they were seeing the "virtual seizure of the city by an unruly tribe." They did not have a better category than ethnicity to define the dangerous. This mode of repression severely disrupted the labor market, drove up wages, and for years to come exacerbated tension between Kikuyu whose exclusion from the city cost them jobs and people from other ethnic groups who moved into certain niches.[111]

Some of the relatively well educated and able leaders who had tried to start a trade union movement were driven across the line. When Kubai came out of jail in February 1951, he turned his attention to KAU, which he had long tried to link to the labor movement, and he became one of the most important leaders of the oathing process in Nairobi. So too did Bildad Kaggia, another Kikuyu labor leader who could not be contained by the boundaries of "industrial relations."[112]

It was virtually on the eve of the declaration of Emergency in October 1952 that the government – as eager as ever to see that EATUC did not rear its head again – decided to make another effort to organize alternatives: industry-specific trade unions and a new central organization, to be named the Kenya Federation of Registered Trade Unions (KFRTU). But with the Emergency, virtually all trade unionists known to be associated with oathing or other radical activity were imprisoned.[113]

The KFRTU remained shaky until officials realized that their ideal of "responsible trade unionism" would go nowhere until potential leaders were allowed enough autonomy to lead. A young Tom Mboya was able to make officials feel, quite honestly no doubt, that he shared their concern for orderly progress at the same time that he understood that unions had to develop militance in their own ways. He learned some of these lessons in a few days in Mombasa in 1955, a year and a half after becoming head of KFRTU: he came to the city after a dock strike, organized behind the back of a new and still ineffectual union, had shut the port and begun to spread beyond the docks. He was initially appalled and frightened by the anger and self-assurance he faced at a mass meeting when he tried to tell the strikers about trade union procedures. Mboya, however, saw his own discomfort as a tool to use against employers, and skillfully brokered a settlement quite favorable to the workers, giving his leadership sudden credibility among workers and labour department officials alike.[114]

The KFRTU, meanwhile, went about its "industrial" business while walking a delicate line on politics. Mboya did not openly denounce the rebellion, but he would not let militants pressure the KFRTU into joining a proposed general strike in Nairobi in 1954. By the mid-1950s, responsible trade unionism was finally launched, and so was the career of a man who would help to bring about Kenya's independence.[115]

Mboya took the central tenet of labour department thinking, stabilization, and – like trade unionists in French West Africa – turned it into an argument about entitlements: migrancy and high labor turnover were caused by "the lack of security at the place of employment and the terribly low wages, poor housing arrangements and inefficient services." Later, as minister of labour in the pre-independence Kenyan government, he would argue that it was better to have a "smaller but satisfied and efficient labour force than a large, badly paid and frustrated labour force." He also saw stabilization as vital to building "a regular dues-paying membership" in the trade unions. Mboya, along with increasingly strong unions in the port and railways, brought concrete gains to many workers, attempted to organize vulnerable workers in the agricultural sector, and developed a clear rationale for promoting a relatively secure, decently paid labor force as Kenya became independent.[116]

The other prong of the labour department's dual strategy of wage-fixing and industrial relations machinery finally made modest progress during the Emergency. The government slowly began to take stronger minimum wage powers in the early 1950s, and in 1954 appointed a committee under Labour Commissioner F. W. Carpenter to review systematically the entire wage question. The Carpenter Report's central argument was the now-familiar gospel: "to increase labour efficiency and productivity" required stabilizing the labor force, and that required "the payment of a wage sufficient to provide for the essential needs of the worker and his family; regular employment; a house in which the worker and his family can live; and security for the worker's old age." The report at last recommended a formula for bringing this about: renaming the old minimum wage as the "bachelor" rate and creating a "family" rate 2.5 times as high to be paid to adult males over twenty-one years of age with thirty-six months continuous employment outside a reserve. The committee considered its plan so radical that it thought it should be implemented over ten years. It also urged extensive efforts to improve housing and to concentrate educational resources on urban areas. Most important of all was the vehement language with which the committee insisted that the labor problem was fundamentally a cultural problem: the state had to take the lead to provide such conditions, both social and economic, as will induce the African to sever his ties with tribal life and virtually start afresh in a new environment... We cannot *hope* to produce an effective African labour force until we have first removed the African from the enervating and retarding influence of his economic and cultural background.[117]

The Kenya government accepted the principles of the Carpenter Report, but wanted to dilute it. It renamed the two wages "youth" and "adult" – now intended to support a wife but not (for now) children – and decreased the intended ratio to 1.67 to 1.[118] The minister for education, labour and land not only invoked the argument about how migrant labor sapped productivity, but played the Mau Mau card as well:

if a return to the chaotic conditions which existed before 'Operation Anvil' is not to be repeated, it seems essential that the main labour force in towns must be given the wherewithal to live a full family life and to dispense with the unnatural and transient features of the life of a migrant labourer which has proved to lead to anti-social practices, crime and vice.

Business interests complained of costs, of the dangers of driving business elsewhere, of the dangers higher wages posed to agriculture. Some insisted that Africans were too ignorant or had too great a love of leisure to respond to the payment of family wages by becoming more stable and diligent workers. Eliud Mathu, on the other hand, argued that higher wages would indeed provide the incentives needed to make Africans better workers: "we are now definitely married to the Western way of life."[119]

That way of life, as most members of Legislative Council saw it, depended on the male wage. One member did raise the possibility of lowering the family wage by calculating in a female contribution, but he hastened to make clear, "I am not considering full employment in factories or homes as domestic servants," but instead "washing for bachelors or other people... looking after other people's children – not necessarily all the time, but from time to time; mending for bachelors, doing their darning and all that kind of thing." Another suggested "spinning and weaving," and the entire argument was so deeply rooted in English images of female labor and stereotypes of the western family that it revealed how far removed white Kenyans were from the realities of women's existence in Nairobi. The majority of the Legislative Council, including its African members, agreed with the Carpenter Committee that the wife's "job is to look after the home and look after the children."[120] Reproduction and production had their own places in the social order.

The settler farms succeeded in protecting themselves from the principles of stabilization and family wages, but in attenuated form the Carpenter Report became policy, often referred to as the "high wage" policy for urban areas – a phrase usually used without irony, even though in Nairobi in 1956 this meant wages and housing allowance of around Shs 100 per month.[121]

In the 1950s, Kenya's appallingly low real minimum wages did move upward – from an index base of 100 in 1951 to 176 in 1956 to 304 in 1964, still not much of a basis for "family" life.[122] More important, continued concerns about strikes in the most vulnerable industries and modest improvement in the capacity of African trade unions led to a more differentiated wage structure: the docks, the railway, and the growing manufacturing sector began to separate themselves from the narrow wage spectrum that had existed in 1945. There was modest progress in constructing housing, and more differentiation in the types of housing provided; the modest family house did not replace but grew up alongside the single room which housed four male laborers. Much housing was provided by African initiative, sometimes in unrecognized urban settlements. Clearly, *some* urban workers could live better in 1958 than virtually any workers could in 1948; some employers had come to accept that long-term workers and stable patterns of industrial relations were desirable and that minimizing wages was not the only way to run a colonial business.[123] But these changes did not make a wholly new society, and the hoped for economic growth was not sufficient to lead to large-scale job creation. The "stable" worker could not be so easily separated, spatially or socially, from the worker who, by necessity if not choice, moved into and out of jobs and who constituted what came to be known as the "informal sector."[124]

But the colonial imagination did not fixate solely on narrowly bounded transformations. The most remarkable document of the mid-1950s was the report of the East Africa Royal Commission, which from 1953 to 1955 conducted comprehensive studies aimed at producing a new blueprint for a Kenyan society. Its report blandly laid out an ideal society – in which class structure replaced racial divisions – at the same time that the psychological terror of the detention camps and the mass round-ups of people of certain ethnic groups constituted African daily life in Central Kenya.

The EARC started from the assumption that East Africa was a "dual economy": "tribal subsistence economies" that were "extremely backward" at the beginning of the colonial era and "just as backward today," set against "modern economic forces" or the "money sector."[125] The EARC rejected any idea that the former could evolve on its own terms. The "static security" which tribal economies provided was a brake on progress, as much for the wage worker who saw it as a safety net as for the cultivator who remained in subsistence production. Indigenous land tenure denied new resources to the producers "who are best able to use it in accordance with its market value" and "perpetuated ideas and practices incompatible with the desire for progress." Backward Africa became an explanation not only for the slow pace of progress, but for Mau Mau itself:

It is this visible opportunity for a new way of life which static tribalism frustrates. And this frustration lies at the root of African discontent. In whatever direction he turns, the African, whether he wishes to become a peasant farmer, a businessman, a permanent wage-earner in the towns or a modern tenant on the land, is hampered by the requirements of his tribal society with its obligations and restraints.

From here, the report endorsed, with a few quibbles, the Carpenter Committee's argument for the stabilization of urban labor. Although the commissioners were still worried enough about the peculiarities of the African "psychological" nature to urge caution in promoting Africans to managerial positions, they thought Africans would do fine as intermediaries between management and labor, in short as a "foreman class."[126]

The stabilization argument was now nested in a wider argument about class. In rural areas, the EARC wanted to see the emergence of individual landownership and a society divided into African landowners and African workers, who without land of their own would work for the property owners. Labor would then be far more efficient in agriculture as well as in industry. In cities, a "responsible African middle class," owning urban property, together with an African working class, would build communities based on "a common level of education or wealth, irrespective of divisions of tribe or race."[127]

As Luise White points out, the closest Nairobi came to anything resembling the vision of the EARC was in the slums, where long-established landlords existed and had catered to the needs of poorly paid workers and who had built something like communities in the midst of the colonial city. Many of these landlords were women; not a few of them had been prostitutes. They were not what the EARC had in mind; it looked to the day when men earned enough so that women did not need to engage in dubious activities.[128] The EARC had imagined for itself a structure of genders as well as a structure of classes, neither of which bore much resemblance to the existing complexities of social relations on a colonial city, let alone to the unknown and unconsidered ways in which different groups of Africans were imagining their own futures.

The EARC had specific suggestions – new initiatives for African house ownership, tinkering with the Carpenter Commission's wage proposals – but they were of such overwhelming modesty in relation to the simple symmetry of its future that they only underscore the pathos of British officials' need to hold an attractive vision of the future before them as they confronted the violence of rebellion and the intractableness of poverty in colonial Africa.[129] These reports contain a crucial nuance: the British government, unlike the settlers, wanted to portray Mau Mau as a particular sort of savagery, not rooted in an unchanging African nature but in the pains of the transition process itself. In these terms, the report of the EARC constituted a necessary work of imagination: a set of images of post-transition Africa, an organization chart of a modern class structure.[130] More clearly than elsewhere in Africa, Kenya exposed the brittle dualism of late colonialism: insistence on the inevitability of western modernity and fear of the power of backwardness.

The political crisis was more acute in Kenya than in, for example, the Gold Coast (where it was serious enough) mainly because Kenya had a rapidly growing landless population, hanging between an urban working class and rural security, driven by desperate necessity as settlers, accumulating Africans, and the state cut out the material and moral ground from under them. Ironically, in view of the stabilization thesis, it was the loss of ties to land that made Kenya's squatters so vulnerable and dangerous, whereas access, however constrained, to both rural and urban resources in other colonies meant that the poor did not feel so much the object of an assault. But officials did not want to read a script about accumulation and disenfranchisement, about the concrete possibilities and limitations within complex processes of economic and social transformation; they saw themselves in a drama of modernity and backwardness.

In Kenya, the transitional savagery of Africans, as portrayed within British elite opinion, gave rise to a particular kind of countersavagery in the camps, justified by the psychology which had diagnosed Mau Mau as madness, by the sociology which provided a guide to the recreation of Kikuyu communities, by the faith in economic development, urban planning, and industrial relations which proved that a rationally organized Kenya lay beyond the crisis of transition. In Kenya, the dualistic thinking of post-war colonialism became a kind of schizophrenia. Like true madness, it had its own meticulous logic and an insistence that it was someone else who was mad.

9　Internationalists, intellectuals and the labor question

The pioneers of new ways of thinking about African labor were bureaucrats – the Inspecteurs du Travail, the labour officers and commissioners, members of investigatory commissions, and a number of governors and ministry officials. As they made their case for stabilization within their governments, they also talked to each other, notably at the ILO and since 1948 at the Inter-African Labour Conferences (IALCs). The international discussions helped to anchor an agenda, giving a global imprimatur to what labor specialists were trying to do inside colonial governments and defining what was a discussable social issue. The ILO had agreed in 1944 and in more specific form in 1947 that the basic standards of labor policy which that organization applied to independent countries should apply to "non-metropolitan" areas as well. From there, a common agenda for the ILO and the IALC shaped discussions well into the 1950s: limiting migration, promoting stability in employment, paying family wages, developing systems of social insurance, establishing institutions to carry out inspections and insure regulations were followed, providing mechanisms for collective bargaining, and increasing the productivity of African labor. That the United Nations should publish in the 1950s a *Report on the World Social Situation* suggests how much the social had become a domain for international surveillance and judgment.

It was only in the first half of the 1950s that there developed a significant body of scholarship on labor and urbanization in Africa. The sequence is important: the new scholarship appeared after the new policies had been decided upon. New labor policy was a direct response, drawing on metropolitan experience, by civil servants to a challenge raised by colonial workers. That governments demarcated "labor" and "urbanization" as distinct social issues helped to create a problem for research, not the other way around. There were "experts" in the 1940s who did their surveys and made their recommendations, but these studies were few in number, limited in duration, and focused for the most part on a series of questions put in technical form – notably, what was the minimum standard of living necessary for an African worker. Scholars' relationship to governmental projects was not simple: some consulted and did research of direct utility to governments; others became advocates of oppositional movements; still others tried to analyze the complex implications of directed social change, opening debates and developing shared paradigms.[1]

For some intellectuals, commitment to change and to improving the lives of Africans implied a wholehearted acceptance of the idea of modernizing the African. This was an anti-racist, and usually anti-colonialist, line of thought: the African, like everyone else, could become industrial man. The emerging modernization theory, which held a universal future before the diverse traditional pasts of the world, was working out in terms of social science the attitudes and visions that had emerged in less analytic form on the front lines of colonial struggles after World War II. On the other hand, researchers – particularly those using ethnographic approaches – were constantly complicating any such picture of transition; their findings did not always comfort the modernizers.

Labor on the international agenda: the ILO and the IALC

The ILO standards of 1944 and 1947, explicitly setting forth metropolitan labor norms as a guide to colonial policy, were elaborated at future meetings, and remained a reference point for British and French officials. The 1952 Convention on "Minimum Standards of Social Security" put issues like medical insurance and old age pensions onto the list of supports countries were supposed to provide their citizens, including those in non-metropolitan territories. A British official in 1957 called this document, which his government had ratified in 1954, the "summit of post-war Beveridgism," just as French officials considered ILO Conventions to be, in effect, the internationalization of their Code du Travail.[2]

This is where the logic of international "standards" reached its limits. British officials could not oppose the principle of social security for workers, but paying for it – and confronting the complexities of African family and community life – was soon labeled "unrealistic" (chapter 8). British officials admitted that "it will be many years before we can conform even to the minimum requirements set out in the Convention." Public contributions to any such schemes would have to come from the individual territories themselves, and hence were contingent on substantial economic progress. The awkward consequence of Britain's boastful assimilation of its own standards to those of the ILO was that the ILO expected annual reports on progress toward implementing its conventions, and "reports are gone through annually before and at the Conference, with a tooth-comb to keep you up to the mark." The British government had to tell the ILO that it "reserved" a decision to implement the social security convention in all its colonies.[3]

So another silence was opened in colonial discourse. The French government reached a similar limit: its Code du Travail did not, for example, mention pensions, and the problem of old age was left to individual trade unions to negotiate in their collective bargaining agreements, something which few of them were able to do until 1958.[4] The ILO itself had to proceed carefully after taking the initiative: subsequent documents referred to the "diversity of conditions" as well as resources in nonmetropolitan territories, but still kept the issue of workmen's compensation, sickness insurance, maternity benefits, disability insurance, old age pensions, child support, and unemployment compensation on the table.[5] The silences were uneasy ones, as had been those into which the ILO forced labor convention of 1930 had placed colonial powers. By 1957 – when the Inter-African Labour Conference took the social security issue to a new level of specificity by calling for government-run pension systems rather than lump-sum retirement benefits – individual governments were in fact appointing committees to look into old age pensions, and action was slowly being taken.[6] France and Great Britain were also discovering that universal conceptions of entitlements coexisted uneasily with the actual results of development initiatives and were beginning to wonder (chapter 10) if the responsibilities and risks of colonial rule were now exceeding the benefits.

ILO conventions on social security, like earlier standards on forced labor, did not *cause* individual governments to act in a particular way, but they helped to lend broader moral and intellectual meanings to complex political processes. Both Britain and France were convinced enough that their labor policies had taken a progressive turn that they welcomed the process of defining standards. After that, the bureaucracy – responding to the flow of events – was also preparing reports or arguing about the language to use at a meeting or in a convention, and thus thinking in one way or another in relation to the international discourse. As different positions were debated, often heatedly, within national institutions, one side could invoke international principles as much as export prices or social danger.[7]

The state's claim to be an agent of modernization – and the dimensions which modernity was held to include – were repeatedly articulated in the last fifteen years of colonial rule. It is precisely because the ties of colonies to a specific metropole were coming to an end that the international dimension of the new discourse was in the long run of special significance.

New African rulers would find themselves as actors in a world with a set of well constituted images – and many specific enactments – of what a modern social policy looked like.

Three interrelated issues were most often discussed at ILO and IALC meetings in the mid-1950s: the need to sustain the families of workers; the need to move from a situation of predominantly migrant labor to one of predominantly "stable" labor, and the cultural and material transformations in African society needed to improve productivity.

At the 1953 Inter-African Labour Conference in Bamako, an agreement on family wage policy was reached: "it is desirable that the wages (which may be in the form of basic wages plus special allowances) paid to the worker taken together with the social services and any other benefits available to him should take account of and include provision for his family responsibilities."[8] France and Belgium wanted to make family allowances a basic standard, but they were opposed by Great Britain, which nonetheless accepted in principle the idea of a family wage. The ambiguous formula bridged the different approaches, and reflected the conference's insistence that its recommendations be "technical" and not "political," that is not make choices among differing policies of its members.[9]

Once accepted by this international organization, the family wage resolution became a reference point for British and French officials in their internal debates, something an Inspecteur du Travail could cite to show that his position reflected international principles, not just a concession to an unruly labor movement.[10] In London, at the same time, the international discussion of family allowances led officials to clarify their opposition to them, and to make clear that they nonetheless supported payment of wages sufficient to sustain a family. Thus Kenya's wage policy of 1954 emerged from a double context of international discussion and territorial rebellion.[11]

Beginning in 1947, the ILO, soon joined by the IALC and some organisms of the United Nations, opened a long discussion of migration and stabilization: international committees of "experts" began to study the question and governments demanded information from their respective territories and wrote position papers for international meetings. From the start the discussion was explicitly in the realm of the social: "Migration affects human beings living in social groups." The character of society at the place of work and at the place of origin of the workers was at stake: family life, "tribal life," and the forging of new forms of urban social structures, with their own institutions, cultures, and notions of community.[12]

As with family wages, the issue skirted the political, but a two-pronged approach achieved wide agreement. Migration was necessary: it reflected seasonal variations in labor supply and demand and brought people previously unfamiliar with wage labor into contact with the possibilities of a new life. But migration necessarily risked fostering social "evils" – family separation, prostitution, the drainage of male labor power from agriculture and the tendency of urban labor to be left in the hands of a "floating population" rather than a disciplined class. A UN document cited the "abnormal mobility of labour in Africa" and associated it with low wages and lower productivity. Migration therefore had to be carefully regulated – this was consistent with ILO resolutions dating to the late 1930s – while its extent should be reduced by inducements to stabilization, such as family wages, family housing, and the provision of social services to urban areas.[13] International bodies were now describing stabilization as a consensus.[14]

For all the efforts to seem apolitical, the international arena was quietly reading South Africa out of its consensus. South African delegates defended migrant labor as it was practiced in their country against the now general critique of migrancy. By the 1950s, in fact, South Africa was not only policing migration with greater intensity than before but was erecting a powerful ideological edifice of "separate development" that directly contradicted the universalism behind French, British, and ILO thinking.[15]

Productivity was only one concern behind stabilization efforts – political order and social disruption were the initial concerns – but by the mid-1950s it was attracting increasing attention, in part due to the higher wages that were part of the stabilization package. The IALC in 1950 discussed the "efficiency of workers," and stressed the need to improve housing and diet, to provide "attractive social surroundings," the "encouragement of normal family life," the provision of "at least the same social security as he would have in his country of origin," and measures to insure "good relations between the worker and the employer."[16] The conference of 1953 began a major study of productivity commenting, "Unfortunately, there would seem to be no expert, either in Africa or elsewhere, capable of examining the enormous field of productivity as a whole." Where the knowledge professionals could not yet help, the international bureaucrats would generate the expertise: they called on member states to undertake wide surveys and research programs, looking at what motivated Africans to work, attitudes to and aptitudes for work in different groups, the effects of labor instability, and the influence of women on attitudes to work and the standard of living.[17] The lack of expert knowledge did not deter the international discussions any more than national ones: an ILO article – without saying how the ratio was calculated – stated that the African produced between one-third and one-eighth the output of the European worker; Northern Rhodesian officials used the figure four to one.[18]

The preparations for and the results of the 1953 Conference led the British Colonial Office and the French Inspection Général du Travail to write papers like "Labour Productivity in Africa" and "Report on the Human Factors of Productivity." This research informed ILO and IALC documents from 1955 to 1958, and a broad consensus emerged about how to pose the problem.[19] P. de Briey of the ILO argued that African workers were caught between two systems, often shocked by the brutality of the changes they underwent upon entering urban labor. But they could adapt to wage incentives and industrial discipline if they could be given security in their place of work, and thus had the opportunity to build "an entirely new and integrated social structure" in urban areas, crossing tribal lines and fashioned out of new forms of association. It was through cultural change that productivity would increase.[20]

This was the international reverberation of the argument made by British and French officials that the African – the male African – could aspire to be universal industrial man, as long as he separated himself from his origins and as long as he brought his wife and children to a home alongside the industrial workplace. "The African woman," the IALC concluded in 1955, "has an essential part to play in the consolidation of family life and in the development and maintenance of social and cultural standards."[21] Indeed, it was the place of women in a spatial and cultural system that more than anything defined what stabilization was all about: they should be in the city, alongside their men, and they should be participating in and transmitting a modern culture, not a "tribal" one. The expectations of the conferees, as the frequent use of the phrase "workers and their wives" suggests, were clear enough: men would produce, and women would reproduce.[22]

These international discussions were simultaneously documenting a social process and calling for government action to help it along. Both aspects were discussed in the language of universality. The opening speech of Mlle Guelfi, chief labor inspector of Overseas France and chair of the 1953 Inter-African Labour Conference made this clear:

Labor law follows from universal rules of justice and of respect for man; they have been powerfully pulled out, over the last thirty years, with enlightenment and authority by the ILO. Whether it is a question of an African worker employed in the mine of Rhodesia or of Tanganyika or whether it is a question of English or French miners working in the coal mines of their countries, there exists among them a community of experience and of life which is born of the similitude of the trade and which calls forth the same protection and similar guarantees.[23]

Such a view of industrial life carried with it a stark separation from African culture. A United Nations document in 1951 was already making the point in a chapter heading: "Dual Nature of Economy." The UN was insisting that the "tribal" nature of the African economy was starkly separated from the modern economy in which wage labor was practiced. Six years later the UN thought "the gulf between the traditional culture of Africans in their own surroundings and the culture of modern cities remains wider and deeper than the rural–urban gulf in any other major region of the world."[24] In the tribal sector, poor nutrition, lack of education, and the absence of a "will to work" consistent with industrial imperatives lowered productivity; the need for stabilization in modern employment was so great because rural Africa was so backward.[25] For all the consensus, the writing on this subject cited virtually no controlled studies of the problem and relied heavily on anecdotal material or general observations from labor inspectors.

But in the dialogue between international organizations and colonial regimes – particularly in reference to "standards" – there from time to time appeared hints that the self-consciously modernizing tone of the discussion was not always convincing and that fears of dangers within African society still penetrated the domain of "labor." This surfaced in the mid-1950s when the ILO considered a tougher convention than its 1939 version, prohibiting the use of penal sanctions to punish laborers who broke labor contracts: such sanctions typically involved the jailing of workers who "deserted," and contrasted to the civil suits to which such violators would be subject in western countries. This was relatively uncontroversial within the ILO, but after it was passed in 1955 British officials had an embarrassing problem.[26] Kenya, Tanganyika, Northern Rhodesia, Southern Rhodesia, and the High Commission territories of Southern Africa (Lesotho, etc.) still had penal sanctions on their statute books and the Rhodesias and the High Commission territories, in particular were "apparently immovable" on the subject. The governor of Southern Rhodesia was still holding to the old justification for penal sanctions: Africans were unreliable workers and, even worse, their way of life meant that they could not be sued. He placed the onus for ending penal sanctions on Africans themselves – as a collectivity – concluding that abolition depended on "the advance made by the indigenous worker and the development of his attitude towards the obligations he assumes under the contract of service."[27]

So Great Britain, the leader in the imperial battle against forced labor, could not ratify one of the final enactments in the tradition of removing government coercion from the labor market. The opposition Labour Party asked an awkward question about this in Parliament in 1957, and the Secretary of State could only reply lamely: "I would certainly like to see such restrictions go, but it is essential if that is done that civil sanctions should be effective."[28] In 1958, an ILO report that penal sanctions were "still a feature" in Central and Southern British Africa caused further embarrassment in the Commonwealth Relations Office and the Colonial Office. In certain colonies, it would seem, it still required the stern authority of the colonial official to keep the African at work.[29] There was not a lot at stake in this debate – Rhodesian workers in the 1950s had reasons other than government compulsion to keep them on the job – but the stubbornness of certain colonial rulers nonetheless reveals that the oft-proclaimed universalism of post-war labor policy was set against a contrary belief about Africans.

At the same time, international organizations – especially as more people from colonies and ex-colonies attended them – could also become embarrassing sites for questioning the seriousness of the modernizing project. Abdoulaye Diallo, Soudanese union leader, CGT activist, and vice president of the WFTU, told a meeting of the United Nations Economic and Social Council that forced labor had been resurrected in the repressive actions of colonial governments in Indochina, North Africa, and the Ivory Coast and in recruitment practices in British Central Africa, Kenya, and South Africa. He turned the forced labor issue into a demand for radical change: "To suppress forced labor it is necessary to assure work for all, to raise the standard of living, to struggle against unemployment and to develop education... To prevent forced labor, it is necessary to condemn colonialism which is contrary to the principles proclaimed in the United Nations Charter."[30] Diallo's radical appeal drew on the rhetoric of standards and of free labor of the ILO and turned it into something else. He and other labor leaders would bring struggles over labor and colonialism into other sorts of international organizations – notably the WFTU and its anti-communist rival the ICFTU – and they would run into the contradictions of proletarian internationalism and African nationalism (chapters 11 and 12).

But even the more consensus-oriented ILO faced debates that tested the limits and the genuineness of the standards/free labor approach. At the ILO meeting of 1956, a trade unionist from Dahomey, Edoh Coffi, began by commending the "excellent" provisions of ILO Conventions, but immediately charged that they were a "dead letter."[31] Forced labor, he said, continued in the hidden crannies of the colonial system and the "coherent and progressive social policy" which followed from ILO initiatives was undermined by colonial states' "predatory economy," in which profits were expatriated rather than reinvested and poverty went unaddressed. He turned the continual reference in discussions of colonies to the standards of social policy in metropolitan countries into a critique of the modernized imperialism of the post-war era:

I will simply ask why countries which can be regarded as mostly highly developed socially, and which give their nationals decent conditions of life and work, are content to keep the peoples under their charge in distant territories in a condition of degrading inferiority.[32]

The highly developed nations would soon give their response: not to remedy degrading inferiority, but to remove the peoples of the colonies from their charge.

Western intellectuals and modern Africans

It was only in the 1950s that the scholarly study of wage labor and African urbanism began to be a sustained enterprise. The intellectual roots of this endeavor were various, but they only came together after the bureaucrats had redrawn the boundaries of the labor question in the late 1940s. Earlier, there had developed a critical literature, from travelers, missionaries, and other intellectuals on forced labor, and later and to a lesser extent on migrant labor. Godfrey Wilson's work, however, stands out as a serious ethnographic investigation of copper miners in Northern Rhodesia: he pointed to an urban society in the Copperbelt of 1940 more deeply rooted and more complex than either officials at the time or scholars at a later date acknowledged. A few other studies published in the 1940s looked at urban society and labor with similar ethnographic specificity. Wilson – along with his wife and fellow anthropologist Monica Wilson – put such findings into a framework that stressed "maladjustments" between a statically conceived "primitive" Africa and a disruptive intrusion. This both continued the earlier criticisms of migratory labor and anticipated the dualism of the 1950s (see below); it was not clear that change in African societies could yet be seen as anything other than external and at least for a time pathological.[33]

The institution best situated to take up Wilson's on-the-spot investigations, the Rhodes-Livingstone Institute, was not allowed to do so. Although it was founded in 1937 in large reason to remedy the ignorance of African life that had made the 1935 mine strike such a shock, the mine companies would not let researchers after Wilson do research among their workers. The RLI was forced back into rural research, although scholars associated with it strayed beyond the mold of anthropological studies of "traditional" societies and studied agriculture and nutrition in the context of a changing colonial situation (chapter 3).

Max Gluckman, who became Director of the RLI in 1943, argued that the mines and rural Northern Rhodesia were two distinct research situations, each of which deserved attention.[34] Gluckman, whose leftist activities as a young man had almost blocked his career in Northern Rhodesia, was eager to see anthropology play an active role in social change and to cooperate with the British government's post-1940 reform agenda. He made this clear in his post-war program – putting the effects of industrialization and labor migration at the center of the institute's concerns, while simultaneously arguing that the RLI had to focus on basic research and retain its autonomy.[35]

From the official side, Lord Hailey was also arguing that research had its role to play in administration. Not just knowledge of the particular ways of African tribes but a much broader set of knowledge was relevant to changing Africa.[36] Hailey pushed successfully for a research agenda for the Colonial Office, using Colonial Development and Welfare Act funding and other sources and leading to the creation of the Colonial Social Science Research Council. The idea of colonial research had found its moment: as Great Britain, like France, tried to modernize imperialism, scientific knowledge was critical both to executing practical projects and to articulating a convincing rationale for colonial tutelage.[37]

Investigation into the lives of migrant laborers had scarcely begun, and for all his interest in research, Hailey had only rather banal things to say about the labor question. The 1945 edition of his *African Survey*, like the 1938 version (chapter 2), recognized that Africans could no longer be treated as "crude manpower," that wage labor had potentially "disruptive" effects on social bonds, and that hesitant moves toward stabilization had not necessarily provided alternative forms of social security and control. He was still stuck in a vague paternalism: workers' contributions to the economy required "a recognition by the community of its social responsibilities towards them."[38]

The first initiative in post-war urban research came not from anthropology's tradition of close observation, but from survey research – directly from the techniques industrial countries had devised for looking at their own poor. B. S. Rowntree's work on poverty in England in the early twentieth century was of particular interest, brought to British Africa via a school of social work that had taken root at the University of Cape Town, under Professor E. Batson. They made use of the concept of the poverty datum line to define basic necessities for survival, supplemented by limited discretionary expenses, which could provide the basis of calculating a minimum wage and adjusting for changes in the cost of living. These techniques were used by locally appointed cost of living committees in Kenya and elsewhere. The *African Labour Efficiency Survey* in 1947, meanwhile, was compiled by a Rowntree-trained British team, which was more concerned with discussing what it saw to be the material and cultural determinants of higher productivity than the labor force as it actually existed (chapter 6). A Ghanaian scholar, K. A. Busia, ran a more down-to-earth social survey of Sekondi-Takoradi in 1948. One of the earliest studies in French Africa, on Douala in the Cameroun, was done by an Inspecteur du Travail, Jacques Guilbot, in 1946–47. In South Africa and the Belgian Congo, where urban labor forces had been around for a longer time, a wider range of issues was studied in urban research, but on the whole urban research in the last half of the 1940s was dominated by the survey: sometimes limited to defining poverty thresholds, sometimes including basic data on the size of the urban population, the extent of migration and the length of time Africans stayed in the city, and on the incidence of marriage and childrearing. These were data which officials desperately needed to know and which in fact confirmed the reality of an urban working population.[39]

The more fundamental break into examining urban working populations as complex, multi-dimensional social entities – which is how Inspecteurs du Travail and labour officers wanted to think of them – came with the work of scholars like J. Clyde Mitchell and Georges Balandier beginning in 1950. Mitchell started his anthropological research on the rural Yao of Nyasaland, but he began a survey of a Copperbelt town in December 1950, defining his object of study as "impact of Western industrialism on their [Africans'] traditional way of life." He went on from there to compile a long record of research on migration patterns, marriage, rituals, attitudes toward the city, cultural innovation among urban Africans, and other such topics.[40] He used his professional knowledge and institutional connections to argue, to the mine corporations among others, not only that labor should be stabilized, but that workers and their families needed improved social services, education, and political rights in order for a productive and orderly urban society to come about. He moved beyond the labour officers' argument that a stable job and decent housing bred contentment, giving officials in Southern Rhodesia the unwelcome advice that Africans' political as much as economic aspirations had to be met.[41]

Mitchell eventually became head of the RLI, and scholars like A. L. Epstein came to work in the Copperbelt as well. Epstein studied law and authority in urban settings, and documented over the course of several research trips the decline of the urban tribal authorities set up by mines and officials to channel politics and administration in acceptable directions, and the rise of the trade union and political parties. The Copperbelt researchers stressed the "situational" nature of the social and cultural patterns they observed. As Epstein put it, the urban African is involved in a number of different sets of social relations which stem from forms of social organization distinct from, and in many respects opposed to, one another. Nevertheless, because they operate for the most part in different spheres of his social life, the African in the towns is able to handle the various sets without obvious difficulty.

Marriage arrangements were made within a "tribe," matters of wages and politics through unions and parties. People were aware both of their tribal and cross-tribal connections, with class becoming increasingly salient as the African population became more differentiated in economic terms.[42] Epstein argued, "the urban African remains a tribesman, and yet is not a tribesman." By decade's end, Gluckman had gone further: "An African townsman is a townsman, an African miner is a miner."[43]

Gluckman in effect proclaimed the reality of the labour officers' fantasy: the African had become industrial man. Epstein wanted to make clear industrial man existed in some respects and not in others. Gluckman, Mitchell, and Epstein all rejected the concept of detribalization, used by Wilson and more importantly a commonplace of official discussions of Africans in cities through the 1940s. Stabilization and urbanization implied quite complex changes, not the wholesale replacement of a "tribal" way of life by a European one.[44] Labour officers hadn't quite got their way.

Georges Balandier also came to Africa at the end of the 1940s, arriving to study Lébou fishermen near Dakar. There he discovered "an Africa different from that which had been taught to me by the *maîtres ès sociétés primitives*."[45] He first discovered the new Africa among Senegalese intellectuals in Dakar, but when he went to Brazzaville he discovered another side to Africa among the workers of the poor neighborhoods of the city. Balandier plunged into a series of studies of that milieu, culminating in his *Sociologie des Brazzavilles noires*.[46] Balandier presented a picture of precarious living conditions, rapid mobility, breakdown of previous kinship structures, individualization, but continued connections with regions of origin. Balandier, like the Copperbelt anthropologists, stressed that this was a particular sort of situation. But he was not just interested in the micropolitics of the city but also in the overall structure of power in which rural and urban Africans were making their lives: the "colonial situation," he called it. Early in his urban research (1951), he criticized, with passion as well as precision, the notion of a primitive society being transformed by a modern economy as well as the culture contact model of Malinowski, arguing instead that the particularity of the colonial situation "as a complex, a totality," stemmed from the exercise of power by a conquering nation. The colonial situation was defined by exploitation, racial domination, and "social surgery" exercised on the conquered people. The post-war era "announces a technocratic phase of colonisation following the politico-administrative phase."[47] The town, Balandier later argued, was where colonial intervention was found at its "maximum stage of development." What he found there was not the colonial planner's dream, but "makeshifts" and "unrest," of Africans struggling to build new communities in their own ways. Balandier used developmentalist rhetoric: social classes were "embryonic," "what might be called a middle class spirit is gaining ground" among certain groups. But counter-evolutionary tendencies were acknowledged as well, and the deepening roots of a working class in some neighborhoods did not, after all, diminish rural connections or the flux and reflux between other neighborhoods and village life or the harsh conditions born of insecurity and instability.[48] The stabilization project was not just incompletely realized, but badly realized and severely compromised by the nature of colonialism itself.

On the whole, social scientists in the 1950s were more eager to see what Africans could do with the opportunities of a decolonizing world than to dwell on the specificity of the colonial situation. The most widely shared theme of 1950s urban anthropology was adaptation. It was a concept that accepted the city – as constructed in Africa by colonial powers – as the object to which Africans had to adapt, but it did not necessarily posit, in the style of Kenya's Commission on African Wages, that Africans adapting to it had to give up everything from their previous experiences and identities. Scholars pointed to new forms of association which cut across ethnic lines, from occupational groupings to mutual aid societies, but also to "tribal" associations that developed among migrants from a particular place and which gave new significance to urban ethnicity.[49]

Two publications of the 1950s say the most about the growing importance and the limits of international discourse about labor and urbanization. When UNESCO, in cooperation with the CCTA and the French government, sponsored a conference in 1954 in Abidjan on the Social Impact of Industrialization and Urban Conditions in Africa, urban studies had matured sufficiently to allow for an extensive exchange of information and the publication two years later of a 743 page book on the subject. Earlier, in 1952, the Pan-Africanist and anti-imperialist journal, *Présence Africaine,* devoted a special issue to "Work in Black Africa." Together, the establishment conference and the anti-imperialist journal marked recognition that the social and cultural significance of work was an issue at the frontiers of public policy, scholarship, and cultural critique. Most contributors to the UNESCO volume wrote in a progressive mold: labor forces and urban populations were growing; women were coming to the cities, if not in numbers equal to those of men; families were being raised in urban environments. No-one seemed to want to resurrect the fantasy of primitive Africa. Although classes were often called "embryonic," at least the metaphor implied they would one day be born. At the same time, most of the papers revealed relentless poverty and insecurity in African cities; they presented evidence of joblessness, which colonial officials were slow to see; they reported on low skill levels among workers and the continued presence of "large floating populations" in cities.[50] Women, according to the first rather general studies from this era, were also not fitting the stabilization model too well: they were both more independent of men and more insecure than their assigned role.[51]

Most scholars lacked the faith of the Royal East Africa Commission that income and class differentials would replace those of race and ethnicity, and some noted the phenomenon of "super-tribalization": being plunged into a multi-ethnic world actually strengthened ties within ethnic groups, sometimes enlarging the scale at which ethnic unity was affirmed. Not only a sense of common language and a common past, but the insecurities of urban life encouraged if not forced the maintenance of rural ties and affiliation.[52] The scholars were at least somewhat less sure than the bureaucrats that the problems of Africans in cities were solely those of transition and that an urban society modelled on the West would emerge at the end. The quest to fit African urbanization and industrialization into a universal model was strong among the urban specialists, but the data on the acute effects of poverty, insecurity, the complexity of cultural change, the countervailing forces which inhibited class formation, and the new meanings of ethnicity were being put on the record.[53]

Most of the authors featured in *Présence Africaine* also saw wage labor as an inevitable trend. They too documented bad working and living conditions, and looked to government and social scientists to show how to make them better. Just as interesting as the overlap with the conventional scholars and the Inspecteurs du Travail is the subtle way in which some intellectuals tried to problematize the concept of work even as they saw it as a necessary category for analysis and reform. Alioune Diop, Senegalese intellectual and editor of the journal, opened the issue with an attempt "to examine the European notion of work with my subjectivity as a black African." He argued,

Europe seems to me to be a continent which organizes itself progressively in an immense "work machine" whose substance expands throughout the world with a force that Europe itself cannot control... The entire European personality is thus a work machine and only finds its most certain joys in work, in the largest sense of the term.[54]

Diop opposed Europe's "militant civilization" to the "natural civilizations" overseas; one was singular and the others plural.

Work, European style, was thus for Diop both something to be taken literally and a metaphor for colonization in both a positive and negative sense – forward-looking, energetic, and exploitative. In the literal sense, his program was very brief: "it is necessary that the worker exercise control over the result of his effort and retains his initiative in work. Hence the vital necessity of the free and redeeming existence of unions. And the no less vital necessity to make all workers equally equipped." That was a program to which a French Inspecteur du Travail would not have taken exception. But at a deeper level Diop was both sadly accepting the inevitability of Europe's bringing its ways to Africa and insisting that Africans had to change them. What was needed was "co-responsibility in the common management of world affairs."[55] This was an argument for an active engagement with the nature of work, labor policy, and economic change. Indeed, it was part of a much broader effort by African intellectuals to come to grips with all the dimensions of European influence, from attacks on colonialism to assertions of the value of African civilizations, to attempts to separate the issue of changing Africa from the model of westernization. Diop's argument constituted neither a passive acceptance of imported ideas nor a rejection of everything that wasn't authentically African.[56]

Several writers had high hopes for the Code du Travail, then under debate; a Dahomean trade union member described what joining the union meant for him.[57] *Présence Africaine*, unlike official reports or the UNESCO volume, contained discussions by African and French authors of work outside the "modern" sector: they provided a picture of work in an African milieu as complex, changing, and not necessarily benign. The labor of women in African societies was discussed.[58] Whereas the UNESCO volume showed that stabilization was an unrealized – if not unrealizable – project and that changing social practices did not fit neatly into a linear model of westernization, *Présence Africaine* gently expanded the boundaries of discourse to suggest that work had multiple meanings and that Africans had something to contribute to defining society and culture in the modern world.

These were important tendencies among scholars and intellectuals working in and on Africa. Meanwhile, some of the most influential theorists within western social science were pushing discussion in a very different direction. The idea of progress – and of the West's vanguard role in it – was hardly new to social theory.[59] The problem of the post-war era was to develop a theoretical apparatus for understanding change in a global, comprehensive way in a rapidly changing political geography, as empires embracing much of the world's population turned into something else. This was a problem that colonial officials had faced in their own ways.

The modernizing discourse of the bureaucrats predates the rise in the academy of what came to be known as modernization theory. This discourse may have been a response to the same sensibilities which affected scholars, but its development within bureaucracies was very much a response to the perceived loss of control within an older form of colonial authority. Officials read recent European social history as the finding of rational solutions to complex social problems, and this gave them confidence that they could apply such approaches generally. In rejecting one form of colonial authority for another, they were rejecting what was "traditional" in their own authority structures – the right to command, the assertion that the good ruler "knew his natives." They accepted that a properly conceived system, be it of industrial relations or of government, would solve problems better than a structure of command. In applying such ideas to Africa, British and French officials were saying that while Africans, like anyone else, could become political actors in legislatures and labor unions, officials themselves had the essential knowledge to build the stage and write the script. Modernizers, after the war, were claiming the right to govern Africa for a time, and they did so on the basis above all of their knowledge; they knew what Africa should be like when it governed itself.

This way of thinking emerged in bureaucracies in regard to labor – it would, I expect, emerge in similar terms if one studied public health, agronomy, or economic development.[60] It emerges as well in the "development" oriented social sciences and most strongly in "modernization theory," a more American, more systematic version of the range of development theories that saw "traditional" society becoming "modern." This is a subject for careful future investigation in intellectual and political history.[61] Here I intend to be no more than suggestive: to try to see the parallels between the ways labor bureaucrats solved their problems in the post-war years and the intellectual trends which arose, a few years later, in the social sciences. Imagining modernity coming to Africa brought coherence, for a time, to intellectuals as well as to officials on the front lines of social change.

Modernization theory had two tenets which went beyond other progress-oriented theories of social change: "tradition" and "modernity" were dichotomous, while modernization could be understood "in terms of the goals toward which it is moving"; and modernity, like tradition, was a package, a series of co-varying changes, from subsistence to market economies, from subject to participant political culture, from ascriptive status systems to achievement status systems, from extended to nuclear kinship, from religious to secular ideology.[62] For some leading American exponents of modernization theory, this conception of change was an explicit alternative to communist progressivism; W. W. Rostow's *The Stages of Economic Growth: A Non-Communist Manifesto* was the best known (and crudest) version of this.[63] It argued that modernization was a much more basic, more universal process than the stages of communist theory, and that the state could help to manage this process in a direction that would avoid the evils associated with communism.

The modernization idea appealed precisely where there was a deep ambiguity regarding how change was brought about. The central tension between modernization as a project directed by those who had already experienced it and modernization as a metahistorical process, driven by deeply seated forces, is evident in the scholarly literature as well as in official discourse.

One of the most relevant examples of a modernization approach is the scholarship on industrialism, notably the work of Wilbert Moore and Clark Kerr. Industrialism, for them, was not simply a way of organizing factories but of organizing life: industrialization and its effects had spread "to virtually every sector of the globe," and even "primitive" societies – as Moore called them – had to respond in some way.[64] Industrialism had its universal "logic" and its imperatives: a "rational" perspective on decision-making, adapting to labor markets, working in a hierarchical structure, adapting to new social situations wherever workers came to reside.[65] But Moore, in his lengthy 1951 study of the social meaning of industrialization in developing societies, did not consider the transition from "primitive" society to industrial to be easy or inevitable: the reason for his inquiry was precisely the uncertainty and complexity of transition. "The world is not peopled by economic men," he wrote, and how people adapted to labor markets and industrial hierarchies depended on the particularities of local cultures, on the mechanisms which brought people into industrial labor markets, and on the way in which social reorganization was managed.[66] Primitive societies were not homogeneous, and out of the fissures within them – the desire of young men to escape control of their elders, the appeal of new alternatives to people of low status, or conversely the adaptation of a traditional hierarchy to an industrial one – came the motivational structure through which workers began to make the transition.

Moore, unlike some modernization theorists, did not ignore the particularities of human experience, but he clearly posited the problem as one of transition from "there" to "here," and variation and complexity appear as "barriers and antipathies" that might obstruct the path between these two given points.[67] Industrialism itself was a bundle of social phenomena which he did not want to unpack: it must be large-scale and hierarchical, and the impetus for it came from the West. To Moore, resistance to industrialism was hopeless romanticism. One could not save "primitive" people for another sort of existence, only assure that they would remain culturally and situationally unsuited for advancement in the industrial hierarchy.[68]

In many ways, Moore was presenting a theorized version of what labor officers, in 1951, were thinking: the socially responsible goal was to prepare Africans for their future in a differentiated, hierarchical structure of labor. Both wanted to foster liveable wages, security, and cultural adaptation.[69] The bureaucrat's and the sociologist's perspectives differed in two ways that seem contradictory at first glance. The labor inspectors were concerned with a boundary question: separating the African working class from the rest of Africa, whereas Moore was concerned with systemic change. At the same time, Moore focused on transition as being both complex and problematic, whereas the administrators thought of transition as requiring expertise – their own – but insisted that the African would, indeed, become industrial man. This faith was an anxious one, and both the desire to bound the domain of change and the need to hold before themselves an unblurred vision of the future reflected the concerns of the men on the front lines.[70]

Industrialism, to Moore and others, was separable analytically from specific economic systems, notably capitalism. That each instance of industrialization involved contestation over the exercise of power was not a point he wished to pursue.[71] Clark Kerr went further: the triumph of "industrial man" eclipsed diversity in human societies. Acknowledging "roads and alleys and even dead ends" along the way, Kerr nevertheless argued in a 1960 article,

The best place to start is with a view of the end result; for industrialism is a great magnet which is drawing all human life to it and ordering the orientation of this life. Whether a society has been matrilineal or patrilineal, whether based on family or tribal ownership of land, whether responding to the Protestant ethic or the Bantu ethic, or whether it goes through a prior commercial revolution or not, it ends up following the logic of industrialism.

Industrialism required certain occupational structures, wage structures, education systems, and labor markets.

There must be managers and there must be the managed... and a whole web of rules governing their relations... The state must be reasonably strong to govern the industrial order, and may perhaps become excessively so. Finally, the men who live within the industrial order must accept its imperatives. There is no place for anarchy in the logic of industrialism.[72]

Kerr did not have Moore's concern with the complexity of transition: "The Bantu of Central, Eastern, and Southern Africa, to give one illustration, are currently being taken straight from the 'bush' and being

turned into mine and factory workers and 'townsmen' almost overnight...
The secret of the Bantu and other rapid and largely successful transitions
to industrialism is the great adaptability of man."[73] Any connection with
agricultural land and "tribal" society – including that of the "target
worker" or the "man on the margin of two civilizations" – was an
obstacle to the "labor commitment" which Kerr saw as fundamental to
effective industrialization. While Kerr thought conflict *within* industrialism was normal, he did not think that conflict *about* industrialism was
more than a futile gesture. Industrialization was not the job of workers,
but of elites; whether they were dynastic, middle-class, revolutionary-
intellectual, colonial, or nationalist, the logic of industrialism was
primary. The real issue remaining was whether the development of industrialism "can be managed well or managed badly."[74]

Inspecteurs du Travail and labour officers needed this fantasy even
more than did Kerr; they had to deal, day by day, with a reality that was
problematic at every level, where neither managers nor workers accepted
industry as a "natural" order of things.

The industrial sociology of Kerr, and in a less extreme way Moore,
exemplify the dualistic thinking that was in vogue in the 1950s in the
academic disciplines trying to come to grips with ex-colonial societies.[75]
The dual economy, divided between traditional and modern sectors,
became a hallmark of 1950s development economics. The most famous
dualistic theory was W. Arthur Lewis' "Economic Development with
Unlimited Supplies of Labour," published in 1954, the same year as
Kenya's Committee on African Wages submitted its report calling for the
separation of the African laborer from "his economic and cultural background." Lewis divided the economy of a less developed country in two,
a traditional sector and a capitalist sector, and he argued that the central
dynamic of development was moving people from one sector to the other.
The rate of savings and hence investment could not be raised in the traditional sector, but it could be raised by the migration of people out of it
into capitalist enterprises and by keeping the wage rate constant. In the
traditional sector, the marginal product of labor was often negligible,
zero, or negative; in any case labor could be released from it at a wage
determined by subsistence needs or by the average product of labor,
rather than by the marginal product of labor as in a developed economy.
Maintaining wages at that level would keep the surplus generated by the
newly employed workers in the hands of capitalists, who would invest
their profits in further production and job-creation, until the traditional
sector was drained of its surplus labor. Then, wages, agricultural productivity, and employment demand would assume a relationship characteristic of developed economies.[76]

Lewis' dual economy is strikingly parallel to the dualistic sociology in which labor was then being discussed: an economist who argues that a society exhibits a zero marginal product of labor is saying something very similar to an industrial sociologist calling a culture "traditional" or to a colonial committee calling it "enervating and retarding." Lewis himself thought of poor countries as having a "low cultural level" and believed that "their kinship and other social patterns, which are such a joy to the anthropologist, are too frail to withstand the ferments of the twentieth century." Against the "economic darkness" of the traditional sector he set the "fructification" that occurred in the capitalist sector.[77]

Lewis was not an apologist for colonial capitalism as it actually existed: early on he had attacked West Indian planters for holding back the advancement of the islands' population; he continued to be critical of rent-seeking and monopolistic behavior by powerful propertyowners. His 1954 model, however, did not address the social basis of production in either traditional or capitalist sector – each was treated as an ideal type. The dynamic of the model lay in the movement of people from one sector to another, first draining surplus labor into a productive sector, then extending the benefits of rising wages.[78] He looked to a liberation in a dual sense: from the backwardness of colonial capitalism toward a more dynamic variant and from the backwardness of tradition into a modern world now open to all. Lewis shared with the Colonial Office a belief that careful state intervention was necessary to move an economic structure from an inhibiting one to a self-sustaining one, and he insisted that political freedom and education were crucial to economic development.[79]

Lewis' argument is particularly interesting because of who he was: a West Indian intellectual, born in St. Lucia, educated at the London School of Economics, teaching in a distinguished British faculty, advising – and not shrinking away from criticizing – the Colonial Office. The failures of modernization theory, disillusionment with the development process, and heightened sensitivity to the imperiousness of western social science should not lead the present-day observer to miss the poignancy of the era of modernization and development in which a young and talented colonial scholar was writing the textbook on how an academic discipline should restructure itself and how the relations of rich and poor should be remade.

Lewis was simultaneously a theorist of the end of empire and a pioneer of an emerging mainstream of development economics.[80] But in the 1950s there was considerable ferment in the field, and other ways of conceptualizing social change were at least for a time open to officials and intellectuals in new states. French social Catholics gave the question of post-colonial economies considerable thought, fearing that independence might lead to "pauperization" and concerned that community values be expressed in economic policy. Latin American economists had since the late 1940s pioneered a "structural economics" that denied the benign role of trade with developed nations. As independent states came into being, their leaders sometimes spoke to one another and began to shape a "third worldism," turning the concept of economic growth into the basis of claims upon the resources of the already developed world. As Mamadou Diouf shows, ideas such as these were invoked by the first leaders of Senegal as it achieved self-governing status, and its first development efforts were led by a French priest whose first act was not to impose a prefabricated plan but to commission a multi-volume study of the economic and social conditions in different parts of the country. The originality of this approach was to lose out before the self-serving actions of Senegal's new elite and the pressures of French firms and officials, but the fact that it was tried at all suggests that economic development, like labor stabilization, could provide the ideological basis for assertion as well as acceptance of French, American, or World Bank versions of directed progress.[81]

The dualistic thinking about backwardness and modernization that arose among colonial officials in the 1940s and captivated the imagination of many scholars and other intellectuals in the 1950s and 1960s must thus be seen in the context of alternative visions of change. But the appeal of modernizing visions must be taken seriously, as much for the anxieties they reveal as the potential for world-wide progress that they asserted. Stabilizing labor appears both as an instance of a wider modernization program and as an admission that modernizing projects could only work within bounded domains, separated from other kinds of worlds. In practice, modernization and stabilization were both cut across by diverse social linkages and conflicting interests; they remained contradictory and unrealizable projects. But such constructs gave an aura of coherence and purpose to a government policy and to scholarly attempts to understand a changing world. The idea of modernization had a liberating element to it which gave it considerable credibility among people emerging from colonial rule and those sympathetic to their aspirations: all people, regardless of origins, could participate in progress and enjoy its fruits. Labor leaders and populist politicians could use these ideas as a basis to claim entitlements, and in so doing they broadened the population with an interest in posing social questions within a modernizing framework. But these were also exclusionary concepts, rejecting modes of life and consigning those who refused modernity's embrace to a marginal status in world history. Leftist intellectuals – the anti-imperialists who wrote for *Présence Africaine* as well as Marxist theorists – shared parts of the progressivist spirit without all of its ethnocentric contents.[82] Nationalist thought was itself divided on this point, at times emphasizing the unique genius of particular cultural traditions and the unique path each needed to take toward its future, at times accepting western modernizers' notions of economic and social progress, while insisting that the colonial state was a false leader and the independent nation-state a true vanguard.[83] International agencies, such as the ILO, provided a forum at which the ideas of a progressive labor policy could be detached from their specifically colonial context, and slowly and subtly shifted from a discourse among colonial powers to a discourse among independent nations.

Conclusion: labor and the modernizing state

The idea of stabilization, like the notion of detribalization which it displaced, was abstracted from the conditions under which workers actually lived. That urban workers in the era of stabilization policies retained rural ties – because of affective relations, because of uncertainties about urban security in ill health or old age, because of the possibilities of families combining wage labor with agriculture or petty trade to enhance collective opportunities – meant that the image of a neatly bounded world of wage labor was an unattainable one. Even had the implementation of stabilization been more thorough-going and the provisions for wages, social security, and housing more attractive, it is not clear that its cultural and social goals would have been attained.

But the power of the model was as much in its unrealistic coherence as in its concrete accomplishments. The model helped colonial officials convince themselves that they were doing more than responding to unruly Africans, even if the strikes of the 1930s and 1940s had set the rethinking of colonial policy in motion. It helped them convince skeptical colleagues first that a progressive imperialism was possible and then that progress in the directions they considered vital could continue in their absence. Trade union leaders used the model to claim entitlements for their members and positions of influence for themselves, even if they emphasized the hypocrisies of colonial rule and the shortcomings of development policy. Social scientists pointed to the inconsistencies and rigidities of models of urbanization, stabilization, and economic development, but most were attracted enough to the overall project of social and economic transformation to join in efforts to train African economists and sociologists, to seek to interject their knowledge into policy debates, and to foster research on many aspects of change. International organizations found in the universality through which issues of work, social security, and living standards were being talked about in the late colonial era a wide domain in which they could claim a privileged voice.

Had colonial governments pursued a more laissez-faire policy in the post-war years – allowing favorable crop prices to bring new prosperity and new investment opportunities to African and European entrepreneurs – economic change might have taken a different course.[1] Alternatively, a more knowledgeable intervention into African society – one giving recognition to the dynamism of Nigerian cocoa farmers or the market women of Accra – might have gone differently from the one which presumed a European-directed "revolution" was necessary (chapter 5). It would be wrong, however, to assume that either of these alternatives would have resulted in a more "natural" evolution of African society: both would have taken place within the context of specific institutions, specific power structures, and their intended and unintended effects would have been as complex as those of the actual policies of the 1940s and 1950s.

The path chosen was not a poorly considered decision. It was thoroughly rooted in the post-war moment: Keynesian arguments for economic management, the consolidation of welfare states in France and Great Britain, the Marshall Plan for reconstructing Europe, the United Nations effort to redesign world order. Social democrats in Europe as much as communist revolutionaries in China, Vietnam, or the USSR had no compunction in seeing their visions of modern and progressive social orders become the basis of government policy even if the contents of those visions were very much in dispute and the self-confidence of European states very much in question. Colonial regimes – in exceptionally frank moments of introspection during and after the war – admitted to themselves that their less interventionist approach to economic change had resulted in woefully inadequate infrastructure, poor educational facilities, inadequate colonial contributions to imperial economies, and anger and discontent among colonized populations. British and French governments believed that leaving investment and decision-making to private capital had failed to produce vigorous economic growth, and that leaving wages and working to the mercies of the labor market had failed to produce a labor force sufficiently stable, healthy, orderly, and predictable to bring about peaceful progress. However uneven the consequences of their interventions, it is not clear that on these last points they were wrong.

The decade after World War II was a time when reformist experiments seemed economically feasible. Export prices for Africa's crops and ores were high, and the stakes in being able to assure continual labor and growing productivity correspondingly great. Yet Europe was ideologically vulnerable, its claims to imperial legitimacy harder to make in an era of "self-determination." The development project – on which new claims to international legitimacy as well as (for a time) imperial economic recovery depended – was at risk economically and politically from demonstrations of African discontent.

The very ethnocentricity of colonial visions of post-war society made them striking targets for an escalating series of claims from African labor and political movements. If the industrial worker was to produce like a European, he should be paid like one; his wife should be able to raise a family without having to engage in her own, distinctly "African," economic pursuits. Indeed, the Inspecteurs du Travail and the labour officers who pushed for stabilization would not necessarily have won the day against less forward looking elements within colonial societies were it not for the active intervention of African leaders in "modern" form and the threat of African action outside those terms. Once the possibility of universal standards for labor was extended from metropoles to colonies – with the colonial regimes willing participants in this discourse – there was no obvious point at which claims to equivalence or equality should stop. The combination of universalistic conceptions of what labor was and what protections laborers needed with political responsibility resting firmly in the hands of European colonial regimes was a volatile one: and it was this linkage which colonial governments eventually sought to break. Meanwhile, the combination of governments' desire to see the emergence of a stable and productive work force and trade unions' claims to entitlements won significant concrete gains for African wage workers, and the general recognition that trade unions had to be a part of the new structure implied that the best organized workers would be well positioned to make further demands.

However, African participation in the discourses of state reform, and the successes they achieved, did much to entrench firmly the frame of reference which colonial officials had tried to develop: the European industrial relations model. That in turn had implications far beyond the labor question: it assumed a particular kind of state, a particular kind of bureaucracy, a particular way of talking about social issues. Positioned between bureaucratic institutions managing the workings of wage labor, international discourse about standards and development, and their culturally heterogeneous constituents, trade union leaders and politicians were coming to grips with their difficult position in global politics and global discourse.

In the vastness of Africa, the modernizing project was a bounded one. That was why the issue of who would fall under the Code du Travail was so crucial, and why the British stabilization model was clearly meant to bring about the separation of African workers and their families from their cultural origins. Rural development – agricultural schemes, education, health care – were of course part of 1950s interventionist policies, but colonial officials did not have too many illusions that they would live to see a modernized countryside. Urban labor was more visible to them, more of a concentrated and immediate danger, more of a potential bottle-neck, and a more plausible model for a modern future. Like many of the sociologists and anthropologists of the era, they thought of social systems having their own coherence, and they sought to bring that integration to the African city. They thought it could be built on notions of economic status, occupational differentiation, and neighborhood akin to those of Europe. European officials wanted to build an African working class, and they clearly stated that such a working class should be separated from all that was African.

In the mid-1950s, the colonial bureaucracies still had their faith in the modernizing experiment. What they were beginning to doubt was their own ability to manage it. African political and labor leaders, some of whom had already turned the modernizing discourse to their own purposes, were there to suggest that others might take up the project.

Part IV
Devolving power and abdicating responsibility

Introduction

Although no-one knew it at the time, the process of African workers laying claim to the entitlements of French workers had reached its apogee when a series of strike threats culminated in the French administration's promulgation of a system of family allowances in 1956. Already, the labor movement was divided over whether it should pursue its demands for equal pay and equal benefits for all members of the colonial labor force or turn its back on the imperial reference point, putting the labor movement at the service of the drive for political autonomy. The new claims to autonomy flew in the face of everything French officials had advocated since the war, but by the mid-1950s so many claims to French entitlements had been made that officials greeted the new direction in unionism with relief.

In British Africa, the experience of partial self-government in the Gold Coast in the mid-1950s eased the worst fears: the one-time Apostle of Disorder seemed to have become the moderate force officials all along had claimed to want. Nkrumah kept the labor movement in check, preventing it from taking the "communist" direction officials most dreaded. But even this – or the suppression of the Mau Mau revolt – left officials feeling unsure of their capacity to handle social disorder and political challenge or even to follow through on their own initiative to superintend an ambitious program of social and economic development. The early 1950s, to be sure, was a period of economic growth and significant social change, but the modesty of the accomplishments paled beside the magnitude of the task of reconstructing imperial economies and beside the political hope of reconstituting the legitimacy of empire. The leadership of the two major empires both lost their confidence that they could simultaneously manage the painful details of directed change and maintain the ideological edifice of imperialism.

The hopes – or perhaps more precisely the illusions – came apart less than a decade after the post-war development drives were launched. The realization that remaking Africa was too great a task for France or Great Britain came on the morrow of independence in India and in the era of violent revolution in Indochina and Algeria. British officials, after the loss of India, had thought that their Africa empire was now more valuable than ever and that they could both legitimately claim that their mission was to prepare colonies for self-government and push the date at which Africa would be ready well into the future. But the quagmire of Palestine, the difficult but successful "counterinsurgency" campaign in Malaya, and the embarrassment at Suez in 1956 shaped the background against which even smaller scale threats in Africa were perceived and in relation to which British interests and powers had to be realistically assessed. France's Algerian quagmire cut to the core of the assimilationist pretensions of the post-war era: Algeria was France and yet its subjects had to give up their status under Islamic law to exercise full French citizenship. The challenges France had for some decades faced in Algeria sometimes took place within a universalistic, rights-centered framework French governments accepted in principle even if they violated in practice, but they spilled outside of such boundaries. The labor movement developed in an assimilationist context – in 1954 more Algerian wage workers were in France than in Algeria – and communist labor movements were bringing them into their internationalist fold. Yet among workers virulent rejection of France and its universalistic assertions contributed to powerful conflicts within Algeria's nationalist movements. What broke out in 1954 was a "war without a name," undeclarable because internal to France yet so brutal that the facade of assimilationist reform – for both liberal and leftist advocates of "un colonialisme de progrès" – was shattered.[1]

Official correspondence in the 1950s is notable for how rarely India and Algeria, formally outside the jurisdictions of the Colonial Office or the Ministère de la France Outre-Mer, are mentioned. Yet the absent presences appear in anxiety that strikes might explode their bounds or that demagogues might mobilize masses, as well as in the growing concern that the costs of stability and progress in Africa might be too much to bear given the burdens of other imperial commitments, cold war rearmament, and national economic revitalization. European governments in subsaharan Africa might well have won struggles with nationalist movements that became violent – as they did in Kenya or the Camerouns – but they had less reason to be sanguine that they could control or contain the daily struggles over work or soil erosion programs. Amidst these anxieties and growing doubts about the prospects for actually realizing goals of social and economic transformation, skepticism about empire began to be voiced well beyond the circles of radical critics (many of whom had themselves been seduced by the idea that progress could be brought to the colonies).

The following chapters explore certain aspects of how two colonial powers thought their way out of the impasse of their reform projects and their loss of confidence in their ability to direct them: both sought to disengage from the management of social change and to remove the metropolitan standard as the reference point for colonial claims to social entitlements, but both held to the belief that their historical experience and the models they had tried to implant in Africa constituted the standard by which their successors could be judged.

10   The burden of declining empire

A French journalist reported on his study of development efforts in West Africa in 1956, "FIDES and its fistful of billions [of francs] amount to nothing in the face of discouraging distances, exhausted land, the routines of Africans, and the immense territories without men and water."[1] The come-down from the high stakes raised in launching development plans was a hard one: too much was expected politically as well as economically. The infrastructure of French and British territories proved incapable of handling even the capital goods imports intended to jump-start commerce; lack of trained economists slowed the planning process and shortages of technical personnel slowed implementation; metropolitan economies could not supply sufficient capital goods or hard currency to buy them abroad; the appropriated funds – small as they were in comparison to Africa's needs – could not be spent at the rate projected; inflation and the high cost of imports and metropolitan personnel nonetheless gobbled up project budgets; ignorance of African conditions led to enormous waste; shortages of housing and consumer goods led to labor conflict and escalating labor costs. The costs of reviving production in the metropoles – which soon proved expensive but more realistic than capitalizing on tropical commodities to save imperial economies – cut into the political support for overseas development, and American advisors did not want too much Marshall Plan aid diverted to imperial preserves partially removed from open world trade.[2] This chapter cannot probe these questions in depth, but it does document the spirit of pessimism which overtook reformist imperialism in the 1950s and which both reflected and affected the posing of the labor question.

A cost-benefit analysis of the British empire

In Great Britain, diminished expectations came out in the debate over the renewal of the Colonial Development and Welfare Act in 1955.[3] Not that the bipartisan consensus on development had come apart, just that

392

its meaning now was being questioned from all directions. The Conservative government insisted there would be "no abrupt change" in colonial development policy, but it admitted that nearly a third of the money approved in 1945 and 1950 had gone unspent, and the carryover was to furnish a third of spending proposed in 1956–60. To do more, given lack of planning capacity and skilled labor, was "physically impossible."[4]

The minister of state for colonial affairs, Henry Hopkinson, added another argument. Colonies, as they neared self-government, "should bear an increasing part of the cost of their own development." Hopkinson was setting something on the record: Great Britain was not going to hold itself responsible for maintaining the letter or the spirit of the Colonial Development and Welfare Act once Africans had claimed the right to govern themselves.[5] Devolving power, as Parliament saw it, implied the abdication of responsibility.

Labour spokesmen lamented, "we are ceasing to deal as generously with the Colonies as we have done under previous Bills." More needed to be spent on social services and education, and the "final stages" of colonial rule actually made it necessary to "step up development."[6] Some MPs on the right replied that development spending was a "terrible burden" for the British taxpayer. They grudgingly asserted that if self-government was what colonial people wanted, they could have it, but they were "responsible" for their own poverty and would have to face the consequences themselves.[7]

Behind the concerns in London was a series of crises in Africa which threatened to pull apart the nexus of development and progress toward self-government on which officials' hopes rested. The Mau Mau Emergency in Kenya (chapter 8) was one instance of economic growth and agricultural "improvement" contributing to political disorder. The linkages were less bloody but equally problematic in Nigeria, where substantial progress had been made toward creating self-governing regions. In Eastern Nigeria, the government of Nnamdi Azikiwe had made social development the cornerstone of its program. But by 1955, British officials were not only convinced that the ministers were corrupt and incompetent, but that the social programs, particularly the attempt to institute universal primary education, exceeded the region's ability to pay. Great Britain stood to pick up the bills if the region went bankrupt and to have to suppress disorder if things went badly wrong. In a self-governing region, however, it could neither kick out the allegedly corrupt politicians nor correct their allegedly unwise policies – unless it suspended the painfully negotiated constitution. The governor, Sir Clement Pleass, put the issue in stark and cynical terms:

so many expectations have been raised of better social services, etc., by the politicians which are, in fact, quite impossible of realisation, that if either the Constitution were suspended or the promise of self-government withdrawn and the Constitution modified, the entire blame for the failure to realise these expectations would fall on us... Inevitably the people are going to be disillusioned, but it is better that they should be disillusioned as a result of the failure of their own people than that they should be disillusioned as a result of our actions.[8]

Over the next four years the regional government was charged with "too ardent pursuit of social services," but each time, officials decided that it was "politically most dangerous even to threaten the use of the Governor-General's power to intervene." In the end, the region did not go bankrupt, but officials remained convinced that Marketing Board surpluses were being looted, that corruption was rampant, and that fiscal management was incompetent. They would only gently raise these issues with Azikiwe: "it is not worth pressing it to the point of making an enemy of Zik." It was with the perception that the political situation was "ghastly," "depressing," "gloomy," and the social development effort a "fiasco" that British officials lurched down the road toward devolving power.[9]

Ever since the Treasury had warned in 1939 against creating a colonial "dole" and Stanley had insisted in 1943 that each territory must in due course pay for its own social services, the British government had sought to avoid any indefinite commitment stemming from the development construct. In Eastern Nigeria between 1955 and 1959, the colonial administration was caught between the pincers of its dual strategy – development and devolution – for managing imperialism in the post-war era.

In 1957, Prime Minister Harold Macmillan called for a dispassionate reassessment of the colonial situation. His predecessors, Churchill and Anthony Eden, did not want to accelerate the unravelling of the British empire even though they would not block the course of events already set rolling in the Gold Coast and elsewhere. They hoped to control the pace and the terms in which constitutional progress was discussed.[10] There was no sharp break from the policies of the Labour government, but the Colonial Office faced continual pressure from the Treasury for restraint. The costs of colonial reform looked more and more questionable as Britain, its economy still sputtering, rearmed itself for the Cold War, while maintaining its domestic welfare state.[11] All the while, the government devoted considerable solicitude to "the many people of our own race who have made their homes in the Colonial Territories." An "instinct... to hang on," as David Goldsworthy puts it, coexisted in the Churchill and Eden governments with the acquired knowledge that one could not.[12]

Macmillan, after the Suez fiasco, cast a much colder light on the problem. The Macmillan of the famous "Winds of Change" speech is rather less significant – the winds had blown the Gold Coast out of the empire before he made the speech in 1960 – than the Macmillan who insisted on a cost benefit analysis of colonialism in 1957. As Chancellor of the Exchequer, Macmillan had already pressed for economies in the colonial, as in other, fields. As prime minister, he asked in January 1957

to see something like a profit and loss account for each of our Colonial posses-sions, so that we may be better able to gauge whether, from the financial and economic point of view we are likely to gain or to lose by its departure. This would need, of course, to be weighed against the political and strategic consider-ations involved in each case. And it might perhaps be better to attempt an esti-mate of the balance of advantage, taking all these considerations into account, of losing or keeping each particular territory. There are presumably places where it is of vital interest to us that we should maintain our influence, and others where there is no United Kingdom interest in resisting constitutional change even if it seems likely to lead eventually to secession from the Commonwealth.[13]

This was most unChurchillian: a calculation of economic and geopolit-ical interest devoid of imperial fervor. As the reappraisal got going, one official felt compelled to assure his colleagues that the prime minister was not "trying to write off any of our Colonial territories in order to save money." Macmillan's colonial secretary, Alan Lennox-Boyd, insisted that Great Britain, while it couldn't make any promises, would hesitate before withdrawing from a colony whose inhabitants wanted her to stay: "nothing is more dangerous than to gain a reputation for forsaking one's friends."[14]

When the Official Committee on Colonial Policy gave the Cabinet its reply to Macmillan's request in September 1957, it concluded that the economic dimension of decolonization was a toss up:

the economic considerations tend to be evenly matched and the economic inter-ests of the United Kingdom are unlikely in themselves to be decisive in deter-mining whether or not a territory should become independent. Although damage could certainly be done by the premature grant of independence, the economic dangers to the United Kingdom of deferring the grant of independence for her own selfish interests after the country is politically and economically ripe for inde-pendence would be far greater than any dangers resulting from an act of inde-pendence negotiated in an atmosphere of goodwill such as has been the case with Ghana and the Federation of Malaya. Meanwhile, during the period when we can still exercise control in any territory, it is most important to take every step open to us to ensure, as far as we can, that British standards and methods of busi-ness and administration permeate the whole life of the territory.[15]

This conclusion followed an assessment of the costs of keeping colonies – £51 million per year for the regular Colonial Office budget, the Colonial

Development and Welfare Act, and the Colonial Development Corporation. Not all this could be saved, since the most advanced territories, like Ghana, received the least and government-to-government aid might well be given after independence, although the government explicitly denied any obligation to do so. On the other side was the contribution colonies made to sterling balances – a major consideration since the crisis of 1947. Colonies held £1.3 billion at the end of 1956. But independence would not necessarily end their importance. Although "standards of prudence" might decline as independent countries "pursued rash policies of over-development and government expenditure," most were expected to stay in the sterling area. Against the danger that balances would be run down or a separate currency regime established if a colony were released too soon was the danger that "postponement and any pique resulting from it would be more likely to lead to abandonment of Sterling Area connections." The argument about trade relations with the United Kingdom was similar: connections born of long-established business relationships would probably continue, unless the independent government made a mess of things or acted spitefully. The conclusion was that Great Britain stood little more risk from devolving power than from trying to retain it.[16]

Here is what the calculation of interest had come down to: Great Britain could in most cases get little more economically out of colonial rule than out of a cooperative post-colonial relationship; the once great empire could not, in these circumstances, risk offending the sensibilities of its one-time subjects, whose good will would hopefully keep ex-colonies in the Commonwealth and the sterling area. Officials' underlying hope was that British discourse and practice had framed the question of governance, and that ex-colonies would become western-style nations.

Although the committee still did not realize how quickly decolonization would proceed, it concluded that some colonies could be sent on their way "without prejudice to the essentials of strategy or foreign relations, and at some modest savings to the Exchequer." Like Lennox-Boyd, it felt compelled to say it would not cut off its loyal subjects prematurely, for fear that would create "a bewilderment which would be discreditable and dangerous."[17]

The detailed responses to Macmillan's inquiry show that officials – finding no compelling reason to hang on indefinitely or at substantial cost – could no longer even see how they could control the pace of decolonization. In Nigeria, the next African country in line behind the Gold Coast, the Official Committee on Colonial Policy thought it best to proceed "as slowly as possible." Loss of Nigeria would result in "a moderate loss of dollar exchange," but that was not the basic problem.

In the eastern part of the country, "a thin red line of British officers stands between the Regions and chaos," which would "most likely" come about within two or three years of regional self-government. The committee took upon itself to comment that Nigerians were loyal to the crown and "have many admirable – and indeed lovable – qualities, in particular a keen sense of humour and the capacity to laugh at themselves... But there is a darker side, which must not be overlooked. Barbarism and cruelty are still near the surface." The problem was, "we are unlikely to have long enough to complete our civilising and unifying mission. The pass in British West Africa was sold when the Watson Commission Report on the Gold Coast was published in 1948." Whether that report so constrained future deliberations in other countries is a moot point, but the language of the 1957 report is an extraordinary commentary on the entire colonial experience as it appeared in the highest reaches of British government. In a region where British missionaries, private enterprise, and government had been operating as long and as intensely as anywhere, savagery had not been conquered. Independence was being recommended by people who expected it to fail: the rapid devolution of power was both dangerous and unavoidable.[18]

Lennox-Boyd put the issue of lack of control over Nigeria even more starkly. Despite the danger of "the country disintegrating," of "administrative chaos," of "corrupt, inept and opportunist rule," the

emotional pressure for independence is strong, certainly in the South... [To] resist too strongly and get all Nigerian politicians against us would be valueless and dangerous for we could hardly control the country if the population were all against us; we must maintain a peaceful and quiet Nigeria, if only to put it no higher, in our ultimate interests as a trading nation (United Kingdom exports to Nigeria run at the rate of £50-60 million annually). To lose the cooperation and affection of Nigerians would be to risk future good relations, when the country is independent.

This is the dilemma with which we are faced: either give independence too soon and risk disintegration and a breakdown of administration; or to hang on too long, risk ill-feeling and disturbances, and eventually to leave bitterness behind, with little hope thereafter at our being able to influence Nigerian thinking in world affairs on lines we would wish.[19]

Lennox-Boyd, like the Official Committee on Colonial Policy as a whole, saw only one thing that could possibly be preserved: British influence on government structure, on "standards," on the Nigerian way of life, on Nigerian trade policy. Lennox-Boyd was not even sure Great Britain could save Nigeria for the West.

In East Africa, Great Britain approached the inevitability of decolonization with even less confidence, aired in a memorandum from the Secretary of State in 1959. The incorporation of Africans into legislative bodies in Uganda and Tanganyika had already gone far enough that "rapid progress to internal self-government is difficult to check." Uganda's divisive politics were "potentially" threatening and Tanganyika posed a "real dilemma" because of its "backward" economy and inexperience of its politicians, yet in the face of "a highly organised countrywide pressure group... it is unrealistic to plan on the assumption that we can hold out against advances which, on strict merits, are manifestly premature." Lennox-Boyd wanted to keep Tanganyika and Uganda under his jurisdiction for another ten years, to guard against demagogues, insure "reasonable standards of living from their own sources at any rate on recurrent account, and retain the confidence of investors." Even in this period, he wanted to avoid "excessive and continued dependence on United Kingdom aid, especially on recurrent account."

As for Kenya, "I have maintained the line that I do not see any prospect in the forseeable future of Her Majesty's government's relinquishing control; but it will become increasingly difficult to maintain this uncertainty once there is a significant transfer of power in the countries on her western and southern flanks." In East Africa as a whole, nationalist forces were demanding "a very early end of colonial status" and "African-dominated States," and the government had to worry about "recourse to organised and widespread violence."

Economically and financially, the situation was getting worse as world commodity prices fell. Kenya was just coming off a special aid program stemming from the Emergency; Tanganyika's budget was in deficit, Uganda's "marginally better." The process of weaning colonies from development funds – pioneered in Ghana – could not be implemented here, lest "the whole aim of trying to secure a planned constitutional development will be gravely jeopardised."

Lennox-Boyd concluded that no general statement on policy in East Africa could be issued. The best that could be done was to launch Tanganyika, with Uganda somewhat behind it, on a ten-year program toward self-government and "maintain ultimate power in the vital matters in Kenya for an indefinite period."[20] The policy collapsed almost immediately: new Conservative ministers in England after 1959 decided there was no point in delaying the inevitable. Tanganyika became independent in 1961, Uganda in 1962. Kenya, bound the closest by ties of settlement, sentiment, and violence, was discussed until the bitter end in the language of impossibility and inevitability. The new colonial secretary, Reginald Maudling, told the Cabinet in 1962 that officials throughout Kenya believed "(i) that the rate of advance to independence... was too rapid, (ii) They could think of no way in which it could now be slowed down." The economy was "running rapidly downhill";

Africans were, in terms of political maturity, "far behind even the West Africans." The Treasury warned, "we could not accept responsibility for additional aid" if Africans mismanaged their affairs and fell into the "complete bankruptcy" officials felt likely. The hope – as a decade earlier in the Gold Coast – was that a "moderate" wing (under Mboya) of the Kenya African National Union could be split from the "men of violence and of communist contact – led by Kenyatta, Odinga and Ngei." The danger of delay was "provoking a violent African reaction."[21]

As the Cabinet was confronting its own inability to control events in Africa, it was making clear its interest in limiting responsibility in the future. As countries became independent they would of course lose their eligibility for assistance under the Colonial Development and Welfare Act and for investment by the Colonial Development Corporation. In case there was any doubt, a number of Cabinet committees recommended firmly that government-to-government financial aid, while a distinct possibility in a post-colonial situation, would not be considered "a regular pattern." Officials did not want to "overstress" these conclusions in public, but a private consensus emerged that Britain's retirement from the state houses of its colonies shifted the basic burden of development finance to the ex-colonies themselves.[22] Officials were well aware that other sources of finance might be problematic: private investment, in West Africa most notably, was weak; the London financial markets were strained by efforts to provide funds to other parts of the Commonwealth; sterling assets were still needed for foreign obligations and reserves and sterling had suffered yet another blow in the aftermath of the Suez fiasco.[23] Some of this had already been rehearsed in the case of Ghana, weaned from the Colonial Development and Welfare Act and pushed toward more intensive use of its reserves from cocoa exporting as it made its way to independence.[24]

The British government, in fact, did provide development assistance to many of its former colonies. But to a very significant extent these countries entered multilateral relationships involving aid, trade, and capital transfer with a wider range of "developed" nations. The argument of the Official Committee on Colonial Policy in 1957 for getting "British standards and methods" to "permeate" the life of the colony represented the best of what authorities could hope for in the late 1950s. In 1959, the foreign secretary and the prime minister could only express the hope that Africa would remain "favourably disposed towards the West" and "oriented towards Western ideals."[25]

The model, in officials' own language, was becoming separated from the men who executed it. The developmentalist ideal plays a crucial role in this picture: that a path lay before Africans toward modernity helped officials to make an imaginative leap, to see their colonies existing without them. Officials in the late 1950s did not look toward the African future with confidence, but the universalism they had espoused for the past decade at least enabled them to imagine a future at all, enough so that the Cabinet committees could see their way to shedding control and responsibility. The labor question was one arena in which the vision of modern, industrial society coming to Africa had been worked out, and for all the inconsistencies, policy actually seemed to be affecting the domain of work. The changes in discourse pioneered by labour officers and commissioners – in unsteady dialogue with African trade unionists – continued during this period of growing pessimism, offering the possibility that in the realm of the social, at least, transformation had been launched and might continue forward.

The bitter pessimism of the Cabinet reports from 1957–59 overlook clear evidence of growth in exports and marketed output, of improved infrastructure and much expanded schools systems, of better paid workers and newly functioning systems of industrial relations in at least some sectors of some colonies – all of which British officials boasted of in other contexts. But the sense of failure has much to do with the way the problem was framed in the first place: a single idea of "development" bringing together the raising of African standards of living and the reconstruction of the British economy, of "responsible" trade unions and respectable politicians, of "scientific" ideas – applied by knowledgeable experts – of public health and agronomy disseminated throughout the African continent. The kinship and clientage networks of Gold Coast or Nigerian cocoa farmers may have been helping to bring in record harvests, but they were not what officials had in mind. The "scientific" approach to social change provided a vision, a highly ethnocentric one, of an endpoint for social change, but no notion of how one got from the complex social situations found in Africa in the 1940s to that ideal "modern" society, and it offered little opportunity to integrate knowledge of actual patterns of change in Africa into deliberations. When British officials were forced to take stock of their progress in the late 1950s, they did not find what they meant by "civilization" and they tended to interpret its absence as chaos and as danger. But African politicians, by virtue of the very insistence of British officials that they had to prove their popular mandates, made their connections with African society as it actually was, with all its particularisms and conflicting forms of affinity. Top officials often read this as demagogy, corruption, and divisiveness. Such observations were not without basis – some of the social and political breakdowns that occurred in the 1960s in Nigeria and elsewhere resemble the predictions of 1957–59 – but the expectations which Africa had failed to fulfill were those of a fantasy of imperial modernization of the 1940s.

The progressive imperialists of the post-war era had had to defend their vision against other officials and settler colonists who thought Africans incapable of social and political advance. From the point of view of preserving the empire, the conservatives had a point: the imperial system which collapsed in the late 1950s and 1960s was imperialism at its most interventionist and transformative. Development had been put forward after the West Indies disturbances as an antidote to disorder. Instead, the increased tempo of change in an era of expanding markets and social engineering – from the intensified production at the expense of squatters on farms in Central Kenya to the heavy-handed interventions of agricultural experts in soil conservation projects – helped to bring about conflicts which strained the ability of the forces of order to contain.

But British officials did not want to give up their dream. They still saw in their own concept of modernity a vision of what the future for Africa must be. They thought they saw some Africans who accepted it too, and they took great pride in the education and the models which they had provided for such people.[26] The post-war bureaucrats had a double image of their role: the system from which they emerged provided a model for the colonies, and their own expertise and wisdom was necessary to implement it. As the latter aspect became increasingly untenable, the former made it possible for British officials to come to grips with the end of empire.

The costs of assimilationist empire: the opening of a debate

The French analogue to the above discussion has been analyzed with considerable skill by Jacques Marseille.[27] The sentimental imperialism of the French elite (in its leftist and rightist versions) came increasingly in the 1950s to reckon with a more calculating variety. One difference lay in the ruling fictions about colonial structure: the claim that the French Union was an indissoluble community versus the British claim that colonization followed a natural course toward self-government. More important still was the fact of the wars in Indochina and Algeria, the latter beginning in 1954 as the former came to an ignominious end. Against that lay the increasing integration of France into Europe, ultimately resulting in the founding of the European Economic Community in 1957, a process which convinced more and more of France's capitalists that they had better investment alternatives than colonies. The human costs of imperial defense – higher than those paid by Great Britain in Kenya or Malaya – made the sentimental argument more strident; the financial costs entered the other side's calculations.

In 1954, Pierre Mendes-France asserted that it was necessary to choose between Indochina and economic reform in France. In 1955 and 1956, some French commentators began to write about what they called "the Dutch complex," the apparent fact that when the Netherlands lost their East Asian colony after the war they quickly became more prosperous. The journalist Raymond Cartier published in a popular journal an influential account of wasted development spending, of territories so vast and so impoverished that they offered little resources or profits to France. He insisted on asking about each of France's African territories, "What is it worth? What does it cost? What does it bring in? What hopes does it allow? What sacrifices does it merit?" With Algeria and Indochina on his mind, he argued that African demands for self-government were growing and could not be blocked, that "It is necessary to transfer as fast as possible as much responsibility to Africans. At their risk and peril."[28] Cartier was in effect taking an old image of colonialist writing – that Africa was poor and backward – and turning it from a rationale for colonizing into a reason for decolonizing.

Such arguments, like Macmillan's demand for a cost-benefit analysis in 1957, forced attention to be paid to questions which progressive and conservative imperialists alike had long avoided. In France, above all because of the Algerian war, they were extremely painful to face, and it took de Gaulle – and only in 1961 – finally to explain why France had to leave Algeria: "Algeria costs us – that is the least one can say – more than it brings us... That is a fact, decolonization is in our interest and, as a result, our policy."[29]

Marseille does not answer the question of why production in the colonies did not become more profitable and why the costs of empire, even in places where colonial wars did not erupt, were so high. The French government had its own post-war development fantasy, and it was not without a success: the Ivory Coast's move from Senegal's shadow into the agricultural vanguard of West Africa. But that success was politically ambiguous, enhancing the prestige and maneuvering room of Félix Houphouët-Boigny, the leader of the planters who drove the colons into irrelevance and grew the cocoa and the coffee and cut the hardwood. The Ivory Coast's leap forward underscored the lack of breakthroughs elsewhere, and many colonial officials would have agreed with the report on Senegal that the "weight of the past and the improvidence" of the peasant "seem to hold [the African mass] prisoner despite all our efforts."[30]

As early as 1951 and 1952, reports were asserting that French developmentalism became caught up in cost overruns, in manpower and equipment shortages, in the inadequacies of existing infrastructure to absorb capital spending, and in the consequent reliance on expensive equipment and technicians from the metropole merely to lay the ground-work for productive investment. As of 1952, a former governor wrote in *Marchés Coloniaux*, that tonnages exported from French West and Equatorial Africa had not regained their 1938 levels.[31] France's principal economic advisory council noted the "disastrous state of affairs" in French West Africa and the "bankruptcy of agricultural policy." The civil service had doubled since 1938 and was absorbing half of the government-general's budget; all budgets except that of the Ivory Coast were in deficit; private investment was not forthcoming; and export possi-bilities were diminishing as world prices were descending from their post-war peak. Given the inability to increase exports dramatically, the development plan allegedly became the "principal factor" in a balance of payments problem, "a disequilibrium inevitable in a start-up period, but whose tendency to get worse is worrisome to contemplate."[32]

A comprehensive review in 1952 of the economic and financial condi-tion of French West Africa by a mission headed by Inspector Monguillot painted a bleak picture five years into the development era. French Africa's production costs were high compared with those of British Africa: wages were double, railway charges were higher, the profits of commercial firms were high, and the bureaucracy was large, well-paid, and growing. Exports had barely reached pre-war levels despite the accomplishments of the Ivory Coast; they did not cover the cost of imports, considering both consumer items and capital. Development projects were often ill-conceived; they often failed to run a profit; and they burdened budgets with high running costs (as well as cost sharing) once they were done.[33]

The accountant's conception of the problem was vehemently contested by the government of FWA. "I believe," said the governor-general, "that technical and social progress cannot be separated and should march together."[34] The finance director acknowledged that equal pay (and benefits) for equal work in the civil services raised the costs of government, but he defended this vigorously in terms that went beyond those of the inspection mission: "Given that the law of 30 June 1950 [the Lamine Guèye law] sought to make all racial distinctions disappear, it would be very delicate to distinguish, as in the private sector, Europeans from Africans, without running into considerable political difficulties. The Administration cannot go backwards in regard to family allow-ances."[35] Nor would the high commissioner pull back from the govern-ment's spending in the "social domain": it was incumbent on the government to concern itself with education, with public health, "with the improvement of the habitat and the conditions of life of the popula-tion, with the perfecting of a large number of political and social institutions still at their beginning and to which the future of FWA is bound."[36]

The governor-general saw the roots of development as deeper than immediate returns to investment: "Progress, in this domain, can only be foreseen, alas! to be slow and difficult. The effort which is incumbent on the Administration, toward this end, must focus on the essential: to augment bit by bit the productive potential of the country."[37] The government in Paris was told that France was going to have to support Africa's productive "potential," not just its production, and France was not necessarily going to get anything out of this arrangement for a long time. The tone of this debate was a far cry from discussions eight years previously at Brazzaville or six years before at the time FIDES was voted, when developing colonial resources was heralded as a way to boost France's economy and image in a single initiative.[38] Elsewhere, the governor-general, Cornut-Gentille, admitted, "the basic objective which was the elevation of the standard of living of the population, has not been attained in a significant fashion."[39]

The inspector's argument about personnel costs and social spending is still made today: that African governments have taken on the state apparatuses and social standards of advanced societies without having developed the productive capacity to pay for them.[40] This had particular meanings in the late colonial context. Officials did not see how productive capacity could be significantly increased without an extensive state intervention and without fundamental changes in African social organization: the African farmer with her hoe was not where the future lay.[41] Less interventionist approaches had been tried before, and it was because of their woeful inadequacy that the current impasse had been reached. A healthy, educated, willing Africa had to be produced and reproduced for the efforts of the future, and it was not apparent that incremental growth in peanut production was going to finance that.[42]

But the social standards question in the French colonial system was getting more complicated. The claim that all colonies were part of a French Union was putting in a more explicit and aggressive form the line which the ILO was promoting – that similar sorts of social standards should apply to workers in dependent and independent countries alike. It was ideologically impossible to separate, overtly, conditions of recruitment for African and metropolitan civil servants, and impossible practically to recruit metropolitan civil servants for overseas service unless they were paid as well as their homologues serving in France.[43] The high-cost bureaucracy, the high-level standards for workers in private and public sectors, could not be turned around or even attenuated without a drastic break in the ideological facade of post-war French imperialism. The individual territory's capacity to pay did not enter into the political equation and the territorial assembly neither set the personnel conditions nor raised the money.

Meanwhile, another bubble was bursting. FIDES was supposed to provoke increased investment by the private sector, which would undertake the export-producing and profit-making sorts of endeavors which FIDES's concentration on infrastructure, social services, and demonstration projects was leaving to others. But this was not happening. The business-oriented periodical *Marchés Coloniaux* published in 1954 a lament that private investment was not following public. Only 20 percent of investment was coming from the private sector, a quarter of that being reinvested profits from FWA. The French taxpayer supplied 55 percent of total investment, the African taxpayer 25 percent.[44] Nor were structural changes among large firms forthcoming: an official study argued that commerce remained dominated by a small number of firms, who left the African producer "disarmed" and maintained high profit margins. A review of the economic situation in Senegal commented on the absence of private investment outside of commerce, leaving the economy "as before the war tributary of the peanut."[45] A distinguished governor saw one of the obstacles to development lay with firms habituated "to earn a lot by producing a little."[46]

The commission studying overseas development in 1953 acknowledged that in the current circumstances France's attempt to "fulfill her strategic, political and social duties in the territories she is charged with administering... risks to lead us to the exhaustion of the Metropole and to growing difficulties in our territories." It still clung to the belief that looking upon France and Africa as a "vast integrated unity" would lead to progress. But that required redoubled efforts "to reform the mores and customs, to lift them progressively from whatever they have of the primitive, and to lead them to a stage closer to civilized conceptions." In the countryside, "sectors of modernizations" would be introduced; in cities efforts would be made to "restructure this new proletariat." In short, the planners were still insisting that Africans remake themselves in the name of Greater France. It all rang hollow, and such an argument opened up the possibility that France should give in to its exhaustion.[47] That was what Cartier and others were soon to argue.[48]

As frustration with development led to calls for a careful calculation of France's true interests in maintaining colonial rule, French officials and politicians did not suddenly call for the termination of FIDES and the abdication of responsibilities only recently taken on under the Code du Travail.[49] No-one seriously challenged the vision of modernity France proclaimed it was bringing to Africa, although left and right might have different conceptions of what that modernity entailed. The question that was beginning to assert itself was that of the metropole's role in the actual management and financing of development.

Developmentalism, in its early phases, fostered centralization: the expertise lay in France; plans had to be coordinated; finance was allocated from Paris. But the sense of burden and exhaustion that entered governmental and public discourse in the period 1953–56 implied a tendency to think that the financing and organization of development should not lie so heavily on French shoulders. Decentralization – the passing of political and above all fiscal responsibility to each colonial territory and eventually to African elected officials – would soon became a mechanism for distancing themselves from the implications of the French model without actually renouncing the modernizing project. This is a subject to which I will turn in the next chapter.

The concept of "development" offered no clear-cut solution to the problems of imperial economic recovery, international legitimacy, and internal order, all of which it was intended to resolve. By the mid-1950s, both governments had discovered they had taken on a burden, not found a solution to multiple problems. African opposition had not been sidetracked; it had in some ways been exacerbated by the tensions unleashed by development efforts themselves as well as by the increasing political salience of the state which development projects had highlighted. In Europe, meanwhile, the Marshall Plan, a decade of recovery from war, and on the continent the prospects of an economic community was making empire a less interesting alternative for leading sectors of business. When officials took stock, they realized that the Africa they had imagined was not to be. They faced the difficulties of ruling Africa as it was.

11   Delinking colony and metropole: French Africa in the 1950s

In 1956 and 1957, a peculiar and unintended convergence of two connected but conflicting ways of thinking about colony and metropole took place. African trade union leaders, having made very good use of the rhetoric of French imperialism to claim for their members a work regime and a standard of living equivalent to those of French workers, pulled away from the French reference point in order to demand autonomy for their union organizations and for their territories. French officials, having insisted that the French Union was an indissoluble whole, pulled away from their unitary vision to press for decentralization, hoping to end the cycle of demands they had been unable to resist.

Both were trying to come to grips with the growing importance of African political parties and to ideologies of nationalism and anti-colonialism. Leading trade unionists wanted their movement to cut loose from the often overbearing tutelage of French *centrales* and to become an expression of African unity and anti-colonialism. In stressing African unity over working class internationalism, the autonomists, in a fierce struggle with many of their comrades, were giving up the organizational and ideological basis of a series of impressive victories.

French officials, meanwhile, were giving up their dream of a Greater France. That they were willing to divest substantial power in each colonial territory to elected legislatures reflected their frustration with the development project, their recognition that African political parties were making demands that could not be ignored, and that their assimilationist and centralized approach to governance was entrapping them in a series of claims to entitlements without providing efficacious means of control.

The autonomist trade union movement broke out at a time when African political movements, especially the RDA, were seizing the modest opportunities of the French system to catapult their leaders into political office and to mobilize African opinion for political action. Sékou Touré became the most dynamic figure in the nationalist phase of the trade union movement, just as he had been a leader of proletarian internationalism. The unions' change of direction climaxed in the formation of a purely African *centrale* in 1955, followed by the fusion of *centrales* into a unified, African labor federation, the Union Générale des Travailleurs d'Afrique Noire (UGTAN). Meanwhile, in 1956, France conceded substantial power to legislatures within each of its territories, keeping little more than the shell of the French Union.

African leaders were divided over decentralization. Some, including Senghor, feared it would "balkanize" French West Africa in a series of small, weak units; others, like Houphouët-Boigny, thought that it would allow his Ivory Coast to make full use of its resources as it wished, without turning over much of them to Dakar. But for all well-placed party leaders, the new framework law of 1956, the Loi Cadre, provided a chance to compete for offices that would give them substantial power. The possibility that French West Africa might be transformed into an independent but unified entity was lost as much to the ambitions of African leaders as to French-fomented divisions.[1]

Almost immediately the policy did part of what French officials hoped it would: by making African officials responsible for budgets, it required them to meet any demands by civil service unions or workers for firms with government contracts with the territory's own fiscal resources, that is with the taxes of voters. "Territorialization" put a damper on unions' strategies in the very year when the extension of family allowances to the private sector marked a final victory for assimilationist trade unionism. Trade union leaders were caught in a trap baited by their own nationalism and sprung by the takeover of state institutions by ambitious men of power. Colonial officials were caught in a trap too: they had deflected the ever rising demands of labor unions onto African leaders but at the expense of turning over to elected African politicians the sites where social change was actually in question.

Autonomy and the French West African labor movement

French African trade unions in the early 1950s were doing well by their mastery of the assimilationist rhetoric of French imperialism. The Code du Travail had been enacted in November 1952 in the wake of a unified strike; the 20 percent increase in basic pay in the private sector had been conceded after a series of strikes in 1953; and family allowances were implemented in 1956 after strike threats in Africa and strong lobbying in Paris by trade union representatives. The CGT unions in FWA had taken the initiative, but the CFTC as well as the still autonomous railway workers had joined these struggles. The union movement in 1956 embraced an impressive 35 percent of French West Africa's 500,000 workers. It had proven particularly adept at organizing widespread –

often interterritorial – efforts to pressure the government and win gains for large numbers of workers; unions were least impressive at firm-level organization, weaker in the private sector than the public.[2]

A number of leading trade unionists were by the beginning of the 1950s becoming irritated at the French CGT's know-it-all attitude and began to raise doubts about African adhesion to the CGT and through it in the World Federation of Free Trade Unions. They began to call for an African labor movement and an African *centrale* voicing distinctly African concerns. In so doing, the autonomist leaders were downplaying class-based claims in order to include workers in a broader claim for liberation. This phenomenon has been studied and debated in scholarly literature.[3] My aim is to focus on the surprisingly strong interaction between a movement taking an increasingly anti-colonial position and colonial officials who saw the autonomist movement as useful to colonial objectives themselves and to ask how this connection affected both sides' thinking as well as their tactics.

The rhetoric of the autonomy faction denied the most fundamental ideological premises of post-war French officialdom. Yet officials realized that the autonomy movement was turning away from the kind of politics which was then giving them the most difficulty: the claim to every entitlement of French workers, based on principles that were solidly French. It was a sign of the extent to which France had lost control over the political agenda that even an anti-colonial alternative to the politics of equality and entitlement was welcomed with relief.

Officials believed that the CGT had become since the late 1940s the sharpest thorn in their side. Following the exodus of the communists from the French government in 1947, the railway strike in France later that year, the government's involvement in splitting off Force Ouvrière (CGT-FO) from the CGT, and the formation of the ICFTU as a rival to the WFTU in 1949, anti-communism became an important theme of French trade union policy.[4] In West Africa, security forces in 1950 were keeping a close eye on Abdoulaye Diallo, Soudanese CGT leader and vice-president of the WFTU, whom they identified as a communist.[5] Sékou Touré was described in 1950 as a "notorious communist," the "star" of the West African CGT.[6] In 1951, officials banned the WFTU from operating in French West Africa and banned as well a WFTU-sponsored Pan-African trade union conference planned for Douala. They were thinking about banning another CGT conference scheduled to meet in Bamako in October 1951.[7]

But by then they had fastened onto the possibility that the CGT might split, and they had already realized that Sékou Touré was the likely agent of its destruction. Intelligence sources reported that he intended to denounce publicly "the utopian and dangerous character of the communist ascendancy over the African masses." He had reportedly come to believe that the French Communist Party "would not penetrate the African soul."[8] In the hope that the Guinean trade unionist would promote a split, officials decided to let the Bamako conference take place: "Sékou Touré would promote secession; union organizations French West Africa would detach themselves from metropolitan CGT," telegraphed Dakar to the governor in Bamako; a circular telegram went out, "Do not refuse leave of absence to civil servants thought favorable to secession."[9]

They got their man right, but the timing wrong: only when union leaders acquired new political ambitions was annoyance with the CGT turned into action. The CGT forces came to Bamako in 1951 prepared for trouble, and most of the conference focused on the usual CGT agenda – demands for the Code du Travail and a widening range of entitlements of French workers. Sékou Touré criticized his rival Abdoulaye Diallo and the CGT. He voted against an organizational resolution, but only one other delegate joined him; Diallo and others tried to cool things down, and a fragile unity was maintained.[10]

Sékou Touré was never a convinced communist, but rather a union leader who thought that the CGT was the best vehicle at the time to lend organizational strength to trade unions. The French CGT's tendency to put its agenda and its rhetoric of proletarian internationalism over the particular concerns of Africans increasingly called the relationship into question.[11] Sékou Touré's rivalry with Abdoulaye Diallo, who had the inside track with the CGT and WFTU, added a personal dimension. Most complicated was Sékou Touré's relationship with Houphouët-Boigny and the RDA. Houphouët-Boigny had broken his marriage of convenience with the French Communist Party in October 1950. French officials felt that as Sékou Touré began to use his trade union base to enter politics – under the auspices of the Guinean branch of the RDA – he came under the tutelage of the RDA's leading figure.[12]

Sékou Touré was reportedly summoned by telegram to Abidjan after the Bamako conference. Houphouët-Boigny, according to French sources, was angry that most CGT conference delegates who had been at Bamako and who were also RDA members did not follow his orders to break with the CGT line, just as the RDA had broken with the French Communist Party. But Sékou Touré was "struggling sincerely, it seems, against those who would not engage themselves in Houphouët's direction." Other RDA leaders were apparently pressuring trade unionists in their respective territories to quit the CGT.[13]

What concerns us here is the interconnections of the labor question and the political question. Some writers think that the shift in the trade union movement requires no explanation: the nationalism of the working masses is self-evident. Yet it is not clear that the move came from the unions' rank-and-file; on the contrary, they frequently continued to push issues like equal wages and benefits. The move came from a union leadership increasingly concerned with its own political advancement and in framing issues consistent with the dominant trend in party politics. The very success of the battles for and around the Code du Travail were redefining the meaning of the labor struggle for politically minded and ambitious men like Sékou Touré, specifying narrowly who constituted the working class and within that zone giving substantial scope to the operation of a labor movement along what French officials called "professional" lines.[14]

The success of the labor movement within these bounds helped to increase the salience of those limits, but the French government was not above using coercion to drive a labor movement back into them. The situation in Cameroun, in contrast to French West Africa, makes this quite clear: there, an especially radical labor movement made common cause with a political party, the Union des Populations du Cameroun (UPC) that quite early made claims for independence. That was where the government drew the line, harassing both the Camerounian CGT and the UPC until the latter (and many of the militants of the former) went underground and into guerrilla action, which was in turn vigorously repressed by 1958. The UPC had taken the opposite fork from the RDA, radicalizing itself where the RDA compromised, and that fork was sharply cut off, bringing down much of the Camerounian nationalist and trade unionist left with it.[15]

But the more precisely defined labor movement and the political movement willing to stay one step inside the boundaries of the permissible in French West Africa posed dilemmas for the politically minded trade unionist. As early as 1951, Sékou Touré was acknowledging that his political career required going beyond his initial base in the labor movement. "The relative success I obtained in the legislative elections," he said, "is not solely due to the progressive ideas which I defended; it is the consequence of the affection which a part of the Guinean masses hold for me, because I am the descendant of an illustrious family."[16]

Ideologically, the movement's claims for equality, for the universal value and universal needs of the working class, were potent within its limits but meant little outside them.[17] Proletarian solidarity was not, in the African context, an ideology that appealed to everybody. The RDA, as well as such groups as Senghor's Bloc Démocratique Sénégalais, were trying to forge a broad political appeal and hoped that labor could become a part of it.

This subsumption of labor struggles under African liberation is precisely what had *not* developed in the railway strike of 1947–48 or in the strikes centered on the Code du Travail. Among leaders seeking to build an African political movement – with their complex attitudes toward relations with France – some, like Houphouët-Boigny, thought workers of much less political importance than agriculturalists and had little sympathy with the major strike movements of the day.[18] Senghor distanced himself from the nitty-gritty of strike movements in Senegal, but worked to coopt its political force once it had achieved success, bringing Abbas Guèye and Ibrahima Sarr onto his party's list of candidates. But he was keeping his labor people as a piece of a broader movement with himself at the apex, hoping to outmaneuver rival leaders for whom labor and urban constituencies constituted a principal base.[19] In the Ivory Coast – home base for the Houphouët-dominated RDA – a Union de Syndicats Autonomes, independent of the CGT, appeared not long after the RDA–Parti Communiste Français split. By 1953, Senghor was himself calling for a strictly African labor organization – African labor should be part of an African liberation movement, not a global proletarian one.[20] As for Sékou Touré, he was in the early 1950s trying to have it both ways. He was talking, carefully, about an independent African labor movement, while carrying on the struggle within existing structures and universalist ideology.

Meanwhile, officials remained convinced that Sékou Touré would be the agent who split the CGT and that the argument for African autonomy would be the vehicle. The governor of Guinea thought his political positions were "rather nuanced," supporting Houphouët-Boigny on RDA matters while carrying on the labor struggle within the West African CGT.[21] In 1953, Sékou Touré was a candidate in a by-election for the Conseil Territorial, following the RDA "ligne Houphouët," and officials predicted he would moderate his trade union followers to establish a cooperative political arrangement. He won his election. But the great 67-day strike of Guinea's workers occurred that September–November and gave a large boost to recruitment and self-confidence within Guinea's CGT union movement. Guinea's branch of the RDA, the Parti Démocratique de Guinée (PDG), was achieving a national mobilization – and working out a broad mobilizing ideology – even as Guinea's working class, growing but still a small percentage of society, was itself mobilizing effectively in the West Africa wide, CGT-led campaigns for equality.[22]

So it continued: Houphouët-Boigny was trying in 1954 to keep RDA members from cooperating with the CGT, but agreed that Sékou Touré could do so as long as he kept the RDA out of discussions, while the latter pushed for the classic CGT causes of equal pay and benefits while criticizing the metropolitan CGT itself and attacking its principal African supporter, Abdoulaye Diallo.[23]

The French government in 1954 was still attributing to the West African CGT "a perpetual spirit of demands," and feared that political parties would feel themselves called upon to match their militance.[24] What was happening, however, was closer to the reverse: unions had to face the consequences of heightened activity in the political sector. The French government was making new efforts to accommodate African demands for political power within its existing structures. In the wake of the French defeat at Dien Bien Phu and the opening of the Algerian war, Paris did not want trouble in Africa, and the new minister of Overseas France, Robert Buron, was going to some length to accommodate the RDA, specifically the "Houphouët tendency."[25] After a CGT-organized conference in September 1954 on the civil service, High Commissioner Cornut-Gentille feared efforts to set loose a protest movement among civil servants. He insisted impressive efforts had been made to end racial discrimination and reorganize cadres in a more egalitarian way, and that the limits of possible reform had been reached.[26] This was the background to the drafting of the Loi Cadre, begun in 1955 and consummated in 1956 (below).

In turn, the sense that a breakthrough to political power was about to be made and that leaders associated simultaneously with unions and parties would share in it affected the atmosphere in which the union question was debated. In 1955, the tensions broke into the open. Some individual unions pulled out of the CGT. Senghor's party machine in Senegal made overtures to trade unionists who thought an alliance with an African party made more sense than a relationship with a French centrale. CGT forces, on the defensive, accused Sékou Touré of betraying some of the strike movements that had been attempted that year.[27] During a trip by Sékou Touré to meetings in Senegal, he defended himself vigorously against his attackers and, according to intelligence services, told supporters that he was standing up to Abdoulaye Diallo and the French cégétistes, opposing strikes that were not in the workers' true interests, and supporting "the new orientation given to the RDA by Houphouët-Boigny in 1951." Within the union movement, he was maintaining his "delicate" position of action in the workers' interest combined with an effort "to liberate [the movement] progressively from exterior influences." Sékou Touré spoke to his Senegalese comrades of the "personality of African trade unionism," while his enemy Diallo fought back against "the so-called African trade unionism."[28] Meanwhile, other RDA leaders, notably Ouezzin Coulibally, were publicly calling for an exclusively African trade union *centrale*. Behind the scenes, the government-general and the minister himself were reportedly using their rapprochement with the RDA to try to get support for the formation of an African union.[29]

The Senegalese CGT, with Sékou Touré chiming in alongside the Senegalese ex-CGT leader Bassirou Guèye, voted in November 1955, by 50 to 17, to form a new *centrale*, the Confédération Générale du Travail-Autonome (CGTA), independent of the French CGT. The CGTA cooperated closely with the Bloc Démocratique Sénégalais as the latter – for all its connections with conservative Muslim leaders – tried to portray itself as a party of workers and peasants. Guinea's Union des Syndicats, closely connected to the PDG, joined the CGTA in May 1956. The organization tried to extend itself, amidst bitter disputes, throughout most of French West Africa, and by year's end had 55,000 members, compared to 60,000 for the CGT, 33,000 in the other *centrales*, and 30,000 in older autonomous unions (notably the railwaymen); Guinea and Senegal remained its real stronghold. The Confédération Française des Travailleurs Chrétiens also spun off, more or less by mutual consent, an African *centrale*, the Confédération Africaine des Travailleurs Croyants (CATC).[30]

The rivalries were hurting the labor movement's ability to conduct strikes, a number of which fizzled as the usual "intersyndical" organizations that had been effective in the past were beset by fragmentation, inconsistency, and jealousy. French officials were pleased by the prospect of the "eventual crumbling of the massive block of the CGT," but worried lest the new *centrale* acquire a "total ascendancy" over workers.[31] The orthodox CGT dubbed its new rival "CGT-Administrative," charging that it "blabbed about the African personality when the plan which it executed with servility came directly from the Federal Building [i.e. the administration]." The two organizations, officials rejoiced, were engaged in a "war of tracts."[32]

The old CGT, battered but still resourceful, now realized that the attractions of autonomy had to be confronted, while the new CGTA saw a unified African trade union movement as necessary to its struggle against colonial authority. The rivals began to talk about a wider fusion as an alternative to their recent fission. Trade union leaders from around FWA organized a major conference at Cotonou.[33]

At Cotonou in January 1957, a new African *centrale* was founded, independent of any metropolitan organization and aspiring to unite all workers of French Africa. It called itself the Union Générale des Travailleurs d'Afrique Noire (UGTAN). Its core was the old CGTA and CGT, plus some autonomes; the CATC, fearing that it might get swallowed up and perhaps sensing the conformacy that the idea of African unity might impose on its members, kept its distance while trying to express approval of UGTAN's goals. The CGT forces, through astute organizational maneuvering, got themselves into leading positions in UGTAN's governing committees, with Abdoulaye Diallo as secretary-general, while the CGTA forces set the ideological tone.[34]

I will return to ideology shortly. Organizationally, the coup through which Diallo of the CGT outmaneuvered Sékou Touré of the CGTA proved to be short lived.[35] In March of 1957 the first legislative elections took place under the Loi Cadre – with a single college and universal franchise – followed by the first Conseils de Gouvernement (Cabinets) in each territory chosen on the basis of these elections. Almost immediately after the Cotonou conference, most of the leading lights of the labor movement dispersed to their respective constituencies and campaigned, as RDA members or otherwise, for elected office. Most did well: labor unions, however small a percentage of the population they represented, were among the best organized launching pads available for campaigns. Victorious party leaders were anxious to have a labor leader in the Conseil de Gouvernement, for purposes of cooptation and constituency building. In eight of the nine territories of FWA, trade union leaders were named minister of labor or minister of the civil service, and seven of these eight were UGTAN members.[36] These included Diallo, who became minister of labor in the Soudan, having resigned the WFTU vice-presidency and shifted his political position closer to RDA lines. His involvement in UGTAN quickly diminished, and Sékou Touré – although himself the vice president of the Council in Guinea – managed to get some of his supporters and allies to take up the slack.[37] Union leaders' decision to follow the route of party politics seemed to be paying off.

Sékou Touré's program of turning the labor movement into an instrument of national liberation also seemed to be working – but at the expense of fracturing the unity he preached. The pan-West African scope which UGTAN's founders had considered crucial had been quickly diffused as each minister in each territory focused on his political base.[38] And the militance which Sékou Touré and his colleagues wanted UGTAN to bring to the anti-colonial cause became problematic and confused as UGTAN's best leaders found themselves part of governments that were exercising real power within their portfolios although they were still under French sovereignty.[39]

French officials expected that the entry of African labor leaders into ministries would tame them: the fox would do a pretty good job of guarding the chicken coop.[40] Throughout most of 1957, they were right: union activity was "very reduced." UGTAN in some instances even intervened to cool off strike movements.[41] But, as soon became clear, much of the conflict was now taking place within UGTAN, as members debated the extent to which their comrades, now in power, were failing to support the union cause. Some insisted that it was inappropriate for union leaders to join the government and that they helped "to oppress the working class." Sékou Touré replied that trade unionism was "incomplete" without "political action."[42]

Pressures from below soon welled up around typical issues – revisions of the minimum wage, equalization of benefits, and the status of the civil service under the "territorialization" policies of the Loi Cadre. UGTAN was torn by debates over what leaders could demand of their comrades in power and whether strikes should be pursued against African governments; UGTAN was forced to press rank-and-file issues and 1958 witnessed considerable strike activity.[43]

In politics, the alliance of party and union for African liberation did not work out smoothly. Rivalries and controversies were serious, none bigger than that over de Gaulle's referendum of September 1958 on whether each territory wanted to remain within a Franco-African community. UGTAN's Comité Directeur followed Sékou Touré in pressing for a "non" vote. The RDA, whose quest for a broad movement of African unity had helped to inspire the formation of UGTAN, split over this issue, and outside of Guinea the RDA favored a "oui" vote. Many workers, including those in UGTAN, apparently thought a "non" vote "not compatible with the defense of their interests as workers," and much of the worker vote went for the "oui."[44]

The entry of union leaders into political power clearly posed a structural dilemma for them: would they act as union men, pressing for the same kinds of goals they had pressed for before, or would they act as government men, trying to contain such demands, maintain order, and keep government personnel costs down? French officials hoped for the latter, and they were not entirely disappointed.

But the structural situation was only part of the story: CGTA and UGTAN, even before the entry into the ministries, had begun to articulate an ideology that subordinated "class struggle" to "national liberation." This ideology denied the labor movement an autonomous space from which to question the actions of the labor leaders/labor ministers. Out of power, this was a call for anti-colonial solidarity; in power, it was a rationale for repression.

Sékou Touré did most to articulate this ideology and he was the first to implement it. At a CGTA meeting in February 1956, he argued for "African solutions" to "African problems." That meant for him the unity of all Africans in a single movement: "Although the classes of metropolitan and European populations battle and oppose each other, nothing separates the diverse African social groups [couches sociales]." Since there was no plurality of interests in African society, he rejected the need for a plurality of unions.[45]

At this time, in 1956, ideological disagreement was open. Abdoulaye Diallo still wanted an alliance with the French working class and saw the French Union as instrumental to that end. He did not altogether reject a *centrale* that was specifically African, as long as it was linked to the international proletarian movement via the WFTU, but he thought the time was not ripe for such a step. He focused on issues like raising the minimum wage, improved family allocations, social security legislation, and an end to racial discrimination. The CGTA, meanwhile, denied that the international working class had any interest in African problems, and wanted "to break with the spirit of assimilation." Trade unions should be concerned with "the evolution of all of Africa... in all domains, political and economic." It claimed, in curiously defensive tones, "this however does not make us forget our industrial demands; increased wages, conditions of work, defense of trade union freedom." The rhetoric was at its most powerful in subsuming the labor movement under a greater cause, at its most vague in discussing issues that were specific to wage earners.[46]

As UGTAN was born, the delegates resolved to work for "the end of the colonial regime, the emancipation of workers and the protection of public and individual liberties." They balked at a resolution proposed by the CFTC's David Soumah calling for struggle not only against "white colonialism, but also against Africans who exploit their racial brothers, like the planters of the Ivory Coast." Even Abdoulaye Diallo, in the midst of his maneuverings for power within UGTAN, urged – successfully – that this be rejected, because the liquidation of colonialism should "take pride of place over the class struggle."[47] This was upsetting to many UGTAN members and at a later meeting one wanted it made clear that the concept of class struggle had only been abandoned "provisionally, so as not to annoy the young government of Black Africa." Sékou Touré was willing to concede that the class struggle was "the fundamental principle of the trade union movement." But the class struggle was not on the current agenda: "the conseils de gouvernement and the territorial assemblies, on the basis of a constructive general program, ask the unions to be patient in regard to certain of their exigencies which will have to cede priority in particular to the claims of African peasants, artisans and fishermen."[48]

The closer Sékou Touré got to power, the more decisively he put his old comrades in their place. In February 1958, some eight months before

Guinea's independence under his leadership, he told trade unionists that unions were "a tool" that should be changed when it got dull. A strike against "the organisms of colonialism" or against employers – such as the 1947–48 railway strike – was "just," but now an elected assembly "is sovereign for all questions relevant to the world of work." A strike against the railway in Guinea would be a different question:

But when it is directed against an African government, it affects African authority, reenforcing by this means, in the relations of force established between the dependent power and the dominant power, the authority of the latter... Trade unionism for trade unionism's sake is historically unthinkable in current conditions, trade unionism of class just as much... The trade union movement is obligated to reconvert itself to remain in the same line of emancipation.[49]

His minister of labor, Camara Bengaly, also lectured UGTAN members on their new duties under African rule:

The workers, without renouncing any of their rights but convinced of the necessity to use them in good earnest, will go through a reconversion to become the precious collaborators of the authentic elected authorities of the people and more particularly to the young Conseil de Gouvernement in its mission to realize the happiness of all Guineans through work done in love... [The] orientation of our trade union movement must necessarily correspond to the general policies desired by our populations. Any conception of trade unionism contrary to this orientation must be discarded, and courageously fought in order to be eliminated definitively.[50]

Coming on the eve of Guinean independence, the words were chilling, a warning that a labor movement's assertion of its members' own interests was not to be balanced against other interests, but was illegitimate and subject to elimination. David Soumah, CATC leader and a fellow Guinean who had worked alongside Sékou Touré in several strikes, sensed what was coming once such ideas would be backed by the might of the state:

Unity for unity's sake makes no sense. And a unity which stifles the voice of free trade unionism sets back the emancipation of the laboring masses instead of facilitating it. A unity which ends up in reality in subordinating trade union action to the good will of governments and employers, which submits trade unionism, the very expression of liberty, to a too narrow obedience toward political parties and political men, neutralizes the action of the masses for social progress.[51]

Although colonialism was the arch villain in the rhetoric of the autonomists, French officials looked positively on CGTA and UGTAN. As noted above, they had encouraged, even lobbied, Sékou Touré and his comrades to form a specifically African trade union confederation independent of the CGT. They welcomed the founding of the CGTA. They recognized that "a form of nationalism" was part of the drive for autonomous union organizations, but the idea of "a specifically African consciousness" had its appeal in that its immediate implication was a rejection of CGT intervention in Africa. Officials associated the trade union split with the split of the RDA from the French Communist Party and with "the support and the precise tutoring given to this leader [Sékou Touré] by M. Houphouët."[52]

The founding of UGTAN in January 1957 led officials in Paris to contemplate the possibility of a new "line" in labor policy. But whatever African motivations in founding their new federation, "the movement could a priori be considered – and it has not failed to be this in effect – as favorable to our future in Africa." They worried that "the organic unity of all the *centrales* of Black Africa" might be too strong and that the CGT might regain influence within such an organization; they wanted the African *centrale* to remain independent of the ICFTU as well as the WFTU. "However, any solution would appear preferable to a reimposed seizure by international communism on African trade unionism."[53]

In Dakar, the high commissioner noted "the accessory character in which the demands habitually expressed by wage workers are reclothed, on immediate or even long term perspectives." Even Abdoulaye Diallo had given up the principle of class struggle in order to forge a movement with teachers, doctors, and others. He still worried that Diallo and the ex-CGT members might take over UGTAN, and for this reason the French administration could not support UGTAN financially, but it should still consider a policy "to put confidence in the new organization in supplying it with material means that would permit it to liberate itself from the control of national and international extremist organizations." In any case, he hoped to establish "as close a liaison as possible" with the Sékou Touré faction of UGTAN, in opposition to Abdoulaye Diallo and Alioune Cissé.[54]

French officials, fearing internationalist communism and worn down by the politics of equal entitlements, thought they had no alternative but to hitch themselves to the cart of African unity. So much did they think they needed an alternative to the kind of trade unionism they had been facing that they convinced themselves that Sékou Touré did not mean what he said about French imperialism and that his call for a radical African consciousness would be less of a threat to French interests than his opponents' call for equal pay for equal work. They badly misestimated Sékou Touré. Most important, the hope French officials vested in African ministers to control the escalating demands of the unions reveals how much the vital force of French colonialism had spent itself by 1956.

Officials were closest to the mark in their prediction that once in government African elected officials would have to act to tame the unions

and that UGTAN would become divided and confused over its relationship to its members' class interests and its own nationalist program. With
Sékou Touré heading the government council in Guinea, with Abdoulaye
Diallo serving as labor minister in the Soudan, and with Gaston Fiankan
– veteran of the railway strike – serving in that role in the Ivory Coast,
the labor question was looking rather strange in the middle of 1957.

The Inspecteur Général du Travail predicted in April 1957 that as
RDA members, with their UGTAN connections, entered ministries, they
would find themselves in the position of providing workers "very meager
satisfaction in regard to the demands they are now expressing." Their
rejection, as responsible members of a government, of union demands
might lead to the creation of a new, extremist, labor movement:

> The question would then be to know if and to what extent such a movement will
> be capable of extending its influence on the mass of workers, caught between their
> search for a rapid and substantial improvement in their material conditions and
> their respectful fear of local African authorities, who will not lack means to make
> their point of view prevail.[55]

The high commissioner, Gaston Cusin, had a similar prediction: the
responsibility of government would weigh on Sékou Touré, "constraining
him to refuse workers much of what he would have demanded himself as
union representative... the ties between the local trade union movement
and the majority political representative in the territory will only deteri-
orate rapidly and end up in the abandonment of the RDA by this same
mass of workers, which had been its first and firmest support."[56] Cusin
did his best to encourage such a split: when a civil servants' strike was
threatened in 1958, he went on the radio to say how "respectful" he was
of the territorial legislatures' will, that the unions' actions risked compromising the political changes which Africans so wanted, and that it no
longer made sense simultaneously to claim "growing governmental
responsibilities for the territories" and "assimilation" of salary scales to
the metropole.[57]

African government–African union tensions had already erupted in the
Ivory Coast following the RDA's rapprochement with the French government and Houphouët-Boigny's assumption of a ministerial position in
Paris in 1956. When Gaston Fiankan led a three-day strike, 99 percent
effective, he was criticized by the RDA leader Ouezzin Coulibally and
replied by criticizing Houphouët-Boigny and other RDA leaders, whose
actions he said were "less and less in accordance with the aspirations of
the mass."[58] But by 1957 Fiankan himself was part of the government.

The ugliest confrontation occurred in Dahomey where the demands of
different groups of workers came together at the end of 1957 into a strike
movement which turned violent. Civil servants in October were

demanding the application of new wage scales from the metropole, with the territorial UGTAN awkwardly proclaiming, "although it has decided to give its support without reserve to the local executives to assure the success of African promotion in democratic and healthy management, it just as much refuses to pay the price of a policy of discrimination." Meanwhile, auxiliaries on the railway staged a wild cat strike over pay; a palm oil factory went on strike; and the employers' attempt to fire strikers led to solidarity strikes with UGTAN involvement. The minister of labor, Guillaume Fagbamigbe – formerly of the Dahomean CGT and later an UGTAN leader – was criticized for having "betrayed the cause of the working class" in regard to the oil factory incidents, and for preaching moderation when he had earlier told union representatives that he would support their demands. Leaders later met with Fagbamigbe who, "very embarrassed, replied that he could make no decision without having referred it to the Vice-President of the Council." Workers, according to police informants at their meetings, were now expressing regret that Fagbamigbe had accepted his ministry. One speaker commented that "it was easier to obtain satisfaction from a European Inspecteur du Travail than it is now from an African Minister."

The disputes led to a one-day general strike in December over the oil factory dispute followed by a three-day civil service strike – part of a FWA-wide movement – followed by more strikes in January 1958, which led to riots on 24 January which resulted in some deaths and the imprisonment of alleged rioters. UGTAN by then was trying to seize the initiative on both private and public sector strikes (trying to outmaneuver the CATC, which was relatively strong in Dahomey). The oil company dispute ended with the factory closing; the civil service issue festered as UGTAN accused the government-general of hiding behind the Loi Cadre to hold back wage adjustments granted to civil servants working directly for the French administration. UGTAN was in the position of demanding, in Dahomey and elsewhere, that "the territorialization of the civil service not translate into a diminution of entitlements acquired, nor into discrimination," while some of its members, serving in government, were exercising power as part of that territorialization. Meanwhile the opposition – this was the RDA, which had lost in Dahomey's 1957 election – was lending support to the unions and criticizing the Dahomean government. These disputes had no ready resolution. They were among the most serious problems facing inexperienced governments, before and after formal independence, as they came to grips with the situation France had placed them in: turning a discourse about African–French equality and universal standards of labor policy into a discourse on the scarcity of local resources.[59]

UGTAN in Dahomey seems to have been caught, despite itself, into organizing opposition to a local government which went a long way toward representing its aspirations for self-government and which included an UGTAN leader. Where the RDA governed and was close to UGTAN local leaders, the relationship could be even more tense.[60] At the territorial level, UGTAN, at least as concentrated in the public sector as the CGT had been, had no choice but to protest on behalf of its constituents against the effects of territorialization on the civil service: "décrochage" (delinkage) became a paramount issue in 1957 and 1958 in the public sector, as unions fought the implications of putting the civil service of each territory under that territory's jurisidiction and on its budget.[61] In various territories, and in some inter-territorial services like Postes-Télégraphes-Téléphones, there were strikes and slow-downs, enough that union and government officials began to talk of the "malaise" in the civil service. UGTAN tried to pin the blame on the "Central government," which it accused of using the financial difficulties of the territorial governments to foment disputes between them and the civil servants. But some union meetings were hearing more and more complaints from the rank and file and shop stewards about the salaries of ministers and "their rich prebends." They questioned whether UGTAN leaders could serve the union membership and the state at the same time. The top leadership of UGTAN, however, kept trying to remind members that strikes threatened schisms and the future of UGTAN itself, and that the local administrations were not "organisms to combat systematically, but organisms elected by the populations, and which should be served to advance the historic march of Black Africa toward its unity and its development."[62] When UGTAN leaders in Senegal took their grievances to Mamadou Dia, Vice-Président du Conseil, he told them that the "particular struggle of the workers to resolve secondary contradictions risks compromising the general struggle engaged by the Conseil de Gouvernement, the Unions, and the Senegalese people" to assure genuine autonomy from France.[63] His words were virtually identical to those used many times by Sékou Touré in defending UGTAN's subordinating the class struggle to the national liberation struggle.

The ideology of nationalism was being used to put a workers' movement in its place. There were difficult issues here: whether workers should aspire to equality across the races within the French Union or to parity with the standard of living of the majority of the local population. Sékou Touré was not trying to open up a debate, but to suppress a discourse. The insistence on unity – from a man in power – was a denial that addressing workers' conditions of life had its own distinct legitimacy.

The French colonial regime had linked its authority to a French reference point, and had no answer, other than evasion or stonewalling, to
ever-escalating demands from workers for the entitlements of French
workers. It was only on conceding power that France made it possible
for "décrochage" to take place, for the French reference point to be put
aside. But the argument for national unity and national struggle by which
the autonomist union movement and the new governing councils of francophone Africa broke the French connection also left workers ideologically as well as politically weak to take on the new governments'
assertions that they and only they served the universal African good.
Equally important, as the public sector unions lost their French reference
point, the connection to private sector unions which the idea of equality
for an entire class had provided, and the benefits of interterritorial solidarity, they became increasingly caught up in the patronage structure
over which each territorial government presided.[64]

When Guinea became independent, the trade union movement became
an arm of the ruling party and alternatives were suppressed: "trade
unionism was forbidden to trade unions." A strike of teachers was
harshly suppressed and its leaders jailed. The governments of Senegal and
the Ivory Coast tried to push all unions into single organizations,
although the Senegalese government never did manage altogether to tame
an often chaotic labor movement. A number of strikes in the early post-
independence era were suppressed: in Senegal for example a civil service
strike in 1959 was followed by massive firings of workers later forced to
plead to get their jobs back, in notable contrast to the gingerly handling
of such an event by officials in 1947–48. Senghor used the power of
patronage and his alliances with conservative rural leaders to try to force
"labor reconversion" that would make labor a collaborator in his development drive. One of the casualties of the push for political power which
UGTAN had encouraged was UGTAN itself: as the territorial governments became the relevant units of political action, it broke (by 1959)
into territorial units.[65] The dream of African trade union solidarity faded
along with it.

An epilogue to the story of unions and parties: in August 1994, a group
of Senegalese graduate students and I interviewed trade union veterans
in Dakar and Thiès. To a leading figure in the Senegalese branch of
UGTAN, Alioune Cissé, the trade union movement deserved credit not
only for what it had won its members but for its contributions to the
independence struggle. Yet Cissé himself had both gained and suffered
from the political connection: he had been given high political office,
including important ambassadorships, but after he helped lead trade
unionists in the general strike of 1968, he (like railway union leader

Ibrahima Sarr previously) was jailed by Senghor's government, a fate he had not suffered under the French. For Cissé, the blame for what went wrong lay with the French Loi Cadre (discussed below), which fragmented Africa, costing it both the possibilities for action on a wide scale and dissipating the moral force that the union movement had garnered. Our interviews with rank-and-file militants disclosed a similar pride in the movement's contributions to the making of Senegal, yet a bitterness about its fate. Union leaders, we were told, took off the "boubou syndical" (the robes of union office) and put on the "boubou politique." The unions became the "auxiliaries" of the political parties – a word which echoes the marginal positions to which French job hierarchies had consigned large portions of the work force (a factor in the deadly railway strike of 1938 and the monumental one of 1947–48). And in the midst of ministerial power and wealth, the material causes of the 1950s were allowed to wither.[66] So, in the memories of some trade unionists, the glory days of struggle for higher wages, equal benefits, and the Code du Travail led to a political victory from which a large proportion of the victors were excluded.

The Loi Cadre and the renunciation of assimilation

As UGTAN leaders demanded that African workers act as Africans first and workers second, they were taking the line the French officials hoped they would. The colonial government had itself stepped back from the ideological framework under which claims to equality had proved so hard to resist and set up – believing it was the best it could do – an institutional framework that refocused attention on the integrity and resources of the individual territory.

When the Loi Cadre was introduced into the French Assemblée Nationale in March 1956, Pierre-Henri Teitgen, the recent minister of Overseas France who had done much of the drafting before leaving office, put the issue in the context of French colonial history.[67] The new law, he argued, would be a complete break with the governing concept in French colonial ideology, assimilation: "We are going to change totally the orientation, the spirit, the objectives of our overseas policy and renounce definitively and solemnly this so called policy of assimilation." It had never been realized, for the French people would never have accepted its consequence – that in a true "Republic one and indivisible," the overseas territories would have more votes in Parliament than the metropole. He then took the argument from the political to the social:

Whether you like it or not, whether you think they are right or wrong, in fact, when you speak of assimilation to our compatriots in the overseas territories, they understand it, first and foremost, as economic and social assimilation and assimilation in regard to standard of living. And if you say to them that France wants to realize assimilation overseas, they reply: Well, give us immediately equality in wages, equality in labor legislation, in social security benefits, equality in family allowances, in brief, equality in standard of living.

It is thus that they understand the policy of assimilation and it is in fact this which it would have to signify if it were to be effectively applied.

What would be the consequences?

Attaining this goal would require that the totality of French people accept a decrease of their standard of living by 25 to 30 percent for the benefit of their compatriots of the overseas territories.

As Teitgen spoke these words, he was interrupted three times by deputies from the overseas territories – Sékou Touré among them – reminding him that the overseas populations were not demanding assimilation, that they were in fact demanding the end to such a policy.[68]

The French colonial establishment and the most militant African nationalists were agreed: assimilation was dead. With it fell the ideological framework within which the most important social questions in French Africa had been contested over the previous ten years: a framework used by colonizer and colonized in their own ways, through which the one claimed that the other should remake his or her way of life and the other claimed equality of voice and standard of living. Assimilation, as articulated at Brazzaville for example, had been a doctrine of politics and culture. The social question had entered through the back door, and French officials had only noticed its presence during the strike of 1946, when for the first time they saw, in a form they could not ignore, that the logic of assimilation and equality was being applied not just by a small elite of évolués, but by the united work force of Dakar. The precise meanings of assimilation and equality were fought over throughout the next decade, but French officials, resisting escalating demands, had not in fact denied the fundamental justice behind the idea of "equal pay for equal work" or the fact that French standards of living and of labor regulations should set the standard for Africa. Now, equality was going out the back door of the house of assimilation just as it had come in, and some of the African leaders who had fought the hardest in its name were happy to see it go.

Most of the debate on the Loi Cadre focused on political institutions. Each territory was to be given substantial power to run its own affairs, under a Conseil de Gouvernement with a majority of elected members from the Assemblée Territoriale, with the governor as president and an elected member – obviously being groomed to be prime minister – as vice-president. The Assemblée would be elected in a single college under universal suffrage. The government told the Assemblée that these reforms were intended to let the people of each territory control their own affairs and would be meaningless unless that territory's government had control over its civil service – including its salaries and benefits – and responsibility for paying the bills.

The corollary of this change was the Africanization of each territory's service.[69] France would help each government push such a goal by expanding the access of Africans to the Ecole Nationale de la France Outre-Mer, which trained colonial officials. There would still be a *service d'état* – now distinguished from the *services territorialles* – whose responsibility crossed territorial lines and covered the continual maintenance of French sovereignty (defense, foreign affairs) and coordination and communication (FIDES, post, telegraph, and telephone). The service d'état would be paid by France, the *services territorialles* by the territories. There would have to be some juggling of tax revenues and continuing aid under the FIDES program, but the reforms were clearly a major step toward transferring the arduous tasks of running a state to elected representatives of individual territories and to civil servants responsible to and paid by them.[70]

The Loi Cadre was controversial – exactly how much power would be devolved was very much in question.[71] So too was the fact that power was passed to territories, not to French West or Equatorial Africa as a whole.[72] But the Loi Cadre promised African activists enough access to real power, with real budgets and real possibilities for patronage, while promising enough of the trappings of French sovereignty to the sentimental imperialists that a coalition for the legislation could be built that went from Sékou Touré to René Malbrant, the most die-hard opponent of previous colonial reforms.[73]

The reform of the public service – "territorialization" or "delinking" (décrochage) was as important symbolically as it was in practice. It cut away the French reference point in a large and influential sector of the labor force, and in making the local budget responsible for paying civil servants helped to make the point that a local standard was morally and politically sound. The government was astute enough to guarantee "to civil servants currently in service the maintenance of all their acquired rights in regard to remuneration, benefits, pensions, and the normal development of careers." Government did not want to induce colonial civil servants to leave or unions to make a fuss.[74] The point was to cut the *future*, largely African, civil service of the territories loose from France and the French standard.

In internal government papers during the period when the Loi Cadre was being drafted, the importance of ending the French standard emerges clearly:

In the current state of affairs, there is no point of support to resist claims when they pass the limit beyond which the cost becomes too heavy for the budgets... The solution consists of giving to those who are in charge of receipts, that is the elected representatives of the taxpayers, the power of decision in regard to the status and remuneration of civil servants in each territory. They alone can accept an increase in budgetary charges for they, alone, have the responsibility to vote the taxes which will pay for them.[75]

Recent progress in bringing Africans into the civil service made the question more difficult: Africans now constituted 85 percent of the cadres, including 23 percent of the *cadres généraux* and 70 percent of the *cadres supérieurs.* For practical reasons, it was impossible to pay metropolitan recruits less to go to Africa than to serve in France, and for political reasons it was impossible to pay Africans less. Décrochage addressed the problem with which the administration had been wrestling for a decade:

It is easy, from here, for the African unions to take on the administration at its own game, and far from demanding the abolition of the privileges of Europeans, to base individual and collective demands on the quest for assimilation to the most favorable situation... The public service in FWA is impregnated by the spirit of pure assimilation: to stay on this base created a misunderstanding that can only become aggravated on the level of race.[76]

The politics of race, equality, and living standards were thus very much in mind as Teitgen told the Assemblée Nationale that assimilation was to be definitively rejected.

These issues resonated especially strongly in French West Africa, because in a large and diverse federation the point at which political pressure was applied and decisions made (Dakar) was distant from the points from which money had to come: FWA had become "a system which generalizes 'claims' after having pushed them to their most extreme expression." The uniting of diverse territories permitted the siphoning of resources to a federal elite, allowing "those who produce nothing to live off those who work, but prohibit[ing] the producer from living better."[77] Such a sentiment, and the appeal of decentralization, may well have gained support from African politicians in the Ivory Coast at the expense of those in Dakar. For French officials, it represented a step away from their own centralizing biases, faced with the frustrations of having others make claims to those centralized resources.

Civil servants' organizations were aware of the danger, but the politics of union autonomy as well as of the Loi Cadre were making concerted action increasingly problematic.[78] Sékou Touré and others were now looking on the Loi Cadre as an opportunity to enter the halls of government, and UGTAN was preoccupied with autonomy. The Africanization promised in the Loi Cadre was attractive to the best trained civil servants seeking better positions, and the law also promised that no current civil servant would lose by its provisions. The CGT unions, which had been in the assimilationist vanguard, took a low-key approach to the pending law, arguing that whatever its objectives it should come into affect only when the equality promised by older laws had taken effect. The CGT expressed fear that inequalities might develop between the colonies and the metropole and among the different territories, but it stopped well short of opposition to the projected reforms.[79] The labor movement, already caught up in the political ambitions of much of its leadership, was not in a position to challenge the administrative decentralization that was the concomitant of political devolution.

Barely had the law been passed when the governor-general replied to a new set of demands from the Comité d'Action des Organisations Syndicales de la Fonction Publique by invoking the Loi Cadre: he would not interfere with the prerogatives of the Territorial Assemblies. A union official charged that the government "is taking refuge behind the texts of application of the loi cadre and refuses to take a position on our demands."[80] Officials repeatedly reassured unions that acquired rights would not be taken away, but future rights would depend on the government of the territory where they served and would be subject to, among other considerations, the "financial potential" of that territory. Privately, officials recognized that this would mean inequality among the territories, but it was parity with the private sector of each territory, rather than the "disastrous" old linkage to the prerogatives of the French civil service, that they now sought.[81] Meanwhile, the new territorial governments, with their African ministers, began to put their own stamp on the regulations of the territorial civil services.[82]

Security officials reported that civil servants were anxious about "delinking from the Metropolitan Civil Service," and there were a number of civil service strikes in different territories in 1956. But the internal battles of the trade union movement were too acute for them to be shaped into a coherent opposition to delinkage, and a number of planned strikes never came off.[83] In 1957 and 1958, civil service unions in various services in the several territories mounted campaigns over the usual sorts of issues – claims that the Lamine Guèye law had still not resulted in equal pay and benefits across the civil service hierarchy.[84] A civil servants' strike, which followed to varying degrees in much of French West Africa, except for Guinea and the Ivory Coast, in January 1958, was one of the results, as was the bitter Dahomey strike in early 1958 (see above) and other disputes. The agitation from the individual unions put UGTAN on the spot: it tried to cool off such disputes, but it had no choice but to take up issues so important to constituent unions.[85]

The Loi Cadre was having its intended effect, putting African politicians in the position of rejecting workers' demands on the grounds that territorial budgets could not sustain them. The vice-president of the Government Council in Senegal, Mamadou Dia, lectured civil servants that they had to give up their aspirations to the salaries of their French predecessors, using the same word – décrochage – that French officials had in advocating the Loi Cadre. UGTAN leadership in the territories was confused, sometimes backing strikes, sometimes trying to derail them, sometimes appealing to comrades in government for "serious study of the situation of workers," sometimes condemning them for "the aggravation of the misery of the laboring masses." A number of unions and local UGTAN chapters bitterly condemned territorialization: "Delinkage in the current conditions of our territories, dependent economically and politically on the Metropole, signifies injustice and flagrant discrimination, diminishing the buying power of the civil servants of the territorial cadres."[86] UGTAN leaders serving in governments replied, as in Dahomey, with embarrassed deference to the Conseil de Gouvernement or, as in Senegal, with arrogant insistence that the problems of workers were secondary (see above).

French officials, who had seemed to think that the tension between African ministers and trade unionists would work in favor of the French government's interests, began to worry that the "wave of demands" was jumping from the territorial to the federal level and "risks totally disorganizing administrative life and causing a failure of the harmonious application of the loi-cadre."[87] But the storm was no longer theirs to weather. Outside of the limited service d'état and the dwindling federal bureaucracy in Dakar, the new territorial governments would make their concessions or resist demands, coopt union leaders or throw strikers in jail in accordance with their own political calculations.[88]

The weakening of the French reference point, as Teitgen had told the Assemblée Nationale, represented an ideological transformation whose implications transcended the conditions of service of the bureaucracy. In discussing the post-Loi Cadre Inspection du Travail, French officials revealed that they expected the bureaucracy to *act* in new ways. The inspection remained a service d'état and the Code du Travail a French law. But instructions went out to the inspectors that they should act in a deferential manner to the minister of labor in each territory and send all correspondence via the local ministry and territorial governor. In case of strikes, the Inspector should "bring with tact his active collaboration to the Minister."[89]

The veteran head of the labor inspectors, Pierre Pélisson, travelled to meet with ministers of labor in the territories in 1958, and claimed that they had "given homage in my presence to the professional competence of the Inspectors and to the loyal cooperation that these civil servants brought them even though they belong to a Service d'Etat." However, "The Ministers desire, over all, the *territorialization* of the Inspection du Travail and the Lois Sociales. In actuality, they do not have at their disposal ministerial services, contrary to the majority of their colleagues." The anomalous situation of having the political direction of the labor ministry be territorial and its bureaucratic arm be under French control gave the labor ministers a "psychological inferiority" vis-à-vis the other members of the cabinets. For now, Pélisson proposed that the nomination of inspectors be done with the "consent" of the minister. He also proposed that Africans be trained as inspectors at the Ecole Nationale de la France Outre-Mer; all inspectors as of 1957 were French. He worried that since the Code du Travail was French law, territories could not amend it and therefore lacked flexibility.[90] Such anomalies would shortly be overcome as the territories moved toward independence, but at the immediate aftermath of the Loi Cadre the universality of labor law which had been the focus of the inspection's existence and its pride since World War II had become an inconvenience in the process of bureaucratic devolution.

Conclusion

The French government had pried open a fundamental contradiction in the African labor movement, between the idea that African workers faced the same needs as workers of any race, and the idea that African workers were part of an Africa-wide struggle for autonomy and power. The assimilationist model of work, however satisfying it had been to the French tendency to identify their own experience with universal human values, had unleashed an escalation of demands which the French government could not control; the African nationalist model, however hostile to French ideological pretensions, offered a way out of a set of practical and ideological problems. The Loi Cadre appears, in this context, like a stroke of political genius, giving African politicians and labor leaders access to power that they could not refuse, while through the same process of territorialization undermining the ideology by which the labor movement made its claims and taking away the French budgetary resources which might meet them.

But the power which the French government gave away was real. The territorial governments now had their budgets and law-making powers, and after 1956 the powers and the trappings of sovereignty which France retained were to be of diminishing interest in France itself. There is no more telling sign of the change in attitudes in the heart of the French colonial establishment than the lamely cooperative stance taken by the Inspection du Travail as its independence, as its claim to the knowledge and skill necessary to superintend labor, as the very claim that French experience with the labor question provided a model of universal validity, were compromised in deference to the political prerogatives of the newly Africanized labor ministries in the territories. The Loi Cadre, from this perspective, was not so much an adroit maneuver as a reconciliation to the fact that the post-war attempt to revitalize the French empire had failed.

12   Nation, international trade unionism, and race: anglophone Africa in the 1950s

Having been backed into accepting African self-government in the Gold Coast, British officials watched – with at least a touch of admiration – as Nkrumah and the CPP sought to tame and mold the labor movement. Like French officials welcoming the rise of the highly nationalist UGTAN and misreading the intentions of Sékou Touré, their confidence to manage their modernizing project had all but dissipated even if they clung to the project itself. Operating in a different institutional framework from the other fading empire, British officials faced similar problems and a similar need to convince themselves that they could leave without admitting that their entire effort to transform Africa was a failure. This chapter considers two manifestations of Great Britain's ambivalent disengagement from Africa: its thinking about trade unionism in relation to newly self-governing regimes and to international labor organizations, and its approaches to government personnel in the transition. Both Great Britain and France were in a sense accepting that social transformation was a global process, not a project for a particular empire. All they could do, in effect, was try to keep Africa in the "West." In the labor field, this meant working with the anti-communist International Confederation of Free Trade Unions as the only viable alternative to the World Federation of Trade Unions. They did this grudgingly and bitterly – the ICFTU was too critical of colonialism for their taste. Trying to navigate between communism and extreme nationalism in regard to labor organizations, transitional regimes were also facing the fact that the largest body of wage workers were their own employees and that the categories of civil servant and worker remained both unclear and deeply racialized.

The ambivalences of responsible trade unionism after colonial rule

For Great Britain, the Gold Coast was the key test. Would its first subsaharan colony to be set irreversibly on the march to independence remain within boundaries of social policy that British rulers could accept as a precedent? In fact, in the six years between Kwame Nkrumah's transit from jail to State House and the pulling down of the British flag, his government gave plenty of signs that authoritarianism – in union affairs as in many others – would be as much a characteristic of the new order as of the old, and British officials chose to read these signs in a tolerant manner, perhaps wishing they could have handled labor with the same authority.

After the failure of the "positive action" campaign of 1950, the Gold Coast's trade union movement – especially its umbrella organization, the TUC – was in disarray, having split over the issue of "political" strikes in support of the CPP. Nkrumah's unexpectedly rapid recovery from the debacle of 1950 to the triumph of the 1951 elections rendered irrelevant the CPP's initial urge to rebuild an anti-colonial workers' movement. After that, as Richard Jeffries puts it, "Nkrumah had no more desire than governor Sir Charles Arden-Clarke to have to deal with serious industrial disturbances." The British model of apolitical trade unionism suddenly seemed more appealing, and the CPP and the labour department now cooperated in reconstituting the TUC as a "more moderate, manipulable, Accra-based labour movement."[1] The Colonial Office described the revived TUC as having been "wrested from the hands of extremists," and hoped that its apparent willingness to follow "a reasonable line" would be enhanced by the "successes" it achieved.[2] The CPP gave crucial support as well to a dissident group of mineworkers opposed to the leadership which had successfully led the 1947 mine strike but which had opposed involvement in the CPP's campaigns. D.K. Foevie, a man sensitive to wind direction, became head of the MEU.[3]

As colonial officials reconfigured their one-time enemies into moderates, their enemies' enemies now became the extremists. The noted militants Anthony Woode and Pobee Biney spearheaded the formation of a rival to the Gold Coast TUC, called the Ghana Federation of Trade Unions (GFTU). British officials observed that the goal of this organization "appeared to be to undermine the authority of the T.U.C. and of the Ministers and to adopt largely Communist tactics; it will undoubtedly try to win over the more irresponsible trade unions and there is a possibility that it may affiliate itself to the W.F.T.U."[4]

Within a few years, the power of the state had taken care of this danger. Nkrumah accused the GFTU of "dividing the workers," maneuvered his men into most of the constituent unions, made some concessions to left-wing trade unionists, marginalized Biney and Woode politically, and eventually folded the GFTU into its better-connected rival in 1953. Initially, the Gold Coast TUC was independent of both the WFTU – which had earlier given it some assistance – and the ICFTU.[5]

Nkrumah stated he would not employ communists in government services, and the GCTUC decided to join the ICFTU. The government, British officials concluded, had "clearly defined its anti-Communist attitude."[6]

Thus by 1953 the trade union question in the Gold Coast had become a "political struggle between Mr. Nkrumah and the Communists," and Mr. Nkrumah was winning.[7] Faced with party and government power, the radical trade unionists faded and the current moderates consolidated their position. Unions were registered within specific trades or industries, as British officials had long advocated, and the labour department congratulated itself on the improved state of industrial relations machinery. Wages and rankings within the civil service were revised with advice from a British specialist and the efforts of a commission under Nkrumah's minister of finance, Komla Gbedemah. When the leading mine magnate of the Gold Coast, Major General E. Louis Spears, complained that driving up the wage rate might force some mines out of business and asked for London's help, the Colonial Office was supportive of Nkrumah's ministers: wage increases were important "for the purpose of keeping labour quiet"; it was the business of "Gold Coast politicians" to make decisions and learn from them if they had negative consequences; "the mining companies must face the fact that the standard of living in the Gold Coast is bound to rise; and that if the rise goes beyond the level at which it has been possible to operate low grade mines in the past, then those mines will simply have to go out of business as uneconomic."[8]

Labor, reported the governor in 1955, was becoming "progressively quieter" and by 1957 it was "remarkably quiet" and labor leaders – presumably those being coopted rather than excluded – had become preoccupied with "possibilities about to open before them." By then, the Colonial Office had presented (in 1956) the case to Commonwealth prime ministers why the Gold Coast should join the Commonwealth, citing not only the ability of an all-African Cabinet "to run its own affairs," but the fact that it was "firmly opposed to Communism" and "since 1951 there had been no major disturbances to public order in any part of the country." The same point would be made two years later about other West African countries moving toward independence.[9]

With independence, the CPP was ready to exert even tighter control over the trade union movement. Twenty-four national unions were established beneath the TUC, but the central organization itself – controlled by a large bureaucracy and by CPP leaders – was responsible for negotiations with employers and for collection of dues, 45 percent of which it would retain. Institution of the check-off made collection easier. The

TUC leader, John Tettegah, did not conceal his centralizing ambitions: the new government-sanctioned TUC would be "a gigantic Labour organisation co-ordinated and centralised with a general staff capable of taking decisions and manoeuvring with monopoly capital in securing for the workers economic independence in an independent Ghana." The TUC and the CPP would be "comrades in arms," parts of a "division of labour" in a common cause.[10] Workers in essential services, including the railway, were forbidden to strike, others could strike only after the exhaustion of "practically inexhaustible" negotiating machinery. This measure did benefit weaker unions, and the TUC negotiated some important wage increases in the private sector, but the strong, militant unions which had played such an important part in the Gold Coast's past, were denied the autonomy to play such a role in Ghana's future.[11]

So union membership grew and strike activity declined, especially after independence.[12] The remaining nucleus of militance remained in the railway unions and most notably with the rank and file in the Mine Employees Union. Foevie, its CPP-connected leader, was under strong pressure in 1952 and again in 1955 to bring home a wage increase, and was forced into aggressive wage bargaining, ending in a 100-day long strike in 1955–56. Nkrumah, now eager to show that Ghana provided a favorable climate for investment, joined the Chamber of Mines in fighting mine union militancy, forcing a weak settlement. After 1956, work stoppages – mostly concerning workers' resistance to "scientific management" – occurred in spite of the union and not because of it. Foevie, in 1958, accepted the restrictive conditions of the new structure of the TUC, and, while still the union's head, joined the board of the State Gold Mining Corporation, eventually becoming its managing director. Nkrumah, meanwhile, was telling the mineworkers that their "former role of struggling against capitalists is obsolete" and that they were now to "inculcate in our working people the love for labour and increased productivity."[13]

Such stories are not unique to the labor question; in agriculture and other spheres autonomous organizations were dismantled or transformed into arms of the CPP, over considerable resistance.[14] British officials were aware of the precedent set by "what had happened in Ghana where the trade unions had been brought under the almost complete domination of the government."[15] But they were not entirely unhappy with the fact that the labor militants – whom they chose to label "communist" – were the victims of authoritarianism in the final years of British rule. Nor were they unaware that Nkrumah was the only hope they had for an orderly transition away from a situation over which they had effectively lost control. An aide to Prime Minister Macmillan, writing a series of confidential papers in 1959 about "the next ten years in Africa," said about one issue what could have been said about the labor question as well: "the experience of Ghana seems to show, if demonstration is necessary, that parliamentary democracy will not survive the end of colonial rule. Ought we not decide what we would like to see in its place instead of going on pretending?"[16] The pretense of a peaceful, managed decolonization was precisely what was so important for the British government to maintain.

Great Britain in the last part of the 1950s was not trying to keep British Africa British, but to keep it western. When it came to labor matters, and particularly to trade unionism, the principal embodiment of this internationalist ideal was the ICFTU.[17] Nevertheless, colonial officials liked the idea of an anti-communist world trade union organization more than they liked the one that actually existed.

Although the WFTU was strongest in French territory (although it was banned from direct activity there after 1951) and the ICFTU in British, both saw the ICFTU as the best means of preventing the WFTU from being the only source of international sustenance to African unions. The ICFTU had a solidarity fund to provide financial aid to fledgling unions; it could send advisors and organize training sessions; it could bring Africans into international trade union circles. The possibility of success in Africa, however, hinged on the ICFTU's ability to distance itself from the taint of colonialism, and the American influence on that organization brought with it an anti-colonial bent.

In French Africa, the ICFTU got off to a slow start, largely because the CGT was so far ahead and the CGT-FO weak, but also because the growing autonomy movement was not enthusiastic about allying with another non-African organization.[18] French officials and CGT-FO leaders – fearful of ICFTU criticism of colonialism and its contacts with politically active North African trade union movements – tried to make the CGT-FO an intermediary between African trade unions and the ICFTU and when CGTA and UGTAN eclipsed all the French-centered union associations, they sent spies to make sure that Sékou Touré was not getting too cozy with ICFTU leaders. In fact, there wasn't much to worry about.[19] It was the autonomist trend in FWA, not the ICFTU, that produced the desired break with the WFTU: even Abdoulaye Diallo resigned from it, took up office with UGTAN, and was soon in a government ministry.[20]

The British connection to the ICFTU was considerably stronger; the TUC had been there at the foundation. Some of the greatest hopes British officials had for "responsible" trade unionism, the revived Gold Coast TUC under Tettegah and the Kenya Federation of Registered

Trade Unions under Mboya, affiliated to the ICFTU. Officials needed this alternative to the WFTU: "It is no use trying to break Communist leaders if there is nobody to step into their places," wrote a Colonial Office official in 1953. To assure international legitimacy – as well as advice and material support which the TUC was too weak and condescending to provide to African unions – the government concluded that the ICFTU had to be "welcomed" into British colonies. Its presence was a mixed blessing: "internal rifts within the ICFTU and the strong 'anti-colonial' tendencies which are likely to cause us difficulty and embarrassment, its general rawness and lack of experience of the conditions and problems in Colonial territories..."[21]

In fact, some of the unions British officials most wanted to help, such as the KFRTU, very much wanted assistance from the ICFTU. An ICFTU mission first came to Kenya in 1951, led by a trade unionist seconded by the TUC, and quite correctly noted the Kenya labour department's hostility to Kenyan trade unions (chapter 8). At the KFRTU's request, another ICFTU delegation visited Kenya – not very warmly welcomed by an administration obsessed with Mau Mau – and later a Canadian trade unionist, Jim Bury, became area representative of the ICFTU. He developed a close relationship with Mboya, whose federation the ICFTU helped to finance.[22] Bury and Mboya organized courses in several Kenya towns for trade union officers; others went to ICFTU trade union courses in the Gold Coast, and the ICFTU sent Mboya as its representative to Tanganyika and Uganda in 1955 to meet union representatives and officials. Mboya's contacts in Africa and Europe grew, and he joined the ICFTU executive and chaired its East, Central, and Southern Africa committee. With help from the ICFTU he was well launched on the circuit of international labor leaders in the "free" world.[23] While this could have been taken as the great success of British labor policy, for Mboya was both a protégé of British officials in Kenya and an articulate defender of trade union democracy, it gave rise to considerable misgivings in London. He appeared to be too successful – and therefore too powerful – and did not take the pledge (which to him made no sense) to build a wall between trade unionism and politics.[24]

British officials were caught between their need to build "responsible" African trade unionism and their fear that any autonomous action by an African leader with his own following would endanger their authority or that an informed Kenyan might tell international organizations more than they needed to know about colonial politics. In 1955, Governor Baring almost lifted Mboya's passport to prevent him from attending an ICFTU meeting in Vienna, at which, it was feared (correctly) that he would bring out embarrassing information about government repression during the Emergency.[25] Even within western-oriented organizations, the passage from a specifically colonial framework was still a painful one.

Meanwhile, the ICFTU ran training courses for budding trade unionists in the Gold Coast and opened a West African office in Accra, paralleling its East African office in Nairobi.[26] On the eve of Ghana's independence, the ICFTU made an extravagant gesture: it held an African Regional Trade Union Conference in Accra, 14–19 January 1957, opened by Kwame Nkrumah and attended by delegates from seventeen countries – British colonies, plus Algeria, the Belgian Congo, Madagascar, and Tunisia – and ten observers. Nkrumah's speech was the focal event. He invoked his own membership in a union when he was working in the United States and proclaimed his support for "independent and free trade unions in the new state of Ghana." But he immediately added, "It would be a mistake, however, if trade unionists were to consider that their duties in regard to Africa consisted merely in helping to establish trade unions." From that point on, almost the entire speech was about development. When he went back to "the narrower aspect of trade unionism," it was to warn unions not to copy the European or American model and to focus on "the particular conditions of Africa." What he had in mind was raising productivity. His final argument was that "Trade unions in Africa are therefore expected to play an active role in the struggle against colonialism and imperialism."[27]

Like Sékou Touré at the same moment, Nkrumah showed little interest in workers as workers, in issues of equality across the races, in the struggle workers had long been waging for decent conditions of life and for recognition that they, like other identifiable groups in society, had the right to organize themselves in their own defense. Both leaders sought instead to persuade workers of the virtues of order and productivity, in the name of a bigger cause, fighting imperialism and developing the economy.

But the rest of the conference was quite different in tone.[28] The resolutions it adopted sound more like the agenda of a CGT union in francophone Africa than like the more narrow goals on which trade unionism in the British territories had by and large focused. "Equal pay for equal work irrespective of sex, race, colour or creed" was inscribed in the "declaration of the rights of the workers of Africa."[29] So too was "the right of the workers to social security and good working conditions," including the 40-hour week (45 hours was the norm in the Gold Coast), minimum wages sufficient for a family, free and compulsory primary education, old age pensions, guarantee of full employment, compulsory recognition of unions. A conference secretariat report criticized the migrant labor system and called for stabilization, family wages, and a system of social security.[30] There was considerable criticism of colonial governments – notably the French in Algeria – but little interest in sweeping condemnation of imperialism. The conference voted its support for self-government and self-determination and for each African territory to pursue economic development in its own way and in its own interest. The conference was strongly agreed – a point which UGTAN accepted formally and in effect undermined – that trade union autonomy was an essential goal.[31] The ominous note in Nkrumah's opening address, made more ominous by what he had already done to subordinate the Ghanaian trade union movement to a vision of the unified nation-state, was scarcely commented upon.

Like other international organizations, the ICFTU operated in an ambiguous middle ground: it could not criticize states too much or it would lose access, but states could not altogether ignore it because it could acquire knowledge about how trade unions were actually being treated and use its anti-communist credentials to make a fuss overseas. Tom Mboya, for one, credited the ICFTU with saving the Kenya labor movement during the Emergency: "our survival at that time depended on the Kenya government's fear that the international labor movement might come in and exert international pressure if we were proscribed."[32]

Great Britain and France in the late 1950s could not prevent the internationalization of imperialism. They might ban one international organization, like the WFTU, from their territories, but they could not keep international organizations in general out, nor could they prevent all such organizations from defining problems in ways that reflected their institutional interests and perspectives. Great Britain and France had, of course, consciously opened themselves up to this sort of scrutiny, going back to the Brussels Conference of 1890, the League of Nations' Anti-Slavery Convention, and the series of ILO conventions on colonial labor policy beginning in 1930. They had thought that the invocation of international standards, if occasionally annoying, would secure the moral position of empire in international politics. But with the rise of political movements on the African continent, colonial powers could no longer control the access of such organizations to information on Africa. In mandated territories, United Nations Trusteeship Council representatives were constantly hearing complaints and evidence from unions or political leaders; Africans had increasing access to international publicity; and the ICFTU – which France and Great Britain accepted because they feared worse – could and did work directly with African trade unionists and give them access to its fora. In the long run, institutions like the World Bank and the International Monetary Fund, plus commercial and aid-giving institutions from other countries, would become part of the daily life of

an ex-colony. Cold-war rivals would enter the picture, and "development" would become the watchword of new but still unequal relationships in the international arena.[33]

A small incident reveals much about the ambivalence of a colonial
regime as its power waned. In 1958, the ICFTU was working on plans to
establish a trade union college in Kampala, Uganda. This was the kind
of training colonial officials had advocated, and to a limited extent
provided, since the early 1940s, and they preferred that such training take
place in Africa rather than England, for fear that Africans would run into
too many left-wingers in metropolitan union circles. But the ICFTU
college raised hackles. Governor Crawford proclaimed himself "strongly
opposed," fearing that its presence would "give a political colour" to the
new trade unions of Uganda and that the college might politicize students
at Uganda's Makerere University. He was worried about "rum charac-
ters" coming to teach, about the college driving "a wedge between our
young trade unions and the Labour Department," and about the presence of an "international establishment" in a British colony.[34] All the
class prejudices, xenophobia, and paternalism of British colonialism
seemed condensed in the governor's opposition.[35]

The Colonial Office shared worries about "subversion," but wrote
apologetically to the governor that Great Britain was trapped by an
understanding worked out among the CO, the TUC, and the American
Federation of Labor-Congress of Industrial Organizations (AFL-CIO).
Allowing the ICFTU a free hand in such activities was "the price of
securing the withdrawal of direct American trade union activity in dependent Africa."[36] The previous year, the AFL-CIO had begun to show
interest in establishing direct linkages with African unions and with
providing support. The Colonial Office and the TUC were appalled by
this, both because it seemed as if another imperial power was taking over
Great Britain's historic role and because they distrusted the African-
American trade unionists who were involved in such projects. They
feared embarrassing questions about the color bar in British colonies and
more doses of American anti-colonialism. The TUC strongly lobbied
their American colleagues and after a fight at the AFL-CIO convention
in December 1957, the AFL-CIO decided to work through the ICFTU
rather than "going it alone."[37]

Part of the settlement was a "gentleman's agreement" between the
TUC and the AFL-CIO that gave the ICFTU entré into British colonies
in exchange for the Americans' agreement not to act unilaterally. That
was why the Colonial Office would not block the college. It feared as well
that obstruction would play into the hands of "those in ICFTU who may
want to run the college as an anti-imperialist mission." Officials hoped to

get a Briton appointed director, but settled for a Swede and considered it "welcome news" when the TUC was asked to nominate a tutor.[38] So the ICFTU opened its college in Kampala, starting in a temporary location and contributing £95,000 for its own building. It began with twenty-four students from West Africa, British East Africa, Somalia, and Mauritius. Reports soon noted that it "proceeds quietly."[39]

That such a fuss should be made over so little suggests how narrow a perspective and how limited the power the British government now had over social questions in its African colonies, even as it was desperately and largely vainly struggling to control the timing of the passages of colonies to independence. It was now hoping that its ex-colonies would stay in the western world, and it was increasingly bound to accept that the institutional manifestations of the the western world would not be distinctly British and might even smack of what London thought of as "anti-colonial."

In 1959, officials learned that John Tettegah, head of Ghana's TUC, had gone to the UGTAN convention in Conakry, bringing together union representatives of subsaharan Africa's two independent nations. At that meeting, there was talk of forming an African Trade Union International, uniting francophone and anglophone regions. Tettegah – already highly placed in the ICFTU – was elected an UGTAN vice-president. The British report on this meeting thought all this was very good: there were still dangers that UGTAN, despite its focus on independence, was still "inclined to the left" and hopefully bringing an ICFTU connection to it would have a beneficial effect.[40] The issue of building an All-African Trade Union Federation in post-colonial Africa would later surface, and promptly get swallowed up in the new rivalries of independence. Indeed, UGTAN itself would soon fall victim to the territorial nationalism it had helped to encourage.[41] The colonial regimes would be bystanders to the resolution of questions such as these, but for now they seemed to prefer the spirit of pan-Africanism in trade union affairs to the spirit of proletarian internationalism.

Just as the international dimensions of trade unionism passed into a realm that British officials could only observe, so too did trade unionism at the national level. Once the advocates of responsible and apolitical trade unionism, British officials noted another sort of politicization of trade unionism in the Gold Coast, as an instrument of a state.[42] In Tanganyika, the labour commissioner surmised that African trade union leaders there thought Ghana's new trade union legislation was "repugnant." The Kenyan labour commissioner thought his colleagues "should have no delusions about the power of African nationalist politicians. They could dispose of opponents and secure the overthrow of union leaders

who were not to their taste."[43] Officials worried if their "rather paternal
trade union laws of the past decade" had not gone too far in giving
governments control over which trade unions would be allowed to register
and participate in industrial relations machinery. Now that such controls
might be exercised in the near future by Africans rather than Europeans,
the problem looked rather different. The Colonial Office thought it wise
to recommend governors "to reduce considerably their powers of statutory control of, or an administrative intervention in, the affairs of trade
unions." The Overseas Employers Federation too apparently had doubts
"about the prospects of the independent governments inheriting and
turning to their own needs a paternalistic system devised by us for laud-
able purposes." The TUC was worried about the same thing.[44]

African trade unionists were not unmindful of the issue and did not
necessarily subscribe to Sékou Touré's or Kwame Nkrumah's view of
trade union subordination to nationalist unity. In 1958 – still some years
from his own ascent into power – Mboya told an ICFTU meeting in Dar
es Salaam, "I would take strong exception to any trade union leader or
trade union movement that compromised with any particular government just because that government happened to be an African government." He thought that the colonial government's attempt to "divorce
trade unions and politics" made no sense, but he would not subsume the
one under the other:

Once industry is created a wage-earning community is created and that is where
we come in, for it is our objective that wherever there exists a wage-earning
community that wage-earning community should be fairly treated, should receive
its due rights, should receive a fair wage for the work or labour itself.[45]

Mboya too would go from being labor leader to minister of labor and
would face the ambiguities of reconciling such roles. Mboya, however,
accepted that workers had distinct identities and distinct interests that
could not be subordinated beneath an ideology of nationalist developmentalism, and while he sympathized with the drive to create an All
African Trade Union Federation, he did not reject the usefulness of an
internationalist approach to labor that went beyond Africa, including the
idea of standards which had been so important to the framing of the
labor question throughout the post-war era. As minister, he continued to
argue that a well-paid, stable work force was conducive to economic
development. Mboya, however, was also trying to define boundaries for
the Kenyan labor movement, to focus on collective bargaining and away
from the kinds of system-changing demands that might discourage the
international firms which were becoming increasingly important to
Kenya as the settlers' star faded.[46]

Party power, national development, and international labor standards would be difficult objectives to reconcile. For colonial regimes – frustrated with the fact that their own reform agenda had been turned into claims to entitlements by African labor movements, unable to keep conflict within the boundaries of their industrial relations machinery, forced to work with national and international organizations whose anticolonialism they feared because they feared alternatives even more – the time had come to pass these problems on.

Self-government and the civil service in British Africa

In both French and British colonies, the civil service was in an ambiguous position: a major part of the wage-earning population, yet also a part of the apparatus which was to preside over social questions. The month-long strike of Nigerian government workers in 1945 and the two-month long strike movement in Dakar in early 1946 – in which government workers in the "cadres" joined daily laborers – served notice that civil servants could use the classic weapons of the trade unionist and that the connection of government workers to other workers was very much in question. It would remain so: whatever mechanisms government leaders used to determine wages and regulate conflict with government workers would have a large impact on the independent state's salary structures, and government workers would play a big role in determining a labor movement's effectiveness. In the colonial context, the ambiguity of civil servants' status as workers inevitably opened up the relationship of workers of metropolitan and African origin and hence the question of race.

If French colonial ideology presumed their empire to be more unified than it could ever be, the British elite treated individual colonies as more autonomous than they were. Whereas the French government emphasized "territorialization" as it sought to separate government workers from metropolitan connections, the separateness of the civil services in British Africa was presumed from the start. In the major colonies, a series of commissions – much like those which had tried to come to grips with the labor question in the era of general strikes – took on the problem of redefining conditions of recruitment, service, and remuneration for civil servants as Africans laid claim to a right to administer their own affairs. Anglophone African unions had no basis in the structure of empire to defend a unified structure of the civil service in which they could claim parity to a British reference point. The process of change was pervious to the tendencies and tensions, in particular those over race, in individual colonies.

Each colony had its own civil service, although the Secretary of State recruited the more senior officers on its behalf. After World War II the Secretary of State made clear that the future direction was toward greater territorial autonomy, even though the increasingly interventionist nature of the colonial state was leading to an escalation in the number of civil servants, particularly in technical fields, sent out from England. This was part of the policy of moving toward self-government – at whatever pace that might be. As the Commission on the Civil Services of British West Africa 1945–46 (the Harragin Commission) made clear, "it is the avowed policy of His Majesty's government to Africanise the Service as soon as suitable African candidates can be found."[47] Previous steps in this direction, notably at the senior level, had been halting and effectively limited to West Africa; the recruitment of two Africans to the senior civil service in the Gold Coast in 1942 had caused a huge controversy and Nigeria had to be pressured to follow suit.[48] The process of finding suitable Africans, reports made clear, was likely to be slow, and educational facilities had to be built up; Nigeria only obtained a decent university in 1948.[49]

The post-war reflections on the civil service came not only from a realization that the implications of self-government actually had to be faced, but from the unrest among African civil servants, most dramatically in the Nigerian civil servants' strike of 1945. Officials feared an "explosion" among functionaries – including European ones – that might extend "throughout West Africa."[50] Officials debated for a time whether a systematic, West Africa-wide study of recruitment and salaries would calm things down or stir them up. One hornet's nest they feared to uncover was the question of "fitting Africans into posts formerly held by Europeans" and whether such Africans "should be given European conditions of service."[51] Opening up high positions, with European-level wages, would have the beneficial effect of breaking up the shared meagerness of government salaries which had caused the Nigerian strike to spread throughout the civil service and railway; it risked letting British colonies slide down the slippery slope that eventually claimed the French – toward making British salary scales the reference point for all government workers.

The Harragin Commission, recognizing that for some time to come British and African civil servants would both enter the colonial service, addressed these issues:

All African Associations have argued with force that there would be equal pay for equal work; an excellent precept but not one which can be accepted entirely in this enquiry. So long as it is necessary for the West African governments to employ persons from overseas, so long will they have to pay an extra amount to induce them to leave their homes and families and spend their lives in less healthy and less congenial surroundings.

Instead of the principle of equal pay for equal work, the commission offered something which sounded like the principle of the market: "If a comparison of terms of service is to be made at all, it would be more correct to compare the terms of service offered to the Britisher in the United Kingdom with those of the Nigerian in Nigeria than to compare the Nigerian in Nigeria with a Britisher in Nigeria."[52] The complication was that British thinking about such comparisons had long emphasized communities more than individuals: "where different sectors of the community at present enjoy standards of living which vary widely the immediate application of the principle [equal pay for equal work] would not be practicable." Qualifications and responsibility were also seen to be collective attributes: getting Africans ready for leadership positions would be "a slow and gradual process governed by the rate of advancement of the general level of the community."[53]

The difference between French and British policy in this regard was not so much the end result – French administrations accomplished the same end by expatriation bonuses and other such prestations – as the rhetorical systems in which decisions were justified: French policy was to emphasize unity and equality in the civil service, expressed by ritual enunciations of the principle of equal pay for equal work and by having a single salary scale based within each cadre; British policy was to deny the principle at the first pass and to emphasize instead that distinct communities had different notions of work and different reference points for salaries.

In East Africa, the structure was explicitly racial. The 1947–48 Salary Commission rejected the notion of racial equality, arguing that even where people from different races approached each other in formal qualifications for a certain post, they differed in "responsibility, judgment, application to duty and output of work." The commission recommended – and this became policy, if not by name – what it called the "Three-Fifths Rule," that a non-European in a senior position should receive three-fifths of the salary paid a European in the same position. In the lower grades, salaries would be set "on an African basis" – that is, in relation to the local economy, although the state was such a big part of the local wage economy that this was a circular argument.

In 1950, Secretary of State Griffiths admitted, "With one exception in Tanganyika, there are no African officers holding higher administrative, professional or technical posts in any of the African territories outside West Africa." Griffiths tried to focus on the issue of qualifications, noting "These East and Central African territories were in an exceedingly primitive state when they first came under British rule some fifty years ago."[54] Racial exclusiveness could no longer be explicitly defended, and the Secretary of State, admitting the Three-Fifths Rule, told Parliament "I dislike the system, and I hope to live to see it abolished. But it does not mean – I must be quite candid – that we can get exact equality of pay between those who are resident in the country and those who have special obligations outside it." In 1954, a new Commission on the Civil Services of the East African Territories and the East Africa High Commission (the Lidbury Commission) threw out the Three-Fifths Rule – making much of the fact that the fixed ratio enshrined a conception of relative wages rooted in race and nothing else – and espoused instead the concept of "inducement." The East African would be comparing a civil service salary with local alternatives; a recruit from the United Kingdom with prevailing salaries in the public and private sectors of the metropole. Hence, the grading and advancement structure of the civil service should become non-racial, but civil service salaries would reflect the dual wage structures of the points of origin of the civil servants. It was a market system, but not quite: it was emphasizing the dual reference points as a principle more than the market as practice.[55]

In the lower grades, meanwhile, Lidbury was caught up in the same debate as that then before the Carpenter Commission (see chapter 8): whether wages should reflect family obligations or the cost of living of the single man. It claimed that lower level workers – in the railway as well as civil service jobs per se – had often separated themselves from rural life and needed to cover the costs of reproduction from the wage, but that others had not. It would not, unlike the Carpenter Commisssion, accept a dual wage structure, separating stabilized and unstabilized Africans. This it regarded as too cumbersome and so found itself setting wage levels that were a compromise between family and "bachelor" levels.[56] In effect, one level of African civil servants (of whom there were very few) were put on a discounted version of European scales, while the pay of the majority was assessed in terms of their ability to reproduce themselves.

As Anthony Clayton and Donald Savage remark, the Lidbury Commission's distaste for explicitly racial classifications and the hope it placed on education indicates an implicit assumption that Kenya was not to remain a "white man's country." The Kenyan government was not so sure. It accepted the non-racial scales, put a great emphasis on keeping the pace of Africanization slow enough so as not to compromise "standards," and offered expatriate pay to anyone recruited from London, even if that person was a white Kenyan. This approach simultaneously ended settler illusions of a civil service that would be white, local, and permanent, and kept up racial differentiation pending Africanization.[57]

Railway workers in East Africa came under the same commissions as civil servants. Their wages jerked upward in 1948 and 1955 when the two Lidbury commissions became alarmed at allowing the wages of such vital employees to be held at levels where they could not reproduce themselves. It was only in 1959 that the railway unions were strong enough to take on management in a major strike, and that one was very major indeed, spreading through Kenya and Uganda, then into Tanganyika. It resulted in yet another commission and another jerk upward in wages and a new impetus to Africanize the more skilled positions in the railway, which had lagged embarrassingly even as politics took its unsteady course toward African involvement in government.[58]

The 1959 strike revealed the extent to which old problems remained unsolved and old fears remained all too real. "A snowballing African strike," minuted the Colonial Office's labour advisor, "can only exacerbate racial feelings in Kenya...[and] create the kind of psychological climate in which the extreme nationalist politicians will gain ground at the expense of moderates." The union indeed charged, "The Railways Administration has always been run and is in practice still run on a racial basis... When an African is in charge of a train, he is known as a Guard, an Asian is an Examiner, and a European for that matter is a Conductor."[59] The strike led to threats of a "general strike throughout the colony" from Mboya, although he brought behind the scenes influence to bear on British officials and was himself subject to their influence to calm things down. There had earlier been talk of a general strike in Kenya, and a messy general strike in Tanganyika two years before.[60]

Race was a very big question in Central Africa as well. Equal pay for equal work was categorically ruled out by a commission in 1947, and the Three-Fifths rule would only apply to rare cases, since virtually no Africans would be qualified for senior posts "for many years."[61] The Northern Rhodesian salary commission of 1952 continued the argument as much in the form of its report as in its contents: two separate volumes, one on African Staff and the other on European Staff. The European volume agonized about the high salaries paid whites in the mining industry and the burdens that put on civil service recruitment. The African volume noted "cases of hardship" among some African government employees and posited as an ultimate goal "that an African Civil Servant should be in a position on, or soon after, confirmation in appointment in his fifth year of service to marry and in due course support a family and maintain a standard of living commensurate with the status of his post in relation to Africans employed in commerce and industry."[62] So while in parts of Africa governments and unions were in a dialogue about the access of Africans to high posts or about equality of pay, in Northern Rhodesia the salary commission thought it a sufficiently ambitious goal to let African bureaucrats marry after five years.

In West Africa, where in 1951 Africans were taking on ministerial responsibilities, this simply would not do. The Gold Coast claimed to have had an Africanization scheme in place in the public service since 1925–26.[63] Yet in 1946, only eighty-nine Africans were in senior positions. Attempts were made to do better after 1944, and in 1948 a Public Service Commission was instructed to give preferential treatment to Africans in competition with expatriate candidates; later instructions were to hire an expatriate only if no "qualified and suitable" Gold Coast candidate was available. In 1953, the Colonial Office admitted Africanization had received "lip service." As the government came under CPP control, efforts at training and recruitment were increased, but officials made clear that promotion would be "by merit alone," to make sure that civil servants of all races would have incentives to perform efficiently. Between 1949 and 1954, the percentage of Africans in the senior service rose from 14 to 38; only in the mid-1960s was Africanization complete.[64]

Civil Service reform and pay revisions were largely done by commissions, and African governments continued this practice. The Gold Coast government did not bring about drastic reform of the structure of the civil service. For a time, the CPP appealed to its potentially biggest (and most aggrieved) constituency, the lowest paid government workers, and permitted significant wage increases. But during the period 1955–66 real wages for African workers increased 10 percent in the private sector and declined in the public sector by 11 percent. What happened to the salary structure under Nkrumah's government, Richard Jeffries argues, was not the development of a "labor aristocracy" of well-organized, skilled workers in public and private sectors, but the singling out of a tiny elite of politicians and top bureaucrats with other workers' incomes stagnating and differentials relatively compressed. Wage increases came especially as a result of union pressure in the early 1950s, and once the CPP consolidated its grip and imposed its institutions on the labor movement, it kept wages in check.[65]

In Nigeria too the politics of Africanization and of wage setting by commission prevailed. A 1954–55 commission insisted that in the civil service, "Structure and remuneration alike should now be measured by the yardstick of Nigerian conditions and requirements, and be designed to attract the best men and women that Nigeria produces."[66] But the slow pace of educating and recruiting Nigerians was outweighed by the growth of the development oriented government itself, and the Colonial Office needed more and more inducements to keep non-Nigerian staff in place as the colonies offered less and less attractive career opportunities.[67] As for Nigerian civil servants, the insistence by British commissions and Nigerian politicians on a Nigerian reference point pushed together the civil service question and the labor question in the private sector. At times, this helped government workers, as political parties competed for an important block of voters. But governments also wanted to bring the patronage apparatus under their direct control, and the dominance of one party in each region lessened the need for such electioneering. The wage-setting commissions became the focus of strike movements – in 1955, 1960, and 1964 – that cut across the public and private sectors, both to get the attention of the government and then to generalize awards throughout the economy. In between, trade unions or civil service associations tended to lack the day-to-day bargaining power to bring about regular wage adjustments. When governments proved unresponsive, this pattern led to compression of wage differentials, common grievances across public and private sectors, pent-up demands for a restoration of real income, and patterns of mobilization and alliance that got around ineffectual or pro-government central organizations of trade unions. The Nigerian general strike of 1964 and the Ghanaian general strike of 1961 followed this script.[68]

There is a certain parallel here with the effects of territorialization in French Africa, the imposing of a sort of closure on the post-war decade when the labor question burst open and when fear of mass strikes and generalized disorder made colonial officials want to promote a better paid, more differentiated, better organized work force. Beginning in the late 1950s, and especially in the 1960s, African governments were trying to check the power of the strongest unions and contain the cycle of demands unleashed upon them. Inflation eroded at least part of the results of earlier efforts to drive wages up. The danger African governments then faced was the same as British officials confronted in the late 1940s, periodic strike movements that would not stay within the boundaries of an industrial dispute.

In comparison with French Africa, British officials had a less wrenching break to make as the imperial center devolved its power to successor states.[69] They did not have to face unions which took the key rhetorical devices of an imperial government – unity, assimilation, equality – and turned them into claims for salaries and rights equivalent to those of the metropole. The difficulty was that many of the problems of public labor in a system that had been built on race remained unsolved. African governments, such as that of Ghana, stepped into the breach, taking over the method of the grand commission studying wages and job structure in the civil service, or in the country generally. The governments used the commissions in their own ways, as had British officials in pursuit of different goals, and they were left with a problem British officials had confronted in the 1940s: keeping the labor question within its boundaries.

Conclusion: the social meaning of decolonization

Why and how Great Britain and France decided to give up their colonies is a complex question. Only recently have historians begun to reexamine the early studies of journalists and political scientists, and a quite different picture is likely to emerge over the next decade. This study makes no attempt to answer the why question, but it does address a part of the how. By focusing on an aspect of what governments did with their power – on how they sought to reshape social organization – it helps to unravel the ways in which colonial regimes reconciled themselves to their conclusion and thought through what they could pass on.

The colonialism that began to come to an end in the 1950s was not the colonialism of the interwar years, which had made a virtue of its own inability to transform African society. Perhaps that form of colonialism could have staggered on for decades longer than the one that ended. What came apart with remarkable rapidity in the decade after World War II was colonialism at its most reformist, its most interventionist, its most arrogantly assertive.

Great Britain just before World War II and France at the war's end began serious soul searching on the subject of empire. Both powers came to see the labor question as a problem which European knowledge and experience could help to bring under control. Through the early 1950s, the project of making the African into industrial man – and more generally of making Africans into modern people – was viewed as one that required precise intervention from the possessors of the relevant knowledge and experience. This section has documented the pulling apart of the process of modernizing society from the issue of direct European control.

As a colonial project, the post-war reforms failed. As an imperial project, their fate was more ambiguous. Officials did, in fact, succeed in part in reframing the labor question, but they could not control the new framework itself. African labor organization proved far more effective in certain ways than expected, even if its record in collective bargaining with different employers was a mixed one. In French Africa, the labor was able to unite on a broad scale in French West Africa-wide protests aimed at government. British African unions, as in the Copperbelt and Gold Coast mine strikes and the Mombasa dock strike, proved capable of mounting big, long, and effective strikes which existing industrial relations machinery could not contain. Even when African union leadership was coopted into such machinery or else (as in the Gold Coast) into an African party structure, it could not hold in the militancy of the rank-and-file. Meanwhile, in East and Central Africa labor issues were constantly being reframed as racial issues, and raising precisely the kind of danger of unbounded anti-colonial agitation which officials so greatly feared.

Such events were not in themselves fatal to colonial rule, but they were part of the failure of development programs to generate predictable and regular progress. Wage labor was a domain that officials thought could be demarcated well enough so that problems within it could be managed, but that domain was neither manageable nor impervious to the economic, cultural, and political influences of the vast parts of rural Africa which officials were unable to transform or even pretend to understand. The encounters with labor – and the inability of officials to separate the labor question from issues of race and politics – contributed to a political process in which fear of militant and demagogic politicians led to actions which empowered the politicians who could now be labelled moderate. Colonial regimes, by the late 1950s, still had the option of resisting nationalist demands, and they did in fact exercise the option of defining the sort of regime they would go to some lengths to combat: the UPC in the Camerouns or the radical nationalists in Kenya, for example. But they were no longer sure what the point would be of a die-hard struggle to maintain empire. They were not in any case able to get the sort of empire they aspired to have.

In the face of the escalating claims being made upon them, French and British governments both disavowed responsibility for raising the colonial standard of living to European levels and moved away from the metropolitan standard as a measure of wages even within comparable categories in the civil service: the legislative debate over the Loi Cadre and the responses to Macmillan's inquiry about the costs and benefits of colonies are explicit on these points. But parallel to the abdication of responsibility was the hope – if not quite the expectation – that ex-colonies would remain in the French or British orbit, or at least in the western world. Here the discourse exemplified by the Inspecteurs du Travail or the labour officers – the insistence that Africans could be brought into the modern workplace and a modern system of industrial relations – was crucial in making plausible the fiction that Africans could, after all, model their administrative structures and their social policies on their colonial tutors. In both their disavowals and their affirmations, the political elites of the two major colonial powers of the postwar era were reflecting the plunge into remaking African society that they had made since the war: metropolitan society could not in the end be the reference point for colonial reform, but it was precisely the claim to universality of metropolitan social norms that made the giving up of colonies imaginable.

There is a tone of bitterness as French officials observed that African labor ministers after the Loi Cadre would now be faced with problems French officials could not solve. One reads a similar bitterness, if not cynicism, in the expectations of the very top British officials on the eve of turning over power that democratic government in Africa would fail. In regard to trade unionism, both powers clearly expected that independent governments would bring about the kind of authoritarianism that neither of them had been able to sustain in the 1950s. Officials' grudging resignation is underscored by their annoyance at the ICFTU's anti-colonialism, accompanied by an acceptance that this sort of organization was the best they could hope for if their ex-colonies were to remain connected to the western alliance.

France and Great Britain had – or so they thought – addressed the fact that wage labor, in Africa as much as in Europe, was a complex social phenomenon. Workers had to be socialized into their new roles and had to be paid enough to encourage stability in the job and to bring up a new generation of workers in a suitable physical and cultural milieu. The proper industrial relations machinery could make the difference between chaotic mass movements and the orderly posing of demands and the negotiating of differences. Governments had to set minimum standards for conditions of labor and regulate dispute settlement. They had pioneered – or so they thought – a path to a modern, orderly future. But that future was not to be theirs.

Conclusion

13   The wages of modernity and the price of sovereignty

Imaginative projects have material consequences. The imagining of an African working class within colonial bureaucracies – and the larger act of imagining that European modernity could be transported to the colonies – affected the conditions of work of a designated segment of the laboring population, and it opened up political possibilities which the African labor movement was to a significant extent able to seize.

The multiple consequences of the experiment thereafter had to be faced by newly independent governments, by politicians, civil servants, and union leaders whose habits and expectations had been affected by the confrontations of the final decade of colonial rule. It is not very fruitful to look for a "legacy" which colonial rule left to future generations, for – important as are the conjunctures when key questions open up to wider debate – the consequences of any historical process are liable to be redirected or seized at any moment along the way.[1] This book has been concerned with the reshaping of a political framework in which a social question is debated, and such a framework was both affected by many specific struggles and itself affected similar struggles. A full analysis of the effects of the reframing of the labor question should take into account the dynamics of post-colonial history and the intricacies of each context in which questions of labor were contested. My goal here is merely to be suggestive, to indicate some ways in which the economic and social conditions of African workers changed in the 1950s and early 1960s and to point to the continued efforts by different groups to frame and reframe the issues of living standards, social rights, citizenship, and sovereignty discussed in these pages.

The African worker unbound

The labor inspectors' dream of a compact, stable, reasonably well paid labor force – set apart from the rest of African society – was of course only one vision in a complex political field. Assessing the impact of government initiatives, or those of the labor movement, is not made

Table 13.1. *Indices of real minimum wages and import purchasing power of wages (1949 = 100)*

Date	Lagos		Accra		Dakar		Abidjan
	Wages	Imports	Wages	Imports	Wages	Imports	Imports
1946					92	106	119
1947		102		80–92	87	105	131
1948		101		98	99	86	79
1949	100	100	100	100	100	100	100
1950	77	102	97	107	103	108	115
1951	82	90	84	90	111	112	120
1952	98	104	113	122	106	113	135
1953	97	119	116	132	112	142	183
1954	101	133	117	136	126	173	213
1955	122	172	112	139	127	175	243
1956	112	159	117	150	140		
1957	111	152	128	161	130		
1958	111	153	136	170	135		
1959	106	141	127	168	148		

Source: Elliot J. Berg, "Real Income Trends in West Africa, 1939–1960" in Melville Herkovits and Mitchell Harwitz (eds.), *Economic Transition in Africa* (London: Routledge, 1964), 220–24.

easier by the inconsistency of categories in which labor departments (as eager for knowledge after 1945 as they were complacent a decade earlier) collected data. The variations in the implementation of labor policies and the strengths of unions and employers are considerable, but the changes and patterns described below begin to suggest some of the effects of the story told above on the material circumstances of African workers.

Elliot Berg has assembled changes in real minimum wages for an unskilled laborer in the central city in select parts of West Africa. His data show movement upward in the 1950s, but not at very impressive rates in the case of Nigeria and Ghana (Table 13.1), rather better in francophone Africa.[2] In British West Africa, despite London's family wage policy, wage revision occurred mostly by ad hoc government commissions, and scholars have debated the effects of union pressure and other factors on minimum wage revision.[3]

In British East Africa, especially Kenya, settler pressure had kept wages low and when government policy finally embraced stabilization in 1954, agriculture was exempted. But urban minimum wages went up more decisively than in British West Africa: economists even refer to the urban wage "explosion" of the 1950s. Taking 1951 as an index base of

100, wages in Nairobi reached 176 in 1956, 304 in 1964; in Kampala 147 in 1956, 343 in 1964. In the public sector, real wages rose 88 percent in Kenya between 1949 and 1959, private non-agricultural wages 73 percent, agricultural wages only 16 percent. One effect of this, predictably enough, was that employment in Kenya, after increasing by a third in the early 1950s, hovered between 490,000 and 560,000 for the next decade, while it essentially stagnated around 225,000 in Uganda.[4] This was itself consistent with government policy – the goal of a compact labor force – and it was only at the end of the colonial period that officials began to think of "unemployment" as a social and economic problem.

Minimum wages in key francophone cities rose somewhat more,[5] reflecting most likely the effective institutional structure of annual wage reviews with union participation. The French West African labor movement organized a quite significant portion of the labor force – 35–40 percent in the mid-1950s. Although Nigeria had a similar percentage of workers in unions, the labor movement was more fragmented. In Uganda, union membership was infinitesimal; in other instances, such as the mines of Northern Rhodesia, unions were large, well organized, and relatively responsive to a militant rank-and-file.[6] In French Africa until 1956, the labor movement and government structure were both more centralized than in British Africa and the effects of collective action cumulated on a regional basis; the government (chapters 7, 11) both feared the labor movement and talked to it.

The minimum wage remains a partial indicator of the extent of change. French policy, the more explicit, sought to attach workers to a career ladder. An official survey from 1958 documents that – as had been the case since the late 1940s – workers received seniority bonuses proportionate to their years of service, peaking at 15 percent of base pay. After 1956, permanent workers – or rather those willing to document their family status and submit to surveillance – received family allowances. In 1958 in the Ivory Coast, for instance, these amounted to 550 francs per month per child. For an industrial worker midway through the hierarchy with two children, that would amount to between 10 and 15 percent of base pay. During his wife's pregnancy and at the time of birth, he would have received as well 18,150 francs (less after three children), equivalent to two to three months pay. Benefits, all told, came to 20-32 percent of wages in French West Africa, or 2.3 percent of the total volume of business. In 1958, commercial and industrial workers at last obtained a decent pension system, a benefit civil servants already had.[7]

The work force had also become more differentiated and skilled, a goal of the Inspection du Travail as well as a consequence of the power of certain unions. In Senegal in 1957, average wages in manufacturing

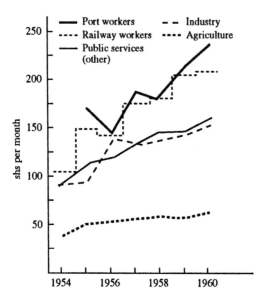

Figure 13.1. Average cash wages paid to adult Africans in Kenya, 1954–1960 (East African Railways and Harbours, Annual Report, 1960: 32. Reprinted from Frederick Cooper, *On the African Waterfront* (New Haven: Yale University Press, 1987), 243.)

industry were 2.2 times what they were in agriculture, in construction 1.9, in commerce 2.3; domestics, however, earned less than agricultural laborers. Each collective bargaining agreement provided six or so hierarchal categories, and the top typically earned four to five times the rate of the bottom.[8] In Senegal in 1957, the labor force broke down as 42 percent unskilled, 30 percent skilled manual workers, 26 percent white collar workers, and 2 percent managerial cadres. But the differentiation among Africans came nowhere close to bridging the gap between Europeans and Africans. In Senegal in 1957, 40 percent of non-Africans from the French Union (the vast majority metropolitan Frenchmen) were in the cadres, and the average metropolitan Frenchman earned 4.2 times the salary of the average black Senegalese.[9]

As usual, systematic data are harder to find for British Africa, but Figure 13.1 illustrates the differentiation in wage rates in Kenya. In the East African railway system, a third of the 39,000 African workers had struggled out of the lowest of the three wage categories into a zone where promotion was possible within a scale ranging from £186 to £1,100 per year, compared to £84 to £156 at the bottom. The shared misery studies of Mombasa had found in 1947 ceased to be shared by the mid-1950s.[10] But as in French Africa, the racial gap remained enormous: half the white workers in Kenya in 1960 earned at least ten times as much as the average Mombasa docker.[11]

In Northern Rhodesia, real wages of underground African miners rose 75 percent between 1949 and 1954, those of surface workers by 82 percent. These rates of increase were over three times those for white miners, but the latter still earned over fifteen times as much in 1954.[12] Africans on the mines increasingly moved into semi-skilled and skilled positions; the percentage of married miners increased from 60 in 1951 to 87 in 1960; labor turnover fell to 9.3 percent in 1962, 6.4 percent in 1969, low by any standards. Studies indicated a large and growing difference between the wages and opportunities in the towns in the Copperbelt or along the rail line from those elsewhere in Northern Rhodesia.[13] In anglophone West African cities, where minimum wage rates did not grow dramatically, studies nonetheless show a highly differentiated wage force, with railway, industrial, and other well positioned workers earning well over minimum wages: a job had become something to struggle for and to keep. With that, managers had acquired a means to introduce tighter labor supervision and to demand steadier labor than in the days of anonymous workers moving into and out of jobs.[14]

At the very end of the colonial era and into the early days of independence, governments and some private sector firms engaged in wholesale Africanization of high level jobs, trying to accomplish in a few years what they had failed to do in decades. The catch was that this was a one-time-only affair and it installed relatively young people into good positions, in skilled labor as well as clerical roles.[15] It probably contributed to the independence euphoria and then the disillusionment that followed.

In the 1960s, independent governments – their ambitions escalating and their means diminished by declining terms of trade – were strongly tempted to let inflation eat away at workers' past gains and to keep, via cooptation, clientism, and coercion, the labor movement from posing a challenge. In Ghana and Nigeria, most notably, governments' allowing grievances over the standard of living to spread throughout much of the urban work force brought back analogous conditions to those which led to the wartime and post-war strike wave: the Ghana general strikes of 1961 and 1966, the Nigerian general strike of 1964, and the Senegalese general strike of 1968 recall the kind of movement that had become rare during the intervening years of stabilization and differentiation.[16]

Organized workers – in the era of decolonization and in some cases into the independence era – did well enough for themselves that some leftist scholars, taking up a page from Frantz Fanon, called them a "labor aristocracy."[17] The argument – as with the more conservative argument about "urban bias" – was misplaced from the start, confusing urban workers with a truly affluent city-based elite of politicians, senior bureaucrats, and others with access to power, and confusing an "interest group" category with the relations of clientage that have in many cases widened the distance between workers and their union leaders from what it was in the 1950s. Yet African workers – as the labor movement's central role in restoring multi-party democratic elections in Zambia and in the general strikes against dictatorial power in Nigeria remind us – can in the 1990s still be the most effective nucleus of opposition to an oppressive regime. For all their failings in firm-level collective bargaining and in institutionalizing the influence of labor on day-to-day policy, urban workers make themselves felt in certain moments – via strikes, general strikes, consumer revolts, and occasionally urban riots – that keep recalling the movements of the 1940s. It is the connections of strategically placed wage workers through wider urban and rural networks, rather than the fact that a working class has been "made" in the sense trade unionists and colonial officials in the 1950s (or scholars in the 1970s) had in mind, that are the key to understanding the uneven but important place of labor in politics.[18]

The central flaw of the labor aristocracy argument as well as the reason behind the volatility of urban politics in Africa today correspond to one of the ways in which the vision of the colonial labor officers was not borne out. Local studies of workers in their milieu have shown that they were never separated – as officials wanted – from rural Africa or from the less stable elements of the city. To be sure, these surveys frequently show a remarkable decrease in labor turnover – although in some cases, notably in the Copperbelt, the trend started even before stabilization became official policy.[19] Urbanization data show that families indeed came to cities: Nairobi's population contained 71 percent adult males in 1948, 49 percent in 1962.[20]

But socially, the pattern did not fit the model: workers retained close connections with their regions of origin, often maintained land and personal connections so that they would be able to return. A study in Senegal revealed the "reconstruction" of family, kinship, and ethnic institutions in which urban jobs became part of adaptive, extended social networks, linking the unevenly stabilized urban population to rural areas; a Nigerian study showed 90 percent of workers sent money, often a substantial portion of their incomes, to parents, brothers, or sisters.[21] These patterns did not imply continuation (if such a pattern had ever been so dominant) of circular migration, but rather varied and complex strategies of individuals and families to combine different sources of income over time.[22] Within cities, there was considerable fluidity between non-wage employment – what became known as the "informal sector" –

and wage employment, as people sold peanuts on the street while trying to find a job, and as skilled workers – the ones firms most wanted to retain – found opportunities in small-scale shops and businesses that enabled them to shorten their wage labor careers.[23] In Kenya, urban wages proved to be a major source of capital for rural development, countering poor credit facilities, inefficient land tenure arrangements, and inefficient labor markets in rural areas and contributing to possibilities for upward mobility.[24] This implies that if one looks not just at individual workers, but at larger groupings of kin, and examines life cycles rather than moments in time, the role of wage earning in social life has turned out to be more complex than intended. In such terms, the "over-privileged" urban worker of some scholarly accounts becomes considerably less privileged, and also becomes less clearly the central figure in the creation in African cities of the "industrial culture" of the modernization theorists.[25]

At the end of the colonial era, wage labor remained a largely masculine affair and was thought about in even more gendered terms. In a survey intended to help plan the family allowance program, French officials in 1954 found that 1 percent of the enumerated wage labor force in both private and public sectors was female. A more precise census of Dakar in 1955 showed that only 7 percent of women had an occupation, around half of those women were in roles like petty commerce, and under 2 percent of the total were classified as "laborers," "skilled workers," or civil servants.[26] In Kenya, women played a major role in agricultural wage labor – 25 percent of the enumerated labor force – but only 4 percent in the public sector and 5 percent in industry and commerce. In Nigeria, women accounted for 4 percent of the workers counted.[27] In general, women workers were concentrated in agriculture and domestic service.[28] But that does not mean that women were quietly living off husbands' family wages or family allowances. Urban studies reveal considerable economic activity – the best known, at least, being that of market women in West Africa – but the categorization of that activity as "informal" made it vulnerable to harassment by bureaucrats and police. Meanwhile, in areas of labor migration women became particularly vulnerable to the fate of men in the job market and the continuity of their relationships, while even the most active market women in West African cities experienced considerable tension with their wage-earning husbands about access to familial resources.[29]

It is not clear that the categories in which the labor question was being posed in the 1950s get to the bottom of wage and welfare issues. Nor is it clear that the categories used today in debates over the appropriateness of urban wages and benefits get very far toward analyzing who has access to what resources, how those resources are shared or distributed, or how social conditions shape the productive process.

The urban labor force that emerged from the social experiments and power struggles of the late colonial era was less bounded than the labor force that either labor inspectors or trade union leaders talked about. How it would contribute to production and to building a new sort of society depended much on the complex patterns and habits that evolved. Mboya, shortly after having joined the government of Kenya, commented that "it is no use paying so many people wages on which they cannot live in order to have many more employed. I think that it is better to pay a few people wages on which they can live and work to maximum production."[30] He was in fact summarizing a lesson colonial officials had only learned a decade before: that predictable, orderly production in urban conditions does not come from the miserable, the malnourished, the sullen, the angry, no matter what – to paraphrase what a British Colonial Secretary (p.333) said in 1954 – the supply price of labor.

Framing the labor question in post-colonial Africa

When the territories of French West Africa became independent states in 1960, they all maintained the basic text and structure of the Code du Travail of 1952. In some cases, like Guinea, the destruction of trade union autonomy rendered meaningless much of the act, although the government's role in setting minimum standards and providing guarantees to workers was maintained. Elsewhere, as in Senegal, the labor code remained formally intact, to be nibbled away by hardball politics with trade union leaders or by the effects of inflation on wages and benefits. In any case, the modernizing conception of the labor question which the code embodied – the idea that the labor question would be the object of regulation and surveillance by a state bureaucratic apparatus, that universal conceptions of work should be imposed on a legally defined category of people – remained viable in radical and conservative, oppressive and pluralistic regimes.[31] That much was true of anglophone Africa too: the ministry of labour, minimum wage boards, surveillance of workplaces, and rudimentary forms of social security for wage workers. Likewise, anglophone and francophone states kept intact some kind of "industrial relations" machinery – sometimes meaningful, sometimes gutted by the repression of trade unions – and that continued the aura of normality which participation in collective bargaining in the late colonial era had imparted to the idea of the particular work organization characteristic of twentieth-century capitalism. All this was reinforced at the international level by African states' participation in the

International Labour Organization, the United Nations, and other such bodies which enmeshed trade unions, employers, and government officials in the kind of discourse that all three parties – with the help of the ILO and the Interafrican Labour Conference – had joined in the 1940s and 1950s.[32]

At first glance, this looks like a telling instance of neo-colonialism, the way in which institutions and institutional cultures built up in the colonial era shaped the possibilities afterward. The problem with this concept is that it provides an answer where a question is needed: what are the external constraints and their articulations with the exercise of domestic political power? I have been arguing that the meanings which "western" notions – including wage labor, citizenship, or modernization – took on in Africa were not attributes of "the West," but products of struggle. Then too, the presence within Africa of a bureaucracy formally constituted like one in Paris or London does not mean that its internal dynamics or the idioms in which its authority is exercised are so derivative. Finally, one must take care (as one must with colonial states themselves) to define the limits within which certain institutions and institutional discourses operate: to a significant extent African states are "gatekeeper states," strong at the point where ex-colonies meet international institutions. State bureaucracies have paraded their modern knowledge and their global connections to their own people while positioning themselves as the representatives of African people before the rest of the world.[33] Developmentalist ideologies are crucial to the gatekeeper state, for they define the terms in which foreign aid is appealed for. The gate faces inward as well and represents a potent source of jobs and patronage. At the same time, local politicians cannot rest on their modernizing claims to authority or on the modern state's patronage apparatus but must mobilize political support and clientage on a variety of fronts, in a variety of cultural idioms. The gatekeeper's alleged modernity does not necessarily constitute a hegemonic ideology much beyond the site of the gatekeeper's toll booth.[34]

For ex-colonial powers (and the United States), the post-war project of development and planned social change defines another sort of power: the power to label.[35] Thus, for example, international agencies and scholars call that portion of the labor market which falls outside the Code du Travail or similar legislative regulation the "urban informal sector." Hawkers, unlicensed beer brewers, self-employed artisans, workers in unregulated sweatshops, prostitutes, and other workers outside state regulation or the formal subsumption of labor to capital fall into this category; it is not incidental that much of what women do in African cities is so classified.

The urban informal sector is not particularly urban – its networks connect city and country. It is not particularly informal – relationships are highly structured. It is not particularly a sector – regulated firms articulate in important and complex ways with unregulated enterprise. That such a category should become salient in public-policy and academic discussion reflects the historical process described in this book: the informal sector is what was left out in the process of defining a bounded working class and integrating that into a process of regulation and surveillance by a state. It is the new term for an old anxiety which colonial policy failed to eliminate and which was once called the "floating population."[36] The dichotomy of informal–formal, like that of market–non-market or modern–backward, arose out of the struggles of a colonial state and labor movements trying to seize control of institutions and of discourse. Such labelling has its consequences: the "irregular" character of those who work without being workers provides an excuse for police harassment and bribe collecting as well as an arena where local entrepreneurs who control urban property or dominate urban networks can exercise unexamined power. The raids against market women in a number of African states are cases in point. Still, one should not take the argument about the power of labelling too far: in much of Africa the informal or "second" economy is more dynamic than the first and impossible for the state to control.[37]

The contradictions of universality

"There are two ways to lose oneself: by a walled segregation in the particular or by a dilution in the 'universal'" – Aimé Césaire.[38]

When colonial states claimed that they would shepherd colonies into the modern world, they were asserting that their own conception of modernity was of universal value. But exposing the parochialism of universality leaves a fundamental issue on the table. A rejectionist stance – condemning everything with a European connection as imperialist – would still allow European categories to define the discourse even if the values attached to each category were reversed.[39] Carried to its logical conclusion, an anti-universalist argument allows no possibility for dialogue about moral issues across cultural borders, even though what those borders are is as much in question as the kinds of social and political practices that can be considered emancipatory.[40]

This study has stressed the dynamics of interchange, even one as power-laden as that of the colonizer and the colonized. The Manichean view of colonialism, as in the arguments of Frantz Fanon, or for that matter Clark Kerr's dichotomy of traditional and industrial, tells us little about the lives people lived in colonies or in places of work, about the ways in which people – from intellectuals to wage workers – came to grips with the power of colonial regimes and capitalism, or of the alliances and coalitions that effectively challenged governments and employers. Fanon's quest for the True Anti-colonialist reduced the complexity with which wage workers engaged colonial states to the stick figure of a labor elite compromised by its colonial referents, while Kerr's dichotomized vision of society took away the space in which political engagement matters most – where different visions of past, present, and future intersect.

When British and French officials tried to frame discussions of social policy in terms of generalizable standards, they were doing so for their own reasons. International conventions which condemned slavery and "analogous" conditions lent an aura of normality to anything that fell outside such bounds, yet under pressure from African workers – organized or unorganized – those limits were pried wider. In the 1940s, France and Great Britain both extended this notion in a fashion somewhat comparable to T. H. Marshall's notion of social citizenship from Europe to their colonies. The ILO became an essential forum for shaping discourse around such standards, and the Conventions of 1944 and 1947 attempted to proclaim that the universal worker, in colony as well as independent country, was entitled to certain basic protections at work, to family life, and to a decent standard of living.[41]

All this appeared as yet another assertion that Europe's peculiar history – and a self-serving reading of it at that – constituted a model for the entire world: a certain definition of a job and of a worker was privileged over other possible conceptions of work. The concept of "employer" and "employee," of capital and trade union, appear as natural, unquestionable, categories in the language of the ILO or the United Nations, of the ICFTU as much as the WFTU. But it was precisely this kind of language that was seized by African trade unionists and turned into something quite specific: demands for equal pay for equal work, for family allowances, for a full role for trade unions in collective bargaining and the setting of public policy. Universal language can be useful, precisely because it provides a reference point outside particular power structures; it is useful, however, in so far as such claims are part of well-grounded political mobilization.

As Nancy Fraser and Linda Gordon argue, the idea of the rights of "man" being steadily extended into new realms ignores the fact that each new right of citizenship carries certain presumptions about who is exercising it, that citizenship discourse excludes as it includes. Their concern is with the gendering of social rights, with the fact that welfare states as they spelled out the form of social protection citizens were to receive in effect treated men as family providers – at risk from unemployment, industrial accidents, etc. – and women as the provided for, at risk of single motherhood.[42] In colonial Africa, the social rights that were extended in the 1950s were gendered as well: family allowances and family wages both presumed a division between production and reproduction, and the union movement of the 1950s was more clearly male-dominated than the general strikes of the 1940s. The social rights of the ILO and labor inspectors also excluded vast realms of society by distinguishing the working class from "customary labor," a category that could be left unexamined. Even in the heart of the stabilization program – the workers' family – there was a basic ambiguity: the African woman was being trumpeted as the key to nourishing and socializing the working class of the future, yet she was not quite to be trusted, so that schoolteachers and nurses were to intervene directly in the realm of the family.

In the end, Great Britain and France were trapped by the logical and political consequences of their universalism. The claims for equal pay and equal benefits that were being made against them came in the form of principles on which they themselves staked their legitimacy and on a conception of the worker which they themselves hoped would prove valid. At the same time, the appeals colonial governments were making to universal ideals clouded the particularist claim of one people to rule another, a claim which was making less sense in international dialogue even as it was being attacked directly by nationalist movements. By the mid-1950s, French and British officials were backing away both from the insistence that only they could manage economic and social development and from the implications of their own universalism. They found in the nationalist assertion of an African reference point for political identity an answer to the demands which presumed a European reference point for social equality.

African labor movements were also caught in an ideological trap, in this case by the logic of nationalism. It became more difficult for them to assert that the metropolitan standard for wages and benefits should apply to all workers, or indeed to frame their political position around the notion that workers – and other groups – existed both within the nation and across the globe and that the condition of "the worker" posed problems that required specific attention, both within and among nations. The tension between workers' claims to globally defined entitlements and Africans' assertions of political rights *as Africans* was, during the 1940s and early 1950s, a creative and empowering one. But when "nation-building" became a state project and national identity was held to subsume all other forms of affiliation, that tension was pushed from the arena of politics. Its loss was part of the tragedy of Africa's mode of decolonization.

The notion of sovereignty itself has its traps, and global acceptance of self-determination as the ultimate value in international politics has often occluded discussion of the content of that sovereignty. In the 1960s and 1970s, the denial of meaningful citizenship to black South Africans was a world-wide concern, just as slavery had been a century before, but the destruction of labor movements in Guinea was not. The poverty of an urban South African posed a political question, while the poverty of a Malian posed a question for experts in famine relief.[43] Yet the silences and exclusions of concepts like sovereignty and citizenship do not necessarily remain that way; political movements seeking to push a shared set of principles in new directions can, and have, used them as points of departure.

Discourse about citizenship is particularly difficult to contain, for appeals from those who are excluded in one situation reaffirm the value which the included attach to citizenship.[44] Indeed, this book has repeatedly focused on discourses of state control that would not stay put: the French government could no more prevent their formalistic notion of citizenship generalized throughout their empire in 1946 from opening questions of material equality than the British government could invoke the concept of development to deflect workers' attention from their specific concerns.

Similarly, the development concept – once intended to solidify the colonial empires ideologically and economically – was deflected by nationalist movements into assertions that true development required self-government and then into assertions that membership in a community of nations implied a kind of universal citizenship, which conveyed social and economic as well as political rights upon all human beings. These arguments linked a rights argument, which implies universal standards, with a citizenship argument, which implies political involvement by those claiming rights. Most recently, Nelson Mandela spoke before the UN of interests in democracy and prosperity that cross national borders, and he asserted that greater knowledge of conditions across the globe was a "force impelling the deprived to demand a better life from the powers that be."[45]

France and Great Britain had, for their own reasons, accepted in the 1940s, through the "international standards" framework of the ILO and the universal human rights framework of the UN that there was a minimum standard of living below which no-one should fall and which better-off societies should help to insure. Even as they abandoned sovereign responsibility for their own colonies and asserted that each territory had to take in charge its own social services, they accepted – in a diluted and non-binding way – that development should become a global process, now shared with the United States, the Soviet Union, the Scandinavian countries, Japan, Germany, and others. The development initiative assumed a kind of universal social citizenship.[46] The ILO – true to its past role in articulating international standards – addressed this issue in a particularly vivid way in the 1970s, through its "Basic Needs" program, a vision of development oriented around a set of minimal provisions – adequate nutrition, sanitation, health care, educational opportunities, etc. – put forth as human rights.[47]

The development framework is in many ways highly problematic, but it has provided a basis on which the people of impoverished, ex-colonial countries could make claims; it opened the possibility that alternative formulations could get themselves heard on a global scale, as indeed happened, within limits, with Latin American structuralist economics, dependency theory, the basic needs approach, and sustainable development.[48]

Both the orthodox and the dissident versions of development imply that economic progress cannot be reduced to allowing markets to function. The very idea of basic human needs that should be met irrespective of output within a given unit has been under strong attack from free marketeers, and since the 1980s these critiques have had a strong effect on policy (more so than leftist or anti-modernist critiques of development). The purists insist that the free market is the only true guide to determining wages within each country, just as the world market is the best means of allocating resources among nations. African states are being told that they have erred in trying to hold wages, benefits, and social services to a standard other than that of the local market.[49] The IMF has used both its financial and its discursive power to persuade many African governments to cut social services, food subsidies, and real wages, to remove the protections in labor codes against arbitrary dismissal in the name of allowing investors flexibility. In short the IMF in the 1980s and 1990s has been trying to undo what the ILO encouraged in the 1950s. Some academics give powerful support to such arguments, and – rather like the French right in its last struggle against the Code du Travail – invoke a kind of populist rhetoric, insisting that the "privileges" of wage workers come out of the incomes of peasants.[50] These arguments may have merit, or they may not: the fact that African economies grew during the 1950s and 1960s, when wage workers were doing relatively well, and declined in the 1980s as real urban wages plummeted does not lend credence to blaming "urban bias" for Africa's economic woes.[51] It may be true that following the IMF's advice could take money out of wasteful bureaucracies and make it available for job-creating investments, but IMF prescriptions may also weaken the social resources that make efficient, stable, orderly production possible. Be that as it may, the argument remains important as moral discourse.[52] The correct wage, the correct price, the correct national income that a country with given resources can attain is determined by the market. That the Ugandan peasant ends up poor and the Swiss farmer rich is an unfortunate fact, but not an injustice.

What goes unquestioned in this argument is that the individual state is the unit in which the correct wage or the correct price should be determined. In this way, the purists of the market are following through the "territorialization" argument made, in their own ways, by French and British colonial officials in the mid-1950s, only to soften its impact through the development initiative. These officials were trying to break away from making the relevant unit be the empire, and the concept that all workers – and perhaps all citizens or subjects – from Wales to Kiambu, from the Touraine to the Niger Bend, were part of the same polity and had claim on the same basis to imperial resources. The development idea, to a more qualified extent, posited the same on a global level. That is the way of thinking which the purists of the market are trying to dismiss from international discourse.

French and British officials in the 1940s and 1950s – followed by the Mboyas of independent Africa – believed that the market price of labor was not its only relevant characteristic: work, as they saw it, was a social process, and the peaceful and successful carrying out of labor required a certain support system. Family life, schools, health services, and a framework for conciliating and containing disputes could determine the difference between a system capable of peaceful expansion and one doomed to stagnant anger. Productivity would only rise if companies and governments took a long-range view of labor, raising the value of "human capital" and giving workers and employees enough confidence in their continued relationship with each other to foster investment, training, and cooperation. The labor inspectors' formula was an ethnocentric vision of the possible and the necessary, put forth as a universal sociology of work. Now, the bounded universalism of industrial sociology is being displaced by a market universalism that is both narrow in what it measures and sweeping in its influence on policy.[53]

But the implications of free market morality cannot be neatly kept abroad. As low-wage producers, particularly in Asia, become successful, the reverse of what happened in the 1940s and 1950s begins to happen now: the standards of wages and benefits of ex-colonies and other countries once labelled backward become a reference against which the workers of ex-metropolitan powers and the United States need to measure themselves.[54] A great deal is at stake, throughout the world, in the terms in which such questions are framed.

Africans have been belittled and disempowered time and time again in the name of some universal notion of civilization or economic development which they did not meet and which knowledge-bearing outsiders could claim to bring to them. The ability of the wealthy and the powerful to shape discourse is not about to disappear, but it can be engaged. In the 1940s, Africans in colonial cities and workplaces forced colonial regimes to confront the uncertainties of their power and their claims to legitimacy. The colonial regimes' desire for a more stable basis of rule and an opportunity to use their rule more productively gave African labor movements an opening, which they seized with at least some success. Colonial governments in turn found that their claim to manage the social affairs of Africans on the basis of European knowledge led to painful problems without stabilizing either the economic or the ideological roots of colonial authority. Colonial officials' insistence that European knowledge could be used to manage social change in Africa gave way in not too long a time to an insistence that Africans would ride to their destiny along a path pointed out by colonizers, whether Europeans remained to guide them or not. They bequeathed to their successors the task of leading the transformation of a continent they themselves could not control, and allocated to themselves the more possible task of sitting in judgment over Africans striving to make their way in a changing world.

Notes

1 Introduction

1 An early and powerful expression of this point of view is Ayi Kwei Armah, *The Beautyful Ones Are Not Yet Born* (Boston: Houghton Mifflin, 1968).

2 For comparison see, among a rapidly growing literature, Sonya Rose, *Limited Livelihoods: Gender and Class in Nineteenth Century England* (Berkeley: University of California Press, 1991), and Ava Baron (ed.), *Work Engendered: Toward a New History of American Labor* (Ithaca: Cornell University Press, 1991).

3 Chinua Achebe has suggested that "the word *universal* [be] banned altogether from discussions of African literature until such time as people cease to use it as a synonym for the narrow, self-serving parochialism of Europe." Quoted in Christopher L. Miller, *Theories of Africans: Francophone Literature and Anthropology in Africa* (Chicago: University of Chicago Press, 1990), 2.

4 For a review of labor history, see Bill Freund, *The African Worker* (Cambridge: Cambridge University Press, 1988).

5 Examples include Achille Mbembe, "Domaines de la nuit et autorité onirique dans les maquis du Sud-Cameroun (1955–1958)," *Journal of African History* 32 (1991): 89–122; Luise White, "Cars out of Place: Vampires, Technology, and Labor in East and Central Africa," *Representations* 43 (1993): 27–50; Luise White, "Separating the Men from the Boys: Constructions of Gender, Sexuality and Terrorism in Central Kenya, 1939–1959," *International Journal of African Historical Studies* 23 (1990): 1–25. An exemplary European study of a belief structure of workers is William Sewell, Jr., *Work and Revolution in France: The Language of Labor from the Old Regime to 1848* (Cambridge: Cambridge University Press, 1980).

6 A good start for examining the post-colonial African state is Jean-François Bayart, *The State in Africa: The Politics of the Belly* (London: Longman, 1993, trans. from French version, 1989).

7 Two excellent studies of how self-consciously modernizing regimes constitute the objects of their interventions and conceive of their own actions are James Ferguson, *The Anti-Politics Machine: "Development," Depoliticization, and Bureaucratic Power in Lesotho* (Cambridge: Cambridge University Press, 1990), and Gwendolyn Wright, *The Politics of Design in French Colonial Urbanism* (Chicago: University of Chicago Press, 1991).

8 The two-way comparison obviously does not exhaust the possibilities. I will also discuss ways in which the two powers influenced each other and in which both interacted with international agencies. In my archival research, I also searched for evidence that Great Britain and France looked toward other

colonial powers for models or shared problems. While early on Belgium was seen as a pioneer of "stabilizing" labor around its mining centers in Katanga, once the other powers began to think of stabilization, metropolitan systems of industrial relations, rather than other colonial powers, became the basic points of reference. Belgium's version of stabilization was seen to demand more administrative control than France or Great Britain wished to undertake and provide less of a chance for taming workers' discontent.

9 The pragmatism with which all this was done is emphasized in Deborah Posel, *The Making of Apartheid, 1948–1961: Conflict and Compromise* (Oxford: Clarendon Press, 1991).

10 This theme characterized much writing by political scientists influenced by modernization theory in the 1950s and 1960s; for a pioneering example, see James S. Coleman, *Nigeria: Background to Nationalism* (Berkeley: University of California Press, 1958). A more radical version from a scholar with strong personal ties to the post-war generation of African political intellectuals is Thomas Hodgkin, *Nationalism in Colonial Africa* (New York: New York University Press, 1957). The triumphalist version emerges most strongly in autobiographies and other publications by leading participants, including Kwame Nkrumah, Nnamdi Azikiwe, Jomo Kenyatta, and Sékou Touré.

11 Frantz Fanon, *The Wretched of the Earth*, trans. by Constance Farrington (New York: Grove, 1966; orig. published 1961).

12 Ibid., 30; Frantz Fanon, *Black Skin, White Masks*, trans. by Charles Lam Markmann (New York: Grove, 1967; orig. published 1952), 226–29. For a fuller discussion of some of the issues raised here and in the following paragraphs see Frederick Cooper, "Conflict and Connection: Rethinking Colonial African History," *American Historical Review* 99 (1994): 1516–45.

13 One of the first American political scientists to point to the implications of ideological systems which combined a singular history of nationalist triumph with a singular notion of the future – the drive for development – was Aristide Zolberg, *Creating Political Order: The Party States of West Africa* (Chicago: Rand McNally, 1966).

14 Partha Chatterjee argues that the nationalist enterprise is fundamentally contradictory: by focusing on the nation-state – and its apparatus – nationalists fall into a political discourse shaped by the imperialists. *Nationalist Thought and the Colonial World: A Derivative Discourse?* (London: Zed, 1986). African philosophers and critics have begun to debate these issues in a complex and stimulating way. For an introduction, see Miller, *Theories of Africans*, chapter 2.

15 The above argument appears in Ronald Robinson, "Andrew Cohen and the Transfer of Power in Tropical Africa, 1940–1951," in W. H. Morris-Jones and Georges Fischer (eds.), *Decolonization and After: The British and French Experiences* (London: Cass, 1980), 50–72, and R. D. Pearce, *The Turning Point in Africa: British Colonial Policy, 1938–1948* (London: Cass, 1982). For a cogent critique, see John Darwin, "British Decolonization since 1945: A Pattern or a Puzzle?" *Journal of Imperial and Commonwealth Studies* 12 (1984): 187–209.

16 Jacques Marseille, *Empire colonial et capitalisme français: Histoire d'un divorce* (Paris: Albin Michel, 1984).

17 Sherry Ortner, "Resistance and the Problem of Ethnographic Refusal." *Comparative Studies in Society and History* 37 (1995): 173–93. For a thoughtful argument about the creative and politically powerful possibilities – for critical intellectuals from colonies and metropoles – of moving between colonized and colonizing cultures and mobilizing interconnected lines of thought against colonial rule, see Edward W. Said, *Culture and Imperialism* (New York: Knopf, 1993).

18 Ann Laura Stoler and Frederick Cooper, "Between Colony and Metropole: Rethinking a Research Agenda," in Frederick Cooper and Ann Laura Stoler (eds.), *Tensions of Empire: Colonial Cultures in a Bourgeois World* (Berkeley: University of California Press, forthcoming); Nicholas Dirks (ed.), *Colonialism and Culture* (Ann Arbor: University of Michigan Press, 1992).

19 Jean and John Comaroff, *Of Revelation and Revolution: Christianity, Colonialism, and Consciousness in South Africa.* Vol. I (Chicago: University of Chicago Press, 1991).

20 Ranajit Guha, "On Some Aspects of the Historiography of Colonial India," in Ranajit Guha and Gayatri Chakravorty Spivak (eds.), *Selected Subaltern Studies* (New York: Oxford University Press, 1988), 39, 40. Emphasis in original.

21 For a critique of *Subaltern Studies*, see Rosalind O'Hanlon, "Recovering the Subject: *Subaltern Studies* and Histories of Resistance in Colonial South Asia," *Modern Asian Studies* 22 (1988): 189–224. For related issues, see Gyan Prakash, "Writing Post-Orientalist Histories of the Third World: Indian Historiography is Good to Think," in Dirks, *Colonialism and Culture*, 353–88, Dipesh Chakrabarty, "Postcoloniality and the Artifice of History: Who Speaks for 'Indian' Pasts?" *Representations* 37 (1992): 1–26, and Cooper, "Conflict and Connection."

22 Ranajit Guha, "Dominance Without Hegemony and its Historiography" in Ranajit Guha (ed.), *Subaltern Studies VI: Writings on South Asian History and Society* (Delhi: Oxford University Press, 1989), 210–309.

23 James Scott, *Domination and the Arts of Resistance: Hidden Transcripts* (New Haven: Yale University Press, 1990).

24 On the sequence of ambitious projects giving way to preservationism, see Anne Phillips, *The Enigma of Colonialism: British Policy in West Africa* (London: James Currey, 1989), and Frederick Cooper, *From Slaves to Squatters: Plantation Labor and Agriculture in Zanzibar and Coastal Kenya, 1890–1925* (New Haven: Yale University Press, 1980).

25 For a valuable discussion of a French hegemonic project of defining the particularities of each of its colonies, set against the universal values of French civilization, see Herman Lebovics, *True France: The Wars over Cultural Identity, 1900–1945* (Ithaca: Cornell University Press, 1992), chapters 2 and 3. Lebovics also notes that it was precisely in these terms that French-educated colonial subjects challenged the regime, claiming that it was they who could speak in universal language for the rights of particular peoples.

26 Ann Laura Stoler, "Making Empire Respectable: The Politics of Race and Sexual Morality in 20th-Century Colonial Cultures," *American Ethnologist* 16 (1989): 634–60; Ann Laura Stoler, "Rethinking Colonial Categories: European Communities and the Boundaries of Rule," *Comparative Studies in Society and History* 13 (1989): 134–61.

27 Discipline and indiscipline are discussed in a stimulating way in Achille Mbembe, *La naissance du maquis dans le Sud-Cameroun: Histoires d'indiscipline (1920–1960)* (Paris: Karthala, 1993).

28 John Lonsdale and Bruce Berman, "Coping with the Contradictions: The Development of the Colonial State in Kenya," *Journal of African History* 20 (1979): 487–506.

29 William H. Sewell, Jr., "Toward a Post-materialist Rhetoric for Labor History," in Lenard R. Berlanstein (ed.), *Rethinking Labor History: Essays on Discourse and Class Analysis* (Urbana: University of Illinois Press, 1993), 15–38, 18 quoted. Sewell does not address the serious epistemological problems involved in reconciling his three imperialisms.

30 The current fashion of identifying positions as post-modernist, post-Marxist, or post-structuralist is another instance of theoretical hubris, a claim to have imbibed all the wisdom of a theoretical tradition and to have moved beyond. The "posts" do not always recognize how much of what they argue has been a part of debates within the school they claim to transcend: "modernist" artists and social scientists have been as eager to destabilize categories as find universal themes.

31 Frederick Cooper, "Urban Space, Industrial Time, and Wage Labor in Africa," in Cooper, (ed.), *Struggle for the City: Migrant Labor, Capital, and the State in Urban Africa* (Beverly Hills: Sage, 1983): 15–18, and the essays in Frederick Cooper et al., *Confronting Historical Paradigms: Peasants, Labor, and the Capitalist World System in Africa and Latin America* (Madison: University of Wisconsin Press, 1993).

32 Dipesh Chakrabarty, *Rethinking Working-Class History: Bengal 1890–1940* (Princeton: Princeton University Press, 1989), xii, 112–13, 166–74, explains the colonial elements of bosses' authority in the jute mills, as well as the way in which Indian notions of authority and personal relations shaped the relationship of managers and workers. He argues that these patterns of authority engendered particular patterns of defiance and struggle (185–99).

33 A conventional Marxist definition of class as a group of people with a particular relation to the production process is reasonable enough. The problem is that terms like "proletariat" or "bourgeoisie" are insufficiently precise class markers to stand for the complex and contingent processes that shaped group boundaries.

34 Gay Seidman argues that in situations where capitalism was particularly "savage," where working classes were concentrated in residential areas surrounding cities, where an authoritarian government affected workers' daily lives and ability to contest workplace issues, and where a relatively skilled industrial labor force was well enough positioned to make capital unsure that coercion would be a sufficient mechanism of control, a particular kind of trade unionism emerged – social movement unionism. Such unions raised fundamental questions about state power and the provision of resources to communities as much as workplace issues. The cases discussed here do not so clearly fall into situations of savage capitalism and industrialism, but they nonetheless reveal a fundamental tension between unions' focus on workplace issues and their cooperation with other sorts of movements in addressing state power. This tension will be a central theme of chapter 11. See Seidman's

Manufacturing Militance: Workers' Movements in Brazil and South Africa, 1970–1985 (Berkeley: University of California Press, 1994).

35 Michel Foucault, *Discipline and Punish: The Birth of the Prison*, trans. by Alan Sheridan (New York: Vintage, 1979); Michel Foucault, *The History of Sexuality*, I: *An Introduction*, trans. by Robert Hurley (New York: Pantheon, 1978). For a stimulating analysis of the exclusions written into the making of bourgeois ideology, see Ann Laura Stoler, *Race and the Education of Desire: A Colonial Reading of Foucault's 'History of Sexuality'* (Durham, NC: Duke University Press, 1995). Other schools of scholarship raise boundary questions, especially the ways in which political and social organizations frame debates and issues. See Erving Goffman, *Frame Analysis: An Essay on the Organization of Human Experience* (Cambridge, Mass.: Harvard University Press, 1974) for a classic study, and Aldon Morris and Carol McClurg Mueller, *Frontiers in Social Movement Theory* (New Haven: Yale University Press, 1992) for a collection of recent ones.

36 Megan Vaughan, *Curing their Ills: Colonial Power and African Illness* (Cambridge: Polity Press, 1991), 10–11. While I think Vaughan is right that early colonial regimes' disciplinary efforts focused on collectivities rather than individuals, she relies overly strongly on a notion of "coercion" as characterizing colonialism and misses the importance of social collectivities in Foucault's analysis of Europe.

37 The timing of shifts in disciplinary regime varied. In British India, work became an object of central government knowledge collection in the 1920s, more than a decade before African governments seriously took to surveillance of labor. Even so, some parts of the Indian governmental structure did not want to ask too many questions and to let the companies maintain a work regime more attuned to modes of subordination rooted in village hierarchies and religious authority. Chakrabarty, *Working-Class History*, 70–73. For a Foucauldian analysis of another knowledge/power regime, see Adam Ashforth, *The Politics of Official Discourse in Twentieth Century South Africa* (Oxford: Clarendon Press, 1990).

38 See for example Alan Fox, *History and Heritage: The Social Origins of the British Industrial Relations System* (London: George Allen & Unwin, 1985); Susan Pedersen, *Family, Dependence and the Origins of the Welfare State: Britain and France, 1914–1945* (Cambridge: Cambridge University Press, 1993); and Peter Baldwin, *The Politics of Social Solidarity: Class Bases of the European Welfare State 1875–1975* (Cambridge: Cambridge University Press, 1990).

39 Michael Mann, *The Sources of Social Power* (Cambridge: Cambridge University Press, 1986), 1: 2, 13.

40 On the difficulties which these issues pose, see V. Y. Mudimbe, *The Invention of Africa: Gnosis, Philosophy, and the Order of Knowledge* (Bloomington: Indiana University Press, 1988), and Kwame Anthony Appiah, *In My Father's House: Africa in the Philosophy of Culture* (New York: Oxford University Press, 1992).

41 Mudimbe, *Invention of Africa*, Miller, *Theories of Africans*. See also Chatterjee, *Nationalist Thought and the Colonial World*, and Said, *Culture and Imperialism*.

42 The interweaving of narratives in this book emphasizes how the contingent resolution of particular conflicts restructures the possibilities and limitations of agency at the next moment. Like all writing strategies, narrative entails losses as well as gains. It poses a danger of losing track of causality as an author directs all actors into a linear script that implies casual linkages without analyzing them. These problems can be addressed in the text by discussion of how categories are constituted and linkages made, but author and reader need to keep in mind the seemingly obvious point that any study is only a partial attempt to cover the issues it raises and its methodologies are intended to complement, not to displace, others. An illuminating intervention in the methodological literature is Larry Griffin, "Narrative, Event Structure Analysis, and Causal Interpretation in Historical Sociology," *American Journal of Sociology* 98 (1993): 1094–133.

43 The title of this section is an obvious play on the typical title of a book in African labor history, Paul Lubeck, *Islam and Urban Labor in Northern Nigeria: The Making of a Muslim Working Class* (Cambridge: Cambridge University Press, 1986), and John Higginson, *A Working Class in the Making: Belgian Colonial Labor Policy, Private Enterprise, and the African Mineworker, 1907–1951* (Madison: University of Wisconsin Press, 1989). All these titles refer to E. P. Thompson, *The Making of the English Working Class* (New York: Vintage, 1963). All are works of considerable merit and at least complicate the linear proletarianization thesis which their titles imply.

Part I Introduction

1 Charles Maier, "Between Taylorism and Technocracy: European Ideologies and the Vision of Industrial Productivity in the 1920s," *Journal of Contemporary History* 5 (1970): 27–61.

2 The labor question unposed

1 These connections are discussed in Frederick Cooper, *From Slaves to Squatters: Plantation Labor and Agriculture in Zanzibar and Coastal Kenya, 1890–1925* (New Haven: Yale University Press, 1980), chapter 2, and more generally in David Brion Davis, *Slavery and Human Progress* (New York: Oxford University Press, 1984), 279–84, 298–306.

2 Suzanne Miers, *Britain and the Ending of the Slave Trade* (London: Longman, 1975).

3 See the studies collected in Suzanne Miers and Richard Roberts (eds.), *The End of Slavery in Africa* (Madison: University of Wisconsin Press, 1988) and Paul E. Lovejoy and Jan S. Hogendorn, *Slow Death for Slavery: The Course of Abolition in Northern Nigeria, 1897–1936* (Cambridge: Cambridge University Press, 1993).

4 Cooper, *From Slaves to Squatters*; Anne Phillips, *The Enigma of Colonialism: British Policy in West Africa* (London: James Currey, 1989); Richard Roberts, "The End of Slavery in the French Soudan, 1905–1914," in Miers and Roberts, *End of Slavery*, 282–307.

5 Ruth Slade, *King Leopold's Congo* (New York: Oxford University Press, 1962); Robert Harms, "The End of Red Rubber: A Reassessment," *Journal of African History* 16 (1975): 73–88.

6 Joseph Folliet, *Le travail forcé aux colonies* (Paris: Editions du Cerf, 1934), 104.

7 On segregationism as a "modernizing ideology," see Paul Rich, *Race and Empire in British Politics* (Cambridge: Cambridge University Press, 1986), 56, and John Cell, *The Highest Stage of White Supremacy: The Origins of Segregation in South Africa and the American South* (Cambridge: Cambridge University Press, 1982).

8 John H. Harris, *Africa: Slave or Free?* (London: Student Christian Movement, 1919); André Gide, *Travels in the Congo*, trans. by Dorothy Bussy (New York: Knopf, 1929); and Folliet, *Le travail forcé*.

9 Vagrancy regulations were among the less subtle means used by states to push people into wage labor, and the more perceptive critics of forced labor attacked them strongly (e.g. Folliet, *Le travail forcé*, 139, 227). Taxation also could serve such a purpose, although it pressured people into entering the money economy rather than into wage labor per se.

10 See for example the "Bishop's Memorandum" – cautiously critical of the Kenya Government's labor policy – in *Parliamentary Papers*, 1920, XXXIII, 81, 8–10. Others – Norman Leys most strikingly – went further, although largely within the language of anti-slavery ideology.

11 Albert Sarraut, *La mise en valeur des colonies françaises* (Paris: Payot, 1923); Stephen Constantine, *The Making of British Colonial Development Policy 1914–1940* (London: Cass, 1984); Jacques Marseille, *Empire colonial et capitalisme français: Histoire d'un divorce* (Paris: Albin Michel, 1984). Milner resigned the Cabinet in 1921 over his colleagues' refusal to support his colonial designs. Sarraut (see below) bent with the wind.

12 Terence Ranger, "The Invention of Tradition in Colonial Africa," in Eric Hobsbawm and Terence Ranger (eds.), *The Invention of Tradition* (Cambridge: Cambridge University Press, 1983), 211–62; Herman Lebovics, *True France: The Wars over Cultural Identity, 1900–1945* (Ithaca, Cornell University Press, 1992), chapter 3; Raoul Girardet, *L'idée coloniale en France de 1871 à 1962* (Paris: Table Ronde, 1972); Alice L. Conklin, "A Mission to Civilize: Ideology and Imperialism in French West Africa, 1895–1930," Ph.D. dissertation, Princeton University, 1989.

13 League of Nations, Slavery Convention, September 25, 1926, reprinted in Leslie Raymond Buell, *The Native Problem in Africa* (London: Macmillan, 1928) 2: 954–57. For an account of the work leading up to this convention by an ILO insider see Jean Goudal, *Esclavage et travail forcé* (Paris: Pedone, 1929).

14 Folliet, *Le travail forcé*, 153–62. The French government tried in vain to stop the Conference from banning the use of conscripted labor for nonmilitary purposes and compulsory cultivation for educational purposes. It opposed, unsuccessfully, restricting the length of service of forced laborers and setting a definite period (five years) for a transition to voluntary labor in public projects. Direction des Affaires Politiques, "Revue trimestrielle de politique coloniale étrangère," deuxième trimestre 1930, 17G 245; Ministère des Colonies, Note Verbale, 14 May 1929, K 64 (19), AS.

15 Members of the Colonial Ministry's advisory board, the Conseil Supérieure des Colonies, strongly criticized the ILO proposals but insisted they were not

"partisans of forced labor." Procès Verbal of meeting of 20 June 1930, 17G 250, AS.

16 International Labour Organization, *Conventions and Recommendations 1919–1981* (Geneva: ILO, 1982), Convention No. 29 of 1930, 29–36.

17 René Mercier, *Le travail forcé aux colonies* (Paris: Imprimerie nouvelle, 1933), 198–203, 207, 217–18. Mercier also argued that French colonies had a less enlightened population than those of Great Britain, and that the British policy of indirect rule allowed indigenous chiefs to do the dirty work while the government claimed it used no coercion. He did not know that although Great Britain had promptly ratified the convention, its Colonial Office quietly decided in late 1932 to stop insisting that individual colonial governments – which were responsible for local regulations – take action to enforce ILO conventions. Mercier, 198–203, 207, 217–18, and P. S. Gupta, *Imperialism and the British Labour Movement, 1914–64* (New York: Holmes & Meier, 1975), 248–49.

18 See also Jules Ninine, "La main-d'oeuvre indigène dans les colonies africaines," Doctoral thesis, Faculté de Droit, Université de Paris, 1932 (Paris: Jouve, 1932), 11, 127, 234. Ninine argued that forced labor – to be used provisionally and for public purpose only – was necessary "to modify the primitive mentality of the native" and to overcome his tendency to be "apathetic, incapable of any regular or sustained effort or labor."

19 For the anti-forced labor case at its most thoughtful, see Folliet, *Le travail forcé*. He argued that forced labor undermined the long-term positive effects of colonization, spreading disease, hurting agriculture, making a mockery of economic incentives and of education.

20 James Duffy, *A Question of Slavery* (Cambridge, Mass.: Harvard University Press, 1967); Ibrahim Sundiata, *Black Scandal: America and the Liberian Labor Crisis, 1929–1936* (Philadelphia: Institute for the Study of Human Issues, 1980).

21 Governor-General Carde, circular to Governors, 11 October 1929, K 95 (26), AS.

22 The few writers willing to defend aspects of forced labor in public lamented the "equivocal and clandestine" manner in which it operated, for this prevented "a rational, methodical and humane organization of obligatory labor." *Europe Nouvelle*, 20 June 1930, quoted approvingly in Ninine, "Main-d'oeuvre indigène," 165.

23 Governor-General de Coppet to Minister, 25 January 1937, K 8 (1), AS.

24 Directeur des Affaires Politiques (Tousset) to Inspecteur Général des Travaux Publics, 12 October 1928, K 95 (26), AS, in reference to the governor-general's request for a note on the effects of mechanization on public works labor.

25 Hélène d'Almeida-Topor, "Recherches sur l'évolution du travail salarié en AOF pendant la crise économique 1930–1936," *Cahiers d'Etudes Africaines*, 61–62 (1976): 103–17; Monique Lakroum, *Le travail inégal: Paysans et salariés sénégalais face à la crise des années trente* (Paris: Harmattan, 1982), 33–34.

26 Sarraut, *La mise en valeur*, 74–76, 94, 339–40, 343. Sarraut was a developmentalist, not an assimilationist: he favored educating an elite, not the mass, in the French manner (94, 96, 101).

27 Eugène-Léonard Guernier, *L'Afrique: Champ d'expansion de l'Europe* (Paris: Colin, 1933), 3–4, 211–12. All he had to say about labor was to call it "indispensible" and praise Madagascar's forced labor corps for giving workers good treatment and good wages until they had evolved sufficiently to work on their own.

28 "Rapport de M. Giscard d'Estaing," 18 April 1932, AP 539/1, ANSOM.

29 Sarraut to Governor-General, French West Africa, 22 August 1932, 17G 364, AS. While Giscard equated useful Africa with coastal regions, Sarraut thought certain parts of the interior were useful as well.

30 "Note; Economie Générale de l'A.O.F.," prepared by Services Economiques, enclosed in Sarraut to Governor-General, French West Africa, 22 August 1932, 17G 364, AS.

31 Delavignette later discussed the aims and effects of his book in the preface to the new edition, *Les paysans noirs* (Paris: Stock, 1947; orig. published 1931), 10, 14 quoted. Delavignette explains how his upbringing in rural France allowed him to see the possibilities of peasant agriculture. See his *Soudan–Paris–Bourgogne* (Paris: Grasset, 1935).

32 The Catholic study group "Semaines sociales" devoted its 1930 meeting to "social problems in the colonies." See Girardet, *L'idée coloniale*, 175–90.

33 The Economic Conference of 1935 backed both peasants and planters. The ministry would not give up its frustrating support of settlers and backed an authoritarian variant of "indigenous colonization," creating a committee to study moving people where they were thought most useful and supervising them closely. Most such schemes came to naught, but the Office du Niger did follow the "indigenous colonization" model, using much forced labor for irrigation works and other projects. République Française, Decree of 5 September 1935, copy in PA 28/1/5, and "Note au sujet de la création dans chaque colonie d'un comité d'action coloniale et de paysannat indigène," 27 May 1936, ibid.; report by Inspecteur Général du Service de Santé des Colonies (Sorel) to Minister regarding a document on "Généralités sur la colonisation indigène," AP 2808/2, ANSOM; Robert L. Delavignette, "Action colonisatrice et paysannat indigène," *Afrique Française* 45 (1935): 526–30.

34 Carde quoted in Conklin, "A Mission to Civilize," 320–28, 323 quoted.

35 Conklin, 343–52, 344 quoted. The decree provided for a ten-hour day, weekly rest, and sanitary protection and medical care for workers. At the same time, the requirement that each contract worker constitute a "pécule" – wages withheld to be paid to him on his return to his village – was both an attempt to prevent desertion and an effort to ensure the reinsertion of workers in village life. Actually, the decree was rarely implemented in "free labor" situations, and mainly served as a very minimal form of protection for forced laborers. Ibid., 355–59. The decree is reprinted in Buell, *Native Problem*, II: 155–75.

36 Report by Inspector Maret "concernant la question de la main d'oeuvre et le régime du Travail en Côte d'Ivoire," No. 125, 25 May 1931, in papers of the inspection mission led by Inspector Kair, AP 3066, ANSOM.

37 Maret report, AP 3066; extracts from transmission of Haranger's report by Kair to Governor-General, AP 2797/11, ANSOM. Kair emphasized that the abuses of the administrator of Kong could not have taken place without the "tacit" approval of the Ivory Coast administration. Kair to Minister, 19 June 1931, AP 3066, ANSOM.

38 An earlier inspection report had also pointed to the use of "administrative constraint" and to its negative consequences. Inspecteur Picanon, "Situation Economique (Main d'Oeuvre), Mission 1924–25," 18 January 1925, AE, Main d'Oeuvre, 23, ANSOM.

39 Carde insisted that labor regulations were satisfactory and private enterprise deserved support. Forced labor was "Illegal, perhaps, this help was justified by reasons which no-one, including people of good faith, disputes." Lapalud's failing was that he "did not pay attention to [the regulations'] strict application." Carde had, however, insisted before the inspection that all was well in regard to labor. He accused the inspector of demonstrating the "grandiloquence of a beginner." The minister also exempted higher authorities and government policy from blame, and pinned all responsibility on the "erroneous ways" of Lapalud's administration. He perhaps revealed more than he meant to when he faulted the local administration for taking 10 percent of a district's population; apparently a lower percentage would have been acceptable. Response of Lieutenant-Governor Bourgines, 3 June 1931, Kair to Governor-General, 4 June 1931, AP 3066, ANSOM; Carde to Governor-General, French West Africa, 25 June 1931, in Dirat Papers, PA 31/2/13, ANSOM; Minister to Governor-General, 18 February 1932, AP 2797/11. For Carde's earlier complacency, see Carde to Directeur des Affaires Economique, Paris, 26 July 1928, AFOM 380, ANSOM.

40 Governor-General to Lieutenant-Governor, Ivory Coast, 31 March 1932, and Governor-General to Minister, 2 April 1932, K 122 (26), AS.

41 Gide, *Travels in the Congo*; Girardet, *L'idée coloniale*, 143–50; Claude Liauzu, *Aux origines des tiers-mondismes: Colonisés et anticolonialistes en France 1919–1939* (Paris: L'Harmattan, 1982); Gilles Sautter, "Notes sur la construction du Chemin de Fer Congo-Océan (1921–1934)," *Cahiers d'Etudes Africaines* 7 (1967): 219–99; Cathérine Coquery-Vidrovitch, *Le Congo au temps des grandes compagnies concessionaires, 1898–1930* (Paris: Mouton, 1972).

42 Resumé of Report of Lejeune, chargé de mission en A.E.F. "sur la main d'oeuvre et le travail indigène en A.E.F.," March 1932, AE, Main d'Oeuvre, 28, ANSOM.

43 In sending out the questionnaire, the minister of colonies (Maginot) served notice of the imperial consensus on the principle in question: "one can say that a unanimous accord has been reached to *condemn* forced labor *for the benefit of individuals* and to *regulate* forced labor *for public ends*, with the will to prepare for the complete disappearance of a system which one can affirm is a remnant of slavery." Minister, Circular, to Governors-General and Governors, 19 September 1929, K 62 (19), AS.

44 Governor-General (Affaires Economiques) to Governor-General (en mission à Paris), 2 May 1929, K 64 (19); Governor-General, Circular to Governors, 11 October 1929, K 95 (26), AS.

45 On Guinea – a somewhat more modest instance of what has been described here in relation to the Ivory Coast and Upper Volta – see Babacar Fall, "Economie de plantation et main d'oeuvre forcée en Guinée française," *Labour: Capital and Society* 20 (1987): 8–33.

46 Governor-General's Reply to questionnaire, c. May 1929, K 64 (19), AS. The

same desire to shift the labor question into an issue of taxation and military service emerged in an international meeting of colonial experts in Brussels in 1929. Members were nervous lest new "social legislation" in Europe be applied to colonies and were thus at pains to turn labor into something else. "Rapport Général" and "Le Régime et l'Organisation du Travail des Indigènes dans les Colonies françaises de l'Afrique," in *Le régime et l'organisation du travail des indigènes dans les colonies tropicales* (Brussels: Etablissements Généraux d'Imprimerie, 1929), I: i–x, 121–25.

47 Babacar Fall, *Le travail forcé en Afrique Occidentale française (1900–1945)* (Paris: Karthala, 1993), 157–227; Myron Echenberg and Jean Filipovich, "African Military Labour and the Building of the Office du Niger Installations, 1925–1950," *Journal of African History* 27 (1986): 533–51, statistics on p. 541 cited.

48 Governor-General, circular to Governors, 11 October 1929, K 95 (26), AS.

49 Governor-General to Minister, 11 March 1930, AFOM 382/61 bis/1/a; Governor-General's replies to questionnaire, 1930, K 62 (19), and Affaires Politiques et Administratives, "Note pour M. le Gouverneur Secrétaire Général, 2 May 1930," K 64 (19), AS.

50 Governor, Senegal, to Governor-General, 11 January 1930, K 62 (19), AS.

51 Governor, Ivory Coast, to Governor-General, 5 January 1930, and Governor, Dahomey, to Governor-General, 31 December 1929, K 62 (19), AS.

52 Governor, Soudan, to Governor-General, 10 April 1930, Governor, Senegal, to Governor-General, 12 November 1930, K 66 (19), AS.

53 Report to Minister by Besson, delegate of Colonial Ministry to meeting of experts of the ILO, incl. Gaston Joseph to Governor-General, 7 February 1929, K 64 (19), AS.

54 The failure is recorded in the Directeur des Affaires Politiques (at the ministry), "Revue trimestrielle de politique coloniale étrangère," 2ème trimestre 1930, 17G 245, AS.

55 Minister, Circular to Governors-General on a document from the ILO's committee of experts on native labor, 28 May 1934, and Note by Affaires Politiques, 22 May 1934, K 131 bis (26), AS.

56 Minister, "Rapport au Président de la République Française suivi d'un décret réglementant le travail public obligatoire aux colonies," 21 August 1930, K 66 (19), AS. The minister's note was filled with claims that France was trying to phase out all forced labor and using it only when absolutely necessary, all this on the eve of scandals about the enormous extent and abusive practice of forced labor for public and private ends. Around the same time, the governor-general – having just defended the regime of prestations – sent around a decree calling them a "feudal" relic, no longer useful, leading to "waste of manpower and abuses," and called for a "lightening" of the system, above all by making it possible for Africans to buy out their labor obligations with cash. Governor-General, circular to Governors, 12 September 1930, K 392 (39), AS.

57 "Rapport sur le danger proche de dépopulation que font courir à l'Afrique Occidentale Française des recrutements excessifs et mal repartis," by Inspecteur Générale des Services Sanitaires et Medicaux, Sorel, 12 October 1931, K 172 (26), AS. A similar set of calculations was performed by the governor of Guinea, the other zone of European plantation development.

Governor, Guinea, to Governor-General, 2 February 1932, K 128 (26), AS. For more on demography in colonial Africa, see Dennis Cordell and Joel Gregory (eds.), *African Population and Capitalism: Historical Perspectives* (Boulder, Colo.: Westview Press, 1987).

58 A report from 1923 cited the emigration to the Gold Coast and claimed that this was a reason why more force could not be used to push people from Upper Volta to the farms of settlers in the Ivory Coast. Cited in Buell, *Native Problem*, 2: 29. In 1927, the governor-general told the governor of Upper Volta to stop the emigration. Governor-General to Governor, Upper Volta, 19 December 1927, 1Q 326 (77), AS. See also report on "L'emploi de la main d'oeuvre française dans les possessions étrangères de la Côte Occidentale d'Afrique" by Direction des Affaires Economiques, 16 April 1928, AFOM 382/61 bis/1/c.

59 Lieutenant-Governor, Haute Volta, to Governor-General, 28 September 1931, K 121 (26), AS. See also A. I. Asiwaju, "Migrations as Revolt: The Example of the Ivory Coast and the Upper Volta before 1945," *Journal of African History* 17 (1976): 577–94.

60 Upper Volta, "Main d'Oeuvre," n.d. [1932], K 128 (26), AS. More common statistical exercises were manpower inventories based on guesses of population in each colony and formulas for estimating the number of able-bodied men of the right ages. For one largely fanciful manpower survey see "Inventaire des ressources en travailleurs de l'Afrique Occidentale Française," for the Sécretariat Permanent de la Défense Nationale, 1934, K 131 (26). A historical study based on interviews with people of a variety of ages in Burkina Faso records that the overwhelming majority of workers in the pre-1931 era recall force as the reason for going to the Ivory Coast and avoiding compulsion as a major reason for going to the Gold Coast. They also recall the escalation of recruitment after 1932. Joël Gregory, Dennis D. Cordell, and Victor Piché, "La mobilisation de la main-d'oeuvre burkinabè, 1900–1974: Une vision retrospective," *Canadian Journal of African Studies* 23 (1989): 73–105.

61 Even members of the colonial business establishment were debunking the reservoir myth. See the speech of J. L. Gheerbrandt, Directeur de l'Institut Colonial Français, "Le problème de l'organisation du travail de couleur," to Redressement Français, 8 April 1930, text in AFOM 380, ANSOM.

62 Minister, Circular to Governors-General of FWA, FEA, Togo, and Cameroun, 27 March 1929, AE, Main d'Oeuvre, 46. He cited reports by Ormsby-Gore on Nigeria stressing the attachment of the African to the soil, and a Belgian report of 1928 calling for "a race of prosperous peasants." Equally interesting, he cited Governor-General Carde as opposing "grandes entreprises."

63 Côte d'Ivoire, Rapport annuel sur la main-d'oeuvre, 1934, 1935, copy in Fonds Guernut 50/B12, ANSOM. See also FWA, IT, AR, 1932–1935.

64 Even when Voltaics began to come to the Ivory Coast in the late 1940s to work for African planters under a complex system that combined tenancy and wage labor, officials tended to think of it as an "African" practice – as something they did not need to examine – rather than as a work regime.

65 Pierre Kipré, "La crise économique dans les centres urbains en Côte d'Ivoire,"

Cahiers d'Etudes Africaines 61–62 (1976): 119–46; Catherine Coquery-Vidrovitch, "La Mise en dépendance de l'Afrique Noire: Essai de périodisation, 1800–1970," *Cahiers d'Etudes Africaines* 16 (1976): 7–58; "L'Afrique et la Crise de 1930," special issue of *Revue Française d'Histoire d'Outre-Mer* 63 (1976); Marseille, *Empire colonial et capitalisme français*.

66 FWA, IT, AR, 1932, 1933, 1934, 1935.

67 In officials' own terms, in any case, unemployment peaked at 3.6 percent of the (very small) wage labor force in 1933, mainly in Dakar, other Senegalese towns, or Dahomey (where palm oil processing had collapsed); by 1935, it had fallen to 1.3 percent. D'Almedia-Topor, "L'évolution du travail salarié," 110; FWA, IT, AR, 1932, 1933. See also ibid., 1936, for a particularly vivid instance of the circularity of official reasoning on the subject: "there are no 'unemployed' in French West Africa." Anyone who so desired could go back to the soil, and any worker who did not "prefers to vegetate in the city which he only will leave at the last extremity. There is thus constituted a floating urban population of 'non-workers' [sans-travail] of a particular nature, seeking daily labor without enthusiasm, living most often at the expense of more favored brethren."

68 A similar argument was made about compensation for job-related accidents: families took care of dependents of an accident victim and wives were married off to a deceased victim's kinsmen, so that insurance would mean "paying money, small sums to be sure, without utility to Africans who will have no need of it and will not understand the goal of our measure." Governor, Soudan, to Governor-General, 16 September 1931, and Governor, Upper Volta, to Governor-General, 10 September 1931, K 67 (19), AS. The government did nonetheless pass in 1932 a very narrow accident insurance program, limited to cases of people injured operating machinery.

69 Monique Lakroum, "Les salaires dans le port de Dakar," *Revue Française d'Histoire d'Outre-Mer* 63 (1976), 640–53; Lakroum, *Le travail inégal*; Dakar, Rapport d'Ensemble Annuel, 1930, 1933. In the early 1930s, the floating population was seen as a positive factor and the reason why officials did not have to think of using force to recruit labor for private enterprise or public works in Dakar. Administrateur de Dakar to Governor-General, 23 March 1931, K 66 (19), AS.

70 d'Almeida-Topor, "L'évolution du travail salarié ," 114.

71 d'Almedia-Topor, p. 105.

72 FWA, IT, AR, 1933, 1934, 1935.

73 Assistant District Commissioner, Kilifi, to Provincial Commissioner, 18 October 1918, CP 38/582, KNA. This argument is not very different from Mercier's attack on the contradiction of free labor ideology and indirect rule (see above).

74 For an insightful analysis of the winding path of official thinking, see Bruce Berman, *Control and Crisis in Colonial Kenya: The Dialectic of Domination* (London: James Currey, 1990), and Bruce Berman and John Lonsdale, *Unhappy Valley: Conflict in Kenya and Africa* (London: James Currey, 1992).

75 See the "Bishop's Memorandum," from missionaries in Kenya, in *Parliamentary Papers* 1920, XXXIII, 81, pp. 8–10; Joseph H. Oldham, *Christianity and the Race Problem* (George H. Doran, 1924), 101; Anti-

Slavery Society, memorandum to the Colonial Office, reprinted in *Anti-Slavery Reporter*, ser. 5, 10 (1920): 52–55.

76 *House of Lords Debates* 41 (14 July 1920): c. 155; revised circular in *Parliamentary Papers*, 1921, XXIV, 433, pp. 3–4. One critic who did go deeper was Norman Leys, a medical doctor with long Kenyan experience. He lambasted settlers and the government, but he too stayed close to free labor ideology: a truly free market would arbitrate, as the government did not, between the claims of different communities for resources. *Kenya* (London: Cass, 1973, orig. published 1924).

77 Charles van Onselen, *Chibaro: African Mine Labour in Southern Rhodesia 1900–1933* (London: Pluto Press, 1976).

78 Robin Palmer and Neil Parsons (eds.), *The Roots of Rural Poverty in Central and Southern Africa* (London: Heinemann, 1977); Leroy Vail, "Ecology and History: The Example of Eastern Zambia," *Journal of Southern African Studies* 3 (1976): 129–55; Elias Mandala, *Work and Control in a Peasant Economy: A History of the Lower Tchiri Valley in Malawi, 1859–1960* (Madison: University of Wisconsin Press, 1990).

79 Frederick Cooper, "Africa and the World Economy," in Cooper et al., *Confronting Historical Paradigms: Peasants, Labor, and the Capitalist World System in Africa and Latin America* (Madison: University of Wisconsin Press, 1993); William Beinart, *The Political Economy of Pondoland, 1860–1930* (Cambridge: Cambridge University Press, 1982).

80 George Chauncey, Jr., "The Locus of Reproduction: Women's Labour in the Zambian Copperbelt, 1927–1953," *Journal of Southern African Studies* 7 (1981): 135–64; Jane L. Parpart, "Sexuality and Power on the Zambian Copperbelt: 1926–1964," in Sharon Stichter and Jane L. Parpart (eds.), *Patriarchy and Class: African Women in the Home and in the Workforce* (Boulder, Colo.: Westview Press, 1988): 115–38. On Belgian policy, see John Higginson, *A Working Class in the Making: Belgian Colonial Labor Policy, Private Enterprise, and the African Mineworker, 1907–1951* (Madison: University of Wisconsin Press, 1989).

81 Munroe to Permanent Undersecretary of State for the Colonies, 30 January 1931, CO 795/43/36043, PRO. Munroe indicated that the companies were willing to make provisions for health and other services and even to consider "some suitable scheme for looking after such of them as, through old age or other cause not due to their own fault, may become unfitted for work."

82 J. F. Green, Minute, 12 December 1930, reacting to earlier conversations on this topic with mine officials, CO 795/40/35696, PRO and Secretary of State (Lord Passfield) to Governor, Nyasaland, 9 March 1931, CO 795/43/36043, PRO.

83 Governor, Nyasaland, to Passfield, 7 May 1931, Minute by J. F. N. Green, 27 July 1931, and by Passfield, 17 August 1931, CO 795/43/36043, PRO. Much migration out of impoverished Nyasaland went on anyway, and officials viewed this as dangerous to people "not yet able to stand by themselves under the strenuous conditions of the modern world." They hoped to restrain the process, above all any definitive out-migration. Nyasaland Protectorate, *Report of the Committee Appointed by His Excellency The Governor to Enquire into Emigrant Labour, 1935* (Zomba, 1936), p. 7 quoted.

84 See chapter 3. Another case of an industry reluctant to confront the social dimensions of production and reproduction is analyzed in Ibrahim Abdullah, "Profit versus Social Reproduction: Labor Protests in the Sierra Leonean Iron-Ore Mines, 1933–38," *African Studies Review* 35 (1992): 13–41.

85 Tabitha Kanogo, *Squatters and the Roots of Mau Mau, 1905–63* (London: James Currey, 1987).

86 Frederick Cooper, *On the African Waterfront: Urban Disorder and the Transformation of Work in Colonial Mombasa* (New Haven: Yale University Press, 1987).

87 Polly Hill, *Migrant Cocoa-Farmers of Southern Ghana* (Cambridge: Cambridge University Press, 1963); Sara Berry, *Cocoa, Custom and Socio-Economic Change in Rural Western Nigeria* (Oxford: Clarendon Press, 1975).

88 Roger Thomas, "Forced Labour in British West Africa: The Case of the Northern Territories of the Gold Coast, 1906–27," *Journal of African History* 14 (1973): 79–103; van Onselen, *Chibaro*; Michael Mason, "Working on the Railway: Forced Labor in Northern Nigeria, 1907–1912," in Robin Cohen, Jean Copans, and Peter C. W. Gutkind (eds.), *African Labor History* (Beverly Hills: Sage, 1978), 56–79.

89 For an overview of Colonial Office discussion on the connection of indirect rule and labor, see G. D. Tarrant, "The British Colonial Office and the Labour Question in the Dependencies in the Inter-War Years," Ph.D. dissertation, University of Manitoba, 1977.

90 Labour departments or labour commissioners had ceased to function in Tanganyika, Uganda, the Gold Coast, Nigeria, and Northern Rhodesia, as well as in the West Indies. Some colonies, such as Kenya, had never had such a department. See the various minutes from 1935 in CO 323/1319/9 PRO. It was only with the greatest diffidence that the Secretary of State – and this was after the Copperbelt disturbances – asked governors to think again about labour departments or other mechanisms to keep an eye on the labor question: "I do not share the opinion, which is held in some quarters, that the object in view *necessarily* requires the establishment of a separate Labour Department." Malcolm MacDonald, Draft Despatch, 9 November 1935, ibid.

91 Governor Hubert Young to Secretary of State, 6 July 1935, CO 795/76/45083.

92 Major G. St. J. Orde Browne, *Labour Conditions in Northern Rhodesia*, Colonial No. 150 (1938), p. 4.

93 This was one of the motivations for seeking to move a permanent labor force from Nyasaland to the Copperbelt. Munroe, "Memorandum concerning the Native Labour Association of Northern Rhodesia," encl. Munroe to Permanent Undersecretary of State for the Colonies, 30 January 1931, CO 795/43/36043, PRO.

94 Although the problem originated with Africans' social behavior, it was exacerbated by the wasteful use of whatever manpower came forth, lack of training, and the need for close European supervision. "Labour and the Economic Development of Tropical Africa," Typescript, Orde Browne Papers, Rhodes House, Oxford University, 2/1, pp. 5, 17–18, 28.

95 FWA, IT, AR, 1935; Ivory Coast, IT, AR, 1936.

96 In British Africa nothing as comprehensive as the French statistics on manpower had been put together, and manpower data from individual

colonies was spotty and inconsistent. Officials did not yet want to think about labor as a continental or imperial issue.

97 FWA, IT, AR, 1936; Lakroum, *Le travail inégal*, 54–55, 58; d'Almedia-Topor, "L'evolution du travail salarié," 112–13.

98 FWA, IT, AR, 1936.

99 FWA, IT, AR, 1935. The minister was more worried about French Equatorial Africa. He asked the acting governor-general there to keep on eye on public works sites, for he had seen reports of people being kept on after their service period was over, of workers not being fed, and other "scandalous abuses." Minister to Governor-General per interim, FEA, 3 August 1935, AP 662/1.

100 FWA, IT, AR, 1935; Dakar, Police et Sûreté, AR, 1935. These worries lay behind periodic efforts to segregate much of Dakar's African population into the quarter known as the Medina, a task officials never could pull off. "L'urbanisme en A.O.F.," n.d. [c 1934], AFOM 377/42bis; Dakar, AR, 1929, copy in AP 579/1, ANSOM.

101 Minister, Circular to Governors-General of AEF, AOF, and Commissioners of Cameroun and Togo, 25 June 1935, PA 28/5/145, ANSOM.

102 J. Merle Davis (ed.), *Modern Industry and the African: An Enquiry into the Effect of the Copper Mines of Central Africa upon Native Society and the Work of Christian Missions Made under the Auspices of the Department of Social and Industrial Research of the International Missionary Council* (London: Macmillan, 1933). The study was financed in part by the Carnegie Corporation and was based on a team's visit to Northern Rhodesia and Katanga between July and December 1932.

103 Ibid., vii, 1–2.

104 Charles W. Coulter, "The Sociological Problem," ibid., 45–46, 87, 103–4; E.A.G. Robinson, "The Economic Problem," ibid., 177.

105 Robinson, 177, 209; J. Merle Davis,"The Problem for Missions," 377–79.

106 For an example of the assimilation of migration to the slave trade, see a pamphlet entitled "The Industrialization of the African" (1937) in which the Anti-Slavery and Aborigines Protection Society argued that labor contracts did not constitute free labor and inevitably led to abuses. In effect the contract laborer was agreeing to be a slave for a set period of time, since leaving a job was not an option and dismissal was not a realistic sanction. Migrancy should at most be a transitional step: "The aim should be deliberately pursued of establishing a free labor market" (p. 8).

107 Another study slightly ahead of its time was I. C. Greaves, *Modern Production among Backward Peoples* (London: Allen & Unwin, 1935). Claiming that labor was the "primary problem of tropical production," Greaves applied economic analysis to explain the work habits of tropical populations. The supposed disinclination of backward people to change resulted from "satisfactory adjustment" to a situation where there were few returns to additional labor. Primitive economies were constantly making adjustments, and wage labor could be attractive if it offered equivalent returns to other activities (33, 40, 53–56, 64). But where taking a job did not mean giving up land, the possibility of opting out of wage labor was always available – people were not *progressively* taken into the labor market. Most

governments therefore would not leave recruitment to market forces. When employers were not disciplined by the market, they tended to keep wages low and conditions bad, and this hurt the development of wage labor over the long term (66, 112, 121, 152–53). The Colonial Office was no more ready for Greaves' economic analysis of African behavior than for Davis' social perspective on migration.

108 If Northern Rhodesia was eager to acquire migrant laborers, Nyasaland was worried about being treated as British southern Africa's reservoir, rather like Upper Volta in French West Africa. See Nyasaland, *Committee to Enquire into Emigrant Labour.*

109 The circular on health and population issued by the Colonial Secretary, Lord Passfield, in 1930, revealed this clearly. Worried that population did not seem to be increasing, he asked governors for more information, commenting that health problems "may in a large measure be attributed to the prevalence of certain native customs which are directly repugnant to European ideas of hygiene and medical knowledge." He thought that if women's status were improved they would become "better mothers and better qualified to rear their children afterwards." Even asking about health seemed to require some language blaming problems on the Africans. *Despatch from Secretary of State for the Colonies to African Governors, 8 March 1930,* Colonial No. 65 (1931).

110 These issues are discussed at length in Megan Vaughan, *Curing their Ills: Colonial Power and African Illness* (Cambridge: Polity Press, 1991), and John Iliffe, *The African Poor: A History* (Cambridge: Cambridge University Press, 1987).

111 Lord Hailey, *An African Survey* (London: Oxford University Press, 1938), 710–11.

112 Irwin Wall, "Front Populaire, Front National: The Colonial Example," *International Labor and Working Class History* 30 (1986): 32–43; Liauzu, *Aux origines des tiers-mondismes.*

113 Norman Leys, "The Labour Party's Colonial Policy," paper for Labour Party Advisory Committee on Imperial Questions, No. 205B, June, 1939, copy in ACJ, Rhodes House. During Passfield's tenure, Drummond Shiels tried to get some basic protections applied to colonial workers but got little support within or outside the Colonial Office. Tarrant, "British Colonial Office," chapters 2, 4.

114 Gupta, *Imperialism and the Labour Movement*; Stephen Howe, *Anticolonialism in British Politics: The Left and the End of Empire, 1918–1964* (Oxford: Clarendon Press, 1993). See also chapter 3.

115 Convention No. 50 concerning the Regulation of Certain Special Systems of Recruiting Workers, 1936, in ILO, *Conventions and Recommendations,* 837–43.

116 A controversy erupted over penal sanctions when Archdeacon W. E. Owen of Kenya interpreted part of Orde Browne's report on Northern Rhodesia as a defense of penal sanctions, and used the phrase cited in the text in reference to Kenya's Employment of Servants Ordinance of 1937. Clipping of Owen's letter to the editor of *The Manchester Guardian,* 11 October 1938, and Minutes of Swanzy and Pedler, 8 November 1938, CO 822/91/4, PRO. See also Tarrant, "British Colonial Office," 218–30.

117 The self-referential quality of critiques of imperialism is pointed out in another context by Edward Said, *Culture and Imperialism* (New York: Knopf, 1993).

3 Reforming imperialism

1 Michael Cowen and James Newman, "Real Wages in Central Kenya," Unpublished paper, 1975; Monique Lakroum, "Les salaires dans le port de Dakar," *Revue Française d'Histoire d'Outre-Mer* 63 (1976): 640–53.

2 The most detailed study is Ken Post, *Arise Ye Starvelings: The Jamaican Labour Rebellion of 1938 and its Aftermath* (The Hague: Nijhoff, 1978).

3 Ian Henderson, "Early African Leadership: The Copperbelt Disturbances of 1935 and 1940," *Journal of Southern African Studies* 2 (1975): 83–97; Charles Perrings, *Black Mineworkers in Central Africa: Industrial Strategies and the Evolution of an African Proletariat in the Copperbelt 1911–41* (New York: Africana, 1979); Jane Parpart, *Labor and Capital on the African Copperbelt* (Philadelphia: Temple University Press, 1983).

4 Governor Young to Secretary of State, 6 July 1935, CO 795/76/45083, PRO. As for Young's efforts to install indirect rule, he later admitted that the results were disappointing, not least because it focused on "tribal organizations which have already fallen into abeyance." Quoted in R. D. Pearce, *The Turning Point in Africa: British Colonial Policy 1938–1948* (London: Cass, 1982), 9.

5 *Report of Commission Appointed to Enquire into the Disturbance in the Copperbelt, Northern Rhodesia* (Lusaka, 1935), 38–40, 59.

6 Governor Young to Secretary of State, 23 October 1935, and Secretary of State to Young, 24 December 1935, CO 795/76/45083.

7 G. St. J. Orde Browne, *Labour Conditions in Northern Rhodesia*, Colonial No. 150 (1938), 4, 45.

8 Ibid., 10, 21–23, 35–40.

9 An industry publication, *Industrial and Labour Information* (22 August 1938) commented on Orde Browne's report, "While I sympathize with the desire to retain sound African customs and to resist the tendency to detribalisation, it has to be recognized that detribalised Africans are now numerous, and that they cannot be expected to return to their original villages to herd goats." Copy in CO 822/91/4, PRO.

10 Minute, P. V. Vernon, 14 June 1937, CO 323/1319/1766/2. The continued use of penal sanctions for contract violators was a sore point, especially when an ILO Convention condemned the practice. One official commented that penal sanctions were "hardly in keeping with modern thought." Settler-influenced legislative councils were convinced that Africans were not modern thinkers and would only fulfill contractual obligations if threatened with jail. Comments of the Secretary of Native Affairs, Northern Rhodesia, to Legislative Council, with replies by elected representatives, 7 June 1940, copy in CO 859/27/9, PRO.

11 J. E. W. Flood, Minute, 4 August 1937, and other minutes in the file, CO 323/1429/1766/1937.

12 Ormsby-Gore, *House of Commons Debates*, 324 (2 June 1937): c. 1081. The Secretary of State was being pressed in this debate to set up separate labor departments.

13 Ormsby-Gore, Circular Despatch, 24 August 1937, CO 323/1429/1766/1937, PRO. For the discussion, see Minutes by J. E. W. Flood, 4 August 1937, J. C. Hibbert, 11 August 1937, and Cosmo Parkinson, 18 August 1937, in ibid.

14 *House of Commons Debates*, 326 (7 July 1937): cc. 331–33; 326 (14 July 1937): c. 1241.

15 Just before the strike, Creech Jones had called for a systematic investigation of labor policy and the elaboration of a "labour code" for Africa; he had attacked the "vicious" conditions of the compounds and the "labour servitude" to which recruitment, contracts, and penal sanctions led. *House of Commons Debates* 324 (2 June 1937): 1052–61. See also P. S. Gupta, *Imperialism and the British Labour Movement, 1914–1964* (New York: Holmes & Meier, 1975), 250–51.

16 Quoted in Gupta, 252. See also "Labour Supervision in the Colonial Empire, 1937–1943," Colonial No. 185, 1943, 4, and G. D. Tarrant, "The British Colonial Office and the Labour Question in the Dependencies in the Inter-War Years," Ph.D. dissertation, University of Manitoba, 1977. Orde Browne had been labour commissioner in Tanganyika until the post was abolished in 1931, and had served on an ILO committee.

17 "Course of Instruction on Labour Problems in the Colonial Empire (October 2nd to 13th 1939), Record of Proceedings," CO 859/28/5, PRO. Orde Browne discussed colonial institutions like labor compounds and indecisively compared migration and stabilization. The anthropologist Meyer Fortes stressed the need to understand the native laborer on his own standards.

18 Anthropology in the inter-war years is associated with indirect rule and the myth of the never-changing tribe, but it was more varied than that and often pushing at the edges of conventional boundaries. Talal Asad (ed.), *Anthropology and the Colonial Encounter* (London: Ithaca Press, 1973); Henrika Kuklick, *The Savage Within: The Social History of British Anthropology, 1885–1945* (Cambridge: Cambridge University Press, 1991).

19 Audrey Richards, *Land, Labour and Diet in Northern Rhodesia: An Economic Study of the Bemba Tribe* (London: Oxford University Press for International African Institute, 1939, 2nd ed. 1961), 398–405. See also Margaret Read, "Native Standards of Living and African Culture Change: Illustrated by Examples from the Ngoni Highlands of Nyasaland," Supplement to *Africa* 11, 3 (1938). A reevaluation of Richards' work in its historical context is an important part of Henrietta L. Moore and Megan Vaughan, *Cutting Down Trees: Gender, Nutrition, and Agricultural Change in the Northern Province of Zambia, 1890–1990* (London: James Currey, 1994).

20 Committee on Nutrition in the Colonial Empire, "First Report: Part I," 1939, *Parliamentary Papers* 1938–39, X, 55, p. 42.

21 Godfrey Wilson, *An Essay on the Economics of Detribalization in Northern Rhodesia*. Rhodes-Livingstone Papers 5 (Livingstone: Rhodes-Livingstone Institute, 1941), 17–18, 21, 27, 42, 69. See also Megan Vaughan, *Curing their Ills: Colonial Power and African Illness* (Cambridge: Polity Press, 1991).

22 Gupta, *Imperialism and the Labour Movement*, 243–44, 262; Michael Cowen and Robert Shenton, "The Origin and Course of Fabian Colonialism in Africa," *Journal of Historical Sociology* 4 (1991): 143–74.

23 Creech Jones, 1938, quoted by Gupta, 237.

24 TUC, "Blackpool Congress Resolution," 7 March 1939, copy in Creech Jones Papers, 14/1. The TUC also emphasized the importance of following the ILO resolutions and of developing Labour Departments and Inspectorates. Stephen Howe terms the TUC's earlier attitude toward colonial workers "almost wholly parochial." *Anticolonialism in British Politics: The Left and the End of Empire, 1918–1964* (Oxford: Clarendon Press, 1993), 77.

25 Gupta, 251–53.

26 W.M. Macmillan's *Warning from the West Indies* (Harmondsworth: Penguin, 1938) first published in 1935 and reissued with an I-told-you-so preface three years later, argued that more democratic institutions, trade unions, and the promotion of economic development were the only alternative to the disorders he had predicted just before they broke out.

27 Creech Jones, speech to Parliament, *House of Commons Debates* 348 (7 June 1939), c. 487; Gupta, 264.

28 Gupta, 264–65.

29 On the limits of the British left's colonial thinking in the 1930s and the beginnings of such organizations as the League Against Imperialism, see Howe, *Anticolonialism in British Politics.*

30 Arthur Creech Jones, "The West Indies Report," New Fabian Research Bureau, 1940, 14.

31 Stephen Constantine, *The Making of British Colonial Development Policy 1914–1940* (London: Cass, 1984), 233–57; J. M. Lee, *Colonial Development and Good Government* (Oxford: Oxford University Press, 1967); D. J. Morgan, *The Official History of Colonial Development* (London: Macmillan, 1980).

32 Malcolm MacDonald to Creech Jones, 7 July 1938, ACJ 25/1, ff. 45–47.

33 Ormsby-Gore to Walter Citrine, 10 July 1937, CO 295/600/70307.

34 The general report on the colonial empire in 1938–39 tried to take the issue of poverty away from the "modern" structures of empire. "In some parts of our Colonial Empire it may be said that, in spite of the peaceful conditions which have resulted from British rule, the populations still live under primitive conditions and suffer seriously from preventable disease." "The Colonial Empire," *Parliamentary Papers* 1938–39, XX, 965, 4.

35 Sam Rhodie, "The Gold Coast Cocoa Hold-Ups of 1930–31," *Transactions of the Historical Society of Ghana* 9 (1968): 105–18; Roger Southall, "Farmers, Traders, and Brokers in the Gold Coast Cocoa Economy," *Canadian Journal of African Studies* 12 (1978): 185–211.

36 Governor Sir Arnold Hodson to Sir Arthur Dawe, CO, 27 May 1939, CO 96/760/31312; Leo Spitzer and LaRay Denzer, "I. T. A. Wallace Johnson and the West African Youth League," *International Journal of African Historical Studies* 6 (1973): 413–52, 565–601.

37 MacDonald to Sir John Simon (Chancellor of the Exchequer), 11 October 1939, and the Colonial Office paper, "Colonial Development; Note for the Chancellor of the Exchequer," included with the above, CO 859/19/7475.

38 "Statement of Policy on Colonial Development and Welfare," February 1940, *Parliamentary Papers* 1939–40, X, 25, 5. The social imperialist purpose of this act was no secret, and MacDonald alluded to its goal being "to bring additional work to idle hands in this country" in explaining to Parliament that the new act had a different purpose. *House of Commons Debates* 361 (21 May

1940), c. 45. For a survey focusing on colonial trade and government policy, see Michael Havinden and David Meredith, *Colonialism and Development: Britain and Its Tropical Colonies, 1850–1960* (London: Routledge, 1993).

39 "Statement of Policy," pp. 6–7.

40 Extract from Conclusions of Cabinet Meeting, 15 June 1938, CAB 28 (38), copy in CO 318/433/1/71168.

41 Memorandum by the Secretary of State, June 1938, CO 318/433/1/71168. Some officials insisted that taking care of the needs of colonial populations now had to take precedence over increasing exports. G. L. M. Clauson, Memorandum on Colonial Development Policy for the Next Few Years, 8 November 1938, CO 852/190/10.

42 Mr. Calder to Meeting with Secretary of State on Colonial Development, 27 June 1938, CO 852/190/10. On class and race in colonial Jamaica, see Thomas C. Holt, *The Problem of Freedom: Race, Labor and Politics in Jamaica and Britain, 1832–1938* (Baltimore: Johns Hopkins University Press, 1992).

43 W. A. Lewis to General Secretary, New Fabian Research Bureau, 12 March 1935, ACJ, 25/1a, f. 18; *The British West Indies*, 1935, and *Labour in the West Indies*, 1939, both published by the Fabian Society.

44 Lewis, *Labour in the West Indies*, 33, 41, 42.

45 G. L. M. Clauson, "The Method of Financing a more Forward Colonial Policy," 7 June 1939, CO 323/1695/7318.

46 Colonial Office to Treasury, 16 December 1938, CO 866/33/1327. Treasury agreed and Gerald Clauson was selected to head the department. Treasury to CO, 21 January 1939, J. E. Shuckburgh to Cosmo Parkinson, 6 March 1939, ibid.

47 G. L. M. Clauson, "The Method of Financing a more Forward Colonial Policy," 7 June 1939, CO 323/1695/7318.

48 George Creasy, Minute, 30 November 1939, CO 859/19/7475.

49 "Colonial Development: Notes for the Chancellor of the Exchequer," incl. MacDonald to Sir John Simon, 11 October 1939, CO 859/19/7475.

50 Sir Horace Wilson, Treasury, to Parkinson, 5 January 1940, Notes of discussion between MacDonald and Wilson and Sir Richard Hopkins of the Treasury, 27 November 1939, CO 859/19/7475.

51 The Colonial Office thought that the Treasury worried that committing Britain to spending on social services while guiding territories toward self-government would commit Britain to paying for services which it did not determine. In Africa at least, the Colonial Office insisted that there was nothing to worry about because the "day when self-governing institutions (other than limited self-government by local authority) would be developed was remote." Creasy to Hale, 11 January 1940, and Notes of a discussion with Mr. Hale by C. G. Eastwood, 11 January 1940, CO 859/19/18, PRO.

52 Eastwood, Notes of discussion, 11 January 1940, CO 859/19/7475.

53 Minutes, Parkinson, Clauson, and Moore, all on 12 January 1940, MacDonald, Minute, 14 January 1940, CO 859/19/7475.

54 *House of Commons Debates* 361 (21 May 1940), cc. 43, 47. There was no real dissent in the discussion of the bill, although MPs backed their pet projects and made various suggestions about refining the administration of the act. The debate can be found at ibid., cc. 41–126 and (third reading, 11 June 1940), cc. 1171–1214.

55 Much of sociological theory in recent decades has been concerned with developing an understanding of social action more complicated than the assumption of a linear relationship between the extent of grievances and the extent of protest. The work of Charles Tilly stands out in this regard.

56 Chambre des Députés, *Débats* 15 December 1936, 3626. The great socialist leader Jean Jaurès had also been an advocate of bringing the French revolution to the colonies.

57 Ibid., 3627. Jacques Marseille (*Empire colonial et capitalisme français: Histoire d'un divorce* (Paris: Albin Michel, 1984, 334–37)) emphasizes the Popular Front's lack of interest in decolonization or industrialization; Irwin Wall stresses the French left's insistence that it knew what was best for colonized people ("Front Populaire, Front National: The Colonial Example," *International Labor and Working Class History* 30 [1986]: 32–43). William B. Cohen stresses coalition politics within the Front: the Socialists favored assimilation within existing colonies, the Radicals favored the civilizing mission and "mise en valeur," and the Communists had been anti-colonial but switched sides on Kremlin orders in order to back the popular fronts in most European countries. "The Colonial Policy of the Popular Front," *French Historical Studies* 7 (1972): 368–93. A strong anti-colonial stance may be found in the leftist groups outside of the Popular Front. Benjamin Stora, "La gauche socialiste, révolutionnaire, et la question du Maghreb au moment du Front Populaire (1935–1938)," *Revue Française d'Histoire d'Outre-Mer* 70, 258–59 (1983): 57–79.

58 Moutet was an Ardechois, from one of the most rural parts of France. In a press conference in 1937, trying to explain why he opposed moving Africans depending on where their labor was needed, he pointed to the self-evident absurdity of moving "peasants" from one region of France to another to harvest beets. Press conference quoted in *Notre Voix, organe du Parti Socialiste SFIO en Côte d'Ivoire* 12 (25 May 1937). Robert Delavignette, another advocate of peasant production, connected his Burgundian origins and his Africa policy. *Soudan–Paris–Bourgogne* (Paris: Grasset, 1935). Herman Lebovics argues that the left bought into the myth of rural France, and found its vision narrowed accordingly. *True France: The Wars over Cultural Identity, 1900–1945* (Ithaca: Cornell University Press, 1992).

59 Moutet, Speech to Chambre des Députés, *Débats* 15 December 1936, p. 3626; *Notre Voix*, 12 (25 May 1937).

60 A law dating to 1900 (but with earlier roots) required each colony to be self-sufficient, although some occasionally needed help with administrative expenses. Even before the Popular Front, some officials argued that the doctrine of self-sufficiency "has paralyzed our colonial effort for a half-century," and on coming to power Moutet called (using the English phrase) for an end to "the politics of 'self-supporting' in the colonies." Claudine Cotte, "La politique économique de la France en Afrique noire (1936–1946)," Thèse de troisième cycle d'histoire, Université de Paris VII, 1981, 128–29, and Chambre des Députés, *Débats*, 15 December 1936, 3628.

61 Such themes are spelled out in a book to which Moutet contributed a preface, Louis Mérat, *L'heure de l'économie dirigée d'intérêt général aux colonies* (Paris: Sirey, 1936).

62 The bill creating a Fonds Colonial, along with a committee to which governors-general could apply for metropolitan funds, passed the Chambre des Députés but languished in the Sénat. Chambre des Députés, *Débats*, 2 July 1937, 2175, and Report of the Commission des Finances, *Documents*, Annexe No. 2857, session of 7 July 1937, 1686–87.

63 Speech to the opening of the Grand Conseil, 23 November 1937, in French West Africa, *Journal Officiel* 1750 (27 November 1937), 1224. A comprehensive labor code for Indochina was enacted under the Popular Front government.

64 Charles H. Cutter, "The Genesis of a Nationalist Elite: The Role of the Popular Front in the French Soudan (1936–1939)," in G. Wesley Johnson (ed.), *Double Impact: France and Africa in the Age of Imperialism* (Westport, Conn.: Greenwood Press, 1985), 107–39.

65 "Pour la Commission d'Enquête. Note sur la colonisation européenne et la colonisation indigène en Afrique Noire Française," 1936, Fonds Moutet, PA 28/5/152, ANSOM.

66 The future governor-general of French West Africa under Vichy, Pierre Boisson – no leftist – shared the Popular Front's sense of the limits of wage labor and white settlement and the importance of peasant production. See chapter 4.

67 "Pour la Commission d'Enquête."

68 De Coppet decided to reestablish the Inspection du Travail in November 1936, with an inspector in each colony except Mauritania and Niger, and to give the posts to relatively high ranking administrators. Governor-General to Minister, 9 November 1936, K 172 (26), AS; FWA, IT, AR, 1936 (citing Circular of 10 November 1936).

69 The second most important nucleus of colons, and hence of forced labor, was Guinea. See Babacar Fall, "Economie de plantation et main d'oeuvre forcée en Guinée française: 1920–1946," *Labour, Capital and Society* 20 (1987): 8–33.

70 Nicole Bernard-Duquenet, *Le Sénégal et le Front Populaire* (Paris: Harmattan, 1985), 70, 82–84. When de Coppet made a formal policy address in December 1936, he said little about labor and nothing about forced labor. He claimed both he and his predecessor shared the same goal: "to make the natives happy and strong." Marcel de Coppet, "Discours du Gouverneur Général de l'A.O.F.," opening session of Conseil du Gouvernement, December 1936, copy in ANSOM.

71 Minister to Governor-General, 22 July 1936, Governor-General to Minister, 28 August 1936, K 191 (26), AS. The wage-reduction decrees were dated 19 December 1935 and 11 April 1936.

72 FWA, IT, Annual Report, 1935. Even after wages were raised again, the governor claimed Africans did not readily seek wage labor because "The natives get from their farms resources which largely assure the satisfaction of their needs and allow them easily to pay their taxes." Mondon to Governor-General, 21 February 1937, K 69 (19), AS.

73 Governor-General, Circular to Lieutenant-Governors, 1 September 1936, K 172 (26), AS.

74 Henri Labouret, "Note au sujet du travail et de la main-d'oeuvre en A.O.F," 28 October 1936 (with marginalia by de Coppet dated 29 October 1936), K 191 (26), AS.

75 Governor-General, Circular to Lieutenant-Governors, 3 November 1936, K 191 (26), AS.
76 Governor, Ivory Coast, to Governor-General, 1 December 1936, and Governor-General to Governor, 12 December 1936, K 191 (26), AS.
77 Governor, Ivory Coast, to Governor-General, 9 December 1936, Governor-General to Governor, 24 December 1936, K 191 (26), AS.
78 FWA, IT, AR, 1936, and Lieutenant-Governor, Ivory Coast, to Governor-General, 20 June 1937, copy in above report.
79 Arrêté of 28 December 1936, copy in K 191 (26), AS; Mondon Letter of 20 June 1937, in FWA, ITl, AR, 1936.
80 Mondon Letter of 20 June 1937, in FWA, IT, AR, 1936.
81 Governor-General to Lieutenant-Governor, Ivory Coast, 7 June 1937, ibid.
82 Ivory Coast, Cabinet et Inspection du Travail, "Notice chronologique et récapitulative de la question de la main d'oeuvre en Côte d'Ivoire," 10 August 1937, K 197 (26), AS.
83 Rapport de Mission du Gouverneur Tap, Inspecteur du Travail, sur la Côte d'Ivoire, July–August 1937, K 217 (26), AS; Lieutenant-Governor to Governor-General, 15 November 1937, AP 2807/3, ANSOM; Lieutenant-Governor to Governor-General, 10 November 1938, enclosed report of labor for first half of 1938, K 191 (26), AS; Lieutenant-Governor to Governor-General, 7 June 1937, K 197 (26), AS.
84 The administration was falling into a trap organization theorists have noted: in a situation of uncertainty, it is the people who control the flow of information who gain power. In a colonial system, the governor-general and the minister were trapped in Dakar and Paris and Governors controlled what they knew about any one territory. Mondon seems to have read the textbook before it was written. James March and Herbert Simon, *Organizations* (New York: Wiley, 1958), 165.
85 Lieutenant-Governor, Ivory Coast, circular to Commandants de Cercle, 21 February 1937, K 191 (26), AS; Lieutenant-Governor, Ivory Coast, circular to Commandants de Cercles et Chefs de Subdivisions, 3 February 1937, AFOM 381/67 bis.
86 Lieutenant-Governor, Ivory Coast, Circular to Commandants de Cercle, 31 July 1937, K 6 (1), AS.
87 Ivory Coast, Bureau Permanent du Travail, Rapport, 1er semestre, 1937, 2G 37-40, AS.
88 Ivory Coast, IT, AR, 1937, and Lieutenant-Governor to Governor-General, 14 June 1938, transmitting the report. On the language of emancipation without barbarism, see Holt, *The Problem of Freedom.*
89 Reports to Governor-General by Mme Savineau, Conseillère Technique de l'Enseignement," Rapport No. 10, "La Basse Côte d'Ivoire," and Report No. 18, "La famille en A.O.F.: Condition de la femme," 17G 381, AS. She reported that women worked well only when they worked for themselves; their wages were "infinitessimal," for example 1.5 francs per day for sorting coffee.
90 Inspecteur du Travail Tap, "Note pour le Gouverneur-Général sur le recrutement de la main d'oeuvre en Côte d'Ivoire," 6 March 1937, and Governor-General to Tap, 18 March 1937, K 6 (1), AS.

91   Transcript of meetings of Comité Régional, Ougadougou, 17, 18, 20, 23 March, 23 April, as well as transcript of meeting of Office Central du Travail de la Côte d'Ivoire, Abidjan, 26 June 1937, and enclosed report by Becq, and incl. Lieutenant-Governor to Governor-General, 5 March 1938; A. Brunel, Note, 6 July 1937, K 236 (26), AS.

92   Lieutenant-Governor to Governor-General, 7 June 1937, and Governor-General to Minister, 13 July 1937, K 197 (26), AS.

93   Governor-General to Lieutenant-Governor, 9 July 1937, ibid.

94   Governor-General to Minister, 9 August 1937, Minister to Governor-General, 16 October 1937, K 236 (26), AS.

95   The most vocal planter, Jean Rose, complained that wages had gone up too much. Rose to Governor-General, 28 September 1937 (telegram), 1Q 326 (77), AS.

96   De Coppet and Mondon encouraged regional committees to keep labor away from employers with a bad record and to sanction them for violations of regulations, but labor inspectors admitted that this was rarely done. Governor-General, Circular to Lieutenant-Governors, 10 August 1937, K 172 (26), AS; Lieutenant-Governor, Ivory Coast, to Governor General, 18 May 1937, enclosing correspondence with the Société des Plantations Réunies de l'Ouest Africain, and Lieutenant-Governor to Affaires Courantes, Abidjan, 25 March 1937 (telegram), K 6 (1), AS; Inspecteur du Travail Casset to Governor-General, 3 October 1937, K 172 (26), AS; Lieutenant-Governor to Governor-General, 14 May 1937, K 197 (26), AS.

97   Jean Rose to Lieutenant-Governor, 24 December 1937, Commandant de Cercle de Man to Lieutenant-Governor, 19 January 1938, Lieutenant-Governor, Ivory Coast, to Governor-General, 8 February 1938, Governor-General to Minister, 21 February 1938, K 6 (1), AS.

98   Governor-General to Minister, 25 October 1937, and Lieutenant-Governor to Governor-General, 2 October 1937, K 6 (1), AS.

99   Rapport de Mission du Gouverneur Tap, Inspecteur du Travail, sur la Côte d'Ivoire, July–August 1937, K 217 (26), AS. Another Inspecteur du Travail visited the Gold Coast and made a similar comparison in favor of its less rigid system of labor organization. He concluded, "it is necessary to create a Kumassi of the Ivory Coast." Becq to Governor, Ivory Coast, 13 November 1937, K 217 (26), AS.

100   Rapport de Mission du Gouverneur Tap, Inspecteur du Travail, sur la Côte d'Ivoire, July–August 1937, K 217 (26), AS. The administrator of Haute Côte d'Ivoire (the former colony of Upper Volta) also raised the issue of adapting work routines to the preferred rhythms of Mossi migrant laborers. He hoped it would be possible to create "the ambiance of the village" – including the presence of women – near work sites. E. Louveau, "Résumé d'ensemble de la tournée effectuée par l'Administrateur Supérieur en Basse Côte d'Ivoire (Visite de la main d'oeuvre originaire de la Haute Côte d'Ivoire employée en Basse Côte d'Ivoire)," 13 May 1938, K 236 (26), AS.

101   Tap Report, 1937, K 217 (26), AS.

102   This might be compared with Laura Lee Downs' argument about the attitudes of French employers in the metal industry towards skill: men's skills were perceived as learned, women's as natural, a consequence of "nimble

fingers" or other feminine virtues. *Manufacturing Inequality: The Construction of a Gender Stratified Workforce in the French and British Metalworking Industries, 1914–1935* (Ithaca: Cornell University Press, 1995).

103 Lieutenant-Governor, Ivory Coast, to Governor-General, 15 November 1937, same to same, 10 November 1938, Inspecteur du Travail Grob, Note sur les incidents survenus à Agboville, 4 June 1938, K 213 (26), AS.

104 Lieutenant-Governor, Ivory Coast, to Governor-General, 10 November 1938, K 191 (26), AS. This letter was transmitting the report on labor for the first half of 1938, and described the events as the only "black point" of the year.

105 Lieutenant-Governor, Ivory Coast, to Governor-General, 10 November 1938, K 191 (26), AS.

106 Speech to Grand Conseil, 23 November 1937, French West Africa, *Journal Officiel* 1750 (27 November 1937), 1231.

107 Moutet to Mandel, 20 March 1939, AP 2807/3, ANSOM.

108 Governor, Ivory Coast, to Governor-General, 15 April 1939, AP 2807/3, ANSOM.

109 R. Delavignette to Moutet, 28 March 1939, Moutet Papers, PA 28/5/143, ANSOM. Notes from the administrators are enclosed.

110 Berlan, "Note personnelle relative à la tournée du Gouverneur," 19 March 1939, and P. Holderer, "La question de la main d'oeuvre en Côte d'Ivoire," incl. Delavignette to Moutet, 28 March 1939, PA 28/5/143, ANSOM.

111 Governor, Ivory Coast, to Governor-General, 15 April 1939, AP 2807/3, ANSOM.

112 Governor to Governor-General, 15 April 1939, PA 28/5/143, ANSOM, Governor Deschamps to Haut-Commissaire, 30 June 1941, PA 36/II/14, ANSOM; Resident Supérieur en Mission Henry Wintrebert to Minister, 3 February 1939, AP 2807/3, ANSOM.

113 Minister to Governor-General, 24 May 1939, K 261 (26), AS.

114 Governor, Ivory Coast, Circular, 22 July 1939, and Governor-General to Minister, 1 July 39, AP 2807/3, ANSOM; Governor to Governor-General, 22 July 1939, K 261 (26), AS.

115 Governor, Ivory Coast, to Governor-General, 22 July 1939, K 261 (26), AS.

116 Mandel had not been particularly interested in colonies before the war, and his French nationalism and Jewish faith – a combination that sometimes went together – meant that he had few compunctions about giving his all, and giving other people's all, to the fight against Hitler. Mandel was murdered by collaborators during the war. John M. Sherwood, *Georges Mandel and the Third Republic* (Stanford: Stanford University Press, 1970).

117 Governor-General Cayla, Circular to Governors, 2 May 1940, K 186 (26), AS.

118 Nancy Ellen Lawler uses documents and oral testimonies to show the harshness of the conscription campaign of 1940 in one rural district. *Soldiers of Misfortune: Ivorien 'Tirailleurs' of World War II* (Athens: Ohio University Press, 1992), 44–56.

119 In 1931 Delavignette chose to open discussion of the peasant possibility by writing a novel; Henri Labouret, in a book originally written in 1938–39, was able to discuss the issue outside of fiction, in an ethnographic survey. *Paysans d'Afrique occidentale* (Paris: Guillmard, 1941).

120 Governor-General to Minister, 25 January 1937, K 8 (1), AS. On the implementation of the alternative tax, see Babacar Fall, *Le travail forcé en Afrique Occidentale française (1900–1946)* (Paris: Karthala, 1993), 220–26.

121 French West Africa, Rapport Politique, 1937; Pierre Vidaud, Acting Director of Affaires Politiques, Administratives et Sociales, Report to Governor-General, 15 December 1938, K 15 (1), AS.

122 Report by M. Lassalle-Sere on the Service Temporaire des Travaux d'Irrigation du Niger (the dam construction project under the Office du Niger), 3 September 1995, AP 2797/12, ANSOM. See also Myron Echenberg and Jean Filipovich, "African Military Labour and the Building of the Office du Niger Installations, 1925–1950," *Journal of African History* 27 (1986): 533–51, and Fall, *Le travail forcé,* 161–99.

123 Governor-General to Minister, 2 January 1938, AP 2808/2, ANSOM; same to same, 24 May 1938, K 301 (26), AS; Mme Savineau, "La famille en A.O.F.: Condition de la femme," February–March 1937, 17 G 381, AS. The Office du Niger was one sordid part of a long hesitation between two approaches to fostering cotton cultivation, one focusing on peasant production, the other on centralized schemes. See Richard Roberts' forthcoming book on cotton and colonialism in the French Soudan.

124 Echenberg and Filipovich ("African Military Labour," 548–49) note that the directors of the Office du Niger had good political connections until they discredited themselves in the 1940s by exceeding the permissible level of enthusiasm for the Vichy regime.

125 Bernard-Duquenet, *Le Sénégal et le Front Populaire,* 91–100; Governor-General to Minister, 12 March 1938, AFOM 382/61 bis/6/e, ANSOM; Governor-General, Circular to Governors, 16 August 1938, AP 2808/1, ANSOM. Officials were aware that "traditional" obligations had a way of rising when chiefs were under French protection. But they feared that "the remedy is worse than the evil" because chiefs might lose authority and using paid labor would require higher taxes. See Governor, Soudan, to Governor-General, 1 August 1939, and other letters in K 246 (26), AS.

126 Governor, Soudan, to Governor-General, 3 August, 16 November 1937, AE, Main d'Oeuvre, 23, ANSOM; "L'emploi de la main d'oeuvre de la deuxième portion du contingent au Soudan français," 26 August 1939, AFOM 381/65 bis, ANSOM; Echenberg and Filipovich, 543, 549.

127 This problem is the subject of an illuminating passage on capitalism and roads in Karl Marx, *Grundrisse,* trans. by Martin Nicolaus (New York: Vintage, 1973), 524–33. My thanks to Aims McGuiness for pointing out this passage to me.

128 Officials also contemplated coming up with a better name for the deuxième portion, such as "un corps de 'pionniers' indigènes." This concept was in fact applied in Madagascar and had a certain appeal in official circles. See the Acting Director of Affaires Politiques, Administratives, et Sociales to Governor-General, 15 December 1938, K 15 (1), AS, and on encouraging emigration to the Niger Valley, Bélime to Governor-General, 9 July 1937, and Ministre des Colonies to Ministre délégué pour le contrôle de la coordination des administrations de l'Afrique du Nord, Affaires Etrangères,

4 January 1938, AP 2808/2; and Ministre des Colonies to Governor-General, 11 July 1936, PA 28/4/113, ANSOM.

129 Governor-General, Circular to Governors, 27 September 1938, AP 2808/1, ANSOM.

130 While Moutet and Delavignette wrote of Africans as natural peasants – as did the more conservative Boisson – de Coppet saw farming and wage labor as two alternatives that Africans could choose between. So too did Henri Labouret, who made the interesting argument that the colonial peace and the opportunity to market crops weakened the importance of the "agnatic community" in favor of "households" and "individualism" and to a certain extent "prepared [Africans] for certain forms of wage labor if they took account of their needs and aspirations." Both cited African labor migration from Upper Volta to the Gold Coast and the Soudan to Senegal as evidence of African flexibility in regard to wage labor. De Coppet, Speech to opening of the Grand Conseil, 23 November 1937, in *Journal Officiel* 1750 (27 November 1937): 1231; Labouret, "Le problème de la main-d'oeuvre dans l'ouest-afrique française," *Politique Etrangère*, 3 (June 1936): 38–39.

131 The outgoing Governor-General of French West Africa, Brévie, thought the better social goal was to allow the African "to develop harmoniously in the context of his traditions and his customs." There was only a "kernel" of men living from wage labor in ports and cities plus seasonal wage labor. He thought labor policy was already consistent with ILO standards and that Africans were "incapable of effectively managing" a union. Governor-General to Minister, 14 July 1936, 17G 253, AS.

132 President, Syndicat de Défense des Intérêts de la Côte Occidentale d'Afrique to Governor-General, 28 August 1936, and Director of CFAO (Compagnie Française de l'Ouest Africain), "Les lois sociales en A.O.F.," August 1936, Report of Chambre de Commerce of Dakar, enclosed in Administrator, Dakar, to Governor-General, 8 October 1936, K 170 (26), AS; Notes of meeting of Chambre de Commerce, Dakar, 19 November 1936, K 7 (1), AS.

133 The government-general's own experiment with a forty-hour week, begun in October, ended in December, when de Coppet decided that productivity in the offices was too low, that correspondence was taking too long, and that the work week had to be extended to forty-two hours. The government-general had tried the so-called "English week," 7:30–11:40 a.m. and 2:00–5:00 p.m., with Saturday afternoon and Sunday off, but reverted to the old week of 7:30–11:30, 2:00–5:00, six days per week. Governor-General, Circular to Governors, 23 October 1936, and Circular to Chefs d'Administration, 19 December 1936, K 7 (1), AS.

134 Administrator of Dakar to Governor-General, 8 October 1936, Governor, Ivory Coast, to Governor-General, 1 October 1936, and other similar letters in K 170 (26), AS.

135 Syndicat des Ouvriers du Bâtiment de Dakar to Minister, September 1936, and EMCIBA to Governor-General, 22 September 1936, K 170 (26), AS; *Périscope Africain* 5, 19 September 1936. On the whole, this newspaper – and even more clearly Lamine Guèye's *L'A.O.F.* – was more interested in the category of "évolué" than in the category of "worker." They frequently ran articles about inequality in education and in access to positions in the civil service.

136 Governor-General to President of Chambre de Commerce de Dakar, 30 October 1936, K 196 (26), AS.

137 Governor-General, Circular, 4 November 1936, K 402 (132), AS. The folder in which this letter appears is entitled "travail des femmes et des enfants, 1936-37."

138 Note on Popular Front social policy, n.d. [fall 1936], and Note from Colonial Ministry, April 1937, Moutet Papers, PA 28/1/3, ANSOM.

139 Directeur des Affaires Politiques, Administratives et Sociales, Note to Directeur des Services Economiques, 20 August 1936, K 169 (26), AS; Minister to Governor-General, 28 November 1936, and Governor-General to Minister, 25 January 1937, K 153 (26), AS; Bernard-Duquenet, *Le Sénégal et le Front Populaire*, 124-25.

140 G. Wesley Johnson, *The Emergence of Black Politics in Senegal: The Struggle for Power in the Four Communes 1890-1920* (Stanford: Stanford University Press, 1971).

141 Bernard-Duquenet, *Le Sénégal et le Front Populaire*, 27-40.

142 Ibid., 42-50; Iba der Thiam, "L'évolution politique et syndicale du Sénégal Colonial de 1890 à 1936," Thèse pour le doctorat d'Etat, Université de Paris I, 1983, 3762-63, 3747-57, 7445-47.

143 "Grèves à Dakar de 1936 à 1940," and "Note," 30 June 1936, K 188 (26), AS.

144 Administrator, Dakar, to Governor-General, 28 August 1936, K 153 (26), AS; Bernard-Duquenet, 123-30; *Périscope Africain*, 19 September, 5 December 1936.

145 Dakar, Inspecteur du Travail, Report on Labor Conflict, 4 December 1936. Fonds Guernut, 50/B12, ANSOM; Administrator, Dakar, to Governor-General, 22 December 1936, Sûreté, Renseignements, 28 December 1936, and Secretary-General to Government-General (Geismar) to Minister, 29 December 1936, K 181 (26), AS.

146 Dakar, IT, Reports, 25, 27 December 1936, Fonds Guernut, 50/B12, ANSOM; Governor-General to Minister, 25 February 1937 (telegram), and Minister to Governor-General, 8 March 1937 (telegram), and "Grèves à Dakar," K 188 (26), AS; Sùreté, "Renseignements donnés a.s. de projets de grèves indigènes à Dakar," 20 January 1937, Sûreté, Renseignements (daily), 20 January 1937, K 181 (26), AS; Administrator, Dakar, to Governor-General, 7 December 1938, K 4 (1), AS.

147 The Sûreté saw the hand of Magatte Coudou Sarr behind them. The leader of an earlier strike of seamen, former director of native personnel for Air France, ex-worker in Marseille, participant in Dakar's electoral politics, and author of a series of articles in the local socialist newspaper, *Périscope Africain*. They thought he had organized unions in many occupations, from building workers to bakers. He may well have been more of an inspiration than an instigator. French West Africa, Direction de la Sûreté Générale, "Renseignments," 25 December 1936, K 188 (26), AS, and idem, "Note relative au mouvement social intéressant la direction de la Sûreté Générale en Afrique Occidentale Française pendant l'année 1936," 9 June 1937, 17G 139, AS.

148 Dakar, Rapport sur l'Inspection du Travail, 22 January 1937, Fonds Guernut, 50/B12, ANSOM; Geismar to Minister, 9 December 1936, K 181

(26), AS. Compare the strikes of 1939 and 1942 in Mombasa (chapter 4).

149 Governor-General, Circular Telegram, 27December 1936, K 188 (26), AS.

150 Secretary-General to Minister, 9 December 1936, K 181 (26), AS. The governor of Senegal made a related point regarding the strikes that spread there in late December: he tried to get each group of workers to choose delegates with whom orderly negotiations could take place. Governor to Governor-General, 21 January 1937, ibid.

151 "Grèves à Dakar," K 188 (26); Governor, Senegal, to Governor-General, 23, 24, 25, 31 December 1936, 6, 8, 15 January 1937, Procurer, Kaolack, to Procurer General, 15 January 1937; Governor-General to Governor, Senegal, 11 February 1937, K 226 (26), AS. The suggestion to use the marabouts came from Secretary-General of Government-General to Governor, Senegal, 14 January 1937 (telegram), ibid. In Dakar, officials called in old debts from Hadj Mahmoudou Baro – they had helped arranged pilgrimages to Mecca – to get him to make the rounds of "worker areas." Renseignements, 20 January 1937, K 181 (26), AS.

152 Inspecteur des Affaires Administratives to Lieutenant-Governor, Senegal, 14 January 1937, K 181 (26), AS; Secretary-General to Government-General to Governor, Senegal, 25 December 1936, K 226 (26), AS; "Rapport sur l'Inspection du Travail," Dakar, 22 January 1937, Fonds Guernut 50/B12, ANSOM.

153 Sûreté Générale, "Mouvement social," 9 June 1937, 17 G 139, AS.

154 Texts collected in file "La réglementation du travail aux colonies au 1er février 1938," AFOM 382/61 bis/3, ANSOM.

155 Governor-General, Circular to Governors, 14 October 1937, K 153 (26), AS.

156 Périscope Africain, 17 April 1937, Africa, May 1937, clippings in K 153 (26), AS, and Note from Paul Vidal, forwarded to Minister by Governor-General, 20 November 1937, ibid.

157 Draft circular to Governors, n.d. [November 1937], K 152 (26), AS.

158 Note by Tap, 23 June 1937, and Draft of a letter (5 July 1937) – apparently written by Tap for the Governor-General to send to Paris to justify revising the March decree and obviously not approved or sent – K 153 (26), AS.

159 Bernard-Duquenet, Le Sénégal et le Front Populaire, 154.

160 Sûreté, "Mouvement social," 9 June 1937; list of unions, as of 1946, with founding dates, K 189 (26); "L'activité de l'Inspection du Travail de l'A.O.F.," 13 November 1937, K 73 (19), AS. For strike figures, see "Grèves en Afrique Occidentale Française, 1936–38," K 4 (1), AS. See also Governor, Ivory Coast, to Governor-General, 8 October 1938, and Governor, Guinea, to Governor-General, 5 October 1938, K 18 (1), AS; Joachim Bony, "La Côte d'Ivoire sous la colonisation française et le prélude à l'émancipation 1920–1947. Genèse d'une nation," Thèse pour le doctorat d'état, Université de Paris I, 1980, 652–57; Léopold Dossou, "Le salariat et le développement des syndicats au Dahomey 1937–1960," Thèse pour le doctorat du troisième cycle, Université de Paris VII, 1981, 52. For more on the desertion of contract workers in the Ivory Coast, see the previous section, and papers from 1937–38 in K 213 (26), AS.

161 Dakar, IT, Report on the First Semester of 1937, 2G 37–141, AS; Bernard-Duquenet, pp. 158–59.

162 FWA, report of Inspecteur des Affaires Administratives Quinquad on the dispute in Kaolack, October–December 1937, K 230 (26), AS; Bernard-Duquenet, 161–67. Dakar unions were able to negotiate contracts: the metal workers in August 1937, the building workers in September, the printers in October.

163 Renseignments, 24 July 1937, K 19 (1), AS.

164 Governor-General to Minister, 14 September 1937, same to same, 24 September 1937 (telegram), Governor-General to Governor, Senegal, 15 September 1937, Gning to Governor-General, 7 October 1937, K 18 (1), AS.

165 Other such dialogues went on with postal workers. Note of Dia Souleymane, 11 October 1937, and reply of de Coppet, 14 October 1937, K 19 (1), AS. An African union defended de Coppet against criticism from a union of white workers. Syndicat du Personnel Auxiliaire des Bureaux et Services du Gouvernement-Général de l'A.O.F. to Secretary of Fédérations des Fonctionnaires de l'A.O.F., 24 June 1938, K 181 (26), AS.

166 Individual disputes, most often over job classifications, also were handled within the inspection. Dakar, Inspection du Travail, AR, 1937, and Administrator, Dakar, to Governor-General, 27 November 1937, K 230 (26), AS.

167 See the annual reports of the Inspecteurs du Travail in the various territories.

168 This was not a universal characteristic of colonial governments under the Popular Front. Although Morocco, for example, experienced unionization on a larger scale than Senegal in the mid-1930s and something of a strike wave in 1936–38, its government considered unions inappropriate for people of this degree of "evolution" and cracked down on them. The Sultan regarded unions as infringing on his authority. William A. Hosington, Jr., writes that this "was the golden moment of the nationalist bourgeoisie, not their proletarian brethren." *The Casablanca Connection: French Colonial Policy, 1936–1943* (Chapel Hill: University of North Carolina Press, 1984), 99–101.

169 Draft Circular, n.d. [1937], from Moutet to Governors-General and Governors, copy in Moutet Papers, PA 28/5/139/E, ANSOM.

170 Dakar, IT, AR, 1937, and Report on First Semester, 1937; Administrator, Dakar, to Governor-General, 18 October 1933, K 392 (39), AS; Report of Inspector Bargues, "sur le niveau de vie des indigènes dans la circonscription de Dakar," 4 February 1939, K 273 (26), AS. The wage ranged from 5–8 francs elsewhere in Senegal to 3–3.50 in the Ivory Coast and 1.5 in Niger. In Guinea minimum wages had more than doubled since 1936; everywhere they had increased substantially in money terms. Table of minimum wages, 1 June 1939, K 261 (26); Governor, Ivory Coast, to Governor-General, 10 November 1938, K 191 (26), AS.

171 At roughly this time, nutritional surveys were also being undertaken. As in the early British surveys, poor nutrition tended to be blamed on African habits and character. Docteur Cazanove, "L'alimentation des indigènes en Afrique occidentale française," *L'Afrique Française* 46 (1936): 288–93, 339–42; Georges Hardy and Charles Richet, *L'alimentation indigène dans les colonies françaises, protectorats et territoires sous mandat* (Paris: Vigo, 1933).

172 Administrator, Dakar (Ponzio) to Governor-General, 29 October 1936, K 16 (1), AS; Dakar, IT, Report on First Semester 1937.

173 A meeting under the Inspecteur du Travail had decided in October 1938 that no adjustment of the minimum wage was necessary, and only one of the five Africans present had voted for a raise. The local administration decided this would not do and added a franc. Transcript of Meeting at the Office du Travail, Dakar, 13 October 1938, K 19 (1), AS.

174 Report of Inspector Bargues "sur le niveau de vie des indigènes dans la circonscription de Dakar," 4 February 1939, and Comment by Governor-General, 8 April 1939, K 273 (26), AS.

175 Pierre Casset, "Note portant exposé des motifs et analyses du projet de décret réglementant le travail indigène," 26 July 1937, K 218 (26), AS.

176 E. Renoux, "Analyse du projet de réglementation du travail indigène en A.O.F. élaboré par le Gouverneur Inspecteur du Travail de l'A.O.F. et communiqué pour avis aux Chambres de Commerce et d'Agriculture de la Fédération," 10 October 1937, Rapport de la Chambre d'Agriculture et d'Industrie de la Côte d'Ivoire, 11 September 1937, and letter of transmission for its president, Jean Rose, to Governor, Ivory Coast, 27 September 1937, K 218 (26), AS.

177 Directeur des Services Economiques, Note pour M. L'Inspecteur du Travail, 16 October 1937, Governor, Senegal, to Governor-General, 14 October 1937, Governor, Ivory Coast, to Governor-General, 9 October 1937, K 218 (26), AS.

178 Governor, Soudan, to Governor-General, 12 October 1937, ibid.

179 In another context, the Syndicat des Ouvriers Métallurgistes et Simulaires de Dakar (Theophile Samuel Baye, Secretary-General) called for paid holidays, the 48-hour week, collective contracts, unemployment compensation, and a pension system that would (unlike current practice) allow for the accumulation of funds by someone who worked for several different firms. Note for the Guernut Commission, 30 October 1937, Fonds Guernut 50/B12, ANSOM.

180 Governor-General to Governor, Ivory Coast, 27 October 1937, Inspecteur Fédéral du Travail, Note, 26 October 1937, ibid. In another context, de Coppet indicated that he did not believe that African workers were quite like other workers. He opposed unemployment compensation on the ground that, "I am not a partisan of unemployment indemnities in a country where the soil can nourish those who wish to cultivate it." Governor-General to Minister, 21 January 1937, K 20 (1), AS.

181 Paper on family allowances filed with Rogier to Governor-General, 19 August 1939, K 4 (1), AS.

182 The African union's request was included in the demands submitted by the Fédération des Fonctionnaires, signed by Rogier, to the Governor-General, 19 August 1939. The above quotation is taken from an undated reply to this by Boisson, and a detailed position paper on the union's demands included in the file, K 4 (1), AS. Another "temporary special indemnity" was discussed in the same correspondence, and this time officials were willing to consider it for "the cadres that include agents whose social habits and manner of life approximate those of European agents (auxiliary doctors for example)."

183 Conseil Supérieur de la France Outre-Mer, Commission des Lois Sociales, 16 December 1938, K 218 (26), AS.

184 "Note relative au mouvement social intéressant la direction de la sûreté générale en Afrique Occidentale Française pendant l'année 1938," 12 April 1939, 17G 127, AS.

185 Compte rendu of meeting of Syndicat des Travailleurs Indigènes du Dakar–Niger, 25 July 1937; Sûreté, Renseignements, 24 July 1937, 30 August 1937, K 19 (1), AS.

186 Governor, Senegal, to Governor-General, 8 October 1938, K 1 (1), AS; Acting Director of Dakar–Niger (Lascanne), Report on the incidents at Thiès, 12 October 1938, K 3 (1), AS.

187 Gning to Governor-General, 11 August 1938, and Geismar to Gning, 17 August 1938, K 1 (1), AS.

188 Lascanne Report, K 3 (1), and Governor, Senegal, to Governor-General, 8 October 1938, K 1 (1), AS.

189 These questions have been explored in a thorough and interesting manner by Iba der Thiam, "La grève des cheminots du Sénégal de Septembre 1938," Mémoire de maîtrise, Université de Dakar, 1972. In any case, it is clear that after the fact the incident was exploited in opportunistic fashion by both the Dioufistes and the Laministes, and worst of all by reactionary European interests who had no sympathy with any of the groups of African workers, but who saw it as an opportunity to get rid of de Coppet.

190 Administrator, Thiès (Cau) to Governor, Senegal, 3 October 1938, K 1 (1), AS; Thiam, 86–95.

191 Cau to Governor, Senegal, 3 October 1938, K 1 (1), Lascanne Report, 12 October 1938, K 3 (1), AS.

192 Cau to Governor, Senegal, 3 October 1938, K 1 (1); Note from Affaires Politiques et Administratives, October 1939, K 226 (26); Lascanne Report, K 3 (1); Reports by Chiefs of Subdivision Exploitation, Dakar and Guinguignéo, September 1938, and Governor-General to Governor, Senegal, 12 October 1938, K 181 (26); Sûreté, Renseignements, 5 October 1938, K 1 (1), AS; Thiam, 178–204.

193 Governor, Senegal, to Governor-General, 8 October 1938, Governor-General to Coulibaly, 30 September 1938, Sûreté, Renseignements, 7 October 1938, K 1 (1), AS.

194 The heads of departments at Thiès told Mandel's emissary that discipline had been undermined since the arrival of the Popular Front; they were particularly peeved that Giran was willing to talk to workers personally rather than hearing their complaints through channels. Renseignements, 19 October 1938, K 3 (1), AS; L'A.O.F., 14 October, 5 November 1938; Sûreté, Renseignements, 5, 6, 7 December 1938, and Note by Directeur de la Sûreté, 17 December 1938, K 2 (1), AS.

195 Sûreté, Renseignements, 5, 6, 7, 8, 9, 10, 12, 13, 14 December 1938, K 1 (1) and K 2 (1), AS; Minister to Governor-General, 8 December 1938 (telegram), K 2 (1), AS.

196 Renseignements, 19 December 1939, K 4 (1), AS.

197 "Grèves à Dakar," 1936–40, K 188 (26), AS.

198 There are no francophone equivalents to the independent investigations of wage labor in the 1930s by Wilson or the Davis team. Aside from short descriptions of Popular Front legislation and the more substantial literature on forced labor, the typical semi-academic study that emerged was Henri Labouret's exposition of what peasants could contribute and his ethnographic description of African peasant societies. He did acknowledge "the existence of a proletariat come in from the bush and with which it is necessary to reckon" but had little to say about it, certainly nothing with the empirical richness of Wilson's study. *Paysans d'Afrique occidentale*, 288 quoted.

4 Forced labor, strike movements, and the idea of development

1 Wm. Roger Louis, *Imperialism at Bay: The United States and the Decolonization of the British Empire, 1941–1945* (Oxford: Clarendon Press, 1977). Creech Jones initially thought that the Atlantic Charter should apply to Africa as well as Europe, but in the long diplomatic struggles that ensued he lent crucial support to Churchill's policy. *House of Commons Debates* 376 (20 November 1941), c. 547 and Louis, 429–30.

2 They wanted to justify, but not to be judged. Churchill remarked at Yalta that he did not want the British empire "to be put into the dock and examined by everybody to see whether it is up to their standard." Quoted in Louis, 458.

3 Cranborne quoted (from FO 371/31526) in J. M. Lee and Martin Petter, *The Colonial Office, War and Development Policy: Organization and the Planning of a Metropolitan Initiative, 1939–1945*, Commonwealth Papers 22 (London: Maurice Temple Smith, 1982), 133, and O. G. R. Williams, "Constitutional Development in West Africa," July 1943, CO 554/132/33727, PRO. Frederick Pedler recalled that when he was a young recruit to the Colonial Office he and his fellows debated such questions as the "25-year theory" versus the "50-year theory" of transition to self-government, and he recalled, "I think that when we discussed independence we were really thinking of internal self-government." Interview for Colonial Records Project, Rhodes House, Oxford University, 3–4. Cranborne's public pronouncement was milder: parts of the empire "are not yet ready for full self-government, and will not be ready for some considerable time." *House of Lords Debates* 125 (3 December 1942), c. 409.

4 C. G. Eastwood, Memorandum, 21 April 1943, CO 323/1858/9057B, PRO

5 Extract, Conclusion of War Cabinet Meeting, 9 December 1942, WM (42)166, CO 323/1858/9057B, PRO.

6 Stanley's major points were not new: self-government had for years been a declared objective, and the privileging of economic over political progress dates to the Colonial Development and Welfare Act debate. That the goal of economic assistance was to enable *each* colony to improve its financial capacities so that it could sustain a measure of social services from its own resources had been made clear to Parliament the previous year by Harold Macmillan, the Undersecretary of State. *House of Commons Debates* 380 (24 June 1942), c. 2019.

7 Oliver Stanley, *House of Commons Debates* 391 (13 July 1943), cc. 48–49, 52, 57, 63–64. Stanley's developmentalist rhetoric was also an educational

rhetoric: he stressed local government over central governing, hoping the former would be a school for the latter and would bring "the progressive improvement element" into harmony with "traditional native authorities." Ibid., c. 60.

8 Ibid., cc. 63–64.

9 Sydney Caine, Minute, 30 March 1940, CO 859/40/12901/Part II, PRO.

10 Caine, Minute, 20 December 1941, CO 852/506/15, PRO. The Secretary of State saw the war as the limiting factor: *House of Lords Debates*, 116 (2 July 1940), c. 724.

11 Lord Moyne, Circular Despatch, 5 June 1941, CO 852/482/6, PRO. Caine noted the irony of the situation: most colonies were accumulating budget surpluses that London would not allow them to spend, since it could not supply necessary goods or permit them to expend sterling abroad. For this reason, the text mentioned plans to spend the accumulated surpluses on development projects after the war. Minutes, T. W. Davies, 24 February 1941, Cosmo Parkinson, 28 March and 30 April 1941, Sydney Caine, 10 April 1941, ibid.

12 Orde Browne to Caine, 13 November 1941, enclosing his memorandum, "Some Notes on Variations in the Cost of Living in the Colonies," and Caine to Orde Browne, 16 November 1941, CO 852/506/15, PRO.

13 Dawe, Memorandum, 17 December 1941; Caine, Minute, 20 December 1941, CO 852/506/15, PRO.

14 Gerald Clauson, head of the social services department created in 1939, made a revealing concession to the weight of Caine's invocation of the laws of economics: "But my own feeling is that if Mr. Caine's thesis is sound, as presumably it is, that disposes of the matter, seeing that it is incompatible with an increase in the 'standard of living' as reflected in an increase in basic wages." Minute, 26 December 1942, CO 852/506/15, PRO.

15 Caine, Minute, 17 January 1942, regarding meeting which agreed on the text of a draft circular, dated 9 February 1942, which is what is quoted above. CO 852/506/15, PRO.

16 J. G. Hibbert, Minute, 26 August 1942, CO 852/496/7, PRO. For extensive data on inflation and supply problems and debates over them in the Colonial Office, see Timothy Sander Oberst, "Cost of Living and Strikes in British Africa c. 1939–1949: Imperial Policy and the Impact of the Second World War," Ph.D. dissertation, Columbia University, 1991.

17 Clauson wrote a draft despatch, which Caine mocked as an attempt to rewrite *Wealth of Nations*. After considerable debate, Caine concluded, "the time is not yet ripe for us to put on paper anything which can form a really effective guidance for Colonial Governments in their economic planning." Clauson backtracked, disclaiming any intention to write a "complete economic treatise." The economics department, he said, was not technically qualified to write it; if economists were asked to help, they would "never agree among themselves what to say"; and if a document emerged, the colonial governments would find it "much too long and difficult." Minutes by Caine, 26 August 1942, and Clauson, 2 September 1942, CO 852/503/17, PRO.

18 Caine, Minute, 26 August 1942, CO 852/503/17; Clauson, Memorandum on Standard of Living, 8 March 1942, ibid.

19 Dawes challenged Clauson on this last point, suggesting that "the people of West Africa would be prepared to take the risk of their own people becoming 'capitalists' rather than be 'exploited' by big white business." Lord Swinton, "Economic Policy in West Africa Colonies," Memorandum for West African War Council, WWAC (CM)(4), 24 February 1943, CO 554/132/33178, PRO; conclusions of West African War Council discussion of Swinton's memorandum at Achimota, 9–10 May 1943, CO 554/132/33712/1, PRO; Clauson, Minute, 5 May 1941, and Dawes, Minute, 10 May 1941, CO 852/430/12, PRO.

20 Lord Swinton, Minute, 14 July 1943, regarding French and British policies, CO 554/132/33727; O. G. R. Williams, "Constitutional Development in West Africa, July 1943," ibid. For an idea of the stereotypes considered acceptable in a debate in Parliament in 1942, see the remarks of one MP, Lieutenant-Colonel Wickham: "The African peasant is a simple, primitive soul whose wants are relatively few. Apart from security and justice, he wants food, shelter, clothing and small luxuries and trinkets with which to delight and bedizen his womenfolk." *House of Commons Debates* 380 (24 June 1942), c. 2063.

21 Orde Browne, "Labour Problems in Relation to Development in West Africa," 31 March 1943, CO 554/132/33178, PRO.

22 Minutes by Pedler, 17 April 1942, and Caine, 26 August 1942, CO 852/503/17, PRO.

23 Pedler, Minute, 17 April 1942, CO 852/503/17, PRO. He acknowledged that thinking realistically about workers as workers meant that the problem of unemployment had to be faced.

24 Still, the pace of change in the early war years was substantial, and the Secretary of State reported that 200 new labor laws had been passed in colonies in the past two years, while the number of labour departments had tripled and the number of labour officers quadrupled since 1937. Lord Moyne, *House of Lords Debates* 121 (26 November 1941), cc. 128, 131.

25 Lord Noel-Buxton, *House of Lords Debates* 121 (26 November 1941), c. 115; Lord Cranborne, *ibid.* 125 (3 December 1942), c. 414. There were occasional references in publications to the point brought up nearly ten years previously in *Modern Industry and the African* (chapter 2), that migrant labor led to "maladjustment" in the rural communities from which it was drawn. Margaret Read, "Migrant Labour in Africa and its Effects on Tribal Life," *International Labour Review* 45 (1942): 605–31.

26 Earl of Listowel and Lord Cranborne, *House of Lords Debates* 125 (3 December 1942), cc. 380, 414; Arthur Creech Jones, *House of Commons Debates* 376 (20 November 1941), cc. 551–52. Even the principled Fabian spokesperson Rita Hinden thought at the end of the war that at the "moment" a consensus existed around development and ILO standards. "Imperialism Today," *Fabian Quarterly* 45 (April 1945): 5.

27 The Colonial Labour Advisory Committee during the war discussed the kind of trade union legislation colonies should adopt, insisting that unions be "responsible." Sierra Leone, for example, acquired a trade union advisor in 1942; others went out shortly after the war. See the transcripts of meetings in CO 888/2, PRO, and "Trade Unionism in the West Indies and West Africa," CLAC memorandum, July 1942, CO 859/49/12254/B, PRO.

28 Governor, Nigeria, to Secretary of State, 26 October 1942, Note by J. Hollsworth and A. Dalgleish, "British Trades Union Congress and Colonial Trade Unionism," Paper for Colonial Labour Advisory Committee, 14 November 1942, and Minute by Hibbert, 30 November 1942, CO 859/49/12254/B, PRO; Governor E. J. Waddington, Northern Rhodesia, to Secretary of State, 30 August 1943, CO 859/93/12254/3/1946, PRO.

29 Another issue revealed officials' capacity to register African anger and then to put it out of mind. When the Colonial Office was considering the amalgamation of Northern and Southern Rhodesia and Nyasaland into a single unit in 1943, local officials warned that many Africans would think of this as an effort to create a giant labor reserve for Southern Rhodesia's whites and that there was a risk of "Native 'trouble'." But Andrew Cohen in London dismissed the warnings as "rather parochial." The supposed universality of the goal of increasing production apparently made him oblivious to analyzing the racial and social lines under which production would be organized. African mobilization would eventually expose his myopia and undo the amalgamation effort. Mr. Barton, "Comments on Colonial Office Memorandum of October 1943, on Future Policy in Central Africa," 8 November 1943, Governor E. Richards, Nyasaland, to Dawe, 31 October 1943, and Minute by Cohen, 14 December 1943, in CO 795/122/45104/1942–43, PRO.

30 Lewis, Minute, 22 November 1943, CO 588/12, and his resignation Minute, 30 November 1944, CO 852/586/9, PRO. The committee shortly before asked the Secretary of State, whose job it was to think about politics, to give it some direction, and his reply suggested he wanted to avoid policies that would produce radical social change, but recognized that forces beyond the Colonial Office could affect how things turned out. Answers to Memorandum from the Economic Advisory Committee, CEAC (44) 46, CO 852/588/2, PRO.

31 Caine, Minutes, 2 November 1944, CO 852/588/2, and 1 December 1944, CO 852/586/9, PRO.

32 Enough was being done on the welfare side for Lucy P. Mair to write a booklet, *Welfare in the British Colonies* (London: Royal Institute of International Affairs, 1944), but not enough for her to have very much to say, particularly as regards Africa. Aside from health and education, welfare seemed to refer to the provision of practical and moral guidance by social workers to people who had become detached from the kinship and village organizations which otherwise were the African welfare organization par excellence. An Advisory Committee on Social Welfare was appointed in London in 1943.

33 Oliver Stanley, "Provision for Colonial Development and Welfare," WP (44)643, 15 November 1944, PREM 4/43A/8, PRO.

34 For these discussions, see Caine, draft report, "Social and Economic Planning in the Colonial Empire," September 1943, CO 323/1859/9092; Caine to Evan Durban, 28 December 1943, ibid. See also D. J. Morgan, *The Official History of Colonial Development* (London: Macmillan, 1980), 1: 96–99, and Lee and Petter, *The Colonial Office, War and Development Policy*, 215–31.

35 CEAC meeting, 19 December 1944, CEAC (44) 46, CO 852/588/2. Stanley asked the Cabinet for £150 million, but settled for £120 after Churchill expressed concern at the "extreme gravity of the financial position with which

we will be faced after the war." Stanley, paper for the Cabinet, WP (44)643, 15 November 1944, and Cabinet Conclusions, 21 November 1944, W.M.(44)152, and 21 December 1944, W.M.(44)173, PREM 4/43A/8, PRO.

36 CEAC meeting, 19 December 1944. Stanley earlier wrote to governors putting "the improvement of productive and earning power (in which health and education services may well play an important part)" ahead of welfare services, "in order that eventually the dependency may be able to support itself without external assistance." Circular Dispatch, 28 April 1944, CO 852/588/2, PRO. The Colonial Office cited Nigeria as a good example of planning which stressed "developmental rather than welfare needs." CO, Detailed Points for Discussion with Chancellor of the Exchequer, November 1944, CO 852/588/11, PRO.

37 WP (44)643, PREM 4/43A/8.

38 Thus even Caine, who adamantly opposed action to raise the standard of living, favored planning and spending for social services. See his Memorandum of 12 August 1943 in CO 852/588/2 and of September 1943 in CO 8523/1959/9092.

39 *House of Commons Debates* 408 (16 February 1945), cc. 541–42, c. 552, c. 543. Such arguments were made in the privacy of Colonial Office discussion as well. The development advisor for West Africa, Noel Hall, warned of negative consequences "if the conscience of the western world demands the premature introduction of costly welfare services. The introduction of these on a large scale without a concurrent expansion of productivity will increase the dependence of the Colonies upon outside financial support and lead to methods of indirect control that may retard the development of political self-reliance." "Development Plans and Procedure," July 1944, CO 554/139/33718/1, PRO.

40 Transcript of radio discussion on the meaning and obligations of empire, 13 April 1943, ACJ, 9/5, f. 70. Creech Jones also warned against treating colonies as "preserves for European enterprise." Report of a Conference on "The Colonies, the War and the Future," Oxford, 18–20 July 1941, FCB, 69/12, p. 2.

41 Hence Creech Jones, replying to Stanley's 1943 address on colonial policy, agreed with the basic thrust of the policy, but deplored "our reliance upon commercial exploitation for the development of our dependencies" and raised specific questions on workers on settler farms in Kenya. In response to Stanley's initiative in 1945, he insisted that Governments receiving assistance under the act should enact "suitable trade union legislation." *House of Commons Debates* 391 (13 July 1943), c. 74; 408 (16 February 1945), cc. 543–44.

42 Ibid., 13 July 1943, c. 73. Compare the choice of words in Stanley's comparison of current policy with "the old, rigid system of Colonial financial self-sufficiency," or his comparison of his approach to mobilizing private finance with "the 'Get-rich-quick' type of industrial entrepreneur." Ibid., cc. 63–64, 68.

43 "My Visit to West Africa," transcript of a radio broadcast, 12 September 1944, ACJ, 9/5.

44 Ibid.

45 Anger over wartime deprivation contributed to the final collapse of the political system Britain had built up in India. Michael Cowen and Nicholas Westcott, "British Imperial Economic Policy During the War," in David

Killingray and Richard Rathbone (eds.), *Africa and the Second World War* (New York: St. Martin's Press, 1986), 33–34; John Gallagher, *The Decline, Revival and Fall of the British Empire* (Cambridge: Cambridge University Press, 1982), 134–41.

46 Colonial Office Memorandum, "Secondary Industries in West Africa, 12 February 1943," and the discussion of it at Meeting of the Africa Committee, A (43)1, 19 February 1943, CAB 95/10, and Memorandum of the Economic Advisory Committee, "The Development of Manufacturing Industries," February 1945, CO 852/578/6, PRO. The latter committee agonized over the disruption that more vigorous development, particularly industrialization, would cause to communities "still organised mainly on a tribal basis." It wanted to "soften the impact," while pushing ahead and accepting that "substantial changes in the social structure must be accepted as a necessary cost of progress." In fact, not enough was done to pose these dangers.

47 A. G. Hopkins calls the price manipulations of Marketing Boards "a forced loan in aid of the war effort." *An Economic History of West Africa* (London: Longman, 1973), 266. See also Barbara Ingham, "Colonialism and the Economy of the Gold Coast 1919–45," and R. D. Pearce, "The Colonial Economy: Nigeria and the Second World War," in Barbara Ingham and Colin Simmons (eds.), *Development Studies and Colonial Policy* (London: Cass, 1987), 229–92.

48 Minute by W. Parkinson, 5 June 1945, CO 583/275/30647/1, PRO.

49 Caine, Memoranda, September 1943, CO 823/1859/9092, and 21 November 1944, CO 852/588/11, PRO.

50 David Killingray, "Labour Mobilization in British Colonial Africa for the War Effort, 1936–46," in Killingray and Rathbone, *Africa and the Second World War*, 71–82.

51 Ibid., 82–90, 82 quoted; Forced Labour Returns, incl. Orde Browne to Grossmith, 21 April 1945, CO 859/91/4, PRO; Kenneth P. Vickery, "The Second World War Revival of Forced Labor in the Rhodesias," *International Journal of African Historical Studies* 22 (1989): 423–37; Bill Freund, *Capital and Labour in the Nigerian Tin Mines* (London: Longman, 1981).

52 He did, however, think it desirable that wives accompany migrant laborers to mines and estates. G. St. J. Orde Browne, "Labour Conditions in West Africa," *Parliamentary Papers*, 1941, IV, 1, 10–14, 16–17, 88–89.

53 Ibid., 10, 19, 22, 35.

54 Governor, Nigeria, to MacDonald, 26 August 1939, CO 859/10/1772, PRO.

55 Gold Coast, Labour Department, AR, 1938–39; Sir Arnold Hodson, Notes of Discussion with the Colonial Office, 3 October 1938, CO 96/749/31247/1, PRO.

56 Governor, Gold Coast, to Sir Arthur Dawe (in the Colonial Office), 27 May 1939, and to Secretary of State, 31 May 1939, CO 96/760/31312, PRO.

57 Gold Coast, Labour Department, AR, 1939–40.

58 Governor Burns to Secretary of State, 27 November, 2, 7, 9 December 1941 (telegrams), 10 April 1943, CO 96/774/31312, PRO.

59 Governor, Gold Coast, to Secretary of State, 29 November, 2, 7 December 1941, Minutes by A. C. Talbot-Edwards, 29 November, 1 December 1941, CO 96/774/31312, PRO.

60 Winston Churchill, Minutes, 2, 21 December 1941, ibid.
61 Richard Jeffries, *Class, Power and Ideology in Ghana: The Railwaymen of Sekondi* (Cambridge: Cambridge University Press, 1978), 31–40.
62 Frederick Cooper, *On the African Waterfront: Urban Disorder and the Transformation of Work in Colonial Mombasa* (New Haven: Yale University Press, 1987), 45–49.
63 District Officer, Mombasa, to Willan Commission, 19 September 1939, printed in *Report of the Commission of Inquiry appointed to Examine the Labour Conditions in Mombasa* (Nairobi, 1939) [Willan Commission], p. 75; *Mombasa Times*, 2 August 1939; Principal Labour Officer to Chief Secretary, Kenya, 9 August 1939, LAB 9/1835, KNA.
64 J. T. Chadwick, Minute, 8 September 1939, CO 533/507/38091/6; F. J. Pedler, Minute, 18 August 1939, Secretary of State to Governor, Kenya, 18 November 1939, CO 533/513/38397/2, PRO.
65 Willan Commission.
66 MacDonald to Governor Moore, 7 March 1940, CO 533/518/38091/6, PRO. Previously, there were labour officers, but no labour department.
67 Cooper, *On the African Waterfront*, 62–66.
68 Batson was cited frequently in the Phillips Report on Mombasa (see below) and he performed the Zanzibar social survey of 1948. See also *Enquiry into the Cost of Living and the Control of the Cost of Living in the Colony and Protectorate of Nigeria*, Colonial No. 204 (London: HMSO, 1946) [Tudor-Davis Enquiry].
69 Northern Rhodesia, *Report of the Commission Appointed to Inquire into the Disturbances on the Copperbelt, Northern Rhodesia* (Lusaka, 1940), 16, 18, 21.
70 Acting Governor, Northern Rhodesia, to Secretary of State, 4, 7 April 1940 (telegrams), CO 795/116/45109/7/pt. I, PRO.
71 Commission Report, 6, 7, 10, 26–27, 29, 32, 41–42, 46, 47.
72 Minute, Arthur Dawe, 15 May 1941, CO 795/122/45109/7, PRO.
73 Jane Parpart, *Labor and Capital on the African Copperbelt* (Philadelphia: Temple University Press, 1983), 101.
74 The delay was termed "disgraceful" by the Colonial Office, and was considered the main cause of the strike threats on the railway and in the civil service. Minutes by F. J. Pedler, 30 May 1942, CO 554/129/33669, and J. G. Hibbert, 3 June 1942, CO 859/59/12284/2, and Governor Bourdillon to Moyne, 24 January 1942, CO 583/262/30519, PRO.
75 Governor Bourdillon to Moyne, 24 January 1942, CO 583/262/30519, PRO.
76 Secretary of State to Officer Administering the Government of Nigeria, 26 March 1942, CO 583/262/30519; Acting Governor to Secretary of State, 9 June 1942, and George Creasy, Minute, 6 June 1942, Pedler, Minute, 9 May 1942, CO 554/129/33669, PRO.
77 Acting Governor to Secretary of State, 21 May 1942, 28 May 1942 (telegram), 9 June 1942, CO 554/129/33669. Pedler called this sequence of events "a classic instance of the effects of appeasement," apparently forgetting that he had recommended appeasement three weeks earlier. Secretary of State to Governor, 15 May 1942, and Minute by Pedler, 29 May 1942, ibid.
78 Acting Governor to Secretary of State, 21 May 1942, 28 May 1942 (telegram), 9 June 1942, ibid.

79 Some officials hoped the money would be saved, and if not go into such items as bridewealth, dance societies, and gambling: anything but the purchase of commodities. Pedler, Minute, 4 June 1942, and Orde Browne, Minute, 5 June 1942, ibid.

80 The fear of further "trouble" was the trump card in another battle within the Colonial Office: the economics department, fearful of the consequences of retrospective payments, suggested awarding them in the form of a savings certificate, but the head of the Africa department – who was supposed to think about politics – quashed this bright idea with the remark, "I think the African would probably regard this as a device to swindle him out of the payment to which he would regard himself as justly entitled." Acting Governor to Secretary of State, 19 June 1942 (telegram); Secretary of State to Acting Governor, 7 July 1942 (telegram); Governor Bourdillon to Secretary of State, 16 July 1942, Bourdillon to Dawe, 18 July 1942, Minutes by Sydney Caine, 26 June 1942, and Arthur Dawe, 26 June 1942, ibid.

81 Governor, Nigeria, to Secretary of State, 29 July, 3, 4, 8, 9, 15 August 1942, and Minute by Orde Browne, 7 September 1942, ibid.

82 Record of discussion among Bourdillon, George Gater, Harold Macmillan, Arthur Dawe, and O. G. R. Williams, 27 May 1942, CO 583/262/30519; Governor, Sierra Leone, to Secretary of State, 26 June 1942 (telegram), and Secretary of State to Governor Bourdillon, 5 June 1942, CO 554/129/33669, PRO. Dawe, although he participated in putting Bourdillon down, took the danger of Nigeria-style troubles spreading seriously. The Gold Coast and Sierra Leone had had labor troubles earlier, and he feared another round in Sierra Leone. Minute, 8 June 1942, ibid.

83 The Colonial Office seemed willing to slow down putting Africans into senior posts so as to avoid the question of what to pay them. The issue was finally faced by the Harragin Commission in 1945–46. Sir Charles Jeffries, "Relationship of European and African Salaries in West Africa," 12 June 1944, CO 554/134/33594/6/1945. The principle of appointing more Africans to the civil service came up occasionally in Parliament, where it was given lip service and described as inevitably a "gradual process." Lord Cranborne, *House of Lords Debates* 122 (6 May 1942), c. 937.

84 Minutes by Dawe and Gater, 11, 21 November 1942, CO 583/262/30519, PRO. Earlier, Bourdillon was privately criticized – with better reason – for failing to establish the labour department on an adequate footing. Minute by J. G. Hibbert, 4 June 1942, CO 554/129/33369, PRO.

85 Acting Governor to Secretary of State, 18 July, 4 August 1945, G. Creasy, Minute, 20 June 1945, Acting Governor to Secretary of State, 9 July 1945 (telegram), CO 583/275/30647/1, PRO; Pearce, "The Colonial Economy," 282.

86 The broadcast speech of the acting governor on June 29 made clear that the strike was illegal, but only vaguely pointed out that the strikers "cannot escape these consequences entirely." Speech incl. Secretariat, Nigeria, to Colonial Office, 29 June 1945, CO 583/275/30647/1, PRO. For Colonial Office caution, see Minutes, by G. Creasy, 26 June and 20 July 1945, and by W. Parkinson, 18 July 1945, ibid. The Secretary of State refused to let the

acting governor issue a notice threatening dismissal on the grounds that he could not make good on it. Secretary of State to Acting Governor, 24 July 1945, ibid. See also Wale Oyemakinde, "The Nigerian General Strike of 1945," *Journal of the Historical Society of Nigeria* 7 (1975): 693–710.

87 Creech Jones to J. O. Erinle, General Secretary of African Civil Servants Technical Workers Union, Lagos, 24 July 1945, incl. Creech Jones to Secretary of State, 24 July 1945; Acting Governor to Sir Arthur Richards, 31 May 1945 (extract), Secretary of State, 14 June 1945 (telegram), and 13 July 1945, and Minute by G. Creasy, 20 June 1945; Acting Governor to Secretary of State, 13 July 1945, CO 583/275/30647/1, PRO.

88 He now claimed that he had just discovered a promise made by Bourdillon in 1942 that the cost of living allowance would be revised whenever justified by a change in the cost of living; this was little more than an attempt to say that the government's honor, not its weakness, was the reason for its giving in. The Secretary of State again insisted that strikers be reinstated without prejudice to pension rights and without any penalty except loss of pay for strike days. Acting Governor to Secretary of State, 15, 23 August, 5, 7 September 1945, Secretary of State to Acting Governor, 9 August 1945, ibid.

89 Governor to Secretary of State, 21 November 1945, Creech Jones, Minute, 3 December 1945, and Colonial Office to Admiralty, 5 December 1945, and Secretary of State to Governor, 17 December 1945, CO 583/275/30647/1, PRO.

90 Governor to Secretary of State, 25, May 1946, CO 583/276/30647/6A, PRO. As Oberst ("Cost of Living and Strikes," 218–25, 249) shows, the Nigerian episode was echoed in other parts of the empire.

91 Unions brought up the inconsistency in the government's position on urban/rural incomes to the enquiry, where the point was noted and ignored. Tudor-Davies Enquiry, 10, 12–14, 17–19; Pearce, "The Colonial Economy," 272.

92 On race and the civil service in this period, see John Flint, "Scandal at the Bristol Hotel: Some Thoughts on Racial Discrimination in Britain and West Africa and its Relationship to the Planning of Decolonisation," *Journal of Imperial and Commonwealth History* 12 (1983), 74–87.

93 I am indebted to Lisa Lindsay for information on the unions' efforts, which will be developed in her forthcoming Ph.D. dissertation for the University of Michigan. See also Tudor-Davies report, 9, 17–19, and *Report of the Commission on the Civil Services of British West Africa, 1945–46* [Harragin Commission], Colonial No. 209 (1947), 19. This broad study of civil service issues had been stalled since 1942 but finally approved for fear that discontent in the civil service would lead to strikes and other problems "throughout West Africa." Memorandum of Charles Jeffries, "Relationship of European and African Salaries in West Africa," 12 June 1944; Governor, Nigeria, to Secretary of State (telegram), 24 November 1944; Minutes of O. G. R. Williams, 10 November 1944, C. Lambert, 26 July, 22 October 1945, CO 554/134/33594/6/1945, PRO. I will take up the unresolved problem of equality in the civil service in chapter 12.

94 Gardner Thompson, "Colonialism in Crisis: The Uganda Disturbances of 1945," *African Affairs* 91(1992): 606. The inquiry report blamed a "political

virus" and thought that "Everywhere the people look well fed and cheerful." Uganda, *Report of the Commission of Inquiry into the Disturbances which Occurred in Uganda During January 1945* (Entebbe, 1945), 31–32.

95 Cooper, *On the African Waterfront*, 67–71.

96 *Report of Committee of Inquiry into Labour Unrest at Mombasa* [Phillips Committee] (Nairobi, 1945), 38, 43, 49, 50–57, 65, 97. The government appointed an expert to assess Phillips' assessment, but he supported its basic arguments. Leo Silberman, *Brief Comments on Certain Sections of the Phillips Report on Labour Unrest in Mombasa* (Nairobi, 1946).

97 Phillips Report, 56.

98 Cooper, 76–78.

99 On Southern Rhodesia at this time, see Ian R. Phimister, *An Economic and Social History of Zimbabwe, 1890–1948: Capital Accumulation and Class Struggle* (London: Longman, 1987).

100 There, the "urbanized working class" was even more of a reality than in Mombasa. A significant fraction of the elite, including manufacturing interests who wanted to be assured a labor supply, favored relaxing urban influx controls to allow workers to become a fuller part of urban life. Farmers and others interested in maintaining tight control over where Africans went and channeling them into cheap farm jobs or regulated migrant labor (as the gold mines wanted) opposed such moves. The question being contested within the government was not simply one of segregation and migrancy versus stabilization – although some saw it in those terms – but exactly what mix of permanent African settlement and migration to allow and what institutions to build in order to enable such a mix to reproduce a differentiated labor force. See Deborah Posel, *The Making of Apartheid, 1948–1961: Conflict and Compromise* (Oxford: Clarendon Press, 1991) and Adam Ashforth, *The Politics of Official Discourse in Twentieth-Century South Africa* (Oxford: Clarendon Press, 1990).

101 Southern Rhodesia, *Report of the Committee to Investigate the Economic, Social and Health Conditions of Africans Employed in Urban Areas*, January 1944. These issues are discussed thoughtfully in Timothy Scarnecchia, "Residential Segregation and the Spatial Politics of Gender, Salisbury, Rhodesia, 1940–56," Ph.D. dissertation, University of Michigan, 1993.

102 Elliot J. Berg, "Real Income Trends in West Africa, 1939–1960," in Melville J. Herskovits and Mitchell Harwitz (eds.), *Economic Transition in Africa* (London: Routledge, 1964), p. 203. See also Ingham, "Colonialism and the Economy of the Gold Coast"; Pearce, "The Colonial Economy"; Freund, *Capital and Labour*; and Michael Cowen and J. R. Newman, "Real Wages in Central Kenya," unpublished paper, 1975.

103 Robert O. Paxton, *Vichy France: Old Guard and New Order, 1940–1944* (New York: Columbia University Press, 1972).

104 Richard F. Kuisel, *Capitalism and the State in Modern France: Renovation and Economic Management in the Twentieth Century* (Cambridge: Cambridge University Press, 1981), 128–51.

105 Circular of Mandel to Governors-General, 5 September 1939, and Circular for Directeurs des Affaires Economiques, 18 September 1939, AE 109 bis/1, ANSOM.

106 Claudine Cotte, "La politique économique de la France en Afrique noire (1936–1946)," Thèse de troisième cycle d'histoire, Université de Paris VII, 1981, 26–28.

107 Bertrand Mounier, *L'organisation de l'économie impériale par les comités coloniaux* (Paris: Pedone, 1942), 75, 161, 165, 167.

108 Jacques Marseille, *Empire colonial et capitalisme français: Histoire d'un divorce* (Paris: Albin Michel, 1984), 340–41.

109 Meanwhile, the Vichy organizations were becoming the object of lobbying by labor-hungry colons. Transcript of Meeting of Bureau Consultatif of Comité d'organisation des productions industrielles coloniales, 11 November 1942, AE 146/A, ANSOM.

110 "Possibilités offertes par l'autarcie: le régime du travail en A.O.F.," 17 September 1942, K 172 (26), AS. This material has the label "Mission Michaux" attached to it: Michaux was a GPC leader in Vichy.

111 Transcript of meeting of the Commission des Questions Sociales of the Comité Central des Groupements Professionnels Coloniaux, 5 February 1943, AE 51, ANSOM. For another Vichyite attack on pro-peasant colonial policy (with more references to Rousseau) and an argument for European capital and a stabilized labor force, see R. M. E. Michaux, Vice-President of the Groupement des Productions Agricoles et Forestières (speech), 21 February 1944, AE 55, ANSOM.

112 There were no fundamental objections with the Commission, only some practical concerns. René Barthes, the future Governor-General of French West Africa, thought the general principle – "any indigène must work" – should be enforced through village chiefs under control of the administration. Commission Sociale, 5 February 1943, AE 51.

113 He added, "The importance of this problem is such that it will apparently be necessary one day to regulate it at an international level to avoid competition or conflicts..." He commented favorably on the methods and results of Nazi Germany and the Stalinist Soviet Union. Comité Central des GPC, Report of the President of the session on programs in program, 10 March 1943, AE 51, ANSOM.

114 Paul Bernard to du Vivier de Streel, 5 February 1943, AE 51, ANSOM. Similarly, see "Observations de la Commission Technique (Séance du 23 mars 1943) sur les conclusions du rapport de M. du Vivier de Streel," and Letter from Comité d'Organisation du Crédit aux Colonies to du Vivier de Streel, 17 February 1943, ibid.

115 Inspecteur Général des Colonies, Commissaire du Gouverneur, to M. le Président du Groupement de la Production Industrielle Coloniale, 15 March 1943, AE 51, ANSOM. The inspector thought that only improved working conditions plus sanctions "to oblige natives to respect their contracts" would improve the labor supply, not "texts obliging indigenous populations to work."

116 Transcript of Session of the Comité Central des GPC, 7 April 1943, AE 61, ANSOM.

117 Transcript of Meeting of 4 May 1943, AE 51, ANSOM.

118 President of Chambre d'Agriculture, Guinea, to President of the Fédération Nationale des Producteurs de Fruits et Agrumes dans les Territoires d'Outre-

Mer, n.d. [late 1941], AE 51, ANSOM. There are many similar letters in this file.

119 Note of Groupement de la Production Industrielle, March 1943, ibid.

120 Speech to Académie des Sciences Coloniales, 16 February 1938, in *Bulletin de Documentation Coloniale* 124 (1–15 March 1938), 2–4; also reprinted in Pierre Boisson, *Contribution à l'oeuvre africaine* (Rufisque, Senegal: Imprimerie du Haut Commissariat de l'Afrique Française, 1942), 14–15.

121 "Trois directives de colonisation africaine," Circular to Governors and Chefs de Service du Gouverneur Général, 21 August 1941, reprinted in ibid., 59–60, 64–67.

122 "Le Devoir de la France: Directives pour un programme d'équipement administrative et économique de l'Afrique Occidentale Française," Report to the Ministry of Colonies, 1942, reprinted in Boisson, *L'oeuvre africaine*, 97.

123 Governor-General to Secrétaire d'Etat aux Colonies, 2 October 1942, AE 51, ANSOM. Officials in Vichy also worried that African peasants were too well off and too independent economically. Note on "Ravitaillement de la Metropole par l'Afrique Française," for the Conférence Economique Africaine, Vichy, 18–20 February 1942, AE 77/3, ANSOM.

124 Governor-General to Secrétaire d'Etat aux Colonies, 2 October 1942, AE 51, ANSOM. Similarly, paring down to size a request from Guinea's banana planters for an enormous increase in recruitment, he wrote, "I intend that the maximum effort be made to bring to the plantations of this European colonization that is in place the number of laborers that are necessary to it." In return, he expected better treatment of those laborers. Governor-General to Governor, Guinea, 24 April 1942, K 277 (26), AS.

125 "Le Devoir de la France," 96, 99. One advantage of relying on recruited labor for public works would be the avoidance of proletarianization. A staff report suggested that each African male could be asked to serve two years in a Service Obligatoire du Travail. Report of 23 July 1941 for Governor-General, 17G 396, AS.

126 Boisson *L'oeuvre africaine*, 74, 77, 92.

127 M. Clastre, for Chambre d'Agriculture de Guinée, to President of Fédération Nationale des Producteurs de Fruits et Agrumes dans les Territoires d'Outre-Mer, nd. [June 1942], K 277 (26), AS; M. de Bressieux, President of the Groupement des Productions Agricoles et Forestières, in transcript of meeting of Comité Central des GPC, 18 March 1942, AE 64 bis, ANSOM, and Note for Boisson, 13 April 1942, K 277 (26).

128 Governor-General to Secretaire d'Etat aux Colonies, Vichy, 22 June 1942, K 277 (26), AS.

129 Transcript of meeting of Comité Central, 4 November 1941, AE 146/A, ANSOM; "Etude sur les possibilités en main d'oeuvre de l'Afrique Occidentale Française" [early 1942], K 296 (26), AS. Boisson's view received backing in Vichy from the Secrétaire d'Etat, Brévie, who himself had held Boisson's position in West Africa. Brévie to President of the Comité Central des GPC, 16 October 1942, and to Boisson, 20 October 1942, AP 639/3, ANSOM.

130 Boisson to Secrétaire d'Etat, 2 October 1942, AE 51; Bernard to Boisson, 19 June 1942, Boisson to M. le Délégué Permanent en A.O.F. du Groupement

Professionel de la Production Industrielle Coloniale, 21 March 1942, Bernard to President of the Comité Central des GPC, 2 April 1942, AE 57/DE, ANSOM.

131 "Note du Président du Groupement des Productions Industrielles Coloniales sur le problème du travail obligatoire en Afrique Occidentale," 6 March 1944, in AE 146/A, ANSOM. This argument on the subterranean nature of forced labor strikingly parallels the inspection report of 1931 quoted in chapter 2 – although the earlier report was arguing against forced labor as much as this one was arguing for it.

132 H. Pruvost, "Rapport de l'Inspecteur des Colonies, Inspecteur Général des Affaires Administratives, sur la main d'oeuvre en Côte d'Ivoire," 10 February 1943, K 123 (26), AS; Governor Latrille, speech to Conseil de Gouvernement, 23 December 1943, 51; Administrateur Supérieur de la Haute Côte d'Ivoire (E. Louveau) to Governor, Ivory Coast, 4 April 1940, and Governor to Governor-General, 24 April 1940, K 288 (26), AS. Louveau, early in the Vichy years, was fired and arrested for engaging in pro-Free French activity.

133 Pruvost Report; Hubert Deschamps, "Etude sur la main d'oeuvre," 23 November 1941, Deschamps Papers, PA 36/II/14C, ANSOM.

134 Governor, Ivory Coast, to Governor-General, 11 January 1942, AP 2808/3, ANSOM.

135 Deschamps, who knew what his readers liked to see, was careful in his reports to quote Boisson's views on the peasant nature of African society and the need to avoiding proletarianization, while exercising careful control of the peasantry. Governor, Ivory Coast, to Governor-General, 30 June 1941, Governor to Governor-General, 21 September 1941, PA 36/II/14B, and "Etude sur la main d'oeuvre," 23 November 1941, Deschamps Papers, 36/II/14C, and Governor to Governor-General, 11 January 1942, AP 2808/3, ANSOM.

136 Commandant de Cercle, Ouagadougou, to Governor, Ivory Coast, 3 January 1942 (telegram), K 296 (26); Inspecteur du Travail Becq, in transcript of meeting of Chambre d'Agriculture et d'Industrie de la Côte d'Ivoire, 15 June 1941, K 288 (26), AS.

137 Letter from Aubin, Administrateur des Colonies, to Cdt. Jean Gracieux, Etat-Major, Saint-Louis, 27 July 1943, letter intercepted 14 August 1943, 17G 121, AS. Aubin submitted his resignation which was sent on with an unfavorable recommendation by his Commandant de Cercle.

138 Remarks of M. Pays, President, and M. Lagrosse, Secretary, Transcript of Meeting of Chambre d'Agriculture et d'Industrie de la Côte d'Ivoire, 15 June 1941, K 288 (26), AS.

139 Governor Rey, "Note sur l'application de la réglementation du travail en temps de guerre en Côte d'Ivoire," 9 July 1943, K 149 (26), AS.

140 Pruvost Report, 10 February 1943, K 123 (26), AS. Labor inspectors' reports made similar points. Ivory Coast, IT, AR, 1943, 1944.

141 Governor to Governor-General, 29 December 1941, AP 2808/3, ANSOM. See also extensive correspondence in K 277 (26), AS, and for a careful study, Babacar Fall, *Le travail forcé en Afrique Occidentale française, 1900–1946* (Paris: Karthala, 1993).

142 Governor-General to Governor, Soudan, 10 December 1940, K 186 (26), AS.

143 The leadership of the Office were cozy with Vichy, and their vision of large-scale, centrally directed agricultural development was about as close to reality as Vichy planning got: it resulted in much brutality and little output. Myron Echenberg and Jean Filipovich, "African Military Labour and the Building of the Office du Niger Installations, 1925–1950," *Journal of African History* 27 (1986): 541; Governor, Soudan, to Governor-General, 23 December 1941, 18G 75 (17), AS; Guinea, IT, AR, 1943.

144 Note by the Directeur des Affaires Politiques et Administratives (Berthet) pour M. le Procureur Général, 30 April 1942, K 304 (26), AS. There was doubt whether French contract law contained sanctions against desertion, since these workers had not entered a contract. Procureur Général, note pour le Directeur des Affaires Politiques et Administratives, 29 June 1942, Governor, Guinea, to Governor-General, 23 November 1943 (citing decision of the Chambre d'annulation de Dakar, 29 January 1942), Procureur Général to Procureur, Guinea, 10 December 1943, Governor-General to Governor, Senegal, 10 June 1944, Directeur des Affaires Politiques, Administratives et Sociales to Procureur Général, 30 December 1944, K 304 (26), AS.

145 Thus the governor of the Soudan, replying to Boisson's survey of the manpower situation in late 1941, noted that there were few firms employing wage labor. "But as soon as it is a question of private or public organisms that use many workers, they can only be recruited with the help of the heads of administrative circumscriptions acting under the orders of the Chief of the Colony." Governor, Soudan, to Governor-General, 23 December 1941, 18G 75 (17), AS.

146 Governor-General, Circular to Governors, 5 November 1942, K 186 (26), AS.

147 When the flow of *navétanes* diminished with the wartime consumer goods shortages, officials used force to keep it flowing. The post-Vichy regime thought it would have to continue to do so, but the voluntary flow of navétanes picked up by early 1945, when labor for white farmers was still in doubt, and the end of the coercive regime – not surprisingly – occurred earlier and with less agony. Governor-General to Commissaire des Colonies, 10 March, 18 April 1945 (telegram), Commissaire to Governor-General, 21 March 1945 (telegram), IGT 75/1, ANSOM.

148 Governor, Senegal, to Governor-General, 14 January 1942, AP 2808/3, ANSOM. Interestingly, the doyen of French ethnographers in Senegal was implying much the same thing. Théodore Monod, head of the Institut Français d'Afrique Noire, wrote a "Rapport sur l'organisation des recherches ethnologiques en A.O.F.," 1 December 1941, 18G 75 (17), AS. He asked, apropos of external influences on African life: "Does this evolution only have happy effects? Is it useful to regard what is usually called 'material and moral well-being' as if the one and the other were forever associated for African populations? Is it desirable to see the rhythm of industrialization accelerate without end, when we know what redoubtable dangers – detribalization, proletarianization, demoralization – can be its ransom?"

149 Cotte, "Politique économique," 93–95; Recensement de la main d'oeuvre, Senegal, 1942, annex to Governor, Senegal, to Governor-General, 14

January 1942, K 296 (26), AS; Enquête au sujet de la main d'oeuvre à Dakar, 1939, K 257 (26), AS. The Dakar census – approximate as it is – showed somewhat over 6,000 permanent workers in private employment and 2,500 on government worksites, plus a similar number of temporary workers.

150 Circonscription de Dakar et Dépendances, AR, 1941, 1943 copies in AP 3450/6, ANSOM. The 1941 report noted a modest increase in artisanal activity because of the decline in imports.

151 Governor-General to Administrateur, Conscription de Dakar, 24 August 1940, and to Secrétaire d'Etat aux Colonies, Vichy, 29 August 1941; idem, Circular Telegram, 24 August 1940, and Circular Letter, 25 October 1940, all in AP 2808/3; Circonscription de Dakar, AR, 1943, in AP 3460/9, and 1944, in AP 3450/11, ANSOM.

152 Amiral Decoux, Hanoi, to Colonial Administration, Vichy, 18 October 1943 (telegram), and Amiral Blehaut, Vichy, to Haut Commissaire, Saigon, 21 September 1943, file on "Groupements: Extension de la Charte du travail aux territoires coloniaux," AE 64 bis, ANSOM.

153 Some of Vichy's verbiage did get the attention of hierarchy-sensitive local administrators. A labor inspector announced his hope to remake the labor regulations "in line with the principles of the hierarchical and authoritarian regime over which the MARECHAL presides." Such action "would attach without doubt the indigène to his work and to his employer, and would insure the cohesion of patrons and workers in the accomplishment of the social task of National Renovation." Dakar, AR, 1941, copy in AP 3450/6, ANSOM.

154 Governor-General, Circular to Governors, 25 September 1941, and Procureur Général (R. Attuly), Note pour M. le Directeur des Contributions Directes de l'A.O.F., 3 December 1943, Draft Circular of Governor General, November 1943, Governor, Guinea, to Governor-General, 7 October 1944, Administrator, Dakar, to Governor-General, 5 November 1943, K 323 (26), AS; Governor-General, Circular to Governors, 3 August 1941, K 255 (26), AS. On Vichy's interest – through its natalist and profamily ideology – in family allowances, see Remi Lenoir, "Family Policy in France since 1938," in John Ambler (ed.), *The French Welfare State* (New York: New York University Press, 1991), 150–51

155 "Note sur la main d'oeuvre indigène dans l'industrie," Dakar, 24 February 1942, K 172 (26), AS.

156 Ibid. Laura Lee Downs notes similar concerns with restraining the labor market in France during World War I. *Manufacturing Inequality: The Construction of a Gender Stratified Workforce in the French and British Metalworking Industries, 1914–1935* (Ithaca: Cornell University Press, 1995).

157 Note by Directeur des Affaires Politiques et Administratives pour M. le Procureur Général, 30 April 1942, and Procureur Général to Directeur des Affaires Politiques et Administratives, 29 June 1942, K 304 (26), AS.

158 Governor-General to Secrétaire d'Etat aux Colonies, October 1942, K 299 (26), AS. The requisition decree of 1939 was intended to prevent people in defense-related industries from accepting higher wages in the civilian sector. Officials noted it was useful in preventing strikes as well. Boisson had

initially warned that it should be used "with the greatest moderation," but by 1942 he was reminding civil servants that if they tended to leave their posts they could be requisitioned. Administrator, Dakar, to Governor-General, 24 October 1940, Governor-General to Administrators, 14 November 1940, Governor-General to Governors, 10 August 1942, K 252 (26), AS.

159 "Coût Normal de la Vie à Dakar," 1943, K 273 (26), AS. These figures are for bachelors. The figures for families and for Africans living European-style show inflation rates of the same order of magnitude.

160 Dakar, AR, 1941, in AP 3450/6, ANSOM; Administrator, Dakar, to Governor-General, 10 July 1942; Directeur Général des Finances to Directeur des Affaires Politiques et Administratives, 5 June 1942, K 273 (26), AS.

161 Brian Weinstein, Eboué (New York: Oxford University Press, 1972); Elikia M'Bokolo, "French Colonial Policy in Equatorial Africa in the 1940s and 1950s," in Prosser Gifford and Wm. Roger Louis (eds.), The Transfer of Power in Africa: Decolonization 1940–1960 (New Haven: Yale University Press, 1982), 173–210.

162 Eboué was not averse to using forced labor for administrative purposes and defended this position at Brazzaville. Weinstein, 116, 300–1.

163 Félix Eboué, circular of 8 November 1941, reprinted as La nouvelle politique indigène pour l'Afrique Equatoriale Française (Paris: Office Française d'Edition, 1945), 11, 12. As an administrative officer in Oubangui-Chari, Eboué had constructed his local empire around close relations with chiefs: he even formed a marriage-like alliance with the most important of the chiefs, paying bride-price for the chief's daughter, by whom he had a child. After a rebellion, Eboué turned prisoners over to this chief and did not ask too many questions about their fate. He continued to rely on chiefly author-itarianism during the 1940s and strongly opposed assimilation and citizen-ship for Africans. Weinstein, 48–50, 227, 272.

164 Eboué, Nouvelle politique, 19, 47, 48, 52.

165 A fuller version of this argument came from the Ecole Supérieure Coloniale, a haven of mildly progressive thinking: cities contained a "kernel" of skilled workers, the "crucible out of which must come the new societies, built on principles which approach ours," living side by side with an "inorganized and moving mass of the floating population," "vagabondes de l'embauche" (vagrants of the job market), "evil doers of all sorts." The former were to be encouraged with better wages and urban living conditions, against an expec-tation that they work at a "metropolitan work rhythm." The latter were to be kept in check or expelled by the police. J. G. Desbordes, "Transformation économique et sociale du monde noire depuis 1914 dans les villes," Mémoire de l'Ecole Supérieure Coloniale, 1944.

166 Eboué, 27, 32, 33, 55. These ideas resemble in some ways those of French writers, notably LePlay, on the dangers of urban crowds: the colonial progressive and the metropolitan reactionary had something in common.

167 Boisson, circular on Youth, 26 April 1939, 17G 122, also reprinted in L'oeuvre africaine.

168 Governor-General to Minister, 3 September 1945, K 324 (26), AS.

169 Discours du Gouverneur-Général Pierre Cournarie, Opening of the Session of the Conseil de Gouvernement, December 1943, AP 872/14, ANSOM.

170 Commissaire aux Colonies to Governor-General, 4 April 1944, and to President of Conseil Français des Approvisionnements, 3 April 1944, AE/Correspondance Economique/141, ANSOM; Secrétaire de la Production, Algiers, to Governor-General, 16 March 1943, K 172 (26), AS.

171 Commissaire aux Colonies to President of the Comité Economique, 22 April 1944, AE/Correspondance Economique/141, ANSOM. The Free French allies were not helping much: available textile supplies were largely going to British West Africa, making it hard for French officials to develop an incentive structure for wage laborers. John Kent, *The Internationalization of Colonialism: Britain, France, and Black Africa, 1939–1956* (Oxford: Clarendon Press, 1992), 104–6.

172 Governor Latrille, speech to Conseil de Gouvernement, 20 December 1943, in Procès Verbal of Conseil (Dakar, 1944), 49–53.

173 Secretary-General (Digo) to Governors of Ivory Coast and Guinea, 13 April 1944 (telegram), K 149 (26), AS. Pleven had shortly before warned Cournarie not to let "foreign opinion ... suspect our will for realization" after it had been stimulated by the reformist zeal displayed at Brazzaville. Commissaire des Colonies, Algiers, to Governor-General, 31 March 1944, ibid. Cournarie, defending the gradualist approach, seemed to equate the peculiarity of the African with the peculiarity of the colon: "The mentality of European settlers, like that of autochthonous workers, will take a long time to reform." Governor-General to Commissaire des Colonies, 26 August 1944, IGT 75/1, ANSOM.

174 This is the conclusion of a study of the Korhogo region, Nancy Ellen Lawler, *Soldiers of Misfortune: Ivorien 'Tirailleurs' of World War II* (Athens: Ohio University Press, 1992), 207–8.

175 Directeur des Affaires Politiques to Governor-General, 27 August 1943, K 299 (26), AS; Governor-General, Circular to Governors, 29 April 1943, K 392 (39), AS; Secrétaire à la Production, Alger, to Governor-General, 16 March 1943, and resolution of the Haut Conseil Economique, session of 3 March 1943, K 172 (26), AS.

176 Report of the Commission Permanente du Conseil de Gouvernement, 15 February 1943, K 299 (26), AS; Secrétaire à la Production, Alger, to Governor-General, 16 March 1943, K 172 (26), AS.

177 Administration de Dakar, AR, 1940, 1941, 1943.

178 Syndicat des Travailleurs Indigènes du Chemin de Fer Dakar–Niger to Governor-General, 12 August 1943; Governor-General to Secretary-General of Syndicat des Travailleurs Indigènes, 30 August 1943, K 299 (26), AS.

179 Directeur du Personnel to Directeur des APAS, 14 November 1942, Directeur des Travaux Publics, Note, 1 July 1942, Directeur Général des Finances, "Note au sujet de la grève des ateliers du Benin–Niger," 25 June 1942, K 273 (26), AS.

180 Directeur des APAS to Governor-General, 27 August 1943, K 299 (26), AS; intercepted letter from a group of auxiliaries of the Benin–Niger, Cotonou, to Directeur Général des Transports, Dakar, 19 June 1943, K 273 (26), AS; Renseignements, Senegal, 16, 27 April 1943, K 273 (26), AS.

181 Sûreté, Renseignements, Senegal, 27 April 1943, and October 1943; Général des APAS to Secrétaire Général of Gouvernement Général, 30 June 1943, K 273 (26), AS.

182 M. Despour, Manutention Africaine, to M. Landiech, Directeur, Manutention Africaine, 8 September 1943, Governor-General to Administrator, Dakar, September 1943, K 273 (26), AS.

183 The Inspection was to insure that unions stuck to "economic, commercial and agriculturalist interests," not politics. Dakar, AR, 1943.

184 Requisitioning workers into the armed forces to prevent them from quitting their jobs was thought to be ineffective in regard to "workers or laborers whose names are uncertain and whose residence is unknown." Sous-Chef, Etat-Major, Commendament des forces terrestres et aériennes, Instructions, 3 July 1943, K 252 (26), AS. The anonymous urban mass did indeed limit the instruments of state control.

185 There was a strike in Conakry in 1943, but the labor movement was still concentrated in Dakar, as it had been in 1936–38. This was about to change.

186 Dakar, IT, AR, 1944.

187 Soldes de Personnel of Gouvernement Général, decision of 12 September 1943, K 273 (26), AS. The adjustment proposed for October 1943 would not have kept workers' wages up with the inflation of 1943–44.

188 Conclusions de la Commission d'Evaluation des Salaires Normaux, 23 June 1943, K 273 (26).

189 Dakar, AR, 1944.

190 Most of the growth apparently took place in 1943, but these figures are highly suspect. Dakar, AR, 1943, 1944; Denise Bouche, "Dakar pendant la deuxième Guerre mondiale. Problèmes de surpeuplement," *Revue Française d'Histoire d'Outre-Mer* 65 (1978): 423–37.

191 Dakar, AR, 1943, 1944; Senegal, Rapport Economique Annuel, 1941, 1944.

192 President of the Syndicat des Entrepreneurs Français des Travaux Publics et de Batiments de l'Afrique Occidentale Française to Governor-General, 15 December 1943, K 273 (26), AS.

Conclusion to Part I: posing the labor question

1 John Kent, *The Internationalization of Colonialism: Britain, France and Black Africa, 1939–1956* (Oxford: Clarendon, 1992), 106, 141, 147–49; Marc Michel, "La coopération intercoloniale en Afrique noire, 1942–1950: un néo-colonialisme éclairé?" *Relations internationales* 34 (1983): 155–71.

2 Kent, 115.

Introduction to Part II

1 Charles S. Maier, "The Two Postwar Eras and the Conditions for Stability in Twentieth-Century Western Europe," *American Historical Review* 86 (1981): 327–62; Peter Baldwin, *The Politics of Solidarity: Class Bases of the European Welfare State 1875–1975* (Cambridge: Cambridge University Press, 1990); Susan Pedersen, *Family, Dependence and the Origins of the Welfare State: Britain and France, 1914–1945* (Cambridge: Cambridge University Press, 1993).

2 This period witnessed democratic openings – followed by closings down – in other parts of the world. See for example Leslie Bethell and Ian Roxborough,

"Latin America between the Second World War and the Cold War: Some Reflections on the 1945–8 Conjuncture," *Journal of Latin American Studies* 20 (1988): 167–89.

3 Benedict Anderson, *Imagined Communities: Reflections on the Origin and Spread of Nationalism*, revised ed. (London: Verso, 1991).

5 Imperial plans

1 René Pleven, "Preface," *Renaissances* (October 1944), 7; Arthur Creech Jones, speech to Summer Conference on African Administration, 19 August–2 September 1948, 21. Looking back at this period a few years later, the French colonial intellectual Henri Labouret saw anti-colonial arguments – from inside and outside colonies – as the crucial force motivating French reformism. He was now arguing that France had to respond gracefully to aspirations of people in its colonies, but he still emphasized France's positive role in education and development. *Colonisation, colonialisme, décolonisation* (Paris: Larose, 1952).

2 Claude Levy, "les origines de la Conférence de Brazzaville, le contexte et la décision," and Charles-Robert Ageron, "La préparation de la Conférence de Brazzaville et ses enseignements," in Institut Charles de Gaulle and Institut d'Histoire du Temps Présent, *Brazzaville Janvier–Février 1944: Aux sources de la décolonisation* (Paris: Plon, 1988), 21–40. See also the testimonies of eyewitnesses to the conference, ibid., 41–73.

3 A Comité Français de la Libération Nationale document in preparation for Brazzaville rejected "self-government" (the English word appears in the text) as goal, and insisted: "Let us affirm without reserve, our absolute desire to give our colonial possessions the most generous status. Let us show ourselves to be, in all international colonial conferences, the most liberal and the least imperialist nation." 20 November 1943, AP 2288/4, ANSOM.

4 Eboué's position was attacked by the other governor of West Indian origin, Raphael Saller, who insisted that "the aim of our colonization is to civilize," and then asked rhetorically, "In these conditions, how can we usefully impose on the African any evolution in a framework other than our own and with limits which will leave him different from us? Will he not be tempted to infer immediately from this that we are opposed to his improvement, that we want to maintain him in a state which gives us superiority over him?" Transcript of Session of 3 February 1944, AP 2295/2, ANSOM.

5 The recommendations of the conference are reprinted in *La Conférence Africaine Française. Brazzaville 30 Janvier–8 Février 1944* (Brazzaville: Editions du Baobab, 1944).

6 This issue was discussed at length at a meeting of the "Commission chargée de l'étude des mesures propres à assurer aux colonies leur juste place dans la nouvelle constitution française," Session of 30 May 1944, AP 214, ANSOM.

7 Transcript of Session of 2 February 1944, AP 2295/2, ANSOM; "Note de la Direction Générale des Services Economiques," AP 2295/1, ANSOM; Direction Générale des Affaires Politiques, Administratives et Sociales, "Programme Générale de la Conférence de Brazzaville," 28 December 1943, and A. Drogue, Reporter, "Rôle et place des européens dans la colonisation," 20 January 1944, AP 2201/7, ANSOM.

8 Anyone who could prove that he had worked 18 months for a private employer was to be exempted from the service. Ibid., and *Conférence*, 55–56.

9 "Programme Générale," 1943, AP 2201/7.

10 "Note de la Direction Générale des Services Economiques" in response to Circular of 29 November 1943, AP 2295/1.

11 "Rapport sur l'industrialisation des Colonies," by Mahe, and Transcript of Session of 7 February 1944, AE 101/5, ANSOM; "Note de la Direction Générale des Services Economiques," AP 2295/1, ANSOM; *Conférence*, 60–61. See also René Mayer, "Politique Economique de l'Afrique Equatoriale Française," Paper for Brazzaville Conference, AP 2295/1, ANSOM.

12 Brazzaville Conference, "Les Grandes lignes de la politique économique," AE 101/5, ANSOM.

13 "Programme Générale," AP 2201/7. See also A. Drogue, "Rôle et place des européens dans la colonisation," ibid., and "L'industrialisation des territoires d'Outre-Mer," Algiers, 28 January 1944, AP 2288/7, ANSOM.

14 Session of 1 February 1944, AP 2295/2, ANSOM.

15 "L'industrialisation des territoires d'Outre-Mer," 28 January 1944, AP 2288/7; AOF, Note du Chef du Service du Commerce, Direction Générale des Services Economiques, "Rôle des européens dans le commerce," AP 2201/7; Commission pour l'Etude des Questions Relatives au Personnel, Rapport Général, AE 101/5, all in ANSOM.

16 M. Poimboeuf, Assemblée Consultative Provisoire, *Compte rendu analytique officiel*, session of 20 March 1945, 1–2.

17 "Rôle et place des européens," 1944, and "Programme générale," 1943, AP 2201/7. Some administrators talked about demography in language more appropriate for cattle breeders: "Faire du noire" or "faire de l'indigène" [make blacks, make natives]. Ibid., and Governor Fortune, session of 2 February 1944, AP 2295/2, ANSOM.

18 Session of 2 February 1944, AP 2295/2, ANSOM.

19 "Everything is to be expected from this policy; increase in population, supervision, stability and political allegiance, production." Drogue, "Rôle et place des européens dans la colonisation," AP 2201/7. Planning was pushed by Georges Peter, Directeur des Affaires Economiques, who had previously served Vichy. See his presentation of the report of the Commission de l'Economie Impériale, session of 1 February 1944, AP 2295/2; "Les grandes lignes de la politique économique," AE 101/5. Self-identified socialists among the conferees also shared the faith in planning and cited the Soviet planning model as a case in point. Hubert Deschamps, "Note sur la politique coloniale," 8 January 1944, AP 2288/1. See also the remarks of Henri Laurentie to the "commission chargée de l'étude...," session of 30 May 1944, AP 214.

20 See, for example, Henri Laurentie, "Les colonies françaises devant le monde nouveau," *Renaissances* (October 1945), 3–13.

21 "Etude des questions concernant la main d'oeuvre en Afrique Occidentale Française en vue de la discussion de ces questions à la conférence internationale du travail de Philadelphia, d'avril 1944," K 24 (1), AS

22 Giacobbi to Governor-General, 27 August 1945 (telegram), 17G 140, AS.

23 Report by M. E. du Vivier de Streel (of Vichy notoriety) on the conclusions of a meeting of the Académie des Sciences Coloniales, 21 September 1945,

encl. in Académie des Sciences Coloniales to Minister, 22 October 1945, IGT 29, ANSOM.

24 D. Bruce Marshall, *The French Colonial Myth and Constitution-Making in the Fourth Republic* (New Haven: Yale University Press, 1973); Rudolf von Albertini, *Decolonization: The Administration and Future of the Colonies, 1919–1960.* Trans. by Francisca Garvie (New York: Holmes & Meier, 1971); François Borella, "La conférence de Brazzaville dans le débat politique français après 1944," in Institut Charles de Gaulle, *Brazzaville*, 327–40.

25 Before the Constituante, the only African representative in the French Parliament was elected by the Four Communes of Senegal. In the first Constituante, citizens and non-citizens from French West Africa each had six seats (although the citizens' seat for Senegal went to an African), French Equatorial Africa two each, and Madagascar two each. Overall, the Constituante included 23 deputies elected by non-citizens, 36 elected by colonial citizens, and 5 by mixed electorates, out of a total of 586. Marshall (141, 162–71) discusses the importance of African deputies in handling colonial affairs.

26 In one debate, Edouard Herriot noted that "citizens of overseas territories will be more numerous than citizens of the metropole," so that "France will become... the colony of its former colonies." To that, Léopold Senghor, now a deputy, replied, "That is racism!" Assemblée Nationale Constituante, *Débats* 2 (27 August 1946): 3334.

27 von Albertini, 392–95. The franchise for colonials gradually expanded, from a highly subjective collection of elites – including "notables," holders of French decorations, veterans, property owners, regular wage earners in legally recognized establishments, holders of hunting or drivers' licenses – to include all those who could read in French or Arabic (1947), heads of taxpaying families (1951), and finally all citizens (1956). In French West Africa, voters as a percentage of the population went from 7 in 1946 to 53 in 1957. Ruth Schachter Morgenthau, *Political Parties in French Speaking West Africa* (Oxford: Clarendon, 1964), 55–56, and Joseph Roger de Benoist, *L'Afrique Occidentale Française de 1944 à 1960* (Dakar: Nouvelles Editions Africaines, 1982).

28 Doudou Thiam, "La Portée de la citoyenneté française dans les territoires d'outre-mer," Thèse pour le doctorat en droit, Université de Poitiers, 1951 (Paris: Société d'éditions africaines, 1953), 48. Thiam notes not only the mystique of citizenship, but also the collective rites in which citizens engaged, the common judicial processes, and the rights – including social rights – attached to the quality of citizenship. He concludes, "To say to an African or a Malagasy that he is a French citizen, is it not to ask him in a sense to grow a new skin, to rid himself of the totality of the traditions that make his personality?" Ibid., 81.

29 Max Glass, "Des colonies, ou pas de colonies," *Cahiers du Monde Nouveau* 4, 7 (1948): 4, 15; Michel Berveiller, "L'Europe d'Outre-Mer," ibid., 50.

30 Senghor pointed out that the concept of tutelage, by which many officials tended to assert that they were first among equals, undid much of what egalitarian rhetoric accomplished. Léopold Senghor, "Défense de l'Afrique noire," *Esprit* 112 (July 1945), 247–48. He was engaging the inclusive, but still

hierarchical, rhetoric of colleagues like Henri Laurentie, "Les colonies françaises devant le monde nouveau," *Renaissances* (October 1945), 10; Robert Delavignette, "L'Union Française à l'échelle du monde, à la mesure de l'homme," *Esprit* 112 (July 1945), 222.

31 Administrator, Dakar, to Governor-General, 16 December 1943, K 273 (26), AS; Note for the General Conference of the International Labour Organization, Philadelphia, 24 April 1944, AP 2288/4, ANSOM.

32 "Etude critique du projet de décret instituant un Code du Travail pour les Territoires Français d'Afrique relevant du Ministre de la France Outre-Mer," incl. Governor-General to Minister, n.d. [1944], K 316 (26), AS.

33 Ibid.; Governor-General to Governor, Guinea, 28 August 1944, K 149 (26), AS.

34 Report of the Direction des Affaires Politiques, Administratives et Sociales to the meeting of the Conseil du Gouvernement de l'A.O.F., December 1944 (Rufisque: Imprimerie du Gouvernement-Général, 1945), 126; IGT, AOF, to IGT, France, 17 December 1945, K 438 (179), AS; Speech of Colonial Minister (Giacobbi), in Assemblée Consultative Provisoire, *Compte rendu analytique officiel*, Session of 20 March 1945, c. 10.

35 Governor-General to Colonies, 14 December 1945 (telegram), Colonies to Governor-General, 17 January 1946, Pélisson to Inspecteur Général du Travail (Paris), 6, 17 December 1945, IGT 75/1, ANSOM.

36 Pélisson to IGT, Paris, 6, 17 December 1945; Governor-General to Minister, 14, 29 December 1945 (telegrams); Minister to Governor-General, 29 December 1945, 17 January 1946 (telegrams), IGT 75/1, ANSOM.

37 Copy of Deputies' Letter to Moutet, 22 February 1946, in AP 960/Syndicalisme, ANSOM. The private letter was indeed much stronger than the public article published some months before by Senghor, in which he simply listed the abolition of forced labor among several demands concluding an eloquent critique of the notion of "evolution" and the idea that Africans had to acquire civilization before they could acquire rights. Senghor, "Défense de l'Afrique noire."

38 Moutet to Senghor, 11 March 1946, AP 960/Syndicalisme, ANSOM.

39 Annexe No. 565, *Documents de l'Assemblée Nationale Constituante*, session of 1 March 1946, 554.

40 Interventions of d'Arboussier, Louis-Paul Aujoulat, and Doula Manga Bell, *Débats de l'Assemblée Nationale Constituante*, 2 (20 March 1946), 900–2, 905, 908.

41 Annexe No. 811, *Documents de l'Assemblée Nationale Constituante*, Session of 30 March 1946, 780–83.

42 *Débats de l'Assemblée Nationale Constituante*, 2 (5 April 1946): 1514 (on forced labor) and 1514–51 (on elections).

43 According to Houphouët-Boigny, Moutet – after the African deputies had submitted their proposed law – offered to issue instead a decree banning forced labor. Houphouët-Boigny refused, and thought that the weaker decree would have been subverted by the colons had the issue not been forced in the Assemblée. Testimony of Houphouët-Boigny, 31 May 1950, in *Rapport No. 11348 sur les incidents survenus en Côte d'Ivoire*, Annexe to the Procès-Verbal of Session of 21 November 1950, Assemblée Nationale, and reprinted by the Partie Democratique de la Côte d'Ivoire, 1: 19.

44 Minister to Governor-General, 2 April 1946, K 355 (26), AS. The government-general revealingly told local officials, "you will be expected to win over, to persuade, to move a mass for whom in too many memories work appeared as servitude, and to make them think of it as the source of material and moral satisfaction." Forced labor had taught the wrong lessons. Governor-General to Minister, 25 May 1946, with text of Circular, 21 May 1946, AP 960/22, ANSOM.

45 Commissaire des Colonies, Algiers, to Governor-General, 31 March 1944; Secretary-General, French West Africa, to Governors of Ivory Coast and Guinea, 13 April 1944 (telegram), K 149 (26), AS.

46 At times, Cournarie seemed to damn planters and laborers with the same conception of backwardness: "The mentality of the European settlers, like that of the indigenous workers, will take a long time to reform." Governor-General to Commissaire aux Colonies, 26 August 1944, IGT 75/1, ANSOM.

47 Extracts of letter of 26 July 1945, Governor-General to Minister, AP 960, ANSOM. Habits of command died hard. Officials in Paris as late as January 1946 were willing to consider a decree allowing the requisition of labor "in exceptional and temporary" situations for works of public interest "in order to assure the execution of plans for economic and social development." They were warned by the director of economic affairs not "to go back on, by a devious route, a clearly established principle." Proposed decree, drafted by the Inspecteur Général du Travail, 24 January 1946, and Notes by the Director of Political Affairs, 9 February 1946, and the Director of Economic Affairs, 4 February 1946, AP 960; Denise Bouche, "La réception des principes de Brazzaville par l'Administration en l'A.O.F.," in Institut Charles de Gaulle, *Brazzaville*, 211.

48 Note from the Inspecteur Générale du Travail for M. le Directeur du Plan, 28 November 1945, AP 960, ANSOM.

49 There were also concerns about maintaining banana cultivation in Guinea as well as the supply of seasonal migrants to Senegal's peanut fields. Officials guiltily pondered using coercive methods in both cases in 1945, but a combination of adequate flows of migrant labor and the abolition legislation of 1946 got them off the hook. See Babacar Fall, "Economie de plantation et main d'oeuvre forcée en Guinée française: 1920–1946," *Labour, Capital and Society* 20 (1987): 8–33; Governor-General to Commissaire des Colonies, 10 March, 18 April 1945 (telegram), Commissaire to Governor-General, 21 March 1945 (telegram), IGT 75/1, ANSOM.

50 Ivory Coast, IT, AR, 1944.

51 Directeur des Affaires Politiques, Administratives et Sociales (Berthet), "Relève des principals affaires en instances intéressantes la Côte d'Ivoire," 10 May 1944, K 288 (26), AS.

52 Governor to Governor-General, 18 April 1944 (telegram), K 149 (26), AS. In fact, the base line was a theoretical labor force, not an actual one. In 1943, officials had been unable to meet the recruitment quotas in the Lower Coast (that is, the present boundaries of the Ivory Coast, excluding the supposed "reservoir" of manpower in the sometime-colony Upper Volta, which was at the time part of the Ivory Coast). Account of Inspecteur du Travail Carrieu to Meeting of officials and planters, 19 December 1944, transcript in K 321 (26), AS.

53 Governor Latrille to Governor-General, 27 June 1944, K 149 (26), and Secretary-General Digo to Governor-General, 22 December 1944, reporting on the Abidjan Conference with officials and planters, 17–19 December 1944, K 321 (26), AS.

54 Ivory Coast, IT, AR, 1944, 1945; Dubled, for Chambre d'Agriculture et d'Industrie, to Governor, Governor-General, and Commissaire aux Colonies, 14 August 1944, and Governor-General to Dubled, 4 September 1944; Saller to Latrille, 27 September 1944, AP 2807/3, ANSOM; Latrille, testimony, 1950, p. 1071.

55 Governor Latrille, Monthly Political Report, August 1944, K 403 (132), AS; Ivory Coast, IT, AR, 1945. Houphouët-Boigny described the birth of the SAA as the result of "cruel disappointments" facing African cocoa farmers: discriminatory marketing policies, denial of recruited labor to Africans, and the "quasi-impossibility" of hiring voluntary laborers because of the extent of flight to the Gold Coast. The SAA specifically agreed on métayage as their solution to the labor problem. "Intervention du Président F. Houphouet à l'assemblée générale extraordinaire du Société Agricole Africaine de la Côte d'Ivoire," 25 March 1944, 71 Syndicats I, (7) Dossier 1, CRDA.

56 Governor Latrille, report, 1944, quoted in Ivory Coast, Political Report, 1946.

57 Testimony, *Rapport ... sur les incidents,* 31 May 1950, 7 June 1950, Vol. 1, 12, 17.

58 Governor Latrille, Monthly Political Report, August 1944, K 403 (132), AS; Ivory Coast, IT, AR, 1944.

59 Houphouët-Boigny, Testimony, *Rapport ... sur les incidents,* 31 May 1950, 9; Ivory Coast, IT, AR, 1944; A. J. Lucas, "Enquête sur la condition des travailleurs en Côte d'Ivoire," n.d. [mid 1945], K 363 (26), AS. Particularly interesting is Houphouët-Boigny's description of the métayage system to an audience of colons who refused to believe that a planter could extend such terms and still make a profit. Transcript of Meeting of officials and planters, Abidjan, 19 December 1944, K 321 (26), AS.

60 Ivory Coast, IT, AR, 1944.

61 "Rapport sur le Régime du Travail Indigène, par le Gouverneur Latrille," 20 February 1945, marked "Very secret. Do not distribute." AE 576/23, ANSOM. See also the reports of A. J. Lucas, Inspecteur des Colonies, "Considérations générales sur le travail en Côte d'Ivoire," 7 May 1945, and "Enquête sur la condition des travailleurs indigènes en Côte d'Ivoire," n.d. [mid. 1945], K 363 (26), AS. Part of the Lucas mission was a study of voltaic migrants to the Gold Coast by the anti-imperialist geographer Jean Dresch and the ethnologist-writer Michel Leris. They looked positively on the situation of migrant cocoa farm workers in the Gold Coast, very critically on that of forced laborers in the Ivory Coast. The administration would be better off encouraging the voluntary migration of entire families to the Lower Coast, and better still should "leave the worker in peace." "Rapport sur les migrations des travailleurs de la Côte d'Ivoire", 21 April 1945, reprinted in Jean Dresch, *Un Géographe au déclin des empires* (Paris: Maspero, 1979), 148–62.

62 Moro Naba to Governor, 23 July 1945, K 149 (26), AS.

63 Governor Latrille to Governor-General, 2 August 1945, and Governor-General to Governor, 25 August 1945; Report of Administrateur Supérieur

de la Haute Côte d'Ivoire (Mourgues) to Governor, 20 July 1945, Commandant du Cercle, Ougadougou, to Administrateur Supérieur, 20 July 1945, Commandant du Cercle, Koudougou, to Administrateur Supérieur, 2 July 1945, Commandant du Cercle, Tenkogogo, to Administrateur Supérieur, 18 July 1945, K 149 (26), AS.

64 At the end of 1945, officials were contemplating ending new recruitment but easing the labor crunch by prolonging the contracts of some 10,000 Mossi currently in the Lower Coast. The acting governor, de Mauduit, wanted to do this by fiat and to defer new regulations on forced labor until 1 January 1947, but Cournarie would only allow contracts to be extended when each individual so chose, and he reminded the governor that "obligatory recruitment effected on the eve of the abolition of forced recruitment would constitute a grave breach of the spirit of new legislation." Draft of "note relative à la main d'oeuvre en Côte d'Ivoire," by the secretary-general (Digo) of the government-general in Dakar, n.d. [January 1946], Governor-General to Governor, Ivory Coast, 10 January 1946 (telegram), Governor-General to Director of Public Works, 18 March 1946, K 363 (26), AS; Ivory Coast, Political Report, 1945.

65 "This wage would correspond to the normal cost of life. This is definitively the solution adopted in Dakar where out of the recent events emerged the idea of the permanent laborer, or the specialized laborer, or the heavy-duty laborer [manoeuvre de force]." The allusion to the general strike in Dakar (chapter 6) undoubtedly reflects the fact that top officials were obsessed by those events. The "permanent laborer" – distinguished from the temporary worker – was a key figure in official minds. Now, he was being put forward not only as a way of resolving a general strike, but as a means to solving the labor problems of agriculture in the Ivory Coast. Draft of "note relative à la main d'oeuvre en Côte d'Ivoire," by the secretary-general (Digo) of the government-general in Dakar, n.d. [January 1946].

66 Marshall, *The French Colonial Myth*, 141.

67 Governor de Mauduit to Governor-General, 6 November 1945, with Governor-General's (undated) marginal note, 17G 146, AS; de Mauduit to Governor-General, 20 December 1945, K 363 (26), AS.

68 Directeur Général des Affaires Politiques, Administratives et Sociales (Berlan), "Note pour M. le Directeur du Cabinet," 14 February 1946, "Note sur la situation politique en Côte d'Ivoire," for Affaires Politiques, 13 July 1946, 17G 146, AS.

69 Governor-General to Minister, 3 September 1945, K 324 (26), AS; Governor-General to Ministry, 19 April 1946 (telegram), AP 960/Travail, ANSOM.

70 A more serious discussion had taken place two years earlier in a more private forum, the "Commission chargé de l'étude des mesures propres à assurer aux colonies leur juste place dans la nouvelle constitution française," 30 May 1944 (transcript in AP 214, ANSOM). Development was seen as an expression of France's universalizing ability, and this justified a highly centralized approach in coordinate development efforts.

71 Assemblée Nationale Constituante, *Annales* 4 (12 April 1946): cc. 1756–58.

72 Inspection Générale des Travaux Publiques des Colonies, Plan d'équipement des Territoires d'Outre-Mer. Afrique Occidentale Française Section I: Dépenses d'intérêt social, et dépenses diverses. Notice Justificative, 8 February

1945, by Ingénieur en Chef des Travaux Publics, 1 Q 162 (74), AS. See also Gwendolyn Wright, *The Politics of Design in French Colonial Urbanism* (Chicago: University of Chicago Press, 1991).

73 FWA, IT, AR, 1946. Ouezzin Coulibaly, in the Assembly of the French Union, referred to the April 1946 law as "the second liberation of the slaves." Assemblée de l'Union Française, *Débats*, 2 February 1949, p. 45. For the portrayal in Ivorian hagiography of Houphouët-Boigny as liberator, see "Il y a vingt ans Houphouet-Boigny faisait abolir le travail forcé," *Bingo* 15, 7 (February 1966), 18–20, 46.

74 FWA, IT, AR, 1946.

75 On Guinea, Senegal, and the Soudan, see Babacar Fall, *Le travail forcé en Afrique Occidentale Française, 1900–1946* (Paris: Karthala, 1993).

76 M. Combier, for IGT, "Rapport sur l'état actuel du problème de la main d'oeuvre en Côte d'Ivoire," 13 July 1946, K 450 (179); Ivory Coast, IT, AR, 1946; Ivory Coast, Political Report, 1945, 1946; FWA, IT, AR, 1946; FWA, Direction Générale des Affaires Politiques, Administratives et Sociales, Note on "La main d'oeuvre en Côte d'Ivoire," December 1946, K 363 (26), AS.

77 IGT, FWA, to IGT, Paris, 18 July 1946, K 450 (179), AS. Anticipating labor problems, the railway had apparently decided in later 1945 to switch to coal, but it had not yet been able to do so. Officials, as early as March, had seen the possibility of ending their dependence on European wood-cutters in favor of the Régie's own woodlots and a hoped-for "indigenous cooperative of wood-cutting." Governor-General to Directeur des Travaux Publics, 18 March 1946, and Directeur des Chemins de Fer de l'A.O.F. to Governor-General, 3 July 1946, K 363 (26), AS. In the Soudan, indigenous entrepreneurs had long supplied firewood. James A. Jones, "The Impact of the Dakar–Niger Railway on the Middle Niger Valley," Ph.D. dissertation, University of Delaware, 1995, chapter 5.

78 FWA, Direction Générale des Affaires Politiques, Administratives et Sociales, Note on "La main d'oeuvre en Côte d'Ivoire," December 1946, K 363 (26); Combier, "Rapport," K 363 (26); IGT, AOF, to IGT, Paris, 18 July 1946, K 450 (179); and report of Mission Berlan, September 1946, K 363 (26), all in AS. Paris was receiving information through a second channel, which told them of the European "sabotage" and the success of African wood cutters – Houphouët-Boigny himself. Houphouët-Boigny to Secrétariat d'Etat aux Colonies (telegram), 13 June 1946, AP 960, ANSOM.

79 Mission Berlan, Compte Rendu, September 1946, K 363 (26), AS; Ivory Coast, Politics, AR, 1946. According to a government survey, coffee farms had 13 percent of their optimum labor force in June–July and 54 percent in December, while banana plantations fell to 26 percent in June–July, but surpassed their usual work-force level in December. FWA, IT, AR, 1946.

80 FWA, Direction Général des Affaires Politiques, Administratives et Sociales, "La main d'oeuvre en Côte d'Ivoire," December 1946, K 363 (26), AS; AOF, IT, AR, 1946; "Aperçu sur l'évolution économique et la situation économique de la Côte d'Ivoire," 1949, 1Q 21 (2), AS.

81 FWA, IT, AR, 1946, 47–49; FWA, Direction Général des Affaires Politiques, Administratives et Sociales, December 1946, K 363 (26); Combier Report, July 1946, K 450 (179), AS; IGT, "Rapport relatif à l'évolution du problème

de la main d'oeuvre en Côte d'Ivoire et à son incidence sur la situation économique locale," 5 November 1946, AP 960, ANSOM.

82 FWA, IT, AR, 1946, 33–34.

83 Combier; Direction Général des Affaires Politiques, Administratives et Sociales, "Note sur la main d'oeuvre en Côte d'Ivoire," August 1946, K 363 (26), AS, with note by Governor Latrille. In any case, the citizenship law of 1946 made controls on Africans' movements obsolete. Governor General, circular to Governors, 2 October 1946, K 363 (26), AS.

84 In 1947, the governor-general told the governor of the Ivory Coast, who had complained about desertion and other familiar sins of African workers, that the concept of desertion no longer made much sense in an era of free labor. Much of the so-called instability of workers, he thought, was really seasonality, and he reminded the governor that "the desire, perfectly understandable, of the black peasant to take care of his own agricultural work must not be contradicted." Governor-General to Governor, Ivory Coast, 23 July 1947, IGT 5/10, ANSOM.

85 Ivory Coast, IT, AR, 1946; FWA, IT, AR, 1946; IGT, FWA, "Rapport relatif à l'évolution du problème de la main d'oeuvre en Côte d'Ivoire et à son incidence sur la situation économique locale," 5 November 1946, AP 960, ANSOM; Mission Bargues, September 1946, K 363 (26), AS; Mission Bargues, 1946–47, AP 950, ANSOM.

86 FWA, IT, AR, 1946; Directeur des Chemins de Fer de l'AOF to Governor-General, 3 July 1946, K 363 (26), AS.

87 FWA, IT, AR, 1947; Ivory Coast, Political Report, 1946; Ivory Coast, IT, AR, 1945, 1946.

88 Report to Governor by Administrateur Supérieur, Haute Côte d'Ivoire, incl. Governor to Governor-General, 28 February 1946, K 363 (26), AS.

89 There was an earlier meeting of the Etats-Généraux in Doula, in the Camerouns, and shortly thereafter French colons had set off a riot in their anger at a strike by African workers and the government's willingness to tolerate it. Richard Joseph, "Settlers, Strikers and Sans-Travail: The Douala Riots in September 1945," *Journal of African History* 15 (1974): 669–87.

90 Report of 6th Commission, "Travail," to Etats Généraux de la Colonisation Française, August 1946, and Closing Speech by Jean Rose, 24 August 1946, AE 576, ANSOM.

91 Houphouët-Boigny to Secrétariat d'Etat aux Colonies (telegram), 13 June 1946, AP 960, ANSOM.

92 Moutet to Governor-General, 11 May 1946, AP 960/22, ANSOM.

93 Combier; IGT, AOF, to IGT, Paris, 18 July 1946, K 450 (179), AS.

94 Myron Echenberg and Jean Filipovich, "African Military Labour and the Building of the *Office du Niger* Installations, 1925–1950," *Journal of African History* 27 (1986): 541; Ivory Coast, Political Report, 1946; Senegal, IT, AR, 1945.

95 The director of the railway used almost the same words, "Such a hotbed [foyer] of disorder cannot be allowed to exist any longer." Délégué du Gouvernement du Sénégal à Dakar to Governor, Senegal, 15 April 1947, and note by Directeur de la Régie des Chemins de Fer, 18 March 1947, K 360 (26), AS.

96   Soudan, Monthly PoliticaL Reports, May 1946, 2G 46–134, AS.
97   Echenberg and Filipovich, 549–50.
98   The political report for the Ivory Coast for 1946 made vague allusions to recruitment still being "far from the free labor which we wanted to install in the Ivory Coast," but made no specific reference to who was twisting whose arm, and comments like this quickly disappeared from official reports.
99   Latrille's speech to Conseil Général de la Côte d'Ivoire, 13 January 1947, from *Journal Officiel de la Côte d'Ivoire*, 15 January 1947, in Agence France Outre-Mer 393, ANSOM.
100 When the stabilization of labor forces became a major issue at the end of the 1940s, it was discussed intensively by senior bureaucrats within the Colonial Office, and one of the most interesting discussions took place in the Legislative Council of Kenya (*Debates*, 21 December 1949), but it wasn't mentioned in Parliament except in laundry lists of colonial topics at the annual debate on colonial affairs.
101 "An old story, that," interjected another MP as Arthur Creech Jones recited the 1948 version. Creech Jones, Gallacher, *House of Commons Debates* 453 (8 July 1948), c. 594. Similar policy declarations were made in ibid., 425 (9 July 1946), c. 238, and 441 (29 July 1947), cc. 266–67.
102 Tony Smith, "Patterns in the Transfer of Power: A Comparative Study of French and British Decolonization," in Prosser Gifford and Wm. Roger Louis (eds.), *The Transfer of Power in Africa: Decolonization 1940–1960* (New Haven: Yale University Press, 1982), 87–155; Miles Kahler, *Decolonization in Britain and France: The Domestic Consequences of International Relations* (Princeton: Princeton University Press, 1984).
103 Ernest Bevin, for example, argued, "What I am afraid of is that if we have to go on pushing manufactured goods into the hard currency areas, in a short time we may find ourselves in another form of collapse, because the rest of the world and ourselves will not be consuming our goods, and the areas in which we are trying to sell them will become a bottleneck." Given the need to "produce the raw material in short supply in the United States," Bevin became "a strong advocate of colonial development, which I regard as more vital than ever now." Minute by Bevin to Prime Minister, 7 July 1947, FO 371/62557/5666, PRO. See also P. J. Cain and A. G. Hopkins, *British Imperialism: Crisis and Deconstruction 1914–1990* (London: Longman, 1993), 276–81.
104 The most explicit defense of a kind of social imperialism came from John Strachey, Minister of Food, who wanted "to look at the world's resources as one economic whole" in which the United Kingdom was one of the key "consuming markets" and the "Colonial Empire is essentially one of the primary producer areas." Memorandum, 6 October 1947, FM 47/22, PREM 8/456, PRO. The empire could save Great Britain (and the Labour Government) from – as a result of the dollar shortage – "going downhill [from] what the Americans believe is the already miserable British diet." Memorandum, "Food Import Programme, 1947–48," 31 May 1947, CP (47) 170, PREM 8/489, PRO.
105 D. K. Fieldhouse, "The Labour Governments and the Empire-Commonwealth, 1945–51," in Ritchie Ovendale (ed.), *The Foreign Policy of*

the British Labour Governments, 1945–1951 (Leicester: Leicester University Press, 1984), 84–88; David Goldsworthy, *Colonial Issues in British Politics 1945–1961: From "Colonial Development" to "Winds of Change"* (Oxford: Clarendon Press, 1971); P. S. Gupta, *Imperialism and the British Labour Movement, 1914–1964* (New York: Holmes & Meier, 1975); Stephen Howe, *Anticolonialism in British Politics: The Left and the End of Empire, 1918–1964* (Oxford: Clarendon Press, 1993). A more positive view of the trade union left in colonial affairs comes from a former Fabian Colonial Bureau member, Marjorie Nicholson, *The TUC Overseas: The Roots of Policy* (London: Allen & Unwin, 1986).

106 Fred L. Block, *The Origins of International Economic Disorder: A Study of United States International Monetary Policy from World War II to the Present* (Berkeley: University of California Press, 1977); Anthony Carew, *Labour under the Marshall Plan: The Politics of Productivity and the Marketing of Management Science* (Manchester: Manchester University Press, 1987). On the way Anglo-American diplomacy and American dollars constrained British colonial policy – eventually making it into an uneasy sort of Anglo-American joint venture – see Wm. Roger Louis and Ronald Robinson, "The Imperialism of Decolonization," *Journal of Imperial and Commonwealth History* 22 (1994): 462–512.

107 Transcript of African Governors' Conference, 12 November 1947, 37–40. Frederick Pedler, the bright young star of the Colonial Office, saw that the British loss of power in Asia, combined with the fact that Africa's potential was so unrealized, implied that "Africa is now the core of our colonial position; the only continental space from which we can still hope to draw reserves of economic and military strength." Creech Jones also saw Africa as the key after the loss of India. Pedler, Minute, 1 November 1946, CO 847/35/47234/1/1947; Memorandum by the Secretary of State on Report of the Chief of the Imperial General Staff on Tour of Africa, incl. Private Secretary to Prime Minister's Office, 6 January 1948, PREM 8/923, PRO.

108 Bevin quoted in Hugh Dalton diaries, 15 October 1948, cited in R. D. Pearce, *The Turning Point in Africa: British Colonial Policy, 1938–1948* (London: Cass, 1982), 95–96. Similarly, Creech Jones telegraphed the Gold Coast about his "anxiety to ensure greatest possible increase in gold production in immediate future." Secretary of State to Governor, Gold Coast, 31 October 1947 (telgram), CO 96/795/31312/1947, PRO. In Southern Africa, copper had "first priority." Memorandum on Supply of Copper by Rhonkana, Nchanga, and Rhodesian Copper Refineries, 27 November 1947, FO 371/62559, PRO.

109 African Governors' Conference, 12 November 1947, 37–40.

110 Secretary of State, special message to the colonies on Britain's economic position, 21 August 1947, ACJ 67/2. Officials told each other that "those overseas should realise" that Great Britain's economic troubles stemmed from the war it fought for "the preservation of the freedom of the peoples everywhere and that the prosperity of Britain is an essential factor in promoting the well being and economic prosperity of the Colonial peoples." Sir T. Lloyd (Colonial Office) to Treasury, 26 July 1948, reprinted in Ronald Hyam (ed.), *British Documents on the End of Empire.* Series A, Vol. II: *The*

Labour Government and the End of Empire 1945–1951, Part 2 (London: HMSO, 1992), 72.

111 Circular Despatch from Secretary of State Hall to Governors, 12 November 1945, reprinted in Hyam, 9–12.

112 Creech Jones was explicit in calling the "importance of increasing production in the Colonies" the reason for creating the CDC. Cabinet Memorandum, "development of colonial resources," 6 June 1947, CM (47) 75, CAB 129/19, PRO. For a fuller analysis, see Michael Cowen, "Early Years of the Colonial Development Corporation: British State Enterprise Overseas during Late Colonialism," *African Affairs* 83 (1984): 63–75.

113 Bevin, Memorandum, 4 October 1947, PM/47/139, PREM 8/456, PRO. There was much handwringing over this issue: Creech Jones, "Prices of Colonial Export Products," draft of a memorandum, March 1947, CO 852/989/3, and T. I. K. Lloyd, "The Colonial Empire and the Economic Crisis," Circular despatch on behalf of the Secretary of State for the Colonies, 26 July 1948, T 229/220, both reprinted in A. N. Porter and A. J. Stockwell (eds.), *British Imperial Policy and Decolonization 1938–64. Vol. I: 1938–51* (London, Macmillan, 1987), 274, 299–300; Sir Frank Stockdale, comments at Meeting of Colonial Primary Products Committee, 29 May 1947, FO 371/62557/7990; Memorandum by Strachey, 6 October 1947, FM 47/22, PREM 8/456; Creech Jones, Speech to African Governors' Conference, 1947, 23, and Transcript of Session of 14 November 1947, 66–68; Creech Jones, Memorandum on "Development of Colonial Resources," 6 June 1947, CM (47)/75, CAB 129/12; Consensus of Meeting of Colonial Labour Advisory Committee, 25 October 1948, CO 888/5, PRO.

114 Report of the Colonial Development Working Party, 1948, 4–5, CO 852/868/5, PRO; Creech Jones, "Development of Backward Areas," 1949, ACJ 44/1, f. 158.

115 Fieldhouse, "The Labour Governments and the Empire-Commonwealth," 95–99. Officials even thought about cancelling sterling balances – confiscating the colonies' accumulated earnings – but decided this was politically unwise and "would look extremely odd as an off-set to our development and welfare policy." Minute by Sydney Caine, 1 July 1946, reprinted in Hyam, *British Documents*, 21. In 1950, a leading scholar of imperialism, W. K. Hancock, pointed out that development spending had been an "anti-climax," while the persistence of the colonial sterling balances amounted to financial aid from the colonies to the United Kingdom. *Wealth of Colonies: The Marshall Lecturers, Cambridge, 17 and 24 February 1950* (Cambridge: Cambridge University Press, 1950), 62–63. See also P. T. Bauer, *West African Trade: A Study of Competition, Oligopoly and Monopoly in a Changing Economy* (Cambridge: Cambridge University Press, 1954), and Yusuf Bangura, *Britain and Commonwealth Africa: The Politics of Economic Relations, 1951–75* (Manchester: Manchester University Press, 1983).

116 Creech Jones to Cripps, 19 November 1949, ACJ 44/1, ff. 133–36 (emphasis in original); "Economic Development in the Colonies: Note of the Secretary of State for the Colonies," 5 February 1948, ACJ 44/2, f. 20. The trouble the Colonial Office had in coming up with these statements can be seen from the various drafts and minutes thereon from February to March 1948 in CO

537/3930, PRO. This human capital theory became the standard line to argue for welfare provisions within colonial development programs. Colonial Development Working Party, "Interim Report," 19 April 1948, and Note by Chairman on "The Future Work of the Colonial Development Working Party," 27 April 1948, EPC (48) 35, PREM 8/923; Memorandum sent by Secretary of State to Prime Minister, "Economic Development in the Colonies," 5 February 1948, PRO.

117 "Some Practical Achievements in the Colonies since the War," Colonial Office Paper, 7 December 1948, ACJ, 44/2.

118 Memorandum by Secretary of State on Report of the Chief of the Imperial General Staff on Tour of Africa, incl. Private Secretary to Prime Minister's Office, 6 January 1948, PREM 8/923, PRO.

119 African Conference, 29 September–9 October 1948, Minutes of Session of 29 September 1948, 18.

120 Report of the Colonial Development Working Project, p. 43, CO 582/868/5; Memorandum by Secretary of State on Report of Chief of Imperial General Staff, incl. Private Secretary to Prime Minister's Office, 6 January 1948, PREM 8/923, PRO.

121 These difficulties were acknowledged by Creech Jones in a Parliamentary debate on colonial affairs. *House of Commons Debates*, 453 (8 July 1948): c. 598. The Colonial Office tried gamely to tell governors how to explain to their subjects why consumption and investment were being held back by the British government in the era of development. Circular letter from Sir T. Lloyd enclosing memorandum on "The Colonial Empire and the Economic Crisis," 26 July 1948, reprinted in Richard Rathbone (ed.), *British Documents on the End of Empire*. Series B, Vol. 1: *Ghana, Part I, 1941–1952* (London: HMSO, 1992), 90–98.

122 This argument was made at the Cabinet level in 1951: Memorandum on the Implications of the Colonial Balance of Payments Position, C (51) 22, CAB 129/48. See also Secretary of State (Griffiths) to Sir Richard Acland, 26 January 1951, CO 537/7598. It was made earlier in reaction to the Accra riots of 1948 in *Report of the Commission of Enquiry into Disturbances in the Gold Coast, 1948*, Colonial No. 231 (London, 1948), p. 38, and in Colonial Office Minutes, 18 November 1947, CO 96/795/31312/1947, PRO. The Nigerian government also explicitly sought to reduce the money in rural producers' hands in order to combat inflation, especially in food prices. Governor, Nigeria, to Secretary of State, 15 September 1950, CO 583/309/30585, and Governor to Cohen, 29 January 1951, CO 583/310/30647/15/1951, PRO.

123 One estimate was that 41 percent of total projected investment in the colonies in 1948 would go to local labor. Colonial Office, "Inflation in the Colonies," 1948–49, CO 852/1052/1, PRO.

124 *House of Commons Debates*, 443 (6 November 1947): c. 2054. Another MP took African agricultural practices back to "Biblical times." Macpherson, *House of Commons Debates* 453 (8 July 1948), c. 632.

125 Creech Jones, Speech to Governors' Conference, November 1947, p. 22; opening address to Summer Conference on African Administration, 19 August–2 September 1948, p. 21. Another high Colonial Office official came back from Africa telling his colleagues "how thin is the veneer of civil-

isation" in West Africa, and that "the West African is nothing like as advanced as the Malay or the Burman and of course far behind the Chinese." Report by Mr Rees-Williams to Mr Creech Jones, "West African tour – 1948," CO 537/3226, reprinted in Rathbone, *British Documents on the End of Empire*, 99.

126 Governor Mitchell of Kenya to Creech Jones, 30 May 1947, CO 847/35/47234/1/47, PRO. This letter, and its enclosed note, is in fact a long diatribe about the primitiveness of Africa, the moral depravity of much of its population, and the corruption and skullduggery of its politicians.

127 C. R. Attlee, *As It Happened* (London: Heinemann, 1954), 191. See also Ronald Hyam's comments on this question in his "Introduction," *British Documents*, Part 1, xxxv.

128 Caine, Minute, 23 April 1946, Cohen, Minute, 6 May 1946, CO 852/1003/3, PRO.

129 Sydney Caine, Minute, 23 April 1946, CO 852/1003/3, PRO. Cohen wrote in the margin next to this passage, "I agree: the Wilson recent book on Central Africa explains this well from the sociological point of view. ABC." His reference is to Godfrey Wilson, *An Essay on the Economics of Detribalization in Northern Rhodesia,* Rhodes–Livingstone Papers 5 (Livingstone: Rhodes-Livingstone Institute, 1941).

130 Caine, Minute, 23 April 1946, CO 852/1003/3, PRO.

131 "Report of the Committee on the Conference of African Governors," Sydney Caine, Chairman, 22 May 1947, "Appendix VI: The Economic Development of Agricultural Production in the African Colonies," CO 847/36/47238, PRO. Cohen, citing his recent visit to East Africa, had previously minuted, "I believe personally that it is the low efficiency of the African farmer more than the limited development of local government bodies which has held back economic advance." Minute, 24 September 1946, CO 852/1003/3. The Parliamentary undersecretary for the colonies also attacked the "wasteful methods of native agriculture and the inertia of the native farmer." Statement of Economic Policy Committee, EPC (48), 18th Meeting, 6 May 1948, PREM 8/923, PRO.

132 Statement made in 1946, quoted by David Throup, *The Economic and Social Origins of Mau Mau, 1945–53* (London: James Currey, 1987), 46.

133 Henrietta L. Moore and Megan Vaughan, *Cutting Down Trees: Gender, Nutrition, and Agricultural Change in the Northern Province of Zambia, 1890–1990* (London: James Currey, 1994), 110–28; Michael Havinden and David Meredith, *Colonialism and Development: Britain and its Tropical Colonies, 1850–1960* (London: Routledge, 1993), 276–83. Throup, *Economic and Social Origins of Mau Mau,* shows the dangerous political effects of both pro-settler and imposed soil conservation policies in Kenya, but misinterprets them as peculiar to the Kenya government rather than shared with London. On the history of conservationism, see William Beinart, "Soil Erosion, Conservationism and Ideas about Development: A Southern African Exploration, 1900–1960," *Journal of Southern African Studies* 11 (1984): 52–83. The quotation is from Economic Policy Committee, EPC (48), 18th meeting, 6 May 1948, PREM 8/923, PRO.

134 Caine, Minute, 24 April 1946, and Cohen, Minute, 6 May, 1946, CO

852/1003/3, PRO. Cohen added, "Compulsion may have to be resorted to, but inducement will I think be a more powerful method..."
135 Secretary of State, Circular Despatch, 22 February 1947, CO 852/1003/3. A later despatch (13 July 1948, CO 852/1003/4) was even more specific on the powers to be given Native Authorities and special boards in water and soil conservation projects.
136 Creech Jones himself called for an "agricultural revolution" in the letter of 22 February 1947, CO 852/1003/3, and again in 1949, adding "The African peasant must abandon his traditional ways...." Address to Summer Conference on African Administration, Cambridge University, 3rd Session, 15–27 August 1949.
137 Compulsion also crept in through the retention into the 1950s of penal sanctions for workers who violated contracts, another way in which the peculiarity of the African justified a coercive approach to labor discipline that had been abandoned in England. Great Britain's failure to implement fully the convention against penal sanctions is duly noted in International Labour Conference, "Report of the Committee of Experts on the Application of Conventions and Recommendations," 33rd Session, 1950, copy in CO 859/182/3, PRO.
138 Throup, *Economic and Social Origins of Mau Mau*, 140–64. Elsewhere, soil erosion projects also led to serious political conflict. Beinart, "Soil Erosion," and Steven Feierman, *Peasant Intellectuals: Anthropology and History in Tanzania* (Madison: University of Wisconsin Press, 1990), 160–203.
139 Creech Jones, Circular Despatch, 25 February 1947, CO 847/35/47234/1/1947, PRO. He recognized that educated Africans would have to fill positions of responsibility, but agonized that this "may result in the creation of a class of professional African politicians absorbed in the activities of the centre and out of touch with the people themselves." See also John W. Cell, "On the Eve of Decolonization: The Colonial Office's Plans for the Transfer of Power in Africa, 1947," *Journal of Imperial and Commonwealth History* 8 (1980): 235–57.
140 G. B. Cartland, Memorandum, "The Political Significance of African Students in Great Britain," July 1947, reprinted in Hyam, *British Documents*, Part 4, 13–17. This memorandum led to a discussion among top officials and to the setting up of a "Consultative Committee on the Welfare of Colonial Students." Editor's note, ibid., 20–21, and report on meeting, 24 March 1948, ibid., 21–24.
141 Ronald Robinson's memoranda, 1947, in CO 847/44/3 and CO 847/38/3, as well as Minute by Cartland, 29 December 1947, CO 847/35/9/3, cited in Ronald Hyam, "Africa and the Labour Government, 1945–1951," *Journal of Imperial and Commonwealth History* 16 (1988): 151. The program for "mass education" was actually a community centered effort at "all forms of betterment." Circular despatch from Creech Jones to African governors, 10 November 1948, reprinted in Hyam, *British Documents* Part 4, 60–62. The Summer Conference on African Administration, 2nd session, 19 August–2 September 1948, Cambridge University, which was largely devoted to education.
142 Colonial Office Paper, "Our Main Problems and Policies," 1950, Attlee comment, CO 1015/770/43, both cited in Hyam, "Africa and the Labour

Government," 153, 169. This kind of language dies hard. See Goran Hyden, *No Shortcuts to Progress: African Development Management in Perspective* (London: Heinemann, 1983).

143 Sir Charles Jeffries, "Memorandum on the Relationship of European and African Salaries in West Africa," 12 June 1944, CO 554/134/33594/6/1945, PRO.

144 W. A. Lewis, "Principles of Development Planning," Memorandum for Colonial Economic and Development Council, 11 April 1948, FCB 67/1, item 1.

145 Ronald Robinson, "Andrew Cohen and the Transfer of Power in Tropical Africa, 1940–1951," in W. H. Morris-Jones and Georges Fischer (eds.), *Decolonization and After: The British and French Experiences* (London: Cass, 1980), 50–72; Pearce, *Turning Point in Africa.*

146 "Constitutional Development in Africa," Papers for the African Governors' Conference, 1947, CO 847/36/47238/14/pt. 1, PRO.

147 Hyam, "Africa and the Labour Government," 152, quoting Cohen and Creech Jones. A good place to study the discourse of demagoguery is in the monthly political reports from the Gold Coast, Nigeria, and other colonies in the late 1940s, mostly collected in the series CO 537. A notable example is a description of a rally in the Gold Coast: "Nkrumah's demagogic skill was widely applauded. There is no doubt that Nkrumah is to an increasing extent capturing the imagination of the youth in urban areas." Political Intelligence Report, 15 January 1949, CO 537/4728, PRO.

148 Pedler, Minute, 1 November 1946, CO 847/35/47234/1/1947, PRO.

149 As Creech Jones put it as late as 1951, "The art of working political institutions has to be learnt, and only over a period of years are the essential qualities and traditions developed.... Admittedly, our African colonies have to travel far before these conditions obtain." Arthur Creech Jones, "British Colonial Policy with Particular Reference to Africa," *International Affairs* 27 (1951): 178.

150 John Kent, *The Internationalization of Colonialism: Britain, France, and Black Africa, 1939–1956* (Oxford: Clarendon Press, 1992). I use the word "imperialism" rather than colonialism because the actual apparatus of rule – that which was specifically colonial – was internationalized a good deal less than the global structure of power.

151 David Halloran Lumsdaine argues in a related context that countries with strong domestic social programs are the most likely to press for international social development. In that sense, the ILO initiatives of 1944 and 1947 can be seen as a reflection of the triumph of the welfare state in Great Britain and France. *Moral Vision in International Politics: The Foreign Aid Regime, 1949–1989* (Princeton: Princeton University Press, 1993), 31.

152 ILO, Governing Body, "Appendix IV: Standards of Social Policy in Dependent Territories," Document prepared for 1944 International Labour Conference, GB 91/2/11, copy in CO 859/57/12, PRO. The key actor within the ILO was Wilfred Benson.

153 Recommendation No. 70 of 1944 concerning Minimum Standards of Social Policy in Dependent Territories," in International Labour Organization, *Conventions and Recommendations 1919–1981* (Geneva: ILO, 1982), 875–95.

154 *International Labour Conference*, 1944, 225–26, 227, 230–31, 236, 239, 240.
155 ILO, Commission des Experts, 1st session, London, 17–26 March 1947, copy in IGT 34, ANSOM.
156 "Les migrations des travailleurs de l'Afrique intertropical française et à Madagascar," submitted by Marcel de Coppet, delegate to experts' committee, n.d. [1947], IGT, AEF, to IGT, Paris, 21 January 1947, IGT 34, ANSOM.
157 Convention No. 82 of 1947 concerning Social Policy in Non-Metropolitan Territories, in ILO, *Conventions and Recommendations*, 896–902.
158 Still other conventions dealt with inspections and the duration of labor contracts. Ibid., Conventions Nos. 83–85, 903–9. In the committee of experts, provision was put forward by the staff at a 1945 meeting calling for collective bargaining procedures, but employer representatives, led by the South African delegate, took the line that Africans hadn't attained a sufficient "degree of social and economic development" to be union members. Worker representatives backed the ILO staff and won their case 40–26, but the issue was postponed to 1947, when it was dealt with in rather weak form. ILO, Commission de la politique sociale, 1947, IGT 34, ANSOM.
159 *International Labour Conference*, 1947, 256.
160 Ibid., 257–59. The French government delegate, Justin Godart, tried to take the substance out of Assalé's speech by saying, "He was a pupil of the French school in his village, and he was thus able to express clearly what I believe to have been his true thought in a form which does great honour to the teaching France and her civilisation have given him." Ibid., 262.
161 Ibid., 258, 314–17. The vote on the application of labor standards was 95–20 (12 abstentions), and on the social policy question 101–3 (25 abstentions). Earlier, there had been a vigorous debate over the right of colonial workers to form trade associations, the crucial (rather weak) clause in favor of such a right winning 48–23 with many abstentions. Ibid., 280–81. The South African employers' delegate, Mr. Gemmill, thought that the true solution to the labor problem was "separation of the races" and the South African workers' delegate, Mr. Venter, compared Mr. Gemmill's views to those of "fascists and nazis" and denounced the cheap labor policy. Ibid., 263, 281–82.
162 Marc Michel, "La coopération intercoloniale en Afrique noire, 1942–1950: un néo-colonialisme éclairé?" *Relations Internationales* 34 (1983): 155–71; Kent, *Internationalization of Colonialism*; Louis, *Imperialism at Bay*. The phrase "sentimentally anti-colonialist" is from "Note de la direction d'Afrique-Levant sur les problèmes coloniaux africains tels qu'ils se présentent à la suite des débats de l'assemblée des Nations Unies (Novembre et Décembre 1946)," 20 January 1947, AE 576/13, ANSOM. For an early cooperative effort – two largely fruitless meetings on how to limit migration from the Ivory Coast to the Gold Coast in 1945–46, see "Conversations Coloniales Franco-Britanniques du 19 au 23 novembre 1945, Compte Rendu Analytique," and Notes of conclusion, Anglo-French Discussions of Migrant Labour in West Africa, 1 March 1946, IGT 5/2, ANSOM.
163 See Michael Adas, *Machines as the Measure of Man: Science, Technology, and Ideologies of Western Dominance* (Ithaca: Cornell University Press, 1989).

164 Minutes by C. A. Grossmith, 30 December 1943, T. K. Lloyd and C. J. Jeffries, 6 January 1944, and Lloyd to Sir Frederick Leggett, 7 January 1944, CO 859/57/12; T. K. Lloyd, Minute, 17 January 1944, C. A. Grossmith, Minute, 3 April 1944, CO 859/99/12263/10/1944; CO, draft speech to UK delegation to ILO Conference, April 1944, CO 859/99/3; Notes on replies to ILO questionnaire, 1945, CO 859/102/12293/A/1945-46; Lloyd, Minute, 12 June 1945, CO 859/102/12293/1945, PRO; "International Labour Conference: Proposed Action," November 1945, *Parliamentary Papers,* 1945-46, XXVI, 167.

165 Orde Browne, Minute, 22 August 1944, Lloyd to Leggett, 28 August 1944, Circular by Secretary of State, 4 October 1944, CO 554/102/1, PRO. Before the Conference, there was considerable talk in the Colonial Office that the proposals represented "pious hopes" rather than anything that could be applied "in primitive territories for a long time to come, if ever." But Secretary of State Stanley was adamant that Great Britain show an international body that it really meant to follow "that progressive Colonial policy which responsible Ministers have so often proclaimed." Draft Memo on "Minimum Standards of Social Policy in Dependent Territories," incl. T. K. Lloyd to F. Leggett, 23 May 1944, Notes of Meeting in CO, 22 March 1944, Stanley to Ernest Bevin, 29 March 1944, CO 859/99/3, PRO.

166 There were more worries about the upgrading of the 1944 resolution to the 1947 convention – the British Employers' Confederation opposed this – but the Colonial Office wanted to stay on the progressive bandwagon, although aware, for example, that color bars and penal sanctions clearly violated ILO principles. The CO was only partly hypocritical; it thought ILO Conventions would be useful pressure on the reactionary elements in certain colonies. Draft CO reply to questionnaire from ILO, April 1946; Secretary, British Employers' Confederation to CO, 28 May 1946, CO 859/102/3; Minute by G. W. Henlon, 21 April 1945, W. Blaxter to Ministry of Labour, 16 June 1945, CO 859/102/2, PRO. In the end, Great Britain was the first country to ratify the 1947 conventions. Director General, ILO, to Secretary of State, 29 April 1950, CO 859/197/4, PRO.

167 Note prepared for Philadelphia Conference, 24 April 1944, AP 2288/4, ANSOM; Commissaire aux Affaires Sociales to Commissaire aux Colonies, 3 Janaury 1944, Report on Philadelphia meeting, 1944, IGT 29, ANSOM; "Etude des questions concernant la main d'oeuvre en Afrique Occidentale Française en vue de la discussion de ces questions à la conférence internationale du travail de Philadelphia d'avril 1944," 22 March 1944, K 24 (1), AS. In the 1947 Convention, as noted above, the African workers' delegate in the French delegation was not so supportive of French achievements.

168 IGT, FWA, to High Commissioner, 16 April 1947, and reports on ILO *Conventions and Recommendations,* 1947-50, IGT 29, ANSOM.

169 Michel, "La coopération intercoloniale," and Kent, *Internationalization of Colonialism*; "Note de la direction d'Afrique-Levant" (op. cit.), AE 576/13, ANSOM. The Nigerian general strike of 1945 particularly worried French administrators, who feared "concerted agitation in all the territories of the West Coast of Africa." Governor Latrille, Ivory Coast, to Government-

General, 12 July 1945, Governor-General to Minister (telegram), 29 June 1945, and Letter, 13 July 1945, K 28 (1), AS.

170 "The Conditions of Indigenous Workers in the Belgian Congo in 1944," *International Labour Review* 53 (1946): 340–48; IGT, FWA, to IGT, Paris, 26 November 1947, Communiqué of Anglo-French–Belgian Labour Conference, Jos, February–March 1948, and "Rapport sur la Conférence Anglo-Franco–Belge du Travail ..." 12 March 1948, K 461 (179), AS. The progressive geographer Jean Dresch used Belgium's stabilization policy as a foil to attack the backward labor regime in French Equatorial Africa, while still insisting that one had to go to French Africa to "breathe the air of liberty." "Méthodes coloniales au Congo Belge et en Afrique Equatoriale Française," *Politique Etrangère* 12, 1 (1947): 77–89.

171 Michel, La coopération intercoloniale,"166–68.

172 Recomméndations de la Conférence Franco-Britannique de Coopération dans les Territoires Africains, 20 February 1948, AE 576, ANSOM. Some officials feared – and not without reason – that too obvious a collaboration would make Africans think they were the victims of an imperialist plot. Direction des Affaires Politiques, "Collaboration Franco-Britannique en Afrique," n.d. [early 1948], ibid. See also Kent, 169–74, 202.

173 Kent, 266–67; Michel, 169.

174 Inter-African Labour Conference, 1st Meeting, Jos, 1948, reprinted in CCTA, *Labour. Inter-African Conference. IVth meeting, Beira, Mozambique, 1955,* 51–55.

175 Susan Pedersen, *Family, Dependence and the Origins of the Welfare State: Britain and France, 1914–1945* (Cambridge: Cambridge University Press, 1993). Pedersen argues that the French model for the welfare state was "parental" – focusing on support for children without trying to change gender relations. The British focus was on the male breadwinner, on ensuring an adequate family wage and making special provisions for his absence. These differences were to have colonial echoes (chapter 9).

176 Peter Weiler, *British Labour and the Cold War* (Stanford: Stanford University Press, 1988), and Carew, *Labour under the Marshall Plan*; Denis Macshane, *International Labour and the Origins of the Cold War* (Oxford: Clarendon Press, 1992).

177 Report of the World Trade Union Conference, London, 6–17 February 1945, 155. See also Report of the World Trade Union Conference, Paris, 25 September–8 October 1945, 4th, 5th, and 6th resolutions, 276–77, and Report by the General Secretary of the WFTU to the Executive Board, "On the Help of the WFTU to the Trade Unions in Colonial Countries and Mandated Territories," June 1946, Archives of the International Institute of Social History, Amsterdam, file WFTU/52. The WFTU worked through national organizations, which meant that in French territories, African unions had an automatic connection through the CGT to the WFTU, but the British TUC's problematic relationship to the WFTU meant that it had little connection to British colonies.

178 WFTU, Documents on the Pan-African Conference, Dakar, 10–13 April 1947, including background papers and resolutions, Archives of the International Institute of Social History, Amsterdam, files WFTU 167 and

168. Rapport présenté par l'Union des Syndicats de Dakar, 10–14 April 1947, and Etude critique des resolutions by Union des Syndicats de Dakar, n.d., K 364 (26), AS. The French administration provided logistic support to the conference, and its spies kept an eye on it. Etat-Major de la Défense Nationale, Section Afrique, 2e Bureau, "Note sur la Conférence Intersyndicale Panafricaine, Dakar 10–14 Avril," June 1947, K 364 (26), AS. The British TUC would have nothing to do with this. As Weiler notes (273), their view of the dangers of "immaturity" in colonial trade unions slipped rather easily at this time into a concern with the dangers of "communism."

179 ICFTU, Official Report of the Free World Labour Conference and of the First Congress of the International Conference of Free Trade Unions, London, November–December 1949, "Manifesto on Economic and Social Demands: Bread, Freedom, Peace," 242–43.

6 Crises

1 The phrases cited come from the then governor-general of Madagascar, the former Popular Front governor of French West Africa, Marcel de Coppet. The minister at the time was Marius Moutet. The repression of the revolt and the representation of it as atavistic and demagogic thus come from people associated with a relatively progressive brand of colonialism. De Coppet was trying to bring Madagascar back into the "normal" mode of discussion of labor questions. Marcel de Coppet, "Manpower Problems and Prospects in Madagascar," *International Labour Review* 59 (1949): 249–70, pp. 261, 263 quoted. See also Jacques Tronchon, *L'insurrection malgache de 1947: essai d'interprétation historique* (Paris: Maspero, 1974).

2 The Enugu incident, where police violence against strikers resulted in fatalities, is the exception that proves the rule. Afterwards, officials had to admit that their failure to heed the advice Creech Jones had given in 1939 (chapter 3) on how to represent a strike had helped to create the kind of incident that they later claimed justified colonial violence: "the fact that those agitators stand poised to strike does not convert an industrial dispute into a political agitation. Indeed, to treat such a dispute as a political agitation very often does, as in our opinion it did in the case of Enugu, play right into the hands of the agitators." *Report of the Commission of Enquiry into the Disorders in the Eastern Provinces of Nigeria*, Colonial No. 256 (1950), paragraph 99; Carolyn Brown, "The Dialectic of Colonial Labour Control: Class Struggles in the Nigerian Coal Industry, 1941–1949," *Journal of Asian and African Studies* 23 (1988): 32–59.

3 Robin Cohen, *Labour and Politics in Nigeria, 1945–71* (London: Heinemann, 1974), 194. For some of the post-war strikes not discussed here, see John Iliffe, "The Creation of Group Consciousness: A History of the Dockworkers of Dar es Salaam," in Robin Cohen and Richard Sandbrook (eds.), *The Development of an African Working Class* (London: Longman, 1975), 49–72; Anthony Clayton, "The General Strike in Zanzibar, 1948," *Journal of African History* 17 (1976): 417–34; and Ian Phimister, *An Economic and Social History of Zimbabwe, 1890–1948: Capital Accumulation and Class Struggle* (London: Longman, 1987), 258–75. South Africa also experienced the strike wave during and after the war. See among other studies, T. Dunbar Moodie, "The

South African State and Industrial Conflict in the 1940s," *International Journal of African Historical Studies* 21 (1988): 21–63; idem, "The Moral Economy of the Black Miners' Strike of 1946," *Journal of Southern African Studies* 13 (1986): 1–35, and Gary Minkley, "Class and Culture in the Workplace: East London, Industrialisation, and the Conflict over Work, 1945–1957," ibid., 18 (1992): 739–60.

4 Dahomey, IT, AR, 1950, Guinea, IT, AR, 1950; and files of the Inspection Général du Travail on the Dahomean strikes, IGT 13/8, the Conakry strike, IGT 13/7, and strikes in Senegal in 1948–49, IGT 13/4 and 13/5, all in ANSOM.

5 This and what follows is based on Frederick Cooper, "The Senegalese General Strike of 1946 and the Labor Question in Post-War French Africa," *Canadian Journal of African Studies* 24 (1990): 165–215. See also Oumar Guèye, "La grève de 1946 au Sénégal," Mémoire de Maîtrise, Université Cheikh Anta Diop de Dakar, 1990.

6 Renseignements, Senegal, December 1945, 17G 138, AS.

7 Resolution, 11 January 1946, enclosed in Governor-General to Minister, 16 January 1946, IGT 13/3, ANSOM, and Renseignements, 11 January 1946, K 328 (26) AS.

8 Governor-General to Minister 10 January 1946 (telegram), IGT 13/3, ANSOM.

9 Minister to Governor-General, 12, 16 January 1946, Télégrammes 903, ANSOM. Officials in Dakar felt in such weak control that they advised their minister, Jacques Soustelle, to cancel a planned visit. He decided that cancelling was riskier than coming and shared a plane with Inspector Masselot. While Soustelle was in Dakar his government in Paris fell and his travelling companion's mission prospered.

10 Transcript of Interview, 15 January 1946, between representatives of the Union des Syndicats of Saint-Louis, and the Director of Personnel and the Director of Finance of the Government-General, K 405 (132), AS.

11 Commissaire de Police to Commandant du Cercle, Bas-Sénégal, February 1946, K 327 (26), AS; Governor, Senegal, to Governor-General, 9 February 1946, incl. Governor-General to Minister, 23 March 1946, AP 960/syndical-isme, ANSOM.

12 Governor-General to Minister, 21 February 1946, 16 March 1946, 17G 132, AS; same to same, 16 January 1946, IGT 13/3, ANSOM; same to same, 23 March 1946, AP 960/syndicalisme, ANSOM; Masselot to Minister, 23 February 1946, AP 960/syndicalisme, ANSOM.

13 The inspectors wanted private enterprises to get used to the fact that they would be inspected regularly, and hundreds were each year. For the growing organizational capacity of the Inspection Générale du Travail in French West Africa, see Pierre Pélisson, "Rapport sur l'organisation de l'Inspection du Travail en A.O.F. et au Togo," 4 February 1946, IGT (AOF), "Rapport Semestriel," 1st Semestre 1947, IGT (AOF), circular to territorial inspectors, 30 September 1948, IGT 75/1, ANSOM.

14 Inspecteur du Travail, Senegal, to Secretary-General, AOF, 13 May 1947, and "Notes d'études sur l'appel de la sentence surarbitrale du 24 avril 1947," 29 April 1947, IGT 13/4, ANSOM.

15 Governor-General to Minister, 30 March 1946, K 327 (26), AS.; Great Britain, *Report of the Commission on the Civil Services of Kenya, Tanganyika, Uganda and Zanzibar, 1947–48* (London: HMSO, 1948), 24–25.

16 The material for this section is distilled from Frederick Cooper, *On the African Waterfront: Urban Disorder and the Transformation of Work in Colonial Mombasa* (New Haven: Yale University Press, 1987), 78–113. There was a fledgling railway union at the time, which participated in some of the pre-strike meetings but in the end opposed the strike.

17 Testimony to the Kibachia hearings by William Kihege, Garrison Mwangi, and DC Foster, as well as interviews done by the author in Mombasa in 1979, all cited in Cooper, 81–82; Port Manager, Testimony to Thacker Tribunal, 27 February 1947, LAB 5/29, KNA.

18 *East African Standard*, 21 January 1947.

19 *East African Standard*, 17 January 1947. Emphasis added.

20 S. V. Cooke, "Mombasa Award Points Way to New Approach to African Problem," *East African Standard*, 27 June 1947. Working statistics may be found in Cooper, 146.

21 The testimony to the Thacker Tribunal may be found in LAB 3/16, LAB 5/28, and LAB 5/28, all in KNA. The survey reference is H. S. Booker and N. M. Deverell, "Report on the Economic and Social Background of the Mombasa Labour Dispute" (cyclostyled, 1947). All this is discussed in Cooper, 93–97.

22 Final Award of Thacker Tribunal, 20 June 1947, LAB 9/1844, KNA.

23 Thacker, Memorandum, 2 September 1947, CO 533/544/30891/6, PRO; Cooper, 176–78.

24 Kibachia to Creech Jones, 12 August 1947, CO 537/2109, PRO.

25 D. W. Throup, "The Origins of Mau Mau," *African Affairs* 84 (1985): 419–20; Cooper, 107–8; John Spencer, *The Kenya African Union* (London: KPI, 1985), 172–73.

26 James Patrick, "Memorandum on Trade Unions – Development and Policy – Kenya," n.d. [1949], FCB 118/1, p. 5. For more on the decision to deport Kibachia, see Cooper, 106–11.

27 The attorney general acknowledged that Mathu's intervention "undoubtedly accelerated a return to work and I hope has had the effect of preventing bitterness which might otherwise have resulted if the workers had been compelled, through economic reasons, to abandon the strike." Kenya, *Legislative Council Debates*, 28 January 1947, cc. 815–16.

28 General Manager to Port Manager, 27, 28 January 1947, EST 13/1/1/3, Railway Archives, Nairobi.

29 Written Answers, *House of Commons Debates* 434 (12 March 1947), c. 182.

30 Kenya, *Legislative Council Debates*, 35 (21 December 1949), cc. 638, 642–43, 646.

31 C. H. Northcott (ed.), *African Labour Efficiency Survey*, Colonial Research Publications No. 3 (London, 1949), 7, 12–13, 15. Northcott, the leader of the survey, was the former labor manager of Rowntree & Co. and a fellow and past president of the Institute of Labour Management.

32 R. E. Robins to Northcott, 12 May 1948, CO 927/82/1, PRO.

33 See for example Jane Lewis, *The Politics of Motherhood: Child and Maternal Welfare in England, 1900–1939* (London: Croom Helm, 1980).

34 The Kenyan investigations might be compared with those following strikes in Southern Rhodesia: *Report of the Commission appointed by his Excellency the Governor to Inquire into and Report on all Matters concerning recent native disturbances in the colony and to recommend any action which may seem desirable to the public interest*, 10 September 1948, and *Report of the National Native Labour Board on its Enquiry into the Conditions of Employment in Industry in Bulawayo, Gwelo, Que Que, Salisbury, Umtali, Gatooma and environs...* 6 November 1948.

35 Trans. by Francis Price (Garden City, N.Y.: Doubleday, 1962). The original French edition was published in 1960. This section is based on my article, "'Our Strike': Equality, Anticolonial Politics, and the 1947–48 Railway Strike in French West Africa," *Journal of African History* 36 (1996). See also Mor Sene, "La grève des cheminots du Dakar Niger, 1947–48," Memoire de maîtrise, Ecole Normale Supérieure, Université Cheikh Anta Diop, 1986–87; Jean Suret-Canale, "The French West African Railway Workers' Strike, 1947–48," in Robin Cohen, Jean Copans, and Peter C. W. Gutkind (eds.), *African Labor History* (Beverly Hills, Calif.: Sage, 1978), 129–54; Joseph Roger de Benoist, "La grande bataille des cheminots (1947–1948)," *Afrique Histoire* 4 (1981): 21–28; and James A. Jones, "The Impact of the Dakar–Niger Railway on the Middle Niger Valley," Ph.D. dissertation, University of Delaware, 1995.

36 Monique Lakroum, "Chemin de fer et réseaux d'affaires en Afrique occidentale: le Dakar–Niger (1883–1960)," Thesis for Doctorat d'Etat, Université de Paris VII, 1987, 1: 300–1.

37 This union was autonomous of any of the *centrales*, in part because the largest of them, the CGT, was tainted by the racism of white railwaymen who belonged to it. The suggestion, made at the time and more recently, that the railway strike was begun at the behest of the French Communist Party – involved in a railway strike in France in late 1947 – is absurd, as has been shown by C. H. Allen, "Union–Party Relationships in Francophone West Africa: A Critique of the 'Téléguidage' Interpretations," in Richard Sandbrook and Robin Cohen (eds.), *The Development of an African Working Class* (London: Longman, 1975), 104–9.

38 Renseignements, 29 May 1946, K 352 (26), AS.

39 Official positions may have hardened after the end of communist participation in the metropolitan government in May 1947, although there was no declared change in colonial policy. France itself was enveloped by October in a series of major strikes. In late April and May, the colonial ministry also renewed its efforts to hold wages and prices down. All the official members of the Régie's board, including those on the Commission Paritaire, voted to reject the Commission's proposals. Sene, "Grève des cheminots," 55–57.

40 N'Diaye Sidya, quoted in Renseignements, 29 October 1947, K 457 (179), AS. See also my article, "'Our Strike'," and J. A. Jones, "Impact of the Dakar–Niger," who shows that new sorts of commercial networks and urban settlements grew up around the railway communities in the Soudan and that they became involved in the strike.

41 IGT to Deputy Dumas, 6 January 1948, in IGT, Report, 24 January 1948, IGT 13/2, ANSOM.

42 *Voix de la R.D.A.*, special section of *Réveil*, 5 February 1948. RDA involvement is also discounted by Allen, "Union–Party Relationships." On Senghor, evidence comes from Amadou Bouta Guèye and Oumar Ndiaye, interviews, Thiès, 9 August 1994.

43 IGT to Governor-General, 12 December 1947, K 457 (179), AS.

44 Grand Conseil, *Procès Verbal*, 23 December 1947, 80–81, and 31 January 1948, 320–21. The strike was later debated by the Assemblée de l'Union Française, but no more effectually. There was much handwringing over the suffering of strikers and a plea by the members for the government to settle the strike, without serious discussion of the issues. The most revealing comment was Momo Touré's claim that the African strikers were acting in accordance with the "French tradition." *Débats* 6, 12 February 1948, 69–73, 78–89, 83 quoted.

45 *Réveil* 268 (15 December 1947), 269 (18 December 1947); Renseignements, Ivory Coast, 5, 18 November 1947, K 379 (26), AS; IGT to M. le Député Dumas, 6 January 1948, IGT 13/2, ANSOM.

46 Léopold Senghor to Minister, 26 November 1947, K 457 (179), AS.

47 Renseignements, 17 December 1947, K 457 (179), AS.

48 Sissoko planned his move with officials, as documented in note by Pillot for the Dakar–Niger region, for the director of the Régie, and sent by the latter to the president of the Conseil d'Administration, 19 January 1948, K 457 (179), and Secretary-General of the Government-General to Sissoko, 29 January 1948, copy in Inspection du Travail, Bamako, to IGT, 7 February 1948, ibid. For the union response, see Moussa Dhirra, on behalf of Comité Directeur, telegram to Sarr, 29 January 1948, Renseignements, 4 February 1948, and Inspection du Travail, Bamako, to IGT, 7 February 1948, K 457 (179), AS. Senghor's success in bringing the militants of Thiès under his political wing in the year after the strike is documented in Renseignements, Thiès, 5 February, 27 June, 12 September 1949, 11 D1/1400, AS.

49 Cooper, "'Our Strike'"; Sene, "Grève des cheminots"; Suret-Canale, "Railway Workers' Strike."

50 Robert Delavignette, "Grève des chemins de fer et des wharfs en A.O.F.," 13 December 1947, IGT 13/2, ANSOM.

51 Governor-General to Minister, 11 October 1947, IGT 13/2; Affaires Courantes, Dakar, Telegram to the new Governor-General, Paul Béchard, 3 February 1948, IGT 13/2, ANSOM.

52 High Commissioner's narrative of the strike, 1 April 1948, K 458 (179), AS; Renseignements, 16 March 1948, K 458 (179); Sene, "Grève des cheminots," 104, 112.

53 IGT, "Règlement de la grève des chemins de fer africain de l'A.O.F.," 24 September 1948, IGT 13/2, ANSOM.

54 IGT to Inspecteur Général des Colonies, 6 September 1948, K 458 (179), Directeur Fédéral de la Régie to IGT, 30 June 1950, K 43 (1), AS.

55 Directeur Général des Finances to Inspecteur Monguillot, 5 May 1952, and High Commissioner to Monguillot, 17 July 1952, AP 2306/7, ANSOM.

56 "La vie syndicale en A.O.F. au cour de l'année 1948," 31 January 1949, AP 3406/1, ANSOM.

57 Report of the Committee on the Conference of African Governors, Agenda

Committee, Appendix III, "Constitutional Development in Africa," 22 May 1947, CO 847/36, PRO.

58 Joseph Engwenyu, "World War II and Labour Protest in the Gold Coast (Ghana)," Paper presented to the African Studies Association meeting, 2–5 November 1989; Anne Phillips, *The Enigma of Colonialism: British Policy in West Africa* (London: James Currey, 1989), 141–47.

59 Gold Coast, Labour Department, AR, 1947–48, 6, 9.

60 Richard Jeffries, *Class, Power and Ideology in Ghana: The Railwaymen of Sekondi* (Cambridge: Cambridge University Press, 1978), 33–43, 50.

61 Lloyd to Acting Governor, 23 October 1947, and Acting Governor (Robert Scott) to Colonial Office, 24, 30 October 1947, CO 96/795/31312/1947, PRO.

62 Creech Jones, Memorandum by the Secretary of State for the Colonies on the memorandum by the Chief of the Imperial General Staff on his tour of Africa, 6 January 1948, PREM 8/923, PRO. Years later, two officials who had been there commented that it was "a quite extraordinary thing that a major strike in a nationalised industry should be settled by a back-bench member of Parliament." Transcript of discussion between G. N. Burden and Sir Kenneth Bradley, 7 August 1971, Colonial Records Project, Rhodes House, 9–10.

63 This and most of what follows is based on Jeff Crisp, *The Story of an African Working Class: Ghanaian Miners' Struggles, 1870–1980* (London: Zed, 1984), chapters 4 and 5.

64 Commissioner of Labour, 1944, quoted in Crisp, 71.

65 Crisp, 72; D. J. Morgan, *The Official History of Colonial Development* (London: Macmillan, 1980): 1: 128–29.

66 Crisp, 87–88.

67 Jeff Crisp, "Productivity and Protest: Scientific Management in the Ghanaian Gold Mines, 1947–1956," in Frederick Cooper (ed.), *Struggle for the City: Migrant Labor, Capital, and the State in Urban Africa* (Beverly Hills: Sage, 1983), 91–130.

68 Great Britain, Colonial Office, *Report of the Commission of Enquiry into Disturbances in the Gold Coast, 1948* [Watson Commission], Colonial No. 231 (London, 1948), 38.

69 Dennis Austin, *Politics in Ghana 1946–1960* (London: Oxford University Press, 1964), 66–72; Joseph Engwenyu, "The Gold Coast Riots of 1948," unpublished paper, n.d.

70 Watson Commission, 10–14, 89–90; Engwenyu, "Gold Coast Riots," 11; Timothy Sander Oberst, "Cost of Living and Strikes in British Africa c. 1939–1949: Imperial Policy and the Impact of the Second World War," Ph.D. dissertation, Columbia University, 1991, 321.

71 Governor Creasy to Secretary of State, 1 March 1948, CO 96/795/31312/2, PRO; Watson Commission, 85.

72 Quoted Watson Commission, 91.

73 Governor to Secretary of State, 22 March 1948, Daily Intelligence Summary, 16, 18, 21 March 1948, CO 96/795/31312/2, PRO; Austin, *Politics in Ghana* 74–75; Engwenyu, "Gold Coast Riots," 24–26.

74 Creasy to Colonial Office, 1 March 1948 (telegram), Minute by Cohen, 4 March 1948, Ministry of Defense to Prime Minister, 3 March 1948, Creasy to

Colonial Office, 28 April 1948 (telegram), CO 96/795/31312/2, PRO; Engwenyu, "Gold Coast Riots," 19.

75 Report by the Colonial Secretary of the Gold Coast, incl. Governor to Secretary of State, 5 March 1948, CO 96/795/31312/2, PRO. On 29 February, Creasy declared that Nkrumah, Danquah, and four others were responsible for the riots, and possibly for the railway and mine strikes as well. Governor to Secretary of State, 29 February 1948, ibid.

76 Text of broadcast incl. Governor to Secretary of State, 13 March 1948, CO 96/795/31312/2, PRO.

77 Creech Jones to Governor Creasy, 9 April 1948, CO 537/3558, PRO. The Watson Commission (12–13) also made much of youth gangs, up to "mischief" in the events of 28–29 February.

78 Colonial Office to Creasy, 18 March 1948, CO 537/3558, PRO. The anthropologist Meyer Fortes noted the contradiction in Colonial Office perceptions, writing "the instigators, leaders and tacit supporters [of the disturbances] have been just those 'advanced' middle-class elements whose support almost all recent policy has taken as the essential thing." Fortes to Rita Hinden, 21 March 1948, FCB 5/1, f. 28.

79 Watson Commission, 17.

80 R. D. Pearce, "Governors, Nationalists, and Constitutions in Nigeria, 1935–51," *Journal of Imperial and Commonwealth History* 9 (1981): 300.

81 Governor to Secretary of State (secret and personal), 22 March 1948, CO 537/3558, PRO.

82 Daily Intelligence Summary, 21 March 1948, CO 96/795/31312/2, PRO. There was a small strike at Kumasi, but it fizzled out. Ibid., 19, 19 March 1948. See also Crisp, *Story of an African Working Class*, 99–100.

83 R. D. Pearce, *The Turning Point in Africa: British Colonial Policy 1938–1948* (London: Cass, 1982), 190.

84 Watson Commission, 24.

85 Ibid., 30–31, 62–68.

86 Ibid., 52, 54, 60.

87 Ibid., 10. The lack of faith in the modernizing project was underscored even more by the government's reaction to the report. On its programatic points, the Colonial Office was generally favorable, but it thought that the report unfairly belittled chiefs and "the strength of the tradition and custom which a large part of the country still regards as essential to an ordered society." It used populist rhetoric to support its greater conservatism: "A European system cannot be imposed arbitrarily on an African society...." *Statement of His Majesty's Government on the Report of the Commission of Enquiry into Disturbances in the Gold Coast, 1948*, Colonial No. 232 (1948), 3.

88 Richard Rathbone notes the CPP's lack of a rural base, but adds that the government was misled by the largely accurate reports of chiefs that all was under control to overestimate the ability of the "moderates," now the UGCC, to constitute a politically viable alternative. "Introduction," *British Documents on the End of Empire: Ghana.* Part I: *1941–1952* (London: HMSO, 1992).

89 Gold Coast, Political Intelligence summaries, 16 May, 15 June, 31 August, 15 October, 15 December 1948, CO 537/3650, PRO.

90 Minute by L. H. Gorsuch, 10 May 1949, CO 537/4638, PRO.
91 Ibid.
92 Scott to Cohen, 13 September 1949, CO 96/797/31312/4/1949, PRO; Gold Coast, Labour Department, AR, 1948–49, 16–17; ibid., 1949–50, 20–22; Officer Administering the Government (T. R. O. Mangin) to Secretary of State, 3 June 1949, CO 537/4638, PRO. The UAC, which had been at the center of things in 1948, realized it had to improve its image, especially with its own staff and hence change old labor practices. David Fieldhouse, *Merchant Capital and Economic Decolonization: The United Africa Company 1929–1987* (Oxford: Clarendon Press, 1994), 339.
93 Acting Governor (Mangin) to Secretary of State, 3 June 1949, CO 96/797/31312/4/1949, PRO. A few days later he wrote that self-government to Nkrumah "is nothing more than the rationalization of the emotional instincts of the irresponsible. Its mainspring is race-hatred..." Nkrumah's first target was "the partly educated," but now "he has made a determined set at organised labour." Same to same, 9 June 1949, CO 537/4638, PRO. Creech Jones' fears were noted in Arden-Clarke's manuscript autobiography, quoted in Rathbone, "Introduction," *British Documents* xlviii.
94 Jeffries, *Class, Power and Ideology,* 53–55.
95 Extract from personal letter of Burden to Barltrop, 28 April 1949, and Officer Administering the Government to Secretary of State, 12 May 1949, CO 537/4638, PRO.
96 Gold Coast, Political Intelligence Reports, 14 July, 24 October, 14, 28 November, 5, 12 December, 1949, CO 537/4728, PRO. Months before, a top official in London had argued that the government of the Gold Coast should undertake a campaign of "positive action" to take the initiative away from Nkrumah. Nkrumah got to the slogan first. T. K. Lloyd, Minute, 12 May 1949, CO 537/4638, PRO.
97 Labour Department, AR, 1949–50, 8; Joseph Engwenyu, "The Working Class and the Politics of Constitutional Independence: The 'Positive Action' and the General Strike of 1950 in the Gold Coast," unpublished paper, Dalhousie University, 1983; Jeffries, *Class, Power and Ideology,* 54–57; Crisp, *Story of an African Working Class* 101–4.
98 Richard Rathbone, "The Government of the Gold Coast after the Second World War," *African Affairs* 67 (1968): 216–17. The Malayan analogy was invoked at length in Governor Arden-Clarke's "Draft Report on Disturbances in the Gold Coast in Early 1950," 29 June 1950, CO 537/5812, 19–27. The Colonial Office was so taken by this comparison that they asked Arden-Clarke to elaborate on it in a separate despatch. Gorsuch to Arden-Clarke, 23 September 1950, ibid.
99 Cabinet Paper CP(49)199, 8 October 1949, copy in ACJ 55/1, along with handwritten notes, f. 4. Some five months earlier, Creech Jones ended a letter to the government of the Gold Coast with a bizarre postscript: "I wonder whether there is any productive and constructive work which can be offered to Nkrumah to divert his energies into better and more helpful ways?" This may have been his idea of a joke, but the acting governor actually replied, saying that there was not. Creech Jones to Mangin, 24 May 1949, and Mangin to Creech Jones, 9 June 1949, CO 537/4638, PRO.

100 Gold Coast, Political Intelligence Reports, 12 February 1951, CO 537/7233, PRO. Arden-Clarke also argued that "political unrest and disturbance" had to be prevented in order for economic development to proceed: "Capital and technical assistance of the high quality required will not be forthcoming from overseas unless there is security and a feeling of confidence in the future of the country." Address delivered by His Excellency the Governor Sir Charles Noble Arden-Clarke, KCMG, on the occasion of the Fourth Meeting of the Legislative Council on the 7th September 1950 (Accra: Gold Coast Colony).

101 Minute by A. B. Cohen on future policy toward the Gold Coast, 11 June 1951, CO 537/7181, reprinted in Ronald Hyam (ed.), *British Documents on the End of Empire*. Series A, Vol. II: *The Labour Government and the End of Empire 1945–1951, Part 2* (London: HMSO, 1992), 74. Governor Arden-Clarke, although he was to develop a positive relationship with Nkrumah, was more cynical about the situation the British government was in: "We have only one dog in our kennel." Letter to Cohen, quoted by Hyam in ibid., 73.

Conclusion to Part II: modernity, backwardness, and the colonial state

1 On the political uses of commissions, see Adam Ashforth, *The Politics of Official Discourse in Twentieth-Century South Africa* (Oxford: Clarendon Press, 1990).

2 Kenya, *Report of the Committee of Inquiry into Labour Unrest at Mombasa* (Nairobi, 1945); Edward Batson, "Report on Proposals for a Social Survey of Zanzibar," unpublished document, 1948.

3 Deborah Posel, *The Making of Apartheid, 1948–1961: Conflict and Compromise* (Oxford: Clarendon Press, 1991); Doug Hindson, *Pass Controls and the Urban African Proletariat* (Johannesburg: Ravan, 1987); Jonathan Crush, Alan Jeeves, and David Yudelman, *South Africa's Labor Empire: A History of Black Migrancy to the Gold Mines* (Boulder, Colo: Westview Press, 1991).

4 One can contrast on this point, Posel, 63–64, 117–18, with the Kenyan case, as discussed in Bruce Berman, *Control and Crisis in Colonial Kenya: The Dialectic of Domination* (London: James Currey, 1990).

5 For a recent application of the "semi-autonomy" argument to a colonial situation, see Berman, *Control and Crisis*.

6 Ibid., 41.

7 Ibid., and Bruce Berman and John Lonsdale, *Unhappy Valley: Conflict in Kenya and Africa* (London: James Currey, 1992).

8 Timothy Scarnecchia, "The Politics of Gender and Class in the Creation of African Communities, Salisbury, Rhodesia, 1937–1957," Ph.D. dissertation, University of Michigan, 1993.

9 Luise White, *The Comforts of Home: Prostitution in Colonial Nairobi* (Chicago: Chicago University Press, 1990).

10 The race question could introduce extraordinary anxiety. When a ship with 417 West Indians – all entitled as British subjects to enter the United Kingdom – docked, officials scurried around for pretexts to ban them. They could not figure out how to reconcile their racial fears with their belief in the unity of the empire. See Cabinet Memorandum by Arthur Creech Jones, "Arrival in the United Kingdom of Jamaican Unemployed," 18 June 1948,

Cabinet Conclusions, "Coloured people from British colonial territories," 19 June 1950, and report by a Committee of Ministers, "Immigration of British subjects into the United Kingdom," 12 February 1951," reprinted in Ronald Hyam (ed.), *British Documents on the End of Empire*. Series A, Vol. II: *The Labour Government and the End of Empire 1945–1951, Part 4* (London: HMSO, 1992), 25–27, 43–46.

11 For a glimpse of how the economic development idea led officials to give an important place to white settlers in the post-war era, see the minute by A. B. Cohen on White Highlands land policy, CO 533/556/7, and Cabinet Memorandum by Secretary of State Griffiths, 14 November 1950, reprinted in Hyam, *Part 3*, 14–15, 26–27.

Introduction to Part III

1 Both administrations recognized their affinities to each other and distinguished their thinking from the Belgian Congo's stabilization policies, which they now considered backward, largely because they excluded trade unions. IGT, FWA, "Rapport sur la Conférence Anglo-Franco-Belge du travail tenue à Jos (Nigeria) en février-mars 1948," 12 March 1948, and IGT, Cameroun, to Haut-Commissaire, Cameroun, 22 March 1948, K 461 (179), AS. Belgian thinking about labor actually deserves study in terms parallel to this one. For one take on the subject, see John Higginson, *A Working Class in the Making: Belgian Colonial Labor Policy, Private Enterprise, and the African Mineworker, 1907–1951* (Madison: University of Wisconsin Press, 1989).

2 See the Annual Reports of Labour Departments and Inspecteurs du Travail.

3 After the strike, Colonial Inspector Masselot, who had helped to resolve it, and the governor-general invoked the "alarming" political situation to ask Paris to strengthen the Inspection du Travail, provide means for the statistical monitoring of living conditions, and add more technical and authoritative personnel in general. Masselot Report, 23 February 1946, IGT 13/3, and Governor-General to Minister, 22 January 1946, Télégrammes 921, ANSOM. For background, see P. F. Gonidec, *Droit du travail dans les territoires d'outre-mer* (Paris: Librarie Générale de Droit et de Jurisprudence, 1958), 291–312.

4 George Hall, *House of Commons Debates* 425 (9 July 1946): c. 251.

5 One of the brakes on the developmentalist initiative was the shortage of such personnel owing to high demand for their skills in metropolitan industry and government. In 1949 the Colonial Office had vacancies for 170 engineers, 248 agricultural and veterinary officers and geologists, 163 doctors, and 160 teachers. Paratha Sarathi Gupta, *Imperialism and the British Labour Movement, 1914–1964* (New York: Holmes & Meier, 1975), 311.

6 Memorandum by Orde Browne, "Qualifications of a Labour Officer," 18 March 1946, CO 859/103/12298/1946, PRO.

7 Colonial Labour Advisory Committee, Memorandum, "Conditions of Service of Labour Officers in the colonies," 3 June 1946, and Circular by Secretary of State, 24 August 1946, CO 859/103/12298/1946, PRO; Hall, Statement to Parliament, *House of Commons Debates* 425 (9 July 1946), c. 251. See also G. D. Tarrant, "The British Colonial Office and the Labour Question in the Dependencies in the Inter-war Years," Ph.D. Dissertation, University of Manitoba, 1977, 309–13.

8 There had been some consideration given to making the Inspection du Travail independent of the governor of each colony, but the governor-general, citing the Dakar strike of 1946, argued that strikes most often had political as well as "professional" elements to them and the governor's overall authority therefore had to be maintained. Governor-General to Minister, 28 January 1946, K 402 (132), AS.

9 "Organisation de l'Inspection du Travail Outre-Mer," by the IGT (Paris), 13 February 1947; Report to the 29th International Labour Conference, and Report to the 33rd International Labour Conference, 1950, IGT 29, ANSOM; Gouvernement Général de l'A.O.F., *Organisation de l'Inspection du Travail* (Rufisque: Imprimerie du Gouvernement Général, 1946); Gonidec, *Droit du travail*, 302; IGT, "Note sur le problème de l'Inspection du Travail," prepared for the Conseil Supérieur du Travail, nd [c 1953], IGT 1, ANSOM.

10 Pélisson to Governor-General, 2 November 1945, K 21 (1), AS. Pélisson initially considered the organization "very mediocre and little capable of allowing systematic action." "Rapport sur l'organisation de l'Inspection du Travail en A.O.F. et au Togo," 4 February 1946, IGT 75/1, ANSOM.

11 See the letter of the Inspecteur du Travail of Guinea (M. Roure) to the IGT, Paris, 31 August 1950 (IGT 13/7, ANSOM) criticizing the governor for making salary negotiations more difficult by publicly taking the employers' side.

12 Minister, Circular to Haut-Commissaires and Governors, 14 April 1949, K 431 (179), AS; Ivory Coast, Annual Political Report, 1947; Dahomey, Annual Political Report, 1946. More generally, see Ruth Schachter Morgenthau, *Political Parties in French Speaking West Africa* (Oxford: Clarendon, 1964) and Joseph Roger de Benoist, *L'Afrique Occidentale Française de 1944 à 1960* (Dakar: Nouvelles Editions Africaines, 1982).

13 Local unions of chiefs were to be grouped into a "Union Fédérale des syndicats des chefs coutumiers de l'A.O.F." Minister, Circular to Haut-Commissaires and Governors, 14 April 1949, K 431 (179), AS; Sûreté, Renseignements, November 1956, 1 December 1956 and 5 July 1957, November 1956, 17G 602, AS.

7 The systematic approach: the French Code du Travail

1 In the aftermath of the strike, the Dakar unions protested against the dual codes. The governor-general and the ministry agreed that a dual code was "inapplicable" where workers of diverse origins belonged to the same unions and that a dual code made no sense after the unification of the unified penal code which followed the abolition of the indigénat. Governor-General to Minister, 18 April 1946 (telegram); IGT, Note pour M. le Directeur des Affaires Politiques, 7 May 1946; Directeur des Affaires Politiques, Note pour M. l'Inspecteur du Travail, 9 March, 29 April 1946, AP 960/Travail; IGT, Note pour M. le Directeur du Cabinet, 27 February 1946, AP 960/2, ANSOM.

2 I am indebted to Laura Lee Downs for this insight. See her *Manufacturing Inequality: The Construction of a Gender Stratified Workforce in the French and British Metalworking Industries, 1914–1935* (Ithaca: Cornell University Press, 1995), as well as Peter Baldwin, *The Politics of Social Solidarity: Class*

Bases of the European Welfare State 1875–1975 (Cambridge: Cambridge University Press, 1990).

3 Officials in the Soudan believed that the Senegalese strike had "strongly attracted the attention of all Soudanese milieux" and was seen as proof that Africans were capable of a "certain solidarity." Soudan, Monthly Political Report, January 1946, 2G 46–134. Soudanese civil servants, organizing themselves into a new union, were soon following their Senegalese brethren in putting forth "demands tending to assimilate them completely from the point of view of salaries and grades to European civil servants." Ibid., June 1946.

4 Inspecteur du Travail Pierre Pélisson, Circular to Inspecteurs du Travail, 4 March 1949, K 414 (144); Coste-Floret, Circular to High Commissioners, 24 May 1949, ibid.

5 FWA, IGT, AR, 1946, 57; 1948, 27; 1951, 41, 52; Senegal, IT, AR, 1951; Ivory Coast, IT, AR, 1949; Inspecteur Desbordes, "Conditions de recrutement, d'orientation, de distribution et d'emploi de la main d'oeuvre par les employeurs publics ou privés en A.O.F." 26 July 1949, K 419 (144), AS.

6 FWA, IGT, "Rapport sur les Salaires en Afrique Occidentale Française," 1 October 1949, 2G 49–58, AS. On wage decoupling, see also FWA, IT, AR, 1951.

7 FWA, IGT, AR, 1948, 18. The IGT is quoting a "very high official," presumably the governor-general, whose words might be compared to those of his predecessor in 1945 cited in chapter 5 (p. 189).

8 Ibid., 17. A published study from this period, based on a rudimentary survey of Douala in the Cameroun and a longer disquisition on social and political issues, saw considerable danger in the "floating mass" of the city, but looked toward "moral education" for a solution. J. Guilbot, *Petite étude sur la main d'oeuvre à Douala*, Memorandum du Centre IFAN Cameroun (Yaoundé: Imprimerie du Gouvernement, 1947).

9 South Senegal, IT, AR, 1950. Report to Governor by l'Inspecteur des Colonies Pruvost, "La main d'oeuvre en Guinée," 13 July 1946, in Guinea, IT, AR, 1946. It did not occur to officials that different work ethics might exist, an idea explored in a stimulating fashion in another context by Keletso Atkins, *The Moon is Dead! Give Me My Money!: The Cultural Origins of an African Work Ethic, Natal, South Africa, 1843–1900* (London: Heinemann, 1993).

10 When African cultivators expanded production, as they were doing in the Ivory Coast, officials tended not to call them "industrious" but "an African peasantry in comfortable circumstances and sometimes wealthy." Ivory Coast, IT, AR, 1949.

11 Roland Pré, speech to the Conseil Général of Guinea, n.d. [1950], printed text in AFOM 393/5 bis, ANSOM. The word "proletariat" was sometimes used as if it meant lumpenproletariat, as opposed to the stabilized wage laborers officials wanted to create. The old term "floating population" was used as well, and labor inspectors frequently warned of its political dangers to be countered by vigilance over the "material and moral situation of these workers." FWA, IT, AR, 1951, 197–98; Soudan, IT, AR, 1948; Soudan, Political Annual Report, 1948; Guinea, IT, AR, 1949.

12 These activities are charted in annual reports, as well as in the reports the ILO required on its Conventions, IGT 75/1, ANSOM. The Inspection Générale in

Dakar was kept so busy that in 1949 and 1950 it was unable to complete an annual report. FWA, IGT, AR, 1951.

13 In Guinea and the Ivory Coast, labor inspectors protested governors' efforts to keep minimum wages down, and got at least some acknowledgement from Dakar that their concern with maintaining social peace was legitimate. On Guinea, see Governor Pré to Governor-General 2 February 1949, 1 March 1949, Governor-General to Governor, 11 February 1949, IGT, FWA, to Governor, 17 January 1949, K 453 (179), plus extensive correspondence on the strike in IGT 13/7, ANSOM. On the Ivory Coast disagreement, see Inspecteur du Travail Connilière to IGT, FWA, 19 October 1948, 15 November 1948, IGT, FWA, Report, 13 April 1949, Governor Péchoux to Governor-General 5 April 1949, Governor-General to Governor, Ivory Coast, 7 January 1949, K 453 (179), AS.

14 FWA, IGT, AR, 1948, 37; 1951, 3, 48. Two of the more bitter strikes were in Senegal at a peanut oil factory in 1949 and in the commercial sector in Dahomey in 1950. See lengthy correspondence on them in IGT 13/5 and 13/8, ANSOM.

15 FWA, IGT, AR, 1948, 36; 1951, 85–86.

16 FWA, IGT, AR, 1946, 22–23.

17 See for example the appeals in FWA, IGT, AR, 1946, 1947, 1948. Even in Upper Volta, the inspector referred to "regulatory chaos" in the absence of a code du travail. Upper Volta, IT, AR, 1948, as well as Ivory Coast, IT, AR, 1950; FWA, "Rapport biannuel sur la protection de la collectivité, de la famille et de l'enfance," 1950–52, 2G 52–53, AS.

18 Speech of Governor E. Louveau to opening session of Conseil Général du Soudan Français, 13 January 1947, Agence FOM 393, ANSOM.

19 IGT, Note, November 1947, K 461 (179), AS. On social security in France, see François Ewald, *L'état providence* (Paris: Grasset, 1986), and Baldwin, *Politics of Social Solidarity*.

20 IGT, Paris, to IGT, FWA, 17 December 1946, K 438 (179), AS.

21 Consistent with its universalist logic, this report concluded that family allowances would have to be paid to the entire population, not just workers, because the "social costs" of children affected all parents. This would be precisely the point on which universalism would retreat. IGT, "Note a/s de la sécurité sociale," Dakar, 26 December 1947, K 438 (179), AS.

22 FWA, Annual Political Report, 1948.

23 Citizenship – political and social – has never been an indivisible notion, and access to its rights have been defined in terms of gender as well as of origins. But those exclusions have been vigorously contested – by feminists and anti-racists among others – by invoking the bounded inclusivity which the idea of citizenship implies, a point to which I will return in chapter 13.

24 The relevance of the history of family allocations in France to the colonies is discussed in High Commissioner, FWA, Circular to Governors and department heads, 18 September 1950, 18G 287, AS.

25 Guinea, IT, AR, 1947; Dakar, IT, AR, 1944; Ivory Coast, IT, AR, 1949.

26 Governor-General's comments to the Conférence des Hauts-Commissaires et Gouverneurs de la France Outre-Mer, 22–27 February 1947 (session of 22 February), Delavignette Papers, PA 19/3/34, ANSOM. See also the comments

of Governors-General Delavignette (Cameroun) and de Coppet (Madagascar).

27 The Lamine Guèye law itself passed unanimously in the Assemblée Nationale, with amendments by the Conseil de la République that were acceptable to all. Assemblée Nationale, *Débats*, 15 June 1950, 4822–26. The costs of equalizing benefits in the public service were raised in the Grand Conseil of FWA, but it was hard to go against the plea of Lamine Guèye himself: "we must march toward the future, establish equality and justice so that all can regard the future with more serenity, persuaded once again that the Frenchman of Brest or of Lille will not be considered more French than the Frenchman of Africa." FWA, Grand Conseil, *Bulletin* No. 12, session of 6 November 1951, 15–36.

28 High Commissioner, FWA, Circular to Governors and department heads, 18 September 1950, 18G 287, AS; FWA, IGT, AR, 1951, 100.

29 FWA, IGT, "Rapport: Possibilités conditions et modalités d'organisation en A.O.F. d'un système d'allocations familiales pour les salariés," 26 July 1949, K 455 (179), AS.

30 Governor-General to Minister, 25 October 1949, IGT 17/4, ANSOM. The head of the Inspection Générale du Travail in Paris was quite well aware of the difference of opinion between her IGT in Dakar and the high commissioner there. "Note pour M. le Docteur Aujoulat, Secrétaire d'Etat de la France Outre-Mer," 11 January 1951, IGT 15/1, ANSOM.

31 Aujoulat, Circular to High Commissioners, 9 August 1950, IGT 15/3, ANSOM. Even the early plans for family allowances linked them to surveillance of how the family was fulfilling its role. Workers would have to produce documentation regarding their jobs, bring expectant mothers and children to medical visits, and prove that their children were attending school. Circular of Minister to Governors-General, n.d. [1950], IGT 15/3, ANSOM.

32 "Rapport Biannuel sur la protection de la collectivité, de la famille et de l'enfance," 1951–52, 2G 52–53. In these terms, the report argued that French policy had long supported the "liberation of the woman." They meant that she was being freed to enter into consensual, European-style marriages.

33 IGT (Mlle Guelfi), "Note pour Monsieur le Docteur Aujoulat," 11 January 1951, IGT 15/1, ANSOM. Mlle Guelfi also argued for a limited program on the ground that "detribalized" Africans lacked the "family insurance" which rural populations had, and therefore needed special help in founding families and raising children. Others made similar distinctions between the "organic traditional" structures of rural Africa and the urban milieu. Meeting of Conseil Supérieur Consultatif des Affaires Sociales d'Outre-Mer, 17 July 1952, IGT 15/2, ANSOM.

34 The pioneering urban anthropologist Georges Balandier joined officials in this argument, claiming that men in the city of Brazzaville were "forced bachelors." "Le travailleur africain dans les 'Brazzavilles Noires'," *Présence Africaine* 13 (1952): 325.

35 Governor-General, FEA, to Minister, 26 May 1951, IGT 17/5, ANSOM; meeting of a study committee in Brazzaville, 12 March 1951, transcript enclosed in Governor-General to Secrétaire d'Etat, Ministère de la FOM (Aujoulat), 13 April 1951, ibid.; Inspector Reynaud, "Note sur l'instauration d'un régime d'allocation familiales en Afrique Equatoriale Française," 16

February 1951, IGT 17/1, ANSOM. From 1949, the FEA territory of Moyen-Congo began on an experimental basis a program of family allowances, although the sum added to wages for each child (100 francs) amounted to little. Transcript of 12 March 1951 meeting, IGT 17/50.

36 Althought the *patronat* generally opposed family allocations, the head of one important employer organization in Equatorial Africa claimed that "No one would dream of contesting the principle of family prestations and allocations." They would "form a healthier and more stable race." And he read into them the possibility of their becoming a "bonus for fidelity and regularity." Y. de Laveleye, President of Chambre Syndicale des Mines d'A.E.F., to IGT, AEF, 20 February 1952, IGT 17/5, ANSOM.

37 High Commissioner's Circular, 18 September 1950, 18G 287, ANSOM. The difficulties posed by polygamy to a program of family allowances were brought up repeatedly, e.g. in Ivory Coast, IT, AR, 1949, Guinea, IT, AR, 1950, and as early as 1951 advocates of allowances were building up a case against this argument, largely on the empirical grounds that "polygamists are not numerous among wage earners" and the hope that European-style allowances would promote European-style families. Statement of IGT (Guelfi) to meeting on "un régime d'aide à la famille africaine," 11 January 1951, IGT, 15/2, ANSOM.

38 Comité de l'Empire Français, Section d'Afrique Occidentale, session of 16 May 1950, Union Coloniale 120, ANSOM.

39 There are a large number of security reports from 1946 and 1947 in K 352 (26). Cited are, Renseignements, Dahomey, August 1946, Soudan, April 1946, 3 August 1947, Guinea, 5 August 1946, 1 July 1947. See also Dahomey, Political Annual Report, 1945–47, Guinea, IT, AR, 1945–47, Ivory Coast, IT, AR, 1946, 1947, Soudan, IT, AR, 1946.

40 FWA, IGT, AR, 1948, 83–84. The 1956 figure is from Georges Martens, "Le syndicalisme en Afrique occidentale d'expression française: de 1945 à 1960," *Le Mois en Afrique* 180–81 (1980–81): 82.

41 FWA, IGT, "Rapport: le salaire minimum en Guinée et les conditions de résorption des séquelles de la grève des 9–10 Juin 1950"; Report by Inspecteur du Travail, Guinea, 31 August 1950, IGT, Paris, to Minister, 18 July 1950, IGT, FWA, Report on "Fixation du salaire minimum en Guinée et grève des 9 et 10 juin 1950," 19 June 1950, Inspecteur du Travail, Guinea, to IGT, FWA, 20 June 1950, all in IGT 13/7, ANSOM. See also IGT, FWA, "La vie syndicale en A.O.F. au cours de l'année 1948," 31 January 1949, AP 3406/1, ANSOM, and FWA, IGT, AR, 1951.

42 For an interesting debate on these questions, see Philippe Dewitte, "La CGT et les syndicats d'Afrique Occidentale Française (1945–1957)," *Le Mouvement Social* 117 (1981): 3–32, Paul Delanoue, "La CGT et les syndicats d'Afrique Noire de colonisation française de la Deuxième Guerre Mondiale aux indépendences," *Le Mouvement Social* 122 (1983): 103–16, and Dewitte, "Réponse à Paul Delanoue," ibid., 117–21.

43 Diallo, born around 1917 in Guinea, was educated at the elite Ecole Ponty and then went to work for the Poste-Télégraph-Téléphone, ending up in Bamako, in the Soudan. He became a full-time trade unionist in 1947, and was the secretary-general of the Union Régionale des Syndicats du Soudan.

He had close personal ties with some French communist labor leaders, and became an activist, and eventually a vice-president, of the WFTU. FWA, Inspection Générale des Services de Securité, "Note d'information," 15 February 1950, 17G 272, AS. For his views, see Abdoulaye Diallo, "The Scourge of Colonialism in French Africa," *World Trade Union Movement* 2 (20 January 1951): 29–34, and "Economic and Social Claims of the West Africa Workers," ibid. 7 (5 April 1951): 17–22.

44 When a modest victory was obtained – a raise in the minimum wage – unions called it, for example, the "fruits" of "persistent action of the Union des Syndicats de Dakar." *Réveil* 349 (31 January 1949).

45 "Les revendications des Africains du Sénégal," *Marchés Coloniaux* no. 164 (1 January 1949), clipping in AFOM 381/63/9, ANSOM. This same organization, bringing its concerns before the World Federation of Trade Unions' Pan-African Conference in Dakar in 1947, put most emphasis on the demand for a "Code du Travail Unique, applicable to all workers without distinction of origin or race." It also insisted, "The Trade Unionists of French West Africa demand the application pure and simple of metropolitan legislation on social security in the overseas territories." Like the labor inspectors, it advocated eliminating occasional and seasonal workers and focusing on the "permanent worker." Report by the Union des Syndicats de Dakar to Pan-African Conference of the WFTU, Dakar, 10–14 April 1947, and "Etude critique des résolutions," by Union des Syndicats de Dakar, K 364 (26), AS.

46 Resolutions of the Conférence Syndicale Africaine (CGT), Bamako, 22–27 October 1951, incl. Governor-General to Minister, 28 November 1951, AP 3408/5, ANSOM. For more evidence of the demands and discourse of unions, especially in Senegal, see the pages of the Dakar newspaper (with RDA connections) *Réveil*, notably: "Chronique de la vie syndicale," 221 (10 July 1947); Resolutions of Union des Syndicats Confédérés du Sénégal et de la Mauretenie, 291 (4 March 1948); motion of Syndicats Confédérés de Dakar, May Day meeting, on "Promulgation immédiate du Code du Travail," 303 (6 May 1948); Sékou Touré, "Unité et action chez les fonctionnaires d'A.O.F.," 398 (9 January 1950); articles on claims of civil servants and railway workers, 399 (16 January 1950) and 403 (13 February 1950), plus coverage of strikes. Similarly, see *Le Prolétaire (Organe de l'Union des Syndicats CGT de Dakar)*, 1949–52, including such articles as "Autour du Minimum Vital," 7 (15 September 1951), and "Il nous faut le Code du Travail," 9 (24 November 1951).

47 *Barakela, organe de l'Union Régionale des Syndicats du Soudan*, 17 September 1951, clipping in 17G 272, AS.

48 Note by IGT, FWA, 17 May 1947, and Inspecteur du Travail, Senegal to Secretary-General of FWA, 13 May 1947, IGT 13/4, plus Guinea, Political Report, 2G 47–22, 1947.

49 "La vie syndicale en A.O.F. au cours de l'année 1948," 31 January 1949, incl. Governor-General to Minister, 2 February 1949, AP 3406/1, ANSOM. There are substantial files on major strikes in IGT 13/5, 13/7, 13/8, ANSOM.

50 George Ross, *Workers and Communists in France: From Popular Front to Eurocommunism* (Berkeley: University of California Press, 1982); Irwin M. Wall, *French Communism in the Era of Stalin: The Quest for Unity and Integration, 1945–1962* (Westport, Conn.: Greenwood, 1983).

51 Morgenthau, *Political Parties*, 186–99.
52 Governor-General to Minister, 22 October 1951, Service des Affaires Politiques, FWA, "Pointe de l'activité syndicale en A.O.F. au 31 Décembre 1950," AP 3408/5, ANSOM. Compare this with the much more alarmist vision of RDA–CGT politicization in "La vie syndicale en A.O.F. au cours de l'année 1948," 31 January 1949, AP 3406/1, ANSOM. French officials' hopes for a split in the labor movement are discussed in chapter 11.
53 FWA, IGT, AR, 1951, 197–98. Officials and key legislators believed that on the code and related issues, their goals were similar to those of the labor movement, and that the latter were willing to strike and agitate for what they wanted. Governor-General to Minister, 10 May 1948; Renseignements, 19, 28 January 1948; Notes of IGT, 7 November 1947 and Affaires Politiques, 7 November 1947, to Governor-General, Governor-General to Minister, 10 May 1948, K 439 (179), AS; IGT, Note pour le Ministre, "Problèmes du travail et de la main d'oeuvre en Afrique Occidentale Française," May 1952, IGT 5/1, ANSOM; M. Donnat, speech to Assemblée de l'Union Française, 27 February 1948, p.148; Grand Conseil, *Bulletin*, 28 January 1948.
54 Assemblée Nationale, *Débats*, 6 November 1952, 4796.
55 Etats Généraux de la Colonisation, records of meeting, Paris, 30 July–24 August 1946, in Ruth Schachter Morgenthau (compiler and editor), *Documents on African Political History* (CAMP Microfilm MF 4408), reel 4. In 1943, the President of the Syndicat des Entrepreneurs Français des Travaux Publics et des Bâtiments de l'Afrique Occidentale Française wrote to the governor-general (15 December 1943, K 273 (26), AS): "We ask that a code du travail be prepared and that the rights of our personnel correspond to its duties and that failings in regard to these duties be followed by just but severe penalties." A code should include wage scales and penalties against employers who paid too much.
56 Comité de l'Empire Français, Section de l'Afrique Occidentale, meeting of 9 May 1946, Union Coloniale 120, ANSOM. When the dual codes were abandoned because of the citizenship law, this group thought that it was the citizenship law which should be thrown out. Session of 11 July 1946, ibid.
57 "Note sur le Code du Travail," by the Comité de l'Empire Français, 27 January 1948, K 439 (179), AS. The lobbying activities are detailed in Comité de l'Empire Français, Section d'Afrique Occidentale, sessions of 16 April 1948, 13 January, 17 February 1949, Union Coloniale 120, ANSOM. On the relationship of organizations such as these to the politics of French imperialism, see Charles-Robert Ageron, *France coloniale ou parti colonial?* (Paris: Presses Universitaires Françaises, 1978), and Jacques Marseille, *Empire colonial et capitalisme français* (Paris: Albin Michel, 1984).
58 Luc Durand-Réville, "Pas de discrimination raciale dans le nouveau Code du Travail," *Climats*, 4 January 1951, clipping in 17G 529 (144), AS.
59 For insight into their social vision, see Robert Delavignette, *Christianisme et Colonialisme* (Paris: Arthème Fayard, 1960), and L-P. Aujoulat, *La vie et l'avenir de l'Union Française* (Paris: Société d'édition républicaine populaire, 1947).
60 John Ambler, "Ideas, Interests, and the French Welfare State," in Ambler (ed.), *The French Welfare State* (New York: New York University Press,

1991), 9–11, 22. The focus on the family within the history of welfare in France is also emphasized in Susan Pedersen, *Family, Dependence and the Origins of the Welfare State: Britain and France, 1914–1945* (Cambridge: Cambridge University Press, 1993).

61 Paul Clay Sorum, *Intellectuals and Decolonization in France* (Chapel Hill: University of North Carolina Press, 1977). For a set of papers illuminating social Catholic views on the morality of colonialism, see *Peuples d'Outre-Mer et civilisation occidentale*. Semaines Sociales de France (Lyon: Chronique Sociale de France, 1948).

62 Assemblée de l'Union Française, *Débats*, session of 27 February 1948, 148–50. The language of a communist deputy, Donnat, provides an interesting contrast: he stressed that the code was demanded "with very great force" by workers and that it would be a piece of "legislation adapted to modern needs." Ibid., 148.

63 "Exposé des motifs," attached to the Dumas–MRP proposed "social code for the overseas and associated territories," submitted to the Assemblée Nationale, 30 December 1948, and sent to the Assemblée de l'Union Française for discussion, in *Documents de l'Assemblée de l'Union Française*, session of 20 January 1949, Annex 4, 3. For similar arguments made within "the universalistic spirit of western civilization and the teaching of the Church," see Charles Flory, "Les conditions nouvelles des rapports de l'Occident et des Peuples d'Outre-Mer," *Peuples d'Outre-Mer et civilisation occidentale*, 31, 34, and Gérard Espéret, "Le syndicalisme dans les territoires africains de l'union française," *Les missions et le prolétariat*, 23e semaine de missiologie de Louvain, 1953 (Brussels: Desclée de Brouwer, 1953), 200–1. Espéret, a top CFTC leader, devoted himself from 1950 onward to colonial trade unionism and in some ways was ahead of his communist and socialist counterparts in encouraging African autonomy. See his obituary in *Le Monde*, 4 November 1995.

64 Soeur Marie-André du Sacré-Coeur, "La situation de la femme en Afrique Noire Française," *Civilisations* 1, 4 (1951): 50.

65 On the announcement and withdrawal of the Moutet code, see Minister to Governor-General (telegrams), 24 October, 18 November, 9, 16, 24 December 1947; IGT, circular to Inspecteurs du Travail, 29 December 1947, K 439 (179), vol. 2. The *patronat*'s opposition to the code is expressed in "Note au sujet du Nouveau Code du Travail," by the President of the Chambre d'Agriculture de la Côte d'Ivoire, 14 November 1947, and "Note sur le Code du Travail," by the Comité de l'Empire Français, 27 January 1948, ibid.

66 Governor-General to Minister 10 May 1948, Renseignements, 19, 28 January 1948, K 439 (179), vol. 2, AS; Directeur des Affaires Politiques (Delavignette), Note pour M. le Ministre, 20 December 1947, AP 2255/1, ANSOM; Assemblée de l'Union Française, *Débats*, 27 February 1948, 148–61, 16 July 1948, 763–68; FWA, *Bulletin du Grand Conseil*, 29 January 1948, 277–78.

67 The Conseil Economique and Coste-Floret decided that the Moutet code had so many problems that a new one had to be drafted. *Avis et Rapports du Conseil Economique*, sessions of 30 April 1948, 102–4, 8–9 June 1948, 141–44, and 22 July 1948, 189–96; Minister to Governor-General, 24 December 1947 (telegram), K 439 (179), vol. 2, AS.

68 Assemblée de l'Union Française, *Documents*, Annexe No. 159, session of 17 March 1948, 184–85. Durand-Réville's code had 14 articles, the composite of the others put together by the Assemblée's Commission des Affaires Sociales had 226.

69 Report of Commission des Affaires Sociales, in *Documents* de l'Assemblée de l'Union Française, Annex no. 12, session of 26 January 1949, 19; *Avis et Rapports du Conseil Economique*, session of 8–9 June 1948, 142.

70 Report of Commission des Affaires Sociales, in *Documents* de l'Assemblée de l'Union Française, Annex no. 12, session of 26 January 1949, 23. The committee divided 16 to 6 over the basic question of whether to write a single code for all of Overseas France or multiple codes for different groups of territories. M. Begarra, Reporter for the committee, to Assemblée de l'Union Française, *Débats*, session of 2 February 1949, 42.

71 Compare the governmental proposal and the committee report in Assemblée Nationale, *Documents*, 1949, Annexe 7072, 686–98, and 1950, Annexe 10913, 1712–31.

72 The rightist alternative to the committee draft was defeated 447 to 135, but numerous amendments to the main bill from conservative legislators amounted to a virtual filibuster. *Débats*, 2 December 1950, 8463.

73 Durand-Réville regarded the text passed by the Conseil de la République as "very imperfect," but he thought that rejecting it would give the Assemblée Nationale a blank check to return to its earlier version, "which would have been even more catastrophic for the economies of our overseas territories." Comité de l'Empire Français, Section d'Afrique Occidentale, session of 14 February 1952, Union Coloniale 120, ANSOM.

74 Assemblée Nationale, 18 November 1950, 4918. See also the written report from the committee Dumas chaired, *Documents*, 1950, Annexe 10913, 1712.

75 Assemblée Nationale, 27 November 1950, 8197. He also hoped that Africa could avoid the conflicts which the metropole had faced over the past hundred years. Ibid., 8195, 8196.

76 Konaté, ibid., 18 November 1950, 7923; Senghor, 2, 9 December 1950, 8464, 8894.

77 Jean-Jacques Juglas, 9 December 1950, 8896.

78 Inspecteur Combier, Note pour M. le Ministre, 16 August 1948, K 439 (179), vol. 1, AS.

79 René Malbrant made a similar argument, 18 November 1950, 7923; 30 April 1951, 4374.

80 Joseph Dumas and Léopold Senghor, 9 December 1950, 8896; Charles Benoist, 18 November 1950, 7925, 2 December 1950, 8461; René Arthaud, 9 December 1950, 8898. The vote is recorded in ibid., 8899.

81 Conseil de la République, *Débats*, 22–23 December 1951, interventions of Durand-Réville, Razac, David, and Aujoulat, 3239–40, 3282, 3284–86, 3288.

82 Assemblée Nationale, *Débats*, 22 November 1952, 5462. There was a tedious debate between those who wanted the code to refer to wage earners (*salariés*) and the advocates of workers (*travailleurs*). Ibid., 5465–66. The committee draft before the Assemblée included a clause that the minister and the president of the Republic would later provide decrees which "will fix for each territory the regulation of work born of customary relations of traditional

societies and the conditions under which the dispositions of the present law will be applied to them." It was deleted on the grounds that the Assemblée had decided on first reading to exclude customary labor from the code. Aujoulat, ibid., 5467.

83 Code du Travail, Article 1. The code was published in pamphlet form in Senegal, in addition to its appearance in the *Journal Officiel de la République Française*: *Loi no. 52–1322 du 15 décembre 1952, instituant un code du travail dans les territoires et territoires associés relevant du Ministère de la France d'Outre-Mer* (Rufisque: Imprimerie du Gouvernement Général, 1953).

84 Paul Catrice, Assemblée de l'Union Française, *Débats*, 9 February 1949, 78.

85 P. F. Gonidec, *Droit du travail dans les territoires d'outre mer*, (Paris: Librairie Générale de Droit et de Jurisprudence, 1958), 644, 693. Accident compensation, updating the very limited law of 1932, finally came into effect in 1959.

86 M. Donnat, Assemblée de l'Union Française, *Débats*, 23 February 1949, 201. The work week issue featured not only in the debate over the article in question, but in the opening statements from various parties. Ibid., 2 February 1949, 40, 44, 56.

87 Bagarra, for the Commission des Affaires Sociales, Union Française, *Débats*, 23 February 1949, 202; Assemblée Nationale, *Débats*: Joseph Dumas, 17 March 1951, 2135–36; René Malbrant, 18 November 1950, 7922–25, Jules Castellani, 2 December 1950, 8459–60; Mamadou Konaté, 27 November 1950, 8188, Léopold Senghor, 27 November 1950, 8182, and 7 April 1751, 2909–10; Conseil de la République, *Débats*: Durand-Réville and Aujoulat, 22–23 December 1951, 3232, 3272.

88 Union Française, *Débats*, 23 February 1949, 201–2.

89 Assemblée Nationale, *Débats*, 22 November 1952, 5502–5.

90 This phrase was used by Senghor in print as well, in "Nous sommes pour la communauté européenne et, par delà elle, pour la communauté eurafricaine," *Marchés Coloniaux* 375 (17 January 1953): 124. It was picked up by Governor-General Cornut-Gentille to refer to a central passion of African elites to which administrators had to accommodate themselves. "Allocution prononcée par Bernard Cornut-Gentille, Haut-Commissaire, à la séance d'ouverture de la deuxième session 1954 du Grand Conseil de l'Afrique Occidentale Française, 13 Octobre 1954," p. 20. It was also picked up by France's leading authority on colonial labor law, who argued that this kind of appeal was what was central to the African campaign for the code. From Gonidec's point of view, this had a positive significance: "The mystique of equality brings us back to the mystique of the law." "Une mystique de l'égalité: le code du travail des territoires d'Outre-Mer," *Revue Juridique et Politique de l'Union Française* 2 (1953): 176–96, 96 quoted.

91 Assemblée Nationale, *Débats*, 7 April 1951, 2923–24. One issue which inspired no comparisons was an article banning forced labor. African delegates wanted the most rigorous possible prohibition; the memory of the battle of 1946 was still strong. Article 2.

92 Assemblée Nationale, *Débats*, 7 April 1951, 2911–19. The maternity provision for women wage earners became Article 116 of the code.

93 In presenting the early draft of the code to the Assemblée de l'Union Française, Bagarra said of the various councils, "But who will animate these

organizations of equal importance? Uncontestably, it is in the unions where the best elements will be trained: unions freely constituted on professional grounds, limiting their action to the interests of the profession, unions engaged in the free play of social democracy, unions in which the best elements will acquire the sense of responsibilities of social duty and, in the context of federations and groups of unions will raise themselves above a certain narrow corporatism." *Débats*, 2 February 1949, 45.

94 Aujoulat, 27 November 1950, 8198. Coste-Floret expressed similar views. Ibid., 8180. Aujoulat elsewhere admitted his fears that trade unions could become extremist, but he considered that it would be worse to leave workers "without a guide." Secrétariat Social d'Outre-Mer, *Code du Travail des territoires d'outre-mer: Guide de l'usager* (Paris: Société d'Editions Africaines, 1953), 17.

95 The Moutet code of 1947, never implemented, had a provision requiring government assent to any collective bargaining agreement. Governor-General Barthes opposed this and other restrictive clauses, arguing that they brought the government into controversies it could well avoid. Governor-General to Minister, 28 November 1947, 17G 529 (144), AS.

96 Aujoulat, Circular to High Commissioners, 16 August 1950. See also Governor, Niger, to Governor-General, 25 November 1950; Directeur Général des Finances, FWA, to IGT, 24 December 1950; Directeur Général de l'Intérieur, FWA, "Note a/s de conclusion des conventions collectives (Project Code du Travail)," 27 December 1950, all in 17G 529 (144), AS.

97 Aujoulat, Dumas, Charles Benoist (for the PCF) Assemblée Nationale, *Débats*, 10 February 1951, 1023–27. The right favored official authority over collective bargaining agreements and close supervision of unions. Jules Castellani, 1025–26.

98 The suspicion, particularly among African deputies, of administrative meddling in trade union affairs remained. Senghor still argued at the very end of the code debate, "Everyone knows that the administration has a tendency to abuse its power in these territories..." Ibid., 22 November 1952, 5491.

99 Assemblée Nationale, *Débats*, 29 April 1951, 4304–8, 30 April 1951, 4370–73, 22 November 1952, 5541–43; Conseil de la République, *Débats*, 6 February 1952, 439.

100 Joseph Dumas argued in the final debate that French legislators should vote for measures which "correspond to that which we would want to find if we as well were wage workers in the overseas territories." Assemblée Nationale, *Débats*, 18 November 1950, 7919, 7921, 22 November 1952, 5555. See also Louis-Paul Aujoulat, preface to Secrétariat Social d'Outre-Mer, *Code du travail des territoires d'outre-mer*, 9–26.

101 Assemblée de l'Union Française, *Débats*, 3 March 1949, 286; Assemblée Nationale, *Débats*, 30 April 1951, 4366; Assemblée Nationale, *Documents*, 1949, Annexe 7072, 698; ibid., 1950, Annexe 10913, 1731.

102 Conseil de la République, *Débats*, 5 February 1952, 418–19.

103 Paul Devinat and Senghor, Assemblée Nationale, *Débats*, 22 November 1952, 5547.

104 Pflimlin, ibid., 5547–48.

105 Dumas, ibid., 5548–49.
106 Pflimlin, ibid., 5549.
107 Pflimlin, ibid., 5551, vote count, 5589–90. Aujoulat and Pflimlin abstained, but social Catholic stalwarts like Dumas and Catrice voted for the amendment.
108 Ibid., 5557, 5590–91. There were 200 abstentions and 59 non-voters. Malbrant, who had led the attack during the second reading on the pro-labor features of the code, abstained. So, for no obvious reason, did the leading socialist Pierre Mendès-France.
109 See for example "Le Code du Travail est en 'panne' devant le Conseil de la République," *Afrique Noire*, 4 (27 December 1951), and articles in *La Condition Humaine*, 12 January, 3 March 1952 on the Conseil debate.
110 Abbas Guèye, letter to Comité de Coordination, 2 July 1952, obtained by Sûreté, Dakar, Renseignements, 15 July 1952, K 418 (144), AS. Another letter from Abbas Guèye to his fellow deputies was reprinted in *Condition Humaine* 107 (22 August 1952).
111 In Guinea, the Comité Intersyndical CGT–CFTC–Cheminots took up the cause and published an appeal, calling for similar territorial organizations to join in a meeting to take action on the code. *Afrique Noire*, 30 (4 September 1952), copy in CRDA, file on Code du Travail, II.
112 *Barakela*, "organe officiel de l'Union Régionale des Syndicats du Soudan," special issue of 13 October 1952, copy in K 418 (144), AS; High Commissioner to Minister, 13 October 1952, AP 3417, ANSOM.
113 Governor, Senegal, to High Commissioner, 21 November 1952, K 418 (144), AS. The strike in Senegal was virtually total in the private sector – which is what was in question in the code debate – but 50 percent of public sector workers struck as well. In Conakry, it was 90 percent effective in the private sector, while some public services like the railway and the post office were shut down and others were not. High Commissioner to Minister, 4, 5 November 1952 (telegrams), AP 3417, ANSOM.
114 *La Condition Humaine*, 110 (10 November 1952).
115 Ivory Coast, Renseignements, 3 November 1952, Upper Volta, 4 November 1952, K 418 (144), AS; Ivory Coast, IT, AR, 1952; Niger, Annual Political Report, 1952.
116 Assemblée Nationale, *Débats*, 6 November 1952, 4794–96.
117 Aujoulat, ibid., 22 November 1952, 5463; Durand-Réville, Conseil de la République, *Débats*, 22 December 1951, 3230; Henri Caillavet, Assemblée Nationale, *Débats*, 6 November 1952, 4803. When the struggle was all over, the colonial business lobby acknowledged that it had lost this argument, quoting Aujoulat on the "profound unity of the *salariat*" and acknowledging, "The code responds to this indisputable reality." "Le code du travail est voté par l'Assemblée Nationale en deuxième lecture par 365 voix contre 0," *Marchés Coloniaux* 368 (29 November 1952): 3029.
118 Minister to High Commissioner, 28 November 1952, K 414 (144), AS.
119 FWA, Grand Conseil, session of 29 October 1952, 42–44; Comité de l'Empire Français, Section de l'Afrique Occidentale, Meetings of 15 January, 12 March, 16 April, 21 May 1953 (President Maurel quoted), Union Coloniale 120, ANSOM; René Moreux, "Les textes d'application du Code du Travail dans les T.O.M. doivent être à la fois loyaux et prudent,"

Marchés Coloniaux 381 (28 February 1953): 609–10; "L'application du Code du Travail des T.O.M. et l'affaire des 20%," ibid., 423 (19 December 1953): 3545–46.

120 Affaires Politiques, Revues trimestrielles, Soudan, 19 March 1953, AP 2230/4, ANSOM.

121 Renseignements, Senegal, 7–8 March 1953, 17G 529 (144), AS.

122 High Commissioner to Minister, 10 April 1953, IGT 11/2, Affaires Politiques, "Note sur le syndicalisme en A.O.F.," n.d. [late 1953], AP 3417, ANSOM; Renseignements, Senegal, 22 April, 20, 22 May, 7 July, 6, 7, 9 August 1953; Soudan, 24 July 1953; Dahomey, 31 July, 1 August 1953; Guinea, 1 August 1953, 17G 529 (144), AS.

123 Affaires Politiques, Revues trimestrielles, Soudan, 3rd trimester 1953, AP 2230/4, ANSOM; High Commissioner to Minister 8 August 1953, Affaires Politiques, Note pour M. le Ministre, 10 November 1953, AP 3417, ANSOM.

124 Affaires Politiques, Senegal, Revues trimestrielles, 1st trimester 1953, 1 April 1953, AP 2230/4, ANSOM.

125 Ibid., and the report on the Soudan, 3rd trimester 1953, ibid.

126 Ibid.

127 Conseil Supérieur du Travail, session of 8 September 1953, IGT 1, ANSOM.

128 FWA, Grand Conseil, session of 20 May 1953, 237, 240.

129 Ibid., session of 10 November 1953, 6–7; "Allocution prononcée par Bernard Cornut-Gentille, Haut Commissaire, à la séance d'ouverture de la deuxième session 1953 du Grand Conseil de l'Afrique Occidentale Française, 10 Novembre 1953," 21.

130 Joseph Dumas and Jean Silvandre used the occasion of a discussion of the ministry's budget to chastise the government for delay on the 20 percent. Assemblée Nationale, *Débats* (23 Novembre 1953), pp. 5419–21. Dumas also took the argument to the enemy camp in "L'application du Code du Travail des T.O.M. et l'affaire des 20%," 428 (23 January 54), 187–88.

131 FWA, Grand Conseil, *Bulletin*, 14 November 1953, 12–16.

132 There is a useful review of these events in the intervention of Diawadou Barry before the Assemblée de l'Union Française asking for an investigation into the application of the Code du Travail. *Débats*, 24 November 1953, 1063–64.

133 High Commissioner to Minister, telegrams 13, 20, 25 November 1953, 17G 529 (144), AS; IGT, FWA, Note on "la situation sociale en Afrique Occidentale Française," 10 November 1953, High Commissioner to Minister 18 November 1953, AP 3417, Affaires Politiques, Revues trimestrielles, Senegal, 4th trimester 1953, AP 2230/3, ANSOM; Dakar, Political Annual Report, 1953.

134 IGT, FWA, Note on "the social situation in French West Africa," 10 November 1953, High Commissioner to Minister, 18 November 1953, AP 3417, ANSOM.

135 High Commissioner to Minister, 20 November 1953 (telegram), 17G 529 (144), AS.

136 High Commissioner to Minister, 25 November 1953 (telegram), 17G 529 (144), AS; Affaires Politiques, Revue trimestrielle, Senegal, 4th trimester

1953, AP 2230/3, ANSOM. For a review of the strikes over the 40-hour rule and official reactions to them, see Michel Rezeau, "Un exemple de la mise en application du Code du Travail Outre-Mer," Mémoire No. 37, Ecole Nationale de la France Outre-Mer, 1954–55, 40–57.

137 Renseignements, 1956, on Sékou Touré, 17G 606, AS; Governor, Guinea, to High Commissioner, 1 December 1953 (telegram), 17G 271, same to same, 16 December 1953, 17G 529 (144), AS. The strike was settled on 25 November, after the governor-general had made his plea regarding the minimum wage, but before the minister had answered. In its aftermath, the houses of some "African personalities" who had not joined the strike effort were stoned by groups of youths. High Commissioner to Minister, 2 December 1953 (telegram), 17G 271, AS.

138 Affaires Politiques, "Note sur le syndicalisme en A.O.F.," n.d. [late 1953], AP 3417, ANSOM. Abbas Guèye was criticized in union circles for accepting the 16 percent. IGT, FWA, "Note au sujet des mesures locales d'application du Code du Travail et de la situation sociale," 14 September 1953, 18G 240 (160), AS.

139 "Note sur le syndicalisme."

140 Renseignements, Ivory Coast, 9 December 1952, 17G 271, AS.

141 Revues trimestrielles, Ivory Coast, 2nd and 3rd trimesters 1953, AP 2230/4, ANSOM.

142 Ibid. The Inspecteur du Travail's annual report for 1953 also noted the conflict between the interests of workers and those of African planters, who were the backbone of the PDCI. Fiankan and other trade unionists, even in the CGT, nonetheless were under the influence of Houphouët-Boigny. "It is for that reason that, at the time of the revision of the tables for the *minimum vital*, the trade unionists, while maintaining their extreme position, accepted definitively the compromise solution proposed by the Administration." Ivory Coast, IT, AR, 1953, 89.

143 Quoted in R. W. Johnson, "Sékou Touré and the Guinean Revolution," *African Affairs* 69 (1970): 351.

144 High Commissioner to Minister, 20 March 1954, IGT 11/2, ANSOM.

145 Renseignements, Ivory Coast, 9 December 1952, 17G 271, AS. See also Joseph Roger de Benoist, *L'Afrique Occidentale Française de 1944 à 1960* (Dakar: Nouvelles Editions Africaines, 1982), 212–14.

146 The phrase is used in Affaires Politiques, "note sur le syndicalisme en A.O.F.," n.d. [1953], AP 3417, ANSOM.

147 Section Afrique Occidentale, meeting of 15 October 1954, Union Coloniale 120, ANSOM.

148 FWA, Directeur Général des Finances, "Note pour le Haut Commissaire," 27 January 1953, K 440 (165), AS.

149 Ibid.

150 J. Debay, "Note sur l'incidence de l'application de l'article 112 du Code du Travail sur l'économie agricole et industrielle de l'A.O.F.," 27 February 1953, 18G 240 (160), AS. R. Bonnal, Directeur Adjoint des Travaux Publics, was also less alarmist than Erhard in regard to budgetary matters. Presentation to a Conference of Directors on "L'incidence du Code du Travail," 24 February 1953, ibid.

151 H. de la Bruchollerie, Inspecteur de la France Outre-Mer, "Note sur la situation économique de la Côte d'Ivoire au 1er janvier 1954," 10 January 1954, 1Q 656 (171), AS.

152 Louis-Paul Aujoulat, "La querelle des 20% ne doit pas compromettre plus longtemps une application franche et loyale du Code du Travail," *Marchés Coloniaux* 425 (2 January 1954): 7–8. The study by Bruchollerie asserted that profits in commerce ranged from 20 to 40 per cent of value in the case of cloth to 30 to 40 percent in the case of tools. "Note sur la situation économique de la Côte d'Ivoire," 10 January 1954, 1Q 656 (171), AS. The argument over the consequences of the code also took place between Joseph Dumas and Paul Devinat in the pages of the Catholic weekly, *L'Afrique Nouvelle*, 326 (4 November 1953) and 330 (2 December 1953).

153 Comité de l'Empire Français, Section Afrique Occidentale, meeting of 14 January 1954, Union Coloniale 120, ANSOM. The business community in FWA did not generally see opportunities deriving from the increased purchasing power of African workers. A partial exception is Luc de Carbon, "L'incidence de l'évolution sociale et du niveau de vie autochtone sur la consommation des produits alimentaires importés," *Marchés Coloniaux* 395 (6 June 1953): 1579–81.

154 Jacques Lecaillon, *Les incidences économiques et financières du code du travail: Contribution à l'étude du mécanisme de la répartition des revenus dans les territoires d'outre-mer* (Dakar: Institut des Hautes Etudes de Dakar, 1954). The point that farmers were not falling behind workers was also made in de la Bruchollerie's report on the Ivory Coast, where the standard of living of cocoa and coffee farmers had, he claimed, nearly doubled since 1938. "Note sur la situation économique," 10 January 1954, 1Q 656 (171), AS.

155 Minister to High Commissioners and Governors, 18 March 1953, 11D 1/1309, AS. Chef du Service Judiciaire, Gouvernement-Général, to Présidents des Tribunaux du Travail, A.O.F., 20 February 1956, K 418 (144), AS. This circular cited Senghor's intervention (discussed above) in the debate to emphasize that the definition of a worker was written so as to include a worker from a traditional community when he was working temporarily or seasonally for wages but to exclude him when the labor in question was in the customary milieu. It admitted that care would have to be taken in judging individual cases.

156 Comité de l'Empire Français, Section de l'Afrique Occidentale, meeting of 12 March 1953, Union Coloniale 120, ANSOM.

157 "Note personnelle et confidentielle pour M. le Ministre," 27 November 1952, IGT 15/1, ANSOM.

158 Aujoulat, "Préface," to Secrétariat Social d'Outre-Mer, *Code du Travail*, 18.

159 Bernard Cornut-Gentille, Speech opening the 2nd session of 1954, Grand Conseil de l'Afrique Occidentale Française, 13 October 1954, 14–15. Much of the speech was spent expressing regret that he could not do more for the legitimate grievances of civil servants given the slowing of growth and problems of government finance.

160 Minister, Circular to High Commissioners, Commissioners, and IGTs, 3 September 1953, IGT 16/1, ANSOM.

161 For critiques from the right, see "Le projet d'institution d'un régime d'allocations familiales aux travailleurs du secteur privé," *Marchés Coloniaux*, 507 (30 July 1955): 2106–7, and "Le Comité central de la F.O.M. proteste contre l'octroi d'allocations familiales aux salariés africaines," ibid. 419 (21 November 1953): 3238. This journal had earlier used the polygamy issue to attack the provision of family allocations to civil servants. The Catholic weekly *L'Afrique Nouvelle* supported family allocations, but not for polygamists. The social Catholic Louis-Paul Aujoulat, however, argued that the state should help the African family "such as it actually is and evolves and not imprint such and such a European orientation on it." See "Le gouvernement ne doit plus encourager la polygamie," *Marchés Coloniaux* 455 (14 June 1952): 1632, Joseph Bonnefoy, "Quelques exemples d'allocations 'familiales,'" *Afrique Nouvelle*, 313 (5 August 1952), Aujoulat in ibid., 255 (21 June 1952).

162 IGT, "Eléments pour servir à l'étude de l'institution d'un régime de prestations familiales en A.O.F.," 1 December 1954, IGT 17/3, ANSOM; FWA, Direction Générale des Services Economiques et du Plan, Bureau d'Etudes, "Note sur les répercussions dans les divers secteurs de l'activité économique d'un système d'allocations familiales," n.d. [1955], 18G 236, AS. The figures in industry amounted to an average of 0.84 child per worker, compared to 0.44 in agriculture, 0.6 in transport, 1.09 in commerce, 1.47 on the railway and 2.29 in the civil service (the last two already had allocations). Officials thought the figures outside of the civil service would come up substantially if one eliminated the lowest ranks of workers. In general, better paid workers had more children, but still only an average of 2.3. Ibid. The statistics in different surveys are somewhat inconsistent.

163 High Commissioner, FWA, to Minister, 16 December 1954; High Commissioner, FEA, to Minister, 10 January 1955, IGT, AEF, "Etude préliminaire de l'institution des prestations familiales," 28 September 1954, IGT 16/1, ANSOM; IGT, "Eléments pour servir à l'étude de l'institution d'un régime de prestations familiales en A.O.F.," 1 December 1954, IGT 17/3, ANSOM.

164 IGT, FEA, "Etude préliminaire," 28 September 1954, IGT 16/1, ANSOM.

165 High Commissioner, FWA, to Minister, 16 December 1954, IGT 16/1, ANSOM.

166 The argument was that the problem of supporting families was primarily an urban problem, while the difficulties of administration – lack of the état-civil, inadequate medical personnel to make the checks which the intended regulations required on pregnant women and children – meant that the city was the best place to begin. See in particular the intervention of David Soumah, Session of 13 November 1954, IGT 2, ANSOM.

167 M. Dubled, Conseil Supérieur du Travail, session of 30 July 1953, and Buron, session of 12–13 November 1954, IGT 1; "Note présenté par M. Dubled relative à l'application d'un régime d'allocations familiales dans les Territoires d'Outre-Mer," July 1954, and transcript of meeting of the Conseil Supérieur du Travail, 21 July 1954, IGT 2, ANSOM.

168 Silvandre had presented an amendment making a token reduction of the overseas ministry's budget to protest the delay in implementing family allocations. The vote was 317 to 287. The Conseil de la République would not

go along. Assemblée Nationale, *Débats*, 17 December 1954, 6486–92, 6490 quoted; Conseil de la République, *Débats*, 2 February 1955, 378–86.

169 High Commissioner to Minister, 17 December 1954, 14 February 1955, AP 2264/8, ANSOM; Affaires Politiques, Bulletins mensuels, January 1955, 2G 55–133, AS; de Benoist, 232; Ivory Coast, IT, AR, 1954. On the strike wave of 1955, see Affaires Politiques, Bulletins mensuels, 1955, 2G 55–133, AS. The issue of equality was also evident in the left wing and union press: N'Diaye Massata, "Le racisme dans les allocations familiales," *Phare du Sénégal*, 34 (November 1954), microfilm copy in Morgenthau, *Documents on African Political History*, reel 1; editorial by Kamara Latyr, *Le Travailleur Africain* 8 (November 1954); resolution of the Conférence Intersyndicale Africaine de la Fonction Publique, Conakry, 3–5 September 1954, in *Le Prolétaire*, 37 (August 1954).

170 High Commissioner to Minister, 17 December 1954, AP 2264/8, ANSOM.

171 FWA, "Synthèse de l'activité syndicale et sociale," 3rd trimester, 1955, 2G 55–134, AS.

172 High Commissioner to Ministry, 22 November 1955 (telegram), K 418 (144), AS.

173 Cornut-Gentille noted earlier that the unions' claims were federation-wide, and while at the time he wanted to move slowly he recognized that he had to move over this area. High Commissioner, Circular to Governors, n.d. [June 1954], AP 3417, ANSOM. The IGT pointed out to Paris the inaction of governors in this regard. IGT, "Note pour le Conseil des Ministres," 21 March 1955, IGT 15/1, ANSOM.

174 The question of applying the program to agriculture was fought out in early 1955. Employer representatives opposed it, arguing that only "European type" enterprises would be affected. On the other hand, union representatives wanted to include agriculture. The separate fund for agriculture was the compromise that emerged. IGT, "Note pour le Conseil des Ministres," 21 March 1955, IGT, Rapport au Ministre, 8 April 1955, IGT 15/1, ANSOM; Assemblée Nationale, *Débats*, 17 December 1954, 6487, 6488, 6491 (interventions of Charles Benoist, Jean Silvandre, and Hammadoun Dicko). The last was emphatic that African employers should pay allocations like everyone else.

175 This "allocation au foyer" was limited to the first three children of a worker's first wife (or a subsequent wife in case of the death of the first). The territorial assemblies of Senegal, Mauritania, and the Soudan opposed this because it introduced discrimination against the children of polygamous households. Employer organizations opposed it on grounds of cost, and unions wanted an alternative form. But the minister stuck to the allocation au foyer precisely because it supported the foundation of monogamous households. A memorandum within the Inspection du Travail noted the "preoccupations of the Minister to struggle against polygamy." IGT, Rapport au Ministre, 26 October 1955, and IGT, "Note pour M. Ergman," 3 June 1955, IGT 15/1, and Minister to High Commissioner, 26 November 1955, `IGT 15/3, ANSOM.

176 Minister, Circular to High Commissioners, 13 June 1955, IGT 15/3, ANSOM.

177 Avis des Assemblées Territoriaux d'Afrique Occidentale Française, with comments from the High Commissioner, 11 October 1955, IGT 17/4; High Commissioner to Minister, 14 October 1955, IGT 15/1, ANSOM; Minister to High Commissioner, 26 November 1955; High Commissioner, Circular to Governors, 24 November 1955 (telegram), K 418 (144), AS. For the *patronat*'s surrender, see Comité de l'Empire Français, Section de l'Afrique Occidentale, meeting of 15 September 1955, Union Coloniale 120, ANSOM.

178 For a discussion of the complicated provisions, see Gonidec, *Droit du travail*, 643–92.

179 IGT, "Prestations familiales: état au 10 mars 1956," IGT 15/1, ANSOM.

180 Procedures are detailed in the draft decrees in 18G 236, AS, for example ones from Senegal and the Ivory Coast.

181 Michel Foucault, *Discipline and Punish: The Birth of the Prison* (New York: Vintage, 1979). On the surveillance of women in another colonial situation, see Nancy Hunt, "Le Bébé en Brousse: European Women, African Birth Spacing and Colonial Intervention in Breast Feeding in the Belgian Congo," *International Journal of African Historical Studies* 21 (1988): 401–32.

182 FWA, Directeur Général des Services Economiques et du Plan, Bureau d'Etudes, "Notes sur les répercussions dans les divers secteurs de l'activité économique d'un système d'allocations familiales," n.d. [1955], 18G 236, AS.

183 While opponents of the code questioned whether men would actually spend the money on children, this was just one of a series of charges made by people who had no sincere stake in perfecting the regulations, and such objections carried little weight. Conseil Supérieur du Travail, Meetings of 21 July, 12, 13 November 1954, IGT 2, ANSOM.

184 Minister to High Commissioner, 25 November 1955, IGT 15/3, ANSOM.

185 FWA, "Prestations familiales résultants des premiers mois de fonctionnement," n.d. [1957], IGT 16/2, ANSOM; Senegal, IT, AR, 1956; "Conférence des inspecteurs généraux du travail et des lois sociales de la France Outre-Mer," 16 March 1957, IGT 16/2, ANSOM. One problem was securing proof that a child was that of the worker who claimed him or her. Officials hoped that the incentive of allocations would be a reason for people to register births. Collecting employer contributions also proved slow.

186 Minister, Circular to High Commissioners and Governors, 13 June 1955, IGT 15/3, ANSOM.

187 The minimum wage in Dakar went from 28.10 francs per hour to 31 in 1956, to 35 francs in 1957, to 38.50 in July 1958 and to 40 in December 1958, following changes in the *minimum vital*. Senegal, IT, AR, 1956, 1958.

188 Pierre Chauleur, *Le régime du travail dans les territoires d'Outre-Mer* (Paris: Encyclopedie d'Outre Mer, 1956), 21; Rezeau, "Un exemple de la mise en application du Code du Travail Outre-Mer," 77. Inspectors could claim at home and abroad that the code was a triumph of social policy, and a former minister credited the code with preserving peace and holding off nationalist challenges in Africa. IGT, "Note pour M. le Directeur des Affaires Politiques," 30 October 1953; Jean-Jacques Juglas, preface to Pierre Chauleur, *Le régime du travail*.

189 A territorial social service had opened in 1950 in two working-class areas of Abidjan, and another office opened in Dakar. The service had minimal

funding. FWA, "Rapport Biannuel sur la protection de la collectivité, de la famille et de l'enfance," 1951–52, 2G 52–3; Rapport sur les Centres Sociaux en Afrique Occidentale Française, 1956, 2G 56–125, AS.

190 This organization was supposed to help with the rapid training of adults. Efforts to promote employer-sponsored programs as well as government-run training programs had failed in part because of an acute case of the free rider problem. The labor market in Africa was so disarticulated, with such tiny numbers of skilled people, that anyone trained by his employer could easily find more lucrative employment elsewhere or become self-employed, leaving the trainer in the lurch. This came up in discussions of the Office d'Etudes Psychotechniques, Assemblée de l'Union Française, *Débats* 13 December 1951, 1079. On the importance of Etudes Psychotechniques in France, see Downs, *Manufacturing Inequality*.

191 *Combat*, 24 December 1954, clipping in K 418 (144), Mission d'Etudes Psychotechniques, "Le facteur humain dans la formation professionelle en Afrique," August 1951, K 456 (179), "Quelques aspects de la psychologie africaine," July 1953, 2G 53–113, AS; Raoul Durand, "La formation professionelle et la psychologie des noirs," *Problèmes d'Afrique Centrale* 24 (1954): 102–8. On the emergence of this sort of thinking in Europe, see Anson Rabinbach, *The Human Motor: Energy, Fatigue, and the Origins of Modernity* (New York: Basic Books, 1990).

192 Office d'Etudes Psychotechniques, "Quelqeus aspects de la psychologie africaine," July 1953, pp. 48–49, 2G 53–113, AS.

193 "Comment vit un travailleur Africain au Sénégal?", n.d. [1953], K 455 (179), AS; *Barakela*, 17 September 1951, clipping in 17G 272, AS. Lamine Guèye used a similar phrase in arguing for equal benefits for African and metropolitan civil servants. Grand Conseil, *Bulletin*, 9 November 1951, p. 35. The critics of the code were obliged to take this argument on. "We know that tropical lands are not the Touraine," said René Moureux, in vain. "Les textes d'application du Code du Travail dans les T.O.M. doivent être à la fois loyaux et prudents," *Marchés Coloniaux* 382 (28 February 1953): 609–10.

8 Family wages and industrial relations in British Africa

1 This was what Creech Jones said to his governors to try to get them to conduct frequent reviews of wages in their colonies. Notes by Grossmith on meeting of 20 October 1949, CO 859/150/12284/1946–48, CO 859/150/12284/1946–48, PRO. At one point, British officials in East Africa wrote of their desire for a "common Labour Code" for Kenya, Tanganyika, and Uganda, but they meant it to apply only to organizations like the railway which functioned on an interterritorial basis. Ad hoc committee on "Co-ordination of Labour Policy," Meeting of 8 December 1949, CO 859/208/12327/1/1950, PRO.

2 At times, colonial legislatures caused considerable embarrassment, when for instance several refused to abolish penal sanctions for laborers' violations of contracts in accordance with an ILO convention which Great Britain had ratified. ILO Draft Report by Governing Body on applications of Convention 65 of 1939, 18 December 1958, C. E. T. Storar (Commonwealth Relations Office) to T. V. Scrivenor, 5 May 1959, CO 859/1183, PRO.

3 Creech Jones, Minute, 3 November 1948, CO 859/150/12284/1946-48, PRO.
4 Minute by Edgar Parry, 28 September 1949, CO 859/150/12284/1946-48, PRO.
5 Draft memorandum (unsent), "Labour's Share in the Product of Colonial Industry," 13 October 1949, and Minutes by A. Emmanuel, 3 January 1949 and W. L. Gorrell Barnes, 25 January 1949, CO 859/150/12284/1946-48, PRO. Meanwhile, the Labour government was asking unions in Great Britain itself to moderate wage demands in the face of economic difficulties, and the Colonial Office wasn't clear what if any implications this had for the colonies – in a period very favorable to tropical exports. Minutes of Parry, 16 December 1949, and G. Foggon, 17 February 1950, CO 859/150/12284/1949, PRO.
6 *Labour Administration in the Colonial Territories 1944–1950*, Colonial No. 275 (1951), 6. This paper also documents the hodge-podge of wage-fixing committees and boards through which the request was answered.
7 *Daily Mail*, 27 July 1948, quoted in Frank Furedi, *Colonial Wars and the Politics of Third World Nationalism* (London: I. B. Tauris, 1994), 233.
8 Social Services Department, "Trade Unionism in the Colonies," CLAC (50)28, 14 October 1950, CO 859/184/12254/F/1950-51, PRO.
9 Parry, Minute, 28 September 1949, CO 859/150/12284/1946-48; Colonial Office, Social Service Department, "Trade Unionism in the Colonies," CLAC (50)28, 14 October 1950, CO 859/184/12254/F/1950-51; Colonial Labour Advisory Committee, "Trade Unionism in the Colonies," Memorandum, CLAC (51)11, 1951, CO 888/8, PRO.
10 Secretary of State, Circular, 26 July 1951, CO 859/183/12254/1951, PRO. This circular was based on a review of labor relations by the Colonial Labour Advisory Committee. Griffiths claimed that trade union development in the past decade had been "broadly successful," but he still referred to the "comparative immaturity of the unions."
11 Some British officials thought the French system of wage fixing was superior to their own and variants on it were proposed for the Gold Coast civil service. The Subcommittee on Wage-Fixing and Family Responsibilities suggested that some might want to ask "a body of elder statesmen" in each territory to prepare a "national wage-structure" that would reflect a minimum standard of family subsistence. Why the wisdom of age was the relevant one for this project was not obvious. Notes on changes in the wage structure of the Gold Coast, arising out of the Lidbury Commission, Colonial Labour Advisory Committee Memorandum, CLAC (W)(53)5, August 1953; Subcommittee on Wage-Fixing and Family Responsibilities, meeting of 28 July 1953, CLAC (W)(53)3, CO 888/10, PRO.
12 Memorandum by C. H. Hartwell, Deputy Chief Secretary, "African Wage Policy," 11 November 1952, CO 822/657. The board at this time included two employers', representatives, two employees' representatives, and three independents. Hartwell pointed out that the government itself was paying at the bottom of its scale "less than is required to maintain the worker *and his family*." Wage systems are reviewed by the British TUC in "Industrial Relations in the Colonies," 29 October 1953, CO 859/748, PRO.
13 M. Phillips, "Wage Fixing and Family Responsibilities," draft paper for CLAC, 9 May 1953, CO 859/257; meeting of the Wage-fixing and Family

Responsibility Subcommittee of the Colonial Labour Advisory Committee, 25 August 1953, CO 888/10; Governor, Uganda, to Secretary of State, 23 December 1955, Governor, Tanganyika, to Secretary of State, 11 July 1955, Governor, Gold Coast, to Secretary of State, 1 April 1955, Acting Governor, Nigeria, to Secretary of State 22 April 1955, CO 859/810, PRO. Officials thought that East African wages would have to be raised by 50 percent to provide for a wife and three children. Subcommittee on Wage Fixing and Family Responsibilities, meeting of 28 July 1953, CO 859/257.

14 Barltrop to Governor, Nigeria, 13 May 1954, CO 554/1340; Report by Labour Commission on Industrial Situation in Sierra Leone during the Early Part of 1951, 30 June 1951, CO 554/223, PRO.

15 G. Foggon, "Industrial Relations in the Colonial Territories," Paper prepared for a conference of heads of Labour Departments, August 1951, LC (51)3, CO 859/210/2, PRO.

16 "Trade Unionism in the Colonies," CLAC (51)11, 1951, CO 888/8, PRO; *Labour Administration in the Colonial Territories*, Colonial No. 275 (1951), 5.

17 Notes on a meeting of heads of Labour Departments, 1951, CLAC (51)31, CO 888/8, PRO; Member for Education, Labour and Lands, in Kenya, *Legislative Council Debates* 69 (5 June 1950), c. 99; E. Parry, "Colonial Trade Unions," *Corona* 1, 7 (1949): 20; Governor, Tanganyika, to Secretary of State, 11 July 1955, CO 859/810; Foggon, LC (51)3, CO 859/210/2, PRO; T. M. Yesufu, *An Introduction to Industrial Relations in Nigeria* (London: Oxford University Press, 1962), 178. Parry at least had the wisdom to add to his comment about infancy, "There is of course no such thing as an infant trade union in law."

18 TUC report, "The TUC and Trade Unionism in the Colonies," July 1950, CO 859/186/12254/P/2/1950–51, PRO. Within the Labour left, the TUC's policy was by 1954 being challenged by the Movement for Colonial Freedom. The movement's emergence owes much to the fact of political mobilization in the colonies themselves. Stephen Howe, *Anticolonialism in British Politics: The Left and the End of Empire, 1918–1964* (Oxford: Clarendon Press, 1993), 182, 281–88, 318–20.

19 The TUC got into this game as vigorously as did the Colonial Office. "The TUC and Trade Unionism in the Colonies," July 1950, CO 859/186/12254/P/2/1950–51; N. D. Watson, memorandum on trade union policy, 9 November 1953, CO 859/748, PRO. There was a degree of tension between the two, as the TUC opposed restrictive trade union legislation and wanted more scope for labour officers who were helping unions organize. Record of talks between CO and TUC, 28 January 1954, ibid.

20 The independence of trade unions in Nigeria was mitigated by their tendency to be "small, ineffective, unrepresentative, and badly led" and by the tendency of the unions to push for government wage tribunals rather than negotiated agreements. Yesufu, *Industrial Relations in Nigeria*, 143–44, 170. See also Robin Cohen, *Labour and Politics in Nigeria, 1945–71* (London: Heinemann, 1974); Richard Jeffries, *Class, Power and Ideology in Ghana: The Railwaymen of Sekondi* (Cambridge: Cambridge University Press, 1978); Anthony Clayton and Donald Savage, *Government and Labour in Kenya 1895–1963* (London: Cass, 1974).

21 Although Frank Furedi provides a useful discussion of how the British language of demagogy and communism gave little scope for legitimate political movements in the colonies, he writes as if all oppositional movements could be assimilated to nationalism and therefore misses a key dynamic: the very obsession with danger could make officials eager to find "responsible" elements and different kinds of movements could become more attractive in certain circumstances, either responsible trade unions (vs. irresponsible politicians) or conservative nationalists (vs. radical labor movements). I will return to these dynamics in Part IV. Furedi, *Colonial Wars and the Politics of Third World Nationalism.*

22 Richard E. Luyt, *Trade Unionism in African Colonies.* New Africa Pamphlet No. 119 (Johannesburg: Institute of Race Relations, 1949), 36, 38; Griffiths, comments to 48th meeting, Colonial Labour Advisory Committee, 5 October 1951, CO 888/8, PRO.

23 Colonial Office, Social Service Department, Memorandum on "Trade Unionism in the Colonies," CLAC (50)28, 14 October 1950, CO 859/184/F/1950–51, PRO.

24 These issues were discussed off and on in the 1950s in the Colonial Labour Advisory Committee. CO 888/8 and CO 888/10.

25 Some African trade unionists were brought to the UK, mainly to Ruskin College, for training as well, but officials did not like this idea for fear that the trainees might meet the occasional British communist. Social Service Department, "Trade Unionism in the Colonies," CLAC (50)28, 14 October 1950, CO 859/184/12254/F/1950–51, PRO. On the TUC's role, see the Minutes and Memoranda in the dossier "Trade Union Policy, 1954–56," CO 859/748, PRO.

26 Minute by Barry Smallman, c. May 1950, CO 859/203/12267/2/1950–51; Secretary of State, Circular, 22 August 1951, CO 859/294; Minute by N. D. Watson, 4 March 1952, on meeting with British TUC; Secretary of State to Governor, 7 April 1952, CO 859/268; Secretary of State to OAG, Kenya, Uganda, Tanganyika, 20 August 1952, 17 February 1954, and Governor, Kenya, to Secretary of State, 23 February 1953, CO 859/294, PRO.

27 In Nigeria, the primitiveness argument – that union members were "uneducated and illiterate" – was invoked to justify government intrusion into union business and restrictions on strikes. In Northern Rhodesia, the "very recent origin" of unions and the "industrial chaos" they caused were evoked to justify restrictive measures. In the Gold Coast, it was labor's recent participation in the illegal Positive Action campaign. Governor's Deputy, Nigeria, to Secretary of State, 26 April 1946, CO 859/92/12254/2/1945–46; Governor, Gold Coast, to Secretary of State, 14 February, 18 October, 1 November 1950 (telegram), Minutes by G. Foggon, 1 November, 13 December 1950, CO 859/187/4; British reply to charges made to the ILO over detention of union officers in Northern Rhodesia, incl. Director General, ILO, to Secretary, Ministry of Labour, UK, 12 March 1957, CO 859/1325, PRO.

28 L. H. Gorsuch, Colonial Office, to F. R. Armitage, Gold Coast Secretariat, 29 March 1950, CO 859/187/4, PRO.

29 For direct British reactions to the international discussion see Colonial Office, "Labour Productivity in Africa," paper for the Inter-African Labour

Conference, Bamako, January 1953, CO 859/304, PRO. On this issue in the metropole, see John Macnicol, *The Movement for Family Allowances, 1918–45: A Study in Social Policy Development* (London: Heinemann, 1980). The growing British welfare state remained attached to the idea of the male breadwinner and the family wage, whereas French policy makers took a more "parental" approach and favored a stronger system of family allowances. Susan Pedersen, *Family, Dependence and the Origins of the Welfare State: Britain and France, 1914–1945* (Cambridge: Cambridge University Press, 1993).

30 Conclusion of a discussion of the Subcommittee on Wage-Fixing and Family Responsibilities, 28 July 1953, CO 859/257, PRO. The subcommittee considered that the French approach – "was an ideological one." Ibid.

31 Sir Frederick Seaford, 55th CLAC meeting, 18 June 1953, CO 859/257, PRO.

32 Similarly, the subcommittee on Wage-Fixing and Family Responsibilities concluded, "It was wrong to confuse an industrial problem, namely the wage-level, with a social problem, the need or otherwise for family allowances." Meeting of 28 July 1953, CO 859/257, PRO.

33 Governor's Deputy, Tanganyika, to CO, 11 January 1954, Governor, Sierra Leone, to CO, 6 February 1954, Governor, Kenya, to Secretary of State, 8 February 1954, Governor, Gambia, to Secretary of State, 7 September 1954, CO 859/850; Labour Commissioner, Tanganyika, to Earl Barltrop, CO, 21 September 1953, survey of opinions of Labour Commissioners, in M. Phillips, "Wage Fixing and Family Responsibilities," Paper for CLAC, 9 May 1953, CO 859/257; "CO, "Labour Productivity in Africa," paper prepared for the Inter-African Labour Conference, January 1953, CO 859/304, PRO. More on this theme will come out in the case study of Kenya, below.

34 Subcommittee on Wage-Fixing and Family Responsibilities, meeting of 28 July 1953, CO 859/257, PRO.

35 M. Phillips, "Wage Fixing and Family Responsibilities," Draft paper for CLAC, 9 May 1953, CO 859/257, PRO. The variety of ways in which women earned income went largely unanalyzed until decades later.

36 Southern Rhodesia, *Report of the Urban African Affairs Commission 1958* (Salisbury, 1958), 6, 10, 19, 120, 132.

37 Lyttleton still preferred that wages be set by collective bargaining and admitted again that this was unlikely to happen. He recommended that governments do better than the bachelor rate in setting minimum wages. There was not much more he could say. Secretary of State, Circular Letter, 2 June 1954, CO 859/810, PRO. He was responding to doubts raised in Minutes from Arrighi Emmanuel, 24 March 1954, and Melville, 3 April 1954, ibid.

38 Conclusions of Labour Administration Conference, 1956, CO 859/810, PRO.

39 For an early foray see Colonial Office Memorandum, "Social Security in the Colonies," 1944, CO 859/12/8, and for later ones, "Social Development in the Colonies," Colonial Office Information Department Memorandum No. 10, January 1953, CO 859/518, PRO; Subcommittee on Social Security in the Colonial Territories (of the Colonial Labour Advisory Committee), meetings of 15 February 1954, 12 January, 10 November 1955; Memorandum for the Sub-Committee, "Social Security in the Colonial Territories." Secretary of State Lyttleton dismissed social insurance schemes in response to a

Parliamentary question on 17 February 1954. These meeting minutes, reports, and statements are in the papers of CLAC, CO 888/10. See also revised report of the Subcommittee on Social Security, 1954, CO 859/1180. The need to avoid future financial responsibility is emphasized in Despatch of the Secretary of State, 12 March 1957, and enclosed report from the Colonial Labour Advisory Committee, CO 859/739. The 1961 comment is from Margaret Maccoll, Minute, 29 May 1961, CO 822/2909, PRO. Unemployment compensation was held to be particularly undesirable, because most officials would not acknowledge that the worker who wasn't working was in fact a worker. 11th Meeting of East African Labour Commissioners, Nairobi, 13–15 November 1961, CO 822/2679.

40 For an exception – which led to no follow-up – see the argument "that the immediate introduction of the old age security scheme for the farm workers would lessen the prevalent tension before the African Political Parties and the Europeans" expressed in Herman A. Oduor, Secretary-General, General Agricultural Workers' Union, to Sir Geoffrey Nye, Agricultural Advisor to CO, n.d. [February 1961], CO 822/2908, PRO.

41 H. A. Fosbrooke, "Social Security as a Felt Want in East and Central Africa," *Bulletin of the International Social Security Association* 13 (1960): 284. Fosbrooke (283) points out that Kenya, Northern Rhodesia, and Southern Rhodesia were at least "worried about social security," whereas Uganda, Tanganyika, and Nyasaland – where the stabilized work force was less of an issue – ignored the problem. For the ILO's continued interest in the question it first raised in 1944, see "Social Security in Africa South of the Sahara," *International Labour Review* 84 (1961): 144–74.

42 The copper mines of Northern Nigeria for example provided a pension to employees reaching age 50 with twenty years of service. Most governments paid pensions or lump-sum retirement benefits. Fosbrooke, "Social Security," 284.

43 *Report of the Social Security Committee* (Nairobi: Government Printer, 1957); C. E. Clarke and S. A. Ogilvie, Report on evaluation of social security, 10 April 1961, CO 822/2908; E. Turner, "Provision for Old Age: A Report," June 1963, CO 822/2909; P. C. Crichton (Ministry of Local Government, Health and Housing, Kenya) to J. L. F. Buist (CO), 25 April 1957, Kenya, Council of Ministers, Report by the Minister for Local Government, Health, and Housing and Report of discussion, 16 July 1957, CO 822/1827; Minute by Sheila Ogilvie, 8 March 1960, Crichton to Director, East African Statistical Department, 22 June 1960, CO 822/2908; Kenya, Council of Ministers, Discussion, 21 March 1962, Ogilvie, Minutes, 19 May 1961, 31 July 1963, CO 822/2909, PRO. The last colonial plan for a Provident Fund (Turner report) was expected to apply to 350,000 men – and only men – who would contribute 5 percent of their wages, to be matched by their employers, and who could collect accumulations (with interest) after age 60.

44 Clayton and Savage, *Government and Labour*, 405–6. While the national fund was in limbo, the labour department pressured private firms to do more. Ibid., 406.

45 See correspondence in the above files, especially Crichton to Director, East African Statistical Department, 22 June 1960, Clarke-Ogilvie Report, 1961,

CO 822/1908, Kenya, Council of Ministers, Discussions, 21 March 1962, Margaret Maccoll, Minute, 29 May 1961, CO 822/2909, PRO. Other examples are similarly edifying. The Northern Rhodesian government asked Kenya for help, and similarly cited "incredible difficulties" in regard to demographic data and population registers. William Clifford (Director of Social Welfare) to Ogilvie, 2 August 1960, CO 1015/2632. When a minister in Eastern Nigeria brought up the possibility of a social insurance scheme in 1954, he was pompously told that such programs were "generally associated with countries whose economy is predominantly based upon wage-earning employment" and presumed capacities which Nigeria did not have. But other officials decided "an expert from this country [i.e. Britain]" was needed. Nigeria kept thinking about and shelving plans, sought more expert advice in 1959, and decided to act in 1960. See Extract from Departmental Conference, Lagos, 23–24 February 1954, N. D. Watson, Minute, 7 April 1955, CO 554/1438; G. Foggon, Note on meeting with Minister of Labour, Lagos, 22 May 1958, CO 554/1998; J. S. Bennett, Minute, 12 November 1959, Governor-General, Nigeria, to Secretary of State, 10 June 1959, CO 554/2107; F. C. Nwokedi, Minister of Labour, to Mathews, 3 May 1960, CO 554/2837, PRO.

46 Kenya's National Provident Fund was finally announced in 1964. For more on the efforts of African countries to expand retirement programs and the limits such programs faced, see the studies of the Association Internationale de la Sécurité Sociale, *Cahiers Africains de Sécurité Sociale* 13–14 (1974).

47 Timothy Scarnecchia, "The Politics of Gender and Class in the Creation of African Communities, Salisbury, Rhodesia, 1937–1957," Ph.D. dissertation, University of Michigan, 1993.

48 Lisa Lindsay is completing a Ph.D. dissertation at the University of Michigan on changing family life among Nigerian railway workers in the era of stabilization. The clash of African entrepreneurship and improvisation with the rigidities of planned urbanism are illustrated in Peter Marris, *Family and Social Change in an African City: A Study of Rehousing in Lagos* (London: Routledge, 1962). For more on housing and the gendered complexities of urban life, see Luise White, *The Comforts of Home: Prostitution in Colonial Nairobi* (Chicago: University of Chicago Press, 1990), and Richard Stren, *Housing the Urban Poor in Africa: Policy, Politics, and Bureaucracy in Mombasa* (Berkeley: Institute of International Studies, University of California, 1978).

49 James Ferguson, "Mobile Workers, Modernist Narratives: A Critique of the Historiography of Transition on the Zambian Copperbelt," *Journal of Southern African Studies* 16 (1990): 385–412, 386 quoted.

50 The diversity of marriage forms and the changing situation of women were observed in 1953–54 by the anthropologist Hortense Powdermaker, *Coppertown: Changing Africa: The Human Situation on the Rhodesian Copperbelt* (New York: Harper & Row, 1962), 151–69. See also the work of Jane L. Parpart: *Labour and Capital on the African Copperbelt* (Philadelphia: Temple University Press, 1983); "Sexuality and Power on the Zambian Copperbelt: 1926–1964," in Sharon Stichter and Jane L. Parpart (eds.), *Patriarchy and Class: African Women in the Home and Workplace* (Boulder, Colo: Westview, 1988); and "'Where is Your Mother?': Gender, Urban

Marriage, and Colonial Discourse on the Zambian Copperbelt," *International Journal of African Historical Studies* 27 (1994): 241–72.

51 As late as 1946, company officials were calling African trade unionism "a real menace," but the possibility that Africans would be organized by the European Mineworkers' Union – and present a united front to the companies – was considered even more of a menace. The Colonial Office sent a British trade unionist to take in hand what it regarded as inevitable and he found considerable enthusiasm for unionization among the more long-term mine workers. Branch unions began to form in 1948 and the African Mineworkers' Union took shape in 1949 and was recognized by the companies. Parpart, *Labour and Capital*, 114–21.

52 Ibid., 122.

53 Northern Rhodesia, *Report of the Commission Appointed to Enquire into the Advancement of Africans in Industry* (Lusaka, 1948).

54 Robert I. Rotberg, *The Rise of Nationalism in Central Africa: The Making of Malawi and Zambia, 1873–1964* (Cambridge, Mass: Harvard University Press, 1965).

55 Thomas Fox-Pitt to Governor, Northern Rhodesia, 5 September 1951, J. W. Stacpoole, Minute, 19 October 1951, CO 1015/338, PRO.

56 Governor, Northern Rhodesia, to Secretary of State, 11 October 1951, Secretary, Rhodesian Selection Trust, to Chief Secretary, Northern Rhodesia, 23 February 1952, CO 1015/338, PRO.

57 Officials were particularly annoyed that the AMWU accepted the equal pay argument, and thought it was a concession intended to avoid conflict with the European union. Lennox-Boyd, Minute on meeting with AMWU leadership, 12 February 1952; Governor to Secretary of State, 11 March 1952 (telegram); report by W. M. Macmillan on visit to Central Africa to meeting of Colonial Labour Advisory Committee, 25 September 1952, CO 1015/338, PRO.

58 Governor to Secretary of State, 30 October 1952 (telegram), CO 1015/338, PRO.

59 Sir Ronald Prain, head of the Rhodesian Selection Trust, concluded that "It was essential... for the Companies to look beyond the present dispute, which whilst ostensibly a simple wage claim, was clearly derived from African frustration. It seemed to him, since it was imperative that progress on 'Dalgleish' should not result from African initiative, that apart from continuing the present drift, which he felt would inevitably end with early African action, the only possible course was for the Companies to give notice to the European Union of their intention to terminate the existing agreements." Draft notes on meeting held at the Colonial Office, 6 January 1953, CO 1015/388, PRO. See also Elena Berger, *Labour, Race, and Colonial Rule: The Copperbelt from 1924 to Independence* (Oxford: Clarendon Press, 1974), 119–23.

60 *House of Commons Debates*, 514 (1 May 1953), cc. 2505–14.

61 Ibid., cc. 2532–34. For other parliamentary stereotyping, see the interventions of C. J. M. Alport and Douglas Dodds-Parker Ibid., cc. 2521–28, 2557–62. The Secretary of State, Lyttleton, argued that "we should place rather more emphasis upon the need for fashioning common society and building up common interest in which the colour bar would naturally disappear than in banishing the colour bar in order to make a common society." He also

brought up the old paternalist justifications for racially specific policies – that Africans would be hurt if land could be bought and sold without restriction. He put great store in local responsibility, arguing that the colonies should "work this matter out for themselves." Ibid., cc. 2573–83. Parliament voted 82 to 65 not to put the question of Brockway's motion. Ibid., c. 2594.

62 Anglo-American was concerned about links between white miners in Rhodesia and South Africa. *Financial Times*, 5, 7 May 1953, clippings in CO 1015/338, PRO; High Commissioner, Southern Rhodesia, to Commonwealth Relations Office, telegram, 4 May 1953, CO 1015/339, PRO. While the high commissioner of Southern Rhodesia feared what the European miners would do, the governor of Northern Rhodesia feared what the Africans might do. Telegram to Secretary of State, 16 May 1953, ibid.

63 *Financial Times*, 31 December 1953, *The Times*, 31 December 1953, clippings in CO 1015/339, PRO.

64 *Northern News*, 9 May 1953, clipping in CO 1015/339, PRO.

65 These were the years when serious research on workers' lives in the Copperbelt was first undertaken (chapter 9). See also Northern Rhodesia, African Affairs Annual Reports.

66 R*eport of the Board of Inquiry Appointed to Inquire into the Advancement of Africans in the Copper Mining Industry in Northern Rhodesia* (Lusaka, 1954), 6, 16–17, 20–22, 27–29. The Board argued that the industry had developed under the assumption of a dual wage structure and therefore any basic change would be a "threat to industrial expansion and the national economy." Ibid., 18.

67 Edgar Parry, Minute, 28 October 1954, CO 1015/925, PRO. Others were predicting that the labor market for Africans would become segmented. The "rationalisation of labour in the Territory" would make urban employment available only to "the best men," leaving the others in the lurch. W. F. Stubbs, Secretary for Native Affairs, in Northern Rhodesia, *African Affairs Annual Report*, 1954, 4.

68 Governor to Secretary of State, 8 October 1954, extract from Governor Benson to Sir Thomas Lloyd, 22 October 1954, CO 1015/925, PRO.

69 The companies were thinking of gradually opening up about 5 percent of the 6,000 European-held jobs on the mines, that is, about 300. The EMU was thinking in terms of 1 percent over a five-year period, that is 12 per year. Governor Benson admitted that "At first sight this seems so small as to be almost monstrous," but in view of "how few Africans really wanted to do harder and more responsible work, it is not so." Governor to J. E. Marnham, CO, 16 July 1954, CO 1015/935, PRO. This contention did not seem outlandish even to the supporters of African advancement in London, who praised Benson's letter in Minutes, e.g. H. Poynton, 22 July 1954, ibid.

70 Berger, *Labour, Race, and Colonial Rule*, 125–29. This issue made strange bedfellows. Oppenheimer "found very great difficulty in not accepting the principle of 'equal pay for equal work.'" It was also a basic principle of trade unionism. Colonial officials, who had often tried to get the TUC and other British trade union organizations involved in colonial politics, thought its participation quite risky in this case, because the TUC too might come out publicly in favor of equal pay and therefore derail advancement. Note of Meeting of Governor of Northern Rhodesia with Oppenheimer, 27 October

1954, CO 1015/925; Governor to Marnham, 1 December 1954, CO 1015/926, PRO.

71 Labour Commissioner, Memorandum on strike, enclosed A.G. William to J. E. Marnham, 5 January 1954, CO 1015/928, PRO. The *Economist* (8 January 1955, clipping in ibid.) saw the strike, although over a wage claim, as arising "directly out of the crisis over the colour bar in employment in the mines."

72 Reports of Meetings of 9 and 11 February 1955 between the Governor, Attorney-General, the Industrial Relations Officer of the Chamber of Mines, and others, CO 1015/929, PRO. Mineworkers were reportedly planting maize and building mud huts outside of the company housing areas in preparation for their eviction. *Manchester Guardian*, 1 February 1955, clipping in CO 1015/928, PRO.

73 Berger, 139–45. There is extensive material on the strike in CO 1015/928 and CO 1015/929, PRO. Governor Benson was criticized for following the "old methods," for acting as if "'Government' is primarily the Provincial Administration and only secondarily the Labour Department... Whatever the Provincial Administration may think and say about the union, it is with and through the union that Government has to effect a settlement." N. D. Watson, Minute, 19 May 1955, CO 1015/929.

74 Berger, 146–48.

75 Prain to Lennox-Boyd, 7 January 1955; Governor to Morgan, Colonial Office, 1 February 1955, CO 1015/926, PRO.

76 Governor to Secretary of State, 30 July 1955 (telegram), 4 August 1955, 12 September 1955 (telegram), 20 September 1955, CO 1015/927, PRO; Berger, 129–30.

77 Governor to Secretary of State, 3 June 1955, 23 June, 11, 21 July, 7, 18 August, 6 September 1956 (telegram), CO 1015/930, PRO. There were again rumors that the wives and children of miners were being sent to villages in preparation for a long strike. Mineowners complained of "political and racial" strike threats. Same to same, 18 August, 6 September 1956 (telegram), ibid.

78 Most of the detained union and party leaders were consigned to the "areas of their chiefs" – a curious reminder of how easily official thinking reverted when challenged to its old conceptions of African authority. Governor to Secretary of State, 8, 10, 12, 14, 17, 18 September 1956 (telegrams), CO 1015/930, list of detainees incl. Governor to Secretary of State, 27 June 1957, CO 859/1325, PRO; Northern Rhodesia, *Report of the Commission Appointed to Inquire into the Unrest in the Mining Industry of Northern Rhodesia in Recent Months* (Lusaka: Government Printer, 1956); Berger, 150–58.

79 *Economist*, 15 September 1956, Governor to Secretary of State, 17 November 1956, CO 1015/930, PRO; Berger, 158–64. Officials even supported granting the AMWU the check-off so as to bolster Katilungu's position. Ibid., 162.

80 Central Africa Department, Colonial Office, Briefing for Secretary of State's Visit to Northern Rhodesia, February 1960, CO 1015/2621, PRO; Morison Commission Report, 1962, p. 8, quoted in Berger, 213–14.

81 Berger, 203–4; Northern Rhodesia, *Commission Appointed to Inquire into the Unrest*, 1956, 7.

82 Northern Rhodesia, *Report of the Commission of Inquiry into Unrest on the Copperbelt July–August, 1963* (Lusaka: Government Printer, 1963); study of

absenteeism by Harry Franklin, 1959, cited by Parpart, *Labour and Capital*, 153. At Roan Antelope, the percentage annual turnover stood at 77 in 1947, 41 in 1952, and 18 in 1957. Ibid., 166.

83 R. L. Prain, "The Stabilization of Labour in the Rhodesian Copper Belt," *African Affairs* 55 (1956): 305–12.

84 In 1962 the government of Northern Rhodesia was only talking about opening up all jobs in the civil service and railways on a nonracial basis and was inordinately proud of the fact that 81 Africans (versus 131 Europeans) were being trained to be locomotive firemen. Governor to Secretary of State, 8 March 1962, CO 1015/2621, PRO.

85 Racial hierarchy remained important within the structure of work, as extra layers of supervisors were put in to compensate for the loss of racial authority with Zambianization, and African workers were continually seen as lazy and undisciplined. Michael Burawoy, *The Colour of Class on the Copper Mines: From African Advancement to Zambianization. Zambian Papers No. 7* (Manchester: Manchester University Press, 1972), 56–57, 82. For another view of post-independence mine labor, see Robert Bates, *Unions, Parties, and Political Development: A Study of Mineworkers in Zambia* (New Haven: Yale University Press, 1971).

86 Carl G. Rosberg and John Nottingham, *The Myth of "Mau Mau": Nationalism in Kenya* (New York: Praeger, 1966); David Throup, *The Economic and Social Origins of Mau Mau, 1945–53* (London: James Currey, 1987); Frank Furedi, *The Mau Mau War in Perspective* (London: James Currey, 1989); Maina wa Kinyatti, *Thunder from the Mountains: Mau Mau Patriotic Songs* (London: Zed Press, 1980). This section is partly based on an earlier essay of mine, "Mau Mau and the Discourses of Decolonization," *Journal of African History* 29 (1988): 313–20.

87 The best analyses accept the complexity of causation. See Bruce Berman and John Lonsdale, *Unhappy Valley: Conflict in Kenya and Africa, II: Violence and Ethnicity* (London: James Currey, 1992), particularly Lonsdale's analysis of writing on Mau Mau, "The Moral Economy of Mau Mau: The Problem," 265–314. In another article, John Lonsdale, echoing a formulation of Adam Przeworsky, argues that Mau Mau was a struggle about class, not a class struggle. He portrays it as an argument within a single moral system, in which the community's virtues were taken seriously, but which men of authority asserted their right to control – to define a path of respectability – while others saw this system of Kikuyu authority as denying them their adulthood. "Mau Maus of the Mind: Making Mau Mau and Remaking Kenya," *Journal of African History* 31 (1990): 417–18. B. A. Ogot emphasizes the clash of "loyalists" and rebels among Kikuyu, and sees it as a clash of moralities. "Revolt of the Elders: An Anatomy of the Loyalist Crowd in the Mau Mau Uprising," in Ogot (ed.), *Hadith 4* (Nairobi: East Africa Publishing House, 1972), 134–48.

88 Bruce Berman, "Bureaucracy and Incumbent Violence: Colonial Administration and the Origins of the 'Mau Mau' Emergency," in Berman and Lonsdale, *Unhappy Valley*, 242.

89 Tabitha Kanogo, *Squatters and the Roots of Mau Mau. 1905–63* (London: James Currey, 1987).

90 John Lonsdale, "The Moral Economy of Mau Mau: Wealth, Poverty and Civic Virtue in Kikuyu Political Thought," in Berman and Lonsdale, 421–36.

91 Throup, *Economic and Social Origins of Mau Mau*; John Spencer, *The Kenya African Union* (London: KPI, 1985).

92 Mitchell to Creasy, 29 August 1945, quoted in Bruce Berman, *Control and Crisis in Colonial Kenya: The Dialectic of Domination* (London: James Currey, 1990), 287.

93 Lonsdale, "Mau Maus of the Mind"; Ogot, "Revolt of the Elders."

94 Ogot; Lonsdale, 418–20; Luise White, "Separating the Men from the Boys: Constructions of Gender, Sexuality, and Terrorism in Central Kenya, 1939–1959," *International Journal of African Historical Studies* 23 (1990): 1–27.

95 Kanogo, *Squatters*, 150. See also Robert Buijtenhuijs, *Essays on Mau Mau* (Leiden: African Studies Centre, 1982), esp. 81–86.

96 If the primary diagnosis of Mau Mau was mental illness, metaphors of infectious diseases also abounded. The Parliamentary Delegation investigating the situation in 1954 referred to the "danger of infection"; Secretary of State Lyttleton referred to "persons who have been contaminated by Mau Mau." Control over trade unions was justified on the grounds that "It was necessary to remove infected elements wherever they were found." Politics and infection mixed in a MP's reference to the "spread of Mau Mau-ism." "Report to the Secretary of State for the Colonies by the Parliamentary Delegation to Kenya. January, 1954," *Parliamentary Papers* 1953–54, XI, 123, p. 5; Draft of Secretary of State's report to Parliament on Labor in the colonies, February 1955, CO 859/851, PRO; *House of Commons Debates* 530 (22 July 1954): cc. 1592, 1584.

97 T. G. Askwith, head of this department, wanted to show that the crisis was a disease of transition, not – as die-hard settlers would have it – an aspect of irredeemable Kikuyu savagery. He invited a British psychiatrist, Colin Carothers, to bring his environmental approach to African psychiatry to Kenya, and it was Carothers who put together a now notorious interpretation of Mau Mau as a collective disease of modernization, of people caught between one system of psychic security and another. The theory, and the camps, offered a way out of the transitional status – on the modern side. See Berman, *Control and Crisis*, 359, Lonsdale, "Mau Maus of the Mind," 410–11, and J. C. Carothers, *The Psychology of Mau Mau* (Nairobi: Government Printer, 1954).

98 As the Parliamentary Delegation to Kenya of 1954 put it, the goal was that Mau Mau should be "separated from the progressive movements, economic, social and political, which seek, now or in the future, to carry the African people forward into a share of a prosperous future. This clear-cut separation of the Mau Mau from the normal, legitimate functions of constitutional bodies is important and urgent." *Parliamentary Papers* 1953–54, XI, 123, 4.

99 Lonsdale, "Mau Maus of the Mind," 411. In Parliament, the government came in for criticism whenever there was an act of unusual brutality in the camps, and there was debate over the position of settlers and the particular reforms that were needed, but the Labour opposition did not on the whole criticize the use of force or the construction of Mau Mau as an atavistic,

savage revolt. "We are all as one in wanting to defeat Mau Mau," concluded Griffiths in 1954. *House of Commons Debates* 530 (22 July 1954): c. 1629. See also David Goldsworthy, *Colonial Issues in British Politics 1945–1961: From "Colonial Development" to "Winds of Change"* (Oxford: Clarendon Press, 1971), 213–14.

100 Interview, 1966, by Alice Amsden, quoted in her *International Firms and Labour in Kenya, 1945–70* (London: Cass, 1971), 49. White farmers were not much more interested in Hyde-Clarke's plans to reform the squatter system, moving it in the direction of full-time wage labor. Clayton and Savage, *Government and Labour*, 306.

101 Frederick Cooper, *On the African Waterfront: Urban Disorder and the Transformation of Work in Colonial Mombasa* (New Haven: Yale University Press, 1987), chapter 4.

102 R. D. Grillo, *Race, Class, and Militancy: An African Trade Union, 1939–1965* (New York: Chandler, 1974), 46–47, 50, 56, and union submission to 1953 wage commission, quoted 61.

103 Cooper, *On the African Waterfront*, 140–41; Michael P. Cowen and James Newman, "Real Wages in Central Kenya, 1924–1974," unpublished paper, 1975. The influence of settlers in watering down wage regulation is recorded in Governor, Kenya, to Secretary of State, 10 March 1950 and 3 October 1951, CO 859/205/8, PRO.

104 Barltrop to Governor, 9 December 1952, CO 822/657, PRO. His predecessor, two years earlier, had said that wage fixing machinery "will, I think, go a long way to fill the gap caused by the ineffectiveness of the trade unions." It didn't. Report by Mr. E. Parry on visit to Kenya, 26 June 1950, CO 822/148/5, PRO.

105 The tale is best told in Makhan Singh's semi-autobiographical *History of Kenya's Trade Union Movement to 1952* (Nairobi: East African Publishing House, 1969), 202–69. See also Clayton and Savage, *Government and Labour*, 325–28.

106 James Patrick, "Memorandum on Trade Unions – Development and Policy – Kenya," n.d. [1949], FCB 118/1, p. 7; Hyde-Clarke to E. W. Barltrop, 25 June 1949, FCB 115/3; Governor Mitchell to Colonial Office, 28 December 1949, Secretary of State, Minute, 4 January 1950, Secretary of State to Governor, 5 January 1950 (telegram), Barry Smallman, Minute, n.d. [early 1950], CO 859/203/12267/2/1950–51; Report by Mr. E. Parry on visit to Kenya, 26 June 1950, CO 822/148/5, PRO.

107 Patrick, "Memorandum," FCB 118/1, 9; *East African Standard*, 14 January 1949, quoted in Singh, *Kenya's Trade Union Movement*, 195. Hyde-Clarke, defender of the stabilization thesis, did not believe that African organizations could defend their own standard of living and that government had to do the job. See his correspondence with a member of the Fabian Colonial Bureau, Hyde-Clarke to Hilda Selwyn Clarke, 14 September 1949, FCB 115/3, PRO. The British TUC was critical of Patrick's nonorganization of trade unions and of the restrictive government policies. Walter Hood to Marjorie Nicholson, 10 September 1953, FCB 119/1, item 3; Minutes of N. D. Watson, 4 March 1952, E. Parry, 19 February 1952, and E. Barltrop, 23 February 1952, CO 859/268, PRO.

108 Governor to Colonial Office, 28 December 1949, CO 859/203/12267/2/1950–51, PRO.

109 Clayton and Savage, 328–32; Throup, *Economic and Social Origins of Mau Mau*, 194–95.

110 Kenyatta and Mbotela are quoted in Clayton and Savage, 333; the shouting incident is cited by Throup, 202 n 74.

111 Nairobi District, Annual Report, 1954; Throup, chapter 8. For another instance of the ideological and political significance of defining the dangerous in particular ways, see Ann Stoler, "Perceptions of Protest: Defining the Dangerous in Colonial Sumatra," *American Ethnologist* 12 (1985): 642–58.

112 Sharon Stichter, "Workers, Trade Unions, and the Mau Mau Rebellion," *Canadian Journal of African Studies* 9 (1975): 270.

113 Kubai was said to be part of the mythic "central directing body" of Mau Mau. Governor to Secretary of State, 19 April 1953 (telegram), CO 822/490, PRO; Stichter, "Mau Mau," 270–72. The round up of trade unionists created suspicion in left circles in Great Britain that the Emergency was being used as an excuse for anti-union actions, but the Undersecretary of State's insistence before Parliament that arrests were based on evidence of violence was hard to counter. Jay R. Krane to Marjorie Nicolson, 13 May 1953, FCB 61/2, f. 45; Henry Hopkinson, *House of Commons Debates* 530 (22 July 1954): c. 1634.

114 Cooper, *On the African Waterfront*, 203–19. For more on the relations between Mboya and Labour Department officials – far more two-way than the concept of "patronage" would imply – see David Goldsworthy, *Tom Mboya: The Man Kenya Wanted to Forget* (London: Heinemann, 1982).

115 Stichter, "Mau Mau," 273. The government soon realized that it had helped to advance a man it could not control. Mboya was watched very closely, and officials constantly feared his federation – which evolved into the Kenya Federation of Labour – would become "political." In 1959, they thought it had crossed "outside the Labour sphere," contemplated sanctions, but pulled their punches for fear attacking Mboya and his organization would only make things worse. Kenya, Council of Ministers, meeting of 9 December 1959, CO 822/1842, PRO.

116 Tom Mboya, "Trade Unionism in Kenya," *Africa South* 1, 2 (1957): 82; Labour Department, AR, 1962, cited in Goldsworthy, *Mboya*, 204; Kenya, *Legislative Council Debates* 89 (19 July 1962), c. 1014. On agricultural workers, see Acting Governor to Secretary of State, 3 May 1960 (telegram), Governor to Secretary of State, 22 June 1962 (telegram), CO 822/2871, and on Mboya's accomplishments generally, Goldsworthy, and Clayton and Savage, *Government and Labour*. The stabilization argument was taken up by other African politicians, for example Eliud Mathu, who saw the purpose of labor reform as insuring that "he [the worker, obviously assumed to be male], his wife and children will live decently without worries in their place of employment and that they will not have one foot in that place and the other foot in their native land unit." See Kenya, *Legislative Council Debates*, 63 (16 December 1954): c. 1231.

117 *Report of the Committee on African Wages* (Nairobi, 1954), 11, 14, 16. The minority report of F. T. Holden rejected the family wage concept, thinking

it would not effectively lead to stabilization and would have serious effects on economic growth, but he too thought that a segment of the African working population should be encouraged to achieve an exceptionally high standard of living. He called them the "upper ten thousand." At the time, there were about 500,000 in the work force. Ibid., 164.

118 African delegates (Mathu and Gikonyo) to the Legislative Council objected to this, but the minister for local government, health and housing replied that by the time any serious worker was of an age to have children he would have earned sufficient increments above the adult minimum wage to support them. Kenya, *Legislative Council Debates* 63 (16 December 1954): cc. 1231, 1264, 1304.

119 Kenya, *Legislative Council Debates*, 63 (16 December 1954), c. 1211, 1223–25, 1234 1267–68, 1276, 1279.

120 Riddoch, Cooke, Tyson, and Awori, *ibid.*, 1239, 1329, 1265, 1277. For another view of gender in Nairobi, see White, *The Comforts of Home*.

121 Clayton and Savage, 374–75; Cooper, 160–61; East African Statistical Department, Kenya Unit, *Reported Employment and Wages in Kenya, 1948–1960* (Nairobi, 1961), 17; Kenya, *Legislative Council Debates* 63 (16–17 December 1954), cc. 1207–355. In this same period, another committee set about devising nonracial wage scales for the civil service and railway. It tended to reproduce via job classifications what previous systems had done with racial classifications and Africanization of higher positions only began in earnest (indeed in panic) on the eve of independence. These issues are taken up in chapter 12.

122 John Weeks, "Wage Policy and the Colonial Legacy – A Comparative Study," *Journal of Modern African Studies* 9 (1971): 361–87.

123 Cooper, 160–61, 243–44; Stren, *Housing the Urban Poor*; Richard Sandbrook, *Proletarians and African Capitalism: The Kenyan Case, 1960–1972* (Cambridge: Cambridge University Press, 1975); Clayton and Savage; Sharon Stichter, *Migrant Labour in Kenya: Capitalism and African Response, 1895–1975* (London: Longman, 1982), 138–49.

124 From rural perspectives, too, stabilization was piecemeal, as a discussion of the continued "instability of African labour" – reflecting the old uncertainties about social security and fears of the autonomy of women – by a group of local officials in Western Kenya in 1957 made clear. Notes of discussion, Kericho, 23 February 1957, Nyanza Deposit, ADM 5/4/3/9 (Microfilm collection, reel 34B), KNA.

125 East Africa Royal Commission, Report, 1953–55, 43, 46 (hereafter EARC). The argument here and in the section on labor (146–48) is closely related to the more systematic argument made in the most important paper on economic development of this period, W. Arthur Lewis, "Economic Development with Unlimited Supplies of Labour," *The Manchester School* 22 (1954): 139–91.

126 EARC, 50–52, 148, 153, 154, 158.

127 EARC, 153, 214.

128 White, *The Comforts of Home*, 212; EARC, 210.

129 As Richard Stren points out (207–8), the recurrence of the word "stability" in these kinds of documents – the stable job, the stable family life, the stable

relation of races – is juxtaposed against the vocabulary of "social unrest" in the reports on Mau Mau.

130 The settlers had become expensive and expendable – they would bargain for what they could get as the government turned to negotiations with African political organizations, but this would not include a monopoly of political power or of land. See Gary Wasserman, *The Politics of Decolonization: Kenya Europeans and the Land Issue, 1960–1965* (Cambridge: Cambridge University Press, 1976).

9 Internationalists, intellectuals and the labor question

1 On the different stances that appeared within one discipline, see Talal Asad (ed.), *Anthropology and the Colonial Encounter* (London: Ithaca Press, 1973), and Gérard Leclerc, *Anthropologie et colonialisme: Essai sur l'histoire de l'africanisme* (Paris: Fayard, 1972).

2 ILO, Convention No. 102 of 1952, reprinted in International Labour Office, *Conventions and Recommendations* (Geneva: ILO, 1982), 533–53; J. S. Bennett, Minute, 22 October 1958, CO 859/1180, PRO; IGT, "Note pour le Directeur des Affaires Politiques," 30 October 1953, IGT 44/5, ANSOM.

3 Bennett, Minute, 22 October 1958, and J. S. Bennett to J. H. Galbraith (Ministry of Labour), 1 September 1958, Secretary of State, Circular, 12 March 1957, CO 859/1180; CO Memorandum, "Social Security Schemes in Overseas Territories," December 1954, CO 888/10, PRO. In the required reports to the ILO, French (and British) officials made numerous apologies about how poverty made providing such benefits difficult. See reports in IGT 29, ANSOM, and CO 859/182/3, PRO.

4 Civil servants and most workers in parastatal corporations like the railway did have pension plans, and employers' and workers' organizations put together the French West African Provident and Retirement Institution in 1958, based on employer and employee contributions and paying up to 40 percent of end-of-career wages to workers over 55 with 30 years service. Inter-African Labour Conference, 5th meeting, Lusaka, 1957, 194; ILO, *African Labour Survey* (Geneva: ILO, 1958), 397.

5 Conclusions of the meeting of Experts on Social Policy in Non-Metropolitan Territories, Dakar, 1955, reported in ILO, *Survey*, 611–16. The ILO noted that the social security Conventions "are applied only to a very limited extent and in a small number of territories." Ibid. 506.

6 ILO, *Survey*, 394–99; H. A. Fosbrooke "Social Security as a Felt Want in East and Central Africa," *Bulletin of the International Social Security Association* 13 (1960): 281, 284.

7 The international dimension provoked anxieties in colonial bureaucracies that too much sovereignty might be given up. As former Governor Bourdillon told a Colonial Office meeting in 1956, setting standards might well show critics of colonialism that the imperial powers were serious about their responsibilities, but it also made them accountable. "We could not use the argument of accountability without admitting our own accountability, and it had been our object in the United Nations to keep out any such admission." Record of meeting in the Colonial Office, 15 February 1956, CO 859/814, PRO.

8 Inter-African Labour Conference, Bamako, 1953, recommendations printed with *Inter-African Labour Conference, Beira, 1955* (London: Commission for Technical Cooperation in Africa South of the Sahara, 1955), 75.

9 A British delegate, Couzens, objected that the original draft of the family resolution, written by the French delegation, was political in that it would commit Great Britain to a policy it had not already adopted. It required considerable drafting work to come up with an acceptable formula. Summary of 7th session of committee on family allowances, Bamako, and final resolutions of plenary session, 4 February 1953, in K 463 (179), AS. The distinction between the technical and the political was also used to keep criticisms of South Africa out of bounds. 5th session of committee on productivity, ibid.

10 The minister, shortly after the Bamako meeting, invoked the international movement toward family aid, as well as the French constitution and the Code du Travail, in urging the territories to get going on their plans for family allowances. Minister, Circular to High Commissioners, Commissioners, and IGTs, 3 September 1953, IGT, FEA, "Etude préliminaire de l'institution de prestations familiales," 28 September 1954, IGT 16/1, ANSOM.

11 Subcommittee on Wage-Fixing and Family Responsibilities, meeting of 28 July 1953, CO 859/257, PRO. This file contains the replies of various colonies to a survey of what different colonies were doing and thinking in regard to family wages – a direct response to the Bamako meetings. See in particular M. Phillips, Draft paper on "Wage Fixing and Family Responsibilities," 9 May 1953, ibid.

12 ILO, Commission of Experts, 1st session, London, 17–26 March 1947, transcript in IGT 34, ANSOM. This committee had been created as a consequence of International Labour Conference resolutions in 1945 and was charged with studying social policy in dependent (a phrase later changed to non-metropolitan) territories. P. de Briey (ILO) to Minister of Colonies, France, 4 April 1945, ibid.

13 ILO, Commission of Experts, 1947, and position papers submitted by France and Great Britain, IGT 34, ANSOM; Recommendations from Inter-African Labour Conference,1950, reprinted with *Inter-African Labour Conference*, 4th meeting, Beira, 1955, 62–63; United Nations, Bureau of Social Affairs, *Report on the World Social Situation* (New York: United Nations, 1957), 154.

14 United Nations, "Economic Development of Under-developed Countries: Question of Methods to Increase World Productivity," E/2440, 22 May 1953, copy in CO 859/304; Director-General of the ILO, Speech to UN Trusteeship Council, March 1950, copy in CO 859/197/12263/6/2/1950–51; United Nations Trusteeship Council, Official Records, 4th Session, Supplement No. 3. "United Nations visiting mission to East Africa, Report on Tanganyika and Selected Documents," T/218 and T218/Add.1, 1948, 137–38.

15 The South African defense of migration, especially in regard to gold mines, began in the first meeting of the Committee of Experts, 17–26 March 1947, transcript in IGT 34, ANSOM.

16 1950 Recommendations reprinted in *Inter-African Labour Conference, Beira, 1955,* 63–65.

17 "Preliminary consideration of methods of initiating the study of productivity," Document for the Third Committee (3rd session), Meeting of Inter-African Labour Conference, Bamako, 1953, K 463 (179), AS.

18 Inter-African Labour Conference, Elisabethville, Report on "Le rendement de la main d'oeuvre africaine et la question des salaires minima," 1950; ILO study prepared for the United Nations General Assembly, "Preliminary study on wages and productivity of labour in non-self-governing territories," A/AC.35/L.108, 3 September 1952, copy in CO 859/304, PRO; P. de Briey, "The Productivity of African Labour," *International Labour Review* 72 (1955): 120–21. On Northern Rhodesia, see chapter 8.

19 De Briey, 119–37; Inter-African Labour Institute, *The Human Factors of Productivity in Africa* (London: CCTA, 1957); ILO, *Survey*, chapter 5. While the enthusiasm for data gathering was often less in the colonies than in London, Paris, or Geneva, research was done. Nigeria funded a productivity study but Kenya and Tanganyika did not. Governor-General, Nigeria, to Secretary of State, 3 January 1959, CO 859/1245; East African Labour Commissioners' Conference, 24–27 August 1959, Minutes, CO 822/1630, PRO.

20 One of the sources he quoted was Carothers' *The Psychology of Mau Mau* (see chapter 8), stressing that one should not dwell on the dark side of Africans caught between two ways of life but to emphasize the good that would come once Africans were able to cut themselves off from rural society and find stability in urban work. De Briey, 131–33. See also B. Gussman, "Industrial Efficiency and the Urban African," *Africa* 23 (1953): 135–44.

21 *Inter-African Labour Conference, Beira, 1955*, 42. Women also had a role to play as consumers. A British delegate to the 1953 Conference expressed the hope that women would spur men to increase their ambitions: "One of the causes of the high standard of productivity in the United Kingdom is the men being stimulated by their wives' asking for dresses, furniture, etc... This factor should work in Africa where workers are very often satisfied with the little they get and do not care about getting higher salaries. A means of increasing productivity should be to make the African want to earn more money." Transcript, Third Committee, 6th Session, 4 February 1953, K 463 (179), AS.

22 The pioneering urban anthropologist J. Clyde Mitchell wrote, "the success of any advancement scheme for Africans will depend ultimately on the extent to which their wives are rooted in the social structure of the community in which they live." "The Woman's Place in African Advancement," *Optima* 9, 3 (1959): 131. An economist, Walter Elkan, wrote in an IALC publication an explanation for the "virtual absence of women in employment" in Uganda. His main point was that women's contribution to agriculture was so strong that their labor would have a high supply price. This article stands out for considering the question of women's participation or lack of it in labor markets to be worth examining. "The Employment of Women in Uganda," *Inter-African Labour Institute Bulletin* 4, 4 (1957): 8–22.

23 First session of Inter-African Labour Conference, Bamako, 27 January 1953, transcript in K 463 (179), AS.

24 United Nations, Department of Economic Affairs, *Review of Economic Conditions in Africa, 1949–50* (New York: United Nations, 1951), 9; United Nations, *World Social Situation*, 147. Dualism was the basis on which the first report (12) explained the paradox that Africa experienced both a labor shortage and low wages. Because most corporations invested on the assump-

tion of low wages, they made use of migrant labor, whose access to resources to supplement wages made them continue to accept low wages. "Thus, considerable effort has been directed towards maintaining the supply of low-priced labour, a supply which did not become exhausted because of the slow pace of internal development in Africa and the existence of a large mass of subsistence agriculturalists."

25 CCTA, Committee of Experts on Further Research into Problems of Productivity, report of meeting in Salisbury, 12–16 November 1956, copy in IGT 52, ANSOM; ILO, *Survey*, 140. A French report invoked the concept of the "underevolved worker." IGT, Service Central du Travail et de la Main d'Oeuvre, "Rapport sur les facteurs humains de la productivité," document for CCTA, 1955, IGT 52, ANSOM

26 British officials had seen a problem coming, but they could hardly oppose tightening the ban on penal sanctions when its proponents were likening it to servitude. Asked in advance of the Convention what they would do, Kenya and both Rhodesias indicated that they would refuse to abolish penal sanctions. Northern Rhodesia had in 1952 prosecuted 277 Africans for labor law violations, mostly desertion (vs. 124 Europeans, mostly for nonpayment of wages), and 42 Africans had been imprisoned, 1 flogged and 172 fined; 94 Europeans had been fined, none jailed. Edgar Unsworth, Northern Rhodesia, to J. E. Marnham, CO, 7 September 1953, Governor, Southern Rhodesia, to Commonwealth Relations Office, 26 September 1953, Governor's Deputy, Kenya, to Secretary of State, 1 September 1953, R. Turner, Minute, 12 September 1953, CO 859/305, PRO. The last official cited concluded that owing to the views of the colonial governments, "we cannot take as liberal an attitude as we should wish."

27 Governor, Southern Rhodesia, to Commonwealth Relations Office, 26 September 1953, CO 859/305; Minute, A. J. Peckham, 8 April 1957, CO 859/1186, PRO. Officials in East and Southern Africa defended penal sanctions because they did not believe "that the African had yet developed a sufficient sense of responsibility to understand the meaning of a breach of contract." Extract from Minutes of East African Labour Commissioners' Conference, January 1952, extract from British Report to ILO, 34th session of International Labour Conference, Item 3, 1951, CO 859/202/4, PRO. On the decision not to ratify the penal sanctions convention, see R. T. F. Scragg, "Penal Sanctions for Breaches of Contract," n.d. [April 1957], CO 859/1183; Memorandum by the Minister of Labour and National Service, "International Labour Organizations," 4 November 1957, CAB 129/10; and Cabinet Conclusions, 6 November 1957, CAB 128/30, PRO.

28 *House of Commons Debates*, 579 (3 December 1957), c. 206. The Cabinet was unable to ratify the new version of the penal sanctions convention. 78th Cabinet Conclusions, CC(57) 6 November 1957, CAB 128/30, PRO.

29 ILO, Draft Report by Governing Body on application of Convention 65 of 1939, 18 December 1958; C. E. T. Storar (CRO) to T. V. Scrivenor, 5 May 1959, CO 859/1183. In addition, Great Britain was criticized at the ILO through charges that forms of "communal" labor – such as efforts to build Kikuyu villages during the campaign against Mau Mau – were in reality forced labor. Colonial Office, Draft paper "Survey of Different Treatment by

Race in the Laws of British Tropical African Territories," June 1956, CO 859/1108; Governor, Kenya, to Secretary of State, 14 November 1956, CO 859/796; M. Phillips, CO, to Hood, TUC, 23 January 1954; Minute, A. McM. Webster, 14 February 1956, Leslie Pritchard, African Affairs, Nairobi, to M. Scott, CO, 11 May 1956, CO 859/847, PRO.

30 Text of speech, 27 February 1950, from a WFTU document and included as annex to Inspecteur Général des Services de Sécurité de l'AOF, Note d'information, 15 February 1950, 17G 272, AS.

31 International Labour Conference, 39th Session, Geneva, 26 June 1956, 443. The session at which Edoh Coffi spoke was devoted to implementation of conventions.

32 Ibid, 44.

33 Ellen Hellmann, *Rooiyard: A Sociological Survey of an Urban Native Slum Yard*, Rhodes–Livingstone Papers 13 (Cape Town: Oxford University Press, 1948) (based on research done earlier); Sheila van der Horst, *Native Labour in South Africa* (London: Cass, 1971, orig. published. 1942); Isaac Schapera, *Migrant Labour and Tribal Life: A Study of Conditions in the Bechuanaland Protectorate* (London: Oxford University Press, 1947); M. Grévisse, *Le centre extra-coutumier d'Elisabethville* (Brussels: CEPSI, 1951); A. Doucy and P. Feldheim, *Problèmes du travail et politique sociale au Congo belge* (Brussels: Librairie Encyclopédique, 1952); Godfrey and Monica Wilson, *The Analysis of Social Change* (Cambridge: Cambridge University Press, 1968; orig. published 1945). For further citations, see the UNESCO volume discussed below.

34 Richard Brown suggests that Gluckman had to look at rural areas as distinct field sites because the mine companies would not let him onto the mines; structural-functional anthropology also emphasized the bounded unity of each social situation. "Passages in the Life of a White Anthropologist: Max Gluckman in Northern Rhodesia," *Journal of African History* 20 (1979): 535. The RLI was funded by the Colonial Development and Welfare Act, the Beit Railway Trust, and the Northern Rhodesian government. Max Gluckman, "Seven-Year Research Plan of the Rhodes–Livingstone Institute of Social Studies in British Central Africa," *Rhodes–Livingstone Journal* 4 (1945): 1. See also Sally Falk Moore, *Anthropology and Africa: Changing Perspectives on a Changing Scene* (Charlottesville: University Press of Virginia, 1994), esp. 41, 59–60.

35 Gluckman, "Seven Year Plan," 4–6.

36 Lord Hailey, "The Rôle of Anthropology in Colonial Development," *Man* 44 (1944): 10–15.

37 J. M. Lee and Martin Petter, *The Colonial Office, War, and Development Policy: Organization and the Planning of a Metropolitan Initiative, 1939–1945*, Commonwealth Papers 22 (London: Maurice Temple Smith, 1982).

38 Lord Hailey, *An African Survey*, 2nd ed. (London: Oxford University Press, 1945), 603, 605, 696, 711. Hailey's diminishing grip on the post-World War II situation in Africa is noted in John W. Cell, *Hailey: A Study in British Imperialism, 1872–1969* (Cambridge: Cambridge University Press, 1992), 296.

39 For a summary of research up to 1956, see Merran McCulloch, "Survey of Recent and Current Field Studies on the Social Effects of Economic Development in Inter-tropical Africa," in UNESCO, *Social Implications of*

Industrialization and Urbanization in Africa South of the Sahara (Paris: UNESCO, 1956), 53–228. For a good example of survey research, see K. A. Busia, *Report on a Social Survey of Sekondi-Takoradi* (London: Crown Agents for the Colonies, 1950).

40 His early article began, "We in Northern Rhodesia are living in a revolution, the intensity of which, as far as we can judge, has not been equalled in thousands of years." J. Clyde Mitchell, "A Note on the Urbanization of Africans on the Copperbelt," *Rhodes–Livingstone Journal* 12 (1951): 20–27, 20 quoted.

41 J. Clyde Mitchell, "Submission to African Urban Affairs Commission," 1957, Rhodes House MP 625/7, ff. 39–41 (with thanks to Timothy Scarnecchia for providing me a transcript of this document); J. Clyde Mitchell, *An Outline of the Sociological Background to African Labour* (Salisbury: Ensign, 1961). This book was first published as a series of articles by the *Chamber of Mines Journal*. Mitchell and other Copperbelt anthropologists were attacked by Bernard Magubane for exoticizing African urban society while neglecting the way it was shaped by colonialism. The attack misses the subtle way African urban life was described in Mitchell's work – avoiding the Manichean alternatives of progressive colonists/backward Africans or oppressive colonists/revolutionary Africans. But it is true that Mitchell's focus was much more on the micropolitics of Copperbelt towns and their cultural complexity than on the macropolitics of colonialism. "A Critical Look at Indices Used in the Study of Social Change in Colonial Africa," *Current Anthropology* 12 (1971): 419–45.

42 A. L Epstein, *Politics in an Urban African Community* (Manchester: Manchester University Press, 1958), 46, 224–40.

43 Max Gluckman, "Anthropological Problems Arising from the African Industrial Revolution," in Aidan Southall (ed.), *Social Change in Modern Africa* (London: Oxford University Press, 1961), 69; Epstein, 229. See also J. C. Mitchell, *The Kalela Dance*. Rhodes–Livingstone Paper No. 27 (Lusaka: Rhodes–Livingstone Institute, 1957).

44 Max Gluckman, "Malinowksi's 'Functional' Analysis of Social Change," *Africa* 17 (1947): 103–21; J. C. Mitchell, "Urbanization, Detribalization and Stabilization in Southern Africa: A Problem of Definition and Measurement," in UNESCO, *Social Implications*, 693–711; Epstein, 224–40.

45 Georges Balandier, *Histoire des autres* (Paris: Stock, 1977), 52. The other French scholar of the 1940s and 1950s most concerned with urban issues in the colonies was Jean Dresch, and he too has written an autobiography, *Un géographe au déclin des empires* (Paris: Maspero, 1979).

46 Paris: Colin, 1955.

47 Georges Balandier, "La situation coloniale: Approche théorique," *Cahiers Internationaux de Sociologie* 11 (1951): 44–79.

48 Georges Balandier, "Urbanism in West and Central Africa: The Scope and Aims of Research," in UNESCO, *Social Implications*, 506, 509, 510; *Sociologie des Brazzavilles noires*; *The Sociology of Black Africa: Social Dynamics in Central Africa*, trans. by Douglas Garman (London: André Deutsch, 1970).

49 Michael Banton, *West African City: A Study of Tribal Life in Freetown* (London: Oxford University Press, 1957) is a good example of the genre. For

a review and bibliography, see Kenneth Little, *West African Urbanization: A Study of Voluntary Associations in Social Change* (Cambridge: Cambridge University Press, 1966).

50 This tone is picked up in Daryll Forde, "Introductory Survey," in UNESCO, *Social Implications,* 13, 22.

51 Tanya Baker and Mary Bird, "Urbanisation and the Position of Women," *Sociological Review* NS 7 (1959): 99–122, and studies cited in their bibliography, 121–22.

52 Forde, 36, 38, 39.

53 At the end of the long summary of survey research on African cities, McCulloch concluded that "Industrialization has had certain broadly similar results wherever it has taken place," but then she summarized the factors which "hinder the development of social classes among urban Africans." "Survey of Recent and Current Field Studies," 209, 215–16. While South African studies were included in the conference, the volume did not draw out the possibility that its longer experience with urban wage labor cast doubt on the assumption that family dislocation and urban pathologies reflected the recent and transitional nature of urbanization. Ibid., 174–208, and E. Hellmann, "The Development of Social Groupings among Urban Africans in the Union of South Africa," 724–43.

54 Alioune Diop, "De l'expansion du travail," *Présence Africaine* 13 (1952): 7, 10. On the journal's role in developing and disseminating African political discourse, see V. Y. Mudimbe, *Surreptitious Speech: PRÉSENCE AFRICAINE and the Politics of Otherness* (Chicago: University of Chicago Press, 1992).

55 Diop, 14, 17.

56 Focusing on a specific issue like labor allowed Diop (and may allow the present reader) to draw out the complexity of these issues in ways that generalized debates over colonialism and westernization did not necessarily allow. The more general debates are the more familiar, and the best known of the era, coming from someone whose own engagement with French institutions was intimate and complex, is Aimé Césaire, *Discours sur le colonialisme* (Paris: Présence Africaine, 1955).

57 Jacqueline Delange, "La discussion parlementaire sur le Code du Travail en Afrique Noire," 377–400; Georges Balandier, "Le travailleur africain dans les 'brazzavilles noires'," 315–330; K. Basile Gnasounou Ponoukoun, "La vie d'un militant syndicaliste," 355–58. See also Pierre Naville, "Note sur le syndicalisme en Afrique noire," 359–67. One of the overseas ministry's official intellectuals wrote about the "instability" of African labor and the need for "a change in the habits and mentalities" of Africans. Henri Labouret, "Sur la main-d'oeuvre autochtone," 124–36.

58 J.-Cl. Pauvert, "La notion de travail en Afrique noire," 92–107; Paul Mercier, "Travail et service public dans l'ancien Dahomey," 84–91; Michel Leiris, "L'expression de l'idée de travail dans une langue d'initiés soudanais," 69–83; A. Serpos Tidjani, "L'Africain face au problème du travail," 108; Denise Palme, "La femme africaine au travail," 116–23.

59 Robert Nisbet, *History of the Idea of Progress* (New York: Basic Books, 1980).

60 Parallels emerge in Randall Packard, "The 'Healthy Reserve' and the 'Dressed Native': Discourses on Black Health and the Language of Legitimation in

South Africa," *American Ethnologist* 16 (1989): 686–703; Megan Vaughan, *Curing their Ills: Colonial Power and African Illness* (Cambridge: Polity Press, 1991).

61 Ironically, the United States had been the locus of a strong cultural relativism before it became linked to the most sweeping theories of modernization. Melville J. Herskovits argued that African societies represented viable and valuable approaches to political and social life. In a much noticed article ("Native Self-Government," *Foreign Affairs* 22 [1944]: 413–23), he not only criticized colonial regimes, but suggested that ending them should mean something other than adopting western forms of government. His relativism, while it influenced the founding of the field of African history, was marginalized in the policy sciences as the need to pose a coherent alternative to communist progressivism became more acute. One must nevertheless be careful about seeing modernization theory solely in terms of cold war politics, as Irene Gendzier for example tends to do; it responded to broader desires for a social science that made sense of a world after empire and appealed to westerners who wished to see progress as open to people of all races and cultures. *Managing Political Change: Social Scientists and the Third World* (Boulder, Colo: Westview, 1985). On the positive view American liberals had of African nationalists as "modernizers" see Martin Staniland, *American Intellectuals and African Nationalists, 1955–1970* (New Haven: Yale University Press, 1991), 80–82.

62 Dean C. Tipps, "Modernization Theory and the Comparative Study of Societies: A Critical Perspective," *Comparative Studies in Society and History* 15 (1973): 204.

63 Cambridge: Cambridge University Press, 1960.

64 Wilbert E. Moore, *Industrialization and Labor: Social Aspects of Economic Development* (Ithaca: Cornell University Press for The Institute of World Affairs, 1951), 3, 6.

65 Clark Kerr, John T. Dunlop, Frederick Harbison, and Charles A. Myers, *Industrialism and Industrial Man* (Cambridge, Mass.: Harvard University Press, 1960).

66 Moore, *Industrialization and Labor*, 48. Moore saw racial restrictions, as in South Africa or the Rhodesias, as a serious obstacle to creating industrialism, and he predicted that the South African system, which effectively forced Africans into industrial labor but denied them access to any but low-wage jobs, was unstable and doomed to collapse. In 1995, it looks as if he had a point, but that does not explain the intervening forty years and how South Africa became a vastly successful industrial economy in the 1950s, whereas the rest of the continent – without those racial rigidities – did not. Ibid., 18–19, 91, 132–33.

67 The title to Moore's chapter 2 is "Barriers and Antipathies."

68 Moore juxtaposed "sentimental cultural pluralism" against his rigorous insistence that industrialism was an inevitability for which the world's people needed to prepare. Ibid., 188, 192–98.

69 Moore's evidence on Africa – reasonably extensive given the state of Africanist research in 1951 – came primarily from Audrey Richards, Monica Hunter, Isaac Schapera, Margaret Read, Lucy Mair, and documents from the

Colonial Office and the ILO. In theoretical terms, Moore's sociological structural-functionalism shared with anthropological structural-functionalism a
focus on systems and on the external origins of change. But the latter were
interested in more than one system.

70 Moore, like the inspectors, thought overly low pay was an obstacle to industrialism, but he was skeptical about too much of the superstructure of modern
industrial relations being transferred prematurely to newly industrializing
societies, lest regulation reduce investment and employment.

71 There are passages to this effect in Moore (e.g. 44–47), but this point of view
is developed much more fully in Neil Smelser, *Social Change in the Industrial
Revolution: An Application of Theory to the British Cotton Industry* (Chicago:
University of Chicago Press, 1959). Kerr et al. (208–10) set out a "natural
history of protest" which locates resistance near the beginning of an industrialization cycle. See the bitter attack on this argument in E. P. Thompson, *The
Making of the English Working Class* (New York: Vintage, 1963).

72 Clark Kerr, "Changing Social Structures," in Wilbert E. Moore and Arnold
S. Feldman (eds.), *Labor Commitment and Social Change in Developing Areas*
(New York: Social Science Research Council, 1960), 348–49.

73 Ibid., 350. "The Bantu" is a misnomer for a unit of population – it is a
language group, and boundaries of language, cultural, and social groups are
in complex relationship to one another. That is only one of the essentializing
aspects of Kerr's argument: he assumed his "Bantu" came from subsistence
economies and lived in secure, small "tribal units," just as he treated the
"industrial" economy of contemporary South-Central Africa as an undifferentiated whole.

74 Ibid., 351, 357, 359, and Kerr et al., *Industrialization and Industrial Man*,
187–92.

75 The dualism of the 1950s drew on an earlier version, but took away its bite.
J. H. Boeke saw dualism as the clash of a forcibly imposed social system
with a conquered indigenous one. Lewis was thinking of the relationship of
two sectors, a general characteristic of an underdeveloped economy.
Boeke's book was originally published in 1942, *Economics and Economic
Policies of Dual Societies as Exemplified by Indonesia* (New York: Institute
of Pacific Relations, 1953, orig. published 1942). The more naturalized
version of the dual economy was already being given a United Nations
imprimatur before Lewis' work: United Nations, Department of Economic
Affairs. *Review of Economic Conditions in Africa, 1949–50* (New York:
United Nations, 1951), 9.

76 W. Arthur Lewis, "Economic Development with Unlimited Supplies of
Labour," *The Manchester School* 22 (1954): 139–91. For an overview of the
intellectual history of economic development, see H. W. Arndt, *Economic
Development: The History of an Idea* (Chicago: University of Chicago Press,
1987).

77 Lewis, 147–48; W. Arthur Lewis,"The Economic Development of Africa," in
Calvin W. Stillman (ed.), *Africa in the Modern World* (Chicago: University of
Chicago Press, 1955), 97–98. Lewis favored stabilization policies, consistent
with his stress on building a productive modern sector labor force. *The Theory
of Economic Growth* (Holmwood, IL: Richard Irwin, 1955), 192–93.

78 Lewis, "Unlimited Supplies," 149, 159; W. Arthur Lewis, *Labour in the West Indies* (London: Fabian Society, 1939). For another view of Lewis' assumptions about the traditional sector – in particular whether repression is needed to maintain a constant wage rate – see John Weeks, "The Political Economy of Labor Transfer," *Science and Society* 35 (1971): 463–80.

79 Lewis' belief that colonized people needed a voice in the state dates to his earliest pamphlets and continues in his later writing. See his *Politics in West Africa* (New York: Oxford University Press, 1965).

80 Among the key ideas of 1950s development economics was the "big push" – a focused intervention intended to escape the vicious circle of poverty; increasing the savings rate; and import substitution industrialization. Experts saw themselves engaged in "creative destruction," removing barriers that prevented peasants and workers from realizing their productive potential and giving them the resources that would enable economic growth to become self-sustaining. See Arndt, *Economic Development*, and for a useful study of how some of those ideas were applied to Africa's first independent state, Tony Killick, *Development Economics in Action: A Study of Economic Policies in Ghana* (New York: St. Martin's Press, 1978).

81 Mamadou Diouf, "L'entreprise sénégalaise de développement: de la mobilisation de masse à l'étatisme technocratique," paper for workshop on "Historicizing Development," Emory University, December 10–12, 1993. A translation of this paper and others relevant to these issues will be published in Frederick Cooper and Randall Packard, *Development Knowledge and the Social Sciences*, forthcoming. See also C. Choquet, O. Dollfus, E. Le Roy, and M. Vernières (eds.), *Etat des savoirs sur le développement: Trois décennies de sciences sociales en langue française* (Paris: Karthala, 1993) and Ulf Himmelstrand, Kabiru Kinyanjui and Edward Mburugu (eds.), *African Perspectives on Development* (New York: St. Martin's Press, 1994).

82 On the French left's difficulties in jettisoning the notion that French colonial rule could itself be a factor promoting socialism – via the efforts of French socialists and communists themselves – see Paul Clay Sorum, *Intellectuals and Decolonization in France* (Chapel Hill: University of North Carolina Press, 1977).

83 Nationalists could simultaneously hold both positions, arguing that the social and cultural path of a people should be unique, but that the nation-state would be the guide. Partha Chatterjee emphasizes that such a position necessarily brought nationalists into a "derivative discourse," since the nation-state was itself the product of a western and imperialist history. *Nationalist Thought and the Colonial World: A Derivative Discourse?* (London: Zed, 1986).

Conclusion to Part III: labor and the modernizing state
1 The argument in favor of following the market – and particularly against government marketing boards – was made at the time by P. T. Bauer, *West African Trade: A Study of Competition, Oligopoly and Monopoly in a Changing Economy* (Cambridge: Cambridge University Press, 1954).

Introduction to Part IV

1 John Ruedy, *Modern Algeria: The Origins and Development of a Nation* (Bloomington: Indiana University Press, 1992), 125; Benjamin Stora, *La gangrène de l'oubli: La mémoire de la guerre d'Algérie* (Paris: Editions la Découverte, 1992), 76.

10 The burden of declining empire

1 Raymond Cartier, "En France Noire avec Raymond Cartier: La France sème ses milliards, les africains disent: c'est bien tard," *Paris-Match* 384 (18 August 1956): 35.

2 D. K. Fieldhouse stresses the loss of domestic political support for "expensive reformist empire." Reviving "empire on the cheap" was not a viable option at the time. *Black Africa: Economic Decolonization and Arrested Development* (London: Allen & Unwin, 1986), 23.

3 Continued economic problems in Great Britain had as early as 1951 given rise to increasing concerns about the financial burdens of empire, setting in motion the reconsideration that culminated in 1957–59. The period is effectively reviewed in A. N. Porter and A. J. Stockwell, "Introduction," to their collection of documents, *British Imperial Policy and Decolonization, 1938–64*. Vol. II: *1951–64* (London: Macmillan, 1989), 3–91.

4 Investments that promised to earn foreign exchange were favored over social expenditures in the new funding cycle, but the commitment to improve the colonial standard of living was reaffirmed. Secretary of State Alan Lennox-Boyd, Circular, 21 February 1953, CO 852/1365, PRO; Cabinet Office, Agreed Minute of Commonwealth Economic Conference, 11 December 1952, ibid.; and Lennox-Boyd, *House of Commons Debates* 536 (2 February 1955); cc. 1117–18, 1123. The Colonial Development and Welfare Act was of course only one funding source for development spending; colonial budgets themselves were the largest, and Lennox-Boyd estimated that a total of £600 million would be invested by the governments in 1956–60, not counting certain large projects. Ibid., c. 1125. One of the biggest problems was that private investment was not following public. A Treasury official wondered, therefore, if "the whole conception of Commonwealth development as the solution to our difficulties is becoming something of a castle in the air." Exchange of Notes between E. Melville, CO, and M. T. Flett, Treasury, 27, 30 June 1952, CO 537/7858, reprinted in Porter and Stockwell, 176.

5 Hopkinson, *House of Commons Debates* 536 (7 February 1955), c. 1609. As the British Government approved the Gold Coast's move to full self-government, the Chancellor of the Exchequer told the Cabinet "it should be made clear to the Gold Coast Government that the proposed advance to self-government would not carry with it a claim to any funds of the Colonial Development and Welfare Corporations." CM (56) 64th Conclusions, 11 September 1956, CAB 128/30, PRO.

6 Arthur Creech Jones, *House of Commons Debates* 536 (7 February 1955); cc. 1590–92, James Griffiths, cc. 1597, 1614–16.

7 Thomas Reid, *House of Commons Debates* (16 July 1953); cc. 2287, 2291–92; Reid, *House of Commons Debates* 517 (2 February 1955), cc. 1149–50, 1152,

1154–55. He complained in particular that colonial people "breed fecklessly," while the British people "who all practice birth control" were asked to "provide for the families of those who refuse to limit their numbers." See also Richard Law. Ibid. (16 July 1953), cc. 2308–9.

8 Governor to Thomas Lloyd, Colonial Office, 6 August 1955, CO 554/1181, PRO. In London, some officials were even blunter: "the fact must be faced: The West African negro is not capable of honest democratic self-government in this generation; and probably won't be in the next either." T. B. Williamson, Minute, 1 July 1955, ibid. The situation was thought dire enough and the possibility of stopping the movement toward self-government was considered sufficiently seriously that efforts were made to consult military officers in case their intervention was needed; but in the end officials decided things had to be even worse to justify such action. Minutes, J. S. Bennett, 27 July 1955, C. G. Eastwood, 5 July 1955, Thomas Lloyd, 11 July 1955; Lloyd to Governor, 26 July 1955, ibid.

9 There were added worries about riots over taxes and school fees. Governor, Eastern Nigeria, to Secretary of State, 13 February 1956, and Minute by C. G. Eastwood, 28 Feburary 1956, CO 554/1182; Secretary of State's comment about "ghastly" situation cited in Eastwood, Minute, 8 January 1958, M. Z. Terry, Minute, 29 January 1958, Governor to Eastwood, 23 December 1957 and 31 January 1958, CO 554/2128; Minutes by M. G. Smith, 28 July 1958, A. Emmanuel, 28 July 1958 Eastern Nigeria Intelligence Report No. 18, January 1958, CO 554/2129; Minute, Eastwood, 19 January 1959, CO 554/2130, PRO.

10 David Goldsworthy, "Keeping Change within Bounds: Aspects of Colonial Policy during the Churchill and Eden Governments, 1951–57," *Journal of Imperial and Commonwealth History* 18 (1990): 81–108.

11 Ibid., 87; D. J. Morgan, *The Official History of Colonial Development* (London: Macmillan, 1980): 3: 1–7; Fieldhouse, *Black Africa*, 6–17.

12 Lennox-Boyd, *House of Commons Debates* 535 (3 December 1954), c. 489; Goldsworthy, 93–99, 102. Labour's opposition took the form of criticizing Lyttleton and Lennox-Boyd for being too pro-settler or too harsh in repressing Mau Mau, although Labour was pro-development and anti-Mau Mau. By 1954, a more militant, anti-imperialist Labour backbench emerged – as did extra-parliamentary anti-imperialist movements – but their influence did not lead the front bench to articulate an alternative colonial policy. See David Goldsworthy, *Colonial Issues in British Politics 1945–1961* (Oxford: Clarendon Press, 1971), 205–78, and Stephen Howe, *Anticolonialism in British Politics: The Left and the End of Empire, 1918–1964* (Oxford: Clarendon Press, 1993), 256–59.

13 Prime Minister's Minute, 28 January 1957, CAB 134/1555, PRO. This review was to be conducted through the Colonial Policy Committee.

14 Minute, Ian Watt, 11 June 1957, CO 1032/146; Secretary of State, Memorandum, 15 February 1957, CAB 134/1555, PRO. For more on how the reappraisal was conducted, see papers from 1957 in CO 1032/144, PRO.

15 "Future Constitutional Development in the Colonies," Report by the Chairman of the Official Committee on Colonial Policy (Norman Brook), 6 September 1957, CPC (57) 30, CAB 134/1556, 5–6, PRO.

16 Ibid., 4–5. With this report is filed a longer and more detailed analysis of these questions by the Colonial Office, "Future Constitutional Development in the Colonies (Economic and Financial Considerations)," July 1957. The most powerful of colonial businesses were reaching similar conclusions: relationships with African governments could be developed as decolonization began to appear inevitable. D. K. Fieldhouse, *Merchant Capital and Economic Decolonization: The United Africa Company 1929–1987* (Oxford: Clarendon Press, 1994), 355.

17 "Future Constitutional Development," 1, 8.

18 "Future Constitutional Development in the Colonies," Note by the secretaries, 30 May 1957, CP (O) 5, CAB 134/1551, PRO.

19 Memorandum by Secretary of State, "Nigeria," C 57 (120), 14 May 1957, CAB 129/87, PRO. Lennox-Boyd wanted to postpone Nigerian demands for independence as far as possible, but not resist "overtly" should Nigerian politicians demand independence in 1959.

20 Memorandum by the Secretary of State, "Future Policy in East Africa," CPC (59) 2, 10 April 1959, CAB 134/1558, PRO. Members of the Colonial Policy Committee, with the prime minister present, raised doubt about a previously sacrosanct goal, "whether the United Kingdom's political system was necessarily the best form of democratic government for these territories, and in particular for those where difficult racial problems were likely to persist." Macmillan admitted that "the long-term future of the African continent presented a sombre picture." The committee approved the plan for an unofficial majority for Tanganyika in 1965 as a first step for the region. CPC (59) 1st meeting, 17 April 1959, ibid.

21 Memorandum for the Cabinet by the Secretary of State for the Colonies, "Kenya," C (62) 22, 6 February 1962, CAB 129/108, and 12th Cabinet Conclusions CC (62), 8 February 1962, CAB 128/36. In 1962, there was a dramatic rise in strike activity, from 167 the year before to 285, with six times as many man-days lost. Renewed social conflict may well have affected official perceptions of political danger. Anthony Clayton and Donald Savage, *Government and Labour in Kenya, 1895–1963* (London: Cass, 1974). See also Bruce Berman, *Control and Crisis in Colonial Kenya: The Dialectic of Domination* (London: Currey, 1990), and Cranford Pratt, "Colonial Governments and the Transfer of Power in East Africa," in Prosser Gifford and Wm. Roger Louis (eds.), *The Transfer of Power in Africa: Decolonization 1940–1960* (New Haven: Yale University Press, 1982), 249–82.

22 These questions were discussed in the Committee on Commonwealth Economic Development, appointed 15 February 1957. See its report to the Cabinet, C (57) 129, CAB 129/87, PRO. See also Morgan, *Official History of Colonial Development*, vol. 3, 14–15.

23 Official Committee on Colonial Policy, 2nd meeting, 5 June 1957, and "Future Constitutional Development in the Colonies (Economic and Financial Considerations)," Note by the secretaries, CP (O) (57) 4, 30 May 1957, CAB 134/1551, PRO. These issues are discussed at some length in Morgan, 3: 21–99.

24 In the Gold Coast, the Volta River dam and aluminum works – one of the most grandiose projects of the post-war era – suffered from British reluctance

to share in "equity risks," the fears of aluminum companies "about the risks of a political and administrative deterioration in the Gold Coast following independence," and the attractiveness of noncolonial alternatives for aluminum smelting. But this "imaginative project of Commonwealth development" epitomized all the hopes the British government had for its global economic role in the era of decolonization, and it kept trying to patch together minimal British funds, the shaky capital resources of the Gold Coast, international funding from the World Bank, and capital from multinational corporations – making deep concessions to outside investors in the process. Sir Francis Lee, President, Board of Trade, Note on the Volta River Project, CP (56) 105, 26 April 1956, CAB 129/81, and Cabinet Conclusions, CM (56)20th Conclusions, 8 March 1956, CAB 128/30, PRO.

25 Foreign Secretary, Minute, 28 July 1959, Prime Minister, Minute, 3 July 1959, PREM 11/2587, PRO. Wm. Roger Louis and Ronald Robinson argue that in the 1950s the British empire was becoming increasingly "informalized" and increasingly an Anglo-American enterprise, as the United States became convinced that development efforts were necessary to ward off communist threats and as it directly and indirectly contributed to development finance. For American leaders, saving Africa for the West was precisely the point, and British collaboration with African leaders was encouraged. Louis and Robinson keep their focus on London and Washington, saying little about the dynamics of politics in Africa and the unintended consequences of developmentalist initiatives. "The Imperialism of Decolonization," *Journal of Imperial and Commonwealth History* 22 (1994): 462–512.

26 One of the leading governors of the decolonization era, Sir Alan Burns, boasted in 1957 of British accomplishments in education, health, transportation, and preparation for self-government, but set the typical list of colonial achievements against "the slavery, the human sacrifices, the cannibalism, and the gross tyrannies which prevailed in various lands before these lands became British colonies or protectorates." The choice of such a crude foil suggests the bitterness with which a man of such experience faced the charges and countercharges of 1950s politics, and the compatibility of post-war developmentalism with older forms of prejudice. He also distinguished between devolving power to peoples who were "fitted for independence" and withholding it from those who were not: his former colleagues were at the time he wrote trying to evade precisely this distinction. *In Defence of Colonies: British Colonial Territories in International Affairs* (London: Allen & Unwin, 1957), 23, 66–67, 293, 301.

27 Jacques Marseille, *Empire colonial et capitalisme français: Histoire d'un divorce* (Paris: Albin Michel, 1984).

28 Raymond Cartier, "En France Noire avec Raymond Cartier," *Paris-Match* 383 (11 August 1956): 38–41 (41 quoted), and 386 (1 September 1956): 39–41 (41 quoted). See also, "Une économie prospère sans colonie: les Pays-Bas: En définitive la perte de l'Indonésie n'a-t-elle pas été un facteur favorable à l'expansion?" *Entreprise* 63 (1 November 1955): 56–57. Although at first, "Cartierism was perceived on the left as too selfish a policy and on the right as too 'petty'," its influence was considerable and applied increasingly to Algeria as well as Africa. See Nathalie Ruz, "La force du 'cartiérisme'," in

Jean-Pierre Rioux (ed.), *La guerre d'Algérie et les français* (Paris: Fayard, 1990), 328–36, 332 quoted.

29 De Gaulle, press conference, 1961, cited by Marseille, 373. De Gaulle's retrospective view was that "On resuming the leadership of France [1958], I was determined to extricate her from the constraints imposed on her by her empire and no longer offset by any compensating advantages." Charles de Gaulle, *Memoirs of Hope: Renewal and Endeavor* trans. by Terence Kilmartin (New York: Simon & Schuster, 1971), 37.

30 Senegal, Rapport Economique, 1951, AS. See also H. de la Bruchollerie, "Note sur la situation économique de la Côte d'Ivoire au 1er Janvier 1954," 10 January 1954, 1Q 656 (171), AS.

31 Charles Jarre, "Malgré les 214 dépensés dans nos T.O.M., leurs exportations globales, sauf au Cameroun, n'ont pas encore retrouvé, en 1952, leur tonnage de 1938," *Marchés Coloniaux* 416 (31 October 1953): 3053.

32 Conseil Economique, *Conjuncture des Territoires Extramétropolitains de l'Union Française* (Paris: Imprimerie des Journaux Officiels, January 1953), 11–12, 18, 127, 139, 146; M. Huet (Inspecteur Général de la France Outre-Mer, Directeur du Contrôle au Ministre de la France Outre-Mer), "Bilan du Premier Plan du Développement Economique et Sociale des Territoires d'Outre-Mer," n.d. [1952], AE 749, ANSOM.

33 Monguillot, Report, 13/D, 28 May 1952, AP 2306/10, ANSOM.

34 High Commissioner (Governor-General) to Monguillot, 17 July 1952, and Erhard, Directeur Général des Finances de l'A.O.F., to Monguillot, 5 May 1952, AP 2306/7, ANSOM.

35 Erhard, Directeur Général des Finances, marginal note on "Rapport concernant l'évolution des dépenses de personnel depuis 1938 et perspectives jusqu'au terme du Plan décennal," 69/D, 22 July 1952, by M. Mazodier, member of the Mission Monguillot, AP 2306/8, ANSOM. These reports were prepared with large margins so that officials of the unit being inspected could comment directly on the inspection.

36 High Commissioner, marginal comment on Monguillot, "Situation financière du Budget Général de l'A.O.F.," 20 August 1952, AP 2306/16, ANSOM.

37 High Commissioner to Monguillot, 5 August 1952, AP 2306/10, ANSOM. Cornut Gentille, the new high commissioner (governor-general) had until recently held the same post in French Equatorial Africa. There, economic prospects were even worse. "And yet at the same time the Territory is provided with, in virtue of the notion of the universalities of Territories of the French Union and the policy of assimilation which we have adopted, the same institutions, the same Assemblies, as the other Territories, which express the same aspiration, the same needs, the same exigencies as Assemblies elected elsewhere." Transcript of session of 9 May 1950, Conférence des Hauts Commissaires, AP 169, ANSOM.

38 For other studies revealing the high costs and delayed benefits of the development effort, see also Conférence des Etudes des Plans, 28 November–1 December 1950, AE 169; M. Huet, "Bilan du Premier Plan du Développement Economique et Sociale des Territoires d'Outre-Mer," n.d. [1952], AE 749, ANSOM; Roland Pré, "Observations et conclusions personnelles du Gouverneur Roland Pré, Président de la Commission d'Etude et de

Coordination des Plans de Modernisation et d'Equipement des Territoires d'Outre-Mer," May 1954, mimeograph in library of ANSOM.

39 "Allocution prononcée par Bernard Cornut-Gentille," Opening of 1st session of the Grand Conseil de l'Afrique Occidentale Française, 7 May 1953.

40 See for example, David B. Abernethy, "European Colonialism and Postcolonial Crises in Africa," in Harvey Glickman (ed.), *The Crisis and Challenge of African Development* (Westport, Conn.: Greenwood Press, 1988), 3–23. Another of the characteristic indictments of post-colonial development policies surfaced in this period: the contention that development policy had an urban bias, focusing on urban investments and thus leading to an excessive growth of the urban proletariat and making administrative careers attractive. Huet, "Bilan du Premier Plan," 1952, AE 749, ANSOM.

41 The highly regarded Governor Roland Pré thought that the first steps toward a modern economic and social infrastructure had to be taken in the face of a population that remained "frozen in anachronistic and archaic concepts and do not see the necessity to participate by a voluntary and reasoned effort in the progress of their country. *On the whole the masses are not yet socially ready to adapt to the norms of a revitalized life.*" "Observations et conclusions personnelles," ANSOM, emphasis in original. Others talked about indigenous agriculture in similar terms. Session of 29 November 1950, Conférence d'Etudes des Plans, Comptes Rendus, AE 169, ANSOM.

42 Officials occasionally came close to lamenting the bygone days of masses of low-wage, involuntary labor as they contemplated the high costs of a stable, voluntary labor force and of mechanization, but they drew back, reminding themselves that the past witnessed "inhuman labor, reprehensible labor." M. Lauraint to session of 1 December 1950, Conférence d'Etudes des Plans, AE 169, ANSOM.

43 This was one of the major problems that the Monguillot mission uncovered. The *cadres généraux* and *supérieures*, as a percentage of the *cadres locaux* and *auxiliaires,* had gone from 16 percent in 1938 to 25 percent in 1952. Wages were up 40 percent in the last two years, and the size of the bureaucracy had grown by 10 percent since 1950, 150 percent since 1938. "Rapport concernant l'évolution des dépenses de personnel" by Mazodier, 22 July 1952, AP 2306/8, ANSOM.

44 "La tendance des investissements et les conditions de l'essor économique de l'Afrique Occidentale Française," *Marchés Coloniaux* 426 (9 January 1954): 65–66.

45 Report on price structures by Chaffanel, Inspecteur des Finances, and Poncet, Chef du Bureau des Etudes à la direction des Prix, n.d. [late 1954], and Governor-General to Inspecteur Général de la France Outre-Mer, 22 March 1955, 1Q 654 (171); "Note sur la situation économique du Sénégal," by Chovard, 7 January 1954, 1Q 656 (171), AS.

46 Pré, "Observations et conclusions personnelles," 1954. Whether French Africa's problems were more the result of oligopolistic commercial firms or overly high government standards is also debated in H. de la Bruchollerie, "Note sur la situation économique de la Côte d'Ivoire au 1er janvier 1954," 10 January 1954, while in the same dossier the opposite case is made in regard to Senegal by Chovard, "Note sur la situation économique du Sénégal,"

7 January 1954, 1Q 656 (171), AS, and studies of the impact of the Code du Travail cited in chapter 7.

47 Commission de modernisation et d'équipement des Territoires d'Outre-Mer, "Rapport général de la sous-commission de l'intégration métropole-Outre-Mer," n.d. [1953], PA 19/3/38, ANSOM. This body was presided over by Roland Pré and included top economic specialists of Rue Oudinnot (Hoffherr, Peter, Moussa) and a former governor-general of FWA, Barthes.

48 Official inspection reports in 1954 and 1955 reiterated the concerns of 1951–53 that "a primitive economic ensemble" was being made to bear the impossible weight of a ponderous political apparatus intended to transform it. The reports seemed to be blaming some Africans for their primitiveness and others for making "claims" on the already overburdened administrative system. R. Lasalle-Sere, "Rapport sur les finances de l'Afrique Occidentale Française," 15 January 1954, and P. Sanner, "Note succinct sur la réforme de la structure de l'Afrique Occidentale Française," 20 July 1955, AP 491, ANSOM.

49 Nonetheless, Louis-Paul Aujoulat was having to defend FIDES against charges that money was being wasted on fruitless projects and to plead with the government not to cut its funding level. Assemblée Nationale, *Débats,* 27 May 1953, 2860–63. Business interests, as Marseille shows in *Empire colonial et capitalisme français,* also got the picture that without colonial rule they could get by through other means. The major British firm, the United Africa Company, in fact tired of the vagaries of French economic policy while it was worried about French social policy, notably the costs imposed by the Code du Travail. Decolonization perhaps had its advantages. Fieldhouse, *Merchant Capital,* 362.

11 Delinking colony and metropole: French Africa in the 1950s

1 Ruth Schachter Morgenthau, *Political Parties in French-Speaking West Africa* (Oxford: Clarendon, 1964), 65–71; Joseph Roger de Benoist *L'Afrique Occidentale Française de 1944 à 1960* (Dakar: Nouvelles Editions Africaines, 1982), 295–319; William J. Foltz, *From French West Africa to the Mali Federation* (New Haven: Yale University Press, 1965).

2 Georges Martens, "Industrial Relations and Trade Unionism in French-speaking West Africa," in Ukandi G. Damachi, H. Dieter Seibel, and Lester Trachtman, *Industrial Relations in Africa* (New York: St. Martin's Press, 1979), 35; Geoffrey Hansen Bergen, "Unions in Senegal: A Perspective on National Development in Africa," Ph.D. Dissertation, University of California Los Angeles, 1994, 150. One point that goes uncommented upon in official, union, and scholarly texts is that the leadership of the growing union movement was entirely male and that (as the family allowances debate suggested) it quietly assumed that the worker was a male with a dependent family.

3 An interesting debate between a "nationalist" interpretation and a *"cégétiste"* version may be found in the pages of *Le Mouvement Social*: Philippe Dewitte, "La CGT et les syndicats d'Afrique occidentale française (1945–1957)," 117 (1981): 3–32, and Paul Delanoue, "La CGT et les syndicats d'Afrique Noire," 122 (1983): 103–16. See also Georges Martens, "Le syndicalisme en Afrique occidentale d'expression française: de 1945 à 1960," *Le Mois en Afrique* 178–79

(1980): 74–97, 180–81; (1980–81): 53–83. The French CGT's penchant to assert Parisian direction hurt its cause, particularly as African trade unionists forged their own interterritorial relationships in West Africa. Bergen, 229–30.

4 Government reports are explicit about their support for the CGT-FO (in Africa, as in France) to try to diminish worker support for the CGT. FWA, Services des Affaires Politiques, "Point de l'activité syndicale en A.O.F. au 31 Décembre 1950," incl. Governor General to Minister, 23 February 1951, IGT 11/2, ANSOM.

5 FWA, Inspection Générale des Services de Sécurité, "Note d'Information," 15 February 1950, 17G 272, AS. The red shoe fit his foot reasonably well – he had worked closely with French communist leaders, had visited the Soviet Union and Eastern Europe, and gave the usual sort of speeches at the usual WFTU conferences – although things got complicated when he got nearer to political power.

6 FWA, Service des Affaires Politiques, "Pointe de l'Activité Syndicale en A.O.F. au 31 Décembre 1950," AP 3408/5, ANSOM.

7 Minister of Overseas France to Minister of Foreign Affairs, 4 August 1951; Minister of Overseas France to High Commissioner, Cameroun, 14 September 1950; Governor-General, FWA, to Minister, 4 September 1951, AP 3408/5, ANSOM; Governor, Soudan, to Governor-General, 25 August 1951, 21 September 1951, High Commissioner's Office, Affaires Politiques, Memorandum, 25 August 1951, 17G 272, AS.

8 FWA, Direction de la Sûreté, Renseignements, 5 October 1951, 17G 272, AS.

9 Affaires Courantes, Dakar, to Governor, Soudan, 16 October 1951 (telegram); Affaires Courantes, Dakar, Circular Telegram, 19 October 1951, 17G 272, AS.

10 A transcript of the conference, 23–28 October 1951, came from Sûreté in the Soudan, 17G 272, AS.

11 Dewitte, "La CGT."

12 Georges Chaffard, *Les carnets secrets de la décolonisation* (Paris: Calmann-Levy, 1967): 2:205

13 Ivory Coast, Services de Police, Renseignements, 2 November 1951; Governor, Soudan, to Governor-General, 6 November 1951; Guinea, Services de Police, Renseignements, 8, 9 November 1951; Soudan, Sûreté, Renseignements, 1 December 1951, 17G 272, AS.

14 FWA, Affaires Politiques, "Note sur le syndicalisme en A.O.F." n.d. [late 1953], AP 3417, ANSOM.

15 Richard Joseph, *Radical Nationalism in Cameroun: Social Origins of the UPC Rebellion* (Oxford: Oxford University Press, 1977).

16 FWA, Sûreté, Renseignements, 5 October 1951, 17G 272, AS.

17 Paul Mercier notes that unions raised considerable interest among intellectual elites precisely because they were "less penetrable by traditional type differentiations – ethnic, religious, etc." than were political parties, and working with unions affirmed the "modernism" of the intellectuals. The converse of this would be that expressions of interests and beliefs from outside the modern sector would have to look elsewhere for affirmation. "La vie politique dans les centres urbains du Sénégal: étude d'une période de transition," *Cahiers Internationaux de Sociologie* 27 (1959): 81–82.

18 See chapters 6 and 7, plus FWA, Affaires Politiques, Revues trimestrielles, Côte d'Ivoire, March–May 1953, AP 2230/4, ANSOM.

19 Affaires Politiques, "Note sur le syndicalisme en A.O.F." n.d. [1953], AP 3417, ANSOM. Bergen, "Unions in Senegal," also emphasizes the importance to Senghor of preventing interterritorial groupings – such as the French West African CGT or later UGTAN – from becoming a force in Senegal, and hence his strong interest in coopting Senegalese trade unionists and marginalizing those he could not coopt. He notes (278 n 58) that the incorporation of Sarr and Guèye into Senghor's political machine may have brought labor into his movement, but effectively neutralized them *as* labor leaders.

20 Martens, "Le syndicalisme," 53; Andras November, *L'évolution du mouvement syndicale en Afrique occidentale* (Paris: Mouton, 1965), 106.

21 Governor, Guinea, to Governor-General, 25 February 1952, 17G 271, AS.

22 Guinea, Renseignements, 1 August 1953, 17G 529, AS; Morgenthau, *Political Parties*, 226–32.

23 High Commissioner to Minister, 20 March 1954, IGT 11/2, ANSOM.

24 High Commissioner to Minister, 20 September 1954, IGT 11/2, ANSOM. French officials remained convinced that Abdoulaye Diallo was "the most dangerous trade union agitator in French Black Africa." Note on stationery of the Cabinet du Ministre de la France Outre-Mer, 3 March 1955, AP 2264/8, ANSOM.

25 Martens, "Le Syndicalisme," 58.

26 High Commissioner to Minister, 20 September 1954, IGT 11/2, ANSOM.

27 High Commissioner to Minister, 26 March 1955, AP 2264/8, ANSOM, reporting on the meeting of the Comité de Coordination des Unions Territoriales CGT AOF-Togo. Later that year, another intelligence report stated that Sékou Touré had been condemned by the Bureau de l'Union CGT de la Côte d'Ivoire for splitting the working class and aiding the "colonialist reaction." Section de Coordination, France Outre-Mer, Renseignements, 13 October 1955, ibid. See also DeWitte, "La CGT," 18, and November, "L'évolution du mouvement syndicale," 93.

28 France, Overseas Ministry, 2nd Bureau, report dated 21 October 1955, on commentaries of Sékou Touré concerning the meeting of the Comité de Coordination des Unions Syndicales CGT de l'AOF et du Togo, 1–14 March 1955, Saint-Louis, AP 2264/8, ANSOM; Dewitte, 24; Martens, 58.

29 Martens, 54–58. He cites Chaffard (*Les carnets secrets*, 181) to the effect that the French administration paid money to Sékou Touré with this in mind and were surprised when he put the funds to organizational rather than personal use. Ibid., 56. Coulibally's initiative is reported in *Liberté* (organ of the PDG), 25 October 1955, clipping in dossier Syndicalisme/4/I/b, 71 Syndicalisme I, CRDA.

30 Martens, 58–61; November, 93–94, 97–100, de Witte, 26; Guinea, Renseignements, 11 May 1956, 17G 271, AS.

31 IGT (Colonna d'Istria), "Evolution de la situation syndicale en A.O.F.," 28 July 1956, 17G 610, AS. Efforts at intersyndical cooperation and their limited success are reported in FWA, Service de Sécurité, Bulletin d'Information, May, June 1956, 17G 627, August, September 1956, 17G 628, AS.

32 Sûreté, Senegal, Renseignements, 5, 31 July 1956, 21G 215 (178), AS.

33 By then, the French CGT, seeing the writing on the wall, was willing to let the African labor movement go out into the world, hoping that a close relation with the WFTU could be maintained. FWA, Service de Sécurité, Bulletin d'Information, August – December 1956, 17G 628; Direction des Services de Sécurité de l'A.O.F., "Bulletin Spécial d'Information sur la Conférence Syndicale Africaine de Cotonou (16–20 Janvier 1957)," 17G 629, AS.

34 FWA, Affaires Politiques, Revue mensuelle des évènements politiques, January 1957, AP 2232/2; Cabinet du Ministre de la France Outre-Mer, Bureau d'Etudes, "Note d'information: UGTAN," 10 January 1958, AP 2264/4, ANSOM. CGT-FO, the weakest of the centrales, remained wedded to its French connection. November, 100.

35 Soudan, Services de Police, Renseignements, 26 January 1957, 17G 620, AS; FWA, Sûreté, Renseignements 28 January 1957, ibid.; FWA, Direction des Affaires Politiques, Revue mensuelle des évènements politiques, January, February 1957, AP 2232/2, ANSOM.

36 Martens, 88–89.

37 FWA, Sûreté, Renseignements, 29 June 1957, 17G 620, AS.

38 French officials picked up on this point immediately. IGT, "Note sur l'évolution du syndicalisme en A.O.F.," 19 April 1957, IGT 11/2, ANSOM.

39 Elliot J. Berg and Jeffrey Butler have argued that trade unions had a relatively small voice in the political movements of pre-independence Africa. In FWA, it is only in Guinea that a union movement was the launching pad for a dominant political party. Nonetheless, in most other territories, organized workers were a constituency that had to be reckoned with, and the early African governments figured it was worth at least a ministry. Labor, however, also acted *outside* the party structure. That was why the labor movement was so important before independence and why it was so often suppressed afterward. "Trade Unions," in James S. Coleman and Carl G. Rosberg, Jr. (eds.), *Political Parties and National Integration in Tropical Africa* (Berkeley: University of California Press, 1966), 340–81.

40 IGT, "Note sur l'évolution du syndicalisme en A.O.F.," 19 April 1957, IGT 11/2, ANSOM. Even earlier, the entry of the RDA into the governing coalition in Paris and the accession of Houphouët-Boigny to a ministerial position contributed to a "return to calm" after the combats over the work week and family allocations in 1953–55. FWA, "Synthèse trimestrielle des faits politiques," January–March 1956, 2G 56–123, AS.

41 Direction des Affaires Politiques, "Revue mensuelle des évènements politiques," September 1957, AP 2232/2, ANSOM. UGTAN's calming efforts were noted in Niger and Guinea. FWA, Service de Sécurité, Bulletin d'Information, May 1957, 17G 630, AS.

42 There was a lively interchange in *Afrique Nouvelle*, 522 (6 August 1957) and 528 (17 September 1957), and at UGTAN conferences, reported in ibid., 569 (4 July 1958) and 599 (30 January 1959). UGTAN leaders' participation in governments was also defended on the grounds that there were no class struggle in Africa, hence no tension between unions and government. Saloum Traoré, "Ministre et militant syndical," *Démocratie Nouvelle* 12, 6 (1958): 52. See also FWA, Direction des Affaires Politiques, "Revue mensuelle des évènements politiques," September, October 1957, AP 2232/2, ANSOM.

43 See the discussion of the varied and complex debates in different territories in
Martens, part 3, as well as recently available archival data in AP 2264/4,
ANSOM, and 17G 598, 607, 610, 627, 628, AS. The agonizing over strike
issues was particularly evident at the UGTAN Conference in Bamako, 8–10
March 1958, chaired by Abdoulaye Diallo, who was also his territory's
minister of labor. Some *militants* denounced the UGTAN leadership for post-
poning a strike in February and reducing the scale of one held the previous
December; Sékou Touré, however, criticized a teachers' union for striking
without considering "all that I have done for you" and other leaders accused
pro-strike activists of "false militance." Soudan, Renseignements, 9, 22 March
1958, 17G 620, AS.

44 Senegal, IT, AR, 1958; November, 106–07; Chaffard, *Les carnets secrets*,
2:205.

45 It was not clear that this message was what a union audience in Senegal
wanted to hear. The spy who reported on this meeting noted that the audience showed signs of impatience, and Bassirou Guèye, the Senegalese CGTA
leader, advised Sékou Touré to cut his remarks short. Senegal, Sûreté,
Renseignements, 21 February 1956, 21G 215, AS.

46 FWA, Service de Sécurité, Bulletin d'Information, February 1956, 17G 627;
Senegal, Renseignements, 2 August 1956, "Rapport Moral et d'Activités" to
Comité Générale de l'Union CGTA of Senegal – Mauretania, 7–8 July 1956,
17G 610, AS.

47 Governor, Dahomey, to High Commissioner, 22 January 1957, K 421 (165),
AS.

48 Transcript of RDA Congress at Bamako, session of 28 September 1957, 17G
605, AS; FWA, Direction des Affaires Politiques, "Revue mensuelle des
évènements politiques," September 1957, AP 2232/2, ANSOM.

49 Exposé de M. le Vice Président Sékou Touré à l'occasion de la conférence du
2 février 1958 avec les résponsables syndicaux et délégués du personnel RDA,
"Le RDA et l'action syndicale dans la nouvelle situation politiques des
T.O.M.," PDG (9)/dossier 7, CRDA. In a later, more formal, statement on
behalf of UGTAN, Sékou Touré was careful to avoid this intimidating
language and acknowledged workers' rights to protect their own interests, but
the basic point was the same: a vision of unity and a determined claim to
represent the African personality (in the singular), as well as an explicit argument that UGTAN's basic role was as part of this wider struggle against colonialism. Sékou Touré, "Rapport d'orientation et de doctrine," in *Congrès
Général de l'U.G.T.A.N (Union Générale des Travailleurs d'Afrique Noire)
Conakry 15–18 Janvier 1959* (Paris: Présence Africaine, 1959).

50 Speech of Camara Bengaly, in name of Conseil de Gouvernement, to Congrès
Constitutif de l'UGTAN, Conakry, 23–25 May 1958, sous-dossier UGTAN,
K 421 (165), AS.

51 Report of David Soumah, Secretary-General, to Congress de la CATC,
Abidjan, 10–12 March 1958, 17G 610, AS. Soumah became more skeptical as
he heard how Sékou Touré and others interpreted unity. Earlier he had withheld judgment, but worried that fusion might imply the "eviction of minori-
ties." David Soumah, "Après Cotonou: Réflexions sur l'unité syndicale,"
Afrique Nouvelle 495 (29 January 1957).

52 "Note sur la situation du syndicalisme C.G.T. en A.O.F.," March 1956, PA 19/3/37, ANSOM; IGT, "Evolution de la situation syndicale en A.O.F.," 28 July 1956, 17G 610, AS..

53 Minister to High Commissioner, draft of a letter, not sent, dated 8 February 1957, AP 2264/8, ANSOM.

54 High Commissioner (G. Cusin) to Minister, 8 February 1957, IGT 11/2, ANSOM.

55 FWA, IGT, "Note sur l'évolution du syndicalisme en A.O.F.," 19 April 1957, IGT 11/2, ANSOM.

56 High Commissioner to Minister, 8 February 1957, IGT 11/2, ANSOM. For similar predictions, see FWA, Affaires Politiques, "Revue mensuelle des évènements politiques," October 1957, AP 2232/2, ANSOM.

57 *Afrique Nouvelle* 548 (7 February 1958).

58 Ivory Coast, Renseignements, 23 November 1956, 17G 610, AS.

59 This section is based on Dahomey, Renseignements, from October 1957 to April 1958, in 17G 588, AS, as well as Governor, Dahomey, to Minister, 30 January 1958, AP 2189/12, ANSOM. Another instance of the discourse of scarcity coming from the new government of Senegal is Mamadou Dia, "Un régime d'austérité accepté par tous," *Afrique Nouvelle* 499 (26 February 1957).

60 See some of the political reports on disputes arising in several territories in the second half in 1957 in 17G 598, AS.

61 Senegal, Synthèse mensuelle de renseignements, July 1957, 17G 598; resolution of UGTAN meeting, Dakar, 15 January 1958, including in Dahomey, Note d'information, nd [February 1958], 17G 588; FWA, Service de Sécurité, Bulletin d'Information, October 1957, 17G 632, AS. Civil servants of metropolitan origin worried about this too. The more senior ones were attached to the Cadres d'Etat, directly under the French Ministry, but others were part of the cadres that came under territorialization. They could only appeal to African politicians in their territories to ask that their scales be made or remain equivalent to those of their metropolitan counterparts. Ministère de la France Outre-mer, Section de Coordination, Renseignements, 25 July 1957, reporting on meeting of Intersyndicat des Fonctionnaires des Cadres Généraux et Communs Supérieurs, Niamey, 17 July 1957, AP 2232/3, ANSOM.

62 Alioune Cissé to UGTAN Congress, Bamako, 8–10 March 1958, reported in FWA, Service de Sécurité, Bulletin d'Information, March 1958, 17G 633, AS; reports on the Réunion Interterritoriale de la Fonction Publique, Dakar, in FWA, "Renseignements d'activités communistes et apparentées," 18 January 1958, 17G 620, AS; *Afrique Nouvelle* 554 (21 March 1958), on conference of Comité Directeur of UGTAN, February 1958. See also ibid., 549 (14 February 1958) on the civil servants' strike of February 1958, called over the opposition of the Comité Directeur and relatively effective except for Guinea and the Ivory Coast.

63 Renseignements, April 1958, 17G 633, AS. UGTAN by 1958 was pleading against the effects of "delinkage" and insisting that there should be no "diminution of acquired entitlements." Resolution of UGTAN meeting, 13–15 January 1958, VP 282, AS.

64 Such issues are illuminated in the detailed narrative of Bergen, "Unions in Senegal."

65 Claude Rivière, "Lutte ouvrière et phénomène syndical en Guinée," *Cultures et Développement* 7 (1975): 53–83, 53 quoted; November, *L'évolution du mouvement syndicale*, 114–17. In the Senegalese strike of January 1959, the government did what its colonial predecessor had threatened but didn't do in 1946, requisition workers into a quasi-military status, fire those who failed to obey, and evict them from housing. A voluminous file reveals workers' painful attempts to get their jobs back. Mamadou Dia to Commandants du Cercle, Circular, 21 January 1959, Diourbel Circle to Bambey Subdivision, 19 January 1959 (telegram), Dia to Commandants du Cercle, Circular, 7 April 1959, 11 D1/0018, and correspondence on rehirings in VP 294, AS. On this and the collapse of UGTAN, see Bergen, "Unions in Senegal," 316–17, 321–22, 329.

66 Interview, Alioune Cissé, Dakar, August 4, 1994, by Oumar Guèye, Alioune Ba, and Frederick Cooper; Interview, Dakar, Moussa Konaté, August 8, 1994, by Ba and Cooper; Interview, Mory Tall, Thiès, August 9, 1994, by Ba, Cooper, Aminata Diena, and Biram Ndour; Interview, Oumar Ndiagne, Thiès, 9 August 1994, by Guèye, Makhali Ndaiye, and Ouseynou Ndaiye.

67 Although the Loi Cadre was drafted under Teitgen's ministry, it was pushed through the legislature by his socialist successor, Gaston Defferre, who was particularly eager to settle the governance issue in subsaharan Africa because of his preoccupation with the Algerian war. De Benoist, *L'Afrique Occidentale Française*, 295, 298.

68 Pierre-Henri Teitgen (with interjections from Sékou Touré and Félix Kir), Assemblée Nationale, *Débats*, 20 March 1956, 1072–73.

69 The minister also informed the high commissioners that one of the main goals of the legislation was to allow each territory to adapt to local circumstances "in order to foster access by civil servants of local origin to the various cadres and to the highest levels." He cited "Africanization" as a major aim, as long as currently serving "fonctionnaires" were protected. Circular to High Commissioners, n.d. [1956], AP 3511, ANSOM.

70 For explication and justification of these features of the Loi Cadre, see the speeches of Paul Alduy, reporter of the Committee on Overseas Territories, Gaston Defferre, Minister of Overseas France, and Paul-Henri Teitgen, former Minister, Assemblée Nationale, *Débats*, 20–21 March 1956, 1965–68, 1072–76, 1108–10. The bill included a clause reaffirming the government's commitment to development assistance and to economic cooperation, and a number of speakers emphasized the importance of economic and social development to the political project of the Loi Cadre. Gabriel Lisette had a particularly interesting take on the issue: "It is necessary to enrich the cultivator so that he does not turn against the city-dweller, so that he doesn't turn against the civil servant." Ibid., 21 March, 1091. See also Robert Buron, ibid., 22 March, 1191–92, and the text of the development clause, ibid., 1189.

71 In the debate, several speakers, from France and from Africa, alluded to the violence then afflicting North Africa, and their desire to reach a definitive arrangement for the restructuring of the French Union in Africa before similar violence broke out there. See, for example, Paul Alduy, reporter of the Committee on Overseas Territories, *Débats*, 20 March 1956, 1065, Gaston Defferre, Minister, 21 March 1956, 1109, Diawadou Barry, 20 March 1956, 1071.

72 African leaders disagreed over this, with some welcoming the control they would get over their own resources and others fearing "balkanization." Officials also had different attitudes, some fearing that territorialization would destroy the ability to the government-general to coordinate economic and social plans and insure that the poorest territories had a share of resources. Draft reply to the Minister's request of 12 May 1956 for opinions on the future role of the Government-General, 18G 273, AS. See also de Benoist, 311–19, 348–51.

73 The debate went from 20 to 22 March 1956 in the Assemblée Nationale and came back for a second and final reading (after minor changes in the Conseil de la République) on 19 June 1956, where it passed 470 to 105.

74 Article 3, Loi Cadre, in *Débats*, 21 March 1956, 1141. For a clear statement underscoring this guarantee, see Paul Alduy, reporter of the Committee on Overseas Territories, ibid., 20 March 1956, 1067.

75 "Mémoire sur la réforme des structures de l'A.O.F.," Dakar, 11 July 1955, AP 491, ANSOM.

76 Direction des Services de Législation Générale de Contentieux et de Liaison, "Mémorandum sur le problème de la fonction publique en Afrique Occidentale Française," 15 January 1955, 18G 268, AS. Unions continued to make claims in these terms. The Annual Congress of the Union Territoriale CGT-FO (Senegal and Mauritania), 22–23 September 1956, for example, demanded the unification for all cadres of the "complément spéciale," a supplementary payment currently varying by a factor of four up the hierarchy and went on to the unification of family allowances. Transcript of meeting from Sûreté in 17G 610, AS. Similarly, the CGTA protested the failure of the administration to unify benefits in the civil service. Secrétaire Général Adjoint, Union Territoriale des Syndicats du Sénégal et de la Mauritanie to High Commissioner, 16 October 1956, K 425 (165), AS.

77 P. Sanner, Inspecteur de la FOM, "Note succinct sur la réforme de la structure de l'AOF," 20 July 1955, AP 491, ANSOM.

78 A poster of the Intersyndicat des Cadres Généraux et Communs Supérieurs en Service en A.O.F. – a basically white union – carried an "Appeal to All Civil Servants" against the rumored plan of the minister and Senghor to create a small *cadre d'état* and larger *cadres territoriaux*. "We will not accept it!" stated the union, claiming African support for their position. African unions, however, were not very interested in cooperation with them. Poster, nd (c. December 1955), and clipping from *Le Monde*, 5 May 1956, in 18G 268, AS.

79 Resolution of Comité de Coordination des Unions Territoriales CGT de l'Afrique Occidentale Française-Togo, 17 February 1956, K 425 (165), AS.

80 High Commissioner to Résponsables du Comité d'Action des Organisations Syndicales de la Fonction Publique, 25 July 1956; Comité Interfédéral des Services Publics de l'Afrique Occidentale Française to secretaries-general of the unions territoriales-FO de l'Afrique Occidentale Française, 11 August 1956, 17G 610, AS. The same argument was used to reject demands of another civil service union in High Commissioner to Secrétaire Général de l'Union Territoriale des Syndicats CGTA du Sénégal et de la Mauritanie, 10 August 1956, K 425 (165), AS.

81 Minister to High Commissioner, 2 July 1956, K 425 (165); Direction des Services de Législation Générale de Contentieux et de Liaison, "Note sur la territorialisation de la Fonction Publique en application de la loi-cadre," 6 March 1957, 18G 268, AS; idem., "Note sur la maintien des droits acquis par les fonctionnaires intégrés dans les cadres territoriaux," n.d. [1957], 18G 270, AS.

82 Not surprisingly, they wanted to keep as many civil servants as possible under their jurisdiction and cut out Dakar, which was congruent with the wishes of French officials too. FWA, Direction des Services de Législation Générale de Contentieux et de Liaison, "Note sur la gestion des personnels actuels des cadres supérieurs jusqu'à leur intégration dans les cadres territoriaux," n.d. [1957], 18G 270, AS.

83 See FWA, Service de Sécurité, *Bulletin d'Information*, throughout 1956 (April 1956 quoted), 17G 627, AS. There was a strike in the Ivory Coast PTT over the Loi Cadre in August 1956, as the *cadres généraux* in particular sought reassurance over its status. Governor, Ivory Coast, to High Commissioner, 31 August 1956 (telegram), 18G 273, AS.

84 These events may be followed in FWA, Service de Sécurité, *Bulletin d'Information*, monthly reports throughout 1957 and 1958. The governor of Upper Volta noted the participation of his territory in FWA-wide protests of UGTAN, the CATC, and FO, intended to lead up to a three-day strike in late 1957. He cited the "impatience" of civil servants, but noted that his territory lacked the means to respond to the "social agitation which the Conseil de Gouvernement would want to avoid." Governor, Upper Volta, to High Commissioner, 1 December 1957, K 425 (165), AS. This was exactly the kind of dilemma territorialization was to bring about: putting the burden stemming from broad issues that crossed territorial boundaries onto territorial budgets of highly unequal capacity to take them on.

85 See FWA, Service de Sécurité, *Bulletin d'Information*, May 1957, 17G 630, AS, for an astute official analysis of UGTAN's dilemma. UGTAN also took up a private sector dispute in Dakar, which resulted in bitter strikes between 6 and 23 August 1957. Ibid., August 1957, 17G 631, AS

86 Mamadou Dia, "Appel aux travailleurs du territoire," n.d., c. Decembre 1958. Records of UGTAN meeting, Dakar, 13–15 January 1958, K 421 (165), AS; FWA, Service de Sécurité, *Bulletin d'Information*, monthly reports, 1957 and 1958, 17G 632 and 633; Senegal, Renseignements, 21 May 1957, 17G 607, AS; *Afrique Nouvelle* 569 (4 July 1958). The hold outs against UGTAN's assertions of trade union exclusivity, the CATC and the CGT-FO, maintained assimilationist demands – notably for equitable conditions for civil servants of African origin – and tried to safeguard their own autonomy from the compulsions of unity. Report by David Soumah to CATC meeting, Abidjan, 1–12 March 1958, 17G 610; Resolution of "Journée d'Etudes" of CGT-FO, Abidjan, 8–9 February 1958, in Ivory Coast, Renseignements, 10 February 1958, 17G 610, AS.

87 FWA, Service de Sécurité, *Bulletin d'Information*, February 1958, 17G 633, AS.

88 On the rise of the territories and the decline of the federal structure (despite the reservations of Senghor and some other African leaders), see Morgenthau,

Political Parties, 69–70; de Benoist, *L'Afrique Occidentale Française*, 311–19, 348–54.

89 FWA, IGT, Circular to Inspecteurs Territoriaux, 24 June 1957, and Minister, Circular to High Commissioners, 5 August 1957, 18G 270, AS; IGT, "Note à l'attention de M. le Directeur du Cabinet," 12 January 1957, AP 2189/5, ANSOM.

90 IGT, Rapport au Ministre, 26 March 1958, AP 2189/5; "Note à l'attention de M. le Directeur du Cabinet," 12 January 1957, AP 2189/5, ANSOM. The absence of African inspectors is disclosed in "Indices et effectifs, Fonction Publique, AOF," incl. High Commissioner, Circular to Governors, 5 September 1957, 18G 628, AS.

12 Nation, international trade unionism, and race

1 Gold Coast, Labour Department, AR, 1950–51, 4–5; Richard Jeffries, *Class, Power and Ideology in Ghana: The Railwaymen of Sekondi* (Cambridge: Cambridge University Press, 1978), 59.

2 For this reason, the CO advocated reinstating government workers who had been fired during the strikes and pushing the private sector to do the same. It was, however, the one-time extremist on whose behalf the strike had been conducted, Nkrumah, who cut through the government's cumbersome reinstatement procedures and rehired 250 victims of the 1950 events. G. Foggon, Minute, 1 March 1951; Reuters despatch, 24 April 1951, CO 96/819/31312/9A/1951, PRO.

3 Jeff Crisp, *The Story of an African Working Class: Ghanaian Miners' Struggles 1870–1980* (London: Zed, 1984), 112–13.

4 Political Intelligence Reports, Gold Coast, 15 August 1951, CO 537/7233, PRO.

5 Jeffries, *Class, Power and Ideology*, 61–63. The absorption of the maverick labor organization by the GCTUC is duly reported in the labour department's annual report for 1953–54 (p. 9), but in the best bureaucratic tradition, there is no hint of the politics of all this. The labour department was headed by a Welsh former mine union official, I. G. Jones, as it passed under control of African ministers in Nkrumah's government.

6 "Note on the effect of outside influence on Gold Coast Trade Union Affairs," n.d. [1954] and draft report on Gold Coast, January 1955, CO 859/891, PRO. London continued to worry that "communist" union leaders were still within the GCTUC and that its leader, John Tettegah, might be playing a double game between the CPP and the communists. See also Jeffries, 79–82, and Jon Kraus, "The Political Economy of Industrial Relations in Ghana," in Ukandi G. Damachi, H. Dieter Seibel, and Lester Trachtman (eds.), *Industrial Relations in Africa* (New York: St. Martin's Press, 1979), 128–32.

7 N. D. Watson, paper prepared for talks with the British TUC, 9 November 1953, CO 859/748, PRO.

8 A. T. Kerr (Ministry of Health and Labour, Gold Coast) to Watson, Colonial Office, 2 April 1952, and Minutes by I. M. Harding, 13 April 1952, and N. D. Watson, 21 April 1952, CO 554/332, PRO; Gold Coast, Labour Department, AR, 1952–53, 2–4, 7. Earlier, the Colonial Office smugly replied to Spears' complaint that a Gold Coast government committee was investi-

gating labor conditions on his mines that this was an "internal matter" for the Gold Coast government. Minute by Maurice Smith, 22 October 1951, CO 554/226, PRO.

9 Governor Arden Clarke to Secretary of State, 28 December 1955, 16 August 1956, 5 March, 1957, CO 554/1162, PRO; Note by CO for Committee on Commonwealth Prime Ministers meeting, 14 June 1956, PREM 11/1367, PRO; Draft of document for Colonial Office print on "Future Constitutional Developments in the Colonies," August 1958, CO 1032/147.

10 John K. Tettegah, *A New Chapter for Ghana Labour* (Accra: Ghana TUC, 1958), 30, 45.

11 Jeffries, 66–69.

12 See the statistics in Kraus, "Industrial Relations in Ghana," 122.

13 Gold Coast, Labour Department, AR, 1955–56, 13–14; Crisp, *Story of an African Working Class*, 115–21, 126–37. The quotation from Nkrumah is from *Osagyefo in Kumasi* (1962), 17, quoted in ibid., 134.

14 Bjorn Beckman, *Organizing the Farmers: Cocoa Politics and National Development in Ghana* (Uppsala: Scandinavian Institute of African Studies, 1976). The most serious opposition, beginning in 1954, originated with a regional nationalism in the former Asante kingdom. British officials were ambivalent about this challenge and about its implications for democratic process, but unwilling to see their project of devolving power derailed. They were anxious, however, that the Asante opposition not link up with the labor opposition, notably the "really bad men" Woode and Biney. The conservative Asantehene was not about to do that. Jean Marie Allman, *The Quills of the Porcupine: Asante Nationalism in an Emergent Ghana* (Madison: University of Wisconsin Press, 1993), 154–55.

15 G. Foggon, Colonial Office Labour Advisor, to Conference of East African Labour Commissioners, 24–27 August 1959, CO 822/1630, PRO. At this time, CO and British TUC officials were worried about international criticism of restrictive trade union registration laws in certain British colonies, and one official wondered why "attention could not be directed also at the much more severe restrictions on freedom of association introduced in Ghana." Notes of a meeting with a TUC deputation, 29 July 1959, CO 859/1111, PRO. The TUC had been aware even earlier of "the attempts by a nationalist government to control the trade union movement." Comments of Walter Hood, on return from a visit to the Gold Coast, to meeting with TUC, Overseas Employers' Federation (OEF), and CO, 10 January 1956, CO 859/748, PRO.

16 Philip F. de Zulueta, Minute, 1 July 1959, PREM 11/2587, PRO. The prime minister's minute, 3 July 1959, ibid., used some of the language from de Zulueta's earlier minute, but not this phrase.

17 Ghana's story has its unique features – especially because of its pioneering role – but the power of parties to rein in unions *after* independence is a general theme of African states. Elliot J. Berg and Jeffrey Butler, "Trade Unions," in James S. Coleman and Carl G. Rosberg, Jr. (eds.), *Political Parties and National Integration in Tropical Africa* (Berkeley: University of California Press, 1966), 380. For a detailed study of another major case, see Robin Cohen, *Labour and Politics in Nigeria, 1954–71* (London: Heinemann, 1974).

18 As late as 1956, only 15,000 out of an estimated 170,000 trade unionists in FWA belonged to the FO and hence to the ICFTU. The FO had made little progress since 1953. Secrétariat Général du Gouvernement, Commission des informations musulmanes, Groupe de Travail Permanent, "La C.I.S.L. et l'Afrique française," Paris, 28 November 1956, AP 2264/9, ANSOM.

19 Ibid; FWA, Direction des Services de Sécurité, "Note de Renseignements," 4 September 1956; FWA, Renseignements, 21 January 1957, 17G 591, AS. Agents were suspicious of Sékou Touré's contacts with a Belgian woman working for the ICFTU and when he was in Brussels spent long hours in hotel rooms with their ears to the walls, hearing nothing from the adjoining room except the obvious. SDECE/AOF, Renseignements, 28 February, 4 March, 15 April, 1 July 1957, ibid.

20 The WFTU tried to work with UGTAN, but the autonomists were not interested. IGT, "Evolution syndicale en Afrique," February 1957, and High Commissioner to Minister, 8 February 1957, IGT 11/2, ANSOM. See also Andras November, L'évolution du mouvement syndicale en Afrique occidentale (Paris: Mouton, 1965), 175–236.

21 N. D. Watson, paper done in preparation for talks with TUC, 9 November 1953; record of talks between CO and TUC, 28 January 1954; draft record of discussion among CO, TUC, and OEF, 12 July 1954, CO 859/748, PRO. When a representative of the OEF complained of the "anti-colonial" tendencies of the ICFTU, Sir Victor Tewson of the TUC replied that his organization had been fighting such tendencies, but the ICFTU had to consider the sentiments of its member unions, some of which were from colonies, and the fact that it was competing with the WFTU for colonial workers. He credited the ICFTU with having influenced Nkrumah to "come down against Communism." Meeting of TUC, OEF, and CO, 20 July 1954, ibid.

22 Anthony Clayton and Donald Savage, Government and Labour in Kenya, 1895–1963 (London: Cass, 1974), 379–81. Earlier, the ICFTU complained bitterly that the Kenyan government, with Mau Mau "as an excuse, was suppressing the kinds of unions it claimed to want." Colonial Office and TUC officials were indeed sensitive to criticism from this quarter. Jay R. Krane to Marjorie Nicolson, 13 May 1953, FCB 61/2, fl. 4; Secretary of State to Governor, 7 April 1952, and Minute by N. D. Watson, 4 March 1952, on meeting with Tewson, Bell and Hood of the TUC, CO 859/268, PRO.

23 Clayton and Savage, Government and Labour, 382, 386–87, 435.

24 Kenya Intelligence Committee Report, October 1959; G. Foggon, Minute, 31 December 1959, CO 822/1842. See also Paul Tiyambe Zeleza, "Trade Union Imperialism: American Labour, the ICFTU and the Kenyan Labour Movement," Social and Economic Studies 36 (1987): 145–70, and David Goldsworthy, Tom Mboya: The Man Kenya Wanted to Forget (London: Heinemann, 1982).

25 Governor to Secretary of State, telegram, 9 May 1955, CO 859/847, PRO; Clayton and Savage, 390–91, 401. The government considered arresting Mboya on his return for engaging in political activities beyond those allowed trade union officials, but thought wiser of it with a little counsel from the TUC. Ibid., 401. In Vienna, Tewson had to defend Great Britain's position in its colonies by arguing, "The colonialism which we find in Britain's territories

today is not the colonialism of 50 years ago," and he asserted that the TUC had contributed to this change. ICFTU, Fourth World Congress, Vienna, 20–28 May 1955, session of 26 May 1955, 347–48, International Archives for Social History, Amsterdam.

26 Gold Coast, Labour Department, AR, 1952–53, 7.

27 International Confederation of Free Trade Unions, *Report of the First African Regional Conference Held at Accra 14–19 January 1957* (Brussels: ICFTU, 1958), 13–18.

28 Sir Victor Tewson, in an obvious response to Nkrumah, told the African trade unionists that they should steer clear of politics. But in private, Tewson indicated that the TUC had no intention of criticizing Nkrumah's attack on trade union autonomy because he feared "driving the Ghana trade union movement into the W.F.T.U." An observer from France's CGT-FO, Marcel Babau, also told delegates they were "wrong" to discuss "general political problems" at such a conference. Accra Conference Report, 19, 55; note of meeting between CO and TUC deputation, 29 July 1959, CO 859/1111, PRO.

29 ICFTU, *Conference*, 176.

30 Ibid., 132–34, 176–77. The report also addressed the argument that wages should be more or less in equilibrium with peasant incomes, insisting that holding workers down to such a standard would only lower the possibility for general improvement in the standard of living and pointing out the impossibility of having workers of different races in the same enterprises receiving different rates of pay. Ibid., 142. An observer from the ILO told the delegates that aims of his organization and the trade union movement were essentially the same. Ernest Bell, ibid., 50.

31 Ibid., 177–87.

32 Tom Mboya, *Freedom and After* (Boston: Little, Brown, 1963), 199.

33 John Kent writes in a narrower framework on *The Internationalization of Colonialism: Britain, France, and Black Africa, 1939–1956* (Oxford: Clarendon Press, 1992).

34 Governor, Uganda, to Secretary of State, 12 April 1958, and 11 May 1958 (telegram), CO 859/1210, PRO.

35 Minutes, W. A. C. Mathieson, 17 April, 16 May 1958, J. S. Bennett, 17 April 1958, C. G. Gibbs, 30 April 1958, CO 859/1210, PRO. Governor Baring in Kenya fully supported his colleague, while the governor of Tanganyika shared his sentiments but thought alienating the ICFTU would lead to "unforseeable but probably unpleasant results." Governor, Kenya, to Secretary of State, 13 May 1958 (telegram), and Governor, Tanganyika, to Secretary of State, 3 June 1958 (telegram), ibid.

36 Secretary of State to Governor, Uganda, 5 May 1958, CO 859/1210, PRO.

37 Minute J. S. Bennett, 2 January 1958 [incorrectly written 1957 in document]; Minute, C. G. Gibbs, 25 September 1957; report on AFL-CIO Convention, 5–12 December 1957, by A. M. Morgan, Labour Attaché to US; Morgan to Wilson, 13 December 1957, CO 859/1210, PRO.

38 Morgan, report on AFL-CIO convention, 5–12 December 1957; Minute, J. S. Bennett, 17 April 1958, and other minutes 17–30 April, 2 May 1958; Minute, G. Foggon, 24 July 1958, CO 859/1210, PRO. British officials were annoyed with the TUC for not taking a more active role itself in Africa, which they

thought might have preempted the ICFTU move. Minute, Foggon, 15 May 1958, Bourdillon, 21 May 1958, ibid.

39 Governor, Uganda, to Secretary of State, 20 November 1958 (telegram); ICFTU *Information Bulletin* 9, 22 (15 November 1958), which says there were thirty-seven students; ICFTU Press Release, 16 April 1959, CO 859/1211, PRO.

40 S. Dawson, Report of ICFTU delegation to UGTAN convention, 15–18 January 1959, CO 859/1211, PRO. By this time, the UGTAN leadership and Tettegah together differed substantially with Tettegah's ICFTU partner Tom Mboya over the issue of trade union autonomy. The Ghanaians, now trying to assume the mantle of anti-imperialism and pan-Africanism, were making a somewhat uneasy rapprochement with the WFTU, and the ICFTU, keeping its rivalry going, promoted the founding of the African Trade Union Confederation. The rival African federations paralleled the division of African states into the "Casablanca" and "Monrovia" blocks. Georges Fischer, "Syndicats et décolonisation," *Présence Africaine* 34–35 (1960–61), 52, and Clayton and Savage, *Government and Labour*, 436–37.

41 November, *L'évolution du mouvement syndicale*, 114–16. There was also an ugly spat among anglophone trade unionists, when a Ghanaian newspaper accused Mboya of being an "imperialist stooge" for organizing an ICFTU conference in Lagos when the Ghanaians were trying to bring together the all-African trade union group in Accra. Mboya's reply was (for the moment) sympathetic to the All Africa Trade Union Federation but insistent that the ICFTU connection be maintained, for the labor movement wanted its message to "project beyond the boundaries of Africa." He acknowledged dangers of "subtle forms of domination" in such relations but insisted that African leaders need not fear that they "might be outsmarted and used." He linked the international connection to the idea of trade union freedom – an indirect warning against the dangers of too rigorous nationalism and too close an association with state policy: Africans must commit themselves to "free and democratic trade unionism based on the fundamentals of freedom of association and human liberties including the dignity of labour." Mboya, as usual, had a point. KFL press release, "Mr. Tom Mboya replies to *Ghana Times*," incl. British Embassy, Brussels, to Colonial Office, 12 February 1960, CO 822/2020, PRO.

42 In a convoluted discussion about the ethics of leaders of trade unions simultaneously serving as ministers in a government, officials acknowledged the "relaxation" of usual standards given the lack of "able and responsible leaders." What they hoped was that trade union leaders, once in government, would distance themselves from unions; what they feared was an official mobilizing labor against capital. Draft Circular, 23 December 1953, enclosed Memorandum on "Ministers' Associations with Trade Unions," and Minute by R. J. Vile, 10 November 1953, CO 1032/124, PRO.

43 Conference of East African Labour Commissioners, 24–27 August 1959, Dar es Salaam, CO 822/1630, PRO.

44 Minutes, J. S. Bennett, 22, 27 October 1959, N. D. Watson, 16 October 1959, W. L. Gorrell-Barnes, 29 October 1959; Note of meeting between CO and TUC, 29 July 1959, CO 859/1111, PRO. Some governors reacted to this issue

by ignoring it in favor of their much-flogged horse, that African trade unions were still in their "infancy" and not yet ready to take on responsible roles. Governor, Uganda, to Secretary of State, 1 November 1959, ibid.

45 Transcripts of speeches at ICFTU African Regional Conference, Dar es Salaam, 26–28 July 1958, incl. Governor, Tanganyika, to Secretary of State, 13 August 1958, CO 859/1211, PRO.

46 Kenya, *Legislative Council Debates*, 89 (18 July 1962), c. 1030; Mboya, *Freedom and After*, 199–201, 256–61; Bruce Berman, *Control and Crisis in Colonial Kenya: The Dialectic of Domination* (London: Currey, 1990), 413; Alice Amsden, *International Firms and Labour in Kenya, 1945–70* (London: Cass, 1971); Goldsworthy, *Mboya*.

47 Sir Walter Harragin, *Report of the Commission on the Civil Services of British West Africa 1945–46*, Colonial No. 209 (1947), 10.

48 Omorogbe Nwanwene, "British Colonial Policy and Localisation: The Nigerian Experience," *Journal of Commonwealth Political Studies* 6 (1968): 206.

49 Nwanwene, 204.

50 Minutes of Meeting in Colonial Office, written by C. Lambert, 26 July 1945, CO 554/134/11, PRO. The most dire predictions came from Governor Alan Burns.

51 Minute, C. J. Jeffries, 13 December 1944 (citing Burns) and C. Lambert, 23 March 1945, ibid.

52 Harragin Commission, 10.

53 Colonial Office reply to ILO questionnaire on minimum standards of social policy, incl. C. A. Grossmith to Secretary, Ministry of Labour, 8 March 1945, CO 859/102/6; Memorandum by Charles Jeffries, "Relationship of European and African Salaries in West Africa, 12 June 1944, CO 554/134/11, PRO.

54 "Employment of native-born administrators in the higher grades of colonial civil services," Cabinet memorandum by Mr Griffiths, CAB 129/41, CP (50) 171, 17 July 1950, reprinted in Ronald Hyam (ed.), *British Documents on the End of Empire*. Series A, Vol. II: *The Labour Government and the End of Empire 1945–1951, Part IV* (London: HMSO, 1992), 38.

55 Great Britain, *Report of the Commission on the Civil Services of Kenya, Tanganyika, Uganda, and Zanzibar, 1947–48* (London: HMSO, 1948), 24–25; Great Britain; *Report of the Commission on the Civil Services of the East African Territories and the East Africa High Commission 1953–54* (London: HMSO, 1954), 18–19, 27–30. The memberships of these committees was overlapping: East and West African salary policies were being shaped by the same elite officials.

56 Lidbury Report, paragraph 141.

57 Clayton and Savage, *Government and Labour*, 376. All the post-war commissions were complicated by uncertainty about how to define the status of civil servants of Asian origin: because officials tended to regard them as not quite native, but not quite as competent as Europeans – and because their pay tended to fall in the middle – they worked themselves into an especially essentialist framework for deciding what communities contributed and deserved in pay.

58 R. D. Grillo, *Race, Class and Militancy: An African Trade Union, 1939–1965* (New York: Chandler, 1974), 44–51.

59 G. Foggon, Minute, 19 November 1959; Railway African Union pamphlet, September 1959, CO 822/1490, PRO. See also correspondence in CO 822/1791 (Kenya), and CO 822/1625 and 1626 (Tanganyika), PRO.

60 Reuter's despatch, 19 November 1959; Governor to Secretary of State, 24 November, 30 November 1959 (telegrams), CO 822/1490, PRO. On the earlier general strike threat in Kenya, see Governor to Secretary of State, 11 June 1959, CO 822/1791, and on the Tanganyika strike, see papers in the file CO 822/1625, PRO.

61 *Report of the Commission on the Civil Services of Northern Rhodesia and Nyasaland* (Lusaka, 1947), incl. Fitzgerald to Secretary of State, 4 September 1947, CO 822/121/4, PRO.

62 Northern Rhodesia. *Report Of The Commission Appointed to Review the Salary Structure, Remuneration and Terms of Service of the Civil Service of Northern Rhodesia* (Lusaka, 1952), Part I – European Staff, 6, and Part II – African Staff, 1, 2.

63 In colonies where mission education had its longest history, the Gold Coast, southern Nigeria, and Sierra Leone, there had been a significant African presence in governmental service in the nineteenth century. Their importance had diminished as colonization became more systematic.

64 "The Africanisation Policy of the West African Governments," Memorandum by M. G. Smith, 13 March 1953, CO 554/400, reprinted in A. N. Porter and A. J. Stockwell (eds.), *British Imperial Policy and Decolonization, 1938–64.* Vol. II: *1951–64* (London: Macmillan, 1989), 209; Gold Coast, *A Statement on the Programme of Africanisation of the Public Service* (Accra, 1954); Robert M. Price, *Society and Bureaucracy in Contemporary Ghana* (Berkeley: University of California Press, 1975): 44–45.

65 Kraus, "Industrial Relations in Ghana," 136, citing *Report of the Commission on the Structure and Remuneration of the Public Services in Ghana* (1967), 29, 31; Jeffries, *Class, Power and Ideology*, 173–74, 221 n 23.

66 Nigeria, *Report of the Commission on the Public Services of the Governments in the Federation of Nigeria 1954–55* (Lagos, 1955), 35. The situation in Nigeria was made complicated by the division of Nigeria into a federal structure in 1954, resulting in three separate civil services for the three separate regions, plus a federal civil service. See Nigeria, *The Nigerianization of the Civil Service*, by Sir Sydney Phillipson and S. O. Adebo, with a Statement by the Council of Ministers (Lagos, 1954); Federation of Nigeria, *Matters arising from the Final Report of the Parliamentary Committee on the Nigerianisation of the Federal Public Service. Statement of Policy by the Government of the Federation*, Sessional Paper No. 2 of 1960 (Lagos, 1960).

67 Secretary of State, "Future of Her Majesty's Overseas Civil Service," Colonial Policy Committee Paper C.A. (56) 6, 14 February 1956, CAB 134/1202, PRO.

68 Kraus, "Industrial Relations in Ghana"; Victor P. Diejomaoh, "Industrial Relations in a Development Context: The Case of Nigeria," in Damachi, Seibel and Trachtman, *Industrial Relations in Africa*, 169–200; Cohen, *Labour and Politics in Nigeria*.

69 The division of Nigeria into three regional governments during the run-up to decolonization came the closest to paralleling the French experience. A Nigerian union, rather like some of its francophone counterparts, warned that

regionalizing the civil service "destroyed the last chords of a Common Nigerian Nationality" and had a "decapitating influence militating against our efforts to build a sound and healthy trade union movement." Officials worried that it compromised efficiency. Gogo Chu Nzeribe, Secretary-General of All Nigeria Trade Union Federation, to Secretary of State, 27 January 1955, CO 859/764, PRO; Nigeria, *Commission on Public Services 1954–55*, 26–27.

13 The wages of modernity and the price of sovereignty

1 I agree with Ruth Berins Collier and David Collier that there are "critical junctures," with regional or global sweep, at which the modes in which labor is incorporated into state structures are rethought and reconfigured. Although I would not follow them in referring to "legacies" of these junctures, my stress on pathways and new points of contestation that emerge from such a critical moment is not far from their argument. Their book provides interesting parallels (with different chronologies) to the incorporative process discussed here. *Shaping the Political Arena: Critical Junctures, the Labor Movement, and Regime Dynamics in Latin America* (Princeton: Princeton University Press, 1991).

2 In the period 1945–50, inflation was so high that even maintaining real wages was a struggle. Militance helped. From a 1938 baseline (index 100), the import purchasing power of wages in Dakar, which had a strike in January 1946, went from 58 in 1945 to 128 in 1946 to 119 in 1949, whereas the comparable figure in more tranquil Abidjan went from 85 in 1945 to 95 in 1946 to 78 in 1949. In Nigeria, wage spurts occurred during the labor agitation of 1942 and 1945 and otherwise declined during the war, rising slowly afterward, whereas Gold Coast wages stagnated throughout the war but increased during the period of crisis after 1945. Elliot J. Berg, "Real Income Trends in West Africa," in Melville J. Herskovits and Mitchell Harwitz (eds.), *Economic Transition in Africa* (London: Routledge, 1964), 205, 207, 209, 215, plus chapters 4 and 5.

3 T. M. Yesufu, *An Introduction to Industrial Relations in Nigeria* (London: Oxford University Press, 1962), 170–75; Peter Kilby, "Industrial Relations and Wage Determination: Failure of the Anglo-Saxon Model," *Journal of Developing Areas* 1 (1967): 489–520; John Weeks, "A Comment on Peter Kilby: Industrial Relations and Wage Determination," ibid., 3 (1968): 9–18, and further exchanges in ibid., 19–26, and 5 (1971): 165–75; W. M. Warren, "Urban Real Wages and the Nigerian Trade Union Movement," *Economic Development and Cultural Change* 15 (1966): 22–36; Robin Cohen, *Labour and Politics in Nigeria, 1945–71* (London: Heinemann, 1974), 197–209. Cohen is the most convincing: wage revisions reflect not just formal trade union action, but government fears of wider unrest, especially 1945-style strikes.

4 Paul Collier and Deepak Lal, *Labour and Poverty in Kenya 1900–1980* (Oxford: Clarendon Press, 1986), 63–64, 275; John Weeks, "Wage Policy and the Colonial Legacy – A Comparative Study," *Journal of Modern African Studies* 9 (1971): 361–87.

5 French West Africa's higher wage rates were noted at the time by French experts, who complained that it made it hard to compete with British West Africa. Director of Finances, FWA, to High Commissioner, n.d. [1953], K 440

(165), AS. Minimum wages, in accordance with policy, rose more rapidly after 1949 in Conakry, Cotonou, and Abidjan than in Dakar. FWA, IT, AR, 1951, "Note au sujet de l'évolution des salaires," n.d. [1957], K 440, (165). Ibrahima Thioub's data also show important if unspectacular gains in laborers' real wages after World War II, but he emphasizes the catastrophic declines earlier. It should be added that the post-war labor force was much larger. "Economie coloniale et rémunération de la force de travail: Le salaire du manoeuvre à Dakar de 1930 à 1954," *Revue Française d'Histoire d'Outre-Mer*, 81 (1994): 427–53.

6 A. November, *L'évolution du mouvement syndicale en Afrique occidentale* (Paris: Mouton, 1965), 77; Yesufu, *Industrial Relations in Nigeria*, 41–42; Walter Elkan, *Migrants and Proletarians: Urban Labour in the Economic Development of Uganda* (London: Oxford University Press, 1960), 58; Robert H. Bates, *Unions, Parties, and Political Development: A Study of Mineworkers in Zambia* (New Haven: Yale University Press, 1971).

7 Family allocation rates were the same in Senegal as in the Ivory Coast, less elsewhere. Employers were charged 5.2 percent of their gross payroll for family allocations (a calculation which obviously assumed a high rate of bachelorhood in the work force) and 2.7 percent for pensions. FWA, Service de Coordination des Affaires Economiques et du Plan, "Les salaires en Afrique Occidental Française, salaires minima hiérarchisés au 28 février 1958"; Ivory Coast, IT, AR, 1957; Chambre de Commerce, d'Agriculture et d'Industrie de Dakar, "Synthèse de la situation économique de l'ex-Afrique Occidentale Française durant la période 1948 à 1958" (mimeographed, 1959), 1: 153–54.

8 In 1947, 72 percent of the labor force consisted of unskilled laborers; in 1957 the figure was 52 percent (55 percent in the private sector) out of a total work force of 487,000. FWA, IT, AR, 1947; FWA, "Effectif des salariés," 1957, K440 (165), AS.

9 Senegal, IT, AR, 1957; FWA, "Renseignements sur la masse des salaires et sa répartition," 1957, K 440 (165), AS.

10 R. D. Grillo, *African Railwaymen: Solidarity and Opposition in an East African Labour Force* (Cambridge: Cambridge University Press, 1973), 23; Frederick Cooper, *On the African Waterfront: Urban Disorder and the Transformation of Work in Colonial Mombasa* (New Haven: Yale University Press, 1987), 158. Collier and Lal (*Labour and Poverty*, 64–66) argue that the rise in the minimum wage in Kenya in 1954 might have for a time compressed skill and seniority differentials, although actual wages were usually ahead of official ones. The skill composition of the work force in any case increased. As Collier and Lal make clear, analyzing causes and effects in the history of wages in even a single case is a complicated business.

11 The number of white workers in the 1950s was increasing over twice as fast as the number of African workers, one of the ironic effects of the developmentalist state. East African Statistical Department, *Reported Employment and Wages in Kenya, 1948–1960* (Nairobi, 1961), 7, 17.

12 International Labour Office, *African Labour Survey* (Geneva: ILO, 1958), 280.

13 Jane Parpart, *Labor and Capital on the African Copperbelt* (Philadelphia: Temple University Press, 1983), 138; Michael Burawoy, *The Colour of Class on the Copper Mines: From African Advancement to Zambianization*, Zambian

Papers No. 7 (Manchester: Manchester University Press, 1972), 2; Bates, *Unions*; Robert Bates, *Rural Responses to Industrialization: A Study of Village Zambia* (New Haven: Yale University Press, 1976).

14 Yesufu, *Industrial Relations in Nigeria*; Adrian Peace, *Choice, Class and Conflict: A Study of Southern Nigerian Factory Workers* (Brighton: Harvester, 1979); Richard Jeffries, *Class, Power and Ideology in Ghana: The Railwaymen of Sekondi* (Cambridge: Cambridge University Press, 1978); Robin Cohen, *Labour and Politics in Nigeria*; Jeff Crisp, "Productivity and Protest: Scientific Management in the Ghanaian Gold Mines, 1947–1956," in Frederick Cooper (ed.), *Struggle for the City: Migrant Labor, Capital, and the State in Urban Africa* (Beverly Hills: Sage, 1983), 91–130.

15 On Africanization in a large, complex labor force, the East African Railways, see R. D. Grillo, *Race, Class and Militancy: An African Trade Union, 1939–1965* (New York: Chandler, 1974).

16 In Ghana in 1966, wages had fallen from their 1950s peak to below the level of 1939. Kraus, "Industrial Relations in Ghana,"140. On the strikes, see St. Clair Drake and Leslie Alexander Lacy, "Government Versus the Unions: The Sekondi-Takoradi Strike, 1961," in Gwendolen Carter (ed.), *Politics in Africa: 7 Cases* (New York: Harcourt, Brace & World, 1966), 67–118, and Cohen, *Labour and Politics in Nigeria*, 159–68.

17 See the debate in Richard Sandbrook and Robin Cohen (eds.), *The Development of an African Working Class* (London: Longman, 1975).

18 Focusing on networks rather than a bounded working class suggests the kind of "social movement unionism" that Gay Seidman writes about, minus the role of industrialization to her argument. *Manufacturing Militance: Workers' Movements in Brazil and South Africa, 1970–1985* (Berkeley: University of California Press, 1994). One of the best recent studies of labor and politics in an African country is Geoffrey Hansen Bergen, "Unions in Senegal: A Perspective on National Development in Africa," Ph.D. Dissertation, University of California, Los Angeles, 1994.

19 The percentage of railway workers in East African depots with five years or more service went from 44 in a 1946 survey to 90 in 1965; in Nigeria, 73 percent of railwaymen surveyed had worked there over five years, 64 percent expected to finish their career there. Grillo, *Railwaymen*, 14; Yesufu, *Industrial Relations in Nigeria*, 116–20. R. H. Sabot concludes that in Tanzania, "The employers and the government may have fulfilled the goals of their wage policy and thus reduced the private and social costs associated with the system of short-term circular migration." *Economic Development and Urban Migration: Tanzania 1900–1971* (Oxford: Clarendon, 1979), 228.

20 Grillo, *Railwaymen*, 15. Sabot, 200, also documents the development of a "normal demographic pattern" in Tanzania's cities.

21 Paul Mercier, "Aspects de la société africaine dans l'agglomération dakaroise: groupes familiaux et unités de voisinage," *Etudes Sénégalaises* 5 (1954): 11–40; Guy Pfefferman, *Industrial Labor in the Republic of Senegal* (New York: Praeger, 1968), 169; Yesufu, 120. See also Sara Berry, *Fathers Work for Their Sons: Accumulation, Mobility, and Class Formation in an Extended Yoruba Community* (Berkeley: University of California Press, 1984), and a forthcoming Ph.D. dissertation for the University of Michigan by Lisa Lindsay, on

changing structures and conceptions of family among Nigerian railwaymen in the era of stabilization policies.

22 Henrietta Moore and Megan Vaughan. *Cutting Down Trees: Gender, Nutrition, and Agricultural Change in the Northern Province of Zambia, 1890-1990* (London: James Currey, 1994).

23 Peace, *Choice, Class and Conflict*, plus a burgeoning literature on the "informal sector" (see below).

24 Collier and Lal, *Labour and Poverty*, 254-58, 264-66.

25 Early studies shedding light on the strategies of individuals, families, and social groups in cities include Michael Banton, *West African City: A Study of Tribal Life in Freetown* (London: Oxford University Press, 1957); Aidan Southall and Peter C. W. Gutkind, *Townsmen in the Making* (Kampala: East African Institute of Social Research, 1957); Kenneth Little, "The Role of Voluntary Associations in West African Urbanization," *American Anthropologist* 59 (1957): 579-96; Peter Marris, *Family and Social Change in an African City* (London: Routledge & Kegan Paul, 1962). See also Frederick Cooper, "Urban Space, Industrial Time, and Wage Labor in Africa," in Cooper (ed.), *Struggle for the City*, 1-50, and Catherine Coquery-Vidrovitch, "The Process of Urbanization in Africa (From the Origins to the Beginning of Independence)," *African Studies Review* 34 (1991): 1-98.

26 IGT, FWA, to IGT, Paris, 26 November 1954, IGT, 16/1, ANSOM; FWA, Haut Commissariat, Etudes et Coordination Statistiques et Mécanographiques, *Recensement démographique de Dakar* (1955), 1: 88. The European labor force was male-dominated, but not so extreme: 83 percent male. Of African male workers in this study, 46 percent were bachelors, 38 percent in "customary unions," and 19 percent officially married. The average married worker had 1.4 children.

27 East African Statistical Department, *Reported Employment*, 8; Yesufu, 16.

28 ILO, *Survey*, 355. On domestic labor, see Karen Tranberg Hansen, *Distant Companions: Servants and Employers in Zambia, 1900-1985* (Ithaca: Cornell University Press, 1989).

29 Claudine Vidal, "Guerre des sexes à Abidjan. Masculin, féminin, CFA," *Cahiers d'Etudes Africaines* 65 (1977): 121-53; Claire Robertson, *Sharing the Same Bowl?: A Socioeconomic History of Women and Class in Accra, Ghana* (Bloomington: Indiana University Press, 1984); Gracia Clark, *Onions Are My Husband: Survival and Accumulation by West African Market Women* (Chicago: University of Chicago Press, 1994); Elias Mandala, *Work and Control in a Peasant Economy: A History of the Lower Tchiri Valley in Malawi, 1859-1960* (Madison: University of Wisconsin Press, 1990). Professor Robertson's current research on women traders in Nairobi is also revealing their vulnerability to harassment and the extent to which women's economic activity – vigorous as it has long been – faces severe obstacles in producing the kinds of security or accumulation that are possibilities for a portion of the male urban population.

30 Kenya, Legislative Council, *Debates* 89 (18 July 1962), c. 1030. The young African politician was saying something rather similar to an argument made by an old colonial intellectual nearly a decade earlier: "No one living in misery is capable of progress, of a view of the future, of lifting his dignity, and the

stagnation of certain societies is generally explained by the persistent impossibility of satisfying the most elementary needs." Georges Hardy, "L'étude des niveaux de vie, base nécessaire d'une politique d'amélioration sociale," *Marchés Coloniaux* 373 (3 January 1953), 3.

31 How an elected African government used the 1952 code as a basis for its own labor policy emerges clearly from the meetings of the "Groupe de Travail pour le 'travail'" in Senegal, 6, 13, 20 November, 4, 11, 18 December 1958, 22 January 1959, VP 91, AS. For more on post-colonial codes see Senegal, Ecole Nationale d'Administration, "Rôle et fonctionnement des Services du Travail et de la Sécurité Sociale en mars 1962," 5 March 1962; République du Sénégal, *Code du Travail. Loi No. 61–34 du 15 juin 1961* (Rufisque: Imprimerie Officielle, 1961); Chambre d'Industrie de Côte d'Ivoire, *Code du Travail (Loi 64.290 du 1er Août 1964)*, from *Journal Officiel*, 44 (17 August 1964); Michel Goyat, *Guide pratique de l'employeur et du travailleur en Afrique Occidentale* (Dakar: Editions Clairafrique, 1960). See also Mar Fall, *L'état et la question syndicale au Sénégal* (Paris: Harmattan, 1989); Bergen, "Unions in Senegal"; George R. Martens, "Industrial Relations and Trade Unionism in French-speaking West Africa," in Ukandi G. Damachi, H. Dieter Seibel, and Lester Trachtman (eds.), *Industrial Relations in Africa* (New York: St. Martin's Press, 1979), 16–72, and Claude Rivière, "Lutte ouvrière et phénomène syndical en Guinée," *Cultures et développement* 7 (1975): 53–83.

32 There is a large literature on industrial relations and trade unions. See Damachi et al., and for references, George R. Martens, *African Trade Unionism: A Bibliography with a Guide to Trade Union Organizations and Publications* (Boston: G. K. Hall, 1977); William Friedland, "African Trade Union Studies: Analysis of Two Decades," *Cahiers d'Etudes Africaines* 14 (1974): 575–89; and Bill Freund, *The African Worker* (Cambridge: Cambridge University Press, 1988).

33 Anthony D. Smith argues that the colonial state became the "mould as well as the target of African nationalisms, and on them it stamped its special character and aims." This kind of state was "gubernatorial, territorial, bureaucratic, paternalist-educational, caste-like." *State and Nation in the Third World: The Western State and African Nationalism* (Brighton: Harvester, 1983), 56. On the thinness of nationalism and the would-be hegemony of development administration, see Aristide Zolberg, *Creating Political Order: The Party States of West Africa* (Chicago: Rand-McNally, 1966).

34 Jean-François Bayart, *The State in Africa: The Politics of the Belly* (London: Longman, 1993).

35 Geof Wood, "The Politics of Development Policy Labelling." *Development and Change* 16 (1985): 347–73.

36 The term was used as recently as the 1955 Dakar census, which put 8 percent of the urban area's population into it. Forty-seven percent of the floating population was female. FWA, Haut Commissariat, Etudes et Coordination Statistique, *Recensement*, 69.

37 Janet MacGaffey, *The Real Economy of Zaire: The Contribution of Smuggling and Other Unofficial Activities to the National Wealth of an African Country* (Philadelphia: University of Pennsylvania Press, 1991); Alejandro Portes,

Manuel Castells, and Lauren Benton (eds.), *The Informal Economy: Studies in Advanced and Less Developed Countries* (Baltimore: The Johns Hopkins University Press, 1987).

38 *Lettre à Maurice Thorez* (Paris: Présence Africaine, 1956), 15.

39 Scholars from the Subaltern Studies collective of Indian historians have issued a valuable call to stress the parochialism of Europe at the same time that the experience of different people within colonies is taken out of the rigid categories of colonial discourse. This point is sometimes weakened, however, by the terms in which Europe is rendered provincial: repeated attacks on liberalism, on "bourgeois equality," on the ideas of citizenship and the nation state, as if these "western" constructs were themselves static and were not subject to continual appropriation, deflection, and redefinition in the process of politics, within colonies as much as within Europe itself. See Partha Chatterjee, *The Nation and its Fragments: Colonial and Postcolonial Histories* (Princeton: Princeton University Press, 1993), 197–98, 237–39, and Dipesh Chakrabarty, "Postcoloniality and the Artifice of History: Who Speaks for 'Indian' Pasts?" *Representations* 37 (1992): 20–21.

40 David A. Hollinger, "How Wide the Circle of the 'We'? American Intellectuals and the Problem of the *Ethnos* Since World War II," *American Historical Review* 98 (1993): 317–37.

41 The 1948 Universal Declaration of Human Rights included social rights, and in the 1950s the United Nations could issue such publications as *Report on the World Social Situation* (New York: United Nations, 1957).

42 Nancy Fraser and Linda Gordon, "Contract versus Charity: Why is there no Social Citizenship in the United States?" *Socialist Review* 22, 3 (1992): 45–67. Their work starts as a critical commentary on T. H. Marshall's 1949 essay reprinted in his *Class, Citizenship and Social Development* (Chicago: University of Chicago Press, 1963).

43 James Ferguson, "Paradoxes of Sovereignty and Independence: 'Real' and 'Pseudo-' Nation-States and the Depoliticization of Poverty," in Kirstin Hastrup and Karen Fog Olwig (eds.), *Siting Culture* (Oslo: Scandinavian University Press, forthcoming); Kathryn Sikkink, "Human Rights, Principled Issue-Networks, and Sovereignty in Latin America," *International Organization* 47 (1993): 411–41.

44 Such possibilities are more easily realized with certain citizenship constructs than others, notably in the territorially focused French system rather than the descent-based German one. Rogers Brubaker, *Citizenship and Nationhood in France and Germany* (Cambridge, Mass.: Harvard University Press, 1992). But as Yasemin Nuhoğlu Soysal argues, the presence of so many migrants in Western Europe and their involvement in the basic institutions regulating work, residence, and welfare – and despite anti-immigrant prejudice – fragments the association of rights with citizenship. She argues that specific rights and entitlements of certain categories of people are debated not just within notions of national citizenship, but in relation to an idea of "universal personhood." *Limits of Citizenship: Migrants and Postnational Membership in Europe* (Chicago: University of Chicago Press, 1994).

45 Speech of 6 October 1994, reported in *New York Times*, October 7, 1994, A3.

46 David Halloran Lumsdaine, *Moral Vision in International Politics: The Foreign Aid Regime, 1949–1989* (Princeton: Princeton University Press, 1993).

47 International Labour Office, *Employment Growth and Basic Needs: A One-World Problem. Report of the Director-General of the International Labour Office* (Geneva: ILO, 1976).

48 One of the best studies of the development construct is James Ferguson, *The Anti-politics Machine: "Development," Depoliticization and Bureaucratic Power in Lesotho* (Cambridge: Cambridge University Press, 1990).

49 P. T. Bauer has been arguing this for many years, but only in the last decade has he moved from dissent to conventional wisdom. *Dissent on Development* (London: Weidenfeld & Nicholson, 1971). See also Deepek Lal, *The Poverty of Development Economics* (Cambridge, Mass.: Harvard University Press, 1985). The revisionists have not gone unrevised; see Tony Killick, *A Reaction Too Far: Economic Theory and the Role of the State in Developing Countries* (London: Overseas Development Institute, 1989).

50 Robert Bates, *Markets and States in Tropical Africa* (Berkeley: University of California Press, 1981).

51 Vali Jamal and John Weeks, *Africa Misunderstood or Whatever Happened to the Rural-Urban Gap* (London: Macmillan for International Labour Office, 1993). Jamal and Weeks stress instead the importance of diminishing terms of trade for Africa's exports. In a "demand constrained" economy, they argue, urban migration and unemployment continue high even when wages decline. People become more enmeshed in moving back and forth between different activities, including "informal sector" production in order to enhance security, and lowered wages reduce incomes throughout the economy. The discussion of "urban bias" has become more nuanced recently, with more detailed case studies and more judicious views of the concept from some of its originators. See Ashutosh Varshney (ed.), *Beyond Urban Bias* (London: Cass, 1993).

52 Market ideology, like the development concept, can also be mobilized by popular forces against monopolistic elites, although in other circumstances market ideology is attacked in the name of popular entitlements. Richard D. Salvatore, "Market-oriented Reforms and the Language of Popular Protest: Latin America from Charles III to the IMF," *Social Science History* 17 (1993): 485–524.

53 See Bergen, "Unions in Senegal," 754–86, for a discussion of how World Bank-IMF efforts in the 1980s to lower the cost of labor in Senegal failed through the inability of their neo-classical models to comprehend the social and political nature of the labor question: their pressure pushed union leadership (as well as businessmen) ever more deeply into clientistic relationships with the state, while productivity enhancing cooperation and investment was discouraged. Over ten years of "structural adjustment" has failed to raise output or eliminate "rent-seeking" structures – deepening the problems it was supposed to alleviate.

54 The impetus behind the ILO was from the start to address the tendency of international competition to favor the most socially regressive producer. More recently, the American labor movement has tried to defend the social gains of its members through a largely futile protectionist approach. Another strategy

would be a vigorous world-wide campaign for more liberal labor legislation, for higher standards of social policies, and for other measures that would drive up wages in poor industrial countries, in other words to go back to the kind of program enunciated at ILO meetings in the 1940s.

Bibliography

ARCHIVES

FRANCE, ARCHIVES NATIONALES – SECTION OUTRE-MER (ANSOM)

AFOM   Agence de la France Outre-Mer
AP   Political Affairs
AE   Economic Affairs
IGT   Inspection Général du Travail
Telegrammes   Telegrams
PA   Personal Archives
Fonds Guernut Investigatory Committee of Popular Front
Union Coloniale

GREAT BRITAIN, PUBLIC RECORD OFFICE (PRO)

CAB Cabinet Office memoranda and minutes
CO   Colonial Office files:
  96 Gold Coast
  295 Northern Rhodesia
  318 West Indies
  323 General
  537 Secret
  554 West Africa
  583 Nigeria
  795 Central Africa
  822 East Africa
  847 Africa
  852 Economic Department
  859 Social Department
  866 Establishment Department
  888 Colonial Labour Advisory Committee
  1015 Central Africa
  1032 General
PREM Prime Minister's Office files

GREAT BRITAIN, RHODES HOUSE

FCB   Fabian Colonial Bureau papers
ACJ   Arthur Creech Jones papers
Colonial Records Project: interview transcripts
Orde Browne Papers

ARCHIVES DU SÉNÉGAL (AS)

Files of the Government-General of Afrique Occidentale Française:
  K Labor
  2G Annual Reports
  17G Political
  18G Administrative
  21G Police
  1Q Economic
Archives of the government of Senegal:
  D Government of Senegal
  VP Office of the Vice President

KENYA NATIONAL ARCHIVES (KNA)

CP   Coast Deposit
LAB Labour Department files
NYA Nyanza Deposit
Provincial and District Reports

KENYA RAILWAYS ARCHIVES

EST Establishment files

MISCELLANEOUS ARCHIVES

CRDA Centre de Recherche et de Documentation Africaine, Paris
Institute for Social History, Amsterdam: material on World Federation of Trade
  Unions and International Confederation of Free Trade Unions

OFFICIAL DOCUMENTS

BRITISH COLONIES

East Africa. East African Statistical Department, Kenya Unit. *Reported
  Employment and Wages in Kenya, 1948–1960.* Nairobi, 1961.
  *Report of the Commission on the Civil Services of the East African Territories,
  1953–54.* Nairobi, 1954.
Gold Coast. Labour Department, *Annual Reports*, 1939–56
  "Address delivered by His Excellency the Governor Sir Charles Noble Arden-
  Clarke, KCMG, on the occasion of the Fourth Meeting of the Legislative
  Council on the 7th September 1950." Accra, 1950.
  A Statement on the Programme of Africanisation of the Public Service. Accra, 1954.

Kenya. *Legislative Council Debates,* 1947–62.

Report of the Commission of Inquiry appointed to Examine the Labour Conditions in Mombasa. Nairobi, 1939. [Willan Commission]

Report of the Committee of Inquiry into Labour Unrest at Mombasa. Nairobi, 1945. [Phillips Committee]

Brief Comments on Certain Sections of the Phillips Report on Labour Unrest in Mombasa, by Leo Silberman. Nairobi, 1946.

"Report on the Economic and Social Background of the Mombasa Labour Dispute," by H. S. Booker and N. M. Deverell. Mombasa, cyclostyled, 1947

Report of the Committee on African Wages. Nairobi, 1954. [Carpenter Report]

The Psychology of Mau Mau, by J. C. Carothers. Nairobi, 1954.

Report of the Social Security Committee. Nairobi, 1957.

Nigeria. *The Nigerianization of the Civil Service,* by Sir Sydney Phillipson and S. O. Adebo, with a Statement by the Council of Ministers. Lagos, 1954.

Report of the Commission on the Public Services of the Governments in the Federation of Nigeria 1954–55. Lagos, 1955.

Matters arising from the Final Report of the Parliamentary Committee on the Nigerianisation of the Federal Public Service. Statement of Policy by the Government of the Federation, Sessional Paper No. 2 of 1960. Lagos, 1960.

Northern Rhodesia. *African Affairs Annual Reports,* 1946–56.

Report of Commission Appointed to Enquire into the Disturbance in the Copperbelt, Northern Rhodesia. Lusaka, 1935

Report of the Commission Appointed to Inquire into the Disturbances on the Copperbelt, Northern Rhodesia. Lusaka, 1940

Report of the Commission on the Civil Services of Northern Rhodesia and Nyasaland. Lusaka, 1947.

Report of the Commission Appointed to Enquire into the Advancement of Africans in Industry. Lusaka, 1948.

Report of the Commission Appointed to Review the Salary Structure, Remuneration and Terms of Service of the Civil Service of Northern Rhodesia. Lusaka, 1952.

Report of the Board of Inquiry Appointed to Inquire into the Advancement of Africans in the Copper Mining Industry in Northern Rhodesia. Lusaka, 1954.

Report of the Commission Appointed to Inquire into the Unrest in the Mining Industry of Northern Rhodesia in Recent Months. Lusaka, 1956.

Report of the Commission of Inquiry into Unrest on the Copperbelt July–August, 1963. Lusaka, 1963.

Nyasaland Protectorate, *Report of the Committee Appointed by His Excellency The Governor to Enquire into Emigrant Labour, 1935.* Zomba, 1936.

Southern Rhodesia, *Report of the Committee to Investigate the Economic, Social and Health Conditions of Africans Employed in Urban Areas.* Salisbury, 1944.

Report of the Commission Appointed by his Excellency the Governor to Inquire into and Report on all Matters Concerning Recent Native Disturbances in the Colony and to Recommend Any Action which May Seem Desirable to the Public Interest. Salisbury, 1948.

Report of the National Native Labour Board on its Enquiry into the Conditions of Employment in Industry in Bulawayo, Gwelo, Que Que, Salisbury, Umtali, Gatooma and Environs... Salisbury, 1948.

Report of the Urban African Affairs Commission 1958. Salisbury, 1958.

Uganda. *Report of the Commission of Inquiry into the Disturbances which Occurred in Uganda During January 1945.* Entebbe, 1945.

GREAT BRITAIN

House of Commons Debates
House of Lords Debates
Parliamentary Papers:

"Despatch to the Governor of the East African Protectorate relating to Native Labour and Papers connected therewith," 1920, XXXIII, 81.

"Despatch to the Officer Administering the Government of the Kenya Colony and Protectorate relating to Native Labour," 1921, XXIV, 433.

Committee on Nutrition in the Colonial Empire, "First Report," 1939, 1938–39, X, 55.

"The Colonial Empire," 1938–39, XX, 965.

"Statement of Policy on Colonial Development and Welfare," February 1940, 1939–40, X, 25.

G. St. J. Orde Browne, "Labour Conditions in West Africa," 1941, IV, 1

"International Labour Conference: Proposed Action," November 1945–46, XXVI, 167.

"Report to the Secretary of State for the Colonies by the Parliamentary Delegation to Kenya. January, 1954," 1953–54, XI, 123.

Colonial Office Number Series:

Despatch from Secretary of State for the Colonies to African Governors, 8 March 1930. Colonial No. 65 (1931).

Major G. St. J. Orde Browne, *Labour Conditions in Northern Rhodesia.* Colonial No. 150 (1938).

Enquiry into the Cost of Living and the Control of the Cost of Living in the Colony and Protectorate of Nigeria. Colonial No. 204 (1946). [Tudor-Davies Enquiry]

Report of the Commission on the Civil Services of British West Africa, 1945–46. Colonial No. 209 (1947). [Harragin Commission]

Report of the Commission of Enquiry into the Disorders in the Eastern Provinces of Nigeria. Colonial No. 256 (1950). [Fitzgerald Commission]

Report of the Commission of Enquiry into Disturbances in the Gold Coast, 1948. Colonial No. 231 (1948). [Watson Commission]

Statement of His Majesty's Government on the Report of the Commission of Enquiry into Disturbances in the Gold Coast, 1948. Colonial No. 232 (1948).

Labour Administration in the Colonial Territories 1944–1950. Colonial No. 275 (1951).

Miscellaneous:

African Governors' Conference. London, 1947.

Edward Batson, "Report on Proposals for a Social Survey of Zanzibar." Cyclostyled, 1948.

C. H. Northcott (ed.), *African Labour Efficiency Survey*, Colonial Research Publications No. 3. London, 1949.

Summer Conference on African Administration, 19 August–2 September 1948, 3rd session, 15–27 August 1949. London, 1949.

Great Britain, *Report of the Commission on the Civil Services of Kenya, Tanganyika, Uganda and Zanzibar, 1947–48*. London: HMSO, 1948.

Great Britain, *Report of the Commission on the Civil Services of the East African Territories and the East Africa High Commission 1953–54*. London: HMSO, 1954.

FRENCH WEST AFRICA

Conseil du Gouvernement. Procès Verbal, 1943–45.

Grand Conseil de l'Afrique Occidentale Française. *Bulletin.*

Governor-General, Speeches opening sessions of Grand Conseil (variously printed)

Gouvernement Général de l'AOF, *Organisation de l'Inspection du Travail* (Rufisque: Imprimerie du Gouvernement Général, 1946).

J. Guilbot, *Petite étude sur la main d'oeuvre à Douala*, Memorandum du Centre IFAN Cameroun (Yaoundé: Imprimerie du Gouvernement, 1947).

Haut Commissariat, Etudes et Coordination Statistiques et Mécanographiques, *Recensement démographique de Dakar* (1955).

Service de Coordination des Affaires Economiques et du Plan, "Les salaires en Afrique Occidentale Française, salaires minima hiérarchisés au 28 février 1958".

Chambre de Commerce, d'Agriculture et d'Industrie de Dakar, "Synthèse de la situation économique de l'ex-Afrique Occidentale Française durant la période 1948 à 1958" (mimeographed, 1959).

République du Sénégal, *Code du Travail. Loi No. 61–34 du 15 juin 1961* (Rufisque: Imprimerie Officielle, 1961).

FRANCE

Assemblée Consultative Provisoire, *Compte rendu analytique officiel*, 1945.

Assemblée Nationale Constituante, *Débats, Documents,* 1946.

Assemblée Nationale. *Débats, Documents,* 1947–56.

Assemblée de l'Union Française. *Débats, Documents,* 1946–56.

Conseil de la République. *Débats.*

Avis et Rapports du Conseil Economique

La Conférence Africaine Française. Brazzaville 30 Janvier–8 Février 1944. Brazzaville: Editions du Baobab, 1944.

Conseil Economique, *Conjuncture des Territoires Extramétropolitains de l'Union Française*. Paris: Imprimerie des Journaux Officiels, January 1953.

J. G. Desbordes, "Transformation économique et sociale du monde noire depuis 1914 dans les villes," Mémoire de l'Ecole Supérieure Coloniale, 1944.

Journal Officiel de la République Française: Loi no. 52–1322 du 15 décembre 1952, instituant un code du travail dans les territoires et territoires associés relevant du Ministère de la France d'Outre-Mer. Rufisque: Imprimerie du Gouvernement Général, 1953.

Roland Pré. "Observations et conclusions personnelles du Gouverneur Roland

Pré, Président de la Commission d'Étude et de Coordination des Plans de Modernisation et d'Équipement des Territoires d'Outre-Mer." Mimeographed, May 1954 (copy in library of ANSOM).

Rapport No. 11348 sur les incidents survenus en Côte d'Ivoire, Annexe to the procès-verbal of session of 21 November 1950, Assemblée Nationale, and reprinted by the Partie Démocratique de la Côte d'Ivoire

INTERNATIONAL ORGANIZATIONS

Inter-African Labour Conference. *Inter-African Labour Conference, Beira, 1955.* London: Commission for Technical Cooperation in Africa South of the Sahara, 1955.

Inter-African Labour Institute. *The Human Factors of Productivity in Africa.* London: CCTA, 1957.

International Labour Organization. *International Labour Conference.* 1944–56.

"30th International Labour Conference," *International Labour Review* 56 (1947): 265–68.

African Labour Survey. Geneva: ILO, 1958.

"Social Security in Africa South of the Sahara." *International Labour Review* 84 (1961): 144–74.

Employment Growth and Basic Needs: A One-World Problem. Report of the Director-General of the International Labour Office. Geneva: ILO, 1976.

Conventions and Recommendations 1919–1981. Geneva: International Labour Office, 1982.

UNESCO. *Social Implications of Industrialization and Urbanization in Africa South of the Sahara.* Paris: UNESCO, 1956.

United Nations. Bureau of Social Affairs. *Report on the World Social Situation.* New York: United Nations, 1957.

Department of Economic Affairs. *Review of Economic Conditions in Africa, 1949–50.* New York: United Nations, 1951.

NEWSPAPERS

L'A.O.F.
Afrique Noire, 1951
L'Afrique Nouvelle, 1948–58
La Condition Humaine, 1951–1952
Démocratie Nouvelle, 1958
East African Standard
Marchés Coloniaux
Notre Voix, organe du Parti Socialiste SFIO en Côte d'Ivoire
Périscope Africain, 1936
Le Prolétaire, 1954
Le Prolétaire (Organe de l'Union des Syndicats CGT de Dakar), 1949–52
Réveil
Le Travailleur Africain, 1954
Voix de la R.D.A., published as a special section of *Réveil*

OTHER PUBLICATIONS

Abdullah, Ibrahim. "Profit versus Social Reproduction: Labor Protests in the Sierra Leonean Iron-Ore Mines, 1933–38." *African Studies Review* 35 (1992): 13–41.

Abernethy, David B. "European Colonialism and Postcolonial Crises in Africa." In *The Crisis and Challenge of African Development*, edited by Harvey Glickman, 3–23. Westport, Conn.: Greenwood Press, 1988.

Adas, Michael. *Machines as the Measure of Man: Science, Technology, and Ideologies of Western Dominance*. Ithaca: Cornell University Press, 1989.

Ageron, Charles-Robert. *France coloniale ou parti colonial?* Paris: Presses Universitaires Françaises, 1978.

Allen, C. H. "Union–Party Relationships in Francophone West Africa: A Critique of the 'Téléguidage' Interpretations." In *The Development of an African Working Class*, edited by Richard Sandbrook and Robin Cohen, 99–125. London: Longman, 1975.

Allman, Jean Marie. *The Quills of the Porcupine: Asante Nationalism in an Emergent Ghana*. Madison: University of Wisconsin Press, 1993.

Ambler, John (ed.), *The French Welfare State*. New York: New York University Press, 1991.

Amsden, Alice. *International Firms and Labour in Kenya, 1945–70*. London: Frank Cass, 1971.

Anderson, Benedict. *Imagined Communities: Reflections on the Origin and Spread of Nationalism*. Revised ed. London: Verso, 1991.

Anti-Slavery and Aborigines Protection Society. "The Industrialization of the African." 1937.

Antoine, Ph., A. Dubresson, and A. Manou-Savina. *Abidjan "côté cours": Pour comprendre la question de l'habitat*. Paris: Karthala, 1987.

Appiah, Kwame Anthony. *In My Father's House: Africa in the Philosophy of Culture*. New York: Oxford University Press, 1992.

Armah, Ayi Kwei. *The Beautyful Ones Are Not Yet Born*. Boston: Houghton Mifflin, 1968.

Arndt, H. W. *Economic Development: The History of an Idea*. Chicago: University of Chicago Press, 1987.

Asad, Talal (ed.). *Anthropology and the Colonial Encounter*. London: Ithaca Press, 1973.

Ashforth, Adam. *The Politics of Official Discourse in Twentieth-Century South Africa*. Oxford: Clarendon Press, 1990.

Asiwaju, A. I. "Migrations as Revolt: The Example of the Ivory Coast and the Upper Volta before 1945," *Journal of African History* 17 (1976): 577–94.

Association Internationale de la Sécurité Sociale. *Cahiers Africains de Sécurité Sociale* 13–14 (1974).

Atkins, Keletso. *The Moon is Dead! Give Me My Money!: The Cultural Origins of an African Work Ethic, Natal, South Africa, 1843–1900*. London: Heinemann, 1993.

Attlee, C. R. *As It Happened*. London: Heinemann, 1954.

Aujoulat, L-P. *La vie et l'avenir de l'Union Française*. Paris: Société d'édition républicaine populaire, 1947.

Austin, Dennis. *Politics in Ghana, 1946-1960.* London: Oxford University Press, 1964.

Baker, Tanya, and Mary Bird. "Urbanisation and the Position of Women." *Sociological Review* NS 7 (1959): 99-122.

Balandier, Georges. *Histoire des autres.* Paris: Stock, 1977.

"La situation coloniale: Approche théorique." *Cahiers Internationaux de Sociologie* 11 (1951): 44-79.

Sociologie des Brazzavilles noires. Paris: Colin, 1955.

The Sociology of Black Africa: Social Dynamics in Central Africa. Trans. by Douglas Garman. London: André Deutsch, 1970.

Baldwin, Peter. *The Politics of Social Solidarity: Class Bases of the European Welfare State 1875-1975.* Cambridge: Cambridge University Press, 1990.

Bangura, Yusuf. *Britain and Commonwealth Africa: The Politics of Economic Relations, 1951-75.* Manchester: Manchester University Press, 1983.

Banton, Michael. *West African City: A Study of Tribal Life in Freetown.* London: Oxford University Press, 1957.

Baron, Ava (ed.). *Work Engendered: Toward a New History of American Labor.* Ithaca: Cornell University Press, 1991.

Bates, Robert H. *Markets and States in Tropical Africa.* Berkeley: University of California Press, 1981.

Rural Responses to Industrialization: A Study of Village Zambia. New Haven: Yale University Press, 1976.

Unions, Parties, and Political Development: A Study of Mineworkers in Zambia. New Haven: Yale University Press, 1971.

Bauer, P. T. *Dissent on Development.* London: Weidenfeld & Nicholson, 1971.

West African Trade: A Study of Competition, Oligopoly and Monopoly in a Changing Economy. Cambridge: Cambridge University Press, 1954.

Bayart, Jean-François. *The State in Africa: The Politics of the Belly.* London: Longman, 1993. Trans. from French version, 1989.

Beckman, Bjorn. *Organizing the Farmers: Cocoa Politics and National Development in Ghana.* Uppsala: Scandinavian Institute of African Studies, 1976.

Beinart, William. "Soil Erosion, Conservationism and Ideas about Development: A Southern African Exploration, 1900- 1960." *Journal of Southern African Studies* 11 (1984): 52-83.

The Political Economy of Pondoland, 1860- 1930. Cambridge: Cambridge University Press, 1982.

Berg, Elliot J. "Real Income Trends in West Africa, 1939-1960." In *Economic Transition in Africa,* edited by Melville J. Herskovits and Mitchell Harwitz, 199-238. London: Routledge & Kegan Paul, 1964.

Berg, Elliot J., and Jeffrey Butler. "Trade Unions." In *Political Parties and National Integration in Tropical Africa,* edited by James S. Coleman and Carl G. Rosberg, Jr., 340-81. Berkeley: University of California Press, 1966.

Bergen, Geoffrey Hansen. "Unions in Senegal: A Perspective on National Development in Africa," Ph.D. Dissertation, University of California, Los Angeles, 1994.

Berger, Elena. *Labour, Race, and Colonial Rule: The Copperbelt from 1924 to Independence.* Oxford: Clarendon Press, 1974.

Berman, Bruce. *Control and Crisis in Colonial Kenya: The Dialectic of Domination.* London: James Currey, 1990.

Berman, Bruce and John Lonsdale. *Unhappy Valley: Conflict in Kenya and Africa.* 2 vols. London: James Currey, 1992.

Bernard-Duquenet, Nicole. *Le Sénégal et le Front Populaire.* Paris: Harmattan, 1985.

Berry, Sara. *Cocoa, Custom and Socio-Economic Change in Rural Western Nigeria.* Oxford: Clarendon Press, 1975.

Fathers Work for Their Sons: Accumulation, Mobility, and Class Formation in an Extended Yoruba Community. Berkeley: University of California Press, 1984.

Berveiller, Michel. "L'Europe d'Outre-Mer." *Cahiers du Monde Nouveau* 4, 7 (1948): 47–51.

Bethell, Leslie, and Ian Roxborough, "Latin America between the Second World War and the Cold War: Some Reflections on the 1945–8 Conjuncture," *Journal of Latin American Studies* 20 (1988): 167–89.

Bingo. "Il y a vingt ans Houphouët-Boigny faisait abolir le travail forcé." *Bingo* 15, 7 (February 1966): 18–20, 46.

Block, Fred L. *The Origins of International Economic Disorder: A Study of United States International Monetary Policy from World War II to the Present.* Berkeley: University of California Press, 1977.

Boeke, J. H. *Economics and Economic Policies of Dual Societies as Exemplified by Indonesia.* New York: Institute of Pacific Relations, 1953; orig. published 1942.

Boisson, Pierre. "Colonisation européenne ou colonisation indigène." *Bulletin de Documentation Coloniale* 124 (1–15 March 1938).

Contribution à l'oeuvre africaine. Rufisque, Senegal: Imprimerie du Haut Commissariat de l'Afrique Française, 1942.

Bony, Joachim. "La Côte d'Ivoire sous la colonisation française et le prélude à l'émancipation 1920–1947. Genèse d'une nation." Thèse pour le doctorat d'état, Université de Paris I, 1980.

Bouche, Denise. "Dakar pendant la deuxième Guerre mondiale. Problèmes de surpeuplement," *Revue Française d'Histoire d'Outre-Mer* 65 (1978): 423–37.

Brown, Carolyn. "The Dialectic of Colonial Labour Control: Class Struggles in the Nigerian Coal Industry, 1941–1949," *Journal of Asian and African Studies* 23 (1988): 32–59.

Brown, Richard. "Passages in the Life of a White Anthropologist: Max Gluckman in Northern Rhodesia." *Journal of African History* 20 (1979): 525–41.

Brubaker, Rogers. *Citizenship and Nationhood in France and Germany.* Cambridge, Mass.: Harvard University Press, 1992.

Buell, Leslie Raymond. *The Native Problem in Africa.* 2 vols. London: Macmillan, 1928.

Buijtenhuijs, Robert. *Essays on Mau Mau.* Leiden: African Studies Centre, 1982.

Burawoy, Michael. *The Colour of Class on the Copper Mines: From African Advancement to Zambianization.* Zambian Papers No. 7. Manchester: Manchester University Press, 1972.

Burns, Alan. *In Defence of Colonies: British Colonial Territories in International Affairs.* London: Allen & Unwin, 1957.

Busia, K. A. *Report on a Social Survey of Sekondi-Takoradi.* London: Crown Agents for the Colonies, 1950.

Cain, P. J. and A. G. Hopkins, *British Imperialism: Crisis and Deconstruction 1914–90.* London: Longman, 1993.

Carew, Anthony. *Labour under the Marshall Plan: The Politics of Productivity and the Marketing of Management Science.* Manchester: Manchester University Press, 1987.

Cartier, Raymond. "En France Noire avec Raymond Cartier." *Paris-Match* 383 (11 August 1956): 38–41, 384 (18 August 1956): 34–37, and 386 (1 September 1956): 39–41.

Cazanove, Docteur. "L'alimentation des indigènes en Afrique occidentale française." *L'Afrique française* 46 (1936): 288–93, 339–42.

Cell, John W. *Hailey: A Study in British Imperialism, 1872–1969.* Cambridge: Cambridge University Press, 1992.

The Highest Stage of White Supremacy: The Origins of Segregation in South Africa and the American South. Cambridge: Cambridge University Press, 1982.

"On the Eve of Decolonization: The Colonial Office's Plans for the Transfer of Power in Africa, 1947." *Journal of Imperial and Commonwealth History* 8 (1980): 235–57.

Césaire, Aimé. *Discours sur le colonialisme.* Paris: Présence Africaine, 1955.

Lettre à Maurice Thorez. Paris: Présence Africaine, 1956.

Chaffard, Georges. *Les carnets secrets de la décolonisation.* 2 vols. Paris: Calmann-Levy, 1967.

Chakrabarty, Dipesh. "Postcoloniality and the Artifice of History: Who Speaks for 'Indian' Pasts?" *Representations* 37 (1992): 1–26.

Rethinking Working-Class History: Bengal 1890–1940. Princeton: Princeton University Press, 1989.

Chambre d'Industrie de Côte d'Ivoire, Code du Travail (Loi 64.290 du 1er août 1964), from Journal Officiel, 44 (17 August 1964).

Chatterjee, Partha. *Nationalist Thought and the Colonial World: A Derivative Discourse?* London: Zed, 1986.

The Nation and its Fragments: Colonial and Postcolonial Histories. Princeton: Princeton University Press, 1993.

Chauleur, Pierre. *Le régime du travail dans les territoires d'Outre-Mer.* Paris: Encyclopedie d'Outre Mer, 1956.

Chauncey, George, Jr. "The Locus of Reproduction: Women's Labour in the Zambian Copperbelt, 1927–1953." *Journal of Southern African Studies* 7 (1981): 135–64.

Choquet, C., O. Dollfus, E. Le Roy, and M. Vernières (eds.). *Etat des savoirs sur le développement: Trois décennies de sciences sociales en langue française.* Paris: Karthala, 1993.

Clark, Gracia. *Onions Are My Husband: Survival and Accumulation by West African Market Women.* Chicago: University of Chicago Press, 1994.

Clayton, Anthony. "The General Strike in Zanzibar, 1948." *Journal of African History* 17 (1976): 417–34.

Clayton, Anthony and Donald Savage. *Government and Labour in Kenya, 1895–1963.* London: Frank Cass, 1974.

Cohen, Robin. *Labour and Politics in Nigeria, 1945–71*. London: Heinemann, 1974.

Cohen, William B. *Rulers of Empire: the French Colonial Service in Africa*. Stanford: Hoover Institution Press, 1971.

"The Colonial Policy of the Popular Front." *French Historical Studies* 7 (1972): 368–93.

Coleman, James S. *Nigeria: Background to Nationalism*. Berkeley: University of California Press, 1958.

Collier, Paul, and Deepak Lal. *Labour and Poverty in Kenya 1900–1980*. Oxford: Clarendon Press, 1986.

Collier, Ruth Berins, and David Collier. *Shaping the Political Arena: Critical Junctures, the Labor Movement, and Regime Dynamics in Latin America*. Princeton: Princeton University Press, 1991.

Comaroff, Jean, and John Comaroff. *Of Revelation and Revolution: Christianity, Colonialism, and Consciousness in South Africa*. Volume I. Chicago: University of Chicago Press, 1991.

Conklin, Alice L. "A Mission to Civilize: Ideology and Imperialism in French West Africa, 1895–1930." Ph.D. dissertation, Princeton University, 1989.

Constantine, Stephen. *The Making of British Colonial Development Policy 1914–1940*. London: Frank Cass, 1984.

Cooper, Frederick. "Africa and the World Economy." In *Confronting Historical Paradigms: Peasants, Labor, and the Capitalist World System in Africa and Latin America*, edited by Frederick Cooper et al., 84–201. Madison: University of Wisconsin Press, 1993.

"Conflict and Connection: Rethinking Colonial African History." *American Historical Review* 99 (1994): 1516–45.

From Slaves to Squatters: Plantation Labor and Agriculture in Zanzibar and Coastal Kenya, 1890–1925. New Haven: Yale University Press, 1980.

"Le mouvement ouvrier et le nationalisme: La grève générale de 1946 et la grève des cheminots de 1947–48." *Historiens et Géographes du Sénégal* 6 (1991): 32–42.

"Mau Mau and the Discourses of Decolonization." *Journal of African History* 29 (1988): 313–20.

On the African Waterfront: Urban Disorder and the Transformation of Work in Colonial Mombasa. New Haven: Yale University Press, 1987.

"'Our Strike': Equality, Anticolonial Politics, and the 1947–48 Railway Strike in French West Africa." *Journal of African History*, 36 (1996).

"The Senegalese General Strike of 1946 and the Labor Question in Post-War French Africa." *Canadian Journal of African Studies* 24 (1990): 165–215.

"Urban Space, Industrial Time, and Wage Labor in Africa." In *Struggle for the City: Migrant Labor, Capital, and the State in Urban Africa*, edited by Frederick Cooper, 1–50. Beverly Hills: Sage, 1983.

Coquery-Vidrovitch, Catherine. "L'Afrique et la Crise de 1930." special issue of *Revue Française d'Histoire d'Outre-Mer* 63 (1976).

Le Congo au temps des grandes compagnies concessionaires, 1898–1930. Paris: Mouton, 1972.

"La Mise en dépendance de l'Afrique Noire: Essai de périodisation, 1800–1970." *Cahiers d'Etudes Africaines* 16 (1976): 5–58.

"The Process of Urbanization in Africa (From the Origins to the Beginning of Independence)." *African Studies Review* 34 (1991): 1–98.

Cordell, Dennis, and Joel Gregory (eds.). *African Population and Capitalism: Historical Perspectives.* Boulder, Colo.: Westview Press, 1987.

Cotte, Claudine. "La politique économique de la France en Afrique noire (1936–1946)." Thèse de troisième cycle d'histoire, Université de Paris VII, 1981.

Cowen, Michael. "Early Years of the Colonial Development Corporation: British State Enterprise Overseas during Late Colonialism." *African Affairs* 83 (1984): 63–75.

Cowen, Michael, and James Newman, "Real Wages in Central Kenya, 1924–74." Unpublished paper, 1975.

Cowen, Michael, and Robert Shenton. "The Origin and Course of Fabian Colonialism in Africa." *Journal of Historical Sociology* 4 (1991): 143–74.

Cowen, Michael, and Nicholas Westcott. "British Imperial Economic Policy During the War." In *Africa and the Second World War*, edited by David Killingray and Richard Rathbone, 20–67. New York: St. Martin's Press, 1986.

Crisp, Jeff. "Productivity and Protest: Scientific Management in the Ghanaian Gold Mines, 1947–1956." In *Struggle for the City: Migrant Labor, Capital, and the State in Urban Africa*, edited by Frederick Cooper, 91–130. Beverly Hills: Sage, 1983.

The Story of an African Working Class: Ghanaian Miners' Struggles, 1870–1980. London: Zed Press, 1984.

Crush, Jonathan, Alan Jeeves, and David Yudelman. *South Africa's Labor Empire: A History of Black Migrancy to the Gold Mines.* Boulder, Colo.: Westview Press, 1991.

Cutter, Charles H. "The Genesis of a Nationalist Elite: The Role of the Popular Front in the French Soudan (1936–1939)." In *Double Impact: France and Africa in the Age of Imperialism*, edited by G. Wesley Johnson, 107–39. Westport, Conn.: Greenwood Press, 1985.

d'Almeida-Topor, Hélène. "Recherches sur l'évolution du travail salarié en AOF pendant la crise économique 1930–1936." *Cahiers d'Etudes africaines* 61–62 (1976): 103–17.

Darwin, John. "British Decolonization since 1945: A Pattern or a Puzzle?" *Journal of Imperial and Commonwealth Studies* 12 (1984): 187–209.

Davis, David Brion. *Slavery and Human Progress.* New York: Oxford University Press, 1984.

Davis, Merle J. (ed.). *Modern Industry and the African: An Enquiry into the Effect of the Copper Mines of Central Africa upon Native Society and the Work of Christian Missions Made under the Auspices of the Department of Social and Industrial Research of the International Missionary Council.* London: Macmillan, 1933.

de Benoist, Joseph Roger. *L'Afrique Occidentale Française de 1944 à 1960.* Dakar: Nouvelles Editions Africaines, 1982.

"La grande bataille des cheminots (1947–1948)." *Afrique Histoire* 4 (1981): 21–28.

de Briey, P. "The Productivity of African Labour." *International Labour Review* 72 (1955): 119–37.

de Coppet, Marcel. "Manpower Problems and Prospects in Madagascar." *International Labour Review* 59 (1949): 249–70.

de Gaulle, Charles. *Memoirs of Hope: Renewal and Endeavor*. Trans. by Terence Kilmartin. New York: Simon & Schuster, 1971.

Delanoue, Paul. "La CGT et les syndicats d'Afrique Noire." *Le Mouvement Social* 122 (1983): 103–16.

Delavignette, Robert L. "Action colonisatrice et paysannat indigène." *Afrique Française* 45 (1935): 526–30.

Christianisme et Colonialisme. Paris: Arthème Fayard, 1960.

Les paysans noirs. Paris: Stock, 1947. Orig. published 1931.

"L'Union Française à l'échelle du monde, à la mesure de l'homme." *Esprit* 112 (July 1945): 214–36.

Soudan–Paris–Bourgogne. Paris: Grasset, 1935.

Dewitte, Philippe. "La CGT et les syndicats d'Afrique occidentale française (1945–1957)." *Le Mouvement Social* 117 (1981): 3–32.

"Réponse à Paul Delanoue." *Le Mouvement Social* 122 (1983): 117–21.

Diallo, Abdoulaye. "Economic and Social Claims of the West Africa Workers." *World Trade Union Movement* 7 (April 5, 1951): 17–22.

"The Scourge of Colonialism in French Africa." *World Trade Union Movement* 2 (January 20, 1951): 29–34.

Diejomaoh, Victor P. "Industrial Relations in a Development Context: The Case of Nigeria." In *Industrial Relations in Africa*, edited by Ukandi G. Damachi, H. Dieter Seibel and Lester Trachtman, 169–200. London: Macmillan, 1979.

Diouf, Mamadou. "L'entreprise sénégalaise de développement: de la mobilisation de masse à l'étatisme technocratique," paper for workshop on "Historicizing Development," Emory University, December 10–12, 1993.

Dirks, Nicholas (ed.). *Colonialism and Culture*. Ann Arbor: University of Michigan Press, 1992.

Dossou, Léopold. "Le salariat et le développement des syndicats au Dahomey 1937–1960." Thèse pour le doctorat du troisième cycle, Université de Paris VII, 1981.

Doucy, A. and P. Feldheim. *Problèmes du travail et politique sociale au Congo belge*. Brussels: Librairie Encyclopédique, 1952).

Downs, Laura Lee. *Manufacturing Inequality: The Construction of a Gender Stratified Workforce in the French and British Metalworking Industries, 1914–1935*. Ithaca: Cornell University Press, 1995.

Drake, St. Clair, and Leslie Alexander Lacy. "Government Versus the Unions: The Sekondi-Takoradi Strike, 1961." In *Politics in Africa: 7 Cases*, edited by Gwendolen Carter, 67–118. New York: Harcourt, Brace & World, 1966.

Dresch, Jean. "Méthodes coloniales au Congo Belge et en Afrique Equatoriale Française." *Politique Etrangère* 12, 1 (1947): 77–89.

Un géographe au déclin des empires. Paris: Maspero, 1979.

Duffy, James. *A Question of Slavery*. Cambridge, Mass.: Harvard University Press, 1967.

Durand, Raoul. "La formation professionelle et la psychologie des noirs." *Problèmes d'Afrique Centrale* 24 (1954): 102–8.

Eboué, Félix. *La nouvelle politique indigène pour l'Afrique Equatoriale Française*. Paris: Office Française d'Edition, 1945.

Echenberg, Myron, and Jean Filipovich. "African Military Labour and the Building of the *Office du Niger* Installations, 1925–1950." *Journal of African History* 27 (1986): 533–51.

Elkan, Walter. *Migrants and Proletarians: Urban Labour in the Economic Development of Uganda.* London: Oxford University Press, 1960.

"The Employment of Women in Uganda." *Inter-African Labour Institute Bulletin* 4:4 (1957): 8–22.

Engwenyu, Joseph. "The Gold Coast Riots of 1948." Unpublished paper, n.d.

"The Working Class and the Politics of Constitutional Independence: The 'Positive Action' and the General Strike of 1950 in the Gold Coast." Unpublished paper, Dalhousie University, 1983.

"World War II and Labour Protest in the Gold Coast (Ghana)." Paper presented to the African Studies Association meeting, 2–5 November 1989.

Entreprise 63 (1 November 1955): 56–57. "Une économie prospère sans colonie: les Pays-Bas: En définitive la perte de l'Indonésie n'a-t-elle pas été un facteur favorable à l'expansion?"

Epstein, A. L. *Politics in an Urban African Community.* Manchester: Manchester University Press, 1958.

Ewald, François. *L'état providence.* Paris: Grasset, 1986.

Fall, Babacar. "Economie de plantation et main d'oeuvre forcée en Guinée française: 1920–1946." *Labour, Capital and Society* 20 (1987): 8–33.

Le travail forcé en Afrique Occidentale française, 1900–1946. Paris: Karthala, 1993.

Fall, Mar. *L'état et la question syndicale au Sénégal.* Paris: Harmattan, 1989.

Fanon, Frantz. *Black Skin, White Masks.* Trans. by Charles Lam Markmann. New York: Grove, 1967. Orig. published 1952.

The Wretched of the Earth. Trans. by Constance Farrington. New York: Grove, 1966. Orig. published 1961.

Feierman, Steven. *Peasant Intellectuals: Anthropology and History in Tanzania.* Madison: University of Wisconsin Press, 1990.

Ferguson, James. *The Anti-Politics Machine: "Development," Depoliticization and Bureaucratic Power in Lesotho.* Cambridge: Cambridge University Press, 1990.

"Mobile Workers, Modernist Narratives: A Critique of the Historiography of Transition on the Zambian Copperbelt." *Journal of Southern African Studies* 16 (1990): 385–412.

"Paradoxes of Sovereignty and Independence: 'Real' and 'Pseudo-' Nation-States and the Depoliticization of Poverty." In *Siting Culture*, edited by Kirstin Hastrup and Karen Fog Olwig. Oslo: Scandinavian University Press, forthcoming.

Fieldhouse, D. K. *Black Africa: Economic Decolonization and Arrested Development.* London: Allen & Unwin, 1986.

"The Labour Governments and the Empire-Commonwealth, 1945–51." In *The Foreign Policy of the British Labour Governments, 1945–1951*, edited by Ritchie Ovendale, 83–120. Leicester: Leicester University Press, 1984.

Merchant Capital and Economic Decolonization: The United Africa Company 1929–1987. Oxford: Clarendon Press, 1994.

Flint, John. "Scandal at the Bristol Hotel: Some Thoughts on Racial Discrimination in Britain and West Africa and its Relationship to the

Planning of Decolonisation." *Journal of Imperial and Commonwealth History* 12 (1983): 74–87.

Folliet, Joseph. *Le travail forcé aux colonies*. Paris: Editions du Cerf, 1934.

Foltz, William J. *From French West Africa to the Mali Federation*. New Haven: Yale University Press, 1965.

Fosbrooke, H. A. "Social Security as a Felt Want in East and Central Africa." *Bulletin of the International Social Security Association* 13 (1960): 279–89.

Foucault, Michel. *Discipline and Punish: The Birth of the Prison*. Trans. by Alan Sheridan. New York: Vintage, 1979.

The History of Sexuality. I: *An Introduction*. Trans. by Robert Hurley. New York: Pantheon, 1978.

Fox, Alan. *History and Heritage: The Social Origins of the British Industrial Relations System*. London: Allen & Unwin, 1985.

Fraser, Nancy and Linda Gordon. "Contract versus Charity: Why is There no Social Citizenship in the United States?" *Socialist Review* 22,3 (1992): 45–67.

Freund, Bill. *Capital and Labour in the Nigerian Tin Mines*. London: Longman, 1981.

The African Worker. Cambridge: Cambridge University Press, 1988.

Friedland, William. "African Trade Union Studies: Analysis of Two Decades." *Cahiers d'Etudes Africaines* 14 (1974): 575–89.

Furedi, Frank. *Colonial Wars and the Politics of Third World Nationalism*. London: I. B. Tauris, 1994.

The Mau Mau War in Perspective. London: James Currey, 1989.

Gallagher, John. *The Decline, Revival and Fall of the British Empire: The Ford Lectures and Other Essays*. Cambridge: Cambridge University Press, 1982.

Gendzier, Irene. *Managing Political Change: Social Scientists and the Third World*. Boulder, Colo.: Westview, 1985.

Gide, André. *Travels in the Congo*. Trans. by Dorothy Bussy. New York: Knopf, 1929.

Gifford, Prosser, and Wm. Roger Louis (eds.). *The Transfer of Power in Africa: Decolonization, 1940–1960*. New Haven: Yale University Press, 1982.

Girardet, Raoul. *L'idée coloniale en France de 1871 à 1962*. Paris: Table Ronde, 1972.

Glass, Max. "Des colonies, ou pas de colonies." *Cahiers du Monde Nouveau* 4, 7 (1948): 1–17.

Gluckman, Max. "Anthropological Problems Arising from the African Industrial Revolution." In *Social Change in Modern Africa*, edited by Aidan Southall, 67–82. London: Oxford University Press, 1961.

"Malinowski's 'Functional' Analysis of Social Change." *Africa* 17 (1947): 103–21.

"Seven-Year Research Plan of the Rhodes-Livingstone Institute of Social Studies in British Central Africa." *Rhodes-Livingstone Journal* 4 (1945): 1–31.

Goffman, Erving. *Frame Analysis: An Essay on the Organization of Human Experience*. Cambridge, Mass.: Harvard University Press, 1974.

Goldsworthy, David. *Colonial Issues in British Politics, 1945–1961: From "Colonial Development" to "Winds of Change"*. Oxford: Clarendon Press, 1971.

"Keeping Change within Bounds: Aspects of Colonial Policy during the Churchill and Eden Governments, 1951–57." *Journal of Imperial and Commonwealth History* 18 (1990): 81–108.

Tom Mboya: The Man Kenya Wanted to Forget. London: Heinemann, 1982.

(ed.). *British Documents on the End of Empire*, Series A, III: *The Conservative Government and the End of Empire 1951–1957.* London: HMSO, 1994.

Gonidec, P. F. *Droit du travail dans les territoires d'outre-mer.* Paris: Librairie Générale de Droit et de Jurisprudence, 1958.

"Une mystique de l'égalité: le code du travail des territoires d'Outre-Mer." *Revue Juridique et Politique de l'Union Française* 2 (1953): 176–96.

Goudal, Jean. *Esclavage et travail forcé.* Paris: Pedone, 1929.

Goyat, Michel. *Guide pratique de l'employeur et du travailleur en Afrique Occidentale.* Dakar: Editions Clairafrique, 1960.

Greaves, I. C. *Modern Production among Backward Peoples.* London: Allen and Unwin, 1935.

Gregory, Joël, Dennis D. Cordell and Victor Piché. "La mobilisation de la main-d'oeuvre burkinabè, 1900–1974: Une vision rétrospective." *Canadian Journal of African Studies* 23 (1989): 73–105.

Grévisse, M. *Le centre extra-coutumier d'Elisabethville.* Brussels: CEPSI, 1951.

Griffin, Larry. "Narrative, Event Structure Analysis, and Causal Interpretation in Historical Sociology." *American Journal of Sociology* 98 (1993): 1094–133.

Grillo, R. D. *African Railwaymen: Solidarity and Opposition in an East African Labour Force.* Cambridge: Cambridge University Press, 1973.

Race, Class and Militancy: An African Trade Union, 1939–1965. New York: Chandler, 1974.

Guernier, Eugène-Léonard. *L'Afrique: Champ d'expansion de l'Europe.* Paris: Colin, 1933.

Guèye, Oumar. "La grève de 1946 au Sénégal," Mémoire de Maîtrise, Université Cheikh Anta Diop de Dakar, 1990.

Guha, Ranajit. "Dominance Without Hegemony and its Historiography." In *Subaltern Studies, VI: Writings on South Asian History and Society*, edited by Ranajit Guha, 210–309. Delhi: Oxford University Press, 1989.

"On Some Aspects of the Historiography of Colonial India." In *Selected Subaltern Studies*, edited by Ranajit Guha and Gayatri Chakravorty Spivak, 37–44. New York: Oxford University Press, 1988.

Gupta, P. S. *Imperialism and the British Labour Movement, 1914–1964.* New York: Holmes and Meier, 1975.

Gussman, B. "Industrial Efficiency and the Urban African." *Africa* 23 (1953): 135–44.

Hailey, Lord. *An African Survey.* London: Oxford University Press, 1938.

An African Survey. 2nd ed. London: Oxford University Press, 1945.

"The Rôle of Anthropology in Colonial Development." *Man* 44 (1944): 10–15.

Hancock, W. K. *Wealth of Colonies: The Marshall Lectures, Cambridge, 17 and 24 February 1950.* Cambridge: Cambridge University Press, 1950.

Hansen, Karen Tranberg. *Distant Companions: Servants and Employers in Zambia, 1900–1985.* Ithaca: Cornell University Press, 1989.

Hardy, Georges. "L'étude des niveaux de vie, base nécessaire d'une politique d'amélioration sociale," *Marchés Coloniaux* 373, 3 January 1953.

Hardy, Georges and Charles Richet. *L'alimentation indigène dans les colonies françaises, protectorats et territoires sous mandat.* Paris: Vigo, 1933.

Harms, Robert. "The End of Red Rubber: A Reassessment." *Journal of African History* 16 (1975): 73–88.

Harris, John H. *Africa: Slave or Free?* London: Student Christian Movement, 1919.

Havinden, Michael, and David Meredith, *Colonialism and Development: Britain and its Tropical Colonies, 1850–1960.* London: Routledge, 1993.

Heisler, Helmuth. "The Creation of a Stabilized Urban Society: A Turning Point in the Development of Northern Rhodesia/Zambia." *African Affairs* 70 (1971): 125–45.

Hellmann, Ellen. *Rooiyard: A Sociological Survey of an Urban Native Slum Yard.* Rhodes-Livingstone Papers 13. Cape Town: Oxford University Press, 1948.

Henderson, Ian. "Early African Leadership: The Copperbelt Disturbances of 1935 and 1940." *Journal of Southern African Studies* 2 (1975): 83–97.

Herskovits, Melville J. "Native Self-Government." *Foreign Affairs* 22 (1944): 413–23.

Higginson, John. *A Working Class in the Making: Belgian Colonial Labor Policy, Private Enterprise, and the African Mineworker, 1907–1951.* Madison: University of Wisconsin Press, 1989.

Hill, Polly. *Migrant Cocoa Farmers of Southern Ghana.* Cambridge: Cambridge University Press, 1963.

Himmelstrand, Ulf, Kabiru Kinyanjui and Edward Mburugu (eds.). *African Perspectives on Development.* New York: St. Martin's Press, 1994.

Hinden, Rita. "Imperialism Today." *Fabian Quarterly* 45 (April 1945): 5–12.

Hindson, Doug. *Pass Controls and the Urban African Proletariat.* Johannesburg: Ravan, 1987.

Hodgkin, Thomas. *Nationalism in Colonial Africa.* New York: New York University Press, 1957.

Hollinger, David A. "How Wide the Circle of the 'We'? American Intellectuals and the Problem of the *Ethnos* Since World War II." *American Historical Review* 98 (1993): 317–37.

Holt, Thomas C. *The Problem of Freedom: Race, Labor and Politics in Jamaica and Britain, 1832–1938.* Baltimore: Johns Hopkins University Press, 1992.

Hopkins, A. G. *An Economic History of West Africa.* London: Longman, 1973.

Hosington, William A., Jr. *The Casablanca Connection: French Colonial Policy, 1936–1943.* Chapel Hill: University of North Carolina Press, 1984.

Howe, Stephen. *Anticolonialism in British Politics: The Left and the End of Empire, 1918–1964.* Oxford: Clarendon Press, 1993.

Hunt, Nancy. "Le Bébé en Brousse: European Women, African Birth Spacing and Colonial Intervention in Breast Feeding in the Belgian Congo." *International Journal of African Historical Studies* 21 (1988): 401–32.

Hyam, Ronald. "Africa and the Labour Government, 1945–1951." *Journal of Imperial and Commonwealth History* 16 (1988): 148–172.

(ed.). *British Documents on the End of Empire.* Series A, Vol. II: *The Labour Government and the End of Empire 1945–1951, Parts 1–4.* London: HMSO, 1992.

644   Bibliography

Hyden, Goran. *No Shortcuts to Progress: African Development Management in Perspective.* London: Heinemann, 1983.
Iliffe, John. *The African Poor: A History.* Cambridge: Cambridge University Press, 1987.
"The Creation of Group Consciousness: A History of the Dockworkers of Dar es Salaam." In *The Development of an African Working Class,* edited by Robin Cohen and Richard Sandbrook, 49–72. London: Longman, 1975.
Ingham, Barbara. "Colonialism and the Economy of the Gold Coast, 1919–45." In *Development Studies and Colonial Policy,* edited by Barbara Ingham and Colin Simmons, 229–62. London: Frank Cass, 1987.
Institut Charles de Gaulle and Institut d'Histoire du Temps Présent. *Brazzaville Janvier–Février 1944: Aux sources de la décolonisation.* Paris: Plon, 1988.
Institut Colonial International. *Le régime et l'organisation du travail des indigènes dans les colonies tropicales.* Brussels: Etablissements Généraux d'Imprimerie, 1929.
International Confederation of Free Trade Unions. *Fourth World Congress, Vienna, 20–28 May 1955.*
Official Report of the Free World Labour Conference and of the First Congress of the International Conference of Free Trade Unions. London, November–December 1949.
Report of the First African Regional Conference Held at Accra 14–19 January 1957. Brussels: ICFTU, 1958.
International Labour Review 53 (1946): 340–48. "The Conditions of Indigenous Workers in the Belgian Congo in 1944."
Jamal, Vali, and John Weeks, *Africa Misunderstood or Whatever Happened to the Rural-Urban Gap.* London: Macmillan for International Labour Office, 1993.
Jeffries, Richard. *Class, Power and Ideology in Ghana: The Railwaymen of Sekondi.* Cambridge: Cambridge University Press, 1978.
Johnson, G. Wesley. *The Emergence of Black Politics in Senegal: The Struggle for Power in the Four Communes, 1890–1920.* Stanford: Stanford University Press, 1971.
Johnson, R. W. "Sékou Touré and the Guinean Revolution." *African Affairs* 69 (1970): 350–65.
Jones, Arthur Creech. "British Colonial Policy with Particular Reference to Africa." *International Affairs* 27 (1951): 176–83.
"The West Indies Report." *New Fabian Research Bureau,* 1940.
Jones, James A. "The Impact of the Dakar-Niger Railway on the Middle Niger Valley." Ph.D. dissertation, University of Delaware, 1995.
Joseph, Richard. *Radical Nationalism in Cameroun: Social Origins of the UPC Rebellion.* Oxford: Oxford University Press, 1977.
"Settlers, Strikers and Sans-Travail: The Douala Riots in September 1945." *Journal of African History* 15 (1974): 669–87.
Kahler, Miles. *Decolonization in Britain and France: The Domestic Consequences of International Relations.* Princeton: Princeton University Press, 1984.
Kanogo, Tabitha. *Squatters and the Roots of Mau Mau, 1905–63.* London: James Currey, 1987.

Kent, John. *The Internationalization of Colonialism: Britain, France, and Black Africa, 1939–1956.* Oxford: Clarendon Press, 1992.

Kerr, Clark. "Changing Social Structures." In *Labor Commitment and Social Change in Developing Areas,* edited by Wilbert E. Moore and Arnold S. Feldman, 348–59. New York: Social Science Research Council, 1960.

Kerr, Clark, John T. Dunlop, Frederick Harbison, and Charles A. Myers. *Industrialism and Industrial Man.* Cambridge, Mass.: Harvard University Press, 1960.

Kilby, Peter. "Industrial Relations and Wage Determination: Failure of the Anglo-Saxon Model." *Journal of Developing Areas* 1 (1967): 489–520.

Killick, Tony. *Development Economics in Action: A Study of Economic Policies in Ghana.* New York: St. Martin's Press, 1978.

A Reaction Too Far: Economic Theory and the Role of the State in Developing Countries. London: Overseas Development Institute, 1989.

Killingray, David. "Labour Mobilisation in British Colonial Africa for the War Effort, 1936–46." In *Africa and the Second World War,* edited by David Killingray and Richard Rathbone, 68–96. New York: St. Martin's Press, 1986.

Kipré, Pierre. "La crise économique dans les centres urbains en Côte d'Ivoire." *Cahiers d'Etudes Africaines* 61–62 (1976): 119–46.

Kraus, Jon. "The Political Economy of Industrial Relations in Ghana." In *Industrial Relations in Africa,* edited by Ukandi G. Damachi, H. Dieter Seibel, and Lester Trachtman, 107–68. New York: St. Martin's Press, 1979.

Kuisel, Richard F. *Capitalism and the State in Modern France: Renovation and Economic Management in the Twentieth Century.* Cambridge: Cambridge University Press, 1981.

Kuklick, Henrika. *The Savage Within: The Social History of British Anthropology, 1885–1945.* Cambridge: Cambridge University Press, 1991.

Labouret, Henri. *Colonisation, colonialisme, décolonisation.* Paris: Larose, 1952.

Paysans d'Afrique occidentale. Paris: Gillmard, 1941.

"Le problème de la main-d'oeuvre dans l'ouest-afrique française." *Politique Etrangère* 3 (June 1936): 37–47.

Lakroum, Monique. "Chemin de fer et réseaux d'affaires en Afrique occidentale: le Dakar–Niger (1883–1960)." Thesis for Doctorat d'Etat, Université de Paris VII, 1987.

Le travail inégal: Paysans et salariés sénégalais face à la crise des années trente. Paris: Harmattan, 1982.

"Les salaires dans le port de Dakar." *Revue Française d'Histoire d'Outre-Mer* 63 (1976): 640–53.

Lal, Deepek. *The Poverty of Development Economics.* Cambridge, Mass.: Harvard University Press, 1985.

Laurentie, Henri. "Les colonies françaises devant le monde nouveau." *Renaissances* (October 1945): 3–13.

Lawler, Nancy Ellen. *Soldiers of Misfortune: Ivorien "Tirailleurs" of World War II.* Athens: Ohio University Press, 1992.

Lebovics, Herman. *True France: The Wars over Cultural Identity, 1900–1945.* Ithaca: Cornell University Press, 1992.

Lecaillon, Jacques. *Les incidences économiques et financières du code du travail: Contribution à l'étude du mécanisme de la répartition des revenus dans les territoires d'outre-mer*. Dakar: Institut des Hautes Etudes de Dakar, 1954.

Leclerc, Gérard. *Anthropologie et colonialisme: Essai sur l'histoire de l'africanisme*. Paris: Fayard, 1972.

Lee, J. M. *Colonial Development and Good Government*. Oxford: Oxford University Press, 1967.

Lee, J. M., and Martin Petter. *The Colonial Office, War and Development Policy: Organization and the Planning of a Metropolitan Initiative, 1939-1945*. Commonwealth Papers 22. London: Maurice Temple Smith, 1982.

Lewis, Jane. *The Politics of Motherhood: Child and Maternal Welfare in England, 1900-1939*. London: Croom Helm, 1980.

Lewis, W. Arthur. *The British West Indies*. London: Fabian Society, 1935.

"The Dual Economy Revisited." *The Manchester School* 47 (1979): 211-29.

"The Economic Development of Africa." In *Africa in the Modern World*, edited by Calvin W. Stillman, 97-112. Chicago: University of Chicago Press, 1955.

"Economic Development with Unlimited Supplies of Labour." *The Manchester School* 22 (1954): 139-91.

Labour in the West Indies. London: Fabian Society, 1939.

Politics in West Africa. New York: Oxford University Press, 1965.

"A Policy for Colonial Agriculture." In *Attitude to Africa*, edited by W. Arthur Lewis, Michael Scott, Martin Wight, and Colin Legum, 70-104. Harmondsworth: Penguin, 1951.

The Theory of Economic Growth. Holmwood, Ill.: Richard Irwin, 1955.

Leys, Norman. *Kenya*. London: Frank Cass, 1973. Orig. published 1924.

Liauzu, Claude. *Aux origines des tiers-mondismes: Colonisés et anticolonialistes en France 1919-1939*. Paris: Harmattan, 1982.

Little, Kenneth. "The Role of Voluntary Associations in West African Urbanization." *American Anthropologist* 59 (1957): 579-96.

West African Urbanization: A Study of Voluntary Associations in Social Change. Cambridge: Cambridge University Press, 1966.

Lonsdale, John. "Mau Maus of the Mind: Making Mau Mau and Remaking Kenya." *Journal of African History* 31 (1990): 393-421.

Lonsdale, John, and Bruce Berman. "Coping with the Contradictions: The Development of the Colonial State in Kenya." *Journal of African History* 20 (1979): 487-506.

Louis, Wm. Roger. *Imperialism at Bay: The United States and the Decolonization of the British Empire, 1941-1945*. Oxford: Clarendon Press, 1977.

Louis, Wm. Roger, and Ronald Robinson. "The Imperialism of Decolonization." *Journal of Imperial and Commonwealth History* 22 (1994): 462-512.

Lovejoy, Paul E., and Jan S. Hogendorn. *Slow Death for Slavery: The Course of Abolition in Northern Nigeria, 1897-1936*. Cambridge: Cambridge University Press, 1993.

Lubeck, Paul. *Islam and Urban Labor in Northern Nigeria: The Making of a Muslim Working Class*. Cambridge: Cambridge University Press, 1986.

Lumsdaine, David Halloran. *Moral Vision in International Politics: The Foreign Aid Regime, 1949-1989*. Princeton: Princeton University Press, 1993.

Luyt, Richard E. *Trade Unionism in African Colonies.* New Africa Pamphlet No. 119. Johannesburg: Institute of Race Relations, 1949.

MacGaffey, Janet. *The Real Economy of Zaire: The Contribution of Smuggling and Other Unofficial Activities to the National Wealth of an African Country.* Philadelphia: University of Pennsylvania Press, 1991.

Macmillan, W. M. *Warning from the West Indies.* Harmondsworth: Penguin, 1938.

Macnicol, John. *The Movement for Family Allowances, 1918–45: A Study in Social Policy Development.* London: Heinemann, 1980.

Macshane, Denis. *International Labour and the Origins of the Cold War.* Oxford: Clarendon Press, 1992.

Magubane, Bernard. "A Critical Look at Indices Used in the Study of Social Change in Colonial Africa." *Current Anthropology* 12 (1971): 419–45.

Maier, Charles. "Between Taylorism and Technocracy: European Ideologies and the Vision of Industrial Productivity in the 1920s." *Journal of Contemporary History* 5 (1970): 27–61.

"The Two Postwar Eras and the Conditions for Stability in Twentieth-Century Western Europe," *American Historical Review* 86 (1981): 327–62.

Maina wa Kinyatti. *Thunder from the Mountains: Mau Mau Patriotic Songs.* London: Zed, 1980.

Mair, Lucy P. *Welfare in the British Colonies.* London: Royal Institute of International Affairs, 1944.

Mandala, Elias. *Work and Control in a Peasant Economy: A History of the Lower Tchiri Valley in Malawi, 1859–1960.* Madison: University of Wisconsin Press, 1990.

Mann, Michael. *The Sources of Social Power.* 2 vols. Cambridge: Cambridge University Press, 1986.

March, James, and Herbert Simon. *Organizations.* New York: Wiley, 1958.

Marie-André du Sacré-Coeur, Soeur. "La situation de la femme en Afrique Noire française." *Civilisations* 1, 4 (1951): 46–54.

Marris, Peter. *Family and Social Change in an African City: A Study of Rehousing in Lagos.* London: Routledge & Kegan Paul, 1962.

Marseille, Jacques. *Empire colonial et capitalisme français: Histoire d'un divorce.* Paris: Albin Michel, 1984.

Marshall, D. Bruce. *The French Colonial Myth and Constitution-Making in the Fourth Republic.* New Haven: Yale University Press, 1973.

Marshall, T. H. *Class, Citizenship and Social Development.* Chicago: University of Chicago Press, 1963.

Martens, George R. *African Trade Unionism: A Bibliography with a Guide to Trade Union Organizations and Publications.* Boston: G. K. Hall, 1977.

"Industrial Relations and Trade Unionism in French-speaking West Africa." In *Industrial Relations in Africa,* edited by Ukandi G. Damachi, H. Dieter Seibel, and Lester Trachtman, 16–72. New York: St. Martin's Press, 1979.

"Le syndicalisme en Afrique occidentale d'expression française: de 1945 à 1960." *Le Mois en Afrique* 178–79 (1980): 74–97 and 180–81; (1980–81): 53–83.

Marx, Karl. *Grundrisse.* Trans. by Martin Nicolaus. New York: Vintage, 1973.

Mason, Michael. "Working on the Railway: Forced Labor in Northern Nigeria, 1907–1912." In *African Labor History,* edited by Robin Cohen, Jean Copans, and Peter C. W. Gutkind, 56–79. Beverly Hills: Sage, 1978.

Mbembe, Achille. "Domaines de la nuit et autorité onirique dans les maquis du Sud-Cameroun (1955–1958)." *Journal of African History* 32 (1991): 89–122.

La naissance du maquis dans le Sud-Cameroun: Histoires d'indisciplines (1920–1960). Paris: Karthala, 1993.

M'Bokolo, Elikia. "French Colonial Policy in Equatorial Africa in the 1940s and 1950s." In *The Transfer of Power in Africa: Decolonization 1940–1960*, edited by Prosser Gifford and Wm Roger Louis, 173–210. New Haven: Yale University Press, 1982.

Mboya, Tom. *Freedom and After.* Boston: Little, Brown, 1963.

"Trade Unionism in Kenya." *Africa South* 1, 2 (1957): 77–86.

Mérat, Louis. *L'heure de l'économie dirigée d'intérêt général aux colonies.* Paris: Sirey, 1936.

Mercier, Paul. "Aspects de la société africaine dans l'agglomération dakaroise: groupes familiaux et unités de voisinage," *Etudes Sénégalaises* 5 (1954): 11–40.

"La vie politique dans les centres urbaine du Sénégal: étude d'une période de transition." *Cahiers Internationaux de Sociologie* 27 (1959): 55–84.

Mercier, René. *Le travail forcé aux colonies.* Paris: Imprimerie Nouvelle, 1933.

Michel, Marc. "La coopération intercoloniale en Afrique noire, 1942–1950: un néo-colonialisme éclairé?" *Relations Internationales* 34 (1983): 155–71.

Miers, Suzanne. *Britain and the Ending of the Slave Trade.* London: Longman, 1975.

Miers, Suzanne, and Richard Roberts (eds.). *The End of Slavery in Africa.* Madison: University of Wisconsin Press, 1988.

Miller, Christopher L. *Theories of Africans: Francophone Literature and Anthropology in Africa.* Chicago: University of Chicago Press, 1990.

Minkley, Gary. "Class and Culture in the Workplace: East London, Industrialisation, and the Conflict over Work, 1945–1957." *Journal of Southern African Studies* 18 (1992): 739–60.

Missions (Les) et le prolétariat. *23e semaine de missiologie de Louvain, 1953.* Brussels: Desclée de Brouwer, 1953.

Mitchell, J. Clyde. *The Kalela Dance.* Rhodes-Livingstone Paper No. 27. Lusaka: Rhodes-Livingstone Institute, 1957.

"A Note on the Urbanization of Africans on the Copperbelt." *Rhodes-Livingstone Journal* 12 (1951): 20–27.

An Outline of the Sociological Background to African Labour. Salisbury: Ensign, 1961.

"The Woman's Place in African Advancement." *Optima* 9, 3 (1959): 124–31.

Moodie, T. Dunbar. "The Moral Economy of the Black Miners' Strike of 1946." *Journal of Southern African Studies* 13 (1986): 1–35.

"The South African State and Industrial Conflict in the 1940s." *International Journal of African Historical Studies* 21 (1988): 21–63.

Moore, Henrietta L., and Megan Vaughan. *Cutting Down Trees: Gender, Nutrition, and Agricultural Change in the Northern Province of Zambia, 1890–1990.* London: James Currey, 1994.

Moore, Sally Falk. *Anthropology and Africa: Changing Perspectives on a Changing Scene.* Charlottesville: University of Virginia Press, 1994.

Moore, Wilbert E. *Industrialization and Labor: Social Aspects of Economic*

Development. Ithaca: Cornell University Press for The Institute of World Affairs, 1951.

Morgan, D. J. *The Official History of Colonial Development.* 5 vols. London: Macmillan, 1980.

Morgenthau, Ruth Schachter (comp. and ed.), *Documents on African Political History.* CAMP Microfilm MF 4408.

Political Parties in French Speaking West Africa. Oxford: Clarendon Press, 1964.

Morris, Aldon, and Carol McClurg Mueller. *Frontiers in Social Movement Theory.* New Haven: Yale University Press, 1992.

Mounier, Bertrand. *L'organisation de l'économie impériale par les comités coloniaux.* Paris: Editions Pedone, 1942.

Mudimbe, V. Y. *The Invention of Africa: Gnosis, Philosophy, and the Order of Knowledge.* Bloomington: Indiana University Press, 1988.

(ed.). *Surreptitious Speech: Présence Africaine and the Politics of Otherness.* Chicago: University of Chicago Press, 1992.

Nandy, Ashis. *The Intimate Enemy: Loss and Recovery of Self under Colonialism.* Delhi: Oxford University Press, 1983.

Nicholson, Marjorie, *The TUC Overseas: The Roots of Policy.* London: Allen & Unwin, 1986.

Ninine, Jules. "La main-d'oeuvre indigène dans les colonies africaines." Doctoral thesis, Faculté de Droit, Université de Paris, 1932. Paris: Jouve et Cie, 1932.

Nisbet, Robert. *History of the Idea of Progress.* New York: Basic Books, 1980.

November, Andras. *L'évolution du mouvement syndicale en Afrique occidentale.* Paris: Mouton, 1965.

Nwanwene, Omorogbe. "British Colonial Policy and Localisation: The Nigerian Experience." *Journal of Commonwealth Political Studies* 6 (1968): 202–18.

Oberst, Timothy Sander. "Cost of Living and Strikes in British Africa c. 1939–1949: Imperial Policy and the Impact of the Second World War," Ph.D. dissertation, Columbia University, 1991.

Ogot, B. A. "Revolt of the Elders: An Anatomy of the Loyalist Crowd in the Mau Mau Uprising." In *Hadith 4,* edited by B. A. Ogot, 134–48. Nairobi: East African Publishing House, 1972.

O'Hanlon, Rosalind. "Recovering the Subject: *Subaltern Studies* and Histories of Resistance in Colonial South Asia." *Modern Asian Studies* 22 (1988): 189–224.

Oldham, Joseph H. *Christianity and the Race Problem.* New York: George H. Doran, 1924.

Ortner, Sherry. "Resistance and the Problem of Ethnographic Refusal." *Comparative Studies in Society and History* 37 (1995): 173–93.

Ousmanne, Sembene. *God's Bits of Wood.* Trans. by Francis Price. Garden City, N.Y.: Doubleday, 1962.

Oyemakinde, Wale. "The Nigerian General Strike of 1945." *Journal of the Historical Society of Nigeria* 7 (1975): 693–710.

Packard, Randall. "The 'Healthy Reserve' and the 'Dressed Native': Discourses on Black Health and the Language of Legitimation in South Africa." *American Ethnologist* 16 (1989): 686–703.

Palmer, Robin, and Neil Parsons (eds.). *The Roots of Rural Poverty in Central and Southern Africa.* London: Heinemann, 1977.

Parpart, Jane L. *Labor and Capital on the African Copperbelt.* Philadelphia: Temple University Press, 1983.

"Sexuality and Power on the Zambian Copperbelt: 1926–1964." In *Patriarchy and Class: African Women in the Home and in the Workforce,* edited by Sharon Stichter and Jane L. Parpart, 115–38. Boulder, Colo.: Westview Press, 1988.

"'Where is Your Mother?': Gender, Urban Marriage, and Colonial Discourse on the Zambian Copperbelt." *International Journal of African Historical Studies* 27 (1994): 241–72.

Parry, E. "Colonial Trade Unions." *Corona* 1, 7 (1949): 19–21.

Paxton, Robert O. *Vichy France: Old Guard and New Order, 1940–1944.* New York: Columbia University Press, 1972.

Peace, Adrian. *Choice, Class and Conflict: A Study of Southern Nigerian Factory Workers.* Brighton: Harvester, 1979.

Pearce, R. D. "The Colonial Economy: Nigeria and the Second World War." In *Development Studies and Colonial Policy,* edited by Barbara Ingham and Colin Simmons, 263–98. London: Frank Cass, 1987.

"Governors, Nationalists, and Constitutions in Nigeria, 1935–51." *Journal of Imperial and Commonwealth History* 9 (1981): 289–307.

The Turning Point in Africa: British Colonial Policy, 1938–1948. London: Frank Cass, 1982.

Pedersen, Susan. *Family, Dependence and the Origins of the Welfare State: Britain and France, 1914–1945.* Cambridge: Cambridge University Press, 1993.

Perrings, Charles. *Black Mineworkers in Central Africa: Industrial Strategies and the Evolution of an African Proletariat in the Copperbelt 1911–41.* New York: Africana, 1979.

Pfefferman, Guy P. *Industrial Labor in the Republic of Senegal.* New York: Praeger, 1968.

Phillips, Anne. *The Enigma of Colonialism: British Policy in West Africa.* London: James Currey, 1989.

Phimister, Ian R. *An Economic and Social History of Zimbabwe, 1890–1948: Capital Accumulation and Class Struggle.* London: Longman, 1987.

Pleven, René. "Preface." *Renaissances* (October 1944): 5–8.

Porter, A. N., and A. J. Stockwell (eds.). *British Imperial Policy and Decolonization, 1938–64.* 2 vols. London: Macmillan, 1987 and 1989.

Portes, Alejandro, Manuel Castells, and Lauren Benton (eds.). *The Informal Economy: Studies in Advanced and Less Developed Countries.* Baltimore: The Johns Hopkins University Press, 1987.

Posel, Deborah. *The Making of Apartheid, 1948–1961: Conflict and Compromise.* Oxford: Clarendon Press, 1991.

Post, Ken. *Arise Ye Starvelings: The Jamaican Labour Rebellion of 1938 and its Aftermath.* The Hague: Nijhoff, 1978.

Powdermaker, Hortense. *Coppertown: Changing Africa: The Human Situation on the Rhodesian Copperbelt.* New York: Harper & Row, 1962.

Prain, R. L. "The Stabilization of Labour in the Rhodesian Copper Belt." *African Affairs* 55 (1956): 305–12.

Prakash, Gyan. "Writing Post-Orientalist Histories of the Third World: Indian Historiography is Good to Think." In *Colonialism and Culture,* edited by

Nicholas Dirks, 353–88. Ann Arbor: University of Michigan Press, 1992.

Pré, Roland. "Observations et conclusions personnelles du Gouverneur Roland Pré, Président de la Commission d'Etude et de Coordination des Plans de Modernisation et d'Equipement des Territoires d'Outre-Mer." May 1954, mimeograph in library of ANSOM.

Présence Africaine 13 (1952). Special issue "Travail en Afrique."

Price, Robert M. *Society and Bureaucracy in Contemporary Ghana.* Berkeley: University of California Press, 1975.

Rabinbach, Anson. *The Human Motor: Energy, Fatigue, and the Origins of Modernity.* New York: Basic Books, 1990.

Ranger, Terence. "The Invention of Tradition in Colonial Africa." In *The Invention of Tradition,* edited by Eric Hobsbawm and Terence Ranger, 211–62. Cambridge: Cambridge University Press, 1983.

Rathbone, Richard. "The Government of the Gold Coast after the Second World War." *African Affairs* 67 (1968): 209–18.

——— (ed.). *British Documents on the End of Empire.* Series B, I: *Ghana, Part I, 1941–1952.* London: HMSO, 1992.

Read, Margaret. "Migrant Labour in Africa and its Effects on Tribal Life." *International Labour Review* 45 (1942): 605–31.

——— "Native Standards of Living and African Culture Change: Illustrated by Examples from the Ngoni Highlands of Nyasaland." Supplement to *Africa* 11:3 (1938).

Rezeau, Michel. "Un exemple de la mise en application du Code du Travail Outre-Mer." Mémoire No. 37 (1954–55), Ecole Nationale de la France Outre-Mer, 1954–55.

Rhodie, Sam. "The Gold Coast Cocoa Hold-Ups of 1930–31." *Transactions of the Historical Society of Ghana* 9 (1968): 105–18.

Rich, Paul. *Race and Empire in British Politics.* Cambridge: Cambridge University Press, 1986.

Richards, Audrey. *Land, Labour and Diet in Northern Rhodesia: An Economic Study of the Bemba Tribe.* 2nd ed., 1961. London: Oxford University Press for International African Institute, orig. published 1939.

Rivière, Claude. "Lutte ouvrière et phénomène syndical en Guinée." *Cultures et Développement* 7 (1975): 53–83.

Robertson, Claire. *Sharing the Same Bowl?: A Socioeconomic History of Women and Class in Accra, Ghana.* Bloomington: Indiana University Press, 1984.

Robinson, Ronald. "Andrew Cohen and the Transfer of Power in Tropical Africa, 1940–1951." In *Decolonization and After: The British and French Experiences,* edited by W. H. Morris-Jones and Georges Fischer, 50–72. London: Frank Cass, 1980.

Rosberg, Carl G., and John Nottingham. *The Myth of "Mau Mau": Nationalism in Kenya.* New York: Praeger, 1966.

Rose, Sonya. *Limited Livelihoods: Gender and Class in Nineteenth Century England.* Berkeley: University of California Press, 1991.

Ross, George. *Workers and Communists in France: From Popular Front to Eurocommunism.* Berkeley: University of California Press, 1982.

Rostow, W. W. *The Stages of Growth: A Non-Communist Manifesto.* Cambridge: Cambridge University Press, 1960.

Rotberg, Robert I. *The Rise of Nationalism in Central Africa: The Making of Malawi and Zambia, 1873–1964.* Cambridge, Mass.: Harvard University Press, 1965.

Ruedy, John. *Modern Algeria: The Origins and Development of a Nation.* Bloomington: Indiana University Press, 1992.

Ruz, Nathalie. "La force du 'cartiérisme'." In *La guerre d'Algérie et les français,* edited by Jean-Pierre Rioux, 328–36. Paris: Fayard, 1990.

Sabot, R. H. *Economic Development and Urban Migration: Tanzania 1900–1971.* Oxford: Clarendon Press, 1979.

Said, Edward. *Culture and Imperialism.* New York: Knopf, 1993.

Sandbrook, Richard. *Proletarians and African Capitalism: The Kenyan Case, 1960–1972.* Cambridge: Cambridge University Press, 1975.

Sandbrook, Richard, and Robin Cohen (eds.). *The Development of an African Working Class.* London: Longman, 1975.

Sarraut, Albert. *La mise en valeur des colonies françaises.* Paris: Payot, 1923.

Sautter, Gilles. "Notes sur la construction du Chemin de Fer Congo-Océan (1921–34)." *Cahiers d'Etudes Africaines* 7 (1967): 219–99.

Scarnecchia, Timothy. "The Politics of Gender and Class in the Creation of African Communities, Salisbury, Rhodesia, 1940–56." Ph.D. dissertation, University of Michigan, 1993.

Schapera, Isaac. *Migrant Labour and Tribal Life: A Study of Conditions in the Bechuanaland Protectorate.* London: Oxford University Press, 1947.

Scott, James. *Domination and the Arts of Resistance: Hidden Transcripts.* New Haven: Yale University Press, 1990.

Secrétariat Social d'Outre-Mer. *Code du Travail des territoires d'outre-mer: Guide de l'usager.* Paris: Société d'Editions Africaines, 1953.

Seidman, Gay. *Manufacturing Militance: Workers' Movements in Brazil and South Africa, 1970–1985.* Berkeley: University of California Press, 1994.

Semaines Sociales de France. *Peuples d'Outre-Mer et civilisation occidentale.* Lyon: Chronique Sociale de France, 1948.

Sene, Mor. "La grève des cheminots du Dakar Niger, 1947–48." Mémoire de maîtrise, Ecole Normale Supérieure, Université Cheikh Anta Diop, 1986–87.

Senghor, Léopold. "Défense de l'Afrique noire." *Esprit* 112 (July 1945): 237–48.

Sewell, William H., Jr. "Toward a Post-materialist Rhetoric for Labor History." In *Rethinking Labor History: Essays on Discourse and Class Analysis,* edited by Lenard R. Berlanstein, 15–38. Urbana: University of Illinois Press, 1993.

Work and Revolution in France: The Language of Labor from the Old Regime to 1848. Cambridge: Cambridge University Press, 1980.

Sherwood, John M. *Georges Mandel and the Third Republic.* Stanford: Stanford University Press, 1970.

Sikkink, Kathryn. "Human Rights, Principled Issue-Networks, and Sovereignty in Latin America," *International Organization* 47 (1993): 411–41.

Singh, Makhan. *History of Kenya's Trade Union Movement to 1952.* Nairobi: East African Publishing House, 1969.

Slade, Ruth. *King Leopold's Congo.* New York: Oxford University Press, 1962.

Smelser, Neil. *Social Change in the Industrial Revolution: An Application of Theory to the British Cotton Industry.* Chicago: University of Chicago Press, 1959.

Smith, Anthony D. *State and Nation in the Third World: The Western State and African Nationalism.* Brighton: Harvester, 1983.

Smith, Tony. "Patterns in the Transfer of Power: A Comparative Study of French and British Decolonization." In *The Transfer of Power in Africa: Decolonization 1940–1960,* edited by Prosser Gifford and Wm. Roger Louis, 87–155. New Haven: Yale University Press, 1982.

Sorum, Paul Clay. *Intellectuals and Decolonization in France.* Chapel Hill: University of North Carolina Press, 1977.

Southall, Aidan, and Peter C. W. Gutkind. *Townsmen in the Making.* Kampala: East African Institute of Social Research, 1957.

Southall, Roger. "Farmers, Traders, and Brokers in the Gold Coast Cocoa Economy." *Canadian Journal of African Studies* 12 (1978): 185–211.

Soysal, Yasemin Nuhoglu. *Limits of Citizenship: Migrants and Postnational Membership in Europe.* Chicago: University of Chicago Press, 1994.

Spencer, John. *The Kenya African Union.* London: KPI, 1985.

Spitzer, Leo, and LaRay Denzer. "I. T. A. Wallace Johnson and the West African Youth League." *International Journal of African Historical Studies* 6 (1973): 413–52, 565–601.

Staniland, Martin. *American Intellectuals and African Nationalists, 1955–1970.* New Haven: Yale University Press, 1991.

Stichter, Sharon. *Migrant Labour in Kenya: Capitalism and African Response, 1895–1975.* London: Longman, 1982.

———. "Workers, Trade Unions, and the Mau Mau Rebellion." *Canadian Journal of African Studies* 9 (1975): 259–70.

Stoler, Ann Laura. "Making Empire Respectable: The Politics of Race and Sexual Morality in 20th-Century Colonial Cultures." *American Ethnologist* 16 (1989): 634–60.

———. "Perceptions of Protest: Defining the Dangerous in Colonial Sumatra." *American Ethnologist* 12 (1985): 642–58.

———. *Race and the Education of Desire: A Colonial Reading of Foucault's "History of Sexuality."* Durham, NC: Duke University Press, 1995.

———. "Rethinking Colonial Categories: European Communities and the Boundaries of Rule." *Comparative Studies in Society and History* 13 (1989): 134–61.

Stoler, Ann Laura, and Frederick Cooper. "Between Colony and Metropole: Rethinking a Research Agenda." Introduction to *Tensions of Empire: Colonial Cultures in a Bourgeois World.* Berkeley: University of California Press, forthcoming.

Stora, Benjamin. *La gangrène de l'oubli: La mémoire de la guerre d'Algérie.* Paris: Editions la Découverte, 1992.

———. "La gauche socialiste, révolutionnaire, et la question du Maghreb au moment du Front Populaire (1935–1938)." *Revue Française d'Histoire d'Outre-Mer* 70, 258–59 (1983): 57–79.

Stren, Richard. *Housing the Urban Poor in Africa: Policy, Politics, and Bureaucracy in Mombasa.* Berkeley: Institute of International Studies, University of California, 1978.

Sundiata, Ibrahim. *Black Scandal: America and the Liberian Labor Crisis, 1929–1936.* Philadelphia: Institute for the Study of Human Issues, 1980.

Suret-Canale, Jean. "The French West African Railway Workers' Strike,

1947–48." In *African Labor History*, edited by Robin Cohen, Jean Copans, and Peter C. W. Gutkind, 129–54. Beverly Hills, Calif.: Sage, 1978.

Tarrant, G. D. "The British Colonial Office and the Labour Question in the Dependencies in the Inter-War Years." Ph.D. dissertation, University of Manitoba, 1977.

Tettegah, John K. *A New Chapter for Ghana Labour*. Accra: Ghana TUC, 1958.

Thiam, Doudou. "La Portée de la citoyenneté française dans les territoires d'outre-mer." Thèse pour le doctorat en droit, Université de Poitiers, 1951. Paris: Société d'éditions africaines, 1953.

Thiam, Iba der. "La grève des cheminots du Sénégal de Septembre 1938." Mémoire de maîtrise, Université de Dakar, 1972.

"L'évolution politique et syndicale du Sénégal Colonial de 1890 à 1936." Thèse pour le doctorat d'Etat, Université de Paris I, 1983.

Thioub, Ibrahima. "Economie coloniale et rémunération de la force de travail: Le salaire du manoeuvre à Dakar de 1930 à 1954," *Revue Française d'Histoire d'Outre-Mer*, 81 (1994): 427–53.

Thomas, Roger. "Forced Labour in British West Africa: The Case of the Northern Territories of the Gold Coast, 1906–27." *Journal of African History* 14 (1973): 79–103.

Thompson, E. P. *The Making of the English Working Class*. New York: Vintage, 1963.

Thompson, Gardner. "Colonialism in Crisis: The Uganda Disturbances of 1945." *African Affairs* 91 (1992): 605–24.

Throup, David. *The Economic and Social Origins of Mau Mau, 1945–53*. London: James Currey, 1987.

"The Origins of Mau Mau." *African Affairs* 84 (1985): 399–433.

Tipps, Dean C. "Modernization Theory and the Comparative Study of Societies: A Critical Perspective." *Comparative Studies in Society and History* 15 (1973): 199–226.

Tronchon, Jacques. *L'insurrection malgache de 1947: essai d'interprétation historique*. Paris: Maspero, 1974.

Union Générale des Travailleurs d'Afrique Noire. *Congrès Général de l'UGTAN (Union Générale des Travailleurs d'Afrique Noire). Conakry 15–18 Janvier 1959*. Paris: Présence Africaine, 1959.

Vail, Leroy. "Ecology and History: The Example of Eastern Zambia." *Journal of Southern African Studies* 3 (1976): 129–55.

Vaillant, Janet. *Black, French, and African: A Life of Léopold Sédar Senghor*. Cambridge, Mass.: Harvard University Press, 1990.

van der Horst, Sheila. *Native Labour in South Africa*. London: Frank Cass and Co., 1971. Orig. published. 1942.

van Onselen, Charles. *Chibaro: African Mine Labour in Southern Rhodesia 1900–1933*. London: Pluto Press, 1976.

Varshney, Ashutosh (ed.). *Beyond Urban Bias*. London: Frank Cass, 1993.

Vaughan, Megan. *Curing their Ills: Colonial Power and African Illness*. Cambridge: Polity Press, 1991.

Vickery, Kenneth P. "The Second World War Revival of Forced Labor in the Rhodesias." *International Journal of African Historical Studies* 22 (1989): 423–37.

Vidal, Claudine. "Guerre des sexes à Abidjan. Masculin, féminin, CFA." *Cahiers d'Etudes Africaines* 65 (1977): 121–53.

von Albertini, Rudolf. *Decolonization: The Administration and Future of the Colonies, 1919–1960.* Trans. by Francisca Garvie. New York: Holmes & Meier, 1971.

Wall, Irwin M. *French Communism in the Era of Stalin: The Quest for Unity and Integration, 1945–1962.* Westport, Conn.: Greenwood, 1983.

"Front Populaire, Front National: The Colonial Example." *International Labor and Working Class History* 30 (1986): 32–43.

Warren, W. M. "Urban Real Wages and the Nigerian Trade Union Movement." *Economic Development and Cultural Change* 15 (1966): 22–36.

Wasserman, Gary. *The Politics of Decolonization: Kenya Europeans and the Land Issue, 1960–1965.* Cambridge: Cambridge University Press, 1976.

Weeks, John. "A Comment on Peter Kilby: Industrial Relations and Wage Determination." *Journal of Developing Areas* 3 (1968): 9–18.

"The Political Economy of Labor Transfer." *Science and Society* 35 (1971): 463–80.

"Wage Policy and the Colonial Legacy – A Comparative Study." *Journal of Modern African Studies* 9 (1971): 361–87.

Weiler, Peter. *British Labour and the Cold War.* Stanford: Stanford University Press, 1988.

Weinstein, Brian. *Eboué.* New York: Oxford University Press, 1972.

White, Luise. "Cars out of Place: Vampires, Technology, and Labor in East and Central Africa." *Representations* 43 (1993): 27–50.

The Comforts of Home: Prostitution in Colonial Nairobi. Chicago: University of Chicago Press, 1990.

"Separating the Men from the Boys: Constructions of Gender, Sexuality, and Terrorism in Central Kenya, 1939–1959." *International Journal of African Historical Studies* 23 (1990): 1–25.

Wilson, Godfrey. *An Essay on the Economics of Detribalization in Northern Rhodesia.* Rhodes-Livingstone Papers, 5. Livingstone: Rhodes-Livingstone Institute, 1941.

Wilson, Godfrey and Monica. *The Analysis of Social Change.* Cambridge: Cambridge University Press, 1968; orig. published 1945.

Wood, Geof. "The Politics of Development Policy Labelling." *Development and Change* 16 (1985): 347–73.

Wright, Gwendolyn. *The Politics of Design in French Colonial Urbanism.* Chicago: University of Chicago Press, 1991.

Yesufu, T. M. *An Introduction to Industrial Relations in Nigeria.* London: Oxford University Press, 1962.

Young, Crawford. *The African Colonial State in Comparative Perspective.* New Haven: Yale University Press, 1994.

Zeleza, Paul Tiyambe. "Trade Union Imperialism: American Labour, the ICFTU and the Kenyan Labour Movement." *Social and Economic Studies* 36 (1987): 145–70.

Zolberg, Aristide. *Creating Political Order: The Party States of West Africa.* Chicago: Rand McNally, 1966.

Index

OTHER BOOKS IN THE SERIES

Printed in the United Kingdom
by Lightning Source UK Ltd.
103675UKS00001B/172

9 780521 566001